Sensations

The Story of British Art from Hogarth to Banksy

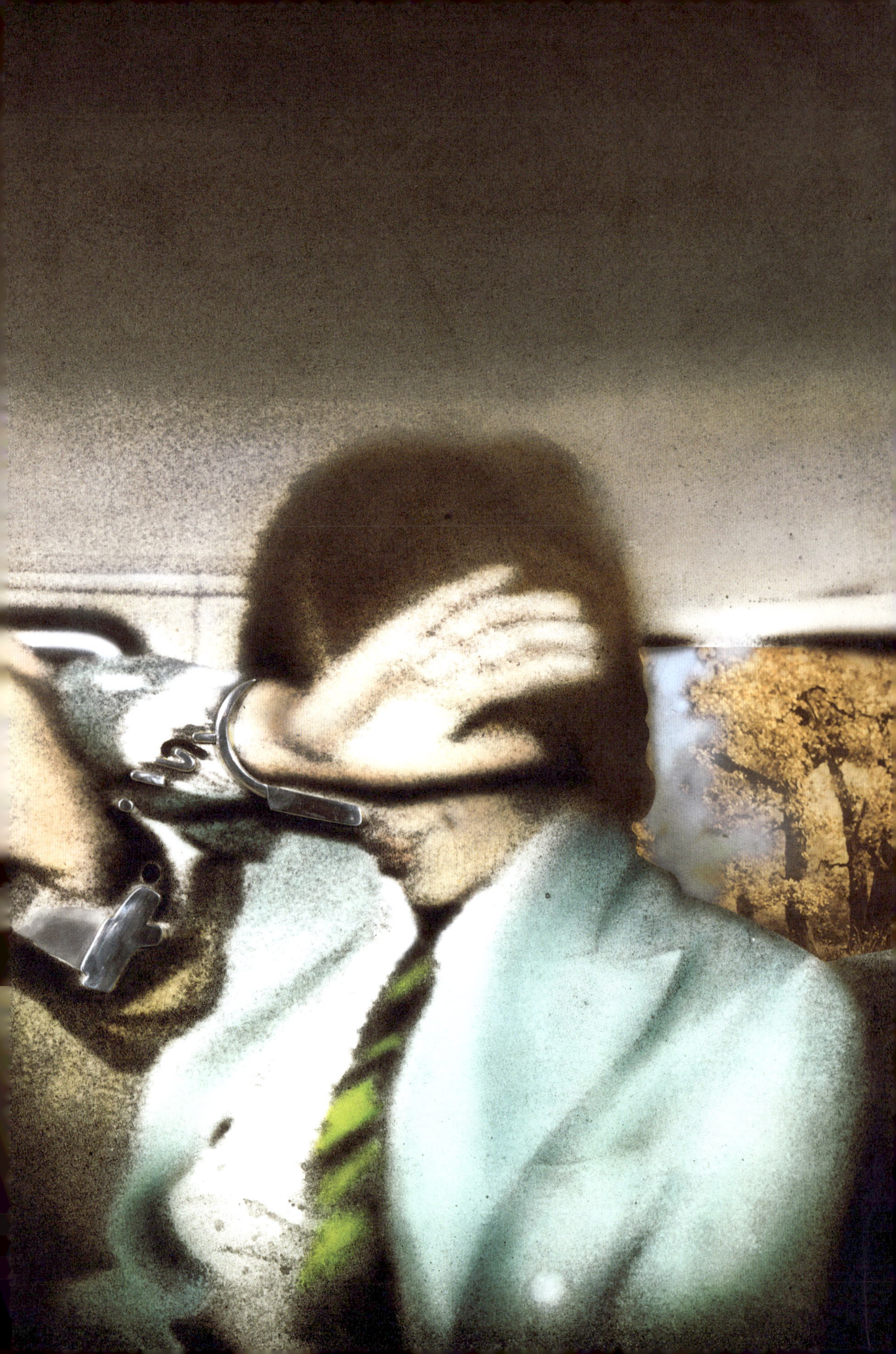

Sensations

The Story of British Art from Hogarth to Banksy

Jonathan Jones

Laurence King Publishing

For my mother-in-law Dr Angela Currie
and in loving memory of my father-in-law
Dr Graham Currie

Published in 2018
by Laurence King Publishing Ltd
361–373 City Road
London EC1V 1LR
Tel +44 20 7841 6900
E enquiries@laurenceking.com
www.laurenceking.com

A catalogue record for this book is
available from the British Library.

ISBN 978 1 78627 297 3
Design concept: Atelier Dyakova
Design: Urban Ant
Printed in Italy

Cover: George Stubbs, *Whistlejacket*,
c. 1762, oil on canvas, 292 × 246.4 cm
(115 × 97 in.), National Gallery, London

Frontispiece: Richard Hamilton,
Swingeing London 67, 1968–69,
acrylic paint, screenprint, paper, aluminium
and metallized acetate on canvas,
67.3 × 85.1 cm (26½ × 33½ in.), Tate

Introduction

A strange fish! Were I in England now (as once I was) and had this fish painted, not a holiday fool there but would give a piece of silver.

Trinculo in *The Tempest*,
William Shakespeare, c. 1611

Rarer Monsters

The comatose seafront opened its hungover windows to bleary August clouds muffling the warm grey Bristol Channel. At one end of the promenade a queue had already formed. Weston-super-Mare's answer to Disneyland was about to open its doors for the first time.

Within the fortress-like concrete walls of a semi-derelict seaside lido, unsmiling staff were waiting to greet the crowds. A ramshackle palace loomed over a dirty pond, surrounded by such attractions as a rickety big wheel, an exhibition of security equipment inside a bus, and a wrecked police van with a slide.

This was Dismaland, a parody attraction created by the pseudonymous British street artist Banksy in late summer 2015. Soon cider was flowing and most visitors appeared to be embracing the ostentatious misery with appropriately ironic zeal. I found it hard to join in. The jokes were too obvious to be funny for long. Banksy's satire seemed to be playing to received ideas rather than digging any real dirt. Great art, surely, should be mysterious, poetic and make you see the world afresh. The popularity of this colossal installation proved that British people, once regarded as conservative philistines who did not 'get' modern art, were up for it by the bucketload in the second decade of the twenty-first century. But what was the value of the art they adored? This grim pastiche was shallow and oddly heartless, a dreary reduction of art to instant entertainment.

Then I saw the unicorn.

It was a young unicorn, an impossible foal. Caught in some far-flung fairytale place, killed by pirates or explorers, floating in a tank in a sideshow tent, its single horn hanging there in the formaldehyde that preserved it, and a white mane flowing with the sort of enigmatic weirdness lacking elsewhere at this insufficiently surreal fairground.

This was a sculpture by Damien Hirst, the leader of the 'Young British Artists' who made names for themselves in the 1990s, and, by 2015, an extremely wealthy man. I had long since given up on ever being surprised or moved by anything he created. Riches seemed to have ossified his talent and turned his imagination to crude pomp. Yet here in Dismaland, his unicorn was a jewel of wonder in an ashtray of the ordinary.

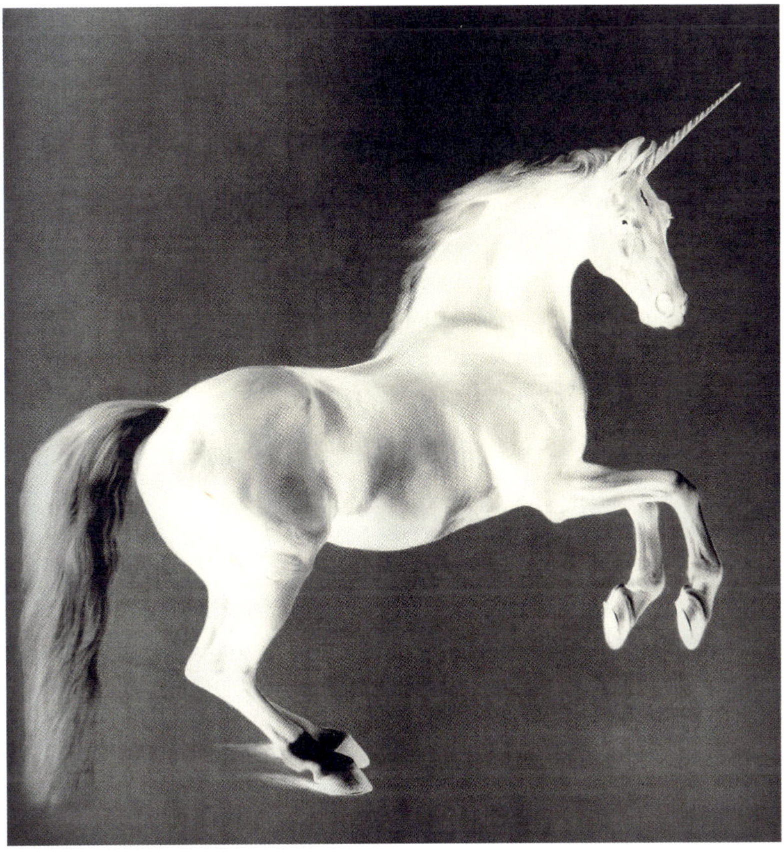

↑Mark Wallinger, *Ghost*, 2001, Scanachrome on translucent PVC, lightbox, 295 × 249 × 18 cm (116 ⅙ × 98 × 7 in.), edition of 3, Tate

Hirst's fairground freak was a smaller version of a unicorn he sold at Sotheby's in 2008 in an auction of his work that raked in £111,576,800. Curiouser and curiouser, some years before that, Hirst's contemporary Mark Wallinger captured a unicorn of his own. Wallinger's 2001 work *Ghost* is a giant negative photograph of a one-horned stallion rearing up on its hind legs, a pale spectre of the fabulous. Like a Victorian spirit photographer, the artist appears to have detected the ectoplasmic shadow of a vanished mythological creature and brought it into the objective world of science.

Wallinger found his unicorn in the National Gallery, whose classical edifice fills the north side of Trafalgar Square in London. Enter that museum and head for its British section, and a marvellous creature meets your eye. George Stubbs's *Whistlejacket*, a life-sized portrait of a thoroughbred horse, was painted in about 1762 (page 105). Alone and magnificent, set in empty space, this beast has one of the most haunting faces in British art. Wallinger's *Ghost* is a negative image of Whistlejacket, out of which a unicorn's tusk has sprouted. It is as if he has taken a photograph of this painting and – like the first photographer to reveal a spooky negative of the Turin Shroud – exposed its secret. Behind Whistlejacket's free spirit, suggests Wallinger, is a secret life as a unicorn.

Hirst too makes a precise allusion to the art of this Liverpool-born eighteenth-century animal artist in his 2008 work *The Incredible Journey*, a zebra in a tank of formaldehyde that restages Stubbs's 1763 painting of the first zebra ever brought to Britain as a three-dimensional taxidermy tableau.

Among the crowds at Dismaland, such echoes of the Georgian age seemed unlikely. Yet there they were. In 1995 Hirst and Wallinger competed for the Tate Gallery's Turner Prize. Twenty years on, the results of contemporary British art's sensational popularization were on show at Dismaland. British modern art by 2015 was a global hit – and a lot of it was crass. But within this fairground of banalities was the ghost of something marvellous. After all, wonders like preserved unicorns were captivating visitors to British fairs long before anyone thought to call them 'art'. Shakespeare comments more than once on Renaissance Britain's appetite for gawping at dried mermaids, two-headed calves, pickled sea serpents and other monstrosities. Trinculo in *The Tempest*, amazed by the monster Caliban, wishes he could show him to the gullible English:

> *A strange fish! Were I in England now (as once I was) and had this fish painted, not a holiday fool there but would give a piece of silver. There would this monster make a man; any strange beast there makes a man. When they will not give a doit to relieve a lame beggar, they will lay out ten to see a dead Indian.*

In *Macbeth* the tyrant is compared with 'our rarer monsters' painted on poles to amaze the crowd. Shakespeare appears acutely aware of freaks of nature as money-making shows, perhaps rivals to his own business of theatre. Above all, these grotesque displays are entertainments of the eye. For as Trinculo puts it, people who never give alms will fork out to 'see a dead Indian': to feast their eyes on strangeness.

Relics of that looking survive. In St Mary Redcliffe Church in Bristol, not far from the Somerset site of Dismaland, a whale's rib – or is it the tusk of a unicorn? – can still be seen, that was brought back to this pioneering port by the fifteenth-century navigator John Cabot. The British Museum owns to this day a 'mermaid' that is part fish, part monkey and all fake. In 1638 a visitor described the various wonders on show at Tradescant's Ark in Lambeth, South London, including:

> *...an ape's head, a cheese, etc; all kinds of shells, the hand of a mermaid, the hand of a mummy, a very natural wax hand under glass, all kinds of precious stones, coins, a picture wrought in feathers...*

Of course, these exhibits were not uniquely English. The collection created by John Tradescant the Elder and Younger, both royal gardeners by trade, was typical of 'cabinets of curiosities' amassed throughout early modern Europe. What is special, however, is the way the British looked at such rarer monsters.

Seventeenth-century Europe saw the birth of modern science. A world of magic and superstition, scarred by witch hunts and plague, found the way forward to a new, experimental, testable form of knowledge that would give humanity a previously unimaginable potential. This intellectual revolution was a Europe-wide phenomenon whose pioneers included Tycho Brahe in Denmark, Andreas Vesalius in Italy and Ambroise Paré in France. Yet it was in Britain, in the anything but promising circumstances of religious conflict, civil war, fire and pestilence, that modern science crystallized. In the second half of the seventeenth century, Britain's Royal Society set the rules of science as they are still followed. A generation of brilliant researchers paved the way for modern thought, and the most inspired of them, Isaac Newton, established the first comprehensive theory of nature to be based on observation and expressed in mathematical laws – the birth of science as we know it.

Natural monsters played a central part in the new science, for this was a revolution in looking. The same freakish exhibits that had only recently nurtured superstition now inspired study. I will argue in this book that British art was born out of the same urge to see that also drove the curiosity of science. It is the child of the scientific revolution – or perhaps its monster twin, pickled in a jar.

The art of Stubbs is one of the most striking proofs that British art has a special connection with science. His paintings of animals isolate them as marvels, as curiosities. In his 1790 painting *The Lincolnshire Ox*, he displays a stupendously sized farm animal with a man beside it for scale. The ox is a true monster, massive and dull-minded, unaware of its uniqueness. Its little human attendant bears witness to its prodigious nature. Yet this is no myth, nor is its scale supernatural. It is a raw and massive empirical fact.

The scientific curiosity that animated art and science in the age of Stubbs delighted in such facts. Long after Shakespeare saw monsters painted on poles, British artists were making records of human wonders. In about 1806 a man whose physical dimensions impressed contemporaries posed for his portrait. The precise observational style of Benjamin Marshall's painting is typical of an age of exactitude in portraiture. What makes his picture memorable is his subject, Daniel Lambert, splayed out in an armchair with his body bursting from his red coat. Lambert's head is tiny compared with his vast stomach. His legs are thick sausages. This painting is an act of medical diagnosis. Lambert's condition was studied by Georgian doctors who believed him the heaviest human being ever recorded. He also put himself on (living) display just like Trinculo's dead Indian. In 1806 this advert for an 'exhibition' appeared in *The Times*:

> *EXHIBITION.—Mr. DANIEL LAMBERT, of Leicester, the greatest Curiosity in the World, who, at the age of 36, weighs upwards of FIFTY STONE.... Mr. Lambert will see Company at his House, No.53, Piccadilly, opposite St. James's Church, from 12 to 5 o'clock.—Admittance 1s.*

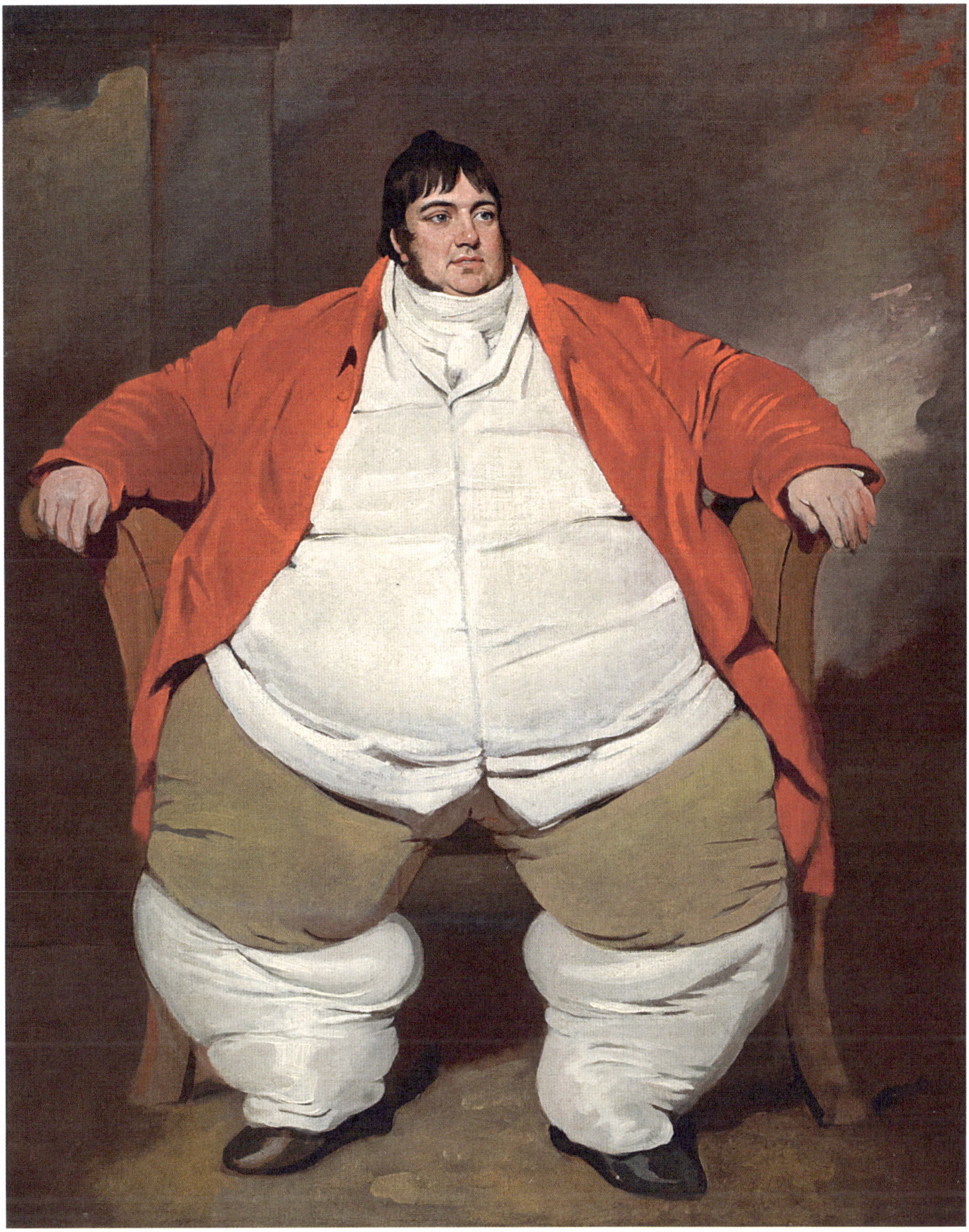

↑ Benjamin Marshall (attr.), *Portrait of Daniel Lambert*, early 1800s, oil on canvas, 75 × 60 cm (29 ½ × 23 ⅔ in.), Hunterian Collection, Royal College of Surgeons, London

British art at its most powerful still exhibits the passion for natural wonders that made Stubbs portray the Lincolnshire Ox and Marshall record the girth of Daniel Lambert – but the stakes are a lot higher than a shilling. In May 2015, three months before Dismaland opened its doors, an extraordinary painting was auctioned at Christie's in New York. Lucian Freud's 1994 canvas *Benefits Supervisor Resting* is a portrait of Sue Tilley sprawled on a sofa, head thrown back, flaunting her generously sized body as she dozes. Her breasts expand over her rolling stomach, her knees and thighs are immense.

Is Freud exhibiting Tilley as a freak? No, she is a unicorn in his eyes – a marvel to admire. The way he admires her is precise and honest. She poses. He paints. The eye he brings to bear is relentlessly empirical and exact. The purpose of art, for him, is always and only to tell the truth. This is the eye for visual facts – ordinary or outlandish – that has driven British art's most powerful talents since the age of Newton.

That spring, four years after Freud's death in 2011 at the age of 88, *Benefits Supervisor Resting* sold in New York for US$56,165,000.

British art in the twenty-first century was plainly at the forefront of cultural fashion, as famous in Manhattan as it was in Weston-super-Mare. Just months after Freud's record sale I was amazed by the unicorn at Dismaland. Perhaps this is where it all started, with curiosities unveiled for a piece of silver by a cynical showman at a fair. And perhaps British art has never stopped its showmanship. The prices just got bigger, the crowds more gullible.

In 1997 the Royal Academy in London staged *Sensation*, a blockbuster survey of Young British Artists collected by Charles Saatchi, from Hirst to Tracey Emin, Sarah Lucas and Chris Ofili. We are still very much in the age of sensationalist art. Yet this book is about another kind of sensation. The new scientific attitude that gripped Britain in the seventeenth and eighteenth centuries held that we are blank slates when we are born. Everything we learn, discover and imagine comes from our senses. In this book I will argue that the greatest British art, from Stubbs to Freud, expresses this empirical or *sensationalist* theory of knowledge. All the greatest artists in the story that follows – with one brilliantly provocative exception – made it their business to look with open eyes at raw fact.

Stubbs, of course, never did paint a unicorn. For him there was wonder enough in real things. What is imagination? We are schooled to think of it as fantasy, wild free thought, uncontrolled mental pictures. Maybe that is just what hucksters want us to think. The greatest art begins in truth. Perhaps it ends there, too.

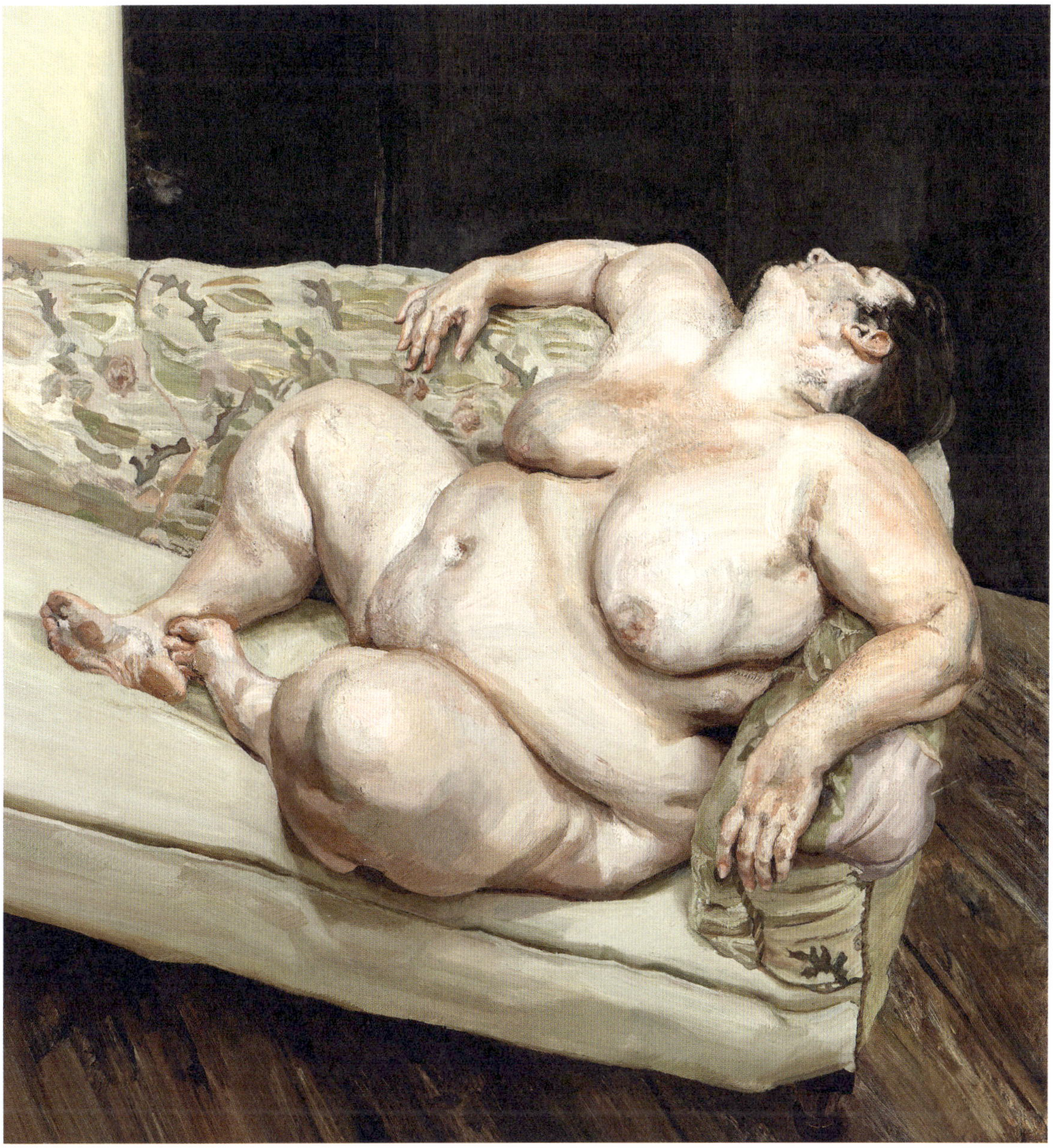

↑ Lucian Freud, *Benefits Supervisor Resting*, 1994, oil on canvas, 160 × 150 cm (63 × 59 in.), Private Collection

1. Let There Be Light

Nature and Nature's Laws lay hid in Night:
God said, "Let Newton be!" and all was light.

Alexander Pope, epitaph intended for Sir Isaac Newton in Westminster Abbey, 1730

The Wedding

William Hogarth, the first great artist born in Britain – and a proudly, self-consciously British one at that – casts a less than romantic eye on marriage in his tough satirical picture serials, portraying it not as the outcome of love but as a hardheaded stratagem for ambitious or impecunious rogues. In *Marriage A-la-Mode* he tells a comic horror story about an arranged wedding between a worthless aristocrat and a merchant's daughter, who do not even look at each other as their fathers make the deal. Two dogs chained together in a corner reflect the brutal nature of the transaction. Yet it is not just in the upper echelons of society that marriage is a cynical calculation, according to Hogarth. When the big-spending Tom Rakewell in *A Rake's Progress* has run out of cash he marries a wealthy older woman so he can gamble away her fortune too. Chained-up dogs haunt this wedding as well. The pair are joined in a City of London church with crumbling walls that more than hint at the ill-made couple's grim future. A happier but no less coolly self-interested arrangement is achieved by the 'Industrious 'Prentice' Francis Goodchild in Hogarth's popular print series *Industry and Idleness*. Goodchild marries his master's daughter, an astute career move that makes him business partner to his father-in-law and sets him on a course to be Lord Mayor of London.

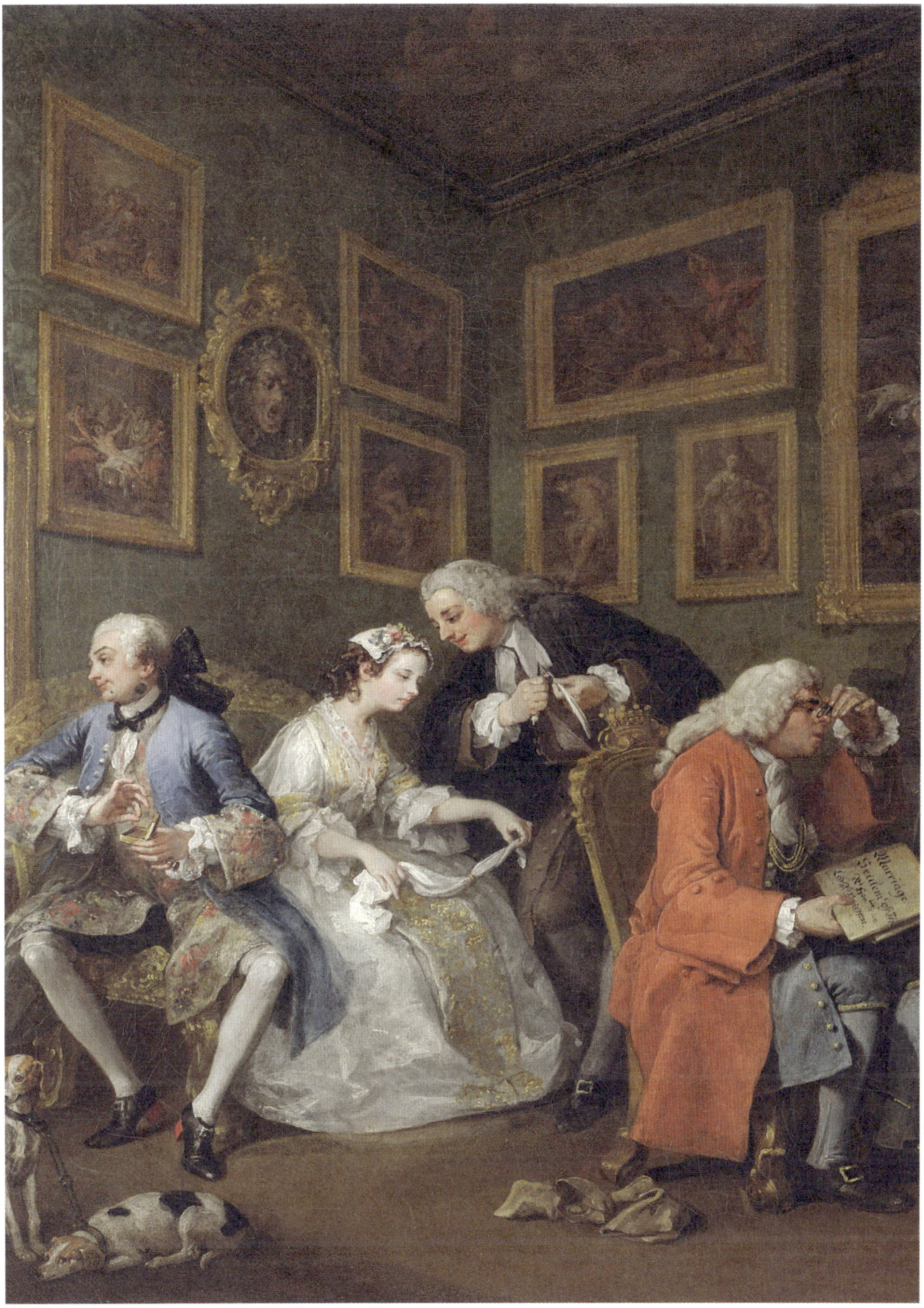

↑ William Hogarth, *Marriage A-la-Mode I* (detail), c. 1743

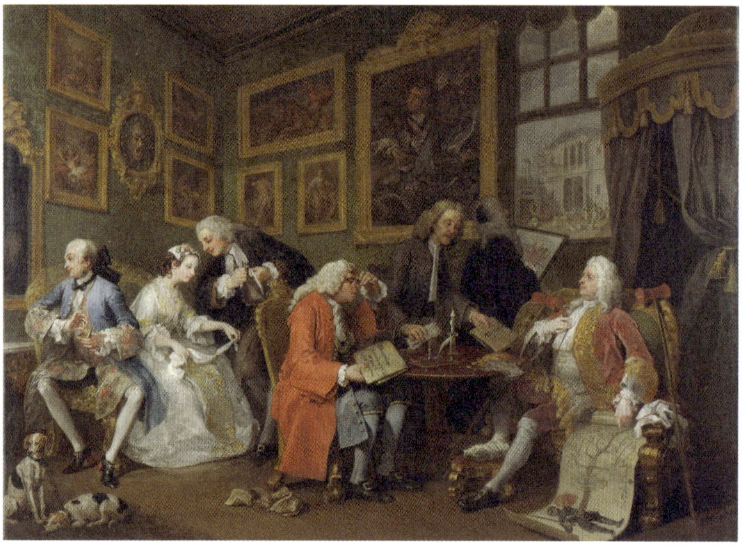

↑ William Hogarth, *Marriage A-la-Mode I*, c. 1743, oil on canvas, 69.9 × 90.8 cm (27½ × 35¾ in.), National Gallery, London

Hogarth's own wedding was a similarly good move. Like the hardworking apprentice, he managed to make a marriage that consolidated his professional future.

On 23 March 1729, the 32-year old William Hogarth married Jane Thornhill, the daughter of Sir James Thornhill, who held the court role of Serjeant-Painter to King George II. Thornhill was – besides being Hogarth's teacher – everything the young artist aspired to become. Not only had his paintings got him knighted but he was even a fellow of the scientific Royal Society. It is entirely possible that William loved Jane deeply, but it is undoubtedly also true that when they married, the brilliant young artist moved up several notches towards the apex of the British art world.

Such a move would have been inconceivable a few decades earlier, for there was no British art world to move up in. There were barely any British artists in the modern sense of the word – and no famous ones, let alone geniuses whose works would live in history. How many people can even name a British-born artist who worked before the 1700s? Art, for the British upper classes, was essentially something that came from abroad.

This had been the case for a very long time. Then, after the Civil War that turned English society upside down in the middle of the seventeenth century, new energies, ideas and modes of thinking took hold that for the first time put the eye, its perceptions and its pleasures at the heart of British culture. By the early eighteenth century it starts to make sense to speak of a 'British School' in art, a distinctive national contribution to European visual civilization.

William Hogarth would soon make British art famous throughout Europe. In 1729, however, he was in trouble. He was just an engraver, and Sir James appears not to have been convinced that he was much of a catch. The marriage went ahead surreptitiously, in the hope that a sceptical father would accept it as a fait accompli. Thornhill had every reason to be fussy. For if today his name rings far fewer bells than Hogarth's, he had earned his elevated rank by quite literally painting British art into new heights.

Those English Beasts

Paul Withypool kneels in prayer, hands palmed together, eyes fixed on paradise, wearing a sombre yet expensively fur-lined coat and his hair fashionably flattened. The realism of his English features and the way he seems slightly out of time with the other figures adds a homely touch to a sophisticated Italian painting, for Withypool's portrait can be found in an early sixteenth-century Venetian picture of the Holy Family by Antonio Solario. Withypool was a merchant from a Bristol family who commissioned this beautiful object in 1514, presumably during a business trip to Italy. The Withypool Triptych is a curious mixture of Italian Renaissance and northern European art styles. Its calm, statuesque figures and view of a Veneto landscape owe a great deal to the Venetian painter Giovanni Bellini, but its folding three-panelled form and the 'donor portrait' that allows a wealthy patron to become part of the sacred action are typical of the artists of Bruges and Brussels. None of it, however, is British – apart from Withypool's presence, and the money he paid Solario.

People who could afford to splash out on luxury art in Britain before 1700 tended to make the same choice as Paul Withypool. They paid for art from continental Europe. From merchants to monarchs, those who aspired to commission a masterpiece looked for masters abroad.

This elite vogue for continental art was already well established in the late Middle Ages, when Edward Grimston, a Lancastrian in the Wars of the Roses, was sent across the Channel in 1446 on a diplomatic mission for the hapless King Henry VI. It took him to Bruges, where he posed for a portrait by Petrus Christus, a great exponent of the new Flemish school of spooky verisimilitude. The fame of Flemish art also reached fifteenth-century Edinburgh. In the 1470s Edward Bonkil, provost of the Scottish capital's Collegiate Chapel of the Holy Trinity, commissioned an altarpiece from the tormented Ghent genius Hugo van der Goes. Only the side wings survive, depicting a visionary image of angels making music and donor portraits of Bonkil and King James III of Scotland – more than enough to show that an artist sought after throughout fifteenth-century Europe sent a very major work to the British Isles.

In Tudor England the Europhilia of Britain's art-buying classes became even more pronounced. The Tuscan sculptor Benvenuto Cellini tells in his autobiography how, as a young man in Florence, he met the artist Pietro Torrigiano, who was looking for assistants on a great work in London, where he now lived. There was something thuggish about Torrigiano, thought Cellini, who was a tough guy himself, 'and every day he boasted of his brave deeds among those English beasts' ('*quelle bestie di quegli Inghilesi*'). What really put him off going to work for this streetfighting sculptor, though, was the tough emigrant's proud confession that as a teenager he had punched Michelangelo in the face and broken the art hero's nose.

Torrigiano, who had indeed studied alongside, and thumped, the young Michelangelo in late fifteenth-century Florence, specialized in a hyperrealistic style of painted terracotta portraiture that makes his bust of Henry VII exceptionally eerie and ghostlike. The ambitious work for which he went back to Florence to find assistants was Henry's tomb in Westminster Abbey, created between 1512 and 1518, the first monumental Renaissance sculpture in Britain, with its quintessentially Florentine putti sitting at the ends of the effigies of the first Tudor ruler and his queen, Elizabeth of York.

After Henry VIII gave his parents this Italianate send-off, Renaissance replaced Flemish as the European style most coveted in Britain. Paul Withypool was not alone in buying Italian in the early sixteenth century. In 1521 Cardinal Wolsey, Henry's chief adviser, commissioned Giovanni da Maiano to create terracotta portraits of Roman emperors on the walls of his new palace at Hampton Court, and in about 1536 Benedetto da Rovezzano made a flamboyantly Florentine fountain for Cowdray House in Sussex.

It was, however, Thomas More, the most learned Renaissance man at Henry's court, who finally hired a truly great European artist to work in Britain. More's friend Erasmus told him about the exceptional talent of Hans Holbein the Younger, one of an Augsburg family of painters who had settled in Basel: Holbein had portrayed Erasmus not only with acute observation but with an intellectual grasp of his Humanist philosophy. He arrived at More's home in Chelsea in 1526 bearing Erasmus's letter of introduction, and stayed to paint a sophisticated portrait of More and his family that is a lost masterpiece of the Renaissance. He went back to Basel in 1528, and returned to London four years later, spending the last 11 years of his life there. Holbein is one of the best painters who ever worked in Britain, but to

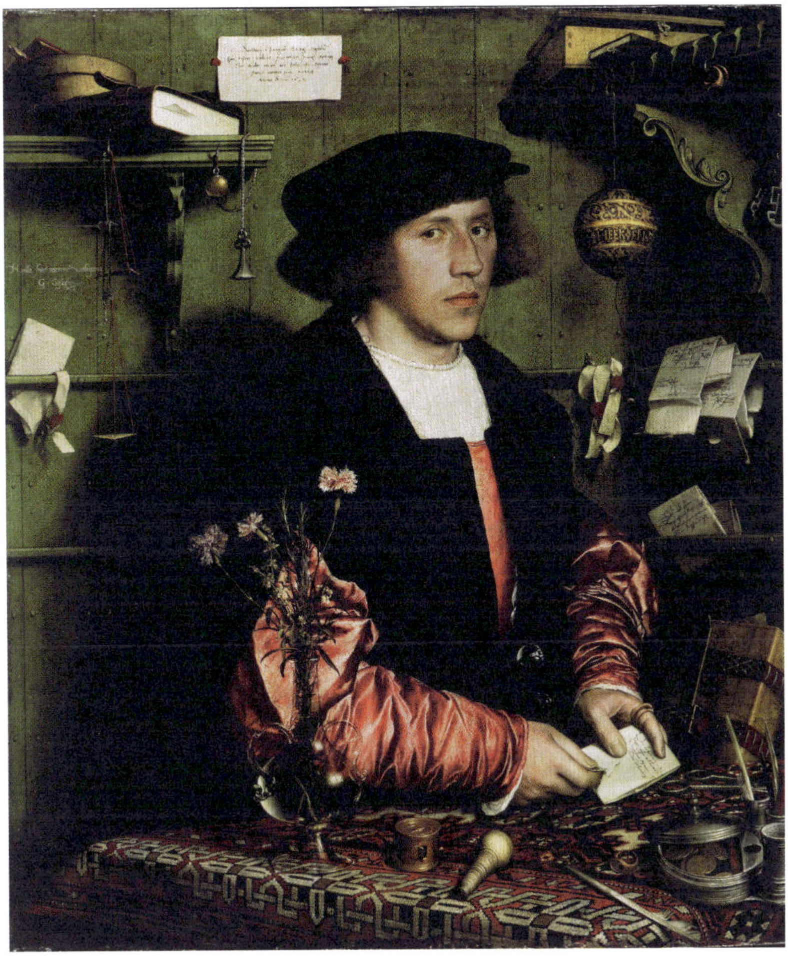

get the true measure of his art you have to understand how German it is. In 1532 he painted a portrait of Georg Gisze, a merchant of the Hanseatic League, posing in his office in London's German enclave, the Steelyard, among precisely observed objects that intricately signify his business, intellect, emotions and affinities – including a vase of carnations, books, letters, quills and coins; it sums up the entire social being of a fellow German in this foreign land. *The Ambassadors*, painted in 1533, is also a portrait of two strangers in England like Holbein himself. The French diplomats Jean de Dinteville and Georges de Selve stand among articles that symbolize Renaissance curiosity and cultivation, while a distorted image of a skull slices through their world, making a mockery of all human pursuits.

↑ Hans Holbein the Younger,
Portrait of the Merchant Georg Gisze,
1532, oil on oak panel,
96.3 × 85.7 cm (38 × 33 ¾ in.),
Staatliche Museen zu Berlin

The Ambassadors is a masterpiece of the German Renaissance. It shares its imagery of learning and its intimation that all is folly with *Melencolia I*, the 1514 engraving by the great Nuremberg artist Albrecht Dürer. It also shares its horror of mortality with Holbein's own *The Dead Christ in the Tomb*, which he painted in Basel in the early 1520s. Holbein's paintings of German and French clients are more intellectually expansive than those of British people. With the exception of Thomas More, his British patrons wanted something simple – an accurate portrait with no philosophical trimmings.

The genius of Holbein was narrowed to straightforward functional portraiture by visually unsophisticated English clients. His portraits of such British subjects as Richard Southwell, Robert Cheseman and Jane Seymour are starkly focused on replicating, with an almost disturbing perfection, the sitter's appearance.

It was as if the English used Holbein as a camera. Henry VIII notoriously put so much faith in the accuracy of his art that he decided he loved Anne of Cleves before he ever met her, purely on the basis of Holbein's portrait of this eligible European noblewoman. The living woman looked nothing like her picture, to the fat, ageing king's disgust.

In Holbein's British portraits we see a meeting between a sophisticated Renaissance master and something more primitive, a raw, perhaps even magical concept of art. This can be felt at its most uncanny in his miniature of Anne of Cleves, painted in about 1539 and enclosed later in the sixteenth century in an ivory box shaped into a Tudor rose. This tiny, bright image has an occult quality, as if by holding it you could exert power over, or through, the person it portrays. It resembles a religious relic or a fetish endowed with supernatural efficacy. Miniature portraiture, introduced to Britain by the Flemish Horenbout family in the 1520s, became a craze. It was one artistic form that produced native British masters, including Shakespeare's contemporary Nicholas Hilliard, whose intense little images radiate sexual enchantment. Yet when Elizabeth I's court needed a grand portrait painting it looked once more to foreign talent. Her former champion Sir Henry Lee of Ditchley commissioned Marcus Gheeraerts the Younger to paint the Ditchley Portrait, in which Elizabeth is a pearly colossus bestriding Britain. In another of this Bruges-born painter's Elizabethan portraits, Sir Henry's relative Captain Thomas Lee poses as a bare-legged noble savage to commemorate martial deeds in Ireland.

Elizabeth's reign was far less distinguished in art than it was in poetry and drama, but the Stuart kings who succeeded her were

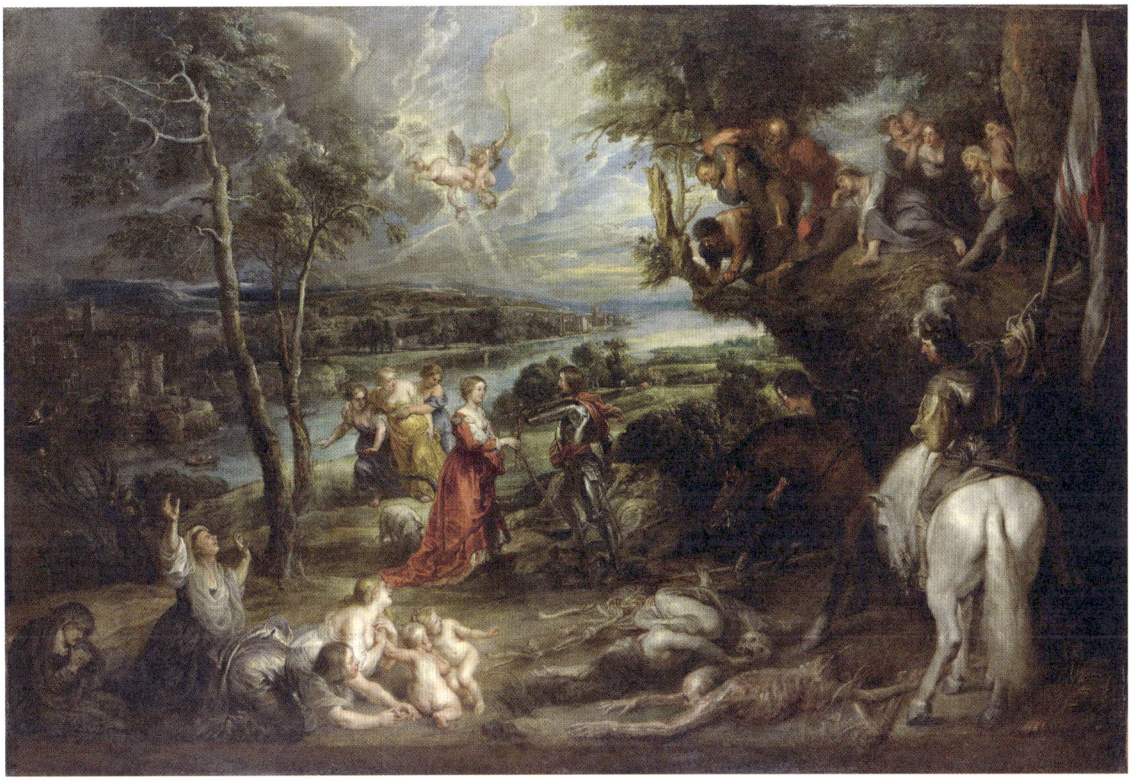

↑ Peter Paul Rubens, *Landscape with St George and the Dragon*, 1630–35, oil on canvas, 152.5 × 226.9 cm (60 × 89 ⅓ in.), Royal Collection Trust

visually aspirational and self-consciously plugged into European art. James VI of Scotland, who from 1603 was also James I of England, lavished huge sums on masques, courtly entertainments in which an allegorical mythology of divine kingship was decorated with sumptuous scenery and special effects, resembling the early operas of Monteverdi's Italy. They were designed by Inigo Jones, the British disciple of the Venetian architect Andrea Palladio. When Charles I attained the throne in 1625 he took the courtly taste for European art to new, almost fanatical heights of aesthetic devotion. Charles was a true art lover. As a prince he went on a crazy *Three Musketeers*-style adventure to Spain, accompanied by his father's favourite, the Duke of Buckingham, to try to secure a dynastic marriage: while there he saw the superb Spanish royal collection with its many masterpieces by Titian. As king he managed to attract many of the leading European painters of his time to London. Sir Peter Paul Rubens, Baroque master and diplomat, decorated the ceiling of the new Banqueting House at the Palace of Whitehall – the only part of this lost artistic treasury that survives

– with allegorical homages to James I that soar with swirling energy, preserving the extravagant spirit of the masques that were staged here. He also portrayed Charles as St George in a visionary scene that happens to be the first great oil painting of a recognizably English landscape. Decaying corpses of a dragon's victims lie in a woodland clearing that overlooks what is clearly intended to be the River Thames. The sun magically illuminates this verdant river scene as St George, looking very like King Charles, meets the princess he has delivered from the monster.

Rubens came and went but other artists were seduced to stay longer. Like Holbein before him, Anthony van Dyck was to die in Britain. This gifted artist from Antwerp, the most brilliant follower of Rubens, worked all over Europe, including at the court of James I, before becoming the star of the Caroline art world from 1632. In Italy he had painted impressive altarpieces. In Britain he found, like other incoming artists before him, that all that the majority of the locals wanted was a nice portrait. In the hands of Van Dyck this could become something as sublimely fantastical as his circa 1638 painting of Rachel de Ruvigny, Countess of Southampton. As Fortune floating in the sky, she is swathed in gleaming heavenly-blue draperies with her foot on a skull, triumphing over Death. Yet sadly it is hard to resist the feeling, looking at portrait after portrait of cavaliers and bishops by Van Dyck, that he might have been a still better artist if he had never come to Britain. As it is, a painter who was clearly as

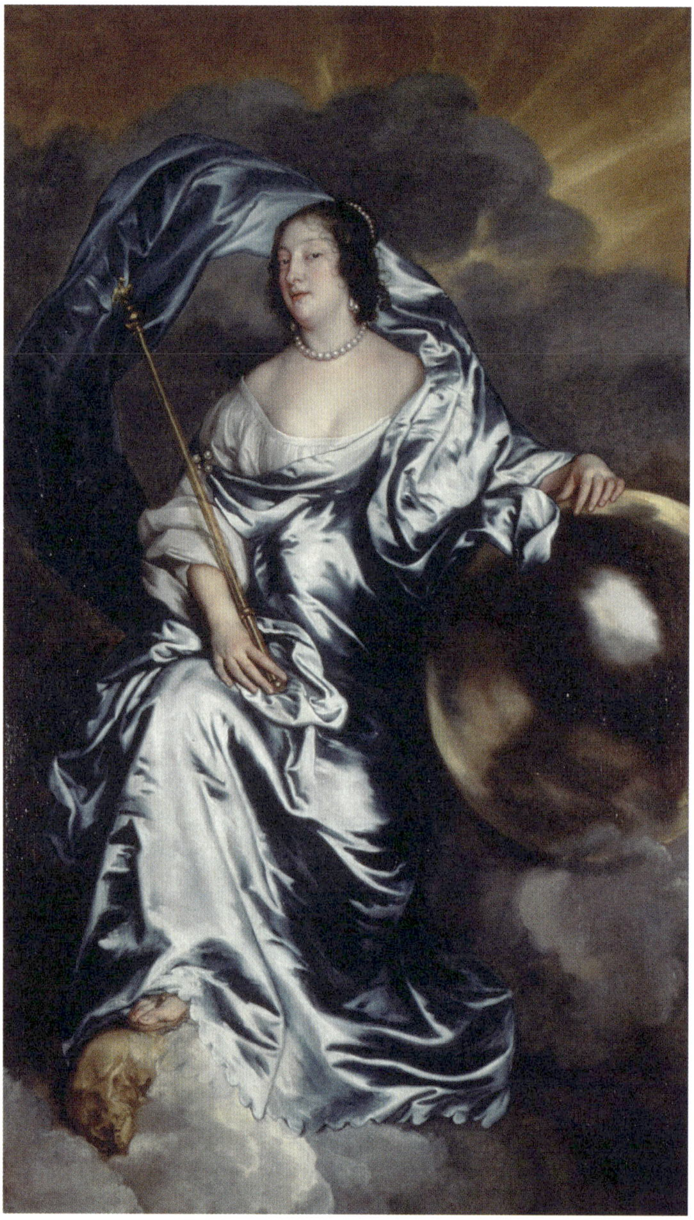

↑ Anthony van Dyck, *Rachel de Ruvigny, Countess of Southampton, as Fortune*, c. 1638, oil on canvas, 219.5 × 132.5 cm (86⅖ × 52⅛ in.), Fitzwilliam Museum, University of Cambridge

talented as Velázquez and Rembrandt never matches their depth of mind.

The same royal generosity that seduced Van Dyck also brought a staggering list of other European masters to the court of Charles I. There was even one mistress: Artemisia Gentileschi, fierce follower of Caravaggio, who joined her father, Caravaggio's close friend Orazio Gentileschi, in England in 1638 at the personal invitation of Charles I. She created her exhilarating vision of creative energy, *Self-Portrait as the Allegory of Painting*, for Charles and it remains in the Royal

→ Artemisia Gentileschi, *Self-Portrait as the Allegory of Painting*, c. 1638–39, oil on canvas, 96.5 × 73.7 cm (38 × 29 in.), Royal Collection Trust

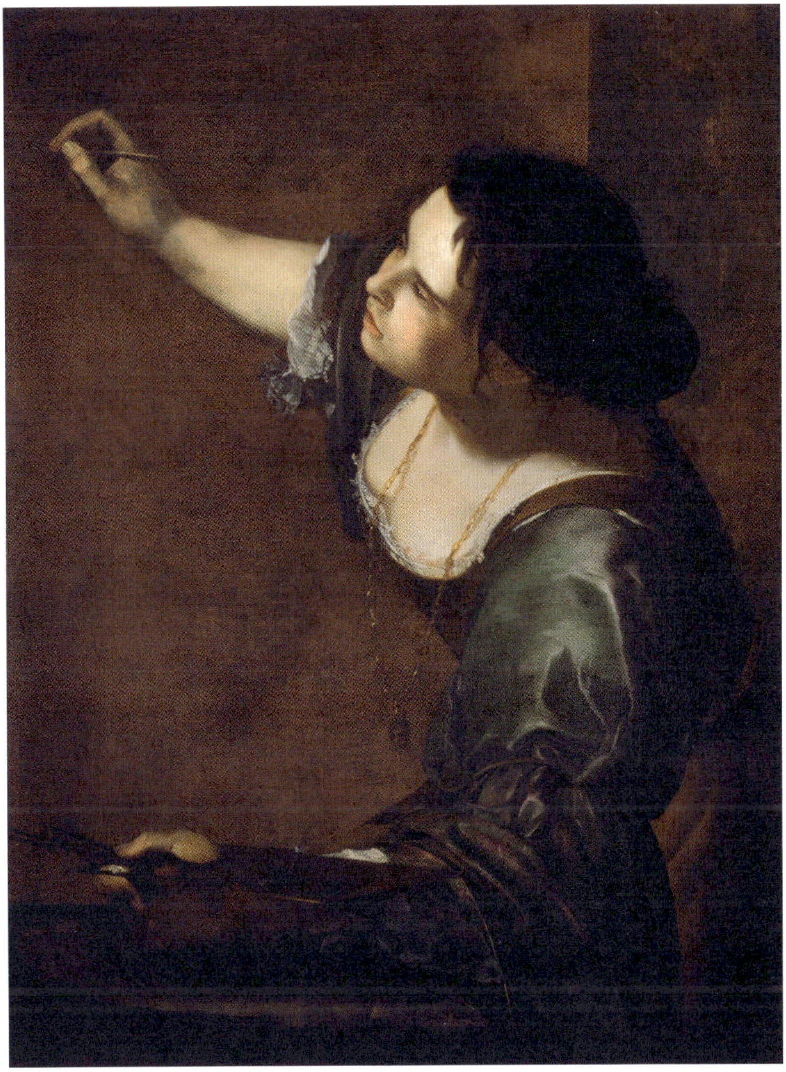

Collection to this day. Jan Lievens, the precocious artist who shared a studio with Rembrandt in the 1620s and was rated equally with him as a young art star in Leiden, also came to the English court in the 1630s, while the Utrecht artist Gerrit van Honthorst – another imitator of Caravaggio – worked for Charles in the late 1620s.

Not only masters but masterpieces flooded in. Charles was a truly avid collector. He bought the art collection of the Dukes of Mantua lock, stock and barrel, including Andrea Mantegna's *The Triumphs of Caesar*, still on view at Hampton Court, and Caravaggio's *Death of the Virgin*. He also persuaded the French king to give him Leonardo da Vinci's painting *St John the Baptist* in exchange for a Titian and a Holbein.

Thomas Howard, 2nd Earl of Arundel, the courtier who most intensely shared Charles's passion for art and was portrayed by Rubens as well as (inevitably) Van Dyck, amassed classical sculptures, even sending emissaries to the Turkish empire in search of ancient Greek works. He also purchased one of Leonardo's notebooks filled with scientific ideas, which became the Codex Arundel, today in the British Library. It is also possible that the world's finest collection of Leonardo drawings was owned by Charles I himself. This mesmerizing hoard of anatomical diagrams, surreal caricatures and sublime deluges was definitely in British royal hands by the end of the seventeenth century and the purchaser may well have been Charles, whose passion for the Renaissance polymath's works is clear from his swap with the French king. Leonardo's caricatures were even reproduced as prints by Wenceslas Hollar, the Bohemian engraver who was yet another artistic immigrant in this period.

Why did this prodigious age of royal patronage not see the birth of a dynamic British art scene? Is it anyway mere bigotry to view Rubens, let alone Van Dyck whose art has become part of the national furniture, as 'foreign' artists instead of celebrating the cosmopolitan character of Britain's artistic heritage? In fact, the sheer lavishness of early Stuart court culture did embrace and inspire local talent, though not to the point of a breakthrough. Jones, designer of the gorgeous court masques, also built the Banqueting House where they were staged, and the Queen's House, Greenwich, for Charles I's Queen Henrietta Maria, with its mind-expanding concept of a completely cubic central space. By the 1640s the boundless royal enthusiasm for art was even starting to kindle British-born portrait painters, including William Dobson and Robert Walker.

Yet it was all utterly fragile. The artistic extravaganza was played out before a hostile public, many of whom saw it as nothing less than evil. The most artistically sensitive ruler in British history would end his days on a scaffold erected outside the Banqueting House on 30 January 1649. The ceiling painted for him by Rubens must have been one of the last things his eyes saw before he went out to be beheaded.

It was not xenophobia that made the royal appetite for European art repulsive to many seventeenth-century Britons – at least not in a form we would recognize today – but a loathing for art itself.

The Reformation cuts through the history of British art like the skull Holbein painted across *The Ambassadors*. Indeed, the melancholy of this painting may reflect the anxiety induced by Henry VIII's decision to break with the Pope and accept parts of Martin Luther's revolutionary rethink of Christianity so he could divorce his first wife. From the moment the Act of Supremacy created a new national church in 1534, the English Reformation physically attacked art. Luther's theology returned to a close reading of the biblical word and to St Augustine's pessimistic argument that human beings are so innately sinful that we

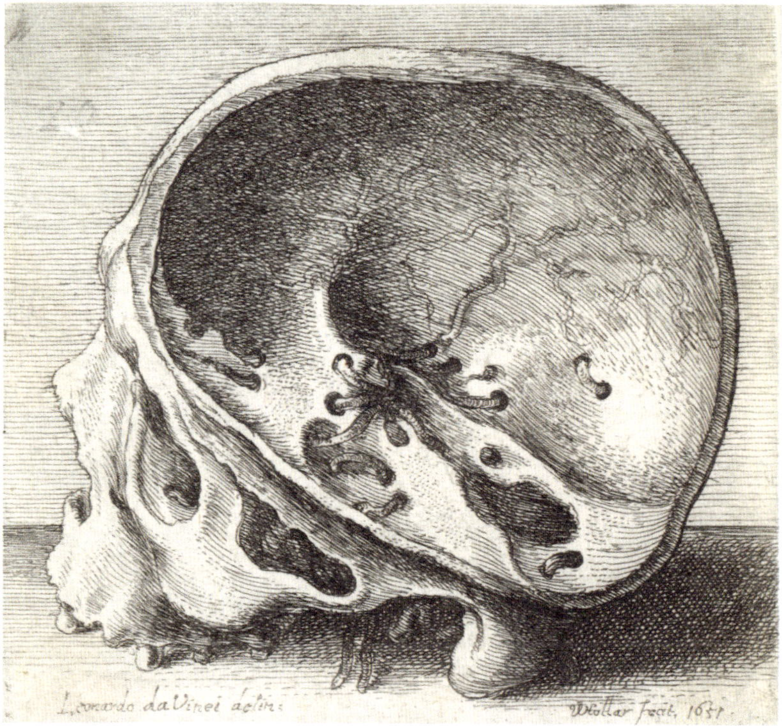

↑ Wenceslas Hollar, after Leonardo da Vinci, *Sectioned Skull in Profile*, 1651, etching, only state, 6.8 × 7.5 cm (2⅔ × 3 in.), The Metropolitan Museum of Art, New York. Rogers Fund, 1920 (20.81.2 [20])

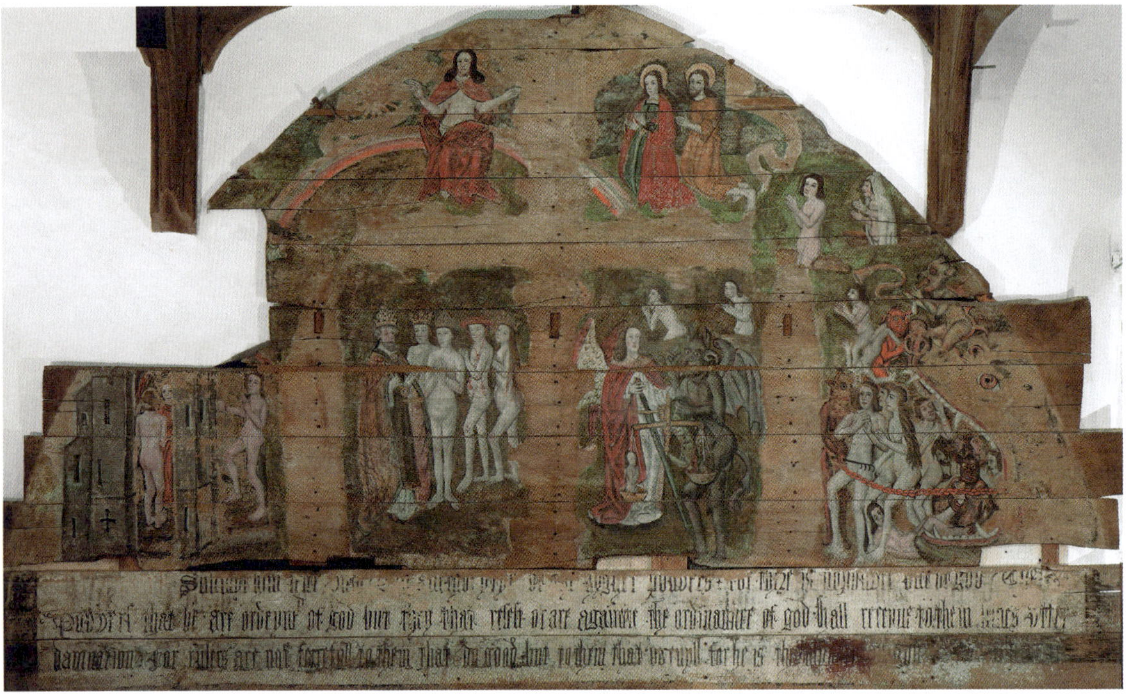

↑ Anonymous, *Wenhaston Doom*, c. 1480, pigment on boards, St Peter's Church, Wenhaston, Suffolk

cannot possibly redeem ourselves. If our souls are saved it can only be thanks to an astonishing act of mercy by God over which we have no control. Therefore, the good works, pilgrimages and relics of the medieval church are worthless – and the stained glass, wall paintings, statues and wood carvings that adorned the old superstitious cult are worthless idols that lull souls into popish credulity.

Lutheran ideas gave Henry's ruthless minister Thomas Cromwell a licence to close monastic houses and seize their wealth for the crown, but the violence done by the English Reformation to 'papist' art and architecture – reducing religious buildings to ruin, smashing stained-glass windows and destroying statues such as those that graced the Lady Chapel at Ely – reeks more of passionate belief than cynical greed. Medieval religious paintings that do at least partially survive were preserved because local officials chose to paint them over rather than destroy them completely. Who painted the raw, primal, expressive Doom, or Last Judgement, rediscovered in St Peter's Church in Wenhaston, Suffolk in 1892? We will never know – although a monk from a local monastery seems a likely guess. The artist or artists who created this image of the saved and the damned, of God, angels and devils, in about 1480 clearly knew nothing of the new realism of Jan van Eyck – but so what? That lack of subtlety does not make this Doom any less effective in the work it sets itself. It was not painted for aesthetes. Its use was as stark as its style – to make the Christian community gathered at mass contemplate the end of the world and each soul's fate after death. Similar Dooms were painted in many English parish churches for the same reason.

The tragedy of artistic destruction marks the British landscape. Romantic ruined abbeys like Tintern and Rievaulx look the way they do because they were closed down, roughly used and left to languish. Medieval cathedrals that have survived intact such as Salisbury and Durham are unquestionably among the most beautiful in Europe, hinting at a lost Britain of sacred grandeur.

Individual artistic genius – the kind of originality that started to be valued in Italy in the early Renaissance and that Charles I coveted for his collection of art and artists – does not leap out from that grandeur. There is no evidence of a British answer to Giotto painting Dooms in Suffolk churches – which is why the British elite were already seeking out continental art, as we have seen, well before the Reformation. That does not stop us mourning, with Seamus Heaney:

> ... *Ely's Lady Chapel,*
> *the sweet tenor Latin*
> *forever banished,*
> *the sumptuous windows*
> *threshed clear by Thomas Cromwell.*

('Leavings', *Field Work*, 1979)

It did not stop Charles I's religious advisers feeling nostalgia for the vanished glories of medieval church art, either. For the aesthetic ambition of the Stuart court was not apolitical. It perfectly mirrored new ideas about church and society that Charles supported.

The keener sort of Protestants in seventeenth-century Britain, who called themselves the Godly and were called by their enemies Puritans, followed the theology of John Calvin. For Calvin, the fate of souls is not only beyond human control but predestined in the cosmic plan. Most are damned, a few are saved, and to know you are one of the Elect is a moment of divine self-discovery. The harsh divisiveness and lack of charity some saw in Calvinism prompted a rebellion known theologically as Arminianism. The Arminians wanted to bring reassurance back into religion. They wanted to make it beautiful again – and that meant re-enchanting churches with art. They insisted on restoring proper altars, vestments, ritual and holy decor, including sculpture and painting in churches that could afford it. Their leader in Britain was William Laud, whom Charles I made Archbishop of Canterbury in 1633.

The Laudian passion for beautifying churches mirrored the sensibility that made Charles I hire Rubens. The royal art collection and the attempt to resacralize places of worship imported the ambitions of the European Baroque. In the Baroque movement that started in Rome around 1600 and renewed Catholic art from Sicily to Brazil, images and spaces work together emotionally and psychologically to embrace, intoxicate, even overwhelm. This overtly manipulative artistic mode was born out of the need for Catholicism to remake its popular appeal against the Protestant threat. It also gave rulers an astonishing style with which to celebrate and glorify their power. Charles I badly wanted to be a Baroque monarch. He even sent a triple portrait of himself by Van Dyck to the sculptor Gianlorenzo Bernini, the definitive genius of Baroque Rome, so Bernini could carve his image.

It was unmitigated folly to try and import the Baroque, for Britain was a Protestant nation always on the lookout for signs of Catholic conspiracy. It was not just extreme Puritans who feared 'popery'. The Spanish Armada and the Gunpowder Plot were defining national memories. Laudian 'idolatry' could be concealing a global Catholic conspiracy. It provoked not a renewal of religious beauty, but a revival of iconoclasm. As relations between Charles I and his Protestant parliament decayed, works of art were attacked once more. Soldiers ripped paintings from cathedrals, mobs bayed for the destruction of Gothic monuments. After Charles lost his war with Parliament, and then his head, his art collection was auctioned off by the new British republic known as the Commonwealth. Many of the European treasures he had brought to Britain went back to continental collections. Leonardo's *St John the Baptist* and Caravaggio's *Death of the Virgin* can be found today in the Louvre, and only a few experts have ever seen the royal mark of Charles I hidden on what was once his Leonardo.

The Optic Glass

The new king was astonished. In his hand he held something impossible. It was both hideous and beautiful. It opened new vistas and most of all filled him with wonder at the young man who had just presented him with this bizarre, brilliant drawing. What kind of genius was Christopher Wren?

Charles II had returned to England from his exile in the Low Countries in May 1660 to reclaim his father's throne and bask in near-universal acclamation. In the end the Commonwealth had been a hollow failure, its Godly elite widely loathed and kept in power only by the military rule of Oliver Cromwell. When the Lord Protector was dead, the restoration of the monarchy was inevitable. In the months before Charles II came, the diarist Samuel Pepys – who would soon be serving him as clerk to the Navy Board – heard boys in the London streets mock the republican Rump Parliament with the season's top joke: 'Kiss my Rump!'

Now, a few months after taking the throne, Charles contemplated the drawings just given to him by a polymath academic still in his twenties. Officially, young Wren was an astronomer – the most brilliant in the realm, everyone said. In February 1661 he was appointed to the top job in the field when he became professor of astronomy at Oxford. Being an astronomer in the seventeenth century was like being a researcher at CERN in the twenty-first. It was to be at the coolest facet of the cutting edge. For astronomy, as every learned and inquisitive person knew, had recently redefined the very nature of human knowledge. When Galileo Galilei turned a telescope on the sky and published his observations of the moon and the solar system, illustrated with his own drawings, in his 1610 book *Sidereus Nuncius* (*Starry Messenger*) he overturned habits of thought that went back to Aristotle and were devoutly institutionalized by every university. The Aristotelian concept of knowledge started from axiomatic beliefs and insisted that nature must obey its assumptions. Galileo demonstrated that observing nature could stand those assumptions on their heads. He had been told the moon was a smooth orb. He could see in his telescope that it had mountains and vast deserts or dusty 'seas'. Galileo put empirical observation at the heart of science. It was like putting an engine in a car or fuel in a rocket. The scientific method made scientific progress unstoppable. Even Galileo's trial by the Catholic Church and his fearful retraction of his support for Copernicus's theory that the

Earth orbits the sun could not stop science. Instead it sent science north. Galileo and his telescope were lionized in Britain. The poet John Milton made a pilgrimage to meet the revered astronomer, now living under house arrest, when he visited Italy in the late 1630s; he preserved the encounter in Book One of his epic *Paradise Lost*, published in 1667, where he compares Satan's shining shield with:

> *... the moon, whose orb*
> *Through optic glass the Tuscan artist views*
> *At evening from the top of Fiesole,*
> *Or in Valdarno, to descry new lands,*
> *Rivers or mountains on her spotty globe.*

Milton was a passionate Godly republican, and in his treatise *Areopagitica*, published in 1644 to urge Parliament to defend free speech, he argues that Galileo's persecution is a warning of how knowledge can be shut down in Catholic tyrannies. He tells of his trip to Italy and his meeting with 'the famous Galileo grown old, a prisoner to the Inquisition, for thinking otherwise than the Franciscan and Dominican licensers thought'.

The conclusion is clear: Catholic oppression silences discovery, but a Protestant state should set it free. By implication, the new Britain being made by the Civil War has the chance to become a utopia of intellectual liberty where the new science will prosper.

This is what happened, though not in the way Milton may have imagined. Britain did become a great centre of science in the aftermath of the Civil War and was ready to spearhead the scientific revolution by the time Charles II took the throne. This unexpected leap to the very forefront of European culture took place to the sound of cannon and in the shadow of Cromwell. Yet its most gifted thinkers were more likely to be Royalists, or sons of Royalists, than Puritan radicals.

Wren, whose father was a Royalist clergyman and whose uncle was a leading Laudian thrown into the Tower of London by the Commonwealth, was one of a generation for whom science offered an escape from the religious madness that had turned the world upside down. The English Civil War is thought to have been proportionately more murderous of Britons than World War I and, unlike Britain's modern conflicts, was fought on home ground, with families divided, every town and county forced to take sides and terrible battles fought on fields with eerily ordinary English names – Edgehill, Bristol, Naseby.

It is hardly surprising that some of Britain's best minds turned from arguing religious dogma to exploring 'natural philosophy'. The empirical pursuit of reality that Galileo had made the heart and soul of science offered an escape from the mental prisons of the fanatics.

Nobody has ever called Charles II a fanatic. In his long exile the son of a beheaded king had become louche and pleasure-loving. The new court he established in 1660 was immediately observed to include royal mistresses and unconcealed amours. Even Pepys, who was not exactly prudish when it came to extramarital sex, was surprised by some of the things he saw. Yet this libertine ethos mirrored the mood of a nation that had been bossed about by the Godly too many times. Restoration hedonism was not mere self-indulgence. It was a rebellion against the devout folly of the Cromwellian years. In this it resembled the new science. Libertine lust and scientific research shared a preference for the facts of life over the cant of religion – and Charles II took an interest in both.

The new mood is presaged in a painting done in the immediate aftermath of the war, when the Godly unquestionably dominated a stunned society. In the early 1650s Peter Lely painted *Nymphs by a Fountain*. a party of sleeping, aristocratic-looking women who drape themselves naked around a fountain somewhere in England, in what seems to be a country park, far from prying Puritan eyes. Lely, a Dutch artist who had come to Britain on the eve of the Civil War, shows a cavalier disregard for religious scruples in this determinedly sensual, secret-seeming study of nude flesh. Lely bought a nude statue of Venus from the sale of the royal art collection. After the Restoration he proved the ideal court artist for Charles II, bringing his own sensuality to portraits of the royal mistresses Barbara Villiers, Countess of Castlemaine, and a naked Nell Gwyn.

Yet the drawings Wren showed Charles II in early 1661 were a great deal less expected than portraits – even nude portraits. They revealed a world nobody had ever seen before. Astronomy, it seemed, was not this whizz kid's only subject. Instead of turning his 'optic glass' on the moon like Galileo, he had made a microscope and used it to examine some of the tiny animals that lived not just around but on everyone in the seventeenth century.

For Wren's drawings recorded massively magnified images of insects, including a flea and a louse.

The king was impressed by Wren's gift, but perhaps careless with it too, for these drawings do not survive. The flea he gave the king

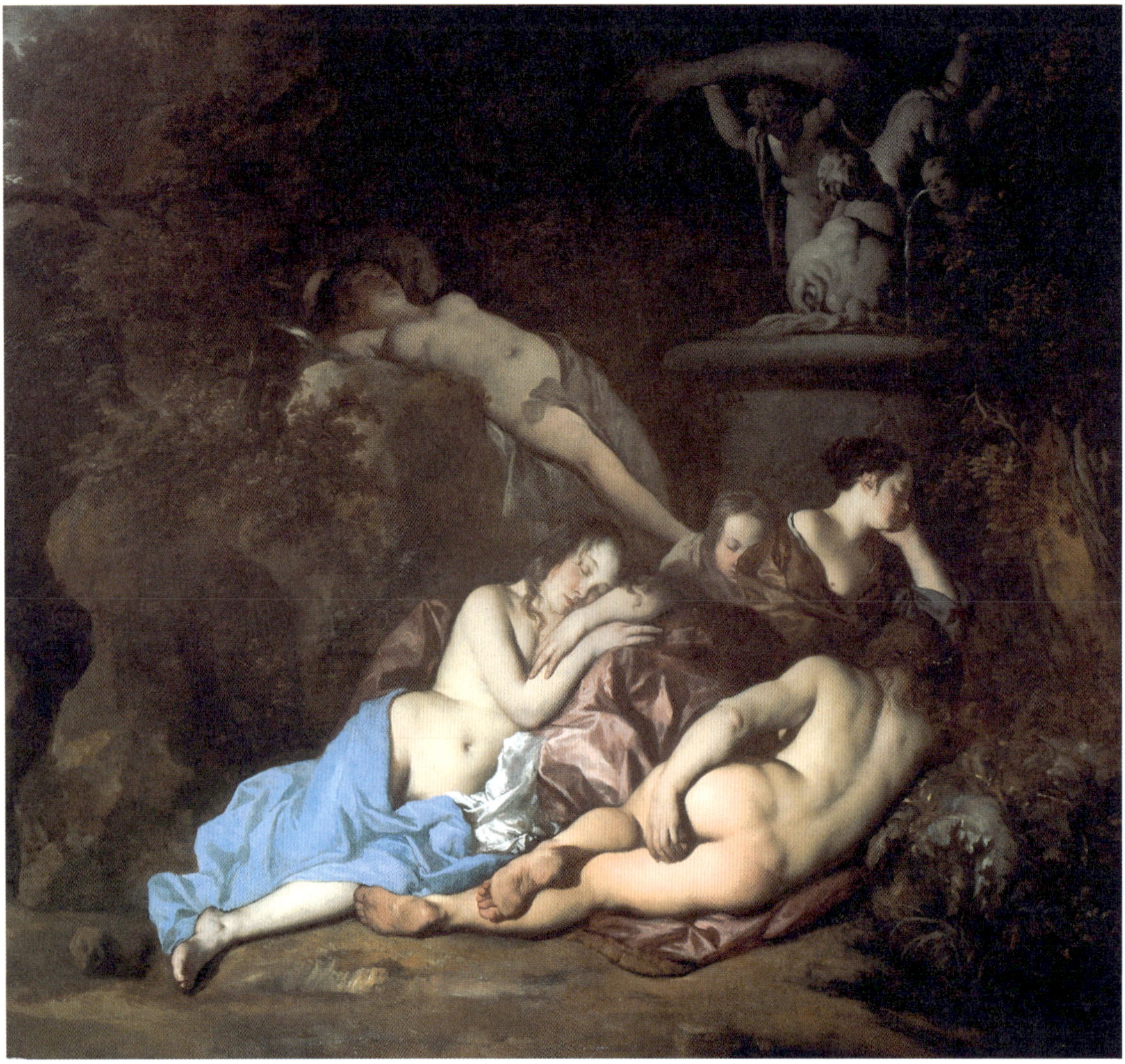

and its tiny brethren were, however, to experience a ghostly artistic afterlife.

It was the second day of January, 1665, and Pepys had already enjoyed a full morning. Despite the severe frost, he dallied with his servant, then 'did sport a good while' with a young woman at the Swan Inn, before going to the house of one Mrs Martin where he enjoyed himself 'very freely'. After a lunchtime banquet, he popped into his bookseller where copies of a spectacular new work were being bound, 'which is so pretty that I presently bespoke it'.

↑ Peter Lely, *Nymphs by a Fountain*, early 1650s, oil on canvas, 128.5 × 144.6 cm (50 ⅝ × 57 in.), Dulwich Picture Gallery

The book was a treatise by Robert Hooke, curator of experiments at the recently founded Royal Society, about a dazzling new invention called the microscope. Yet it was not the book's text that initially entranced Pepys, who, although he was soon to join the Royal Society and would eventually become its president, confessed that he found some of the scientific detail in lectures hard to follow. The reason he fell in love at first sight with 'Hookes book of the Microscope' was that it was a gorgeous visual artefact – a 'pretty' science book that he enjoyed as if it were a work of art.

The strange beauty that struck Pepys is still arresting today. Acutely drawn, faithfully engraved images burst unexpectedly from the pages of *Micrographia*, as Hooke named his book. A freakishly large ant seems to crawl across a page. A pair of compound eyes glare out at you. The two most startling pictures, of a louse and a flea, are printed on large fold-out sheets. These grotesquely detailed marvels of nature escape the book's confines in their unfolded monstrosity.

Seen through the microscope, these tiny animals, barely differentiated to the naked eye, display formidable armour plating, articulated limbs and fierce faces. The flea has hard spiky hairs on its smoothly segmented exoskeleton. Horrible hooks extend from its legs. Its eye is cruel – a rare moment of anthropomorphic sentiment in images that aim at complete objectivity. These are not fanciful pictures of dragons or sea monsters. They are patient renditions of real creatures revealed in all their alienness by the power of lenses. These 'monsters' are natural and this is exactly what they look like. As the louse lies on its back, holding a twig, it casts a shadow beneath it, indicating how light and its laws have exposed these wonders.

On 20 January Pepys returned to the bookseller and 'took home Hooke's book of microscopy, a most excellent piece, and of which I am very proud'. Later that same day he bought a hare, because he had been told the hare's-foot charm that he carried against sickness was inadequate. It needed the ankle joint in order to work. The world into which Hooke's *Micrographia* was published lacked antibiotics, or even a concept of bacterial infection. It also lacked any source of power greater than windmills and water, or any way of getting about that was faster than a horse. Magical charms like a hare's foot were taken seriously in this world where modern science and technology did not exist, except as the dream of a few intellectuals.

As Pepys sat down to enjoy his luxury volume of cutting-edge science – 'I sat up till 2 a-clock in my chamber, reading of Mr Hooke's

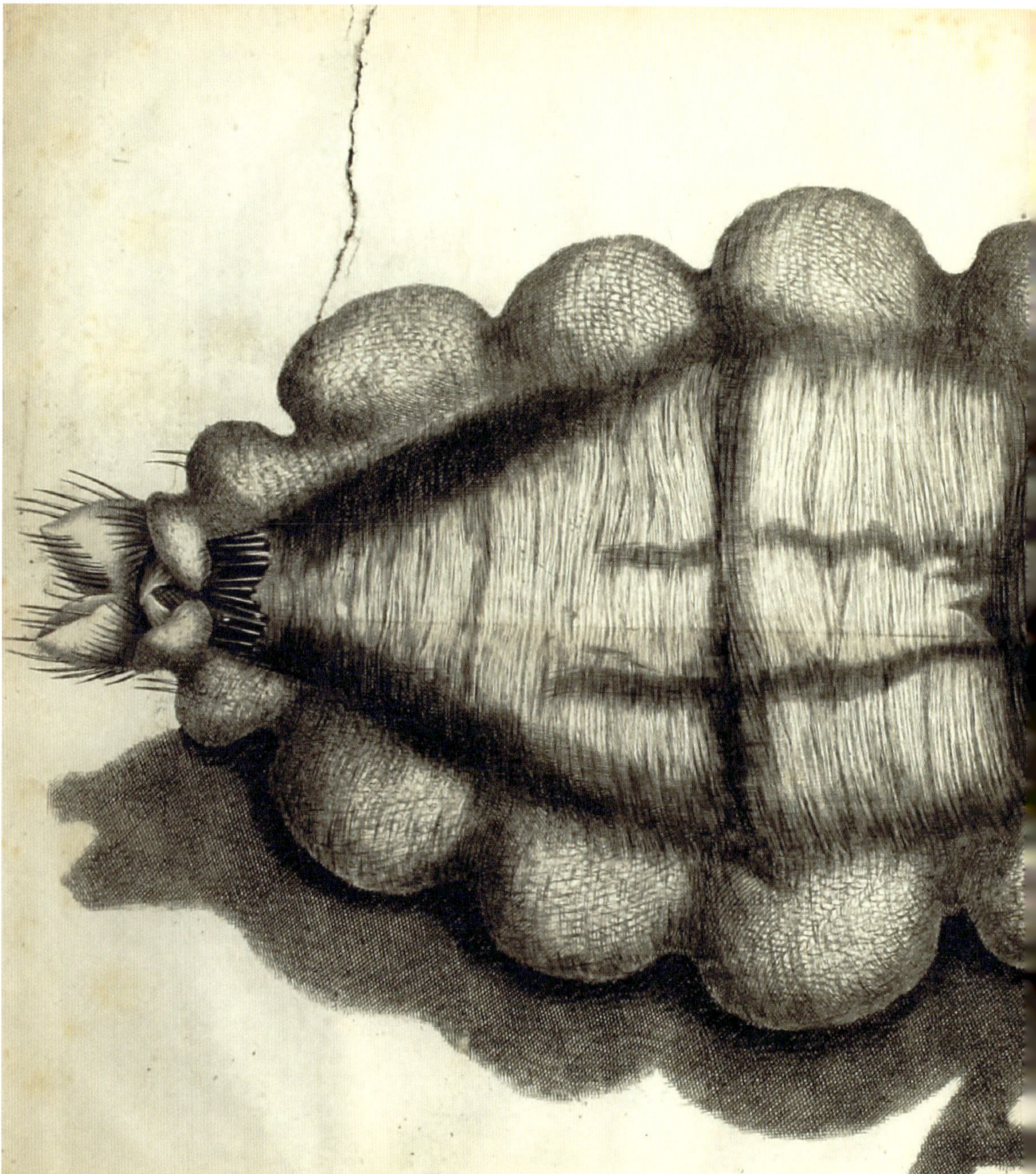

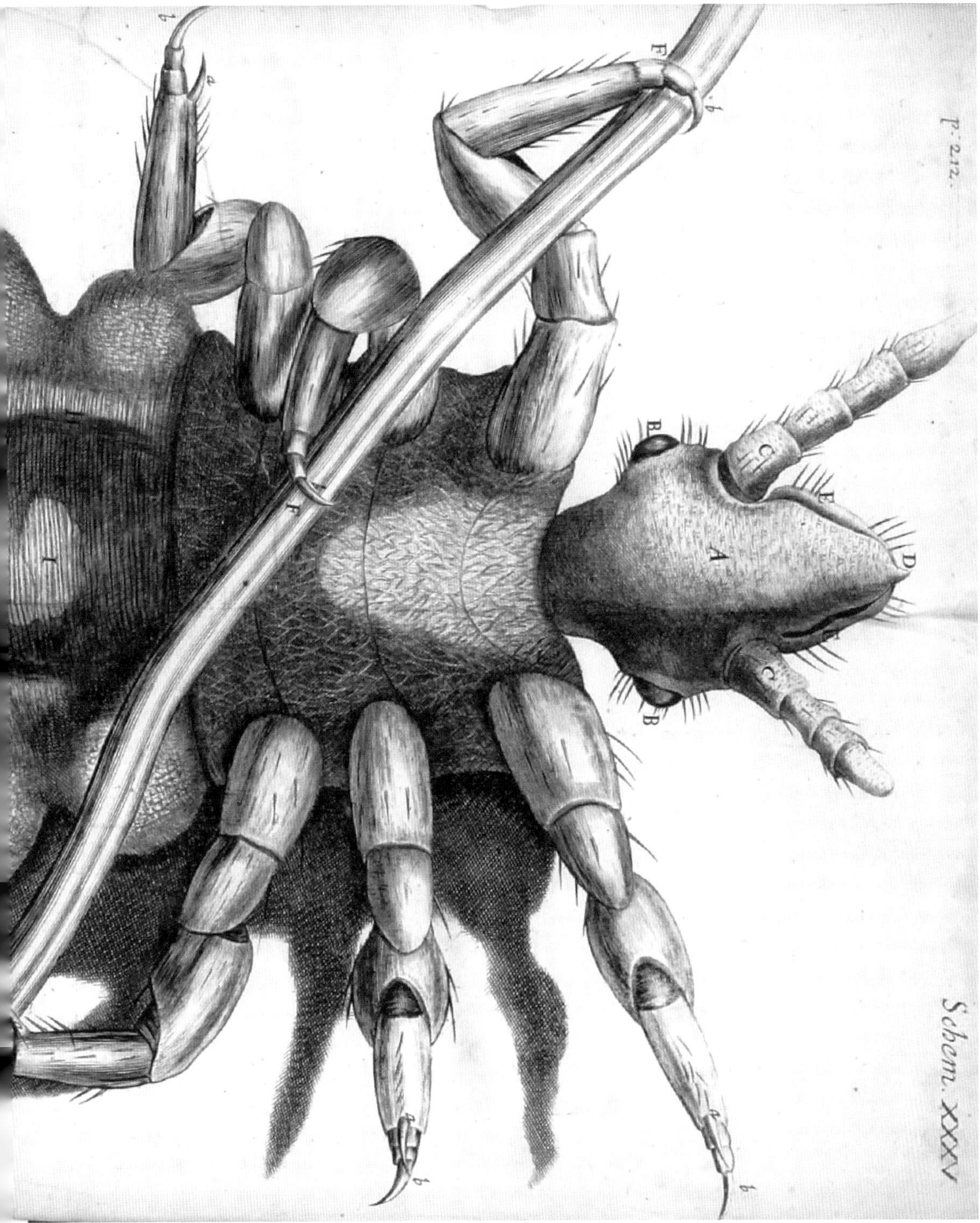

↑ Robert Hooke, *The Louse,* from *Micrographia*, 1665, Duke University Libraries, Durham, NC (QH271 .H66 1667 4to c.1)

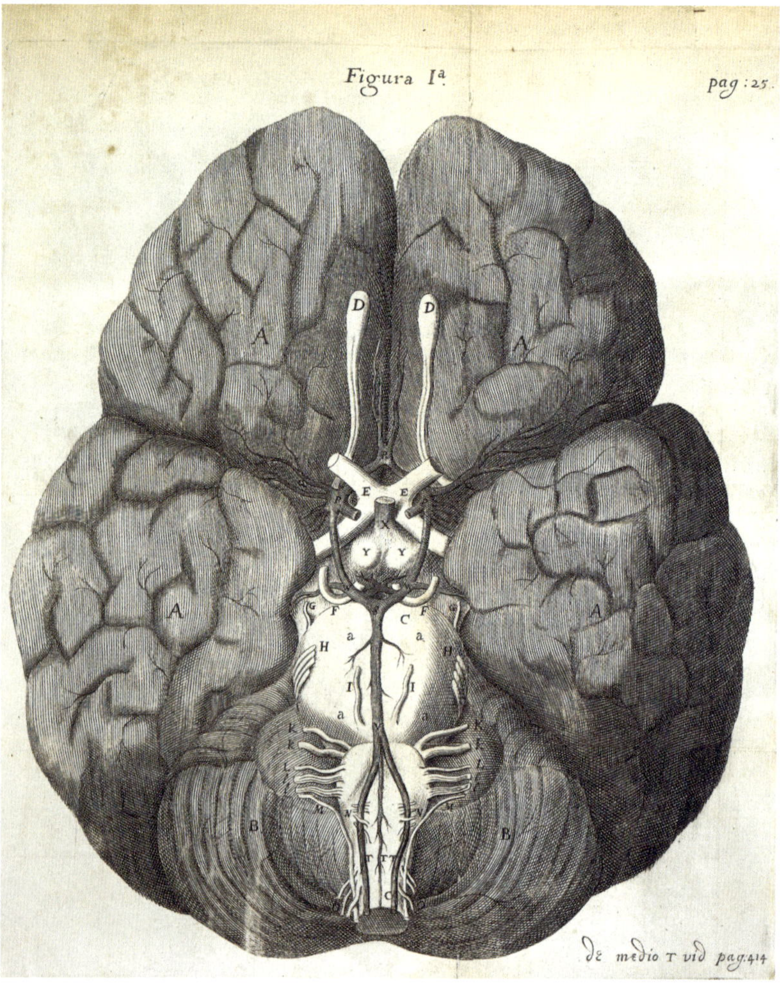

← Christopher Wren, *The Human Brain*, illustration to *The Anatomy of the Brain* by Thomas Willis, 1664, engraving, Wellcome Library, London

Microscopical Observations, the most ingenious book that ever I read in my life,' he writes for 21 January – nature was preparing one of its regular reminders that human beings have no real power over their fate. For 1665 was a plague year. The frosts that made the streets slippy in January were a boon, killing off microbes. It was the hot summer that would see tens of thousands die as the bills of mortality inexorably rose through June, July and August. Houses had crosses painted on them to show the inhabitants were shut inside to die. No one had any means of understanding that so much suffering was due to an organism even smaller than the creatures Hooke saw in his microscope.

Hooke pays tribute in *Micrographia* to his friend and fellow scientist Christopher Wren, to whom he credits the first triumphant use of a microscope to draw insects. It is impossible to know exactly how similar the now-lost drawings Wren gave to Charles II were to the wondrous illustrations in *Micrographia*. It may even be that Wren provided Hooke's illustrations – although a surviving scientific drawing by him of a human brain is not as precise or as beautiful as the flea and the louse in Hooke's masterpiece.

What is impossible to miss – it glares at us like a compound eye seen in a microscope – is that something new, original, astounding is happening here. Wren showing his insect drawings to the king, Hooke publishing *Micrographia*, and Pepys staying up all night to study it – all are caught up in a revolution. The scientific revolution, of course. Yet also a revolution in British art. This moment in the early 1660s when the 'virtuosi' of the fledgling Royal Society are poring over the new visions of nature that their painstakingly constructed instruments reveal and recording those images in brilliant drawings and engravings is literally the first time Britain shows the world something new. British art suddenly comes to life, leaps off Hooke's workbench, and buzzes out of the window to begin its living history.

The Eyes of Reason

The network of experimenters who exchanged ideas and observations at Gresham College (the newly formed educational establishment in London) and at Oxford University during the Commonwealth, and formed themselves into a society following a lecture by Wren in 1660, becoming the Royal Society three years later, put more credence in their eyes than their ears. The Royal Society's motto, 'Nullius in verba' – accept nobody's word for anything – says as much. The new science exemplified by Galileo and theorized by the far-seeing English Renaissance thinker Francis Bacon refused to trust ancient textbooks or accept venerable orthodoxies preached in endless, worthless words. Don't tell me, demanded the seventeenth-century scientific avant-garde – show me.

In Britain, where the art-hating Reformation had so long held the word sacred and the image suspect, and where Shakespeare, Marlowe, Spenser, Donne, Milton and the King James Bible all made it seem that verbal expression was the true national talent, this was a revolutionary reorientation from reading to looking, a revelation of the power of the eye.

Experiments were stirring, visual events and the virtuosi loved to gawp at them. A particular favourite was the experiment with the air pump. Joseph Wright of Derby was to portray an audience fascinated and appalled by this experiment in one of Britain's greatest paintings (page 123). Yet it was more than a century old by then. The first air pump, or vacuum chamber, was constructed at Oxford in the 1650s, during Cromwell's Protectorate, by Hooke and his employer Robert Boyle. This pioneering scientist best known today for discovering Boyle's Law – which states that the pressure on a gas will increase proportionately to a decrease in its volume – was the son of a stupendously wealthy landowner in Ireland. He used his income to pursue a preoccupation with scientific knowledge among Oxford's investigative community, employing the dexterous Hooke as an assistant. The pump they made could remove most of the air from a glass chamber. The best way to see the effect was to put an animal inside – and this produced experiments guaranteed to shock and amaze.

In Wright's painting, a beautiful white cockatoo is being deprived of air. The Royal Society in the 1660s, however, did not leave it at one kind of animal. They gathered to see an impressive range of creatures killed or nearly killed in the vacuum chamber. The diarist John Evelyn records a varied show on 25 April 1661:

> *I went to the Society where were divers Experiments in Mr Boyls Pneumatique Engine. We put in a Snake but could not kill it, by exhausting the aire, only make it extremely sick, but the chick died of Convulsions out right, in a short space.*

It sounds more art than science – experiment as a morbid piece of theatre – and Evelyn's diary is full of such sensations. This founder member of the Royal Society goes to Southwark Fair and ogles 'a monstrous birth of Twinns, both female and most perfectly shaped, save that they were joyn'd breast to breast, and incorporated at the navil, having their arms throwne about each other thus', and Evelyn provides a sketch of the dead conjoined twins preserved in a mutual embrace. At the same fair he sees a 'deformed' living child, and dancing apes, and acrobats. Many of his diary entries are records of things seen. He is all eyes. At the College of Physicians he looks at bones and a preserved fish. Back at the Society, he sees:

> *... a Bird of Paradise or Manucodiata, that had both large wings and feete, confuting the vulgar error: Also two death-Watches as those Insects are cald... Also 2 puppies, no bigger than the top of ons fingers, perfectly shaped both within and without: which were preserved in Spirit of Wine.*

Some relics of this age of curiosity survive. In Padua, renowned for its advanced medicine, in 1646 Evelyn purchased four 'anatomical tables' that can still be seen in London's Hunterian Museum. The nerves, arteries and veins have been removed from a real human body and glued to wooden boards to create these carnal diagrams. The stained wood has a blood-like hue.

It might seem as if early science was almost too addicted to looking. Was anything really being discovered by these connoisseurs of marvels? Another wonder that Wren showed the king was a model he had made of the moon, mapping its surface. It was said to be extremely detailed and difficult to make, but was it a real aid to knowledge or an awe-inspiring scientific sculpture? When Charles II gave the go-ahead to build a Royal Observatory in 1675 it promised even more opportunities for natural philosophers and their fellow travellers to peer into telescopes, before heading off for convivial drunken dinners.

Yet work really was being done. The sociable entertainment and philosophical voyeurism was not shallow at all. Hooke's *Micrographia* not only opened new perspectives on the natural world but also put forward ideas on the nature of light itself. Meanwhile in Cambridge, a lonely, formidable genius was grinding lenses and even inserting a 'bodkine' behind his own eyeball to understand light and perception more fully.

Isaac Newton carried out his eye-popping experiment with a needle in the winter of 1663–64, as he records in his notes accompanied by a diagram:

> *I took a bodkine ... put it betwixt my eye [and the] bone as near [the] backside of my eye as I could ... there appeared severall white darke [and] coloured circles...*

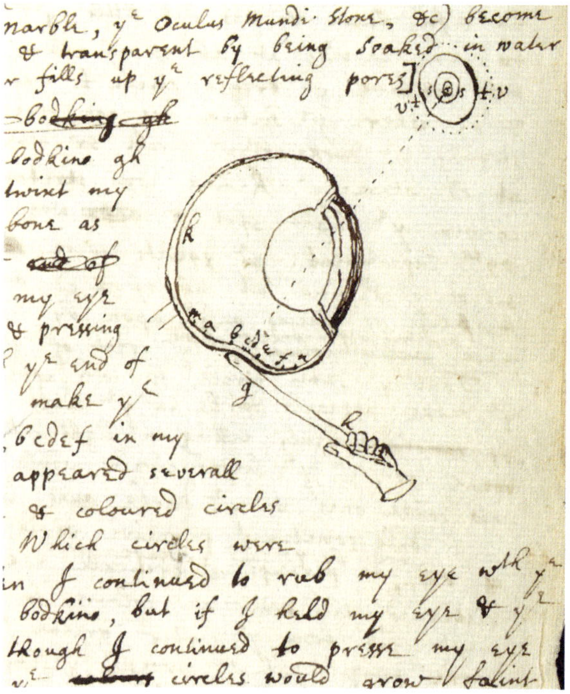

↑ Isaac Newton, diagram of the experiment with a bodkin on his eyeball, page from laboratory notebook, c. 1669–93, Newton manuscripts, Cambridge University Library

This experiment touched (quite literally) on the psychology and physiology of perception, for Newton saw colours produced in his own eye and mind. He was testing reality just like the more sociable London crowd, but his experiments were private, even secretive. There was another difference too. While Boyle, Hooke and Wren were making important progress in establishing the scientific method, it was Newton, in his vast mental palace that nobody else was invited to enter, who progressed through empirical observation to a grand theory of the physical universe.

Newton went far beyond Galileo or Copernicus. He redesigned heaven and earth, conceiving natural laws so fundamental that they structured all physics up to the late nineteenth century, and even in the twentieth were still useful enough to get astronauts to the moon and back. His discoveries begin with the simplest experiments and observations about phenomena we all experience – studying rays of sunlight that pierce a darkened room or even, in legend, an apple falling from a tree – and advance laws that reveal a grand order behind these everyday occurrences. It is not hard to make a glass prism project the colour spectrum on a wall. Newton's genius was to explain it. He could not achieve this by empirical observation alone. He was a gifted mathematician, so gifted that he invented calculus to advance his thoughts, and then, because he was not ready to share it, did the sums all over again in a more traditional way. Think about that: Newton had to fake having a more conventional mind simply to communicate with his cleverest contemporaries. That is why the historical fashion for claiming that the Newtonian revolution owes just as much to others, especially Hooke, is misguided.

Newton's laws of motion and gravity and his analysis of light established science as we know it. When members of the Royal Society crowded around to see a snake writhing in an airless jar or a pickled foetus they were displaying a curiosity somewhere between scientific enquiry and wonder. The word 'science' was not even the one they used for their endeavours – they were 'natural philosophers'. Newton, just as much as Evelyn or Pepys, inhabited a world still shaped by what later scientists would call superstition. Famously, he took a keen interest in alchemy. Yet Newton's laws immediately transformed science from a brave experiment into a new way of understanding everything that exists. Nature was no longer an incomprehensible mystery. Newton showed that it had laws capable of being rationally discovered.

In August 1684 the astronomer Edmond Halley – another of the Royal Society's leading lights – visited Newton in Cambridge to ask him a question. Halley, Hooke and Wren had been arguing about the way planets move. If an inverse-square law of gravity governs the planets in their courses around the sun, how can their orbits be conceived? It was complicated stuff and they all, including Wren, claimed to have the best and earliest grasp of it without actually providing an answer.

Halley made the journey from London to East Anglia to ask Newton. The enigmatic philosopher said he had long ago calculated that the planets orbit the sun not in circles but ellipses. He promised to write explaining the maths.

The eventual result was Newton's book the *Principia*, his comprehensive masterpiece of physics, published by the Royal Society in 1687. Together with his *Opticks*, which took until 1704 to appear, it established Newton as much more than the genius of the age. His affirmative and inspiring vision of a cosmos that can be understood, and laws that make nature predictable, gave birth, not only in Britain but throughout Europe, to an age of reason: a veritable Enlightenment.

The Cupola

It is remarkable that Christopher Wren even had time to chat about the movement of the planets in the summer of 1684, for he was engaged on a colossal work of his own. While Newton fathomed the cosmos, Wren was building a model of it in stone.

Wren was seen by his contemporaries as a new Leonardo da Vinci, a polymath who moved freely between art and science. Perhaps he was conscious of the comparison. As we have seen, it was in the seventeenth century that many of Leonardo's notes and drawings came to Britain. There was something reminiscent of the Renaissance genius who delighted courts with his ingenuity about the way Wren presented his drawings of insects to Charles II. Why distribute them in this way, instead of publishing them as Hooke did? It sold Wren as a man of genius, a multifaceted mind at the king's service.

If Wren did aspire to be seen by Charles as a Renaissance man, the stratagem worked. He soon had to find an excuse – he claimed to be ill – when Charles offered him the exciting, honourable but extremely risky job of creating fortifications for the British colonial enclave of Tangiers in North Africa. Instead he cut his teeth as an architect designing ingenious buildings for the more congenial climates of Oxford and Cambridge. When disaster struck London in 1666, he was poised to be the man of the hour.

Wren might have rebuilt St Paul's even if that spark in Pudding Lane had not ignited the timbers and straw of London's vulnerable old buildings on the night of 2 September 1666. The Gothic cathedral that soared above the capital's narrow overhung streets had been falling apart for a long time. An attempt by Inigo Jones to modernize it by adding a classical portico had done nothing to save the structure. The tower had to come down before it fell down. On 27 August 1666 John Evelyn was on the committee that went along to survey the ramshackle church. He and 'Dr Wren' mocked sentimentalists among the company who tried to argue that its visibly warping stonework was a deliberate perspectival effect and claimed the steeple was still viable:

> *... we totally rejected it and persisted that it required new foundation, not onely in reguard of the necessitie, but for that the shape of what stood was very meane, and we had a minde to build it with a noble Cupola, a forme of church building, not yet known in England, but of wonderful grace...*

There was no nostalgia for old England here. The Gothic beauties of medieval Britain held no sway whatsoever over the men from the Royal Society. Wren and Evelyn dismissed the venerable time-hallowed architecture of old St Paul's as 'very meane'. They wanted to replace its dreary old steeple with something never seen in Britain before – a 'cupola', a dome.

Evelyn's use of the Italian word reflects the fact that he had seen domes in Italy. Wren had never been as far, but he had seen domes in Paris in 1665. Once again Britain was trying to catch up with the culture of the Continent – but it would result in something as native as it was universal.

The fire that struck London just a few days after he and Evelyn argued the case for a new domed St Paul's meant that Wren would not only build his cupola but become the prime architect of a new London. Hooke also turned architect and urban planner to take on the immense task of rebuilding the capital, designing among other structures the Monument to the Great Fire, perhaps with Wren's collaboration.

It was to take decades to rebuild the new St Paul's. The idea of a dome was a given, but Wren submitted many designs over many years for its construction and how it would relate to the body of the church. His drawings propose everything from a vast hemisphere to a small dome with a steeple on top. Unlike Michelangelo, who had died before the completion of his dome on St Peter's and so could not stop it being altered from his original vision, Sir Christopher Wren saw the creation of his masterpiece right through into the eighteenth century. The dome of St Paul's is Wren's glory. It is also Newton's, for this is the scientific revolution preserved in stone.

The reason domes have such 'wonderful grace', as Evelyn put it, is that they resemble the heavens. Uniquely among architectural forms, a dome resembles the sky's canopy as we see it from Earth. That is why if you visit a planetarium, you will find yourself gazing up at a dome with stars, nebulae and planets projected onto it. In Florence, where the defining dome of the Renaissance was built by Brunelleschi, another fifteenth-century dome by him in the Old Sacristy of San Lorenzo, somewhat smaller than his famous one for Florence's cathedral, is painted with the constellations in the night sky. The astronomer Dr Wren could hardly have failed to be aware of this. His dome was the perfect monument to the early days of the Royal Society, to all those nights looking through telescopes, those arguments in the upper rooms of inns about gravitation, optics and star catalogues, that age of coffee houses and comets. The vision of the sky it creates is a calm and grand statement about the cosmos and our place in it.

Look up from the floor of St Peter's basilica into the confounding immensity of Michelangelo's dome and your sense of logic melts. The sublime image of heaven created by its majestic architecture is too vast for the mind to penetrate. It is a mystery that passeth all understanding.

The dome of St Paul's is astonishing too, but its proportions are more human. It is for one thing considerably smaller on the inside

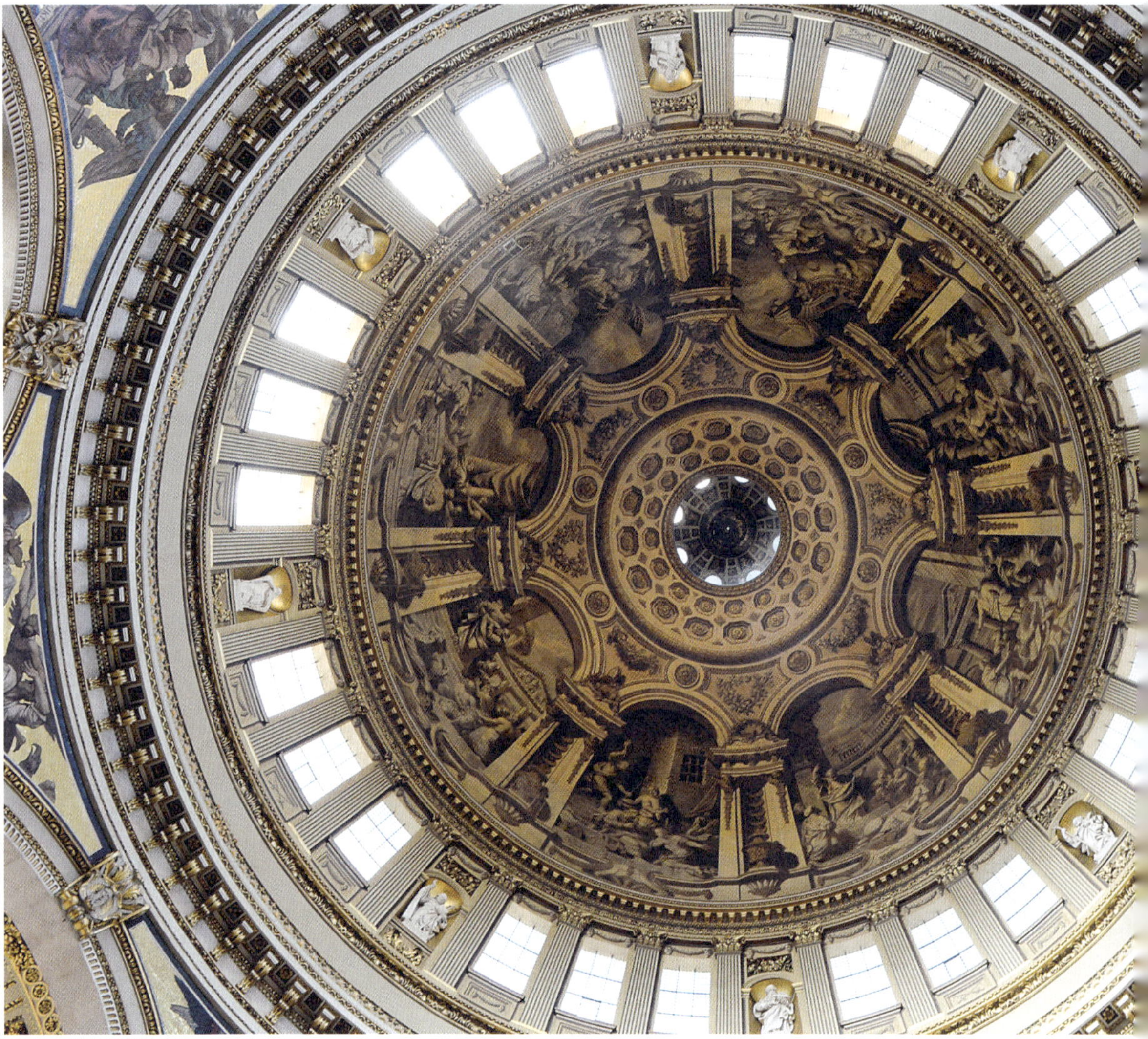

↑ Sir James Thornhill, *Eight Scenes of the Life of St Paul*, 1715–17, grisaille mural on the interior of the dome, St Paul's Cathedral, London

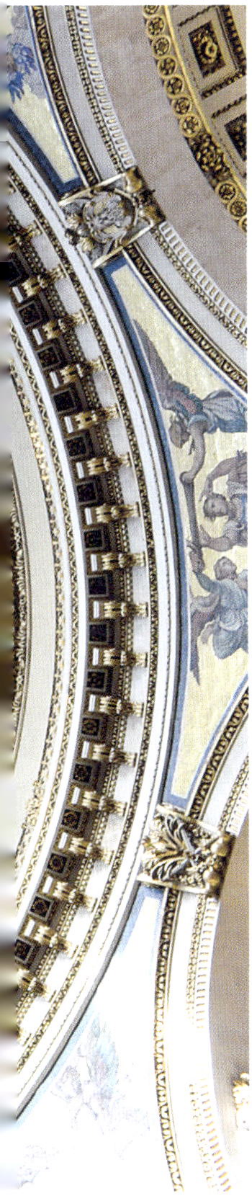

than the outside. Wren built a miniature dome inside his larger one, which helps to make its grandeur more accessible to the light of reason. That light floods in. Looking up from below, the light that reaches you is primarily not that of the distant lantern in the building's heights but even, calm sunshine coming through very tall rectangular windows in the circular drum that supports the dome itself. In other words, it is not a miraculous beam direct from God: it is the prosaic light of nature. Wren's architecture – of which those big windows are a recurring trait, seen too at the Royal Observatory – makes you more aware of the light of nature that is everywhere around us.

For Wren as for Newton the cosmos is of course the work of God, but the laws of science – revealed by Newton to possess a startling explanatory power – reveal a nature that God has left to work without any need for supernatural intervention, as efficiently as a clock that has been properly wound up. That is the vision of the universe and humanity's place in it that Wren put in London's sky. It is a happy vision, because it says we can solve every problem with reason. That confidence in a universe governed by Newton's laws shines from the heights of St Paul's. To this day it makes a glimpse of the Royal Society's great artistic gift to the future on the London skyline a moment of contentment and optimism.

Wren wanted his dome decorated with mosaics, but in 1715, unpopular with a new monarch, he was overruled and a painter was given the hair-raising but noble task of decorating the inside of the cupola. In yet another novelty of a revolutionary age, this painter was British. His name was James Thornhill.

Hogarth really did marry upward.

2. The Real Thing

Sweepings from butchers' stalls, dung, guts, and blood,
Drown'd puppies, stinking sprats, all drench'd in mud,
Dead cats, and turnip-tops, come tumbling down the flood.
Jonathan Swift 'A Description of a City Shower', 1710

The Walls of Newgate

He looks pathetically young to be sitting in a death cell; his hair cropped short, his face almost adolescent, he is preparing for his inevitable fate, knowing he will not escape this time. All of a sudden the hero of the London crowd shows the vulnerability of his 22 years.

His life was an adventure story squeezed into a microscopic moment. For a few short months in 1724 the bold burglar and thief Jack Sheppard led the authorities a merry dance through the alleys and hideouts of the capital. Every time he was caught and thrown in prison, he managed to escape: four vanishing acts all told, each more theatrical than the last, with an ever-growing audience delighted by his death-defying feats. And they really were death-defying, for he faced the noose. Finally, like a parody of Christ, he let himself be taken after going on a final drunken progress through the city, dressed in stolen finery, flaunting diamond and carnelian rings. This time he was heavily chained and shackled to secure him in the most formidable cell in Newgate.

You can see those chains in the portrait Sir James Thornhill drew from life during Sheppard's final time on this earth. The king's painter bribed Sheppard's guards for access to the celebrity criminal as he awaited execution in November 1724. It was more than worth the shilling and sixpence. From Thornhill's gentle and sympathetic sketch

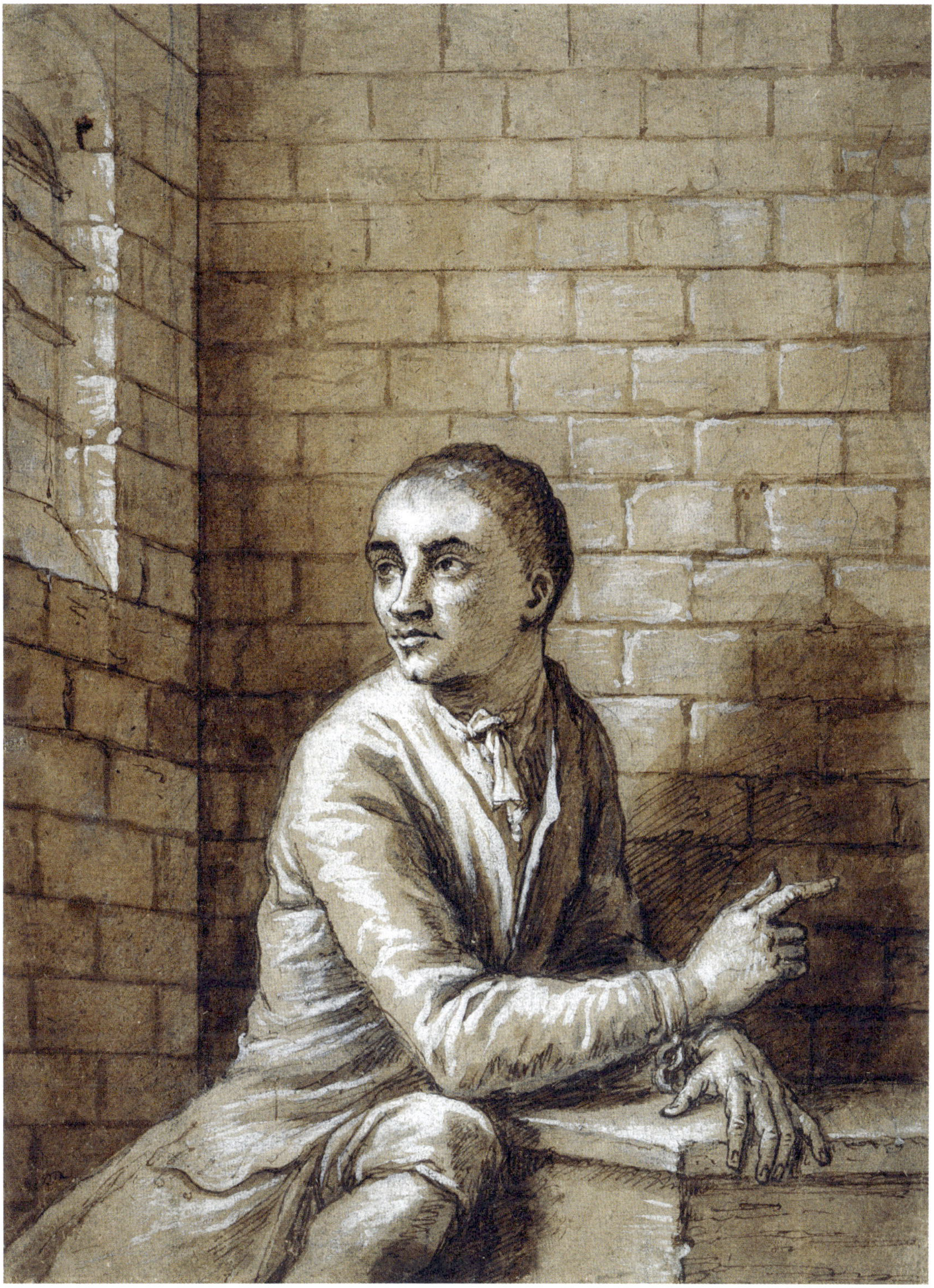

↑ Sir James Thornhill (attrib.), *Jack Sheppard in Newgate*, 1724, ink and wash drawing with white highlights, 33.6 x 25.2 cm (13¼ x 10 in.), Museum of London

the engraver George White created a bestselling printed image whose sombre shadows emphasize the sadness and waste of a young life cut short. For all his dedication to crime the Jack Sheppard that Thornhill preserves looks like a promising character who could have done more, could have put his courage and intelligence to better use. Why not enroll him in the army? Instead he was hanged at Tyburn. His image lived on, pinned up in the coffee shops and inns of a city in mourning for his criminal good looks.

The London that made an icon of Jack Sheppard was not the elegant paradise you might have thought from standing on Greenwich hill with a spyglass, contemplating the lofty dome of St Paul's and the spires of the new churches built by Wren and Nicholas Hawksmoor. Below these brilliant images of cosmic order, the labyrinthine streets, the gambling dens and brothels, the pubs and stinking overstuffed graveyards of the capital had less to do with heavenly calculus than with human chaos. London became the biggest city in the Western world in the 1690s. With a population of 600,000 and growing, it was a new kind of metropolis, its commerce and consumerism unprecedented, its people infinitely various, turbulent, individualist, violent, fashion-conscious, witty, cruel and loud. The appeal and excitement of this precocious modern city can be measured by the fact that it achieved its population growth even though every year, more people died than were born in London. The expansion was due to migrants pouring into the capital from all over Britain. They came from other places too – Huguenots from France, black people from slave colonies or directly from Africa. Britain was becoming a global power and building a world empire. The age of Newton was the age of expansion. At the heart of this imperial Britain was a 'monster city' that nurtured a new kind of art.

London had to be seen to be believed. It was a sinister fairground full of marvels. If the scientific revolution taught the British to look, London gave them plenty to look at.

James Thornhill was far from the only artist or writer to see the fascination of Jack Sheppard. The journalist, novelist and spy Daniel Defoe wrote up his adventures, and may even have been involved in a plot to free him. Yet the most brilliant and successful attempt to cash in on Sheppard appeared in 1728. *The Beggar's Opera* is a subversive confrontation of high art and low life, a punk musical in which traditional ballads are given provocative new words – 'Our Polly is a sad slut,' sing the heroine's parents – and the criminal underworld of London is presented as if it were the norm. John Gay, who also wrote libretti for 'real' operas, including Handel's *Acis* and *Galatea*, created a comedy so uneasily modern that in the twentieth century it could be adapted by Bertolt Brecht and Kurt Weill as *The Threepenny Opera* without really changing it at all. The hero of *The Beggar's Opera* is Captain Macheath, a dashing highwayman with multiple wives and a knack for escaping the noose. He is manifestly modelled on Jack Sheppard. The relationship between Macheath and the thief-taker Peachum, who betrays him to the law, parodies that between Sheppard and the two-faced crime boss Jonathan Wild. The analogies between art and real life do not end there.

In a series of paintings of the play in performance that were done between 1728 and 1731, the world itself is exposed as a ludicrous theatre. The players on stage are hard to tell apart from the wealthiest members of the audience, for in the early eighteenth century the great

↓ William Hogarth, A Scene from *The Beggar's Opera, VI*, 1731, oil on canvas, 57.2 × 76.2 cm (22½ × 30 in.), Tate

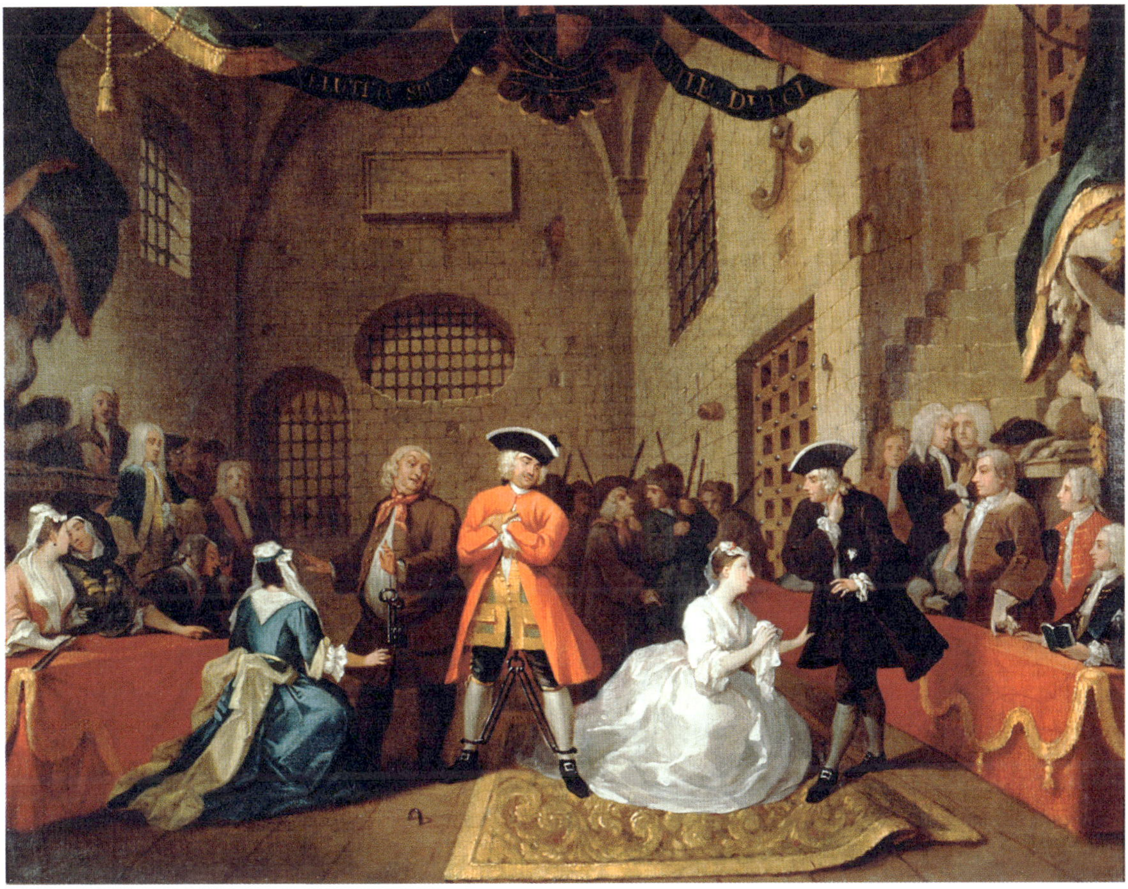

could purchase seats on the sides of the stage. Redcoated Macheath and pleading Polly in her white dress thus perform their parts cheek by jowl with top people who seem confident they are the real stars. Art and life merge. In their wigs and courtly clothes, whispering to one another conspiratorially, conscious of how they look and of their place in the world, the 'real' people are all consummate actors. Their relationship with the play is far from disinterested. John Gay himself is in the audience, chatting with the theatre entrepreneur John Rich. In the version of the painting that belongs to Tate, the race-horse breeder Sir Robert Fagg stands in amorous contemplation of Polly. Lavinia Fenton, who played her, attracted many admirers and ended up marrying a duke.

None of the audience appears aware that looming over them are the walls of Newgate, with heavy chains and manacles hanging from massive stones. This is the painted set of the opera's final act, yet it looks uneasily real and embraces audience as well as actors, fact as well as fiction. The whole of society seems to have been incarcerated, like poor Jack Sheppard, awaiting execution.

It was of course Thornhill's gifted son-in-law who milked the popularity of *The Beggar's Opera* by painting no less than four canvases of it, in which potential buyers could see themselves as part of the action. For if Thornhill recognized the potential of London as a subject, it took William Hogarth to dive into its low life and resurface with great art. In an age of science he invented a new kind of truth-telling. His art is a lens magnifying every pore of the world's skin.

The Palaces of Britannia

Thornhill's simple sketch of Jack Sheppard is a tiny thing compared with the vast paintings that made him rich and eminent. He literally got paid by the yard for decorating walls, domes and ceilings, not just in St Paul's but in a constellation of starry new structures that rose up in the wake of Wren's achievement. This was a golden age of British building, and the British school in painting started out as architecture's handmaiden. The great English houses of this period are so extravagant they make the cosy term 'stately home' seem inadequate. The scale of Blenheim Palace in Oxfordshire is truly stupefying. Designed by Sir John Vanbrugh and built between the 1700s and 1720s, it is a Baroque behemoth whose titanic columns, epic façades, mighty towers and flamelike pinnacles create a daunting sense of power and glory. Inside its lofty entrance hall floats Thornhill's vertigo-inducing ceiling starring the goddess Britannia. Her helmet, shield and spear make explicit the overwhelming meaning of Blenheim itself – welcome to Great Britain.

In 1688 the rule of the Stuart dynasty was overthrown in one of the most bloodless yet epoch-making revolutions in world history. Keen patrons of science they might be, but Charles II and his brother James, who succeeded him in 1685, were also wedded to the mystical sensuality of the Catholic faith. When James II actively tried to defend and promote Catholicism in Britain, an alliance of political grandees who had already started to be called 'Whigs' (their devoutly Royalist enemies were Tories) invited the Dutch Protestant William of Orange – husband of James's daughter, Mary – to enter Britain and accept the crown. James fled and his last stand in Ireland was crushed by William at the Battle of the Boyne in 1690. This final victory for the Parliamentary and Protestant cause in its struggle against the arrogant Stuarts redefined Britain as a country ruled by 'the king in Parliament'. The Bill of Rights was passed and a British monarch would never again try to rule absolutely. Ministerial governments reporting to Parliament were the future.

The new science shaped this revolution. The intellectual voice of 1688 was that of John Locke, a radical thinker whose Whig beliefs forced him to live in exile until James was overthrown. He returned equipped with two books that were to turn the rational thinking of Newton and the Royal Society into a political and philosophical creed. Locke's *Second Treatise on Government*, published in 1689, argues that in the state of nature we are free and equal, so the only legitimate basis for government is consent. Meanwhile in his philosophical masterpiece *An Essay Concerning Human Understanding*, published in the same year, he says with false modesty that because he cannot rival such great scientists of his time as Robert Boyle, Christiaan Huygens and 'the incomparable Mr Newton... 'tis ambition enough to be employ'd as an under-labourer in clearing ground a little, and removing some of the rubbish that lies in the way to knowledge', which he does by philosophically clarifying and justifying the Royal Society's belief that empirical evidence alone is worth anything.

Newton, Locke and the 'revolution principles' of 1688 became the totemic holy trinity of the European Enlightenment. Throughout the eighteenth century the self-consciously 'Enlightened' from Paris to

St Petersburg would see Newton and Locke as the twin founders of a new age of reason. Britain itself was hailed as the most Enlightened of nations, a place happy in its constitution, science and prosperity.

Whig landowners who revered Locke dominated British politics from 1688 until the era of the French Revolution a century later. Fatally condemned as 'Jacobites' loyal to the exiled Stuarts, the Tory faction rarely sniffed power. It is the augustness of the Whig elite that Blenheim expresses. William III was succeeded by Queen Anne, whose favourite, John Churchill, the Duke of Marlborough, proved one of Britain's most talented generals. At the Battle of Blenheim in 1704 he humiliated the seemingly all-conquering Louis XIV of France and gave Britain its debut as a global power. A grateful monarch and nation gave Blenheim Palace as a gift to Marlborough. In Thornhill's painting in its grand hall, Britannia accepts his battle plans as tribute. Thornhill's most accomplished architectural painting of all is a tour de force of illusion and optical fun that simultaneously celebrates Newtonian science and British power.

The Painted Hall in Greenwich was built as part of the Royal Hospital for Seamen, designed by Wren and completed by Nicholas Hawksmoor to give navy veterans the same kind of support that old soldiers got at Wren's Chelsea Hospital. This grandiose dining hall stands at the heart of the new science, downhill from the Royal Observatory where Wren's Octagon Room still creates a luminous sense of the beauty of discovery. A portrait of John Flamsteed, who lived at the Observatory in his cushy job as the first Astronomer Royal, appears in Thornhill's Painted Hall along with the founding fathers of astronomy, Copernicus and Tycho Brahe.

It is known simply as the Painted Hall because Thornhill's decorative scheme not only completes the architecture but somehow replaces it, piercing a fairly plain rectangular shell with illusory columns, carvings, doorways, niches and garlands in such excess that what seems a simple hall from the outside becomes fantastical within. A nautical theme predominates with eye-fooling sea shells adding a surreal salty tang.

High above looms a dauntingly real warship. From its mighty galleried stern flies the flag of the Union. Thornhill started to paint at Greenwich in 1707, the year England and Scotland were politically conjoined by the Act of Union to forge Great Britain. His painting is a complex allegory that attributes the glory of this new nation to two powers – the Navy and science.

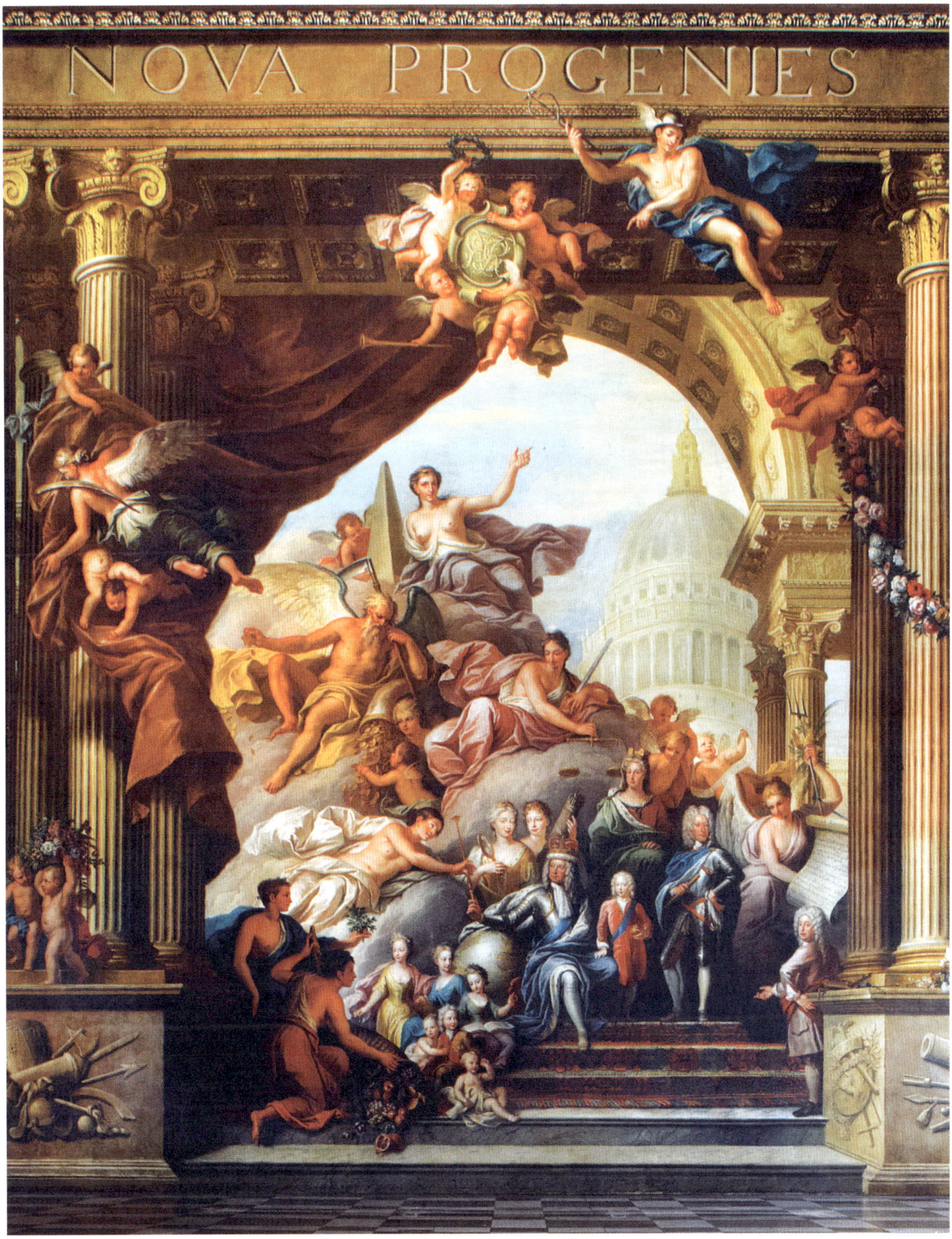

↑ Sir James Thornhill and assistants, Mural on the west wall of the Painted Hall, Old Royal Naval College, Greenwich

Navigation and astronomy in Thornhill's painting are mutually dependent. Scientists counted on the Royal Navy to help them observe the stars in the southern hemisphere. Edmond Halley even commanded his own Navy ship on a voyage of astronomical discovery. The Navy, meanwhile, needed astronomy to navigate. Britain's national success rests on the application of science, proclaims the Painted Hall.

If this room of paint propagandizes for astronomy, then Newton's *Opticks*, published in 1704 and containing a lifetime's thought about the nature of light, going back to those youthful experiments with bodkins and prisms, more subtly shapes it. As in St Paul's, Thornhill uses deep crisp shadows to heighten the reality of his illusory architecture. At the west end of the room, a gigantic painted triumphal arch is given astonishing depth by the strong shadow defining its interior. Light and darkness and the power of optics are the instruments that let Thornhill create his British utopia.

It took almost 20 years for Thornhill and his assistants to finish the Painted Hall, not least because an entire new dynasty had to be accommodated. On the death of Queen Anne in 1714 the Elector of Hanover was brought in from Germany to ensure the Protestant succession and the 'revolution principles' of 1688. Having started out to apotheosize Queen Anne, Thornhill expanded the scheme to praise the peace and prosperity guaranteed by George I and his family. The new royals gather by the triumphal arch on the west wall under a pyramid whose mathematical form promises an age of reason.

As rarely happens, the propaganda of the Painted Hall proved true. The Hanoverian dynasty would reproduce itself in a string of Georges and rule for more than a hundred years. Georgian Britain would prosper and grow and apply the discoveries of Newton and Boyle to give birth to the industrial world in which we live.

It would also be the first golden age of British art.

Poor Players

Horace Walpole's family seat was filled with expensive paintings, but he had no illusions about the creativity of palaces. As an adult he rebelled against the ethos of domestic grandeur that led Britain's aristocracy to raise vast piles of stone. Instead he created for himself a daydreamer's folly of a house named Strawberry Hill, in Twickenham, southwest London, with medieval panelling, eerie lighting and clanking armour, where his mind could wander enough to concoct in the 1760s the first 'Gothic' novel, *The Castle of Otranto*.

It was a more personal and warmly eccentric place than the majestic home his father had built. Houghton Hall in Norfolk is a perfect monument to the vogue for the architecture of Andrea Palladio that captivated early Georgian landowners. The Palladian style – already imported to Britain once by Inigo Jones but emulated more systematically in the eighteenth century – calls for a distilled harmonious classicism, precisely designed and crafted to the highest standards. Houghton has those qualities in abundance, from its almost square portico to its marbled interiors – all surrounded by a gracious park in what seems a timeless balance of nature and design. In Walpole's youth it also boasted a superb art collection. The paintings amassed by his father, Sir Robert Walpole, first prime minister of Great Britain, hang today in the Hermitage in St Petersburg, for they were bought as a job lot later in the century by Catherine the Great of Russia.

The luxury of Sir Robert Walpole's house and the extravagance of his art collection did nothing to allay relentless claims that he was a corrupt schemer whose dominance of British politics from 1721 to 1742 created an oligarchic Whig one-party state. Yet Walpole's appetite for art was not entirely confined to expensive European Old Masters. In 1728 or 1729 he commissioned the up-and-coming William Hogarth to paint a portrait of his ten-year-old son Horace, already looking quite the aesthete in his grey, blue and gold suit as he gestures to a fountain adorned with a statue of Cupid. It was not only keen-eyed of Walpole to hire Hogarth so early in his career but broad-minded, since the painter and printmaker was one of many satirists doing well by railing against the corruption of the prime minister. Walpole was widely believed to be the true target of *The Beggar's Opera*, whose blurring of art and life is so vividly preserved in Hogarth's paintings.

Hogarth's involvement in satire at Robert Walpole's expense cast no shadow on Horace Walpole's lifelong passion for his favourite modern artist. He had no great admiration for British art in general, even though he wrote the first history of it. *Anecdotes of Painting in England*, published in a series of handsome volumes by his own Strawberry Hill Press from 1762 onwards, begins by warning the reader against the dullness of his material and the dearth of genius among British artists. He sees nothing special in the voluminous decorations of James Thornhill, for example, observing merely that he was 'a man of much note in his time'.

It is a different story when he writes about 'that great and original genius, Hogarth'. In his eyes the man who portrayed him as a child was not just an artist but a moral philosopher and visionary:

> *Mirth coloured his pictures, but benevolence designed them. He smiled like Socrates, that men might not be offended at his lectures, and might learn to laugh at their own follies.*

Walpole is correct in his enthusiasm. In Hogarth, Britain produced for the first time an artist who needs no special pleading or patriotic sentimentality to make him seem important. He truly was important, on a European scale. In the Paris of the great sceptical thinker Voltaire it showed savoir faire to know about 'Hogard'. In Spain in the early nineteenth century, where hopes of reform were drowning in the blood of the Napoleonic Wars, Goya imitated Hogarth's Bedlam in his own depiction of an asylum, *Casa de locos*. Hogarth cast such a long and wide shadow that it oppressed the Norwegian Modernist Edvard Munch, who complained that:

> *Hogarth painted vice and Bohemians in London. He was himself a wealthy citizen who died happily in the bosom of his family... A Hogarth and a Shakespeare. The result of a kind of British hypocrisy.*
> (Translated in Poul Erik Tøjner,
> *Munch In His Words*, 2003)

Hogarth would have shrugged and happily accepted the comparison with Shakespeare. He suggests it himself in his 1745 *Self-Portrait with a Pug*, resting his picture on the works of Shakespeare as well as those of Milton and Swift. Walpole thought Hogarth's visual dramas resembled the comedies of Molière and Congreve, the erudite choice revealing his expensive education. Yet in hailing Hogarth as an 'original genius' Walpole recognized that real creativity came not from the smoothness of aristocratic culture but from the noise and mess of socially dynamic London. The serenity that prevails to this day at Houghton is glorious yet sterile.

Hogarth's London is an endlessly shifting stage. Its scenes can change quickly from a noble house to a quack doctor's seedy shop, from a church to a gambling den. More than one drama can happen in the same scene. In one of his most captivating paintings a pious-looking lady walks towards St Paul's Church at Covent Garden on a frozen winter's morning, followed by her shivering page boy. Her respectable demeanour is at odds with a group of all-night revellers warming themselves with kisses by an open fire. These rakes and harlots have been indulging in London's pleasures through the small hours and are still at it at daybreak under the church-goer's uneasy look. What is the moral? There does not appear to be one. This is a picture of London as a veritable universe of humanity where people inhabit worlds of their own, side by side. For the party-goers Covent Garden is a garden of earthly delights; for the woman on her way to church it is a chilly path to heaven. Who knows which of them is right? This painting belongs to a series of London scenes, *The Four Times of Day*, that take delight in the restless contrasts of big city life. While another group of fashionable church-goers leave a service in *Noon*, a little boy weeps over a pie he has dropped and a waitress is embraced by her black boyfriend. In *Night*, homeless people huddle in St Martin's Lane unnoticed by a drunk on his way home.

In Hogarth's print *The Enraged Musician*, published in 1741, a violinist who has been trying to rehearse puts his hands over his ears at the racket outside his window. On the street everyone is making as much noise as possible without any order or coherence. A boy beats a drum, a girl spins a rattle, a pregnant pauper sings a sad ballad while her baby bawls, a fish-seller cries his wares, and people play all kinds of horns and pipes. It is pretty obvious where Hogarth's sympathies lie. The violinist represents a lofty conception of culture that is dull and lifeless compared with the music of the streets. Like Palladian architecture, the musician embodies a civilized ideal that pales beside the raucous reality of life.

The dirty laughter of realism convulses Hogarth's knowing images. He cannot see an illusion without shattering it. Love? His paintings *Before* and *After* portray a youth making passionate proposals to an apparently shocked sweetheart, then the two of them red-faced in exhaustion, the man's white shirt spilling out. Religion? *The Sleepy Congregation* sees that off. Even science gets its come-uppance in his depiction in *Marriage A-la-mode* of a sleazy doctor whose collection of grotesque artefacts perhaps parodies that of Hans Sloane, benefactor of the British Museum.

Born in Bartholomew Close near Smithfield in 1697, Hogarth grew up among, and lived, the contradictions of London. His father was a Latin scholar who scraped a living as a schoolteacher. Such an

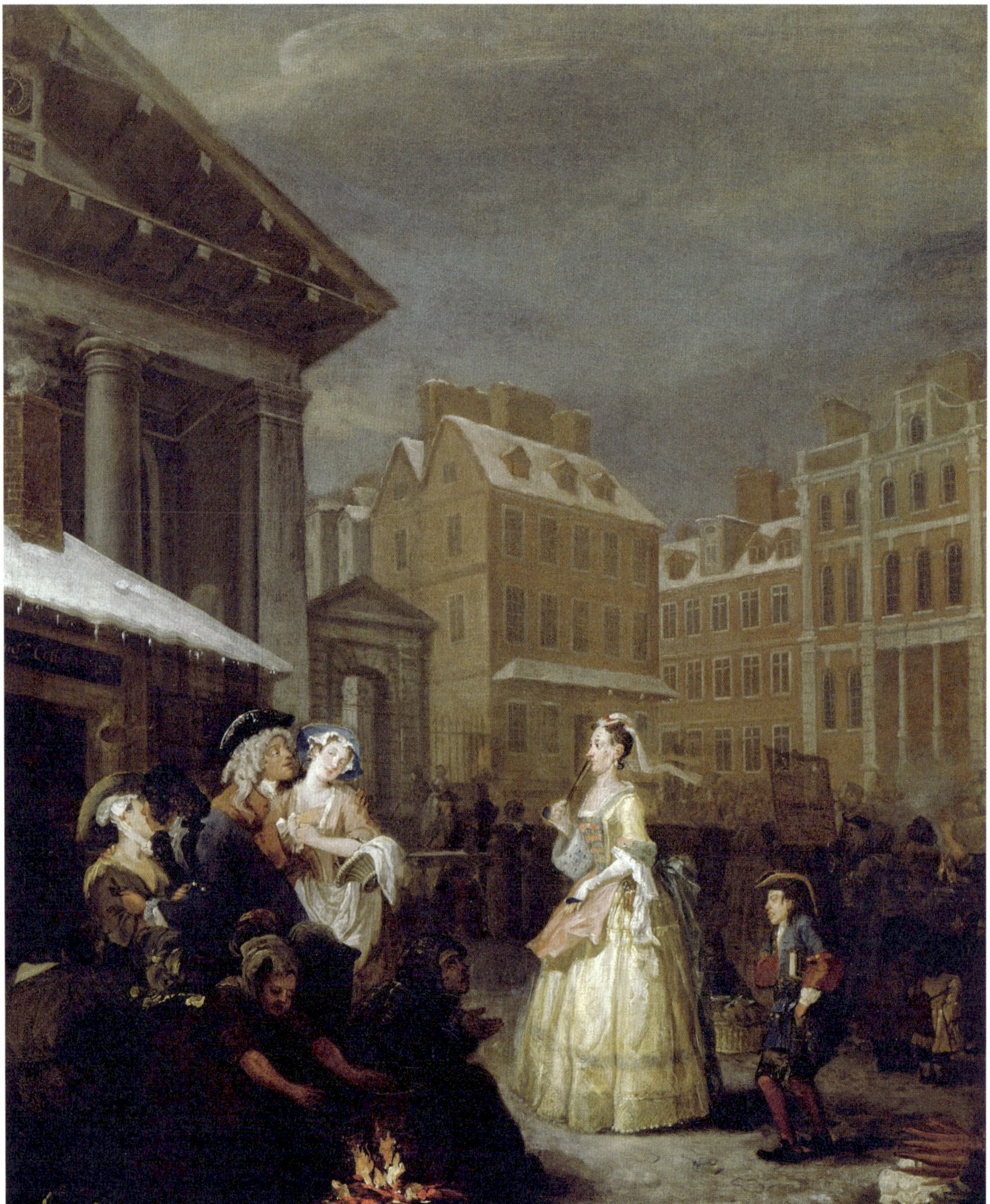

↑ William Hogarth, *The Four Times of Day: Morning*, 1736, oil on canvas, 73.7 × 61 cm (29 × 24 in.), Upton House, Warwickshire (National Trust)

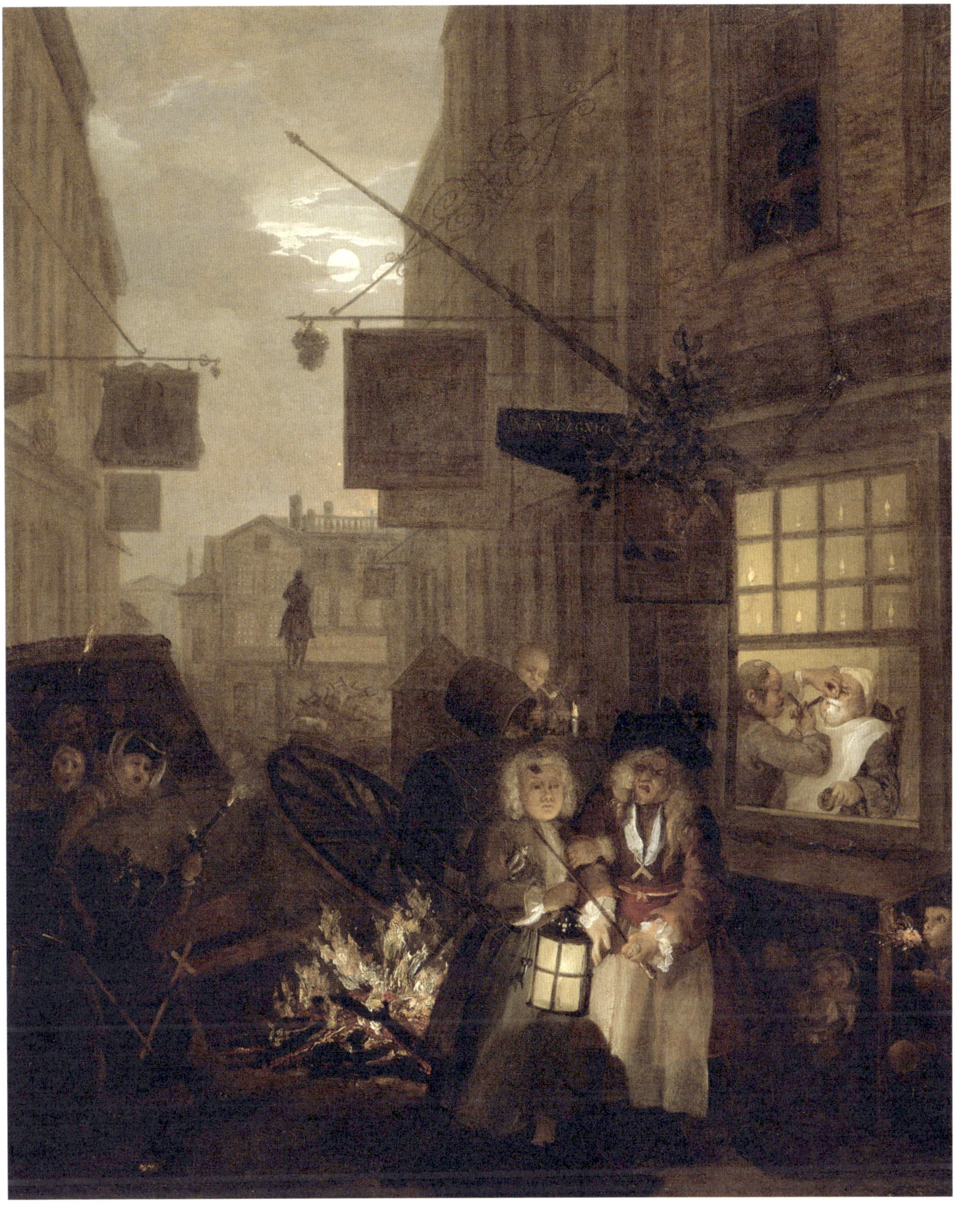

↑ William Hogarth, *The Four Times of Day: Night*, 1736, oil on canvas, 73.7 × 61 cm (29 × 24 in.), Upton House, Warwickshire (National Trust)

educated yet impoverished character is mocked and mourned in his print *The Distress'd Poet*. When Hogarth senior was sent to debtor's prison his son learned the value of money so well that he never stopped thinking up ways to earn it. His art is economically as well as aesthetically versatile. In a city where aristocrats rubbed shoulders with the mob and the middling sort prospered or struggled in between, Hogarth did not rely on any one market, let alone a patron, to provide his living. Trained as a goldsmith, learning to engrave images on copper plates that could be inked and printed to produce a multitude of copies of the same picture, he did not stop there. He learned to paint, absorbing what he could from Thornhill at the noted man's academy in Covent Garden. He pioneered a completely new way of selling art. Hogarth produced his major works as both paintings and prints, advertising for subscriptions for forthcoming 'modern moral subjects' that he also executed in oils, selling the prints like hot cakes then auctioning the paintings to connoisseurs.

Did the print advertise the painting, or the painting the print? Horace Walpole claims that Hogarth's circa 1736–38 painting *Strolling Actresses Dressing in a Barn* was 'the best of all his works'. It is long lost, yet it would be fatuous to see the print of it that survives merely as a grey copy of a colourful original. For one thing it does not look grey, or 'black and white'. If anything its finely nuanced shades look silvery and shimmering. Hogarth constructs an entire world from thousands of interwoven straight lines. The varying densities and weights of his inimitable cross-hatching give the image extraordinary richness and subtlety. It is sharp, sensitive, detailed. Hogarth's precise network of marks creates a powerful perspective view of a barn's ramshackle interior where actresses pose as the gods of ancient mythology. At the centre stands Diana maiden goddess. Behind her is Apollo, to one side Juno, while Flora, Aurora and Ganymede can all be spotted in the rollicking crew. Hogarth remembered his father's classical education after all. Yet of course these are not real gods. They are poor players, putting on costumes for a rustic play. Diana looks none too virginal. Juno is having her stocking darned. A boy is peeping at them through a hole in the roof.

Hogarth created this ballad of life on the road as a memorial to a lost era, for it marks the new Theatre Licensing Act of 1737. Sir Robert Walpole would stand for only so much satire. Stung by the personal jokes of John Gay and Henry Fielding, he cracked down on theatres and actors. The Licensing Act permitted only two legitimate theatres

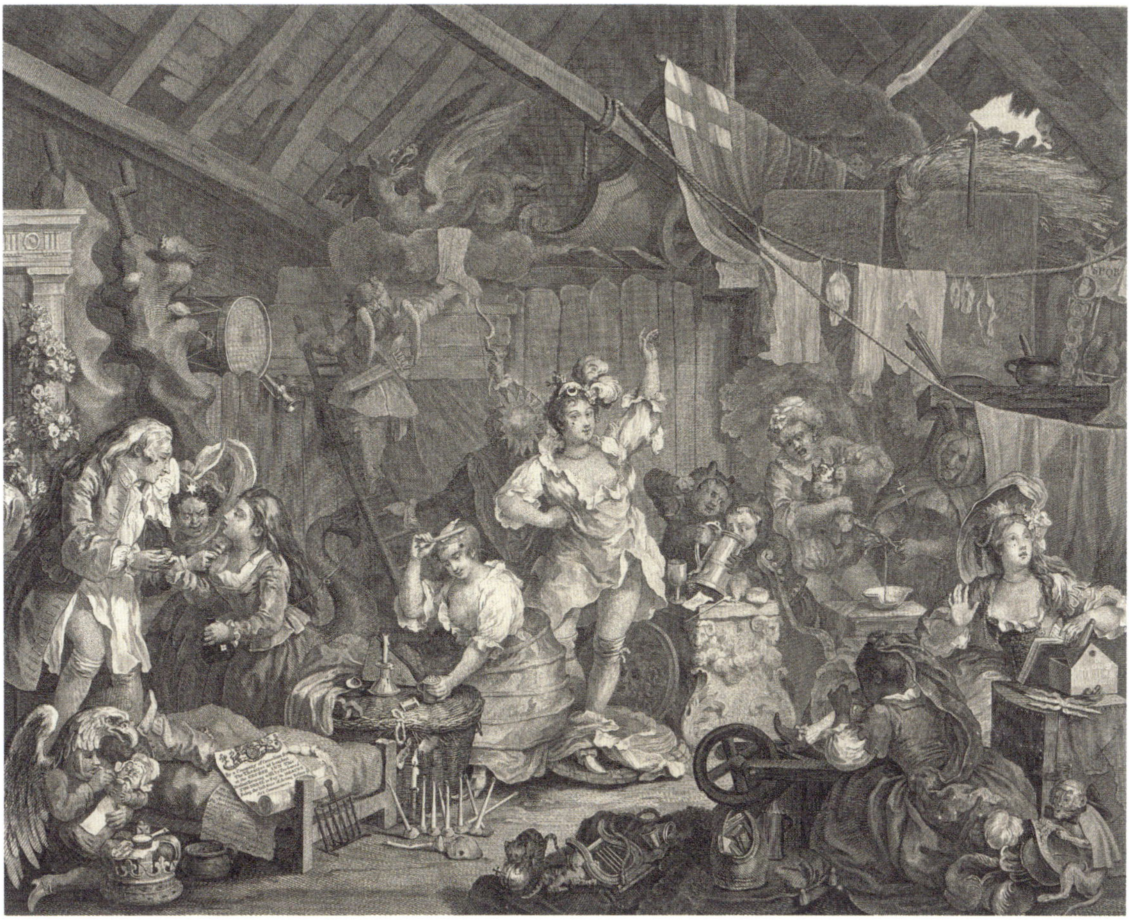

↑ William Hogarth, *Strolling Actresses Dressing in a Barn*, 1738, engraving, 41.9 × 53.8 cm (16 ½ × 21 ⅙ in.), Yale Center for British Art, New Haven

in London, strengthened the Lord Chamberlain's power to censor new plays, and allowed actors to be prosecuted as 'vagrants'. Hogarth's crumbling barn is a last refuge of laughter and liberty. For Walpole's son it was more lovely than all the lawns of Houghton.

Rakehell

A house topples in front of our eyes, bricks cascading a second before the whole thing goes; the wall of a nearby building has already disintegrated to reveal a suicide hanged within. London is falling. Around the unmistakable spire of Hawksmoor's St George's Church, with its stepped pyramid inspired by the Mausoleum of Halicarnassus and crowned by a statue of George I, houses tilt and totter and a solitary chimney rises from hollow ruins. Not that anyone notices. They are all dead drunk, from a woman having gin poured down her throat as she sits helpless in a wheelbarrow to an emaciated blind corpse of a man, more dead than alive, still just about holding on to his empty glass. One woman has already succumbed and is being dumped in her coffin. Horribly, a mother is feeding gin to her baby. Still more horribly, another is so drunkenly impervious that she has let her child fall from the top of a flight of steps as she reaches for some snuff.

These people are desperately poor. The blind ballad-seller is barely clothed at all, the snuff-taking mother clad in rags and covered in sores. The only people prospering are a pawnbroker and the owner of the local gin distillery, a Mr Kilman.

Hogarth's *Gin Lane*, published in 1751, is one of the most powerfully delineated nightmares in European art. It compares with the works of the Northern Renaissance visionaries Pieter Bruegel and Hieronymus Bosch – and not by accident. When Hogarth created *Gin Lane* he was undoubtedly looking at Bruegel. His apocalyptic vision of death consuming an entire city is inspired by Bruegel's 1562–63 painting of a landscape overwhelmed by mortality, *The Triumph of Death*. Yet there is a difference.

When Bruegel, Bosch and similarly brooding artists who lived before the eighteenth century portray poverty, death and apocalypse they do so in resigned acceptance of the inevitability of suffering. Plague, fire and war are not avoidable. The only salvation is in the next life. In medieval Doom paintings in Britain the same fatalism prevails – what matters is the eternal life beyond this mortal one.

Gin Lane plunges into horror yet offers a solution in this earthly life. Quite simply, do not drink gin. Quaff healthy beer instead. Hogarth published *Gin Lane* alongside a companion print, *Beer Street*, that shows a much pleasanter corner of London. Instead of skin-and-bone paupers we see plump, healthy, laughing folk relaxing outside an inn. Everything is reversed. The city looks pristine. Business booms in tall clean buildings and a gang of happy roofers salutes the Union Jack. One of the inn-goers waves an entire leg of beef as he holds up a pewter mug of foaming beer.

This comical contrast between extremes, pitting a fat, happy, amorous crowd against a starving, dying one, is itself consciously modelled on Bruegel's 1559 *The Battle between Carnival and Lent* and the 1563 Bruegelian prints *The Fat Kitchen* and *The Thin Kitchen*. In fact, a man with a huge belly who sits back to enjoy his ale in *Beer Street* is directly borrowed from *The Fat Kitchen*. Hogarth uses the folkloric archetypes of Bruegel's art – themselves rooted in the imaginations of pre-modern peasants for whom the good life is fat, because thinness denotes the ever-present spectres of disease and hunger – because he wants to address directly the illiterate, the uneducated and indeed, the blind drunk. *Beer Street* and *Gin Lane* are popular prints, made and sold more cheaply than his earlier masterpieces because he is genuinely trying to reform the habits of the poor.

Hogarth's moral ambition – part of the 'bourgeois' personality Munch disliked in him – is the most awkward aspect of his art for moderns to love. We would rather see him as a surrealist or socialist than a forerunner of Victorian humbug. Some admirers of *Industry and Idleness*, another of the cheap sets of didactic prints from 1747 that he aimed at a 'low' public, cannot accept that it is as severe a lecture to the young as it seems to be. *Industry and Idleness* tells the tales of two apprentices, Tom Idle and Francis Goodchild. One sleeps at his loom, gambles in the churchyard during services, gets sent away to sea and ends up hanged at Tyburn like Jack Sheppard. The other works hard, wins his master's trust and becomes Lord Mayor. Does Hogarth lace his images with ambiguities that undermine their purported message, as some claim? It is true that Francis looks a prig and Tom's fate is pitiable – as he is rowed away to become a sailor, a hard-faced thug shows him a gibbeted body bleakly swinging at the mouth of the Thames. But the first scene contains the entire parable. It is not smug but realistic. Discipline yourself and you can become rich. Fail to do so and you will instead be the object of discipline from above: beaten, arrested, hanged. Hogarth is not a preacher but a hardheaded observer sharing his knowledge of how people rise or fall. He is giving honest advice.

We need to understand the reforming passion of Hogarth because it is what makes him truly an artist of the Enlightenment. Horace Walpole saw him as a wise philosophical artist smiling 'like Socrates' to laugh his audience into changing their ways. This belief in rational improvement is the essence of the Enlightenment and rests on its commitment to science. Before the scientific revolution there seemed no way of making any aspect of life safer, faster, healthier or more efficient. The pessimism of Bruegel's *The Triumph of Death* was totally justified, for humans were helpless in the shadow of sickness and mortality. Yet the discoveries made and publicized by the Royal Society led to rapid change and raised the prospect of a world

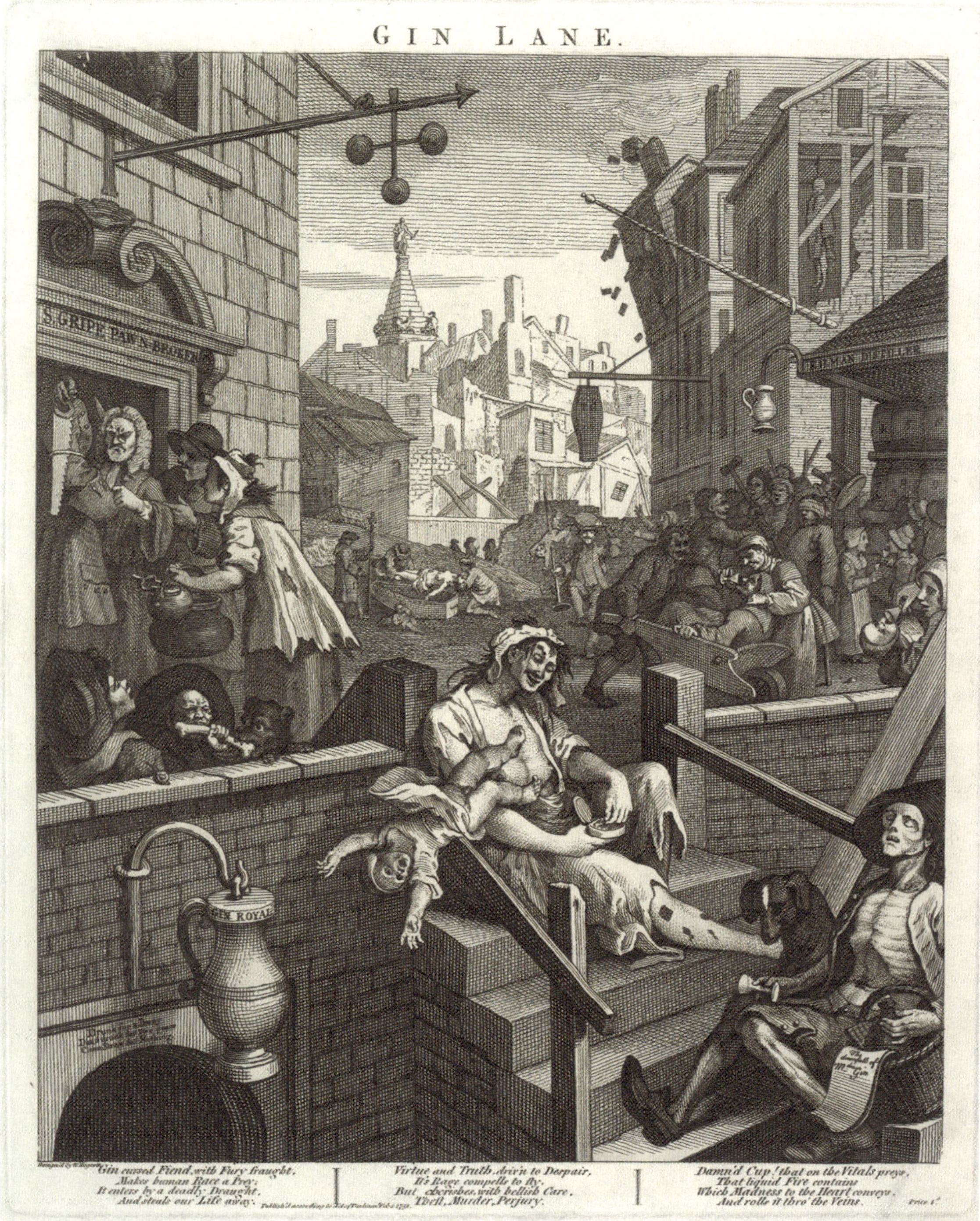

↑ William Hogarth, *Gin Lane*, 1751, etching and engraving, 38.9 × 32.2 cm (15 ⅓ × 12 ⅔ in.) The Metropolitan Museum of Art, New York

transformed. Across Europe and above all in Britain, ingenious applications of science, or optimistic new attitudes inspired by it, stimulated improved ways of doing things. In 1712 Thomas Newcomen constructed the first steam engine. Diseases could be fought with improved medicine, as Lady Mary Wortley Montagu proved when she introduced inoculation against smallpox to Britain after encountering it in Turkey. There was a long way to go but using your head was clearly a good idea.

Hogarth's mordant satires warn what can happen if you fail to do that. *A Harlot's Progress* of 1731 and *A Rake's Progress* of 1734 are blackly comic novels told in pictures. The former survives only as a set of six claustrophobic prints, in which the walls close in on a hapless London prostitute until she is nailed in her coffin. The eight paintings of *A Rake's Progress* still exist and are among the most compelling works of art ever made in Britain.

We are transported back in time to a world of shaven heads covered by filthy wigs, beauty spots that hide venereal sores, guttering candles in smoky cellars, a sedan chair stopped in the street so its owner can be arrested. You can almost smell the tallow, must, tobacco and bodies. The raw way *A Rake's Progress* is painted is almost shocking; Hogarth would later work much harder on his paintings, but the street-art energy of these early pictures is incomparable. The colours are bright and fierce. Reds, blues, gold and silver suggest the sheer lust for life that is the rake's downfall. Tom Rakewell inherits his father's estate, a run-down house bursting with hidden cash. The old man was evidently a miser. In a sadly inevitable cycle of human folly, his son rebels by living like a lord. Fobbing off his former fiancée as a tailor measures him for a fancy new suit, he embarks on a high-spending odyssey. A fencing teacher with the face of Hogarth, a jockey to ride his expensive racehorse, a dancing master and an opera composer are among the hired experts and parasites he gathers around him in his townhouse furnished, inevitably, with fine European paintings. Yet his cultural pretensions are skin deep. In the third painting he finds a more animal way to indulge himself, sprawled in dissipation amid a company of prostitutes in a back room of the Rose Tavern. He is completely unaware that the woman with her hand in his clothes is robbing him and passing his cash to an accomplice.

From here on it all starts to fall apart. The rake is seized in the street for debt, marries a rich old woman to recover his fortunes, then immediately, in Scene VI, heads for a gambling den, where he kneels, wig thrown off in despair, shaking his fist at heaven for his bad luck. His ever-loyal sweetheart follows him to debtor's prison and then, after his mind breaks, to the madhouse.

In its harsh comedy *A Rake's Progress* has an acute psychological realism. Hogarth is experimenting with the idea of a visual novel at a time when the written novel was just taking off. Like Daniel Defoe in *Moll Flanders* he tells a tough story of modern life. Yet there is more pathos and truth in *A Rake's Progress* than in most eighteenth-century novels. Not until the first volume of Laurence Sterne's *The Life and Opinions of Tristram Shandy* appeared in 1759 would a literary novel be as human and insightful as this. *A Rake's Progress* is not a cold moral lesson but an all too plausible tale of everyday disaster. Tom Rakewell just has no self-control. In a city like London he is ripe for the plucking. The debtor's prison is a brutal punishment: instead of helping him to reform, it smashes his mind. We see the moment reason breaks.

'Luxury' was condemned by eighteenth-century moralists, who feared the fatal temptations of an economy in which there was more and more stuff available to consume. Hogarth diagnoses a modern sickness and offers his pictures as its cure. Take a dose of *A Rake's Progress*, young man, before you buy that racehorse. The improving value of these eight scenes arises from their compassionate clarity.

Yet thoughts of improvement give way to fear and pity when you look at the final painting. The Rake in Bedlam takes us beyond sensible advice. That would be like looking for practical suggestions in *King Lear*. In this chilling vision of a young man writhing semi-naked on the floor of a cell in London's notorious Bethlehem Hospital, while other hurt minds pursue fantasies of being the pope, a poet or a musical genius, Hogarth suddenly assumes the mask of tragedy.

One lunatic even seems to think he is playing the Fool from *Lear*. In a final cruelty, two fashionable women have paid to look at the lunatics. Hogarth shows us the depths of human suffering, and the failure of compassion that can allow real people to be watched as if they were clowns on the stage.

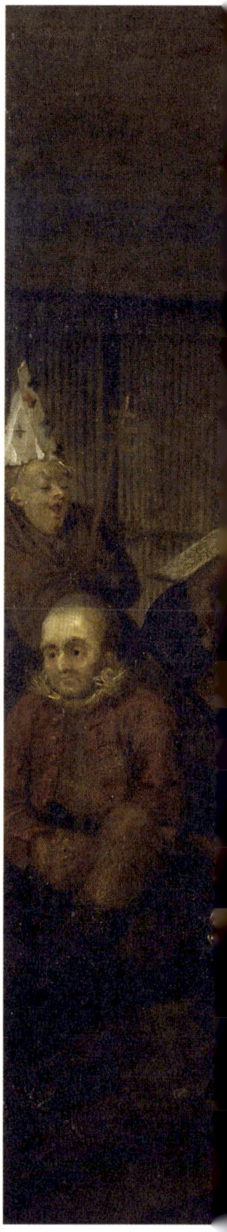

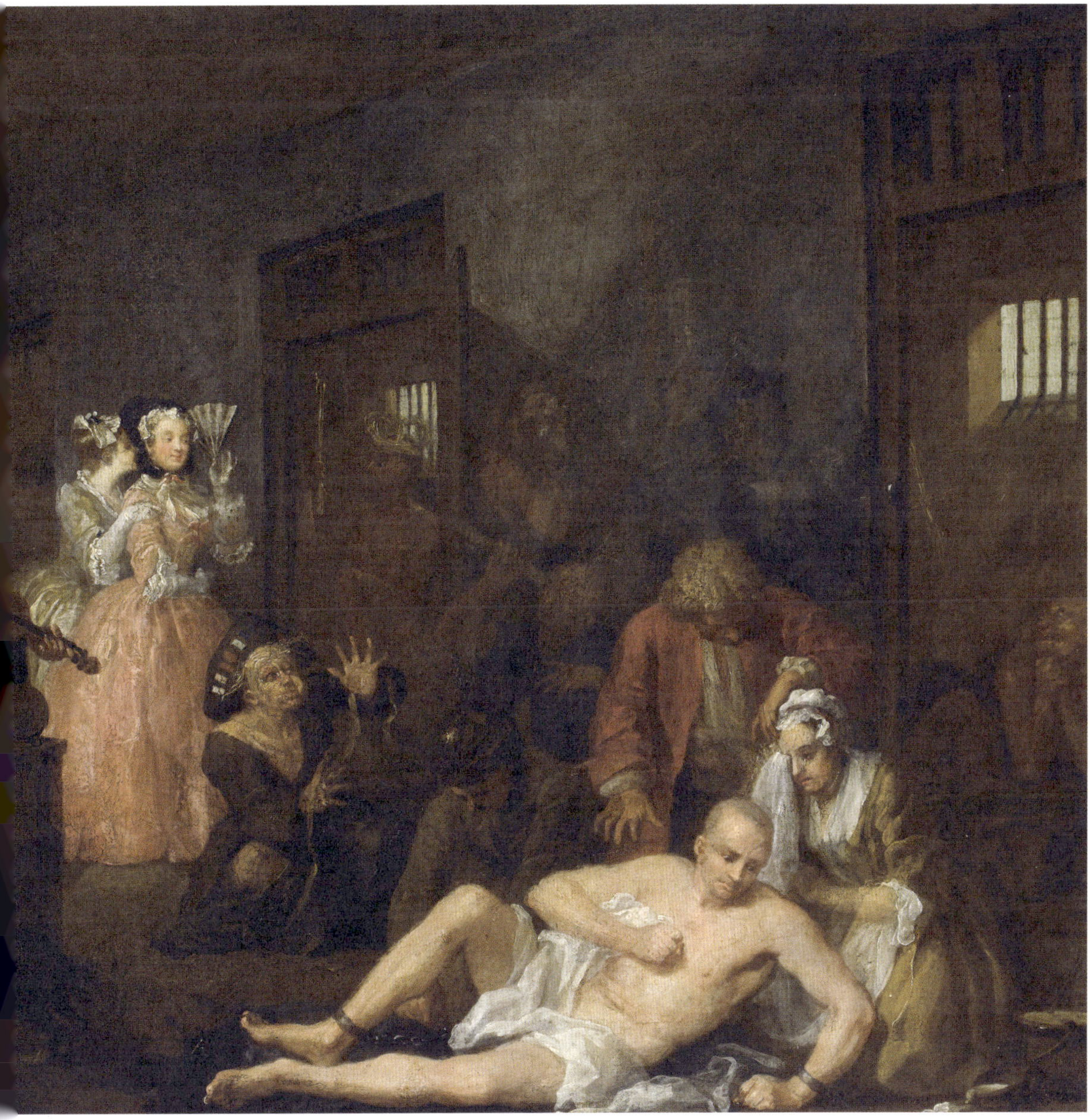

↑ William Hogarth, *A Rake's Progress VIII: The Madhouse (Bedlam)*, 1734, oil on canvas, 62.2 × 75 cm (24 ½ × 29 ½ in.), Sir John Soane's Museum, London

3. Chasing Butterflies

It is with considerable difficulty that
I remember the original era of my being;
all events of that period appear confused
and indistinct. A strange multiplicity of
sensations seized me, and I saw, felt, heard...

The Monster in Mary
Shelley's *Frankenstein*, 1818

The Butcher of Horkstow

He began by slitting their throats. That was not only the quickest way but the best for his purpose, because it killed without leaving marks. Blood jetted out of the jugular vein and they fell. Then he had to inject the arteries and veins with wax, as he had learned to do at the hospital. The strangest and most exhausting part of it all, however, was the suspension of the body. For this he devised a sort of machine. He suspended an iron bar from the ceiling with hooks hanging from it, and below that slung a wooden platform for their feet. Once he somehow stood them on the platform, with Mary helping as best she could, the hooks were applied to hold them upright in a surprisingly elegant, even statuesque pose. Then he flayed them.

The work took 18 months, and for that whole time George Stubbs and his partner Mary Spencer lived in a rented farmhouse near the village of Horkstow in Lincolnshire, undisturbed and isolated in their dreadful work. It was the turning point of his life, a bloody rite of passage that changed him forever.

Stubbs dissected about 12 horses altogether. With a preliminary analysis of a boiled-down skeleton out of the way, he proceeded methodically to investigate every part of equine anatomy. First he exposed one by one every layer of the muscles that covered the

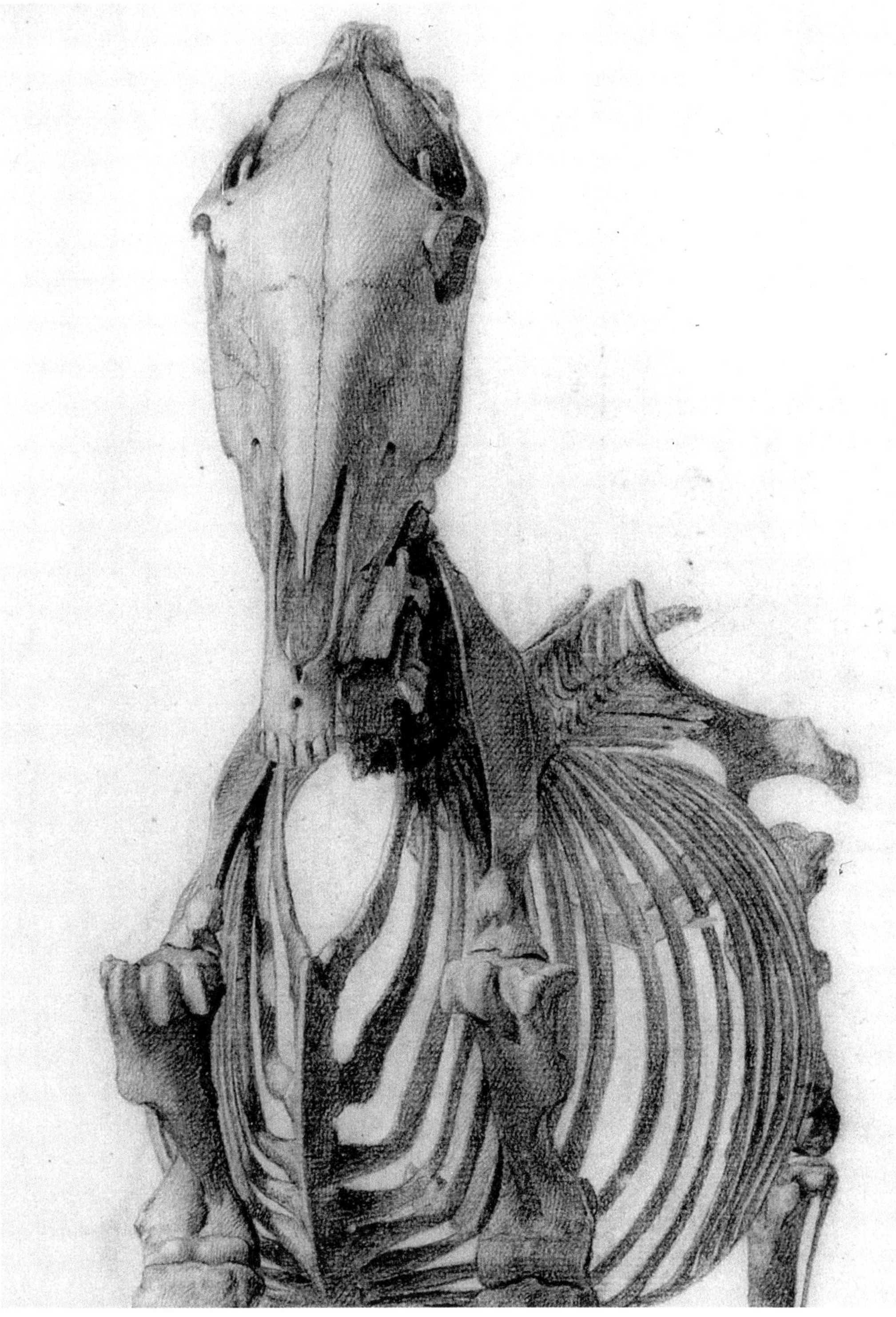

↑ George Stubbs, working drawing from the tenth 'Anatomical Table of the Muscles … of the Horse' (detail), 1756–58

abdomen, cutting deeper and deeper until he reached the lungs and intestines. The stinking bowels 'were taken out, & Cast away'. Next he stripped the skin from the head, before gradually exposing the muscles of an entire body. It gave him great professional satisfaction that his preparation with wax (or perhaps tallow) worked so perfectly that 'by means of the Injection the Muscles, the Blood vessels, and the Nerves, retain'd their form to the last without undergoing any Change of position'.

The skills that Stubbs brought to his project had been acquired with human bodies. At York County Hospital in the 1740s, he studied anatomy with the surgeon Charles Atkinson and got so good at it that he was allowed not only to dissect cadavers but even to lecture on anatomy and dissection. His skills were sought out by another York doctor, John Burton – satirized as Doctor Slop in local clergyman Laurence Sterne's novel *Tristram Shandy* – to illustrate the human foetus in his 1751 book *An Essay Towards a Complete New System of Midwifery*. Dissecting horses was not so ghoulish when you consider that for hours on end he had drawn dead babies in the wombs of dead mothers to produce these superb scientific engravings.

The idea of dissecting horses and producing the greatest ever study of their anatomy started to obsess him in his twenties, probably with encouragement from medical friends, and not even the adventure of a Grand Tour to Rome distracted him. Finally, when he was 32, in the year 1756, he found the perfect place in rustic Horkstow and set to work.

It was, for all its strangeness, research of real scientific value. Yet Stubbs was not a surgeon or a veterinarian. He was a painter. Born in Liverpool in 1724, the son of a leather currier, he was one of many young talents competing for attention in the suddenly highly energetic British art world. What on earth drove him to embark on a slightly sinister experiment in the depths of the English countryside, slinging up carcasses with his hooks and chains, cutting into them by lamplight in the loneliness of the Lincolnshire night to the hoot of an owl, for all the world like an early sketch for Mary Shelley's Dr Frankenstein?

Stubbs was driven to it by empiricism, the mentality of modern science, that holds all true knowledge to be derived from direct experience. In science, that can mean anything from dissecting the dead to capturing gravitational waves. In eighteenth-century British art, as we shall see, it meant both studies as obscure as those undertaken by Stubbs in his rustic retreat, and the patient observation of silvery clouds and emerald grass.

The Silken Empiricist

Nothing shows the Enlightened nature of Hogarth quite so much as the support he gave to Captain Thomas Coram and the Foundling Hospital. This benevolent eighteenth-century institution still exists as a playground near St Pancras in central London, where goats live in old Georgian outbuildings and, in the nearby Foundling Museum, Hogarth's portrait of Coram, red-coated and rosy-cheeked, attests to their friendship.

The nightmare image in *Gin Lane* of a baby falling from a destitute mother's arms into the abyss is a revealing symbol of life and death in eighteenth-century London. With only the barest of public provision, still managed by an outdated system of parish care that was centuries old, poor children were vulnerable to all the violence and brutality of the metropolis. Coram, a civic-minded sea captain, campaigned fiercely to set up Great Britain's first foundling hospital, where babies could be safely left by mothers who felt unable to care for them. It was about time too – some cities in continental Europe had institutions like it centuries earlier.

Hogarth's compassion for poor kids was heartfelt. In all his self-portraits he shows the scar on his forehead that he got from a childhood accident. He knew how tough a London childhood could be – and how damaging. His deliberately hideous 1751 series of popular prints *The Four Stages of Cruelty* (page 84) begins with boys torturing animals in the street – hanging cats, impaling dogs and staging an impromptu cock-fight. This unsupervised childhood of easy violence leaves Hogarth's anti-hero Tom Nero with a damaged personality that will turn him into a murderer. Coram's hospital could hopefully save potential Tom Neros and make useful adults of them. Hogarth became one of its governors, translating his images of good and evil on the streets of London into a genuine attempt to sweeten the lives of the most helpless.

He naturally could not resist bringing it together with his other great project: promoting British art. Hogarth made the Foundling Hospital into a public gallery as well as a philanthropic institution. This made perfect charitable sense because by attracting wealthy people to see art at the hospital, he also helped to get them involved with its real work.

Hogarth had inherited Thornhill's art academy in St Martin's Lane and made it a centre for what he was determined to push as a new British movement in art. British patriotism riotously rampages through his work, especially as he got older and came to see himself as leader of a distinctively British school. In *The Gate of Calais*, painted in 1748–49, he mocks a miserable group of starveling Frenchmen slavering hungrily over a side of British beef. In *The March of the Guards to Finchley* of 1749–50, he does what Shakespeare did in *Henry V* and creates a comic yet patriotic image of red-coated troops heading off under the British flag to defend London from Bonnie Prince Charlie.

In the Court Room at the Foundling Hospital, Hogarth got a chance to create a permanent display of the British artists associated with his St Martin's Lane Academy – and what duffers most of them were. Hogarth took responsibility for decorating this fine Rococo chamber with large history paintings and small roundels by a variety of painters he knew and liked. His own work *Moses Brought before Pharaoh's Daughter* (1746), like other attempts by him at a grand, serious manner, has a bright, sincere strength but none of the dazzling energy of his comic art. Other paintings in the room by Joseph Highmore, Francis Hayman, Richard Wilson and more are competent but unmemorable. Was British art really taking off in the eighteenth century or were there just more mediocre homegrown artists around?

Then your eyes alight on a tiny miracle. The small round paintings placed between the big biblical ones all depict London's hospitals and charitable institutions. Most are fairly unambitious topographical studies. Yet one leaps out as different – and that is not a figure of speech. Clouds appear to pass through the edges of the little circular canvas as they float exuberantly across a city sky. Instead of being studied from a safe distance as a piece of architecture, the painting's purported subject, Charterhouse School, is seen up close, with a walled pathway hurtling towards us in a bold yet very believable perspective. We are seeing a living moment in a real world. Two boys are absorbed in play on the path. Other figures lounge further away, dark against the bright sunlight caught on the pink wall. Trees blow in the breeze, the leaves caught by soft mobile sunbeams. Most of all it is the clouds that catch your heart, those silken parachutes that take up almost half the painting, their colours dappled from pewter to gold. Their movement makes the day live. This is a painting of nature as an ever-changing, infinitely complicated variety of phenomena, at once the setting for human life and mysteriously oblivious to it.

Thomas Gainsborough, who painted it in 1748 when he was 21, shows himself in this little manifesto to be an extraordinary

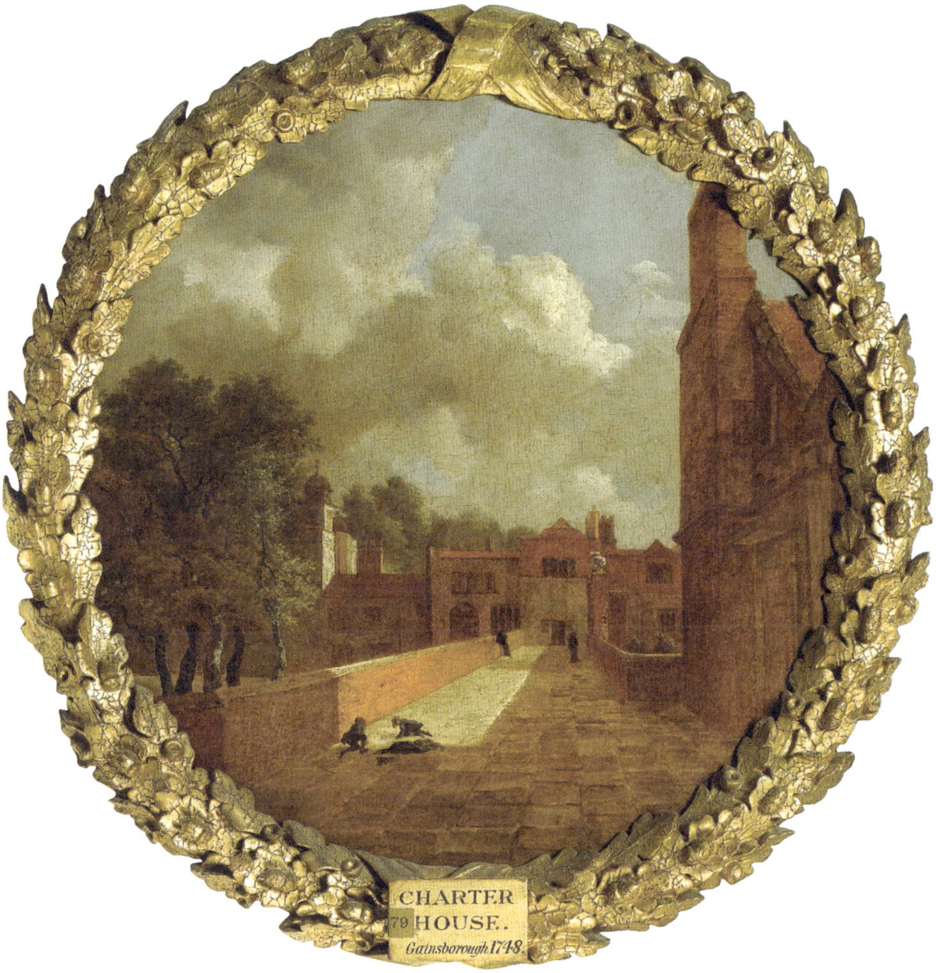

↑ Thomas Gainsborough, *The Charterhouse*, 1748, oil on canvas, diameter 56 cm (22 in.) Foundling Museum, London

observer of the natural world. Even in a picture of London it is clouds, trees and sunlight that make his brush scintillate. There is nothing artificial about his painting, nothing stiff – it has the flow of the spontaneous and the unruly. It is clear he has looked at seventeenth-century Dutch landscape art, yet there is a freshness here that has no model in art, only in life.

Hogarth could not paint nature like this – his skies are blue blanks. He was a city boy to his bones. Gainsborough was not, and a year after painting *The Charterhouse* he left London with his wife Margaret and returned to his home town, Sudbury, in Suffolk, to spend the next few years bringing nature into art in a completely new way.

Part of the newness is the simple fact that it is British nature. There had never been a great British landscape artist before, so there had never been any truly riveting paintings of the rainy skies of England. Yet it is not just that. Gainsborough looks at the shifting sunlight that he loves with eyes opened by science.

Looking hard at nature had been a driving passion of European art since the fifteenth century, but it took the Royal Society to bring such habits of perception to Britain. The Society's belief that science was a visual rather than a verbal way of thinking encouraged researchers not just to display and dissect curious specimens but to draw them, too. In one of the most notorious incidents in its history, the Society could not afford to publish Newton's *Principia* because in 1686 it had exhausted its finances by publishing a sumptuous book of pictures of fish. Samuel Pepys was president at the time. His love of the pictures in Hooke's *Micrographia* had inspired his love of science in the first place (pages 34–35). Yet John Ray's book *De historia piscium* was far from a folly. Its drawings of such creatures as a hammerhead shark, flatfishes and a halibut attempt to record veraciously the natural world. The shark's hammer-like head is impressively accurate even if its fins are fanciful. Ray adds a lifelike 'portrait' of it poking its weird face above the waves.

British curiosity about the natural world blossomed. Collections of plants and animals were hailed as wonders of the age. To be Enlightened was to look at, and attempt to understand, natural phenomena. Yet,there was a magical and mysterious quality to such collections that connects them with the Wunderkammers, or cabinets of curiosities, of Renaissance princes. This lingering sense of the marvellous did the appetite for discovery no harm at all. Museums were born out of it. In 1683 Elias Ashmole's collection of man-made and natural curiosities went on display at a purpose-built museum in Oxford. In 1753 Hans Sloane's equally broad-minded but much bigger collection became the basis of the British Museum, the world's first free public museum. When it opened, this great invention of the Enlightenment included natural history as well as culture. Sloane bequeathed it everything from stuffed snakes to medicine made from crushed mummy.

It is easy to see early natural history as eccentric blundering or, if you are a relativistically minded historian of science who is sceptical about modern Western thinking, as proof that the scientific revolution is overrated. Yet a modern way of looking at nature was evolving fast. That word 'evolving' is a clue. A period that starts with Newton and culminates in Charles Darwin deserves respect.

For what mattered most in the culture of Enlightenment Britain was the widespread acceptance of the scientific method itself. The Royal Society's rejection of traditional authorities and insistence on experiment as the basis of all sound knowledge about nature had vast implications about how we see and experience the world. Those implications did not stay in the lecture room and the library. They pervaded Georgian culture, from the tinkerings of James Watt to the novels of Jane Austen.

The most influential teasing-out of what the scientific method meant in everyday life was Locke's 1689 masterpiece *An Essay Concerning Human Understanding*. This revolutionary book takes the ethos of the new science to its most radical conclusions. Locke dismisses any idea that human minds can possess inherent, pre-existing knowledge given by God. We cannot know anything by mystical inner light. Everything we know or think, says Locke, every idea we can ever have, comes from 'sensation'.

There are no 'innate ideas' implanted in us. The mind of a newborn child is like a blank slate, or a white sheet of paper:

> *Let us then suppose the mind to be, as we say, white paper, void of all characters, without any ideas; how comes it to be furnished? Whence comes it by that vast store, which the busy and boundless fancy of man has painted on it, with an almost endless variety? Whence has it all the materials of reason and knowledge? To this I answer, in one word, from experience...*

The explosive nature of Locke's 'empiricist' claim that not only our impressions of the world but all the ideas with which we understand them, in short everything that happens in our heads, derives from perception (and as understanding grows, from observation of our own mental processes) outraged many contemporary philosophers and social theorists for whom the human mind was fitted, by God or ideology, with a pre-existing cognitive framework. In 1710 the philosopher George Berkeley tried to stand Locke's essay on its head by claiming our observations cannot confirm the existence of the world around us at all.

When James Boswell claimed it was impossible to refute Berkeley, his friend and hero Samuel Johnson kicked his foot hard against a stone and replied: 'I refute it *thus*!' Johnson was not simply displaying common sense but also the immense popularity of Locke's empiricism in the eighteenth century. You did not need to have read his *Essay* to know its gist. As W. H. Auden was to say of Freud in the twentieth century, the man and his ideas had become 'a whole climate of opinion'.

Anyone who has ever enjoyed the gradual realization by Elizabeth Bennet in Austen's *Pride and Prejudice* that Mr Darcy is a completely different man from the caricature towards whom she formed an instant dislike has had an education in Lockean empiricism. Indeed, so pervasive was this philosophy that only someone original and bloody-minded enough to reject it can awaken us to how widely it was disseminated.

William Blake was just such an obstinate rebel against the dominant ideas of his time. In the furious annotations he wrote in his copy of Sir Joshua Reynolds's *Discourses on Art* in about 1808, he disgorges a memory of his eighteenth-century youth:

> *Burke's Treatise on the Sublime & Beautiful is founded on the Opinions of Newton and Locke; on this Treatise Reynolds has grounded many of his assertions in all his Discourses. I read Burke's Treatise when very Young; at the same time I read Locke on Human Understanding & Bacon's Advancement of Learning; on Every one of these Books I wrote my Opinions... I felt the Same Contempt & Abhorrence then that I do now.*

Born in 1757, the young Blake's reactions of 'contempt and abhorrence' to Locke and Bacon, and the Lockean ideas of Burke, were not formed from set readings at university, for he never attended any such establishment. After being largely home-schooled by his artisan family in London's Soho, he was apprenticed to an engraver at the age of 15. And while he obviously was not typical, it is safe to say that in the 1760s and 1770s he would have read the intellectual bestsellers of his time.

Gainsborough's flutteringly sensual and immediate art does not give the impression that he was much in the habit of reading philosophy. Nor do his surviving letters wear knowledge heavily. Yet the very fluency of the way his art lives in the moment is joyfully empirical, as if he were a white sheet of paper waiting to be filled. Locke's ideas and the scientific outlook they proclaim appear to have entered his mind like a fiddle tune heard through an open window as he sauntered by on his morning walk.

In about 1750 Gainsborough painted a landscape of truly eye-opening empiricism. Free from preconceptions of what nature should look like, open to what his eyes can see, he captures a reality as elusive and fragile as a hovering butterfly.

A rolling procession of clouds moves across the countryside. Blue-grey messengers of rain are eclipsing distant mountains of harmless golden-white vapour. Glimpses of eggshell blue peep through the ceaselessly shifting spectacle that appears at once misty and solid. Gainsborough offers no theory of what clouds are, let alone any hint of allegory – he simply, subtly, sensitively shows what they look like. Yes, those are English rain clouds all right. The land beneath them is so real it makes me shiver. There is a thin dark sliver of a hill on the horizon, dotted with trees and sheep. In front of it is a band of lime green, a slender glimpse of a distant field. The view of it is closed off by a tapering line of dark green blobs – a thin woodland at the crest of a low ridge whose shadowed slope leads down to hedges enclosing a sheep pasture. A bright grassy curving meadow rises towards us beside a freshly harvested wheatfield.

Under the old tree where he has stopped to survey his land, Mr Andrews poses with his gun under his arm. Mrs Andrews is sitting on a piece of finely wrought Rococo outdoor furniture, her wide blue skirt spread out across the landscape. She has a blank space on her lap where Gainsborough has not painted the bird shot by her husband.

We are a long way from Hogarth's epics of the London streets. As a portrait, *Mrs and Mrs Andrews* has struck some observers as such a quintessential image of the English ruling class that they cannot see its artistic originality through a red mist of rage. It is a fact that Mr Andrews owned this land. He was a keen capitalist farmer, not only making good use – as Gainsborough shows – of his variegated lands to grow grain and keep sheep but even taking an interest in the new agricultural science that was making farming more productive and profitable. In 1768 the agriculturalist Arthur Young published a letter from him in which he observes how impurities can enter wheat through seeds being spread accidentally by reapers.

So the bundles of wheat in the foreground are neither accidental nor shrouded atavistic symbolism but speak to Mr Andrews' close interest in the economics and even science of farming. The highly profitable rationalization of agriculture by landowners was as important in the economic transformation of eighteenth-century Britain as the early development of the factory system.

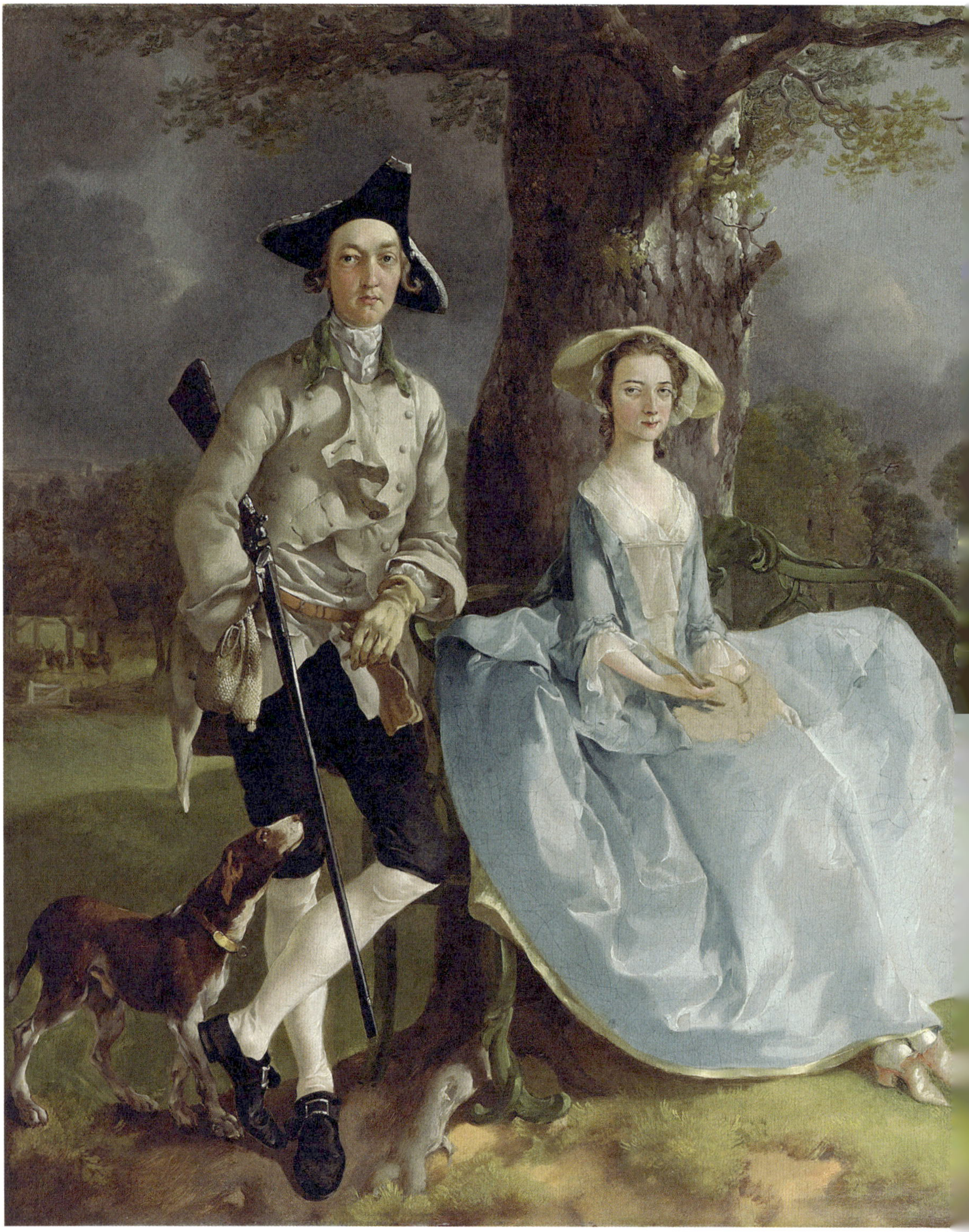

↑ Thomas Gainsborough, *Mr and Mrs Andrews*, c. 1750, oil on canvas, 69.8 × 119.4 cm (27 ½ × 47 in.), National Gallery, London

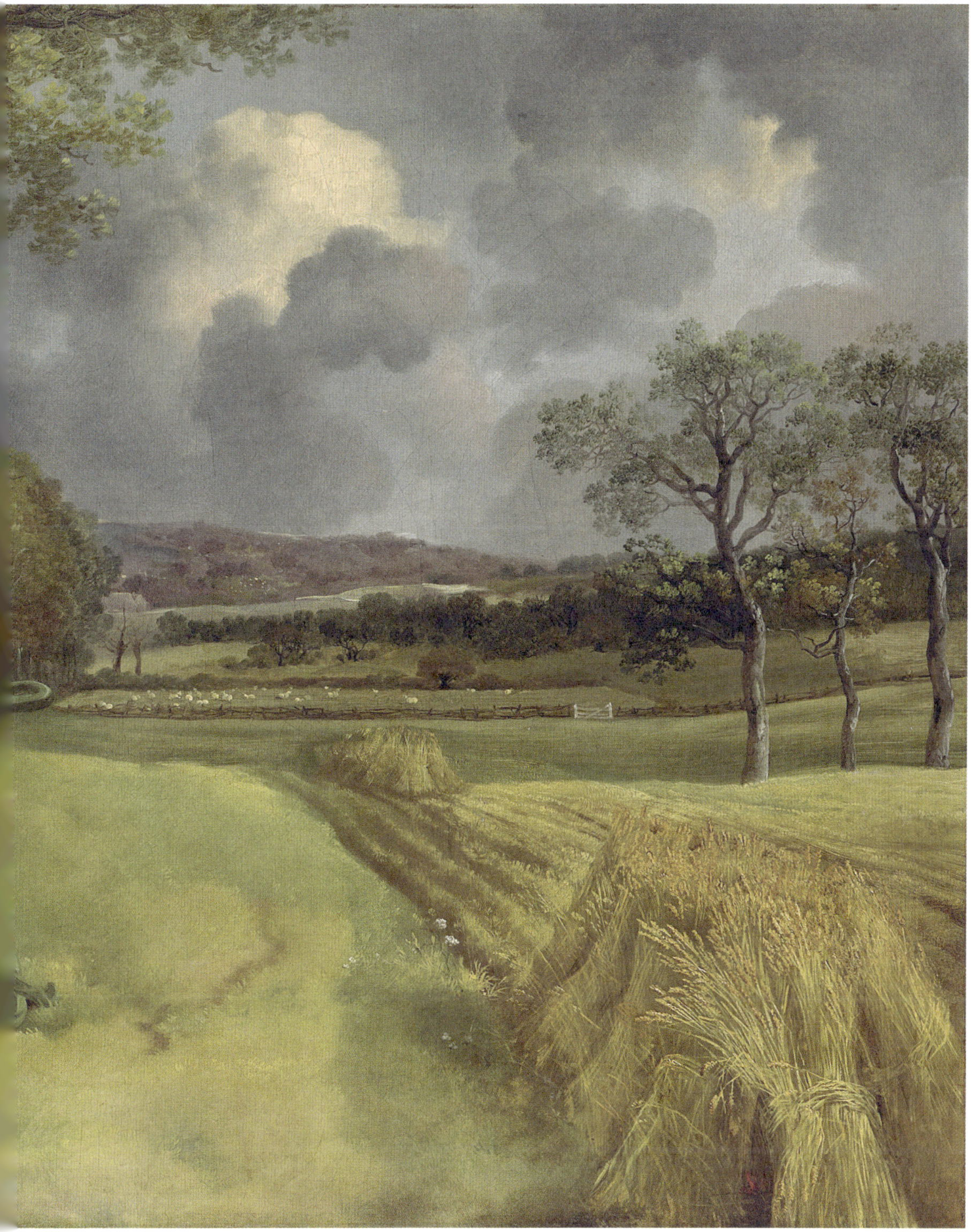

Perhaps there was a sympathy between Gainsborough and his clients, for there is nothing in this picture of the timeless classical dream. Nature is alive and unpredictable here in southeastern England – will it rain? – and bears no trace of the kind of eternal Mediterranean idyll that Palladian houses impose on their landscapes. Surely it is significant that Mr and Mrs Andrews do not want to be painted in front of their house (which was elegant enough). Instead they are out in nature. They have even got a special chair whose curving lines fit naturally into the landscape instead of imposing rectilinear classicism on it.

We are not so far from Hogarth after all. In 1753 this ever-fertile mind published his own book on aesthetics, *The Analysis of Beauty*, in which he rejects the straight lines of the classical ideal and proposes instead a 'serpentine line of beauty', curving and twisting its way through space. Hogarth bases his argument on empirical observations from everyday life as well as art, like a good Lockean Enlightenment thinker. The twisting lines of Mrs Andrews' green wrought-iron seat are nothing if not serpentine.

The serpentine line of beauty is simply an image of the unruly variety of nature itself. The revolutionary genius of Gainsborough's painting is in the way it opens its eyes to that variety. Shifting light, sudden shadows, haphazard vistas hit his eyes, and he paints them. This painting breaks with all the conventions of previous landscape art. Claude's paintings of imaginary classical landscapes had been popular with British landowners since the late seventeenth century. Gainsborough completely ignores the ideals of composition they uphold. He has instead put himself in an actual place, drawn what he saw, then recreated it in the studio on canvas. The tree where Mr and Mrs Andrews posed can still be found. The contours of this view can still be made out. Locke would have been delighted. Gainsborough has let himself be open to impressions like a white piece of paper waiting to be sketched on.

The Child's Mind

Gainsborough did philosophize about seeing, after all. Instead of writing down his understanding of how the visual world gets into our minds he explores it in a painting.

In *The Painter's Daughters Chasing a Butterfly*, of about 1756, Gainsborough's daughters Mary and Margaret are caught in a golden light as they rush through a rocky landscape after a white-winged

→ Thomas Gainsborough, *The Painter's Daughters Chasing a Butterfly*, c. 1756, oil on canvas, 113.5 × 105 cm (44 ⅔ × 41 ⅓ in.), National Gallery, London

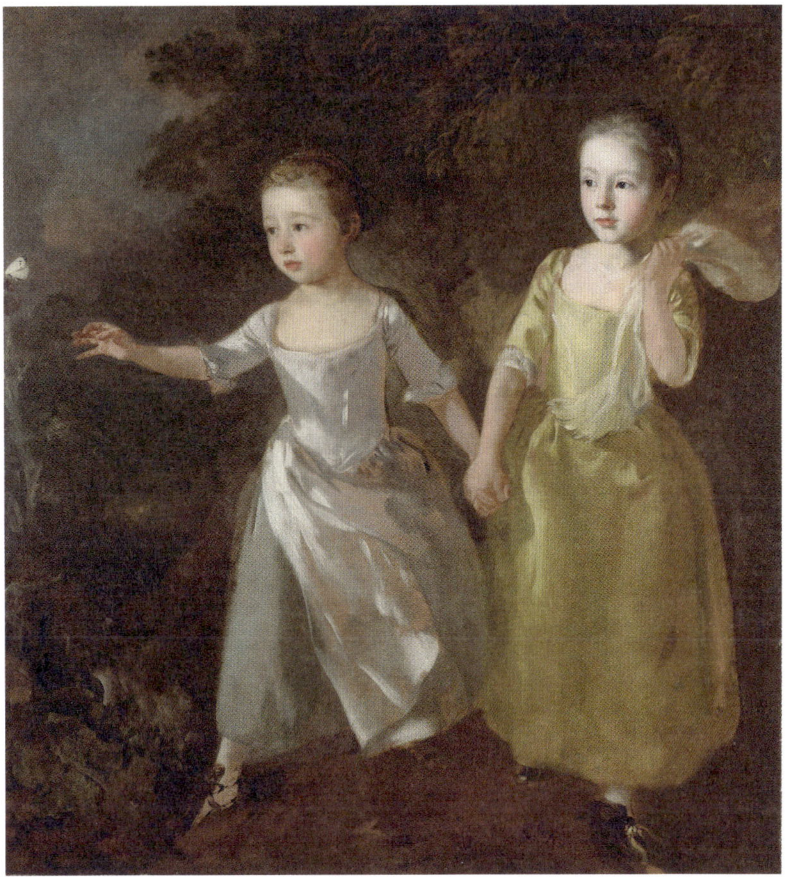

flutterer. Margaret, the younger, reaches out to try and catch it, as small children will. Her slightly older and wiser sister – it is thought they were born in 1750 and 1752 – gazes a little more contemplatively at the bright fast-moving creature.

It is a profoundly loving portrayal. Gainsborough's parental awe at his daughters' beauty and his anxiety for their future are poignantly expressed by making them form the wings of a bigger, even more wondrous butterfly as they hold hands and their shimmering, multicoloured clothes spread out to complete the fragile silhouette.

Childhood blooms in eighteenth-century art. No longer seen as tiny adults, children play in trees, show off toys, dress up and put on theatrical performances. In the 1730s Hogarth painted a cast of children putting on a performance of Dryden's play *The Indian Emperor, or The Conquest of Mexico*, in a miniature theatre constructed in the fine house of John Conduitt, Master of the Mint. It is a rich game of a picture in which an audience of adults watch children pretending to be grownups. Their pleasure in such a performance depends on their understanding that children are, in fact, children. By the time Johann Zoffany painted the children of the Earl of Bute in the 1760s, it would have seemed odd to even refer to adult virtues in this context. One of the earl's sons has climbed into a tree, his brother looks up at him laughing and the third is playing with a bow and arrows. Not to be outdone by the boys, his daughters too are playing by and on a tree in their matching portrait. In about 1768–70, Joseph Wright of Derby painted two girls who are spending their evening trying to put a dress on a kitten by the light of a candle. It is not an allegory of sin – as it would have been in seventeenth-century Dutch art – just an observation of children at play.

Such paintings clearly show, and help to create, a new veneration for the idea of childhood. It was not confined to the children of the rich – the new sentimentality towards children also lay behind the foundation of Coram's Hospital and can be seen in Hogarth's painting of Moses in its Court Room.

Yet something more interesting and precise than tenderness can be seen in Gainsborough's painting of his daughters. Doting dad that he undoubtedly is, he is looking at them with great clarity. He paints not only how children act but how they think, and learn. Even in the 18 months or so between their ages, Mary has become visibly more reflective than Margaret: she holds back from chasing the butterfly, perhaps even slightly restraining her younger sister's enthusiasm. Yet she looks at it even more intently than Margaret does. Margaret's eyes are pained and desperate as she literally yearns to catch the beautiful elusive creature. Mary's gaze is calmer and more perspicacious. She has learned to take pleasure from looking at nature instead of needing to grab it.

Gainsborough wanted his daughters to become artists like himself. In a later portrait that he did of them at the ages of about 12 and 14, both have sketching albums. They have been drawing a plaster cast of a Roman statue of Flora. Mary is by far the more engaged in her work: she sits with porte-crayon in hand and her portfolio on her lap, looking lucidly at us. Does her intent gaze at the butterfly mean Gainsborough already thought he saw an artist in her?

In *The Painter's Daughters Chasing a Butterfly*, Gainsborough ponders the way children learn about the world. This is at the very heart of Locke's philosophy. Children are the proof that we are not born with innate ideas, but must learn everything through sensory perception, argues Locke:

> *He that attentively considers the state of a child, at his first coming into the world, will have little reason to think him stored with plenty of ideas... 'Tis by degrees he comes to be furnished with them: and though the ideas of obvious and familiar qualities, imprint themselves, before the memory begins to keep a register of time and order, yet 'tis often so late, before some unusual qualities come in the way, that there are few men that cannot recollect the beginning of their acquaintance with them...*

And the first things we become aware of are shown us by our eyes:

> *Light, and colours, are busy at hand everywhere, when the eye is but open...*

Gainsborough's young children chase the light they see, and their father, who has learned to notice and to preserve colours with the nuance of art, paints a bright moment of their childhood in which he celebrates the growth of the mind.

The Guts of Science

Hogarth's print series *The Four Stages of Cruelty* makes graphically clear the liberal implications of Locke's theory of child development. If the child starts as a blank slate it must be nurture, not nature, that makes good or bad people. The anti-hero of Hogarth's series is not born bad but corrupted by the callous, banal cruelties he sees every day as a child. Better first impressions could have formed a better person.

The final image, *The Reward of Cruelty*, shows what happens after Tom Nero is hanged. His body has been handed over to the anatomists to be eviscerated for the supposed good of science. One doctor pokes a knife into his eye as his head is raised by a pulley connected to his skull by a screw driven straight into the frontal bone. Another anatomist has sliced open his stomach with a vicious-looking blade. Guts are sliding out on to the floor. A dog sniffs at them even as

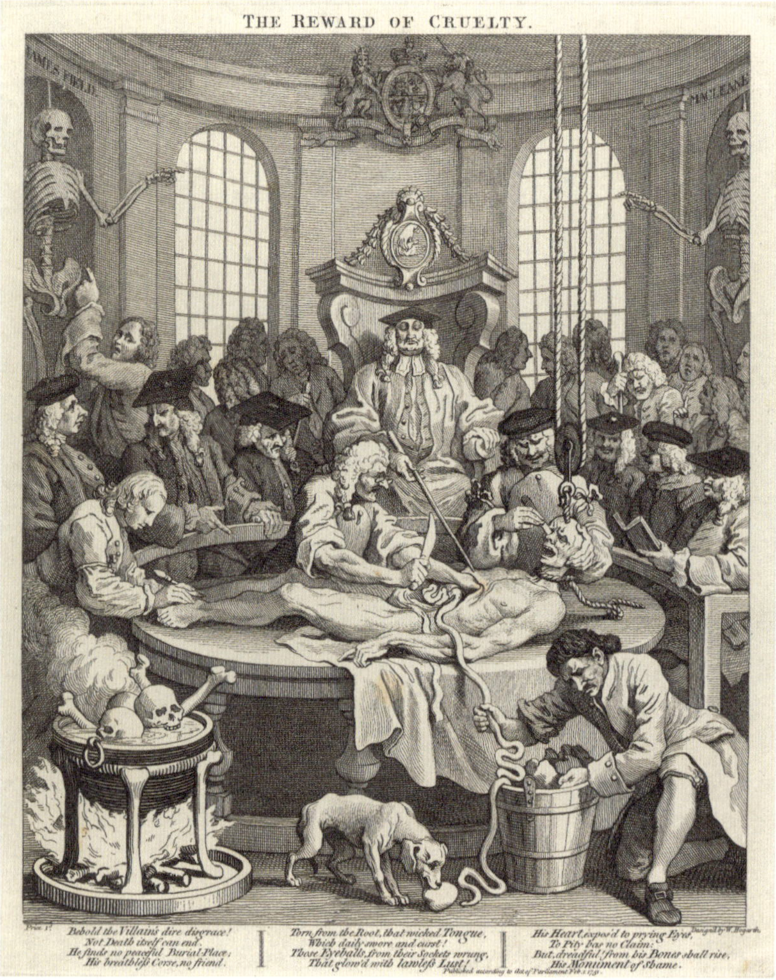

← William Hogarth, *The Reward of Cruelty (Anatomy Theatre)*, from *The Four Stages of Cruelty*, 1751, engraving, 35.6 × 29.8 cm (14 × 11¾ in.), Yale Center for British Art, New Haven

a servant is trying to shove everything into a bucket. The eyes of the audience – many of whom pay little attention to the brutish dissection – are dark and lightless. They have supped full of horrors.

Anatomy was the most spectacular of all the theatrical exhibitions of early science, yet also the most bloody and shocking. Cutting into dead bodies and studying them with fresh eyes was established by Andreas Vesalius in sixteenth-century Italy as the only way to – literally – see beyond the 2,000-year-old hand-me-downs of ancient Greek authorities. It became one of the quickest-developing sciences, with Vesalius and other Italian pioneers including Gabriele Fallopio, discoverer of the fallopian tubes, making rapid progress.

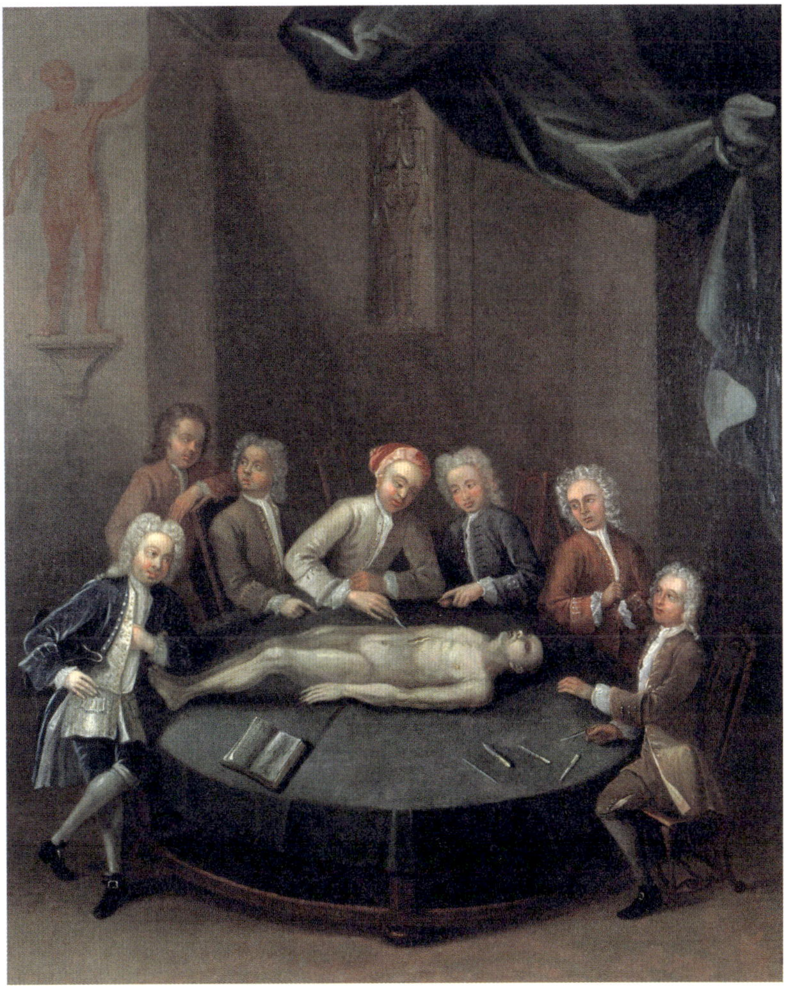

→ Charles Philips attrib., *William Cheselden giving an anatomical demonstration to six spectators in the anatomy theatre of the Barber-Surgeons' Company, London*, c. 1730–40, oil on canvas, 79.7 × 60.5 cm (31⅓ × 23⅘ in.), Wellcome Library, London

Leonardo da Vinci had beaten them to it by doing superb drawings from his own dissections at the very beginning of the sixteenth century. Yet anatomy was always controversial and fraught with moral ambiguity. There was something disgraceful about it – even something criminal. Hogarth's *The Reward of Cruelty* turns the law upside down. The practice he depicts – the use of criminal bodies for dissection – was permitted precisely because it was horrible and un-Christian. To be denied a proper church burial and instead have your body sliced up by surgeons was to put your very soul at risk. Those who believed in draconian punishments to terrify the poor actively promoted the nightmare of dissection. The Murder Act of 1752 formally permitted and encouraged it. This became law a year after Hogarth's print was published. Whose side is he on? His friend the novelist and legal reformer Henry Fielding was concerned that being hanged at Tyburn simply was not deterrent enough. The primitive spectacle of capital punishment made stars of the likes of Jack Sheppard. Hogarth shows that it is no carnival: you will end up with a dog sniffing at your entrails as the anatomists take you apart.

Yet this gory rite loomed large in early modern Britain's love affair with science. The setting of Hogarth's *The Reward of Cruelty* is a purpose-built anatomy theatre created by Inigo Jones in 1636 at the hall of the Guild of Barber-Surgeons. Designed to maximize the visibility of the dissected body, the architecture of Jones's anatomy theatre puts looking at the centre of science. One of the first important British contributions to European science came when Charles I's doctor William Harvey observed the circulation of the blood. Impressive poking about was also done by Edward Tyson, who in 1699 published a work entitled *Orang-Outang, sive Homo Sylvestris: or, the Anatomy of a Pygmie Compared with that of a Monkey, an Ape, and a Man*. Its engravings lay bare the muscles and skeletons of primates, revealing their resemblance to humans: a highly disconcerting comparison in a Christian society that was taught to think of man as King over the Beasts. Tyson's book with its eerie illustrations typifies both the power of anatomy and its spectacularly visual nature. Like astronomy, it showed new knowledge to the human eye in a bold, undeniable way. This was the real, solid, pungent stuff of discovery – the guts of science.

Anatomy became one of Georgian England's favourite blood sports. The early eighteenth-century surgeon William Cheselden gave much-admired shows to the scientific cognoscenti. A painting from about 1730 shows him at work in the Barber-Surgeons' anatomy theatre. Bewigged gentlemen are seated around a grey corpse laid out on the same oval dissecting table depicted by Hogarth. Instead of dead eyes in haggard faces, this is a portrait of polite curiosity as Cheselden points out an interesting detail. Cheselden took an active interest in illustrating his own observations. A painting of a human skull said to be his handiwork survives in the Hunterian Museum. An illustration in his 1726 work *The Anatomy of the Human Body*, of a man who had his arm ripped off at the shoulder, depicts both the amputee and his severed limb as if they were fragments of ancient Roman sculpture. This book was a bestseller, but in his *Osteographia or The Anatomy of the Bones* of

1733, Cheselden takes the analogy between anatomy and art into pretentious territory. In one of its plates, three skeletons contemplate their own mortality, adopting pensive poses next to a marble sarcophagus.

George Stubbs had no such pretensions about anatomy being a fine art. When he dissected horses in his lodgings at Horkstow he was not setting out to show that science could be art, but that art could be practised scientifically. His aim was to understand nature exactly, in order to paint it with precision. Early in his career this enigmatic, single-minded artist fell out with a Liverpool painter who was giving him lessons. The young Stubbs – he later told a friend – swore then that he 'would for the future look into Nature for himself and consult and study her only'.

Few artists have ever taken that aspiration quite so literally. Stubbs challenged himself to understand the nature of horses better than any previous artist, from the inside out. His plan was to publish a book of engravings that would unveil equine anatomy more completely and exactly than any previous study. The drawings that survive from his strenuous enterprise prove that he looked as deeply as he cut. One remarkable analysis resembles a ghost horse materializing on an empty page. Tendons and muscles in the horse's neck and legs are painstakingly detailed, their tangled stillness revealing how perfectly his wax injections have frozen them in place. Yet even as he coolly and carefully observes each taut sinew and expansive muscle, he also notices the closed eye of the horse with a tender compassion for this beautiful creature. Its empty rib cage is pale and spectral, and at the same time a structure of awe-inspiring perfection. Stubbs exposes and sees the complexity of nature, the intricacy of a single animal.

Then he draws it again. Some sheets record the bones of the horse with a translucent, almost digital precision. He shows the skeleton from all sides, exploiting the empty space between the bones to look straight through this majestic cage from front, back and side and see its internal structure in a three-dimensional perspective. In another drawing the horse at first sight appears intact and alive: on closer inspection you see that it has been flayed and what we are looking at is the outer surface of the muscles covering its internal organs. Why does he once again make it seem almost ghostly?

Stubbs is not just being sentimental. He is trying to learn about life by studying the dead. His aim is to comprehend in complete internal detail how a living horse is constituted. Always, he keeps that ultimate

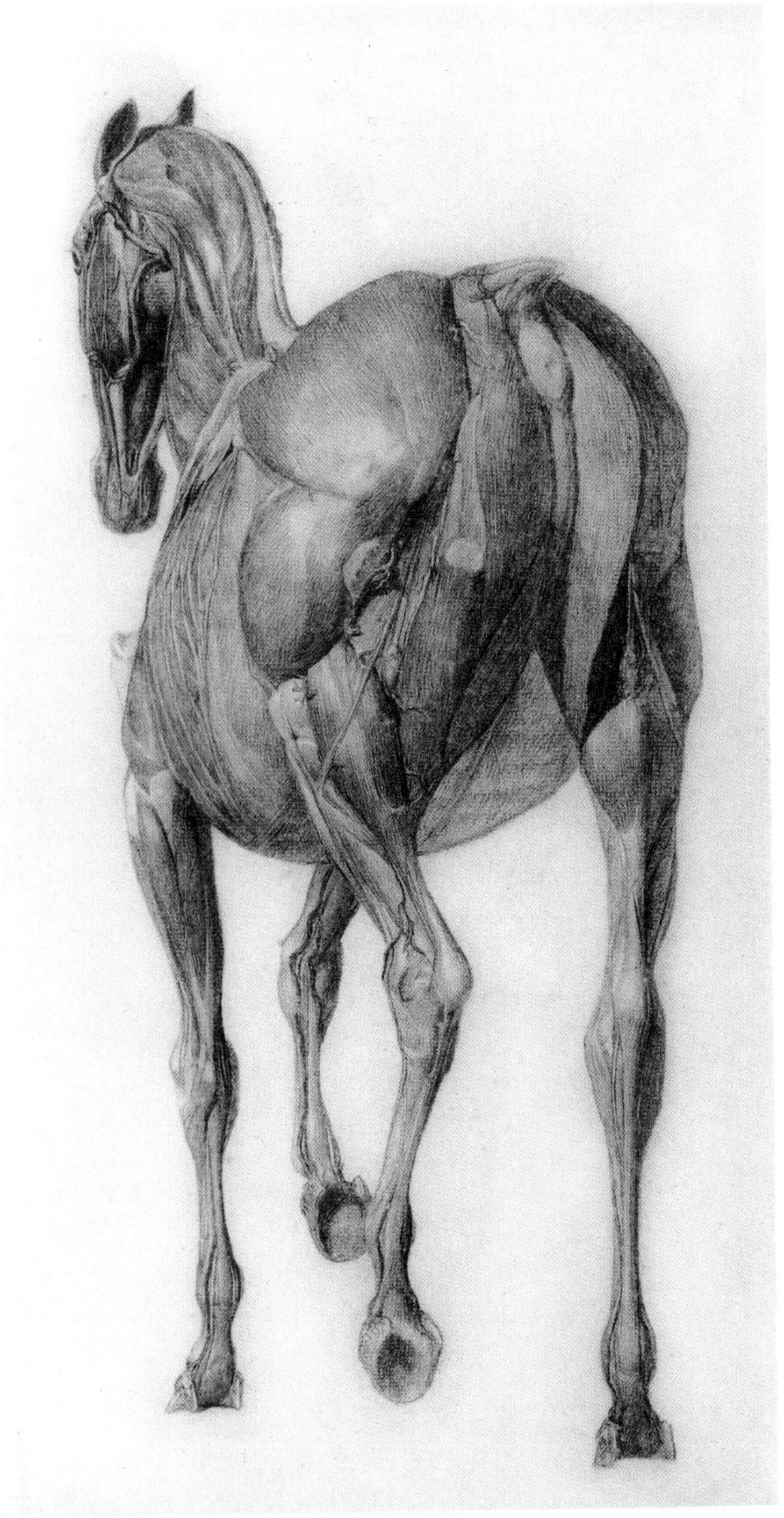

↔ George Stubbs, two working drawings from the seventh and tenth 'Anatomical Table of the Muscles ... of the Horse', 1756–58, pencil, black and red chalk, red-brown ink, 48 × 30.5 cm (18 ⅚ × 12 in.) and 48 × 31.2 cm (18 ⅚ × 12 ¼ in.), Royal Academy, London

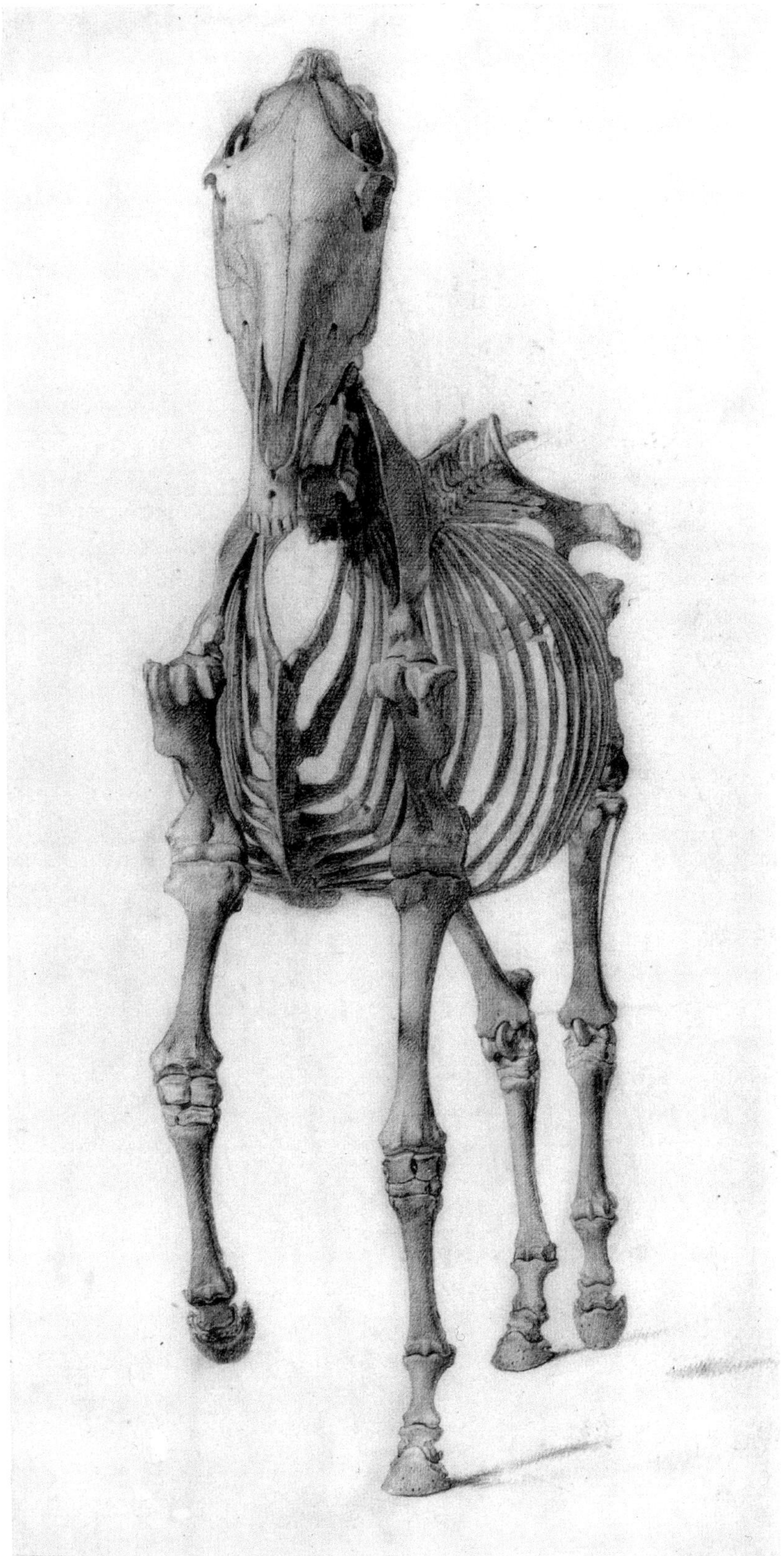

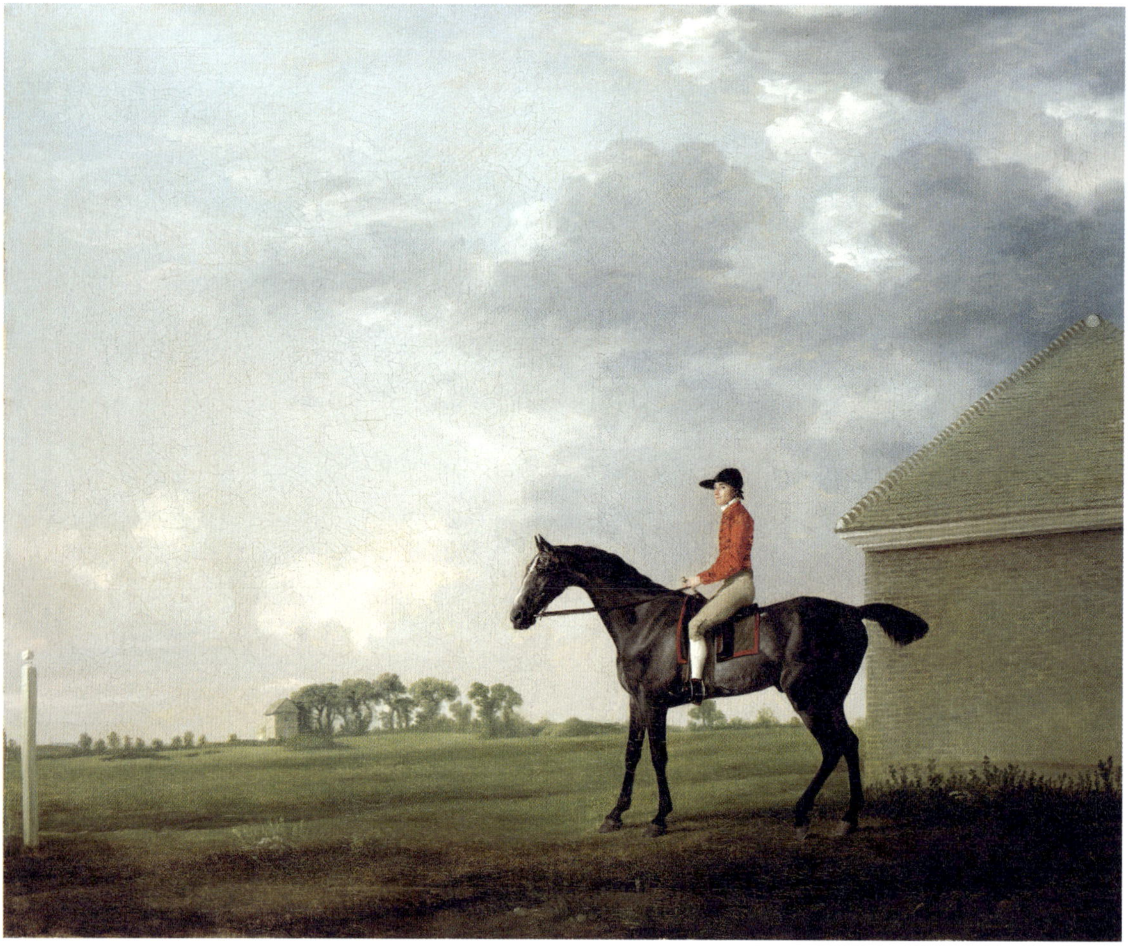

↑ George Stubbs, *Gimcrack, with John Pratt up on Newmarket Heath*, c. 1765, oil on canvas, 100 × 124 cm (39 ⅜ × 48 ⅘ in.), Fitzwilliam Museum, University of Cambridge

purpose of understanding the living animal in mind as he draws the dead one. Yet it is bloody work. The muscles that cover the horse begin to be stripped away. In the next drawing the tendons of the neck are exposed. No illusions about this creature being alive. Its ribs protrude through its skinned flank. Then he cuts away more flesh, to see another layer of muscles. More arteries appear. At last there are just bits of dark nerves and tendons stuck to bare bones.

He draws this entire process from three angles – with the horse facing him and its body turned to the right; with its rump facing him and the body similarly turned; and as a simple side view. The gradual removal of each layer of the horse's muscles can be seen from each of these perspectives. Put them all together and you have a complete three-dimensional picture of the structure of an animal.

Eventually, in 1766, Stubbs published his eye-opening book *The Anatomy of the Horse*. Yet its superb engravings are just a small part of what his dissection gave him. From the moment he completed his anatomical adventure it shaped his art. Before the dissection he painted very little that is known of, and nothing much to speak about. An ungainly but powerful portrait of a Liverpool gentleman with a double chin shows his eye for truth. Did people want that in portraits? Perhaps they valued it more in pictures of their horses. The horse was a rock star in eighteenth-century Britain. Horse racing had become a national sport that combined many aspects of this complicated society. Spectatorship, horse dealing, race reporting and above all gambling captured the energy of an expanding commercial nation. At the same time aristocratic ownership of famous horses showed who was still in charge. Even the obsession with the genealogy of thoroughbreds was a mirror of snobbery. Yet through all this there shone a growing fascination with the natural world as British eyes fixated on horses in the landscape.

We see all that in the art of George Stubbs. Knowing horses from the inside gave him an edge over every competitor in the field. From the late 1750s onwards it seems he must have painted every thoroughbred horse in the country. One landowner after another commissioned him to paint stallions, foals and mares. No wonder, for his paintings exhibit the empirical exactness only anatomy can give them. He often paints them standing quite still, posed like his anatomical specimens. We seem to see into them. Their muscles and nerves pulse under the skin. Stubbs paints the horse as a scientific wonder. Locke's philosophy of empiricism bears strange fruit in his frozen, isolated portraits of animals whose anatomical exactitude makes them more real than the folk who ride them. In his circa 1765 painting *Gimcrack, with John Pratt up on Newmarket Heath*, a racehorse poses with the same sombre dignity Stubbs depicted in his flayed, eviscerated horses. The knowledge he got from his dissections enables him to paint nature with uncanny factuality. Gimcrack is perfectly preserved in paint, his body a dark sleek fact under the vast Newmarket sky, entering our mind as firmly as a pencil mark on white paper.

4. The Sublime Zoo

But I must freely confess, that the many virtues of those excellent quadrupeds, placed in opposite view to human corruptions, had so far opened my eyes and enlarged my understanding, that I began to view the actions and passions of man in a very different light ...

Jonathan Swift,
Gulliver's Travels, 1726

Stranger in the Park

A zebra stands in an English park. Its black and white stripes have been acutely observed and meticulously painted by George Stubbs. He is delighted by this unexpectedly formal and artificial-seeming pattern – as gaudily exquisite as the designs of Georgian textiles – on an animal. His thorough knowledge of equine anatomy enables him to give it a real and solid structural presence. He had never seen inside a zebra, but it looks as if he has been studying this animal for a lifetime. Yet what makes this a masterpiece is the sympathy for his subject that shines through all the purported objectivity. This exotic mammal has the same dignity as his thoroughbred horses. It stares blankly, as if wondering where on earth it is. Caught in bronze sunlight that flows mistily through a leafy woodland, it stands absolutely still as if it has just heard a twig break. A nervous uncertainty ripples through its stripes. It is anxious, alert and alone.

Stubbs has put almost as much observation and effort into painting the leaves overhead and the soft colours of the woodland as he has into getting the zebra's stripes just so. This very English-looking location is a wild spot in St James's Park, where the first zebra ever transported to Britain was put on public display by its owner, Queen Charlotte, consort of the new King George III, in 1762. The following spring Stubbs revealed his superb and strange portrait in the annual

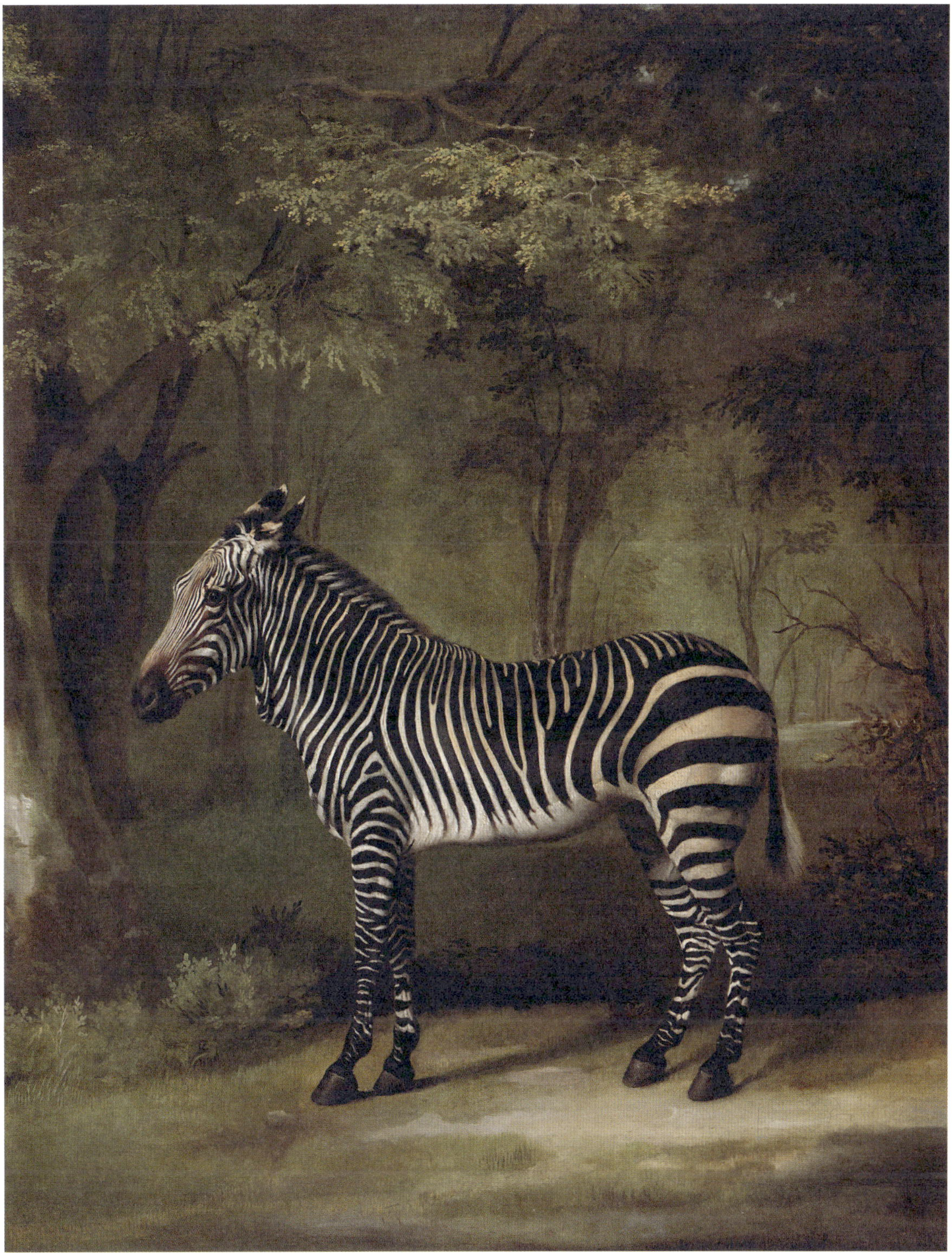

↑ George Stubbs, *Zebra* (detail), 1763

exhibition of the Society of Artists. His empirical regard is so realistic that it becomes utterly surreal. The contrast between the black and white zebra and the surrounding greenwood is outrageous. The woodland is the quintessence of English rusticity: nature as it is supposed to appear if you come from a temperate European climate. Greens, browns, and uneven sunlight. The zebra by contrast does not seem 'natural': it resembles some outlandish new invention. Yet this too is nature. It seems the natural world has many shocks in store for the honest empirical eye.

The zebra comes from a different landscape, a different world. It has been uprooted, stolen, taken to sea; it was in fact transported from Cape Town. Stubbs knew about such cruel displacements. He came from Liverpool whose growth into an important city in the eighteenth century rested on the slave trade. Does this African stranger in St James's Park share the melancholy of the enslaved?

The art of science that flourished in the reign of George III is not only perspicacious and informative but estranging. It is an art that travels to new worlds and returns forever changed.

The World's End

Perhaps everyone equates their own demise with the end of the world, but few have done so as wittily as William Hogarth. Britain's first homegrown artistic genius died on 26 October 1764. That spring he had published his final engraving, a satirical vision of the apocalypse in which an inn sign for a pub called the World's End, with a painting of the globe on fire, sags in a comically overstated landscape of ruin and decay. The pub itself has collapsed, as has a church tower. Lifeless blackened trees recede through the desolate countryside, leading the eye to a hanged man on the horizon. Father Time himself has wilted, uttering the word 'FINIS' (The End) among a heap of cultural detritus that includes a blazing copy of a print in which Hogarth had satirized the radical new 'Liberty' politics of John Wilkes and hailed the reign of George III.

In the sky, the sun god Apollo is asleep in his chariot as gloom covers the land. It is not only death that Hogarth mocks with his dying breath but the current trends in the art market. Hogarth, who had spent his life campaigning for modern British art, expresses his despair at a booming trade in continental Old Masters, a vogue for their

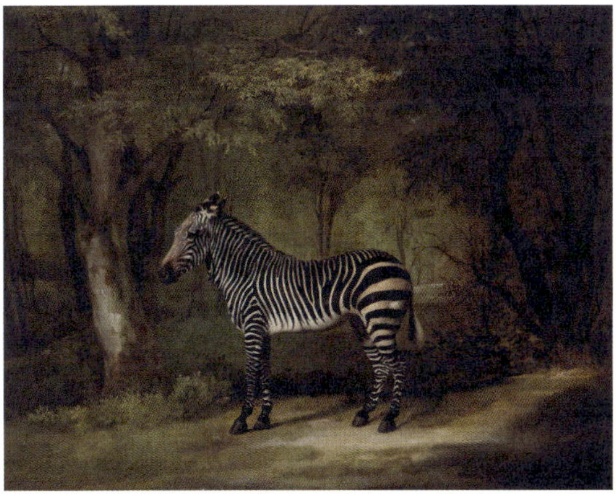

↑ George Stubbs, *Zebra* 1763, oil on canvas, 102.9 × 127.6 cm (40½ × 50¼ in.), Yale Center for British Art, New Haven.

time-smoked, over-varnished shadows, as well as a disturbing new tendency in modern British art. In the subscription he laughs sardonically at the 'Manner of Sinking in Sublime Paintings, inscribed to the Dealers in Dark Pictures'.

Hogarth had begun his career in a Britain that had hardly any artists of its own. He played a leading role in the creation of an original and energetic British art. By the time George III took the throne in 1760 there were plenty of busy British painters, if not many decent sculptors. Some of these painters were doing well financially and a handful were genuinely gifted. In addition to Hogarth and Gainsborough, there was the tireless Joshua Reynolds, friend to Dr Johnson and other luminaries, an intellectual in his own right who attempted to combine profitable portraiture with lofty classicism. Thomas Hudson, Arthur Devis and Allan Ramsay also helped raise the beloved British art of the portrait to such heights of classy cool that when the remarkable German artist Johann Zoffany moved to Britain in 1760 he joined an Enlightened local art world confidently taking its place on the European cultural stage. Proper exhibitions were becoming part of the London cultural mix, with the Society of Artists putting on popular shows of contemporary art from its foundation in 1761.

Yet Hogarth in his old age was cynical. Was it not all getting a bit above itself? The slumbering Apollo is a clue to his feelings about where British art was headed. This reclining figure in a chariot led astray by headlong horses resembles a painting Stubbs exhibited at the Society of Artists in 1762. Stubbs's painting shows Phaeton, the foolish son of Apollo who thought he could drive his father's chariot, falling back in despair as he loses control of his wild stallions of the sky. Hogarth clearly has this recent British painting in his sights, as an example of the fashionable cant he rails at. Stubbs's doomed chariot, while far from his best work, was undoubtedly striving to be a 'sublime painting'.

Edmund Burke was not convinced there could be any such thing. In 1757 this young Irish writer and aspiring politician published his first book, *A Philosophical Enquiry into the Origin of Our Ideas on the Sublime and Beautiful* (one of the texts for which William Blake felt contempt and abhorrence). It has become famous as a work of artistic theory. Yet in Burke's opinion visual art is incapable of generating 'sublime' sensations. Pictures are too clear, too prosaic to exact the requisite awe. Real natural phenomena such as a pitch-black night, a terrifying mountain or a vast ocean are much more likely to fill you with that very special sense of dread, fear, smallness and unease.

To understand Burke's book and its impact we need to escape our own puritan disdain for aesthetic pleasure. Art is rarely praised nowadays for giving pleasure. Instead it is admired for being thought-provoking or challenging or politically subversive. Enlightenment attitudes were the opposite. Art was to be enjoyed. More precisely, beauty was to be enjoyed. Writers on art, from the Whig aristocrat Lord Shaftesbury, who was taught by Locke and pioneered the concept of the aesthetic in works published in the early 1700s, to Hogarth in his *Analysis of Beauty*, are concerned with what beauty is and how to enjoy it. Yet we don't need to read these books to see that eighteenth-century people took wildly uninhibited pleasure in sheer beauty. We just need to look at Gainsborough's portraits.

In 1759 Gainsborough moved to Bath, where he set up a portrait studio catering to the beautiful people who flocked to this stylish spa town. He left behind not only his native East Anglia but his crisp empiricist early style. Nature still wafts through his art but now it is bathed in fancy, a pastoral stage for gorgeous individuality. Instead of the Suffolk sky it is silks and velvets that fill his eye. Gainsborough blossoms into one of the most hedonistic painters to have ever lived.

His hedonism is that of a painter in love with paint and – it cannot be ignored – a man in love with women. Desire shimmers through his portraits in lacy layers of flirtation. Pleasure in the subtleties of his art mingles with delight in female company. It is a cliché to assume that a commercial portrait painter like Gainsborough suppresses his own subjectivity as he 'flatters' the rich. I suppose the grand portrait of Mary, Countess Howe, that he painted in Bath in about 1763–64 is a work of flattery – although we do not have the original to compare it with – and yet it manifestly indulges the artist's own technical delight and amorous fantasy. Standing tall and proud, hand on hip, in a straw hat, pink skirts, and pointy shoes, Countess Howe looks formidable, powerful, wondrous. The painting's allure has a lot to do with the play of light between the stormily smouldering sky Gainsborough has invented and the gleaming shiny rose of her dress, the pallor of her

→ Thomas Gainsborough, *Mary, Countess Howe*, c. 1763–64, oil on canvas, 244 × 152.4 cm (96 x 60 in.), Kenwood House, London

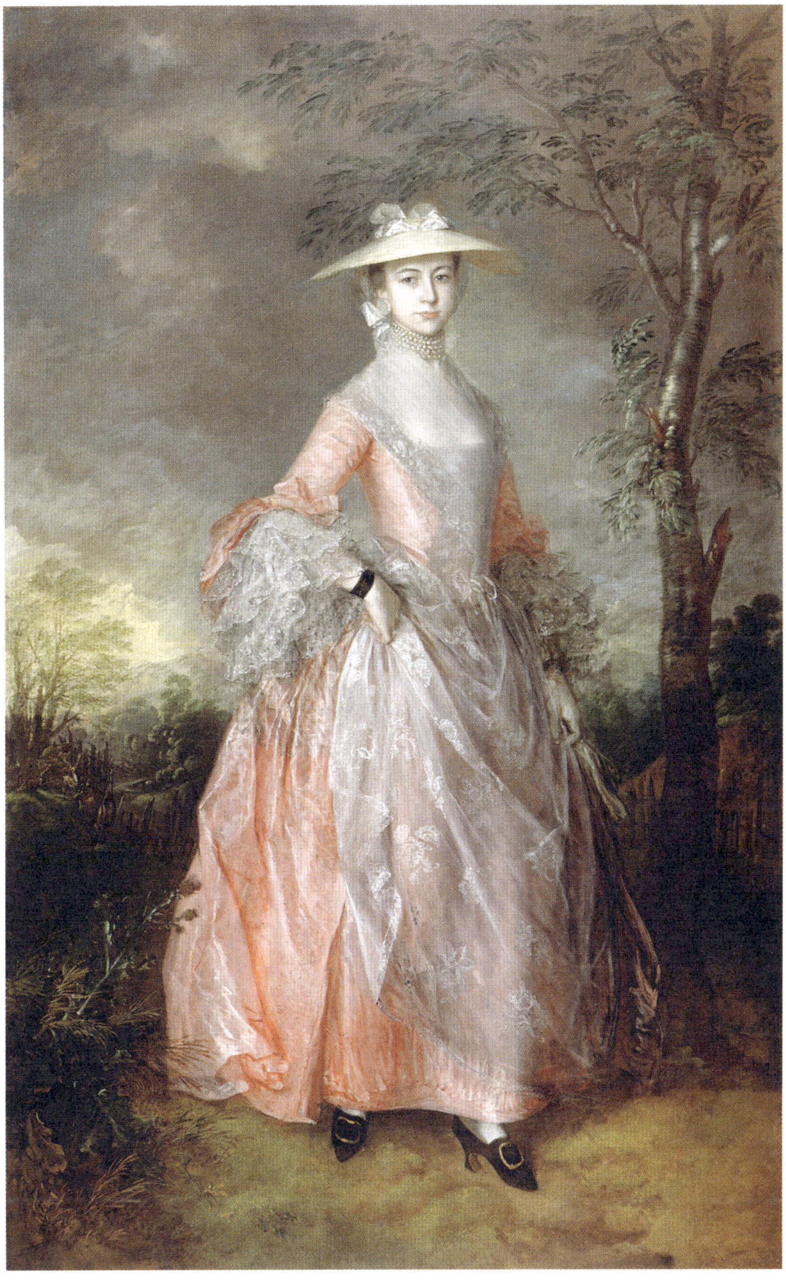

razor-sharp face, the fluffy white mists of lace and gossamer silk falling over her breasts and artfully leading the eye on a wild-goose chase through apparently infinite visual layers.

Eighteenth-century eyes loved to be teased by complexity. For as Hogarth put it:

> *Pursuing is the business of our lives, and even abstracted from any other view, gives pleasure. Every arising difficulty, that for a while attends and interrupts the pursuit, gives a sort of spring to the mind, enhances the pleasure...*

Even the highly urban Hogarth, this passage reveals, enjoyed the quintessential eighteenth-century country sport of hunting. The pleasures of the chase also shape our optical experience, he claims:

> *The eye hath this sort of enjoyment in winding walks, and serpentine rivers, and all sorts of objects, whose forms, as we shall see hereafter, are composed principally of what, I call, the waving and serpentine lines.*

Gainsborough's paintings are a perfect illustration of Hogarth's claim that our eyes enjoy 'winding walks'. He gleefully turns painting itself into a game, playfully threading what often looks like a powerful sexual desire into lush layerings of translucent colour. To put it another way, Gainsborough's paintings and Hogarth's idea of serpentine beauty both transpose to Britain the unabashedly sensual style of the French Rococo that expresses the freedom of Enlightenment culture in a flirtatious theatre of ambiguous looks.

Bath itself is testament to the eighteenth-century capacity for enjoying beauty without guilt or inhibition. The development of this resort town as a place where polite society could play cards, dance, bathe and broker marriages brilliantly merged social function and aesthetic splendour. John Wood senior's splendidly imaginative classical architecture combines Roman rules handed down by Vitruvius with the mystery of southwest England's prehistoric monuments. His masterpiece, the Circus, a magical disc of lofty terraces, created between 1754 and 1768, takes inspiration from Stonehenge as well as the Colosseum. At the nearby Assembly Rooms, you could either take part in the dances or gossip and gamble. Afterwards you might go and see Mr Gainsborough and let him work on your portrait. This theatre of gentility was also a place where talent flourished and where some freedom was possible for women, who played, acted or sang. In Gainsborough's great portrait of Elizabeth and Mary Linley, he portrays

→ Thomas Gainsborough, *Elizabeth and Mary Linley*, 1771/72, retouched 1785, oil on canvas, 199 × 153.5 cm (78 ⅓ × 60 ⅖ in.), Dulwich Picture Gallery, London

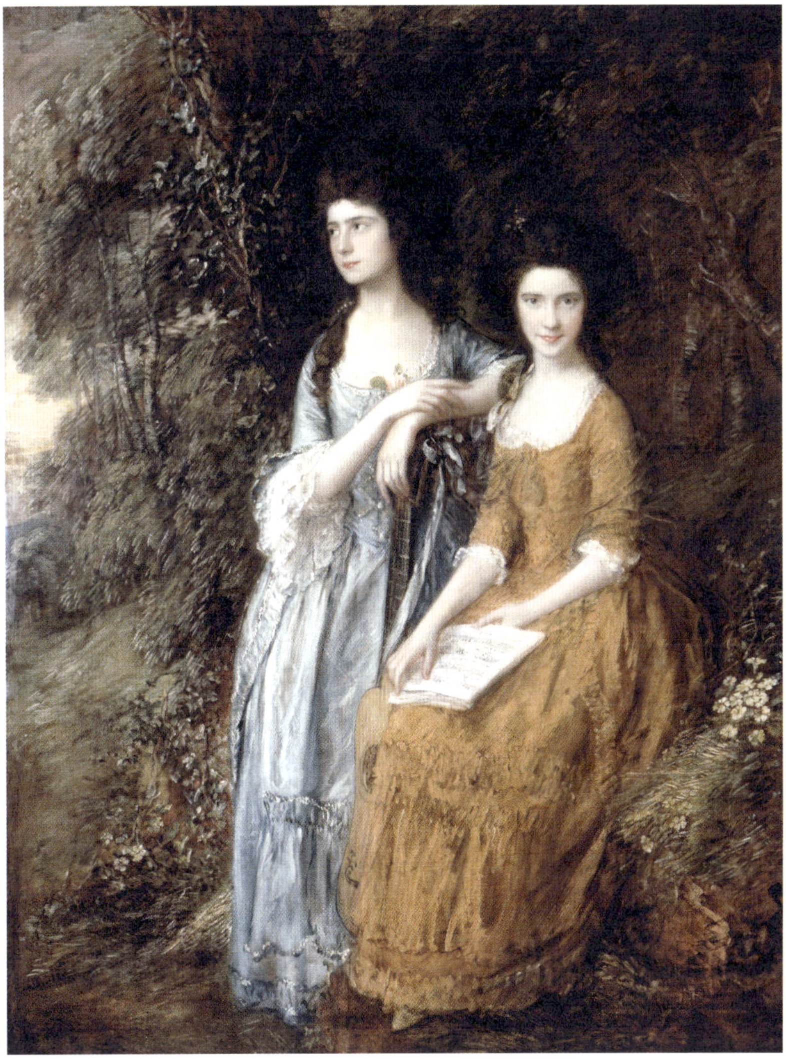

two professional singers who had recently started their careers in Bath. By the time he finished it, Elizabeth had eloped with the dramatist Richard Brinsley Sheridan. She looks off romantically into Gainsborough's poetic velvety landscape while her sister gazes directly at the onlooker. It was the romantic dreaminess of Elizabeth Linley that contemporaries found more fascinating. Sheridan had to fight two duels against a rival for her love.

It was not embarrassment or moral disapproval of the Enlightenment's joy in beauty that made Burke start to think about the dark side of aesthetic experience. It was rather that he sometimes found himself enjoying fear and horror more. He was a student at Trinity College, Dublin, when he started meditating on the sublime and beautiful. It is easy to account for our delight in beauty – anyway, fans of Elizabeth Linley felt no need to theorize what made them fight each other at dawn – but what is it that draws us to a tragic play or a roaring abyss?

Burke's exploration of his feelings in his *Enquiry* is an empirical adventure, rooted in the philosophy of Locke. Yet he finds, analyzing his responses to different stimuli, that reason does not always prevail. Often our minds are 'hurried on' by a powerful 'passion' that inspires:

> *Astonishment; and astonishment is that state of soul, in which all its motions are suspended, with some degree of horror.*

This paralysis is 'the effect of the sublime in its highest degree'. Its most potent source is sheer terror: when we are truly terrified we lose the ability to act or think. We surrender to that strange psychological narcotic, the sublime. A poisonous snake will do as well as a vast cavern to create this dread. What is difficult is to create it by art, for as Burke points out, you can put on the most harrowing tragedy ever written, but if you tell the audience before it begins that a hanging is about to take place next door, the theatre will empty.

Milton's *Paradise Lost* is one work of art that is truly sublime for, Burke argues, it creates 'obscure' and tantalizing images of infinite space and darkness that are limited only by the imagination of the reader. Milton describes the place where Satan and his army of fallen angels find themselves cast down as completely lightless – a black night so inky you can see it, a 'darkness visible' – and so vast that its walls and ceiling are undiscoverable, incomprehensible. In Milton's satanic images, claims Burke, 'all is dark, uncertain, confused, terrible, and sublime in the last degree'.

Milton stands with Newton and Locke as a cultural pillar of Enlightenment Britain. This pillar is ornate and orotund and too lofty for its heights to be seen. Milton is the poet of the seventeenth-century scientific revolution. As we have seen, he met Galileo and prophesied a new age of Protestant science. In *Paradise Lost* he creates a daunting Baroque vision of the cosmos, cleverly avoiding any need to choose between Copernicus and older models of Earth's place in the universe as he unfurls fiery vistas of space and time. *Paradise Lost* is astronomical.

It pictures the sheer glory of cosmic being. For eighteenth-century readers this science-fiction epic was, as Burke expresses it, 'sublime in the last degree'. Other fans included Hogarth, who painted Milton's Satan meeting Death and Sin; and Blake, for whom the blind poet was secretly of the Devil's party.

Burke doubted that painters in their pedantry – as opposed to poets – could ever produce the sublime. How can a picture generate the necessary sense of limitless space and mystery?

It was a horse painter from Liverpool who would show exactly how this might be done.

The Startled Horse

Horace Walpole stood utterly transfixed. He felt pity, compassion, horror. He felt, in his own soul, the poor dumb animal's dread. It was able to convey its fright without uttering a whinny, let alone any words.

Walpole stumbled out of the Society of Artists in 1763 in a trance. A painting by George Stubbs had shaken him so much that when he got home to the shadowy alcoves of his Gothic retreat Strawberry Hill he had to release his feelings in a poem. It is one of Britain's first newspaper art reviews, headlined:

> *November 4th, 1763.*
> *For the Public Advertiser.*
> *On seeing the celebrated Startled Horse,*
> *painted by the inimitable Mr. Stubbs.*

The painting that moved Walpole to verse is one of a series in which Stubbs depicts horses either spooked or actually being devoured before our eyes by a merciless big cat. The action takes place in a bleak landscape of daunting rocks and scrubby trees under a sky whose brightness suggests remote exotic climes – but which is in reality the long, wild gorge of Creswell Craggs on the border of Derbyshire and Nottinghamshire. Stubbs became fascinated by the solitude and silence of this landscape, painting it frequently, and as he walked under its overhanging masses of ancient limestone his fancy peopled it with savage beasts.

In the painting Walpole saw, the dark dreadful form of a lion paces quietly and murderously from the shadow of a stone outcrop. A wild horse with a light-brown coat and white mane has just seen it and recoils in terror, leaping backwards, its eye fixed on the mortal threat that lurks so close, as its legs push it back in sharp reverse. The horse expresses intense fear in its thunderstruck stance, its helpless face. That dumb eloquence makes a mockery of anyone who thinks words are more powerful than pictures, argues Walpole in his fervent poem. What need of language:

> *When startled nature rushes through the eyes,*
> *In all the force of terror and surprise!*

This is sometimes interpreted as a refutation of Burke's pessimism about paintings ever being truly sublime. Walpole explicitly calls Stubbs's picture a 'sublime essay', making it clear, in case of any doubt, that the artist really has released the demonic majesty of the sublime from the unearthly shadows of Cresswell Crags. Yet Walpole goes far beyond artspeak in his response to Stubbs. He sees in this painting a challenge to the traditional belief in human superiority to 'brute creation'. For him Stubbs has painted not just a scary picture but a new vision of nature itself. Sublime art, sublime science.

It challenges, he claims, the anthropocentrism of the French scientist and philosopher René Descartes, for whom animals, lacking a soul, are like machines: 'Is that an engine! that a mere machine!'

Descartes had, in the seventeenth century, constructed a rationalist system of philosophy and physics that proceeds from the one certain fact that we know we exist because we are aware of our own consciousness. He proposed that animals lack that divine conscious spark and so do not feel pain. This was a new way of stating a very old theological prejudice. God appointed man lord over creation. As Adam reminds Eve in Milton's *Paradise Lost*, the human species enjoys:

> *...dominion given*
> *Over all other creatures...*

In eighteenth-century Britain this dominion was being questioned. Hogarth said he engraved his *Four Stages of Cruelty* 'in hopes of preventing in some degree that cruel treatment of poor Animals ... the very describing of which gives pain'. Walpole was at the forefront of this compassionate movement. When his pet cat passed away in 1747 he asked his friend the poet Thomas Gray to compose a memorial verse for her: Gray's 'Ode on the Death of a Favourite Cat Drowned in a Tub of

Goldfishes' belongs to a half-serious, half-embarrassed genre of classical epitaphs for animals that also includes a noble tomb in the gardens of the Palladian masterpiece Chiswick House inscribed: 'Under this stone lies Lilly, my dear hound.'

It is patronizing to glibly sum up this new attitude to nature as part of a culture of 'sentiment'. There is nothing especially sentimental about the brilliant portrayal of a yellow-eyed pet cat digging its claws into the upholstery of a chair as it hunts a caged bird in Hogarth's 1742 painting *The Graham Children*. Nor is there anything conventional, trite or cosy about the painting by Stubbs that Walpole found so shattering. It is not some fey sensibility Walpole sees in it but a tragic art that makes him helplessly share the horse's frozen terror:

My fibres tremble, and my sinews slack;
I feel his feelings: how he stands transfix'd!

To share this awe today it is better to contemplate not so much Stubbs's paintings of horses attacked by lions, which time has turned into documents of the sublime rather than generators of it, as his great equine portrait *Whistlejacket*.

When the Whig politician the Marquess of Rockingham commissioned Stubbs in 1762 to portray his Arabian stallion Whistlejacket in a painting that would take pride of place in a grand room in his house Wentworth Woodhouse, Yorkshire, this daring artist created a masterpiece that looks disconcertingly modern. Instead of setting the mighty rearing chestnut form of Rockingham's racehorse against the green expanses of his estate, Stubbs gives Whistlejacket no context at all. He is framed by a light-brown blankness. His rear hooves, the only parts of him that are in contact with the ground, cast shadows in this otherwise undifferentiated space: this is a paradox, since there is no sign of a division between 'horizontal' or 'vertical' parts of the emptiness.

Moves as radical as this by pre-modern artists inevitably have the experts reaching for prosaic explanations. One that goes back to the eighteenth century (in fact it was recorded by Walpole) has it that Rockingham originally wanted Stubbs to paint an equestrian portrait of George III but changed his mind after falling out with the king. It does not really explain very much. Nor is it enough to see this as an imitation of Roman sculptures or cameos, although Whistlejacket's pose is magnificently statuesque.

To really understand *Whistlejacket* we need to ask what the effect is of isolating this animal infused with energy and electrified by sensibility in a vast empty space, a featureless limbo. Does Whistlejacket know he is in limbo? His eye rolls anxiously at us while the hairs on his mane stand on end. Lost in a mysterious nowhere, he engages all our compassion as we sense not just power but sensitivity in this highly keyed creature.

Featureless wastes are, says Burke in his *Enquiry*, sublime. So is repetition. So is infinity. All these ideas are conjured by Whistlejacket's blank surroundings. Most of all this fellow being of silent inner passion has been cut adrift from place, context, role. Like the people spinning off into imaginary orbit in Joseph Wright's painting of the Orrery (page 119), he has been sent into space. He is almost entirely airbound, the closest thing to a flying machine that then existed, the fastest thing on the mid-Georgian earth. Except he has left it to soar in this no-place. He gazes at us with speed, freedom and a kind of dizziness in his eye.

Deep Waters

If the painted horse that moved Horace Walpole to verse appeared to him to possess an almost human consciousness, the monster that terrorized visitors to the Royal Academy Exhibition in 1778 can never be seen in that way. It is as alien to human thoughts and feelings as any animal conceivable, its yellow eye tiny and moronic in comparison to its huge grey head and immense gaping jaws as it surges towards a wounded teenager who floats helplessly in the fatal green waters of Havana Harbour.

John Singleton Copley exhibited his painting *Watson and the Shark* to a public increasingly fascinated by art. The foundation of the Royal Academy of Arts in 1768 elevated British painting and sculpture officially, with monarchical sanction, into the front rank of polite pursuits and tastes. The following spring it opened its first annual show. George III came and so did everyone who wanted to be anyone. In Thomas Rowlandson's bawdy vision of the *Exhibition Stare Case* (page 163), the spiralling stairs of New Somerset House, where the Academy based itself from 1779, become a voluptuous sprawl of underwear and flesh as London society literally falls over itself to get into the annual exhibition. Copley made a big splash at this crowded art show with his painting of a youth about to be eaten by a shark. The fate of the victim seems inevitable. Even as his fellow sailors in a skiff that has raced to

→ George Stubbs, *Whistlejacket*, c. 1762, oil on canvas, 292 × 246.4 cm (115 × 97 in.), National Gallery, London

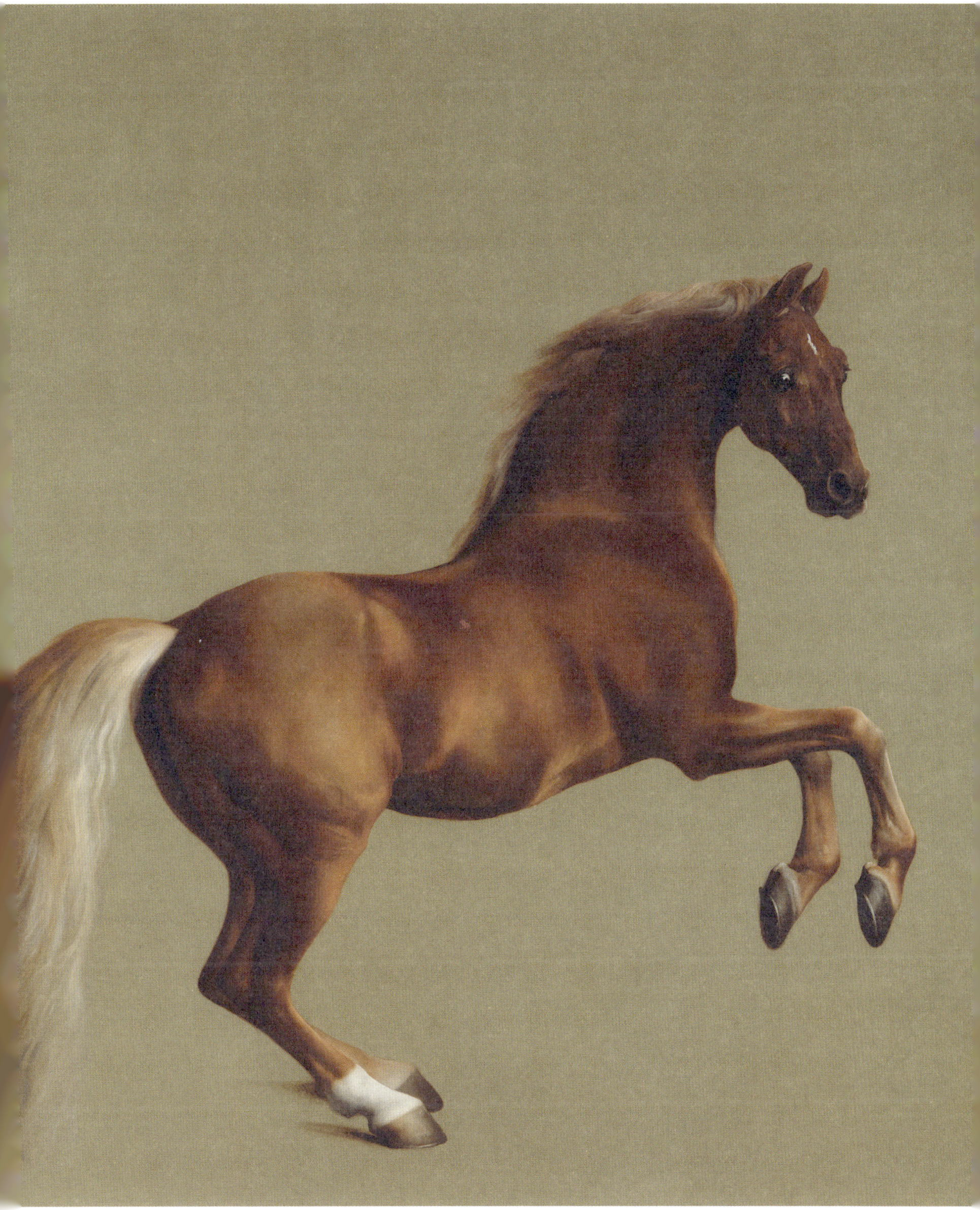

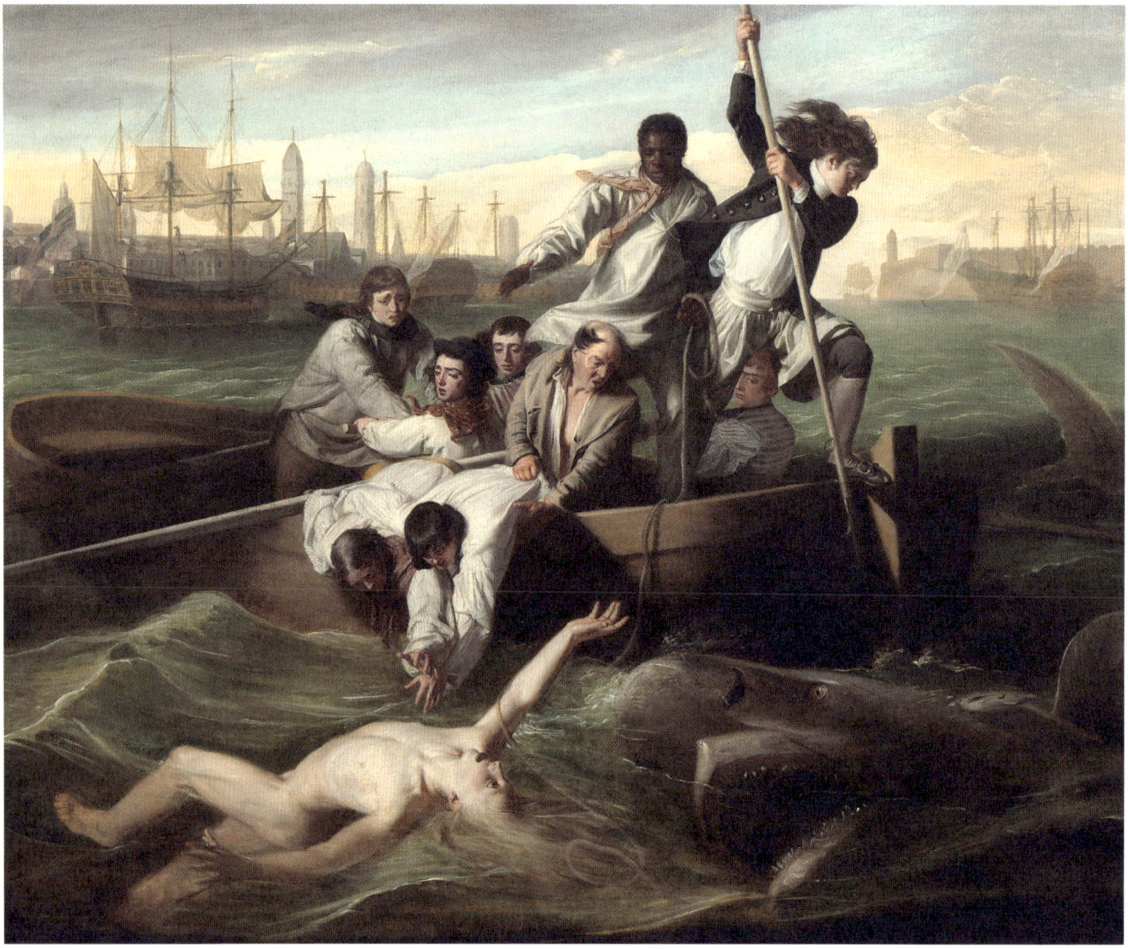

the scene try desperately to help, he is about to fall prey to those merciless teeth. Two friends reach into the water bravely attempting to pull him out, while a third stabs at the shark with a boathook. Others look on in consternation and compassion. At the summit of the statuesque human pyramid, a black sailor shows the greatest empathy of all for his white friend.

↑ John Singleton Copley, *Watson and the Shark*, 1778, oil on canvas, 182.1 × 229.7 cm (71¾ × 90½ in.), National Gallery of Art, Washington, D.C.

Fourteen-year old Brook Watson survived his encounter with a shark off Cuba in 1749. Thanks to the shipmates who plucked him from the water just in time, he lived to become a wealthy merchant and Lord Mayor of London. Like a luckier version of Hogarth's idle apprentice, this orphan sent away to sea came back a man of substance, in spite of his grim ordeal.

The huge success that Copley scored at the Royal Academy in 1778 is not hard to understand. His painting still works as an essay in the sublime because we are still scared of sharks. The factuality of his painting adds to its power: like a modern docudrama it tells a true story about something incredible that happened to an ordinary person. No wonder Copley made pots of money selling prints of his shock-horror hit. And yet there is another dimension to it. At the time it was painted, Great Britain itself was staring into the abyss.

The loss of Britain's proudest imperial possession, the mainland of North America, had been coming on for some time, like a sinister shadow in the water. Two years after Stubbs painted *Whistlejacket* for the Marquess of Rockingham, that sublime thinker Edmund Burke himself became Rockingham's political secretary. In Sir Joshua Reynolds's evocative unfinished portrait of them at work, Burke writes while his patron sits back pensively. There is something noble and tragic about the pair, perhaps even a shadow of the sublime. Together they opposed the Stamp Act that sparked American colonists' rage in the 1760s. Burke proved one of the mightiest speakers Parliament has ever seen, but not even his eloquence could stop George III's ministers provoking the colonists. In 1776 the first of the revolutions that were to shake the late eighteenth century began.

Copley felt the anguish personally. He was born in New England in 1738 but moved to Britain during the revolutionary war. The chances of a future for a purely American artist probably looked slim. London's art scene was booming – but how could he break into it? *Watson and the Shark* proved his transatlantic passport: it not only made him rich but launched him into the establishment by getting him elected a Royal Academician.

It is a vision of the first British empire bloodied by horror. Copley's ambivalence is all too apparent. He offers a mirror of anxiety in which the horror of war and the tensions of liberty are seen through shark-infested waters. The natural world of the Americas has its dangers: like Americans themselves, it can bite back.

Watson and the Shark sinks its teeth deep into Georgian psychology. Young Watson got into trouble because he indulged in a new leisure pursuit that was becoming popular in eighteenth-century Britain: swimming for fun. He stripped off and leapt into Havana Harbour for a bit of healthy exercise, not realizing he was making himself shark food. This image of what can happen when you swim in the sea struck a chill into audiences who were themselves increasingly

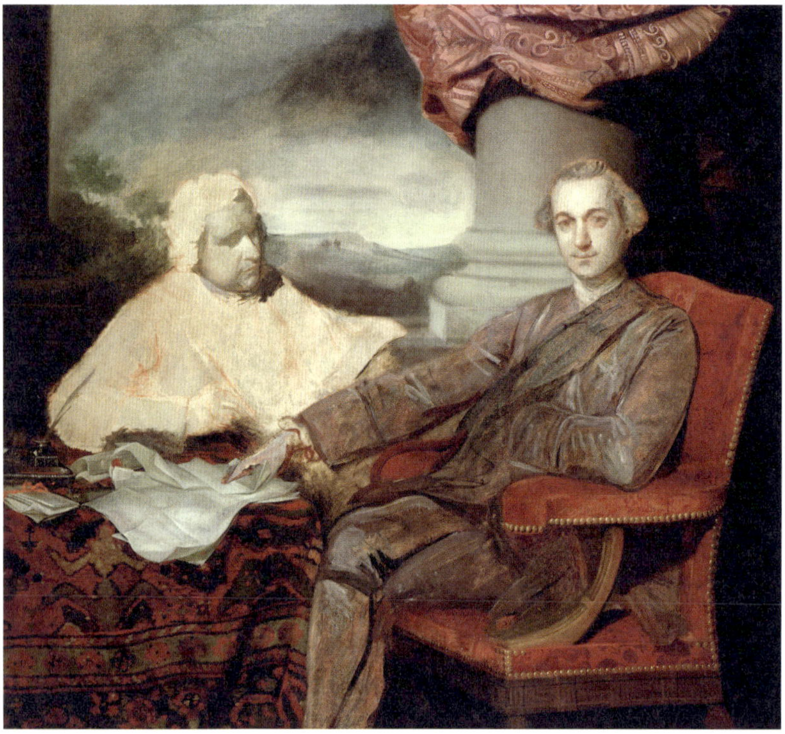

← Joshua Reynolds, *Lord Rockingham and Edmund Burke*, c. 1766, oil on canvas, 145.4 × 159.1 cm (57 ¼ × 62 ⅝ in.), Fitzwilliam Museum, University of Cambridge

likely to spend time in the water on their holidays. Visitors to Bath were safe enough when they sank into its warm spa waters, but its maritime rival Brighton was on the edge of what Burke might call the sea's unknowable sublimity.

Brighton, a declined fishing town in the early eighteenth century, started to be praised by entrepreneurial doctors from the 1730s for its healthy salt water. These quacks recommended swimming in the sea or even drinking it as a cure-all. The less dignified members of George III's family, his brother the Duke of Cumberland and son George, Prince of Wales, became regular visitors and made gambling, drink, dalliance and high dining part of the Brighton scene. Women were known to gather in crowds on the sea front to observe young men stripped to bathe, scientifically scrutinizing their anatomies.

Then disaster hit.

In September 1785 on a fine day with a calm sea, a swimmer off Brighton struck out well beyond the shallows. Here, in the pleasant mild setting of a south of England resort, he suddenly found himself in the same peril as Brook Watson as 'he heard a noise, and discovered the fins of a fish above the surface of the water, which he soon perceived approached him very fast'.

The swimmer desperately headed for land, mercifully making it to the beach. But the horror was not yet over, reported the *Morning Herald*. Something astonishing happened:

> *...a large tiger shark plunged after him with that violence, that it forced itself entirely out of the water on dry land.*

The swimmer gathered fellow beachgoers and they chopped up the man-eating shark with axes. The most gruesome shock was still to come. Inside its stomach, not yet digested, they discovered a human head.

Can a lethal tiger shark, usually found in much warmer waters and never recorded near Britain in more recent times, really have appeared off Brighton in 1785? Or were the swimmer, his companions and the newspapers collectively haunted by seeing prints of Copley's sublime painting? For Copley observes his shark with some care. The blunt shape of its head is unmistakably that of a tiger shark, still common in the Caribbean today. The jaws are particularly accurate. The way he shows them almost as a separate structure below the animal's massive snout suggests he must have directly studied a tiger shark's jaws as he planned his painting.

Perhaps the success of Copley's painting, like Steven Spielberg's *Jaws* in more recent times, gripped imaginations so tightly they imagined a man-eating shark where there could be none. If so this was part of a new familiarity with the exotic in a Britain whose ships were criss-crossing the planet as far-flung colonies offered new varieties of plants, herbs, fruits and fascinating fauna. Before this period no one would have been scared of anything so precisely defined as a 'tiger shark', whether the one off Brighton was real or imagined. Earlier generations had feared sea monsters and mermaids. Now people knew enough of nature and the world to have nightmares about a very real species.

No such terrors disturb the calm of Oaite Peha Bay in Tahiti in the painting that William Hodges showed at the Royal Academy Exhibition in 1776. It is a vision of paradise. A Tahitian woman swims naked, lazily doing a backstroke. Her breasts rise plummily out of the pale blue water. Two more local women rest on shore, one of them unselfconsciously showing the artist her nude behind. Hodges paints this Pacific island as a place of golden skies, breathtaking mountains, swaying palm trees and sensual sunbathing. Yet it is not pure fantasy.

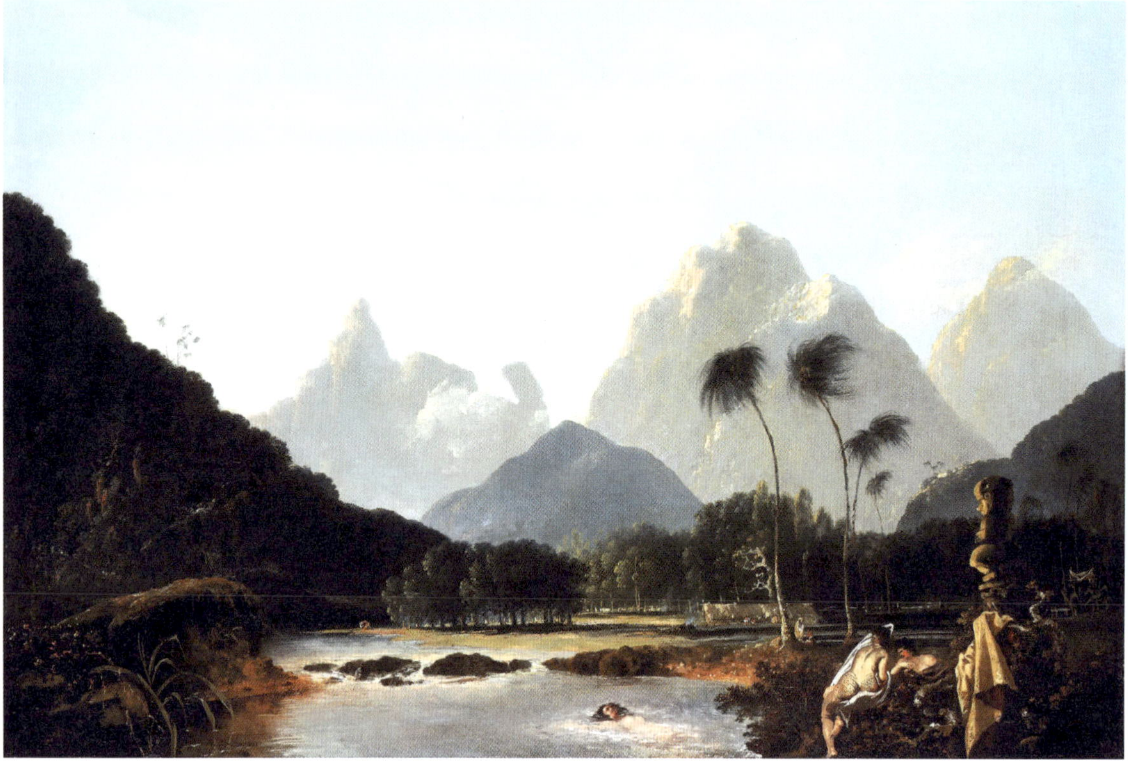

↑ William Hodges, *A View taken in the bay of Oaite Peha [Vaitepiha] Otaheite [Tahiti] (Tahiti Revisited)*, 1776, oil on canvas, 92.7 × 138.4 cm (36 ½ × 54 ½ in.), Ministry of Defence Art Collection on loan to the National Maritime Museum, Greenwich, London

He had really been there. In 1772 he set sail aboard HMS *Resolution* as official artist on Captain James Cook's second voyage of discovery. It was a career opportunity that came with risks. Two painters who sailed on the first of Cook's Pacific adventures in 1768 both died before HMS *Endeavour* got home three years later. Hodges was more fortunate. Back in England, with his reputation made, he could bask in the memory of Tahiti's relaxed sexual customs and sublime landscapes.

Hodges based this painting of a dreamlike South Sea scene on an oil sketch he did on the spot in August 1773. Some of the works he made while aboard the *Resolution* have the harsh immediacy of true empiricism. Huge clouds mass above Table Mountain and the sea churns in a view of Cape Town painted from the deck of the *Resolution* in November 1772. This painting gives a real sense of being on a fragile wooden ship swayed ceaselessly by restless waters. That vulnerability to the wild ocean is even more powerfully conveyed in a watercolour of the deathly white enormity of an iceberg observed as Cook explored the edge of Antarctica. The huge walls of black water that mass and crash are sharply observed, convincingly recording an inhuman Antarctic seascape in which a mountain of ice floats impossibly.

No wonder Tahiti seemed like paradise when Cook moored in Oaite Peha Bay on 16 August 1773. The on-the-spot view Hodges painted that month lacks the nude bathers he later dreamed of nostalgically, but is nevertheless a bewitching vista of tremendous mountains, glowing sky, lush forest. He had seen a living Eden with his own eyes.

A more foreboding mood hangs over the statues of Easter Island (Rapanui) that Hodges painted after the *Resolution* moored there in March 1774. Stormclouds gather above a bleak bay. Exploring the island, Hodges has come across human bones scattered among its stark heaps of stone. This is no paradise. Yet it must have seen a great civilization once, for colossal carved figures stand in rows looking blindly out to sea, brooding on the immensity of time and the loneliness of the ocean.

The Leaping Quadruped

The strangest animal Cook and his companions beheld on the great explorer's first voyage was a big bouncing creature that stood up on its inflated and hugely powerful hind legs. Unable to compare it easily with anything they knew of, they translated its local name as 'The Leaping Quadruped'. This creature dominated the vast landscape of New Holland, later to become Australia. On the voyage home, Daniel Solander, a British Museum botanist, member of the *Endeavour*'s science team and former pupil of Carl Linnaeus, the inventor of systematic taxonomy, transcribed its indigenous name as 'kangaroo'. He and his boss, the wealthy aristocratic naturalist Joseph Banks, brought back skins and skeletons of kangaroos they had eaten, a complete specimen of a young female, and studies made by the ship's artist Sydney Parkinson before he died. All this was enough to reconstruct the animal as it looked in its natural habitat for the eyes of the learned and curious.

They called for the admirable Mr Stubbs. If horse owners were insatiable for Stubbs's expertise in the equine, more Enlightened patrons sought out his powers to portray newly discovered species. His portrait of the zebra in St James's Park was a superb demonstration of his powers of zoological observation (pages 93 and 95). Painted without a commission and shown at the Society of Artists, it beautifully advertised

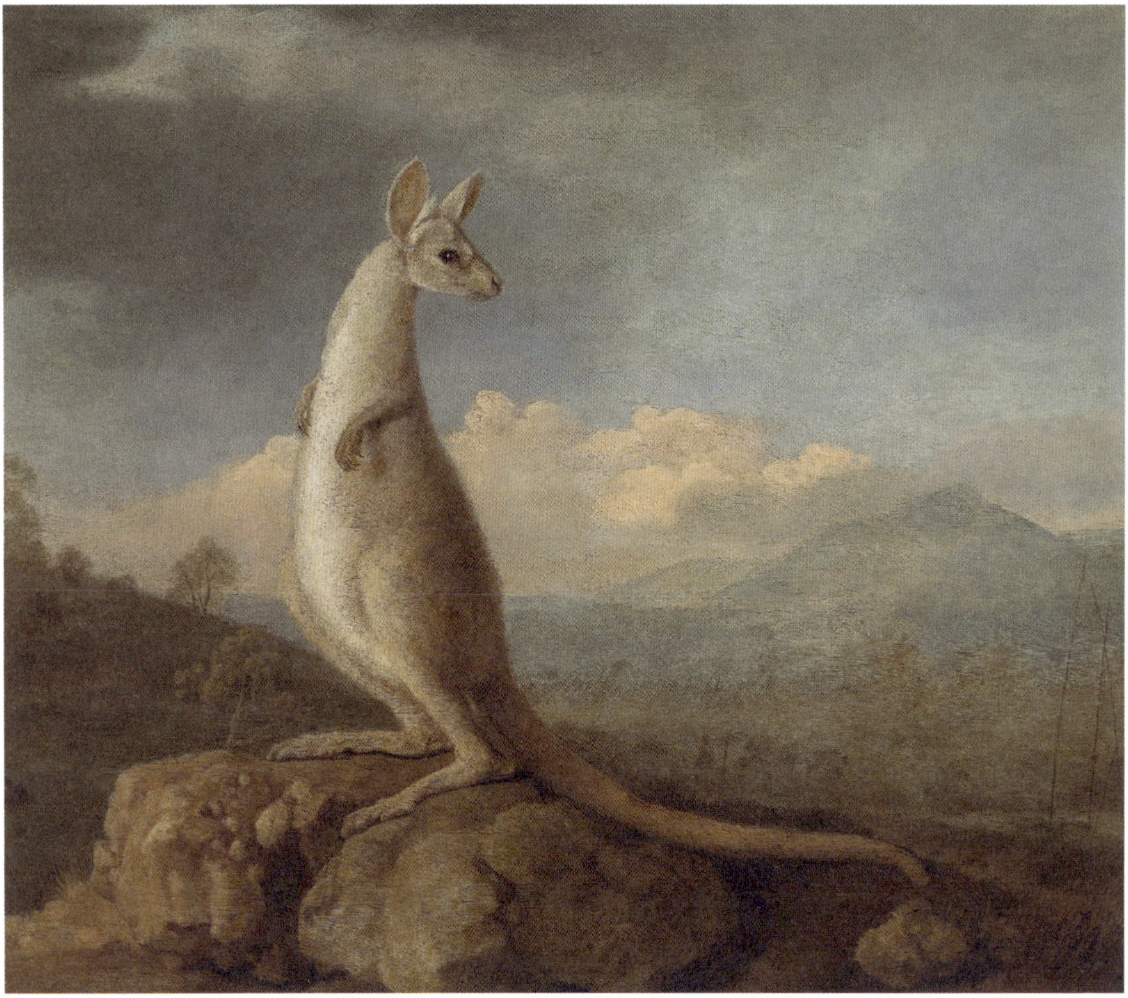

↑ George Stubbs, *The Kongourou from New Holland*, 1772, beeswax on mahogany panel, 60.5 × 71.5 cm (23 4/5 × 28 1/6 in.), National Maritime Museum, London

its creator's capacity to reproduce exotic nature. Addressing the Royal Society in 1770, the Scottish physician, anatomist and all-round man of science William Hunter praised Stubbs for painting a Nyl-ghau, 'an Indian animal not hitherto described', so accurately that anyone who had seen his painting would instantly recognize the animal in the wild.

Hunter lectured the Royal Society on the Nyl-ghau with Stubbs's painting of this Asian antelope behind him as his visual aid. He argued to the Society that 'good paintings of animals give much clearer ideas than descriptions'. In other words, a painter as good as Stubbs was worth a whole team of experts. The painting proved his point. Stubbs brought genuine artistic genius to bear on the expanding field of natural history at a time when an endless stream of foreign specimens was rapidly filling up and testing the classifications mapped out by Linnaeus. It was not curiosity alone that made Britain a natural history powerhouse. Art, science and the colonies were intertwined. The Nyl-ghau that Hunter commissioned Stubbs to paint came from India, where the East India Company spectacularly built up British power and influence in the eighteenth century, pushing out rival European traders as it undermined or corrupted local rulers.

For Edmund Burke, the tactics of the East India Company were a national scandal. He and other critics spent seven years trying to impeach Warren Hastings, Governor of India, between 1788 and 1795. After the loss of North America, the new British Empire needed to be purer than pure. The impeachment of Hastings ultimately failed, and India grew ever more central to a global network of British commerce and control that also encompassed the slave-dependent sugar islands of the Caribbean, the wilds of Canada and the penal colony that was established in Botany Bay in 1788. The very name of the site recommended by Cook as Britain's first Australian base is a reminder of the intimacy of natural history and empire: it was named in honour of Banks and his team.

In a characterful portrait by Joshua Reynolds, Warren Hastings wears a silvery waistcoat embroidered with flowers straight out of Mughal court miniatures and has a sample of Persian script on his writing table. He and other officers of the East India company took an interest in the culture and nature of the continent they were fleecing. Some Company officers commissioned Indian as well as British artists to fill albums with precise botanical and zoological illustrations. Watercolours of lotus flowers, magnolias, Asian coin leaf, peafowl, pheasants, a purple-faced langur and an Indian rhinoceros were among the natural history images commissioned by the East India Company in the 1700s.

If on-the-spot artists could create invaluable scientific illustrations, the eye of Stubbs brought something special to specimens that reached Britain. In 1765, after the success of his zebra, Stubbs was commissioned to paint a 'Portrait of a Hunting Tyger'. Inspired by a real event when a cheetah sent from India as a gift to George III was set upon a deer in Windsor Great Park in 1764 in front of a hearty crowd, Stubbs's painting sees in this unedifying episode an instance of the nobility and mystery of animals. The cheetah in the royal park refused to hunt at all. Apparently spooked by the loud audience, it completely ignored the prey that was offered it. Stubbs portrays two Indian animal handlers

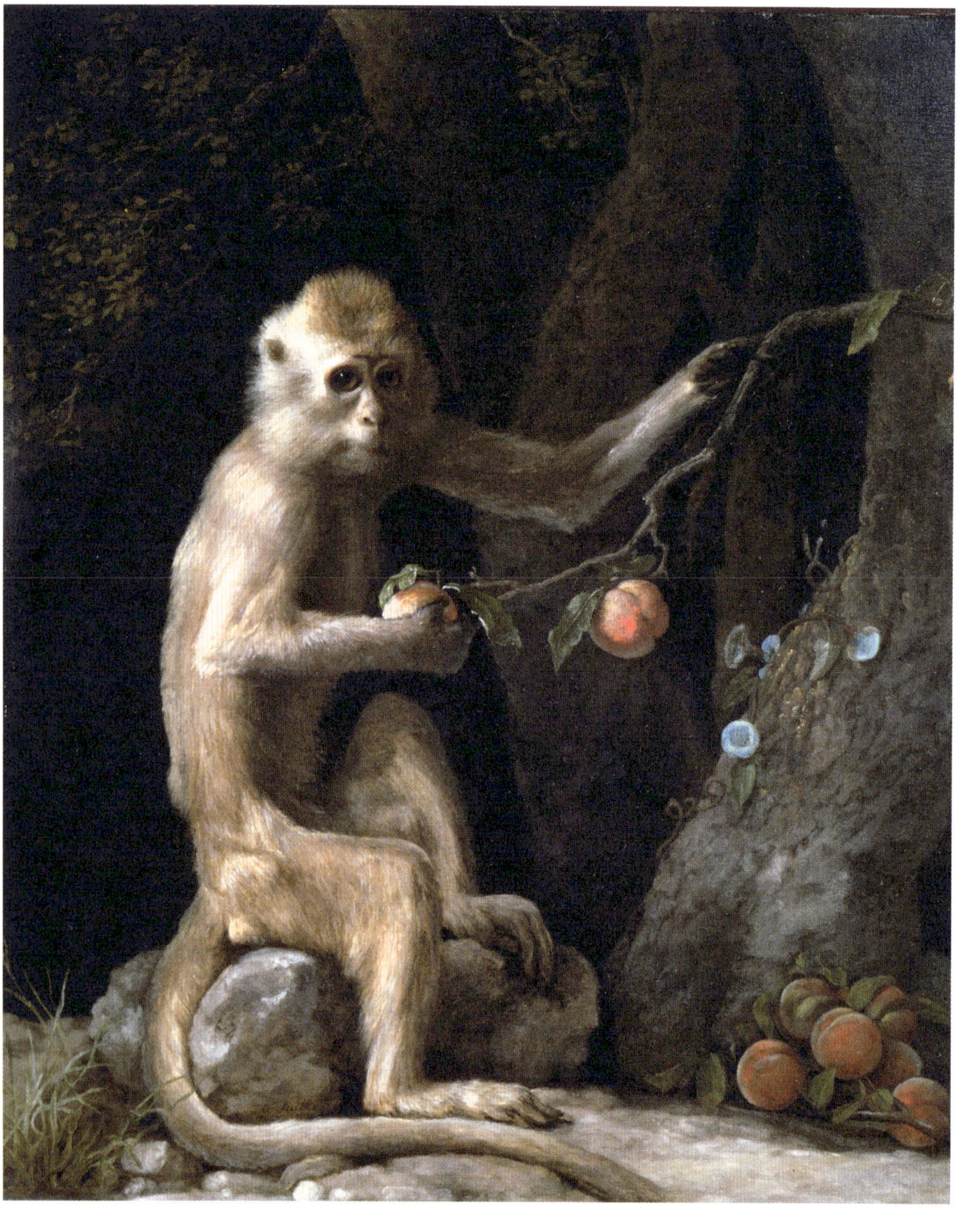

urging it on. Their pleas are pointless. For whatever reasons of its own, the golden cat with its beautiful black spots stands stock still, shying away from a puzzled deer. It is a reversal of his paintings of lions attacking horses: far from a monstrous killing machine, this big cat is sensitive, complex, out of place. It will not serve. It will not entertain.

↑ George Stubbs, *A Monkey*, 1774, oil on canvas, 70.5 × 60.3 cm (27¾ × 23¾ in), Private Collection

Stubbs himself was a complex man with a subtle relationship to his world: he took little part in the social rituals of this clubbable age, refusing to become a full member of the Royal Academy and instead preferring the company of scientific types like William Hunter and his brother John. Do his animal portraits reveal his own inner life, his own wildness?

Painting a kangaroo from a stuffed specimen and trying to make it look alive was a tricky job even for him. Using Parkinson's drawings to flesh out his mental picture, he imagines the brutal landscape through which it leaps. Its eye is on us, taking note of our alien presence in its domain.

It is this look, this regard, that makes the natural world painted by Stubbs so unsettling and mesmerizing. Art, claimed Hunter, got the measure of animals better than any written description. It could help to classify and order nature. Stubbs more than satisfies that requirement, yet his animals look back at us, they study us. We see not just their outer but their inner being. He does not sentimentalize. He looks hard, he looks empirically – and sees the behavioural subtleties as well as the anatomies of wild creatures. Two 'tygers' – or rather cheetahs – fix their eyes on us from a cave in a painting he sold to Burke's boss Rockingham in the 1770s. Their sublimity is in their golden eyes.

Most hauntingly of all, a monkey that he exhibited at the Royal Academy in 1775 stares at us reproachfully from its seat on a stone beside a tree whose fruit it is picking with an adept hand. This animal's regard is very different from the nervous eye of a horse or the lightless eye of a shark. It is much more human. It seems critical, intelligent and melancholy as it watches him paint it. Wisdom and experience inhabit its small face and big brown eyes. It even seems to pose, as elegantly as the great men portrayed by Reynolds, with one leg raised and its tail neatly laid along the ground. Stubbs's paintings make animals look soulful and conscious without anthropomorphizing or trivializing them. He does not attribute a human mind and feelings to them, but tries to capture the mobility of their own distinct intelligence. With his portrait of a monkey we reach a fascinating border. This creature is close to looking human. Its eyes hold a question. How are we related?

5. Into the Volcano

No particular Providence is necessary
to roll this Planet round the Sun.

Erasmus Darwin,
letter to Dr Okes, 1754

Dangerous Thinking

The theorist of evolution holds a quill in his right hand, its awkward angle emphasizing the physical work of writing. Darwin was as prolific as this image of a pen permanently affixed to his hand suggests. The brain that kept his words and ideas pouring out is made visible by the power of concentration evident in his face. His eyes dark with intellectual labour under heavy eyebrows are those of a scientist with no respect for authority, whose vision of nature is so honestly observed, so forthrightly expressed, that it threatens the very foundations of religion, custom and social hierarchy. Erasmus Darwin, atheist, medical man and natural scientist appears the quintessential hero of Enlightened thought in his portrait by Joseph Wright of Derby.

It is consciously a record of a great thinker whose works catch the pulse of an age of revolution. When this portrait was painted in about 1792–93, Darwin had recently become famous for his set of scientific poems *The Botanic Garden*, in which he speculates on the sex life of plants. He was now planning his next book, *Zoonomia; or The Laws of Organic Life*, in which he dares to ask whether:

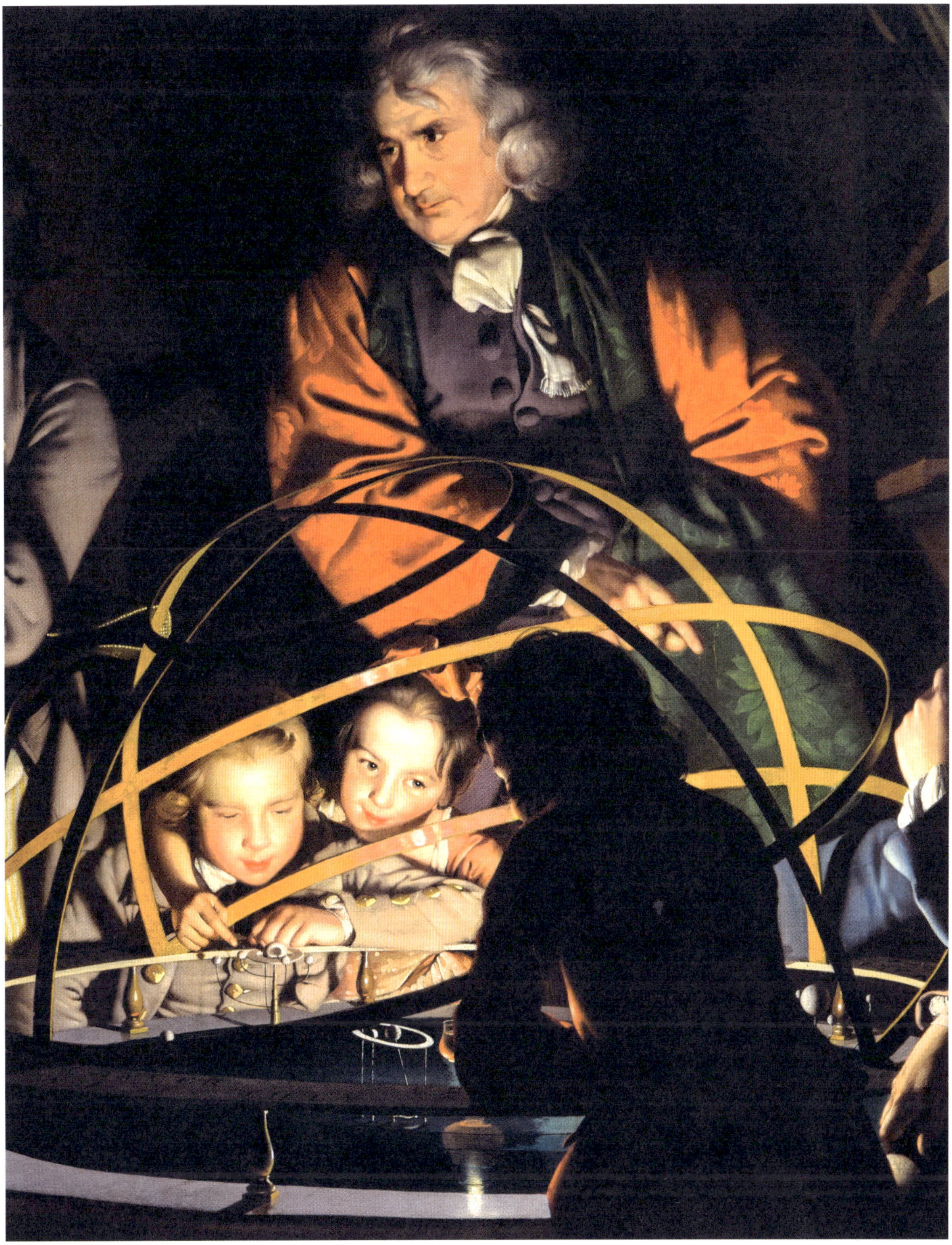

↑ Joseph Wright of Derby, *A Philosopher giving that Lecture on the Orrery, in which a lamp is put in place of the Sun* (detail), 1764–66

> *...in the great length of time, since the earth began to exist... would it be too bold to imagine, that all warm-blooded animals have arisen from one living filament [?].*

As natural history developed in the eighteenth century it gave rise to shocking thoughts. Erasmus Darwin was an enthusiast for Linnaeus, whose system for classifying animals and plants had put biology on a scientific footing. Yet to map the diversity of nature was to ponder its underlying order. Could this immense tapestry of vegetable and animal forms have been individually created? Could the living world really be frozen in a pattern set in the Garden of Eden? And how long had nature existed anyway?

These were questions more disturbing and radical than those asked by the seventeenth-century scientific revolution. The very appeal of Newton's universe lay in its grand vision of a cosmos designed by God as a clockwork machine. Once started, nature ran itself. Questions about exactly how it started could be left aside. In the age of Newton the theologian James Ussher, Bishop of Armagh, worked out the exact age of the Earth from his study of the Bible. According to his calculations, published in a new authorized Bible in 1701, the Earth was created in 4004 BC. Erasmus Darwin's notion that perhaps all animal life evolved from a single ancestor was not only a contradiction of Genesis but could only possibly make sense if the Earth was far older than Ussher claimed.

It would be Erasmus Darwin's grandson Charles who made evolution the most provocative of all scientific theories in his 1859 book *On the Origin of Species*. Before that was possible, the Earth needed to shake. Time needed to stretch. Artists as well as scientists would help to see life on Earth in a new way, as far older and much less eternal than previous generations had imagined it.

Is it too much to see the daring of such ideas in Joseph Wright's portrait of Erasmus Darwin? Not at all, for this is no simple commissioned portrait by a hired hand. Wright and Darwin were friends. About 20 years previously, Wright had stressed that friendship in a considerably less formal portrait. In this earlier painting the young Erasmus looks frankly and with relaxed companionship across a polished table at the artist – and at us. It is a gregarious portrait, a friendly study of a man whose face is warm and welcoming. It bears witness to Wright of Derby's thrilling familiarity with the boldest ideas of his time.

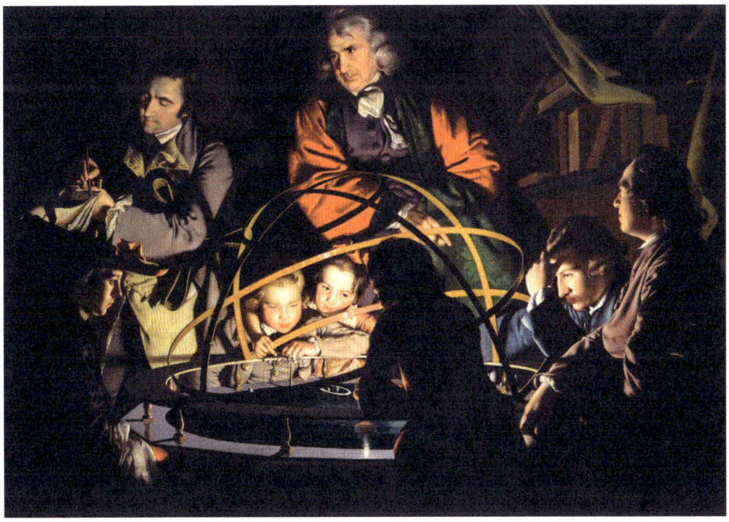

↑ Joseph Wright of Derby, *A Philosopher giving that Lecture on the Orrery, in which a lamp is put in place of the Sun*, 1764–66, oil on canvas, 147.3 × 203.2 cm (58 × 80 in.), Derby Museum and Art Gallery

Full Moon

The children gaze at a model solar system, their faces made golden by discovery. We are witnessing a moment of pure enlightenment. As is explained by the full title of the picture Wright exhibited at the Society of Artists in 1766, this is *A Philosopher giving that Lecture on the Orrery, in which a lamp is put in place of the Sun*.

At the centre of a large clockwork solar system, a natural philosopher – as scientists were still called – has set up a lamp that imitates the light and heat of the sun, illuminating the little planets and their moons in this artfully fabricated and grand scientific toy. The light does not stop at the brass rail on lathe-turned wooden columns that closes off this artificial system of worlds. After transfiguring the metal boundary into a shining ring of ethereal fire, it continues to radiate, illuminating the onlookers. Next to the red-robed Philosopher, a younger man assiduously takes notes. His violet coat with the crimson silk flare in its sleeve and waistcoat decorated with vertical lemon lines are brilliantly lit up. A still younger man sits on the right, resting his forehead on his hand, engrossed, astonished. A gentleman standing by him, half in shadow, ponders the meaning of it all. A young woman seems perturbed. As she stares into space, the circular shape of her hat comically mirrors the orbits of the planets and the metal spherical cage that enfolds them.

Yet it is the children who most innocently express their delight. Two rapt young faces are caught in the lamplight. They are seeing for themselves that we live on a spherical planet orbiting a star. A third child is seen only as a black silhouette against the light – but that shadowy figure speaks volumes. This onlooker too is held by awe and reverence of cosmic reality.

This is the most moving of all eighteenth-century images of perception. It is unsurprising that Wright of Derby's great painting appears on the covers of so many books about the European Enlightenment and the history of science. Yet it does not only show us the amazement of discovery. It makes us share it. Because it uses a single light source in an otherwise darkened room, it subtly disrupts space. The walls of the room are almost invisible. The people are all in orbit, as it were, around the orrery, disconnected from everything else. Their concentration is infectious. To look long is to share the exhilaration of these eighteenth-century people at the sheer beauty and power of the solar system – to float off among cosmic thoughts.

In *A Philosopher giving that Lecture on the Orrery, in which a lamp is put in place of the sun*, Wright turns a toy into a sublime vision of outer space. The orrery was a Newtonian educational plaything whose ingenious clockwork solar system allowed the orbits which gravity imposes on the planets to be shown and explained. It started as an aristocratic luxury, named after Charles Boyle, Fourth Earl of Orrery, who in the early eighteenth century amassed a fine collection of scientific devices, from telescopes to camera obscuras, as well as patronizing this contraption. By the 1760s, orreries were available to a wider public. The cheapest were hand-pushed models that just showed Earth and the inner planets. At the top end of the market were miracles of detailed craftsmanship, 'grand' orreries, like the one that engrosses the people in Wright's painting.

Wright bears witness to the popularization of science in the eighteenth century. He goes out of his way to mix young and old, women and men, in his portrayal of an astronomical lecture as a public event. There are mirrors within mirrors in this masterpiece, all heightening the drama of discovery. The painting itself was conceived as a public spectacle to be shown in the competitive and theatrical context of the Society of Artists exhibition. Like Stubbs's *Startled Horse* a few years previously, it sets out to astound. Yet the way it does so is intellectually intricate. Wright studies the orrery with the same intensity as his human subjects. He delineates its technological refinement, and the spheres orbiting within. His picture can substitute for the orrery itself. It teaches what the model teaches – that we do not live in a fixed place at the centre of the universe but on a rocky sphere orbiting a star.

The man who exhibited this enthralling work was in his early thirties and based in the Midlands. Wright was born in Derby in 1734. He trained as a portrait painter with the fashionable London artist Thomas Hudson; by the 1760s he was back home in Derby, painting local faces for a living. Many of Wright's paintings are still in the city. His career is marked by polarities as stark as that between the lamp at the heart of his orrery and the surrounding darkness. He charted a highly individual path between localism and internationalism, practicality and ambition. His attempts to become rich by painting portraits took him to Liverpool and Bath, but he always gravitated back to his home region. Walpole dismissed him as a surly provincial who could not see that by staying out of London he isolated himself from the art world. It is true that he fell out with the Royal Academy. Yet Walpole did not see how much Wright gained from being in Derby.

One of the most influential scientific communities in eighteenth-century Europe flourished in the Midlands. Erasmus Darwin was a leading member, along with the potteries entrepreneur Josiah Wedgwood, the engineer James Watt and Watt's business partner Matthew Boulton. Other members were the clockmaker and geologist John Whitehurst and the pioneering chemist Joseph Priestley. They met monthly by the light of the full moon – hence their name, the Lunar Society. Wright was closely associated with these experimentalists. He was especially friendly with Darwin and Whitehurst, who wrote riskily about the origins of the Earth.

The Lunar Society were not ivory-tower academics. They were not academics at all. Darwin made a good living as a doctor, trying out innovative treatments on his patients, first in Lichfield and later in Derby. Whitehurst, who lived a few doors from Wright's parents in Derby, was a skilled craftsman by day, making fine clocks, watches and barometers, and a geologist by moonlight. Wright was a natural companion to these enthusiastic characters who shared his own middle rank in society. In 1766 when the *Orrery* was painted, the experimental culture led by the Lunar Society was already gripping the Midlands. There was nothing 'provincial' about it. In 1763 the celebrated American experimentalist and politician Benjamin Franklin wrote to Whitehurst in Derby about his geological ideas.

Wright's *Orrery* is not a literal portrait of the Lunar Society, but an exploration of its intellectual universe. It shares the Lunar sensibility. For it is a poem not only to physics, but to technology.

The shiny polished brass parts of the orrery are painted in hypnotic detail. Its arcs and orbits move in clockwork perfection. Wright loves this machine. What a modern miracle, to reproduce the system of the worlds in clockwork! Surely he must have explored the mechanics with Whitehurst, who was a master clockmaker, manufacturing a novel three-wheeled clock invented by his friend Franklin. The Lunar Society loved high-tech wizardry. Birmingham, Derby, Coalbrookdale and Josiah Wedgwood's ceramic works, 'Etruria', were the Silicon Valley of their time, fusing physics and engineering to remake the world. The *Orrery* is not only a vision of science. It is a window on the Industrial Revolution.

Those precisely turned wooden columns and accurately bent metal pieces have the mechanical sublimity of the steam engines Watt and Boulton started to produce commercially in the 1770s. For Britain's energy in scientific experiment since the seventeenth century was no abstract exercise. The discoveries of Newton and Boyle were put to practical use. Their physics made the steam engine possible. The Lunar Society was studying not just the laws of nature but how to use them to revolutionize everyday life.

It is worth a quick reminder of how people still lived in the mid-eighteenth century. Instead of plumbing, the elegant life of well-off Georgians was kept clean(ish) by 'nightsoil men', who took excrement away in carts. If you wanted a break from your cesspit, in 1780 it took two days to travel between London and Chester. This was in contemporary eyes a modern miracle, for earlier in the century, before turnpike roads improved the journey, it had taken six days. This was still a world where mortality was high. Wright's painting *The Old Man and Death* is a grimly comic image of the skeletal figure of mortality arriving in broad daylight in an eerily beautiful landscape to keep its grisly tryst with a man whose time has come.

The Lunar Society believed the application of science could abolish age-old constraints on human achievement. As Boulton boasted, like a modern-day Faust, when James Boswell visited his steam workshop: 'I sell here, Sir, what all the world desires to have: POWER.' The same insight – with more ambivalence – is at the heart of Wright's second great painting of a scientific spectacle.

In 1768 he exhibited *An Experiment on a Bird in the Air Pump* at the Society of Artists. Once again a natural philosopher is giving a visually powerful demonstration of physics. The full moon is bright, cold and pale outside the window. The luminosity that shows us a variety of reactions to the experiment is bizarre and uncomfortable, and a jar containing a hideous organic specimen has got between us and the light. Divided reactions trouble this gathering. We too are anxious. For the apparatus is a beautifully constructed air pump, the machine invented by Boyle and Hooke in the seventeenth century to prove the existence of a gaseous atmosphere – the same experiment that had fascinated John Evelyn at the Royal Society a century earlier. Now it has become the kind of science entertainment you might see at a country house or a town hall. A glass orb on top of a wooden pillar is

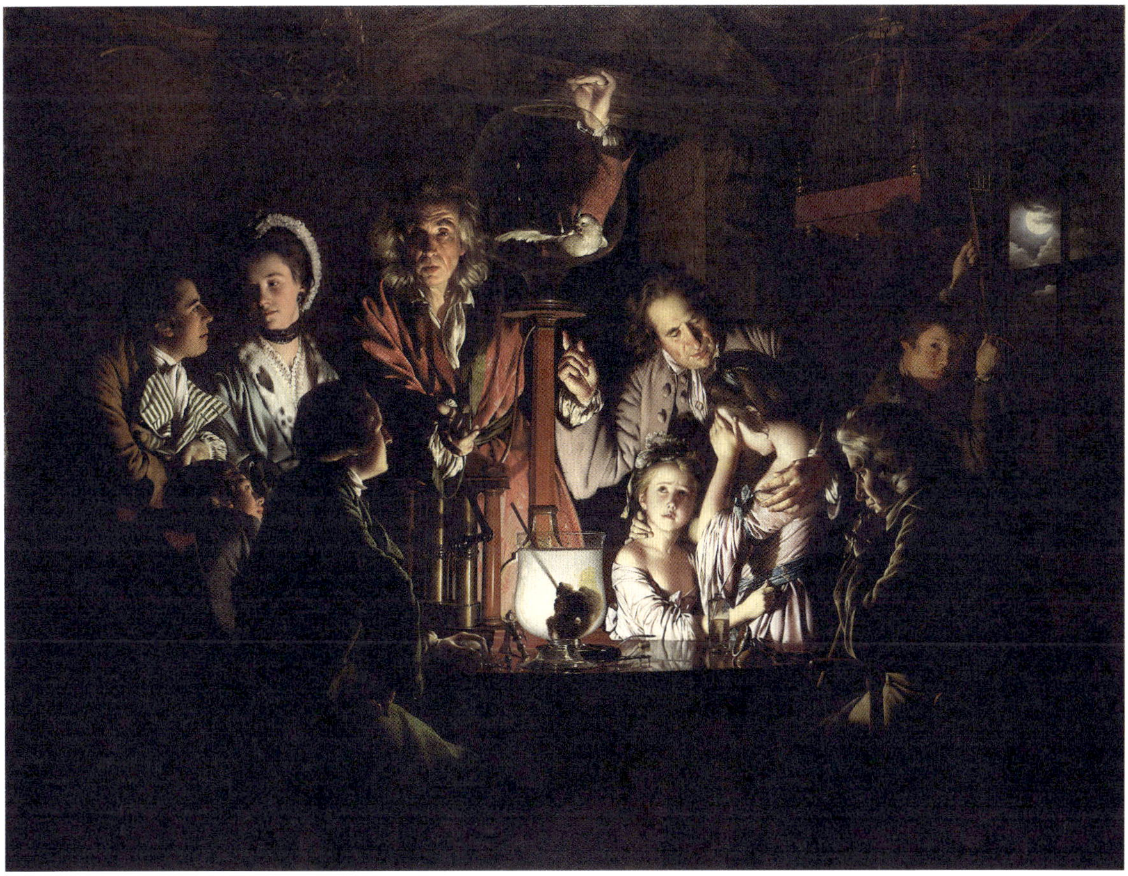

↑ Joseph Wright of Derby, *An Experiment on a Bird in the Air Pump*, 1768, oil on canvas, 183 × 244 cm (72 × 96 in.), National Gallery, London

being deprived of air. In a moment the splendid white cockatoo trapped inside the transparent chamber will suffocate. Science claims a mighty power here over life and death. The wild-haired scientist exults in that power, deaf to the sobs of the girl whose pet has been taken out of its cage and sentenced to death for the sake of science.

It is a grave and shocking scene, full of foreboding. The classical door of the chamber is grey and sinister. Darkness lies beyond. Only one audience member, a youth, seems enthused by what is about to happen. A man in green looks on critically, while an older man lowers his eyes in thought. A child comforts her sobbing sister while she makes herself watch, in spite of her fears.

There is horror here, but Wright is not repudiating science. Far from it. Even more sensationally than his *Orrery*, this painting makes its onlooker feel the excitement and risk of science. It is not the lecturer who will murder the cockatoo. The laws of nature will do that. This is empiricism in action: Boyle's air pump visibly demonstrates a singular and essential fact about nature. Unfortunately it must kill to reveal it.

The atmosphere we breathe contains something essential to life, this experiment harshly proves. What is it?

Joseph Priestley, the Birmingham dissenting minister who was one of the most brilliant members of the Lunar Society, would get close to the answer in the 1770s when, in a series of experiments that went much further than Boyle's air pump, he isolated the gases of which air is composed. He called the atmosphere's most flammable ingredient 'phlogiston'. The French scientist Antoine Laurent Lavoisier would build on Priestley's discoveries to name the critical gas 'oxygen'.

So the experiment painted by Wright is no mere gratuitous act of cruelty. The Lunar Society and its wider network were at the forefront of experimentation on the nature of gases. What we actually see in this painting is the birth of chemistry. It is also a scene from the beginnings of industry, for the improved steam engine Watt was developing at Glasgow University in the 1760s made use of a vacuum to achieve its power. Presumably Wright saw a demonstration of the air pump – examples of Georgian air pumps like the lovingly crafted one in his painting survive – yet this painting does more than just record a popular experiment. Wright was clearly au fait with avant-garde discussions of chemistry in Lunar circles. In 1771 he unveiled a Gothic-looking looking picture of a medieval alchemist. A silvery full moon peeps into the gloomy shadows of a vaulted chamber. While his young apprentice looks on, the grey-robed alchemist kneels before his brightly illuminated glass apparatus. It may seem at first sight a backward-looking scene but Wright's elaborate title reveals a more sophisticated intention: *The Alchymist, in Search of the Philosopher's Stone, Discovers Phosphorous, and prays for the successful Conclusion of his operation, as was the custom of the Ancient Chymical Astrologers.*

The mystical alchemists of the Middle Ages and the Renaissance had pioneered experiments on substances as they searched for chimerical secret knowledge. The greatest of them, Paracelsus, made real contributions to early science. Wright obviously sees alchemy as a primitive ancestor of modern science. The alchemist has accidentally isolated phosphorous. This is a painting of chemistry's prehistory. The boy watching the alchemist does not join in his prayers. Instead he looks and learns. Perhaps he will become a true chemist.

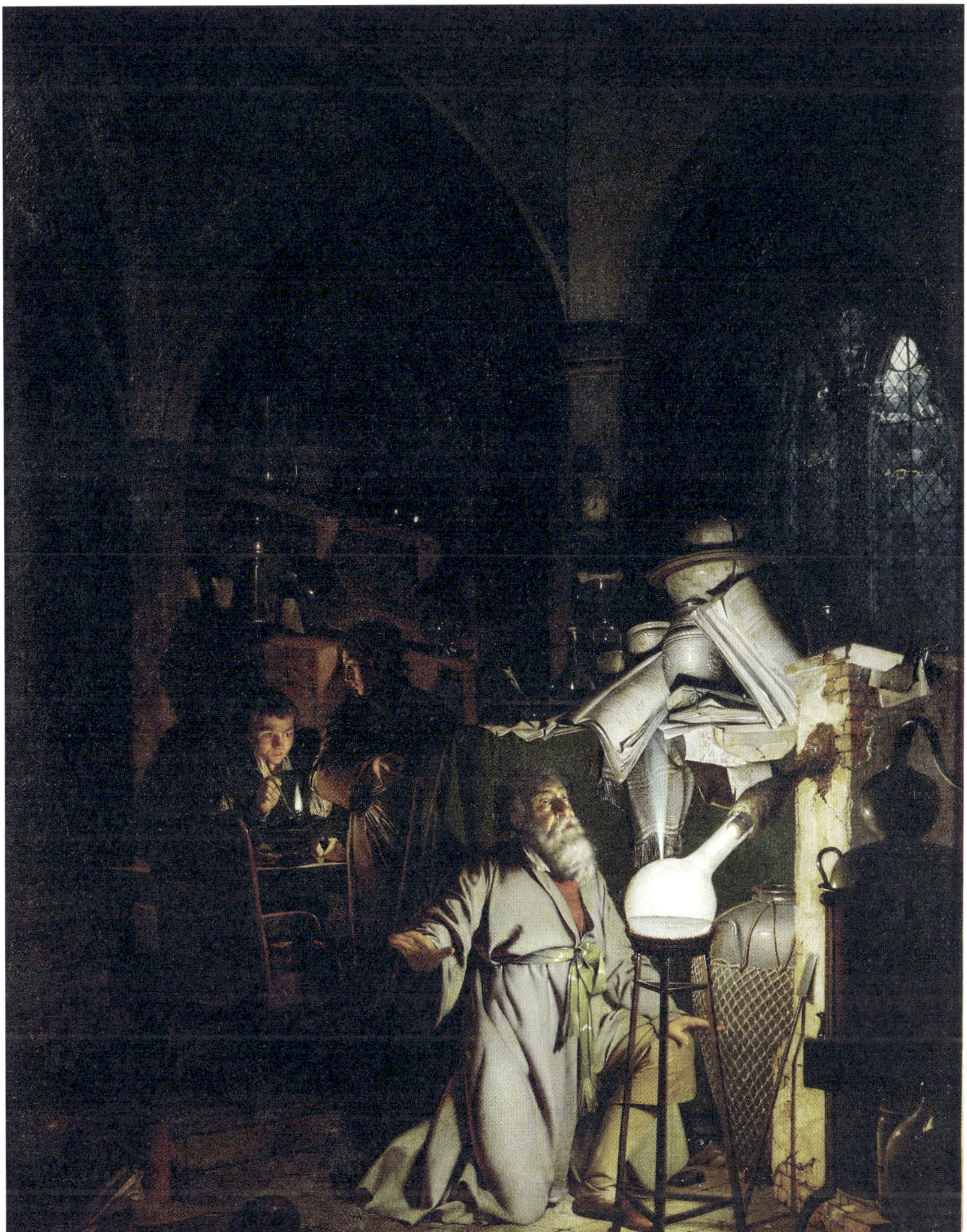

↑ Joseph Wright of Derby, *The Alchymist*, 1771, oil on canvas, 127 × 101.6 cm (50 × 40 in.), Derby Museum and Art Gallery

Wright was painting these scenes – *An Experiment* in 1768, *The Alchymist* in 1771 – in the very milieu in which modern chemistry was leaving behind its alchemical past for good. *The Alchymist* reveals a typically Enlightened belief in human progress. Out of superstition the truth blazes. Wright can mock the superstitions of the 'Ancient Chymical Astrologers' so knowingly because he is conversant with the new 'chymical' thought that was at the cutting edge of 1770s science, in a research network that extended from Priestley's Birmingham to Franklin's America to Lavoisier's France.

That mockery of superstition may reflect the unbelief of one of Wright's known associates in the Lunar Society, its founding member Erasmus Darwin. Some scientific enthusiasts in the Midlands were religious dissenters: Priestley was a Unitarian who doubted the divinity of Christ, as was Wedgwood. Darwin went further, into full-blown atheism. Did Wright share his scepticism?

It can be argued that his art replaces God with Science. The sublime, as Burke argued, is a religious or quasi-religious feeling of awe before something bigger than ourselves. In Wright's two great manifesto paintings of the 1760s it is scientific truth that is sublime; instead of revering God we should bow down before Nature. Even his spectacular lighting may have something blasphemous about it. Earlier artists who explored such extremes, from Caravaggio to Georges de la Tour, used their optical daring to intensify sacred scenes. Wright is secular in his subjects and their illumination. There is nothing mystical about the glow on the faces of his scientific spectators. A lamp has been put in place of the sun – that is all.

Not only does the terror of the experiment with the air pump preserve the atmosphere of nights of fervent scientific discussion, but its effect depends on our sharing that interest. The psychological drama Wright shows makes no sense unless you know what an air pump does. Only with a basic understanding that air is to be removed from the chamber can you share the dread of the cockatoo's imminent death.

An Experiment on a Bird in the Air Pump therefore does the same work as a real scientific demonstration. In a sense, Wright is saving the lives of future animal victims because his painting can substitute for the experiment. And the new understanding of nature's laws that was developing on moonlit nights like these in the Midlands was about to transform human existence. Wright brings the alarming and inspiring news that revolution is in the air.

The Social Contract

The tension of *An Experiment on a Bird in the Air Pump* depends on the new feeling for nature that grew in the eighteenth century. We have already encountered it in Hogarth and Stubbs. It had not at all upset John Evelyn in the 1660s to see a whole menagerie of animals killed in Boyle's chamber. By the 1760s Wright can take it as read that a cockatoo's death is distressing. He does not despise the girl who cries. The figure of wisdom who sits looking downward seems equally perturbed by the paradox that in learning how nature works, we sometimes harm it.

The love of the natural world that bloomed in the Enlightenment was by no means confined to Britain. Its most eloquent enthusiast of all was the *philosophe* Jean-Jacques Rousseau. Born in Geneva, Switzerland, in 1712, Rousseau exerted a titanic influence that grew even more pervasive after his death in 1778. He spent time in Britain – including Staffordshire in the Midlands – after his books were banned in France and Geneva. Kindness to animals is, for Rousseau, part of the compassion for nature and our fellow humans that we should try to nurture in ourselves. For the state of nature is innocent, an Edenic paradise. Human society by contrast is corrupt and unjust, and to live in it is to become wicked. The only hope for humanity lies in reclaiming the goodness of primal nature. Rousseau himself became increasingly solitary as he sought a pure way of life.

Joseph Wright had a way of painting programmatic statements. His art shows him to be an intellectual who took the ideas of his time seriously, and gave them visual form. His images of scientific gatherings reveal his fascination with the researches of the nascent Lunar Society. He also, in the heart of England, painted a manifesto for Rousseauism.

Wright's portrait of Brooke Boothby, painted in 1781, shows a man surrendering to nature. Even though he is fully dressed in the height of fashion, with even his hands covered, Boothby has lain down to read in a wild woodland. The waning day reddens the sky and illuminates the shady glade where he meditates, looking up from his book. The contrast between his refined clothes and the natural pose is significant. Boothby, like all moderns, is ensnared by civilization. His fancy costume literally imprisons him, enclosing him totally except for his friendly, sensitive face. He is confined by custom but wants to change. Wright makes Boothby's discipleship of the radical thinker explicit. On the spine of his book is 'Rousseau'. And Boothby was not just any reader of Rousseau.

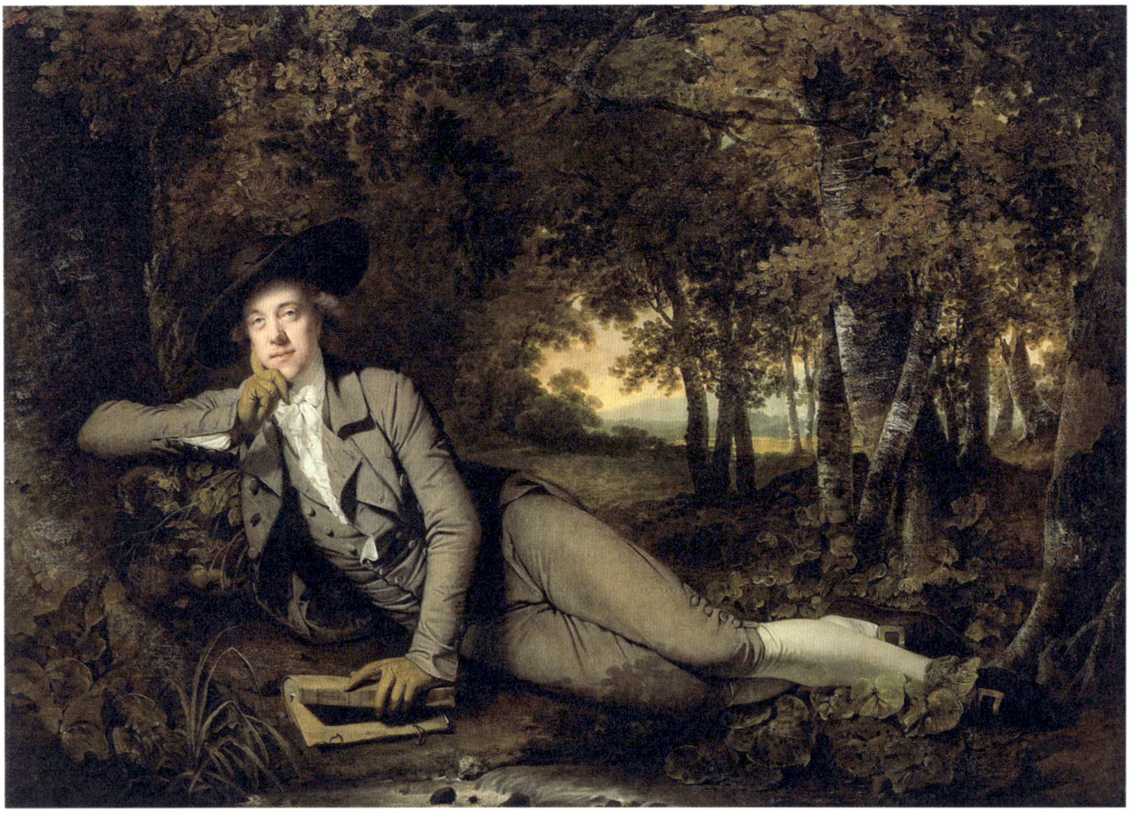

↑ Joseph Wright of Derby, *Sir Brooke Boothby*, 1781, oil on canvas, 148.6 × 207.6 cm (58½ × 81¾ in.), Tate

Boothby, a country gentleman who lived at Ashbourne Hall in Derbyshire, got to know Rousseau when the exiled thinker was staying in Staffordshire in the 1760s. Passing through Paris, where Rousseau now lived, in April 1776 he paid this feted and persecuted icon of the age a call at what proved a critical moment. Rousseau was desperate to entrust his latest work, the first volume of his autobiographical *Dialogues*, to someone who could protect the manuscript and get it published. He chose well. Boothby got the book safely to Britain and paid for it to be printed, in French, in Lichfield in 1780 before donating the manuscript to the British Museum.

It is a remarkable window on Wright's world that a work by one of the greatest minds of the European Enlightenment was first published in the Midlands town of Lichfield. A new force was electrifying the world. The year in which Rousseau entrusted his *Dialogues* to Boothby, 1776, was just a year after the American Revolution began. Franklin, its star intellectual, was still in touch with his friends in Birmingham and Derby. Their own political sympathies were clear. They were on the side of liberty and the Rights of Man. Wright's painting *The Captive*, painted in 1774 and inspired by an image in Laurence Sterne's impulsive, spontaneous travel book *A Sentimental Journey*, portrays a prisoner chained up in Paris's notorious Bastille prison. Naked and starving, he waits to die, entombed among its massive stone walls and arched ceilings.

'And as for the Bastille,' wrote Sterne, 'the terror is in the word.' This venerable French prison was held to symbolize all that was loathsome in arbitrary monarchical government. Its storming by the Paris crowd on 14 July 1789 would be the decisive moment in the French Revolution. Fifteen years before that, Wright was already urging his audience to shudder at the inhumanity of this foul dungeon.

It was not only in France that people behaved in vile ways towards their fellow human beings. Cruelty existed much closer to home. The Declaration of Independence proclaimed by the American colonies in 1776 stated that:

> *We hold these truths to be self-evident, that all men are created equal, that they are endowed by their Creator with certain unalienable Rights, that among these are Life, Liberty and the pursuit of Happiness.*

That begged more than one question. In 1792 Mary Wollstonecraft finally vindicated the Rights of Woman alongside the Enlightenment's omnipresent 'Man'. Still more grotesque was the ability of many of the American rebels to overlook the contradiction between their proud affirmation of universal rights and the exploitation of slaves. English radicals were quicker in seeing this. In 1787 Josiah Wedgwood, member of the Lunar Society and friend of Erasmus Darwin – (Darwin's son Robert would marry Wedgwood's daughter Susannah in 1796) – created a ceramic medallion in the style of ancient Roman cameos, with a black figure against a light background; in different versions that survive the colour ranges from cream to brilliant white. In each, the African slave kneels, almost naked, holding up his chains as he speaks the words inscribed around the oval medallion:

> *AM I NOT A MAN AND*
> *A BROTHER?*

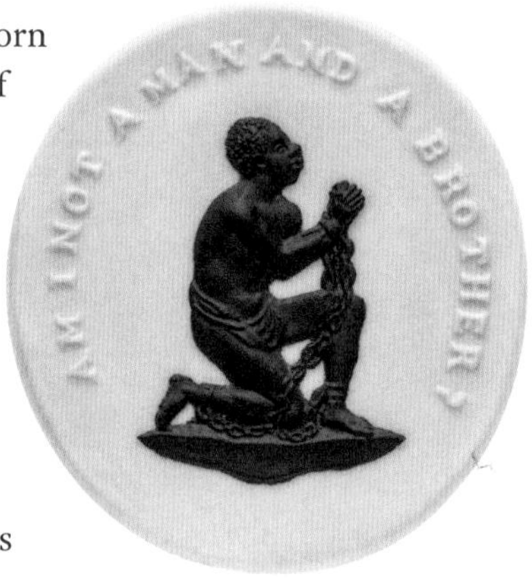

Wedgwood's medal was a spectacular success, worn like a modern political badge by supporters of the Abolitionist movement. He was uniquely qualified to create this masterpiece of political art. Born into a ceramics business near Stoke-on-Trent, he had organized his craftsmen to produce large numbers of identically elegant objects for the middle-class market. The style of his medallion shares the Neoclassical gravity of his 1789 copy of the Portland Vase, the ancient Roman blue and white glass masterpiece that was one of the most exquisite archaeological treasures to reach Georgian Britain. This noble style was perfectly suited to Wedgwood's medallion, with its reasoning plea for universal human dignity.

↑ Josiah Wedgwood, *'Am I Not A Man And A Brother?'*, 1787, black-and-white jasperware (porcelain) cameo, 3.5 × 3.5 cm (1⅜ × 1⅜ in.), Private Collection

It might be asked why, if they felt so strongly about prisoners in the Bastille and slaves transported across the Atlantic by Liverpool ship-owners, the Enlightened progressives of the Midlands failed to question the factory system they were themselves inventing. Wedgwood boasted that in organizing his workforce in an assembly line he would 'make such *machines* of the Men as cannot err'.

The Industrial Revolution simply did not look to its pioneers like our hackneyed image of it. Historians now debate the very usefulness of the term 'Industrial Revolution' for a complex process that took a long time. Yet in the Midlands by the 1770s productivity and the very nature of work were truly being revolutionized. In about 1782–83, Joseph Wright painted a tranquil, silvery nocturnal landscape. His beloved full moon is momentarily half-hidden by grey clouds. Its glow whitens another bank of cloud. Trees are silhouetted against this lunar beauty. Nestled under low hills are two big rectangular buildings with repeated rows of windows. These are the cotton mills of Joseph Arkwright at Cromford in Derbyshire. This lyrical landscape is a painting of the birth of the factory.

Has Wright cleaned up reality to make it more aesthetic? Where is the smoke?

There was none. Arkwright's first two mills – where the factory system crystallized, building on Wedgwood's innovative experiments in production-line assembly – were powered by water from the River Derwent. Yet their radicalism can be seen clearly in this painting. It is true that Wright loved to paint nocturnes, but he has a precise reason to show this industrial complex by night. For he lets us see the crucial fact that all the windows are lit. People are working through the night. It is not steam that is making a new world in this painting. It is the control of workers' time.

Hogarth had shown the Idle and Industrious Apprentices, one toiling at his loom, the other slacking. Wright's painting shows how Arkwright has abolished that choice for his workers. Factory life is a new kind of discipline, not only separating work and leisure by removing labour from the home environment but even abolishing night and day.

In a warmer vision of the future, Wright portrays an iron-founder basking in the glow of a heated bar of metal as it is pounded by a massive mechanical hammer. No longer needing to hammer it by hand, he has leisure to pay attention to his wife and daughters who have come to see the sublime spectacle of the new machinery. Up to now, virtually all craft and manufacture had taken place at home, in family businesses or labourers' cottages. Wright here shows how mechanization might enrich that lifestyle. Yet the real future would look like Arkwright's mills – with pollution added.

Back to Nature

On the face of it Joseph Wright could not be more different from Thomas Gainsborough. One is hard-edged, cerebral, the other lushly sensual. Yet in about 1781, contemporaneously with Wright's portrait of Boothby, the brilliant society painter created a similarly Rousseau-like vision of naturalness and solitude. A longing to get away from it all rustles through Gainsborough's great portrait of 'Perdita', as Mary Robinson was known. This renowned beauty, actor and talented poet was nicknamed Perdita because she had played the role in a hit production of *The Winter's Tale*. Gainsborough takes Mrs Robinson's alter ego seriously. She is indeed Perdita, the lost one, seated under a shady tree in her rustic retreat, free from the cynicism and malice of modern society.

She had plenty of cruel gossip to get away from. Gainsborough's portrait was commissioned by George, Prince of Wales, one of Mary Robinson's lovers. She is holding a miniature of him, although their relationship was over and she had also had a fling with the liberal-minded Whig politician Charles James Fox. Gainsborough allows her to slough off such stuff. She almost seems to sink into the painting. Her

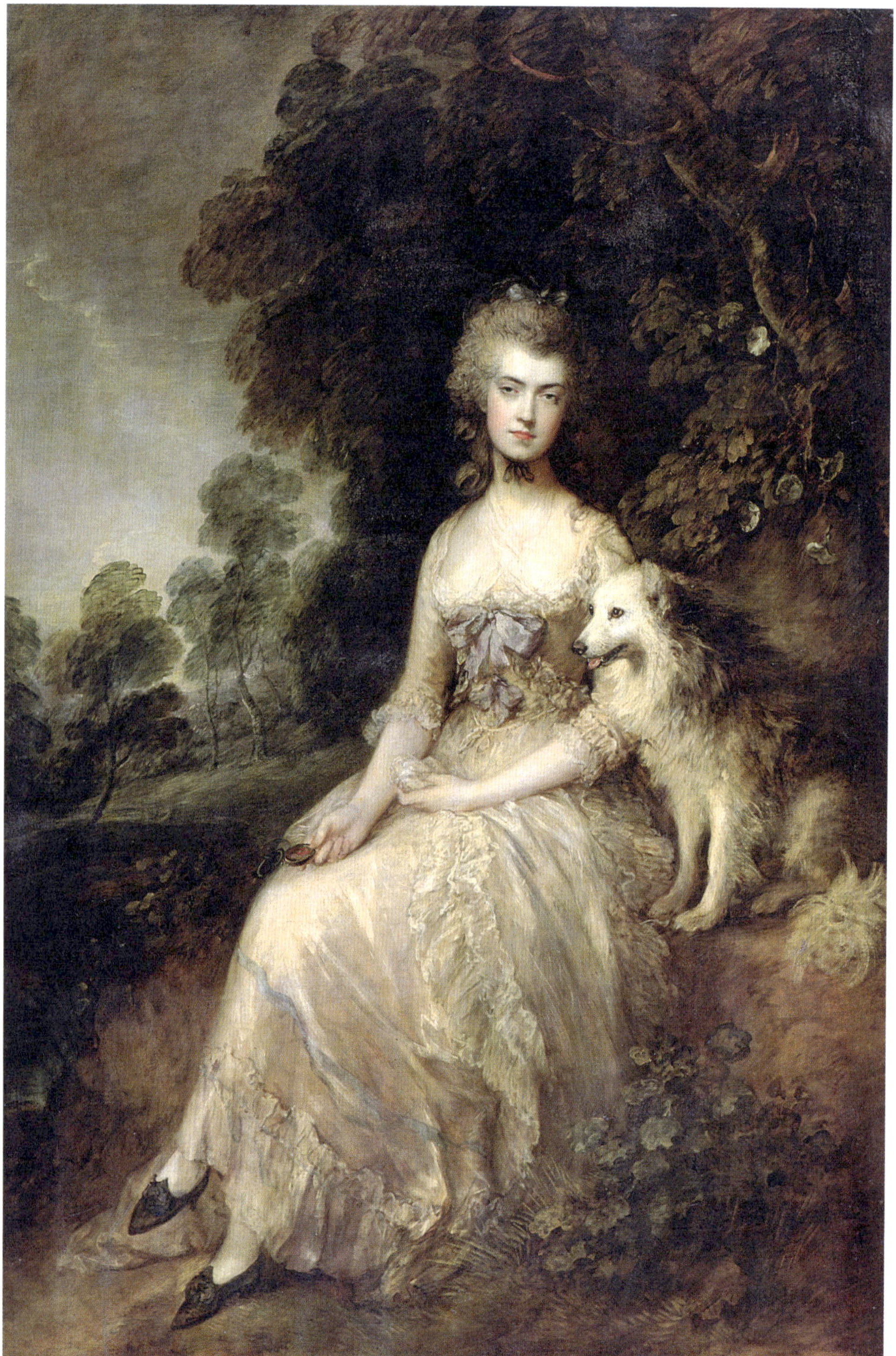

↑ Thomas Gainsborough, *Mrs Mary Robinson (Perdita)*, c. 1781, oil on canvas, 233.7 × 153 cm (92 × 60 ¼ in.), Wallace Collection, London

pale body melts into its greenish light. She is a leaf on the breeze, a rumour in the air. Her darkly intelligent eyes are away in poetic thought. She appears about to vanish forever, to become one with the sympathetic murmur of wind-ruffled trees. And of course she has a loyal pet. Robinson had published her first book of poetry in 1775 with the support of the Whig patroness Georgiana, Duchess of Devonshire. Gainsborough captures her romantic sensibility: 'The birds breathe bliss! light zephyrs kiss the ground…', as she writes in her 1796 verse sequence *Sappho and Phaon*.

The pastoral escapism of this ethereal pan-pipe portrait is no minor note in Gainsborough's later work. For all his sophistication he was still a country boy at heart. He shows this most unequivocally in landscape paintings that completely reject the ultra-civilized, upper-crust world that provided his living. In his big 1786 pastoral *The Market Cart*, a rural family are taking their produce to town in a meandering journey through a woodland. The muddy track has just vanished into a deep pool. Their horse hesitates. A man looks up from gathering wood. Above these little figures, immense trees create a shadowy web of brown-leafed mystery – and higher still, in a moving burst of soft brightness, float puffy clouds. These clouds are as empirically precise as anything he ever painted. Here is a wonderful instance of his eye for nature, alive and keen in one of his very last works. He died in 1788.

Landscape was establishing itself as a genre whose generosity of scale suited it to country houses, yet was capable of poetry intense enough to satisfy the most ardent soul. It combined the legitimacy of tradition with the newness of observation. It had been elevated into a high art in the seventeenth century by Claude Lorrain and Nicolas Poussin, French artists based in Rome whose works were particularly popular with wealthy Britons. An important Claude already hung at Petworth House in West Sussex in the 1680s – one of at least three of his paintings in Britain by that time.

The first British painter to try to raise landscape to the levels of Claude was Richard Wilson, who helped Hogarth decorate Coram's Hospital. Wilson's paintings do not always hold the eye but he led the way in showing the possibilities of landscape. In the 1750s he emulated Claude by making his own artistic pilgrimage to Rome. He spent about six years in Italy, painting such scenes as his *View of Tivoli: the Cascatelle and the 'Villa of Maecenas'*, in which a landscape artist perches on a hilly eminence painting the very view we are contemplating. Above a

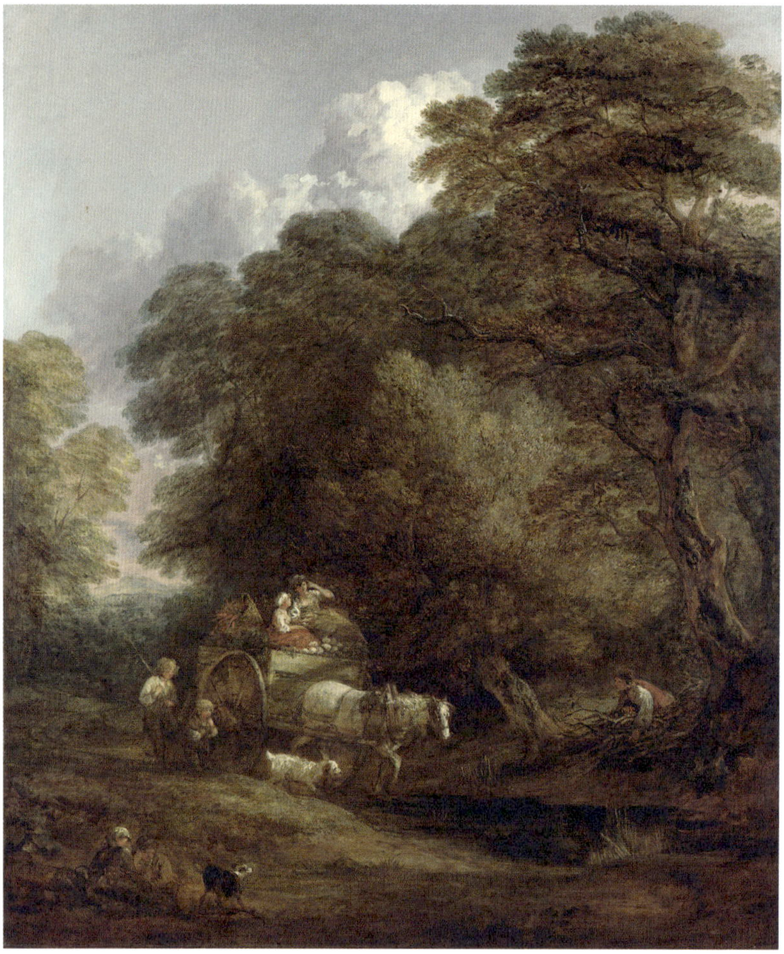

← Thomas Gainsborough, *The Market Cart*, 1786, oil on canvas, 184 × 153 cm (72 ⅖ × 60 ¼ in.), National Gallery, London

crashing waterfall and a hill encrusted with grandiose ruins opens the golden emptiness of the sky. It takes up half the painting.

Wilson's most original paintings were made back in his native Wales. There he could see beyond Claude's grand example. When he painted in Snowdonia he found a genuinely remote natural world. His vista of Cader Idris, exhibited in 1774, dwells on an isolation that verges on the brutal. No trees are in sight, only sheep-cropped grass, bare rock, black water. The mountain's exposed heart is the empty shell of an extinct volcano, long ago blown open to the cold sky. Here is a place primal enough to satisfy the most solitary walker.

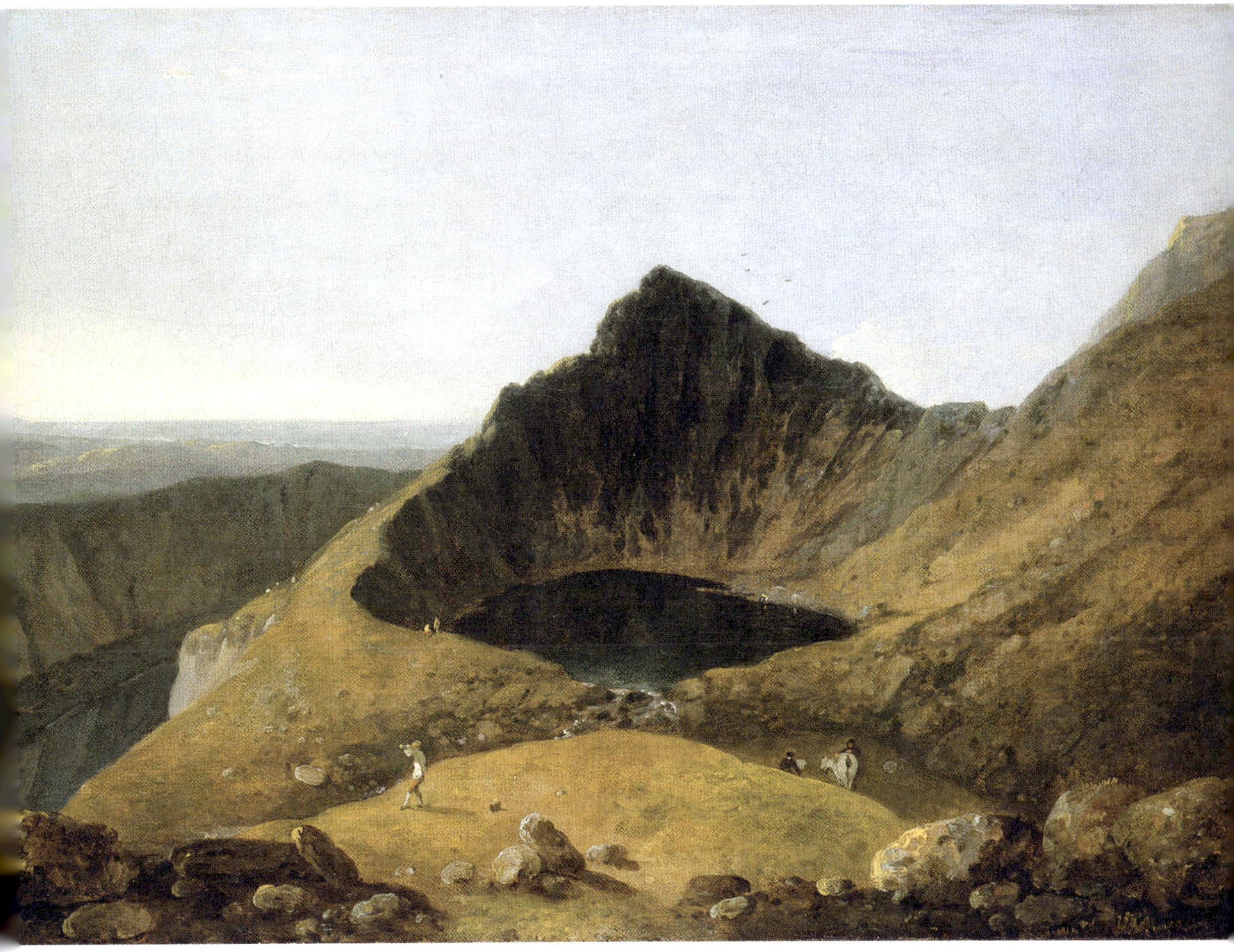

The Bowels of the Mountain

Nothing was going to prevent Joseph Wright from making his own journey to Italy in the footsteps of Wilson, not to mention of Stubbs and Reynolds – not even a pregnant young wife. In October 1773 he and his new bride left Derby on the long journey south. They got to Rome the following February. Their first daughter, born that June in Italy, was named Anna Romana. What impressed Wright most in Rome – to judge from his blazing paintings of it – was the traditional 'Girandola' fireworks display, when Castel Sant'Angelo by the Tiber appeared to explode in yellow fire. Yet the most fruitful part of his tour turned out to lie further south. In a month-long visit to Naples that autumn he found

↑ Richard Wilson, *Llyn-y-Cau, Cader Idris*, c. 1774, oil on canvas, 51.1 × 73 cm (20 ⅛ × 28 ¾ in.), Tate

a strange cocktail of ancient history and geology that was to feed his imagination for years to come.

The Kingdom of Naples, ruled by a branch of the Bourbon family, was a truly unlikely place. Naples itself was one of the biggest cities in the world, comparable in size to London yet utterly foreign in its Baroque Catholicism. The lost cities of Pompeii and Herculaneum were starting to be excavated, and further south lay the sublime ruins of Paestum. Subterranean passageways, fantastical sea caves and sepulchres were everywhere.

Most astounding was the fiery mountain that overshadowed it all. Vesuvius, the volcano that had buried Pompeii and from whose wrath Neapolitans hoped the liquefying blood of San Gennaro would protect them, was no dormant crater. When Wright reached Naples in October 1774 it was erupting. Boulders burst into the smoky sky and glowing rivers of lava flowed slowly towards defenceless vineyards. Wright did not just watch from a safe distance but climbed the volcano as it spewed superheated rock. Any painter would have been thrilled. This one happened to be able to see it as a geological wonder as well as a picturesque event. Climbing the unstable slopes he thought of his friend John Whitehurst, the clockmaker who was the Lunar Society's resident geologist; volcanoes were one subject Whitehurst pondered in his researches on the history of the Earth. In November 1774 the artist wrote to his brother:

> *... when you see Whitehurst, tell him I wished for his company when on Mount Vesuvius, his thoughts would have center'd on the bowels of the mountain, mine skimmed over the surface only; there was a very considerable eruption at the time, of which I am going to make a picture. 'Tis the most wonderful sight in nature.*

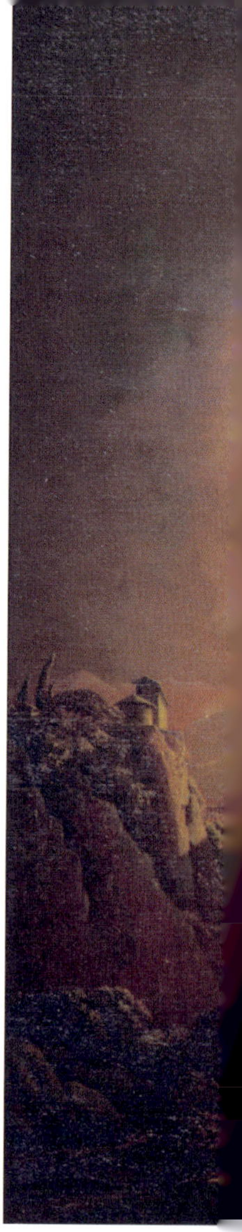

In spite of his deferral to Whitehurst, it is clear from Wright's paintings that his imagination did penetrate 'the bowels of the mountain'. He painted as many as 30 canvases of the eruption. It becomes in these paintings an orgy of the sublime, an opera of light – or as he put it 'the most wonderful sight in nature'. Wright's volcano paintings attracted Enlightenment scientific curiosity far beyond the Midlands. In 1778 he sold one to Catherine the Great of Russia: today it is in the Pushkin Museum in Moscow. The red mountain vomits up Earth's molten innards, turning the sky around it bright yellow and orange, while the

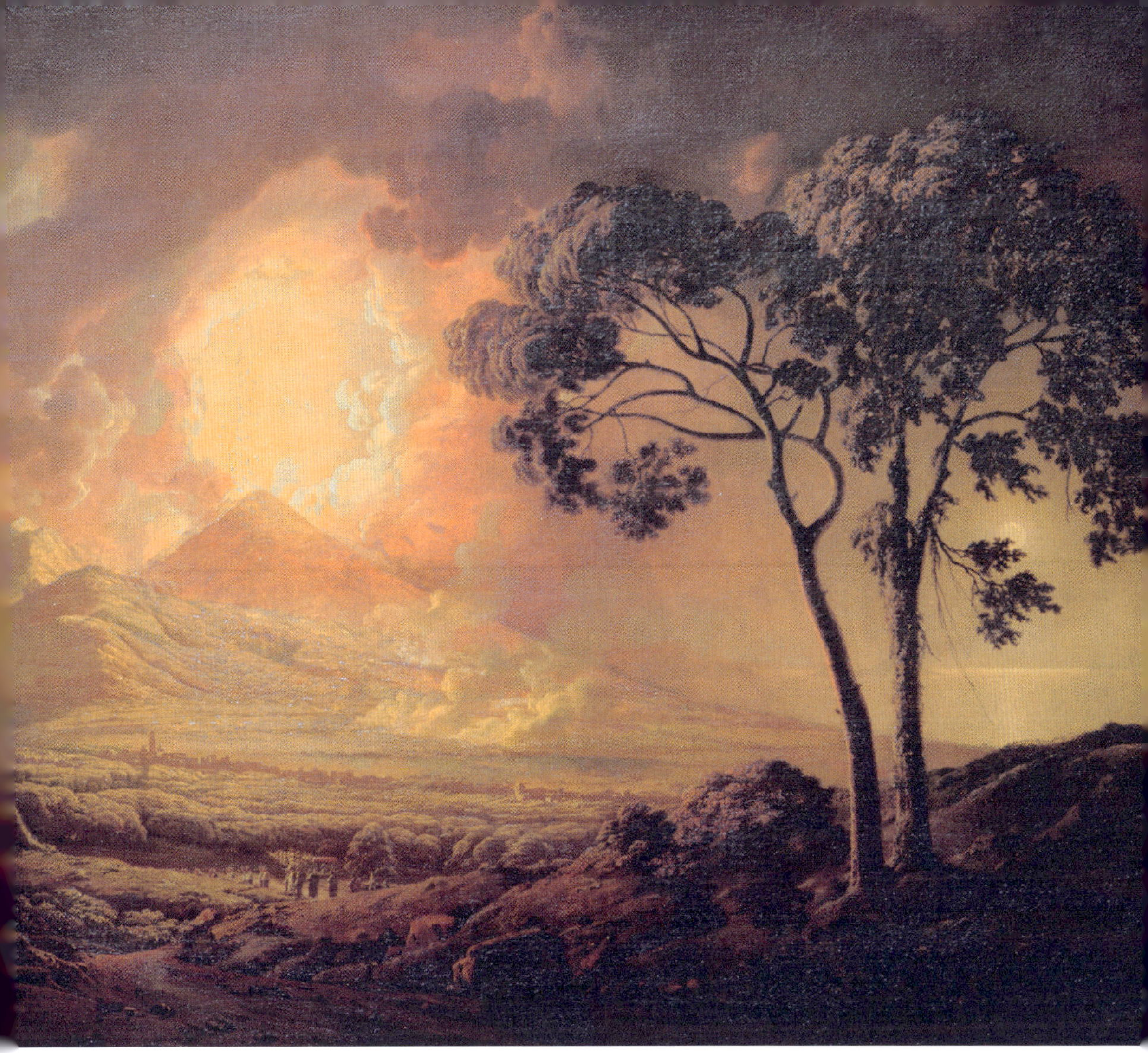

rest of the atmosphere is so thickened by ash that we cannot see if it is day or night. A tree in the foreground has turned to blackened ashy velvet. Across the nightmarish landscape, alternately enflamed and charred, processes a pious crowd carrying San Gennaro's head.

In a version in Tate Britain, the intensity of the eruption sends a golden candle of blinding light vertically upward. Baroque clouds of ash form an airborne grotto around this superhot column. Its light creates subtle shades of pink inside this dusty bower, while the mountain itself has turned a luminous red and burning lava flows across the land below. The disturbing beauty of it all is accentuated by cool blue moonlight on the calm waters of the Bay of Naples.

↑ Joseph Wright of Derby, *Vesuvius eruption with a procession in honour of St Januarius*, c. 1778, oil on canvas, 162 × 213 cm (63 ¾ × 83 ⅚ in.), Pushkin Museum, Moscow

→→ Joseph Wright of Derby, *Vesuvius in Eruption, with a View over the Islands in the Bay of Naples* c. 1776–80, oil on canvas, 122 × 176.4 cm (48 × 69 ⅖ in), Tate

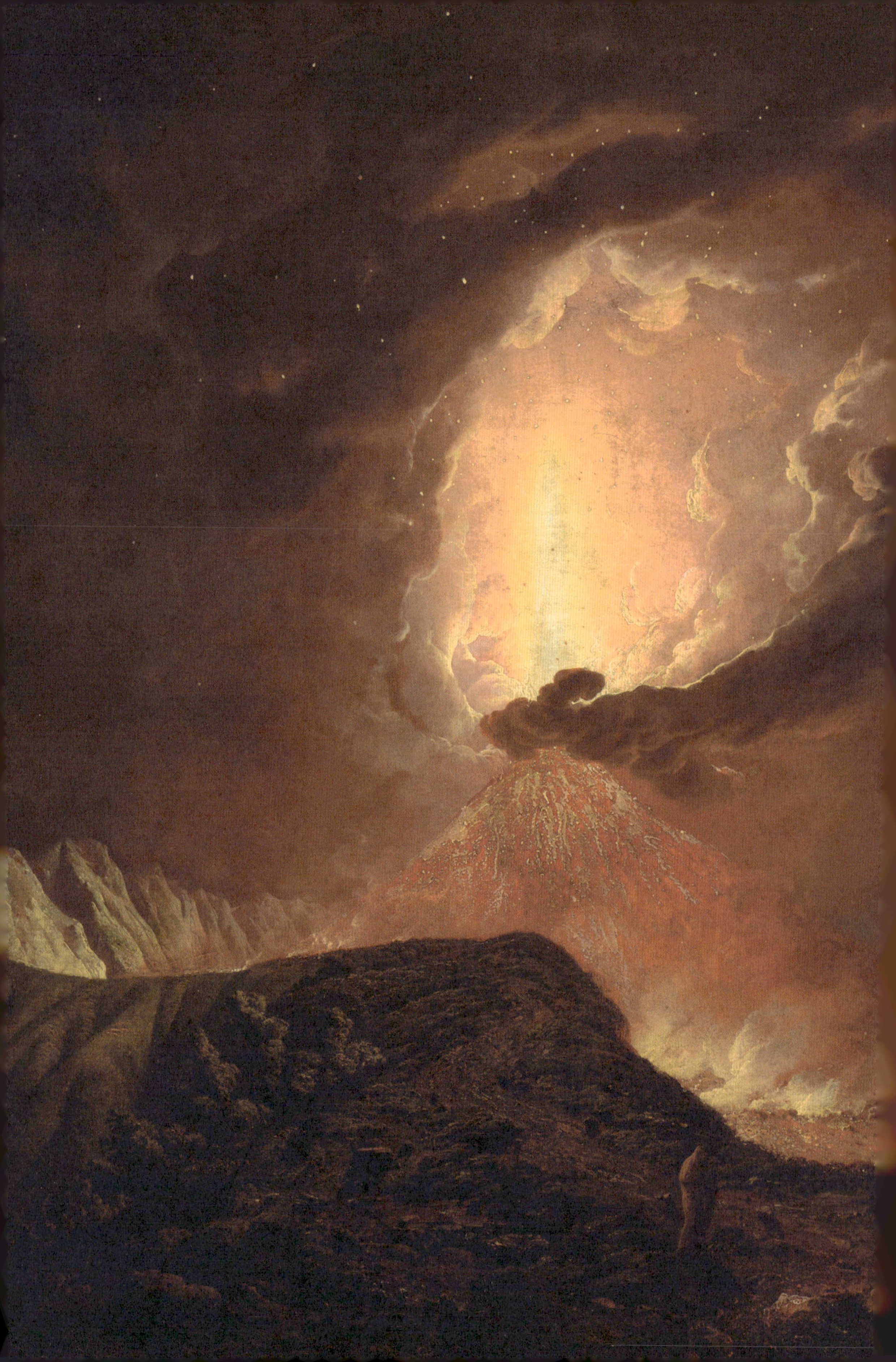

It is the ash cloud that separates two kinds of light, stopping the blaze of the volcano from blotting out the pallor of the moon. In another view, seen from further across the bay, Vesuvius gives the sea a deep russet glow. Only further away from the shore does the moon still peep out on this appallingly beautiful night.

The spectacle of Vesuvius was equally fascinating to art and to science – and showed how closely the two were entwined. Science was still 'natural philosophy', still open to amateurs. Wright understood clearly that looking into a volcano's majestic horror was an insight into the nature of the Earth. He expresses this in a sensitive portrait of Whitehurst as an old man, which includes a view of Vesuvius to symbolize his friend's lifetime's work in geology. Conversely, pioneers of vulcanology could not help wanting to capture the power of the Earth in vivid images. This led to one of the most luxurious science books of all time, Sir William Hamilton's *Supplement to the Campi Phlegraei. Being an Account of the Great Eruption of Vesuvius in the Month of August 1779*.

Everything about the Bay of Naples intrigued Hamilton. In 1764 this member of the nobility continued a family tradition of public service – his father was governor of Jamaica – by becoming Britain's envoy to the Kingdom of Naples. He turned himself into more of a cultural attaché than an ambassador, hosting Grand Tourists, diving into archaeology. He collected huge amounts of ancient pottery; what survived the journey is now in the British Museum. The Portland Vase itself passed through his hands. Why not amuse himself with science too? Hamilton's book *Campi Phlegraei* describes not only Vesuvius but the ominous landscape to its north, the Phlegrean Fields, including the Solfatara, a vast open crater in which it was and still is possible to walk among bubbling hot jets of water and sulphurous smells. An industrial landscape created by the Earth itself.

Then, in August 1779, Vesuvius erupted with massive force. Hamilton's *Supplement* to his earlier book is a report addressed to Joseph Banks, president of the Royal Society, on what occurred. It is sumptuously illustrated with coloured illustrations commissioned by Hamilton from a locally based artist, Pietro Fabris. These pictures lack Wright's passion for fire. Instead they emphasize the surreal stillness of the immense column of ash hanging over Naples.

Vesuvius erupted with gratifying frequency during the Enlightenment. It was as if the god of hellfire had read Burke on the sublime and wanted to oblige, with explosions that were regular and exciting without being the murderous cataclysms of 79 CE or 1631. As Hamilton put it, since 1767:

> *Vesuvius has never been free from smoke, nor ever months without throwing up red hot SCORIAE [igneous rocks], which increasing to a certain degree was usually follow'd by a current of liquid Lava...*

Wright too had seen one of these outbursts – it was more than enough to set his imagination alight.

The Welsh painter Thomas Jones had a similarly earthshaking experience. He arrived in Naples in a crowded coach in September 1778 to see Vesuvius belching ash high in the air. They had just missed an eruption, he was told. That night, he witnessed 'a large stream of Melted Lava running down the Side of the Mountain'. He could not resist getting closer. Hiring mules and guides, he and a friend set off up the slopes, teaming up with two German artists they met on the way. They saw a vineyard that had been overwhelmed by lava just days before. Its grapes had been 'shrivelled up like raisins' by the heat. Still-moving lava set leaves alight as they watched.

They kept climbing. With a casual daring that seems almost unbelievable, these eighteenth-century travellers in their buckled shoes and stockings stepped over the encrusted surface of a lava stream that was still flowing to reach the mouth of the eruption, which was a little below the summit:

> *Here we met several other parties. And we all returned by Torchlight – The whole Scene having a grand and wonderful Effect.*

Was it all just sublime tourism? Vesuvius was attracting artists by the cartload and Hamilton's scientific report looks more like a gorgeous art book than research. Yet the combination of art, history and hot rocks that brought the curious flowing to the Bay of Naples laid the foundations of modern geology. In the early nineteenth century, Charles Lyell paid particularly close attention to three mollusc-eaten columns of what he believed to be the Temple of Serapis – actually an ancient Roman market – by the sea in the town of Pozzuoli. He deduced that within the last two millennia this part of the Earth had been cast down under the waves, then raised up again. It was a crucial piece of evidence that

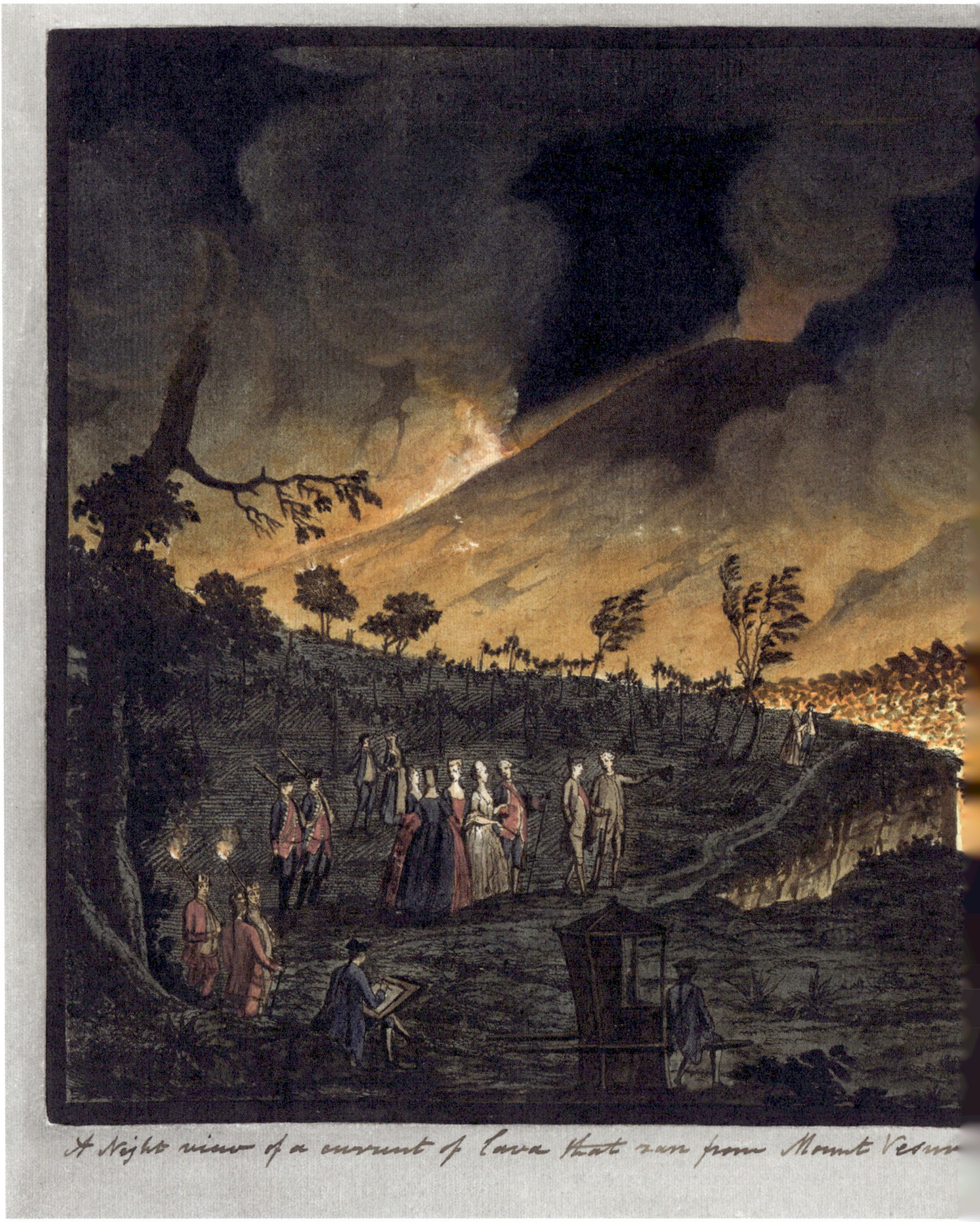
A Night view of a current of Lava that ran from Mount Vesuv

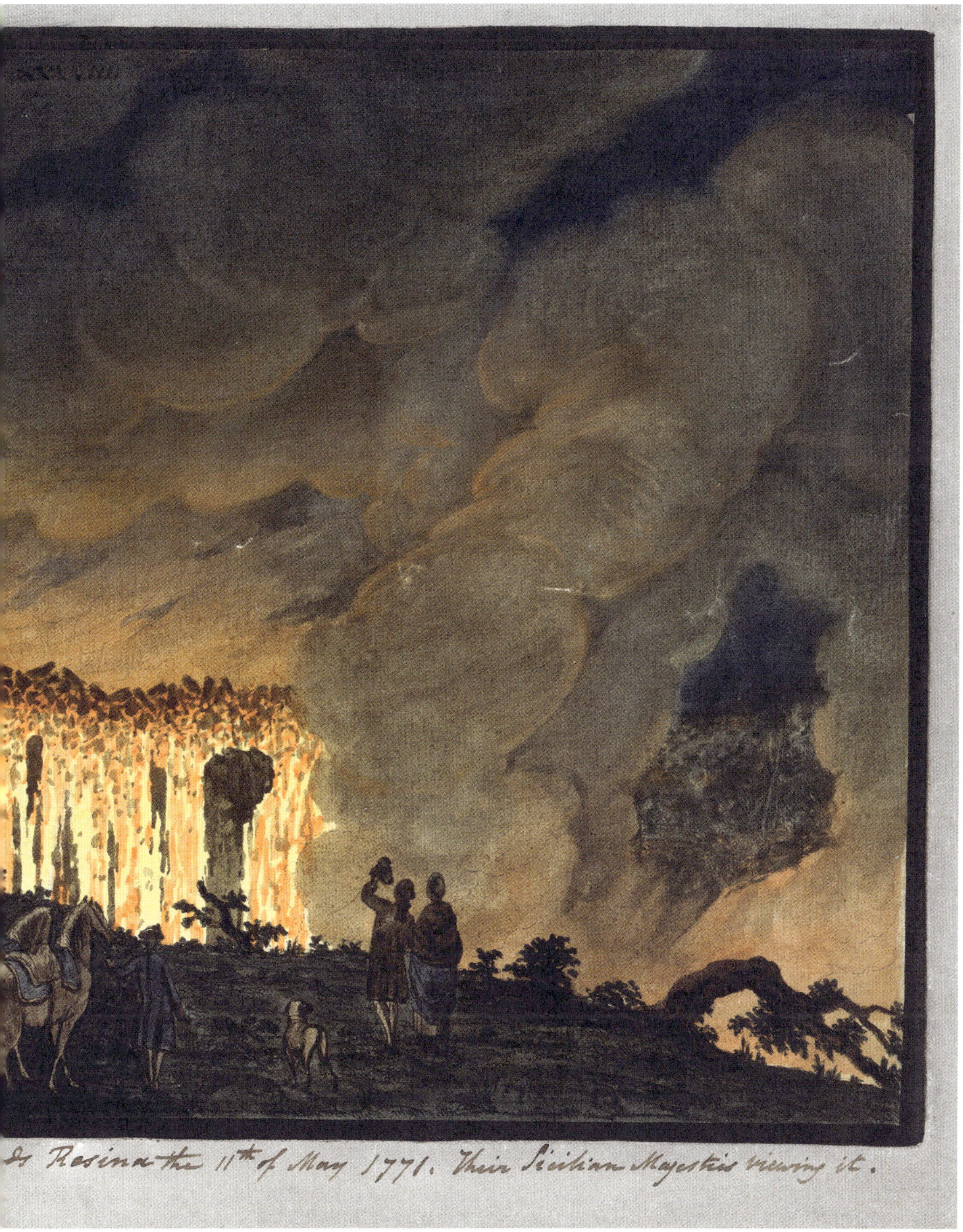

↑ Pietro Fabris, *Sir William Hamilton conducting their Sicilian majesties to see the current of lava from Vesuvius in May 1771* (plate XXXVIII of Sir William Hamilton's *Supplement to the Campi Phlegraei. Being an Account of the Great Eruption of Vesuvius in the Month of August 1779)*, c. 1771–76, etching, hand-coloured on paper, 21.3 × 39.4 cm (8⅖ × 15½ in.), British Museum, London

the Earth's fabric was neither set forever in Edenic times nor shaped by one-off catastrophes, but is constantly changing. The dramatic shifts in Pozzuoli's height were – are – caused by the immense underground volcano it stands over.

An evocative engraving of the 'Temple of Serapis' became the frontispiece to Lyell's book *Principles of Geology*, published from 1830 to 1833, in which he shows that changes in the Earth are continually happening and are governed by natural laws. Lyell's work was crucial in demonstrating the antiquity of the Earth and the slow processes by which it has been formed. It made an impression on Charles Darwin.

Thomas Jones found vulcanism more diverting than artistically inspiring. Born in 1742, this second son of a Welsh squire who grew up in Pencerrig, near Builth Wells, went for a while to Oxford before getting two years' training from his countryman Richard Wilson. His chatty journal is a unique document of an artist's Grand Tour. After climbing Vesuvius he found lodgings in Naples with a Swiss host and his English wife:

> *Where we took two small Apartments at 4 carlines a day and boarded with the family, drinking Punch Dorchester beer and living much in the English manner.*

After returning to Rome he would come back to Naples in 1780 for a three-year stay. He met Hamilton and saw all the sights, even the 'Grotto del Cane', where he 'saw for the first time the cruel and silly experiment performed on a Dog'. This experiment had echoes of the air pump. A dog was forced into a cave notorious for its toxic fumes. It dropped dead, proving vulcanism was releasing deadly gas into the cave.

Fascinating stuff, but it did not bring gripping art out of Jones, even though he was an accomplished painter of Welsh landscapes and spent years in Naples. His views of Vesuvius and the Bay are calm and placid, overshadowed by his teacher Wilson and Wilson's hero, Claude.

Jones was adrift. Why did he spend so long in Naples if the landscape only mildly excited him? It was a competitive place, where artists came and went. He stayed until he must have seemed slightly pathetic, a directionless Welshman in the hot sun. Then one day he started painting small oil sketches of Naples itself, with a distant, curious eye, like an alien portraying a puzzling planet.

Only someone stuck in a foreign city on a long afternoon, disengaged and bored, a little lonely, finding a bit of stability and sanity in the steady work of carefully observing and patiently recording his

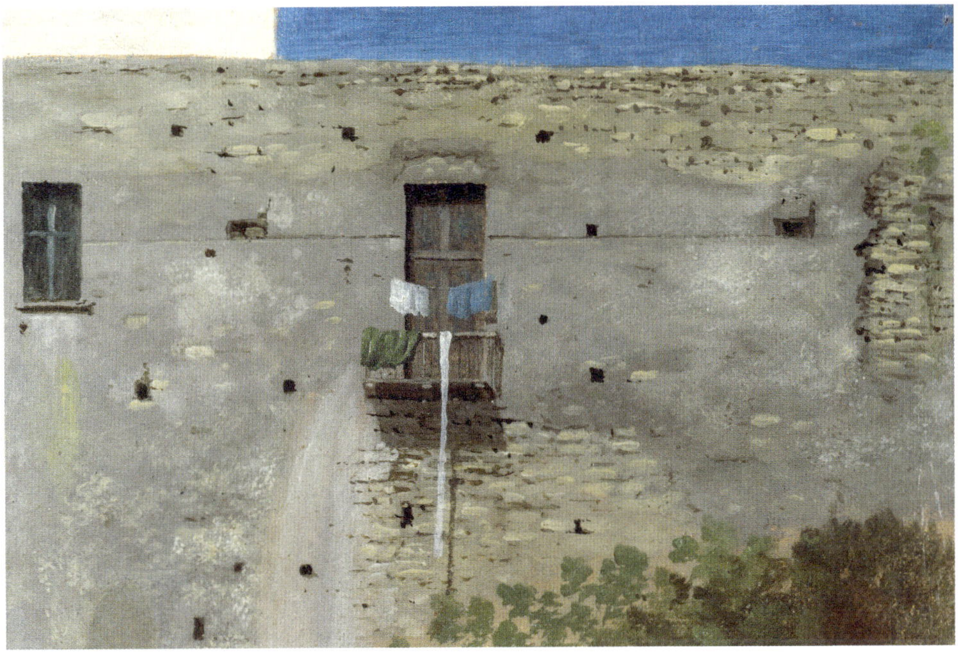

surroundings, could paint the masterpiece that is Jones's little painting *A Wall in Naples*.

He had been living continuously amid the poverty of Naples for two years when he painted it in about 1782. Living like other travellers in an 'English' way he was not part of its tumultuous life. That estrangement is clear in the view he takes. Ignoring all notions of the picturesque, he concentrates on a worn and battered wall. The windows in it are closed and inscrutable. Washing hung out to dry in the sun is the only trace of Neapolitans. They are shut away, resting in the heat. Life is elsewhere. Jones is too British to take a siesta so he paints, and having no ideas, he paints what he can see. He is a blank slate.

British people gazed with similar estrangement at other walls all over the world when Jones was painting this. Company officers watched the sun on walls in Calcutta and Bombay. Planters watched the light on a whitewashed wall in Jamaica. Slavers stared at the stones of Cape Coast Castle in West Africa while they waited for a Liverpool ship to appear on the metal-hard sea in the stifling heat.

Jones paints with the lonely eye of a stranger whose mind has been drained by the sun. All he has left is pure empiricism.

↑ Thomas Jones, *A Wall in Naples*, c. 1782, oil on paper laid on canvas, 11.4 × 16 cm (4 ½ × 6 ⅓ in.), National Gallery, London

6. The Doors of Perception

If the doors of perception were cleansed everything
would appear to man as it is, infinite.
For man has closed himself up, till he sees all things
thro' narrow chinks of his cavern.

William Blake, *The Marriage of Heaven and Hell*, 1790–93

Mind-forg'd Manacles

The most powerful image ever released by the anti-slavery movement in the eighteenth century was a stark printed diagram. In 1788 the Plymouth chapter of the Society for Effecting the Abolition of the Slave Trade produced a drawing of the 'cargo' deck of a British slaver, the *Brookes*. This wooden sailing ship based in Liverpool had been assessed that year by a parliamentary investigation of the slave trade. Under new regulations made law by the 1788 Slavery Act the *Brookes* was now allowed to carry up to 454 slaves across the Atlantic – a 'reform', given that it had previously squeezed in more than 600.

The emblem designed by Josiah Wedgwood bearing the phrase 'Am I Not A Man And A Brother?' (page 130) appears below the *Brookes* in a broadsheet of the diagram published in Bristol in 1789. The view of the ship's deck from above shows how far British slavers were from treating Africans as brothers or sisters. It makes a mockery of the new halfhearted parliamentary 'regulations' by showing exactly how 454 people can be squeezed into the *Brookes*. They lie flat on their backs, unable to move, crushed close together. The most evil thing about this carefully packed cargo of human beings is its rational, even scientific, orderliness. Like any good Enlightened entrepreneur, the captain of the *Brookes* has accurately calculated the ship's capacity and efficiently

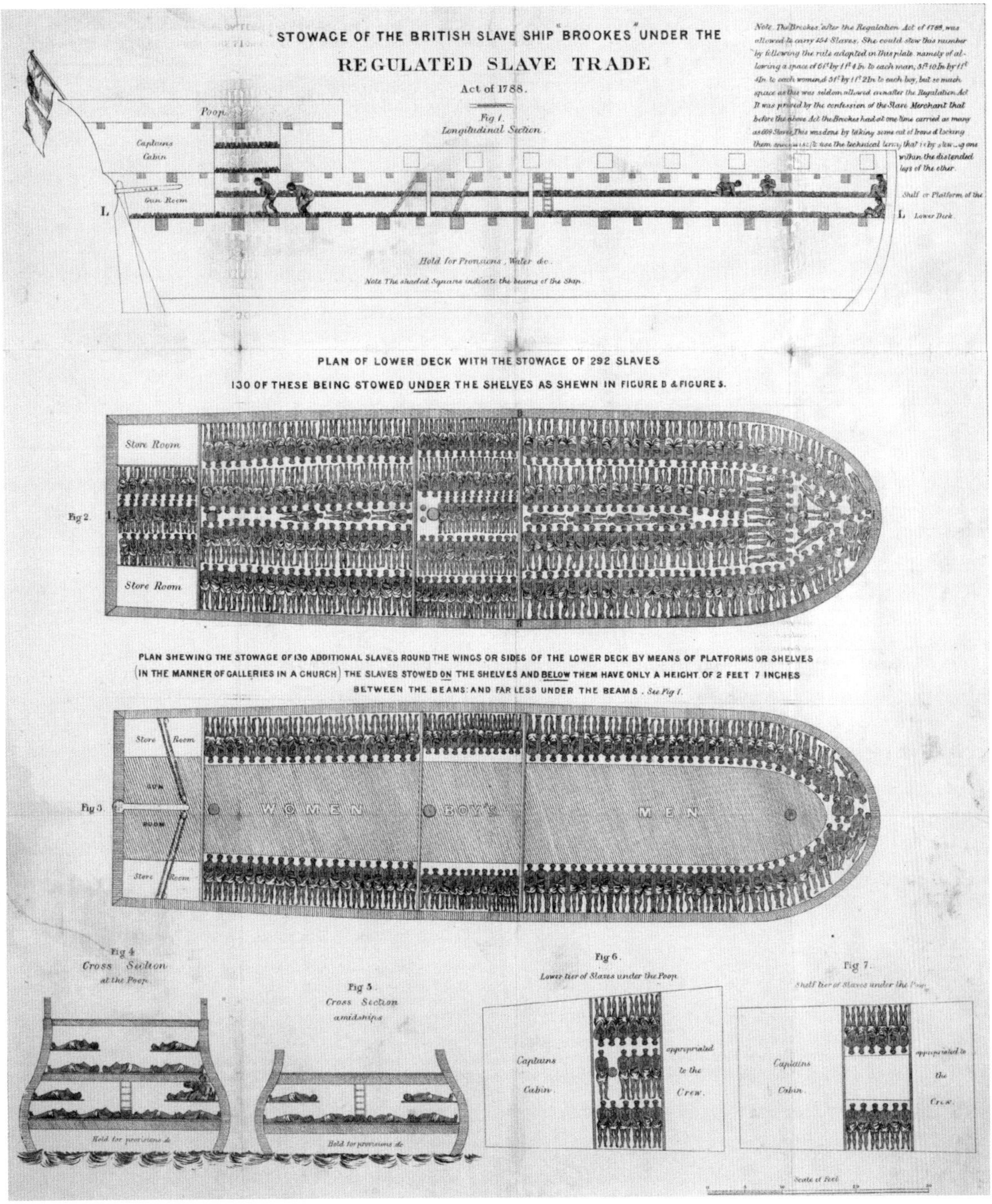

↑ Diagram of slave ship 'The Brookes' drawn in 1788 and issued as prints from 1789, etching, Library of Congress Rare Book and Special Collections Division Washington, D.C.

maximized its load. This is no chaotic dungeon but a very modern system of persecution.

The horror this drawing inspired in 1790s Britain – the horror it still inspires – lies not only in its mapping of inhumanity but its aura of perverted reason. Medieval barbarity did not create this cruelty. Modernity and progress did.

William Blake was surely one of those moved and angered by the image of the *Brookes*. In any case there is no doubting his revulsion at slavery. In his poem 'The Little Black Boy', published in 1789 in his tiny hand-coloured book *Songs of Innocence*, he asserts a common humanity in deliberately childlike language. In the glowing illustration to this poem an African mother and her child sit under a tree contemplating the rising sun, free from slavery's chains. Those chains clank through his art, weighing down souls that strain to be free. On a page of his illustrated book-length poem *Europe: a Prophecy*, published in 1794, a naked, muscular prisoner sits chained by the feet as a shadowy jailer departs, key in hand. In *The Book of Urizen* from that same year, Blake's invented patriarchal deity Urizen is manacled hand and foot.

The first picture in *Visions of the Daughters of Albion*, first published in 1793, is of a naked man and woman chained to a rock, back to back by the cold dark sea under a red sun, while a third figure crouches in despair beside them. The poem begins with the word 'Enslaved' in extra-large letters. The enslavement he means is that of women: 'Enslaved, the Daughters of Albion weep...'

For Blake sees slavery in British homes and streets as well as in the Atlantic trade. A year before he wrote, engraved, and hand-coloured *Visions of the Daughters of Albion*, Mary Wollstonecraft had published *A Vindication of the Rights of Woman*. Blake illustrated a children's book for Wollstonecraft and they were both part of the same circle around the radical publisher Joseph Johnson.

Ultimately, however, the chains Blake defies are not physical. They are mental. Human liberation depends for him on breaking the fetters of what he sees as a system of intellectual enslavement that limits the very way we see. In his poem 'London', which appeared in *Songs of Experience* in 1794, Blake wanders the streets of his city seeing 'Marks of weakness, marks of woe'. The 'chartered' streets of commercialized London are full of misery, the cries of the wretched, but it is 'The mind-forg'd manacles I hear'.

Blake's writings and art make it abundantly clear what system of mental enslavement he is talking about. He means the science of

→ William Blake, frontispiece to *Visions of the Daughters of Albion*, c. 1795, relief etching, ink and watercolour on paper, 17 × 12 cm (6¾ × 4¾ in.), Tate

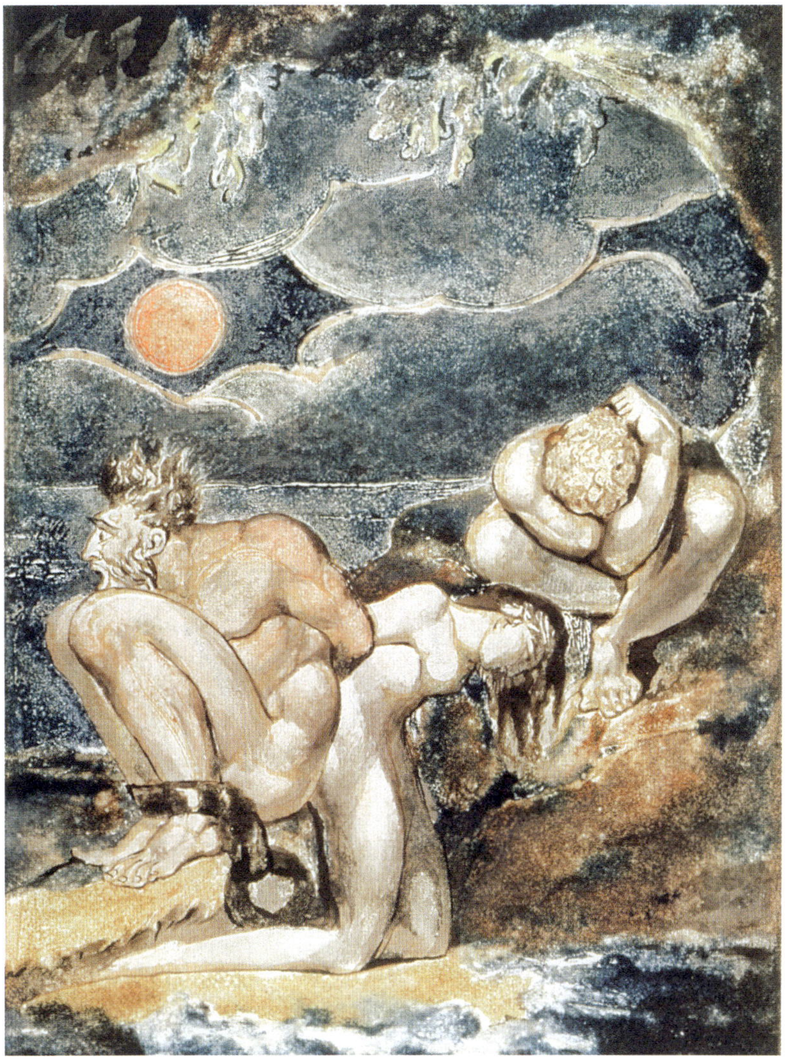

Isaac Newton and the empirical philosophy of John Locke. For Blake, these intellectual pillars of the Enlightenment are titans of oppression. Newton's mechanical understanding of nature and Locke's claim that all knowledge comes through sensory perception sustain a narrow, superficial notion of rationality that imprisons humanity's true potential in the iron chains of industry, empire and war.

Blake, who was born in Soho in London in 1757, the son of a hosier, and apprenticed to an engraver near Covent Garden in 1772, claimed that he read and rejected Locke when he was a youth, and this is probably true because his critique of the scientific and empirical world-view is already fully formed in his early work *There is No Natural Religion*:

> *Mans perceptions are not bounded by organs of perception, he perceives more than sense (tho' ever so acute) can discover.*

Europe: a Prophecy begins with the spectacular image of a white-bearded divine being, who for Blake is the embodiment of tyranny and control, crouching inside the blazing orb of the sun, surrounded by belching smoky clouds, reaching down into the void to map and plan the universe with a pair of golden dividers. To survey the cosmos is to place boundaries around it, to calculate its shape, to limit the infinite. In Blake's richly hand-coloured print *Newton*, created between 1795 and 1805, it is the nude, muscular spirit of the famous physicist who leans forward with a pair of dividers, reducing reality to a triangle, while behind him strange corals and sea creatures swarm in a blue-green reef of nature's mystery.

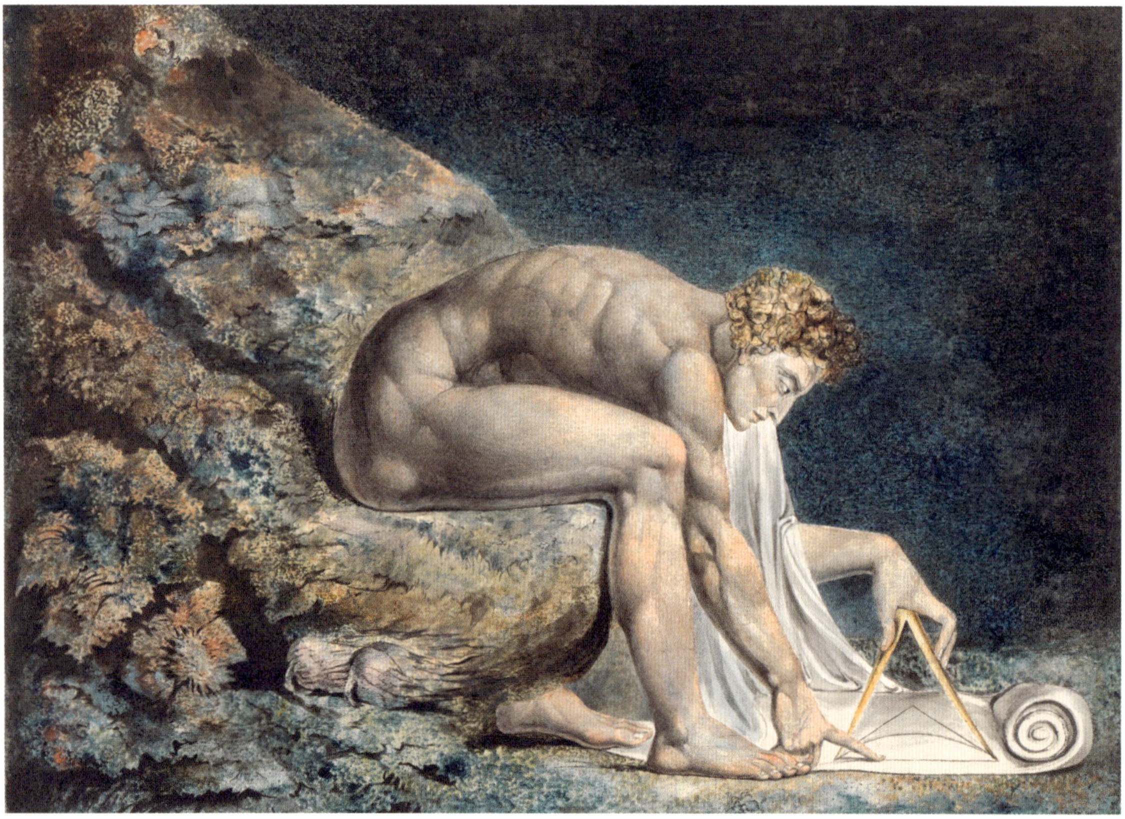

↑ William Blake, *Newton*, 1795–c. 1805, colour print, ink and watercolour on paper, 46 × 60 cm (18 ⅛ × 23 ⅝ in.), Tate

Satan is, according to Blake's 1804–11 work *Milton*, the ultimate engineer of Newton's laws:

> *O Satan, my youngest born, art thou not*
> *Prince of the Starry Hosts*
> *And of the Wheels of Heaven, to turn*
> *the Mills day and night?*
> *Art thou not Newton's Pantocrator,*
> *weaving the Woof of Locke?*
> *To Mortals thy Mills seem every thing...*

'Pantocrator' is not exactly a common word, but Newton himself uses it in a theological appendix to the *Principia*. In this essay Newton defines the supreme yet remote place of God in his system. As it appeared in an English translation from the original scholarly Latin in 1729:

> *This Being governs all things, not as the soul of the world, but as Lord over all: And on account of his dominion he is wont to be called Lord God Pantokrator, or Universal Ruler.*

It seems Blake was not just raging blindly at Newton – he had actually read him. Newton's view of God as a distant absolute ruler of the universe – the Greek word *pantokrator* means 'lord over all' – matches both the image of Newton delineated by Blake, as a distant surveyor of abstract space, and Blake's own myth of the tyrannical divine patriarch Urizen. Or, as he puts it in *Milton*, it means that Satan, the dark prince, not the biblical God, is Newton's true 'Universal Ruler'.

Yet what are the 'mills' where Satan applies Newton's laws to weave 'the Woof of Locke'? (The woof or weft are the horizontal threads on a loom.) Satan's mills are not mere metaphors. They resemble those of Arkwright (page 130), applying the laws of mechanics to make an industrial revolution, and like the disciplined workforces of the new factory age, Satan's mills turn 'day and night'.

Blake's contempt for Enlightenment science is not mysticism. It is a cogent critique of the systematizing, organizing, mechanizing rationality that crammed slaves to neatly fill a ship and employed children in the new cotton mills. It is Satan who works the grinding wheels of commerce and cranks the enslaving gears of materialism: 'To Mortals thy Mills seem everything...'

The Bastille Trembles

The visual art of William Blake is a cosmic theatre of oppression and liberation. Body and soul are one. Like his hero Michelangelo, he expresses the agony and ecstasy of the spirit in bulging muscles and strained sinews, contorted poses and dynamic leaps. The physical is the heart and lungs of his vision. Yet he is portraying inner states, for as the Devil explains in *The Marriage of Heaven and Hell*:

> *Man has no Body distinct from his Soul; for that call'd Body is a portion of Soul discern'd by the five Senses, the chief inlets of Soul in this age.*

↓ William Blake, plate 17 from *Europe: a Prophecy*, 1794, colour-printed relief etching with ink, oil and watercolour on paper, plate 23.2 × 16.5 cm (9 ⅙ × 6 ½ in.), Yale Center for British Art, New Haven

Extremes of confinement and escape, lamentation and joy are expressed by his spiritual bodies. While *Visions of the Daughters of Albion* begins with a man and woman chained back to back, *Europe* ends with a powerful picture of a naked hero rescuing a woman and child from an inferno. The words above this fiery image blast a call to arms:

> *... his head he rear'd in snaky thunders clad;*
> *And with a cry that shook all nature to the utmost pole,*
> *Call'd all his sons to the strife of blood.*

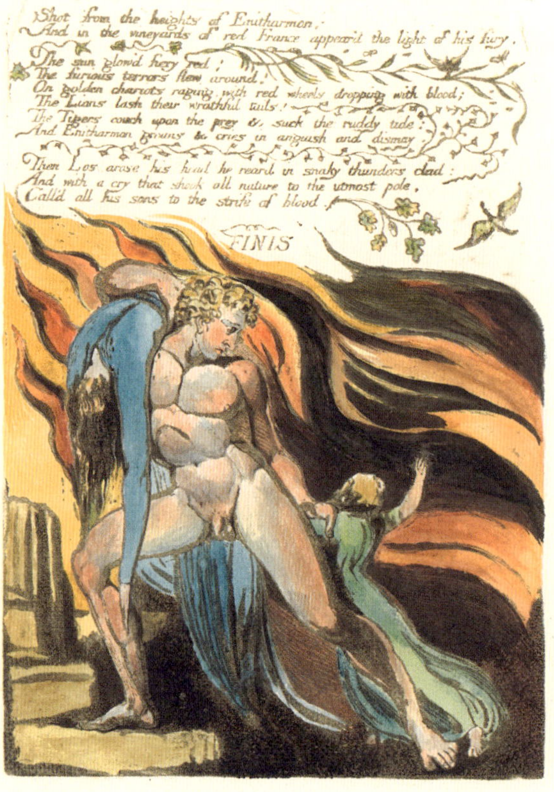

With its epic dramas that span space and time while denying they even exist, its heroic struggles between Universal Rulers and self-liberating innocents, its vortices of energy and unrest, this is an art of revolution.

The French Revolution was hailed by many Britons as an epoch in human liberation. Bliss was it in that dawn to be alive – as William Wordsworth would remember. It was hailed as the next step in a transformation that had started with the American Declaration of Independence in 1776, was taken further in the ideas of Rousseau and now climaxed in the fall of Europe's most powerful absolutist monarchy. In Britain, the demand for democracy had begun in the 1760s among a widening political public. As we have seen, the industrial pioneers of the Midlands were champions of liberty, friends of Franklin, supporters of Rousseau. The campaign to abolish slavery was passionately supported from Wedgwood's Etruria to cities such as Bristol and Manchester. The French Revolution was surely the beginning of the long-awaited age of universal rights.

The French monarchy's repeated failures to reorganize its finances, depleted partly by wars with Britain, forced Louis XVI in 1788 to summon the Estates General, the closest thing France had to any kind of representative body. It had last gathered in 1614 – and it broke up in chaos that time. As soon as the Estates assembled on 5 May 1789, the Third Estate – theoretically representing everyone who was not part of the higher-ranking Estates of the nobility of land and office and the priesthood – started calling for fairer representation. By the 17th of June it broke away to form a National Assembly and three days later, ordered by Louis to disperse, its members met in an indoor tennis court at Versailles and swore to stay together until France got a constitution. On the 14th of July the Bastille was stormed; less than a month later the Assembly formally abolished 'feudalism'; and on 26 August it adopted the Declaration of the Rights of Man and of the Citizen.

In Britain the joy was not confined to Lunarticks and poets. Charles James Fox, leader of the oppositional faction of the Whigs in Parliament, one of the lovers of Perdita (page 132) and a gambling, drinking aristocrat of the old school, matched the most ardent romantic youth in his acclaim for the storming of the Bastille:

> *How much the greatest event it is that ever happened in the world, and how much the best!*

Fox frequented Parliament unshaven and unkempt to show solidarity with *les citoyens*, while Blake is said to have wandered the streets in a red French-style liberty cap.

One former friend of liberty refused to join in the congratulations. Edmund Burke begins his *Reflections on the Revolution in France* with a reply to a French correspondent:

> *You imagined, when you wrote last, that I might possibly be reckoned among the approvers of certain proceedings in France...*

Burke, theorist of the sublime, champion of American rights and critic of imperial corruption, was not an 'approver' of the French Revolution. Not by a long stretch. In his *Reflections*, published in 1790 when enthusiasm for the new age was at its height, he asserts that far from sharing the reasonable ideals of liberty and rights asserted in Britain since 1688, the French Revolution is a violent and irrational assault on tradition. The imagination he showed in his youthful essay on the sublime seeps into the way he sees the French Revolution as he paints a blood-curdling picture of popular madness unleashed, the crazed rule of extremists. Locke based liberty on property rights. In France these are being erased, says Burke. He sees no end to the 'fanaticism' that has overthrown both monarchy and church.

It was a time that summoned prophets. Blake started a poem in seven books called *The French Revolution* that matches Burke's dramatic fantasy without sharing his pessimism: for Blake, the gigantic figures of Louis XVI, his minister Necker and other actors in the events in France are like Milton's fallen angels debating in their hellish capital Pandaemonium. What a shame he never illustrated it. The majority of Blake's books were self-published, but the radical publisher Joseph Johnson, for whom he worked as an illustrator, showed interest in bringing this one out. The failure of any but the first of its planned seven volumes even to be set in type is revealing. For by 1791, when Blake's vision was ready for publication, Burke's cheerless warnings were coming true. After trying to flee Paris that June, the king and queen were placed under close arrest. Tom Paine's attack on Burke, *Rights of Man*, published at the start of the year, already looked dated in its confident equation of American and French constitutionalism by autumn 1792, when aristocrats and priests were being massacred. On 21 January 1793 Louis XVI was executed.

James Gillray's print *The Blood of the Murdered Crying for Vengeance*, published a few weeks after the monarch's death, is a Gothic vision of this decisive moment of the Revolution. Gillray shows the British public how Louis died in the machine that was already coming to symbolize the descent of French liberty into violence. His depiction of the guillotine is as accurate as any eighteenth-century diagram of an ingenious device. This efficient killing apparatus was a perversion of Enlightened science. Joseph-Ignace Guillotin proposed to the National Assembly in 1789 that the barbarity of traditional execution should be replaced by a modern, clean and quick decapitation machine: yet as Gillray shows, the very efficiency of this mechanism results in

→ James Gillray, *The Blood of the Murdered Crying for Vengeance,* 1793, hand-coloured etching, 34.8 × 25.7 cm (13 ¾ × 10 ⅙ in.), Yale University Libraries, New Haven

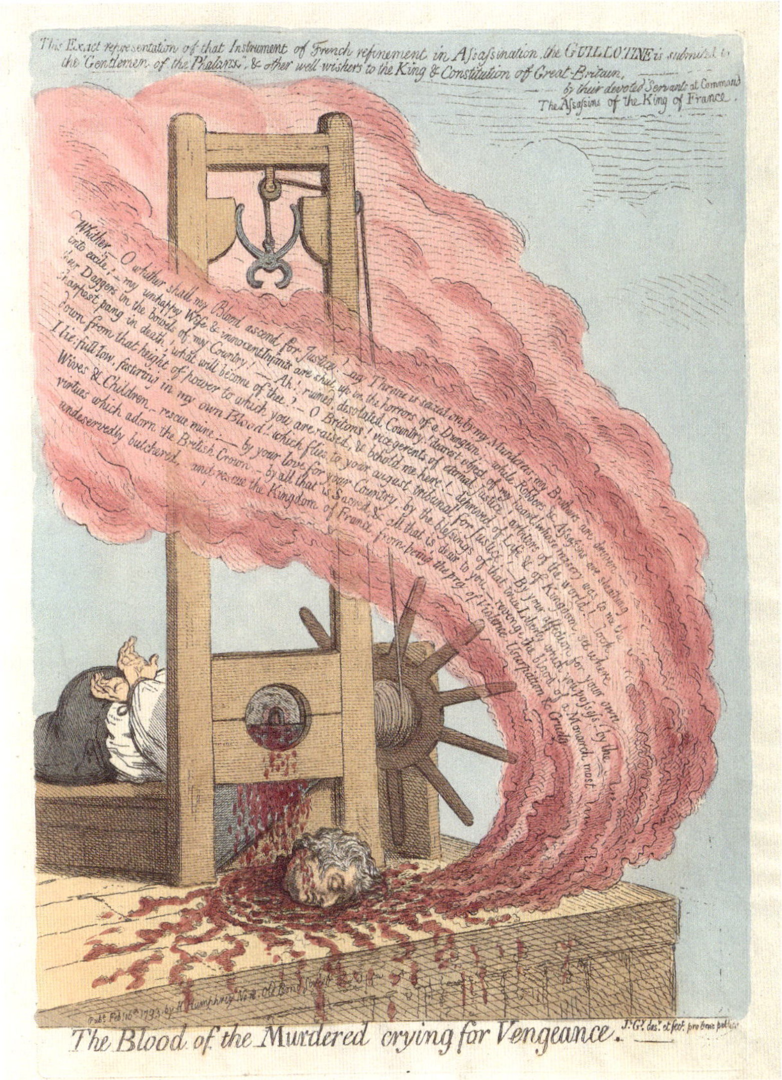

unprecedented horrors. Like the slave ship with its neatly crushed people (page 147), the guillotine is what happens when scientific reason is applied to inhuman ends.

Gillray shared with Burke and Blake an imagination unfettered enough to encompass these historic days. Blake was called mad by some: 'There was no doubt that this poor man was mad,' said Wordsworth, adding in true Romantic fashion that there was that in Blake's madness 'which interests me more than the sanity of Lord Byron and Walter Scott'. Tom Paine mocked Burke as a hysteric who ranted against the French Revolution and its British friends 'in a phrenzy of passion'. Yet of these three it was Gillray who went insane. He spent his final years confined and cared for by his publisher Hannah Humphreys after trying to kill himself by leaping from the top floor of her premises. His art is truly drunk on the macabre and grotesque. It was a surrealism the government of William Pitt the Younger found very useful, and it paid Gillray a secret pension of £200 a year for part of the 1790s.

Gillray's 1795 print *Presages of the Millenium* is as eschatological as any of Blake's visions. Pitt has become Death: his naked bony form rides on a pale horse over the cast-down Opposition, including the fat, unshaven Fox and a red-nosed Richard Brinsley Sheridan, the theatre manager and author of such great comedies as *The Rivals* and *The Critic* who was also a leading pro-revolutionary Whig MP. They both wear red liberty caps. The herd of pigs that Pitt is scaring away is a visual

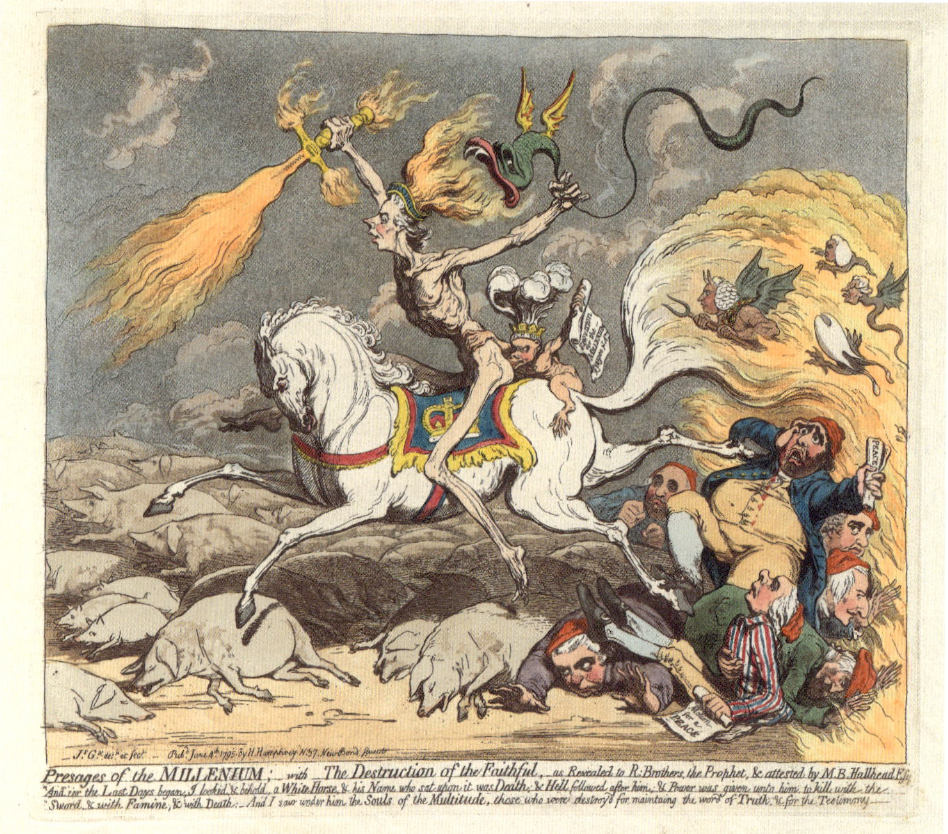

↑ James Gillray, *Presages of the Millenium*, 1795, hand-coloured etching, 32.5 × 37.4 cm (12 ¾ × 14 ¾ in.), Yale University Libraries, New Haven

quotation from Burke, who called the revolutionary crowd 'a swinish multitude'.

By this time Britain was at war with revolutionary France. Pitt made himself the voice of that war, and would be remembered as an unbendingly martial prime minister, bringing death to Britannia's enemies. He was practising his own 'terror' at home, with troops on the streets purportedly to defend against French invasion but, in the eyes of radicals, menacing British liberties. As Blake writes in 'London':

And the hapless Soldier's sigh
Runs in blood down Palace walls.

Toryism had more or less vanished in the later eighteenth century, tainted by its treacherous Jacobite past. Now the Whigs themselves were split into authoritarian and libertarian tendencies as Pitt and Burke forged what would come to be seen as modern Conservatism. Meanwhile the foundation of the London Corresponding Society in 1792, with its rule that 'our members be unlimited', brought shoemakers, weavers and tailors into politics as never before. Pitt attempted and failed to convict its leaders of treason in 1794, on blatantly false claims of a plot to kill the king.

Modern political ideology was born, and in Gillray's splenetic output, so was the modern British political cartoon. Printmaking had been one of Britain's most original contributions to Europe's art since the days of Hogarth. It could create images that reached far beyond the stately homes of the aristocracy. Gillray was the same age as Blake and, like him, trained to join the flourishing craft of the engraver. Unlike Blake he had an eye for the market. His 1808 print *Very Slippy Weather* is both a brilliant advert for his employer and protector Humphreys – her name is boldly displayed over the shop door – and a window for us on the democracy of art in Georgian Britain. A variety of people, from a top-hatted gent to a street urchin, gawp at Gillray's latest caricatures: while they are laughing at the pictures in the print-shop window they do not notice a bit of real-life slapstick going on behind them.

Blake never found the audience that delighted in Gillray. Did he ever expect a comparable following? It is hard to tell, but the prophetic style of his voice implies he felt he had something urgent to say. Prophets cry out in the wilderness but get heard at the last moment. Apocalypticism was the current mood: Gillray's image of Pitt on a pale horse is partly a parody of the prophecies of Richard Brothers, whose

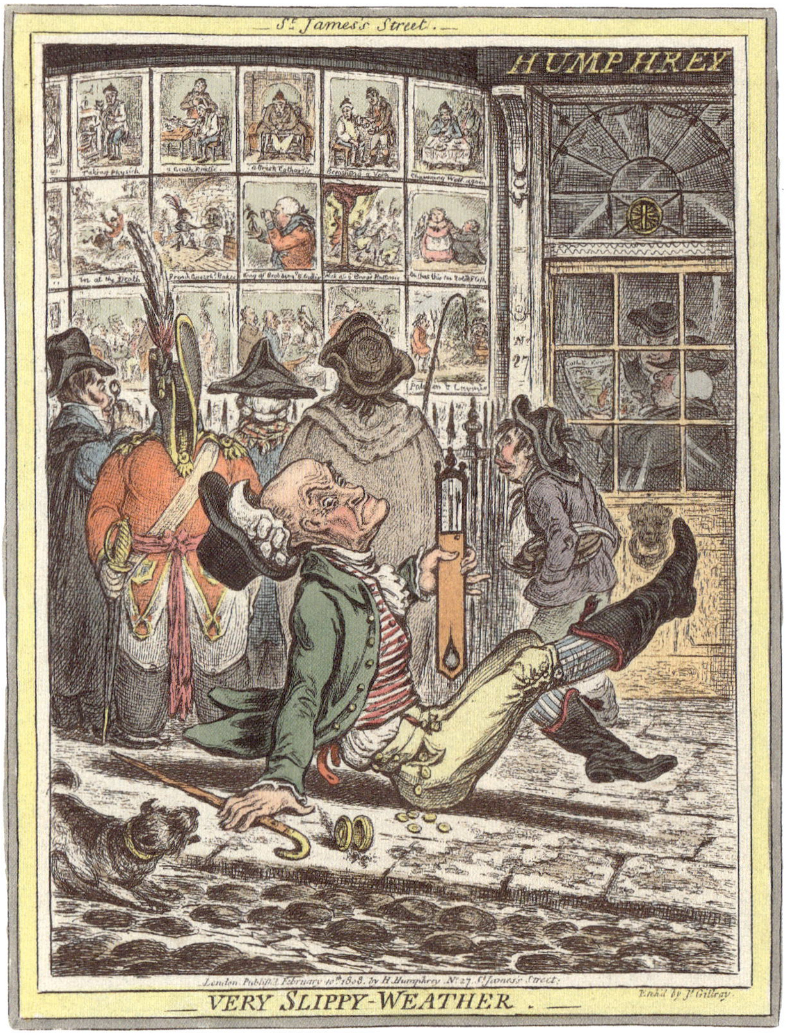

← James Gillray, *Very Slippy Weather*, 1808, hand-coloured etching, 25.2 × 19.4 cm (10 × 7⅝ in.), Yale University Libraries, New Haven

rants drew big crowds in the 1790s. Gillray dates his print 'June 4th 1795', the birthday of George III, mocking Brothers for predicting the king's death. George III might have been mad but he remained very much alive. Another prophet with a popular audience was Joanna Southcott, who claimed to be the Woman of the Apocalypse mentioned in the Book of Revelation.

Soon after dying in 1787, Blake's brother Robert appeared to him in a vision and showed him how to make books in a revolutionary way. Instead of cutting images into a copper plate, the poet experimented with using acid to burn away everything around the image, which was protected with a greasy, acid-resistant layer. The raised image that resulted could then be printed and hand-coloured. Most audaciously of all, Blake was able to write his poetry directly in his own hand on the copper plate. He and his wife, Catherine, hand-coloured the printed pages, resulting in books of dreamlike beauty and intensity. A prospectus for his works that Blake addressed in 1793 'TO THE PUBLIC' suggests he really did see himself as a popular artist:

> *The Labours of the Artist, the Poet, the Musician, have been proverbially attended by poverty and obscurity; this was never the fault of the Public, but was owing to a neglect of means to propagate such works as have wholly absorbed the Man of Genius... This difficulty has been obviated by the Author of the following productions now presented to the Public...*

Blake sees himself as cutting out the middle-man between visionary and public, publishing his own works – as if on an internet of the fancy – to reach directly the eyes and souls of multitudes. In reality his self-published books only reached a tiny audience and his paintings and single prints, such as *Newton*, were equally obscure. A further refinement in the method of colouring his prints – a process of compressed watercolour resembling the Surrealist technique of decalcomania – that produced the subaquatic realm of *Newton* and the subterranean labyrinth in which his clawed primeval Nebuchadnezzar crawls on his hands and knees, could not win over the masses.

This had one lucky effect. Blake's art and writing are enthusiastically subversive yet his political rebelliousness was cloaked by the accidental invisibility as well as the intentional mystery of his work. His tempera painting *The Spiritual Form of Pitt Guiding Behemoth*, from about 1805, portrays the warlord prime minister as an angelic figure leading forward the bestial madness of war. Blake gets away with literally demonizing Pitt. His obscure prophetic style makes the image appear at first sight anodyne. In reality it is a vision of despotism and sabre-rattling, visualizing the fear in Blake's book-length poem *Jerusalem* that 'Humanity shall be no more, but war and princedom and victory!'

Priests in Black Gowns

On a page of Blake's *Europe* a black-scaled, horned satanic figure stands wielding a sword between two yellow-clad angels. One of the angels is praying, the other has her arms folded. Good and Evil, Heaven and Hell seem surprisingly relaxed in each other's company. To read the words printed in cursive script beneath this eerie picture is to enter the psychological depths of Blake's heretical vision:

> *Go tell the human race that Womans love is Sin*
> *That an eternal life awaits the worms of sixty winters*
> *In an allegorical abode where existence hath never come:*
> *Forbid all Joy, & from her childhood shall the little female*
> *Spread nets in every single path.*

On the facing page, in what by Blake's standards is almost a realist scene, two women mourn a dead child in what might be a Georgian drawing room. One sits in a blue Neoclassical chair, baring her ample throat and breasts as she raises her face skyward. On the floor in front of her is the pallid body of a dead child. Another woman is bent double in grief. Above them rears a cast-iron fireplace that is just a little too large to be realistic. Crimson flames burst out of it. This does not after all seem simply a portrayal of death and lamentation. What is it really that has been lost? While the fire rages, the baby lies frozen. Most arrestingly of all, the first woman is sexualized in her fleshy sadness. It is not just a child that has died: this is a funeral for Eros. As the words nearby warn, it is deathly to accept, instead of earthly fulfilment, 'the worms of sixty winters'. For as Blake writes in *The Marriage of Heaven and Hell*: 'Sooner murder an infant in its cradle than nurse unacted desires.'

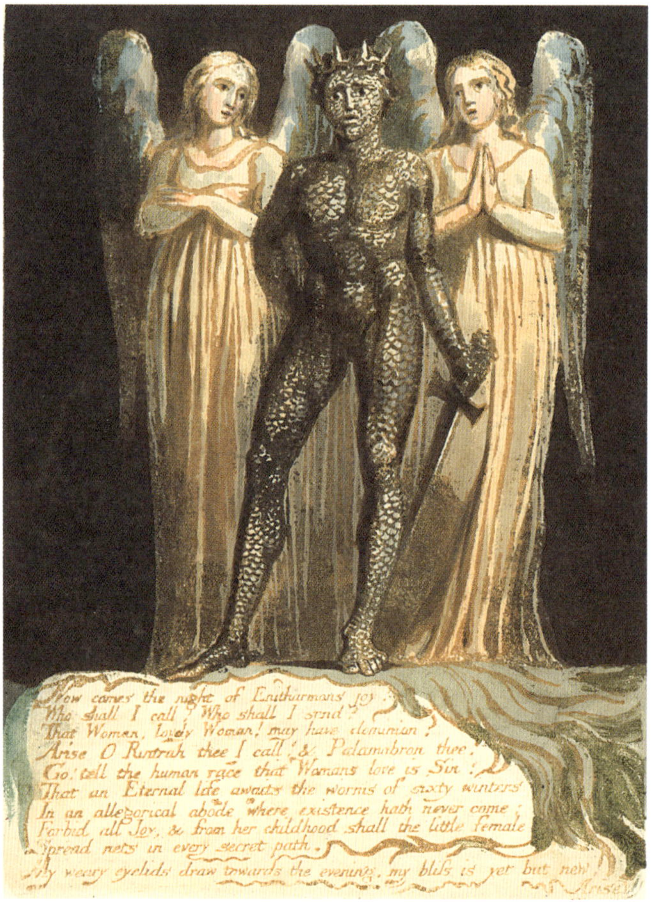

↓ William Blake, plate 5 from *Europe: a Prophecy*, 1794, colour-printed relief etching, 23.8 × 17.1 cm (9 ⅓ × 6 ¾ in.), New York Public Library, New York

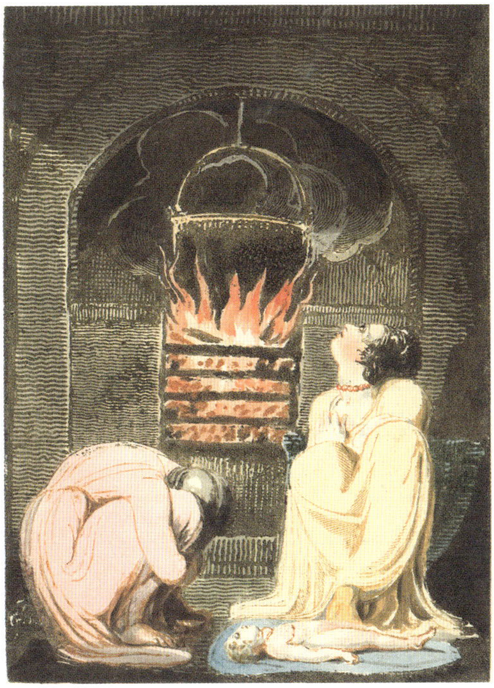

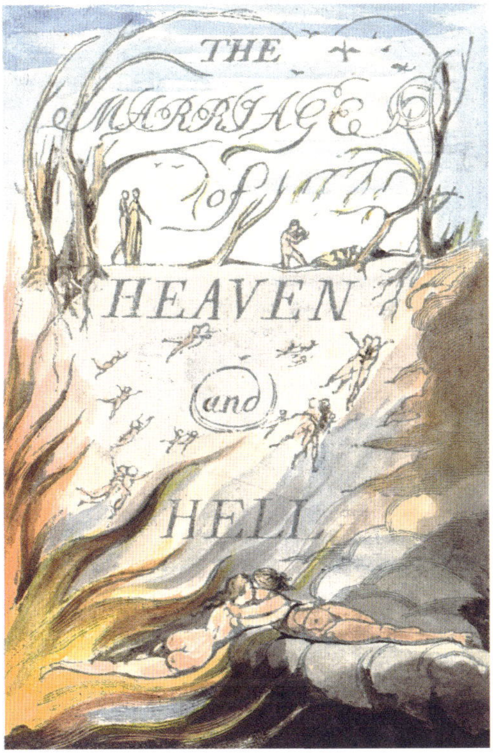

Blake's revolutionary visions of the 1790s are concerned less with constitutional rights than with euphoria. As the Bastille falls and Pitt's spiritual form rises up he dreams of a revolution of desire. This is why it is inaccurate to call Blake a 'religious' artist and poet without also recognizing his systematic heresy against the Christian doctrine of sin.

Because, as he claims in *The Marriage of Heaven and Hell*, soul and body are not separate, the body cannot be dismissed as a sinful vehicle for the soul. The carnal is both humanly and divinely good. Love is born free, yet everywhere it is in chains:

And Priests in black gowns were walking their rounds,
And binding with briars my joys and desires.

Blake is at his most subtle and insightful when he writes about sexuality. He preaches freedom for desire, but excels at describing the vicissitudes and corruptions that result from its denial: the rose that is sickened by an 'invisible worm' and its 'dark secret love'; the nurse who resents the joys of youth:

Your spring & your day are wasted in play,
And your winter and night in disguise.

On the title page of *The Marriage of Heaven and Hell*, demons and angels pair off and fly together in mutual joy: there is no separating good and evil in the garden of love.

Christianity was enjoying a revival in late eighteenth-century Britain. The Methodist movement led by John Wesley had created a new popular Protestantism. Evangelicals were urging a religious intensity and reforming manners. As a spiritual man Blake was part of this resurgence, yet in his heretical insistence that 'The road of excess leads to the palace of wisdom' he sides with tolerant Enlightened hedonists.

The fleshy nudes who glide curvaceously through Blake's dream world have a surprising affinity

↑ ↑ William Blake, plate 6 from *Europe: a Prophecy*, 1794, colour-printed relief etching, 23.5 × 17.1 cm (9 ¼ × 6 ¾ in.), New York Public Library, New York

↑ William Blake, title page from *The Marriage of Heaven and Hell*, 1790–94, relief and white-line etching with hand colouring and rudimentary colour printing, 38 × 26.8 cm (15 × 10 ½ in.), Library of Congress

with the robust figures celebrated by that most rollicking of all Georgian artists, Thomas Rowlandson. Born in 1756, a year before Blake, Rowlandson produced reams of robust pornography alongside good-humoured skits on every aspect of his times, from Bath to Bonaparte. His erotica range from a portrayal of Emma Hamilton, wife of the collector and vulcanologist William Hamilton and lover of Horatio Nelson, posing naked to be sketched by an artist, to a more down-and-dirty picture of sailors having sex with prostitutes as the fleet sails away. He does not feel any need for the religious justifications that Blake provides for free love.

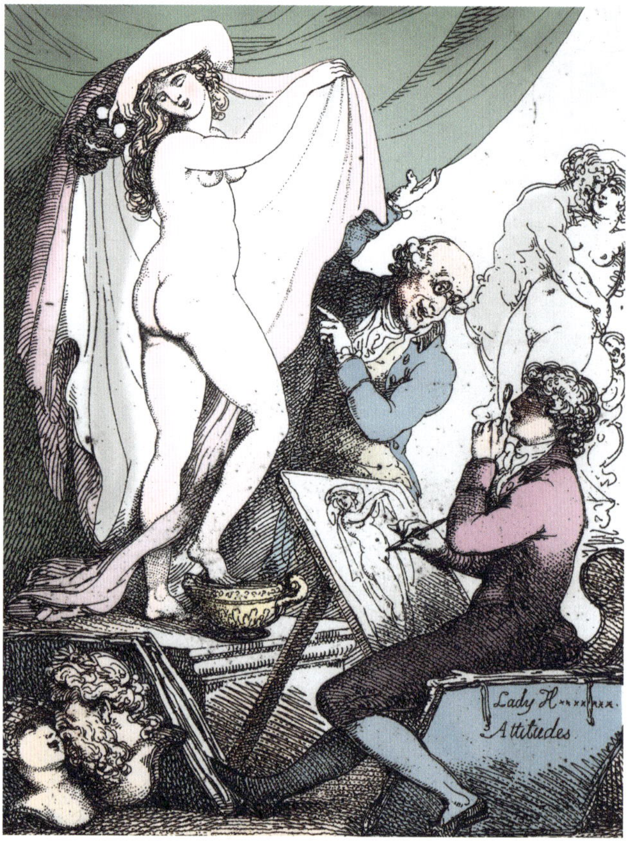

↑ Thomas Rowlandson, Lady H***** Attitudes, mid-1810s, etching and aquatint, 23.7 × 17 cm (9 ⅓ × 6 ¾ in.), Private Collection

Another artist who delved deep in crimson joy was Henry Fuseli, born in Switzerland in 1741, and one of Blake's most loyal friends. Fuseli seems to have been able to laugh gently at Blake without incurring his wrath. He drew erotic scenes – a lot less hearty than Rowlandson's – of bizarrely dressed courtesans and strange couplings. Blake and Fuseli worked together to illustrate Erasmus Darwin's scientific poem *The Botanic Garden*, creating an arresting image of *The Fertilisation of Egypt* that could be one of Blake's own visions.

The closest of Fuseli's concoctions to the visions of Blake is his 1781 painting *The Nightmare*. A woman sprawls as if in ecstasy, but her swoon is a dreamer's paralysis. A homunculus perches on her chest; a ghostly horse stares out of blind eyes. Fuseli's manifestation of an evil dream appeals to the cult of the sublime, yet is different from Copley's shark (page 106) or Wright's volcanoes (pages 136–39), for this is not a depiction of nature but a painting of the unconscious mind. Fuseli lets us 'see' the monsters that visit this helpless woman in her sleep. Are they real phantoms or fevered creations of her brain?

Fuseli is still remembered for *The Nightmare* because it appears to anticipate the theories of Sigmund Freud and images of twentieth-century Surrealism. To see that human beings are formed by unconscious

→ Thomas Rowlandson, *Exhibition 'Stare' Case*, 1811 (?), hand-coloured etching, sheet: 47.6 × 33.2 cm (18¾ × 13 in.), The Metropolitan Museum of Art, New York. The Elisha Whittelsey Collection, The Elisha Whittelsey Fund, 1959 (59.533.573)

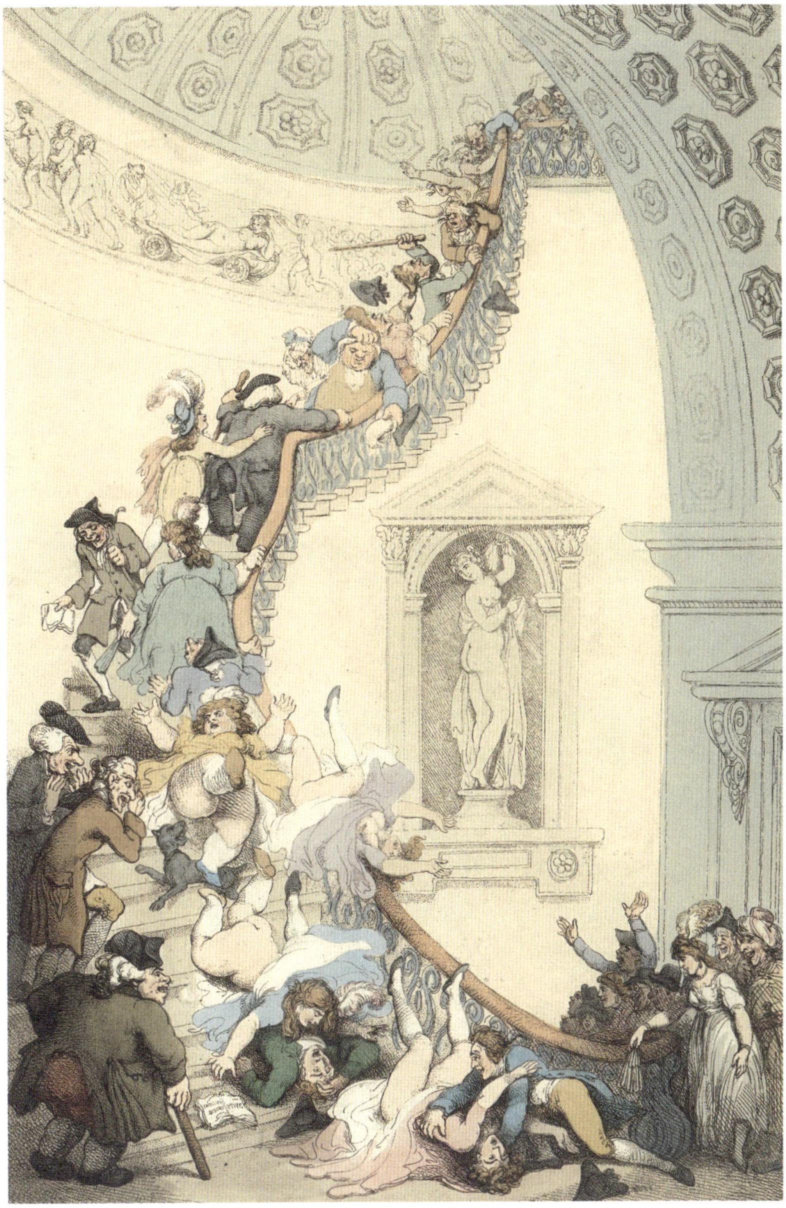

as well as conscious mental phenomena is a precocious perception. And to recognize the power of sexual instincts is an act of scientific observation, just as Erasmus Darwin did when he included, in the volume Blake and Fuseli illustrated, a long meditation on nature's reproductive processes called *The Loves of the Plants*.

What made eighteenth-century British art so advanced in its grasp of the contradictions of the psyche? Fuseli's painting *Titania and Bottom*, painted in about 1790, is a dazzling and disturbing exhibition of this probing analysis of psychology and sexuality in the age of revolution. As in some radical twentieth- or twenty-first-century stage production, Fuseli portrays the fairies from Shakespeare's *A Midsummer Night's Dream* not as gentle, rustic, fluttering sprites but sinister and perverse embodiments of depravity. Shadowed eyes stare out of the night. A beautiful female fairy holds a tiny bearded man on a lead like a little dog. A child-fairy stares with coal-black dots of eyes out of a porcelain face. Her companion has an evil witchlike mask on a child's body. It all adds up to a flesh-crawling picture of malevolence and madness.

This is the sensibility of the Gothic. When Horace Walpole built his neo-medieval house Strawberry Hill in the 1760s he launched a new kind of cultural appetite. Nothing reveals the modernity of eighteenth-century Britain so clearly as its enjoyment of the Middle Ages. Only a society confident it had left the past behind could cultivate that past as a stage-set for fantasy. Walpole's *The Castle of Otranto*, which claims to be a translation of a medieval Italian manuscript, sets the scene for the Gothic novel with a dreamlike tale of a youth crushed by a gigantic helmet in a house full of haunted portraits and worm-eaten by secret passages. In the age of the French Revolution, the Gothic novel, with its macabre tales of sex and power, is a sensational mirror image of Blake's visions. In *The Monk*, first published in 1796, Matthew Lewis tells how sexual represssion and religious hypocrisy breed violence as a Catholic zealot in seventeenth-century Spain, renowned for his purity, becomes a rapist and murderer. Ann Radcliffe's *The Mysteries of Udolpho* two years earlier is a less grotesque but equally thrilling narrative of a young heroine kidnapped by a charismatic brigand.

Gothic novels were fancied as being read primarily by women. Gillray's 1802 print *Tales of Wonder!* portrays a seance-like female gathering reading Gothic fiction by candlelight as if communing with sinister forces in a spine-tingling rite. This dangerous Gothic craze was not only associated with the rise of women as readers – and writers – but with revolution. Jane Austen's *Northanger Abbey*, written in the late 1790s, satirizes Gothic novels and their enthusiastic readers for follies that are ultimately political. In mistaking innocent events for conspiracies, the novel's fiction-addled protagonist seriously misunderstands British society. She thinks it is a place of extreme injustices and abuses of power – just as revolutionary sympathizers

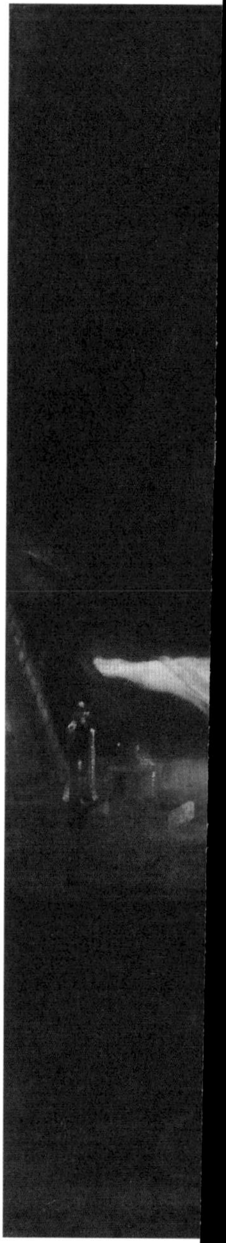

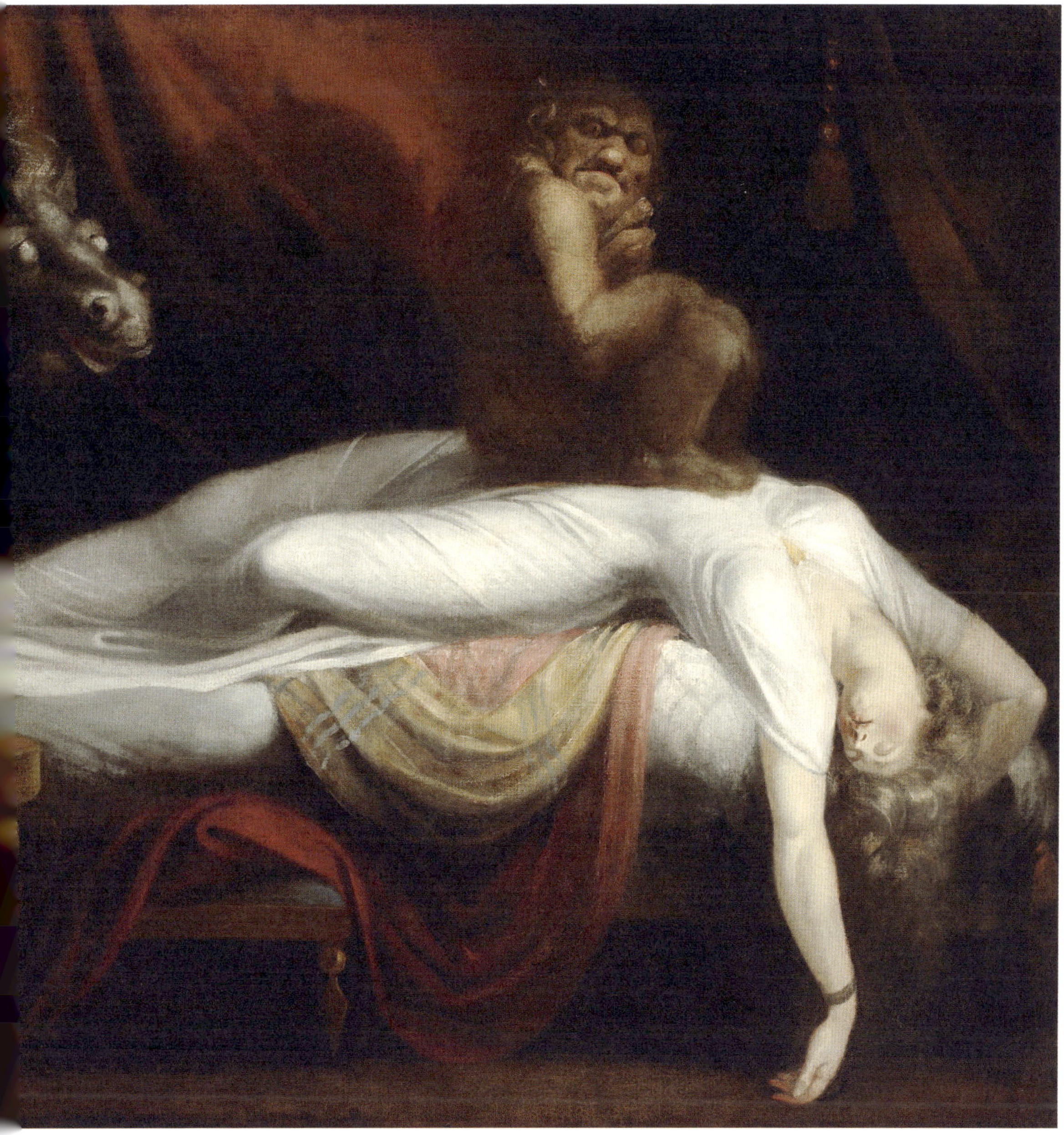

such as Blake believed. Catherine comes to accept that nothing malign is going on in the well-ordered and civilized south of England.

↑ Henry Fuseli, *The Nightmare*, 1781, oil on canvas, 101.6 × 126.7 cm (40 × 50 in.), Detroit Institute of Arts, Detroit

In What Distant Deeps or Skies

Newton leans forward with his compasses outside the British Library in London, cast in bronze from Blake's design by the modern artist Eduardo Paolozzi. He adopts the same intent pose in a reproduction from Blake on the cover of an anthology of science classics, including the *Principia*, edited by Stephen Hawking. These are evidently not intended as attacks on Newton. Blake's portrayal of the seventeenth-century father of physics appears to have been completely misunderstood by the modern world. Instead of a study in cosmic villainy it has been adopted as a heroic image of scientific endeavour. Surely Blake put it clearly and frequently enough that Newton is, for him, a circumscriber of humanity's limitless potential. To add to all his other verbal assaults he tells in *The Song of Los* how, when the immortals created the 'mind-forg'd manacles' of 'a Philosophy of Five Senses', the patriarch Urizen, weeping, 'gave it unto the hands of Newton and Locke'.

How can Blake's image of a scientist whose belief in empirical reality he disputed be cherished today as a monument to reason? One answer lies in Blake's claim that when Milton wrote about devils he was inspired, but when he wrote of angels he was dull. For Milton, he claims in *The Marriage of Heaven and Hell*, was 'of the devil's party without knowing it'.

Blake was made by the scientific age that he rejected. His *Newton* is a passionate homage, despite itself. The insistence with which Blake attacks the Newtonian system in his writings is an acknowledgement of Newton's adamantine hold. His use of Newton's own rare word for the deity, 'Pantokrator', suggests he wrestled closely with his works. When we look at Blake's images of nature and the cosmos, what we see is not antithetical to science. Even as Blake scorns empirical observation, his art conveys the enigma and grandeur of the natural world, and even the energy and sublimity of the Industrial Revolution.

'I want! I want!' says the inscription below his emblematic image of a man climbing a ladder to the moon. It is a captivating depiction of the infinity of human longing – and of space travel. A hundred-and-fifty years before the moon landings, Blake's traveller climbs the rungs of a ladder to space, among the glittering dots of distant stars. His choice of the moon as an example of boundless longing surprisingly allies him with the members of the Lunar Society, meeting by its pale light, as well as with the artist-astronomer John

→ John Russell, *The Face of the Moon*, 1793–97, pastel on board, 64.2 × 47 cm (25 ¼ × 18 ½ in.), Birmingham Museums and Art Gallery

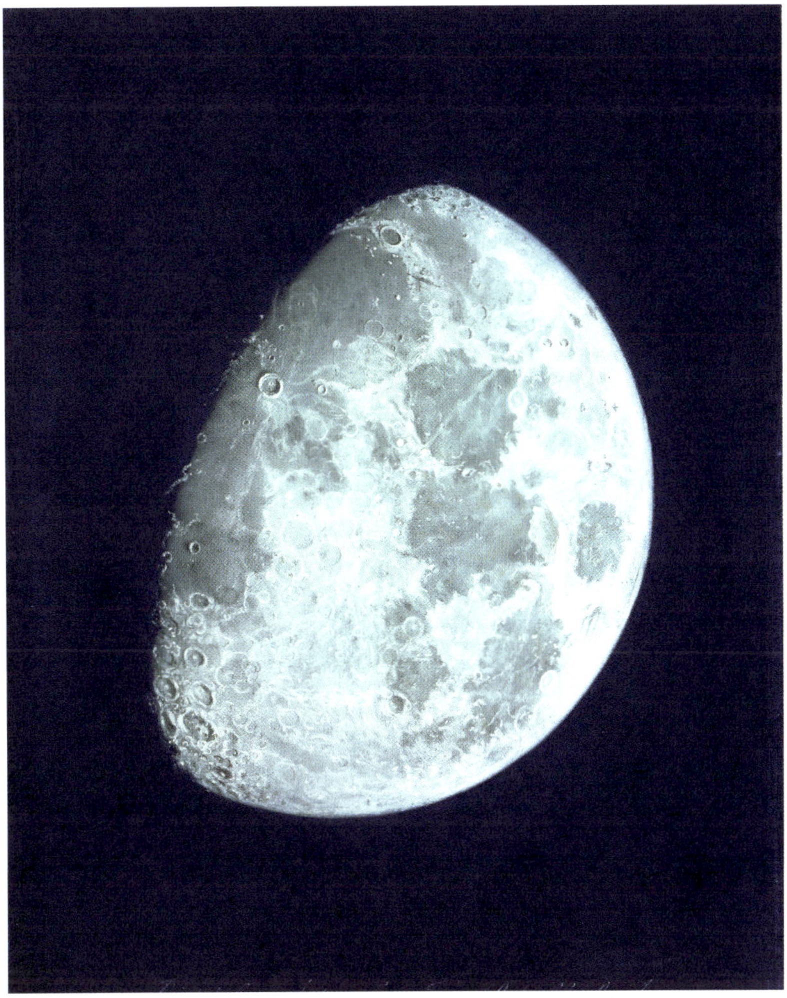

Russell, who invented a mechanized model of the moon that he called the Selenographia. In the 1790s Russell recorded every detail he could see of the moon's surface in a series of silvery pastels. He was as mystically minded as Blake; he saw the moon's beauty as a message from God. Yet his studies are so acute they resemble photographs taken by Apollo astronauts.

Blake mocked the Copernican system as 'the same dull round', but the crimson orbs and billowing clouds that blaze in his unearthly skies resemble red dwarfs and nebulae, forms almost impossible for astronomers to see in 1800 yet unmistakably 'Blakean' when photographed by this century's Hubble Space Telescope.

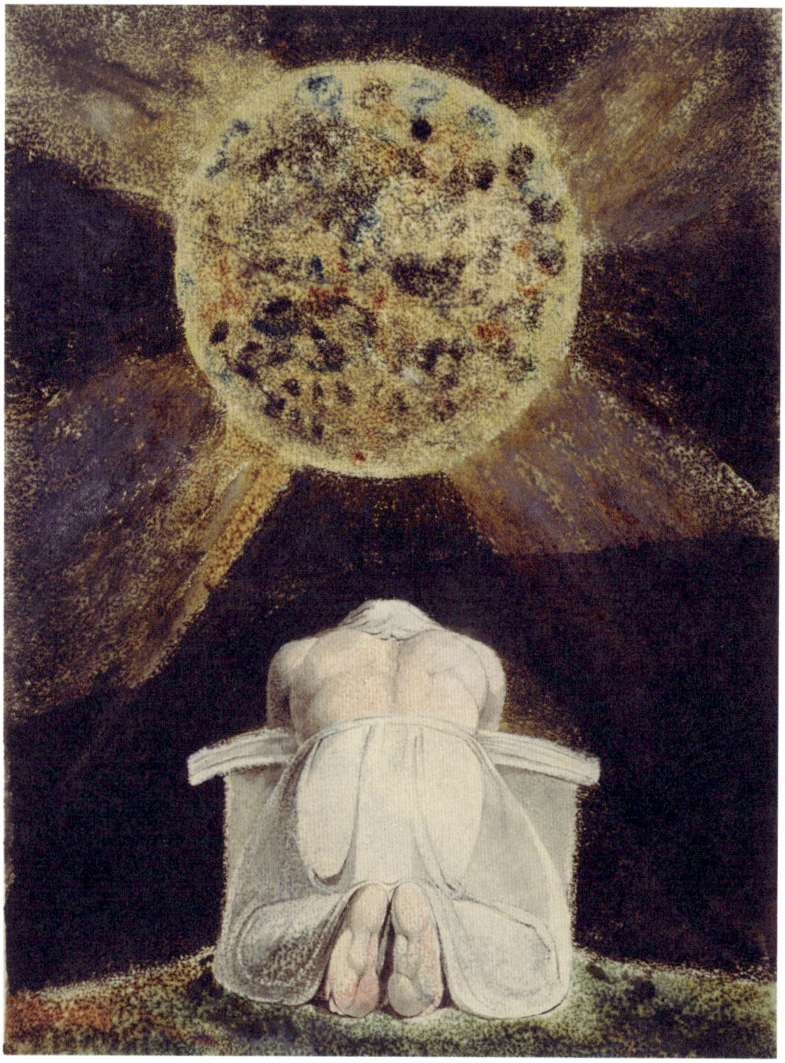

↑ William Blake, object 1 from *The Song of Los*, 1795, relief etching with colour printing and hand colouring. 23.6 × 17.9 cm (9 ⅓ × 7 in.), Library of Congress, Lessing J. Rosenwald Collection

The frontispiece to *The Song of Los* depicts an astral body whose golden glow is perforated by green and brown spots. It is plainly a star, sending out its rays into a dark void. A kneeling figure is crushed by its pulsing power. What it most resembles, to an eye familiar with modern astrophotography, is a detailed image of the sun's surface, swarming with sunspots and fiery corona. Of course I am not attributing to Blake actual powers of prophecy. It is rather that his rejection of observational art allowed him to create abstract images that anticipate the amplitude of later scientific discoveries.

Even that is not quite correct, for Blake is not as blind to nature as he is sometimes said to be. Surely, what he has really done in this work of unsettling beauty is to merge the sun with a sunflower. The brown florets on the sunflower's head become the 'sunspots', while the rays shining out of it resemble the giant flower's yellow petals. The result is a hybrid of botany and cosmology.

This is nature as mind-expanding shock, not so different after all from Wright's volcanoes or Stubbs's animals. In 'The Tyger', Blake gives the sublimity of nature that fascinated them its most perfect poetic expression:

In what distant deeps or skies
Burnt the fire of thine eyes?

The Echoing Green

In spite of Blake's assaults, the empirical method did not vanish from British art in the Romantic age. On the contrary, the keen art of observation that had started with Hooke's *Micrographia* (page 33) was sharpened by an intense, rapturous cult of natural beauty. As poets such as Wordsworth and Samuel Taylor Coleridge wrote of landscape, artists turned their eyes on nature more acutely than ever before. The doors of perception were indeed cleansed, but not by turning away from visible reality. Artists opened their eyes wider, saw more, and recorded it with heightened sensitivity.

The perfect counterblast to Blake's contempt for Newton is Wright of Derby's 1794 painting *Landscape with a Rainbow*. This lovingly precise depiction of a rainbow after a country shower may well be a conscious homage to Newton's analysis of light. His rainbow is not a vague painterly arc of colour. It is a true Newtonian spectrum. Its colours are sharply and accurately banded from red to indigo – but they are not imposed on the scene as if in some abstract diagram. Wright has studied this particular rainbow and seen Newton in it. This is perhaps the most scientific of all eighteenth-century paintings, yet it is also a passionate romantic pastoral. Wright has registered not only the colours of a rainbow after rain but the moist atmosphere of the brown sky filled with a coppery light. The very electric taste of the air, the odour of the fields after rain, seems to cling to this lovely painting of the countryside.

This is one of Wright's final masterpieces. He would die in 1797. Yet in his feel for the English countryside he is at one with a younger generation. Fuseli, who was much less at home with this pastoral mood, said of struggling newcomer John Constable that 'he makes me call for my greatcoat and umbrella'. Constable, born in 1776, aspired to paint with complete fidelity to the natural world. He literally took his art outward into nature to achieve this. It was a Romantic act. In Coleridge's great poem 'This Lime-Tree Bower My Prison', written in 1797, the poet sits in his garden, unable to go for a walk with his friends because of injury, dreaming of their ramble, finally recognizing the beauty in front of his eyes:

> *... and I watch'd*
> *Some broad and sunny leaf, and lov'd to see*
> *The shadow of the leaf and stem above*
> *Dappling its sunshine!*

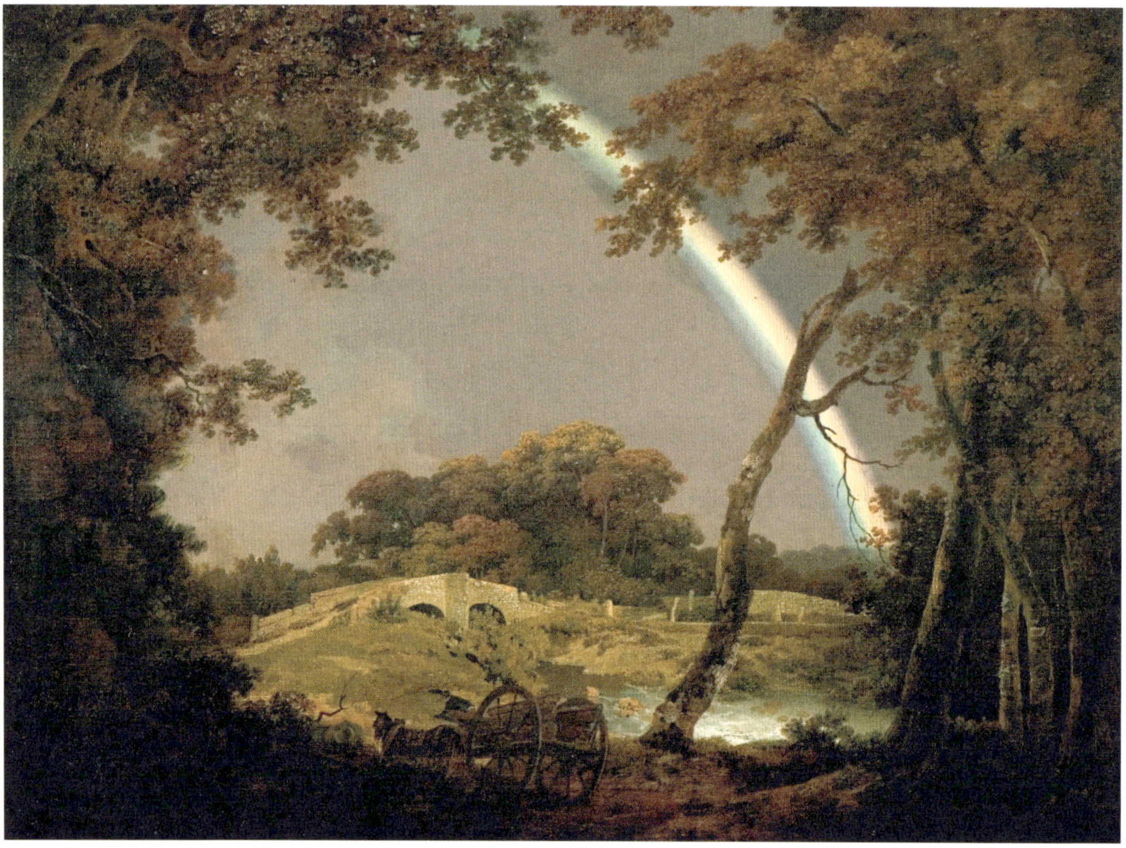

↑ Joseph Wright of Derby, *Landscape with a Rainbow*, 1794, oil on canvas, 81.2 × 106 cm (32 × 41¾ in.), Derby Museum and Art Gallery

Constable took his working materials out into the fields to paint nature from direct sensory observation. A little oil sketch by him of a cottage nestling among blotches of dark-leafed trees under a swathe of clouds does give some credence to Fuseli's joke that his art makes you reach for your umbrella. There is a patch of blue sky, but it is almost obscured by clouds. This is a reverie of British temperate weather – rain promised. It is also a revolutionary work of art. Blake and Fuseli looked inward to see Gothic nightmares and sexual dreams. Constable's acute attention to the outward appearance of nature outdoes them in lyrical sensitivity.

The idea of painting in the open air, catching the randomness of reality in direct oil sketches or watercolours, originated in Renaissance Italy but was taken to daring new heights by Georgian artists. We have seen how Thomas Jones painted unadorned empirical street views of eighteenth-century Naples. He also caught windswept open-air views of the Welsh countryside. In about 1795, another Thomas, the gifted young watercolourist Thomas Girtin, travelled to Wales to execute a view of Beddgelert in Snowdonia that is at once delicately observed and hallucinatory. The mountains become giant mythic forms. According to Blake's anti-Lockean theory of the imagination, the hard work of empirical looking that Girtin and Constable put in should make their pictures dull and plodding. Instead, they are inspired, revelatory, majestic. Their close looking produces poetry, not prose. In Girtin's masterpiece *The White House at Chelsea*, done in 1800, the ethereal veil of a white building is like a single piano note against the orchestral wash of the sky and river. Golden rays dazzle the eggshell sky, turning clouds to pale fire. Trees look like blue stains and the river itself is a dappled surface of turquoise and brown. Everything is observed from nature yet everything looks as if it has to be there – as if it has been composed. The play between chance and apparent design creates a tremulous tension, for it seems the slightest action will destroy this hypnotic trance. The world floats for a moment in equipoise. It is like Chinese painting, and after all chinoiserie was everywhere in Georgian houses and gardens.

Girtin had a real Romantic's lifespan. Born in 1775, he was dead by 1802. His images of nature are prodigious. Constable took far longer to hit his stride. He studied long and hard to find his way. Yet he always knew he wanted to bring air and light and, yes, rain straight from the fields into the art salon.

Many destructive myths flourish about Constable. Supposedly he came from the 'elite', and is 'conservative'. He 'nostalgically' hymns

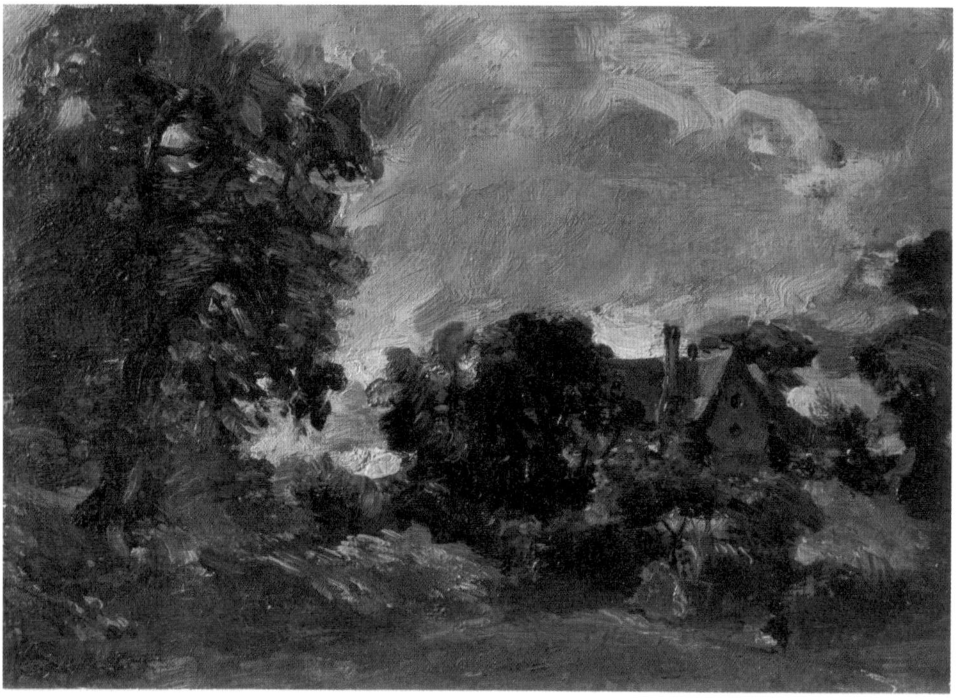

the traditional social order of a timeless English countryside. Fans of Blake are unlikely to enthuse about Constable. Yet the reality of his life and art is not so easy to fit into Marxist fable. Constable was not a member of the gentry. His father was an agricultural entrepreneur who owned water mills, including Constable's famous subject Flatford Mill, and windmills near Dedham in Suffolk. His mother socialized in polite society – but the world in which Constable grew up was a real, working place and his art records it as such. The economic and technological transformation of Britain between 1760 and 1840 was not a sudden, single replacement of a land of villages with a bleak urban skyline of factories. Change in the countryside itself was just as dramatic, yet looked slower and more 'natural' because that is the way things do look in the country. New ways are depicted with matter-of-fact honesty in Constable's art, from the water mills whose antiquity does not damage their practicality to the river transport that so greatly improved the economy.

In *Flatford Mill ('Scene on a Navigable River')*, painted in 1816–17, we do not see an ageless idyll at all but practical modernity, with a barge tethered near a well-kept lock. Boys are playing by the river, just as the artist played by it when he was growing up here. As Blake might

↑ John Constable, *A Cottage and Lane at Langham (study for The Glebe Farm)*, c. 1810–15, oil on canvas, 19.7 × 28 cm (7 ¾ × 11 in.), Victoria and Albert Museum, London

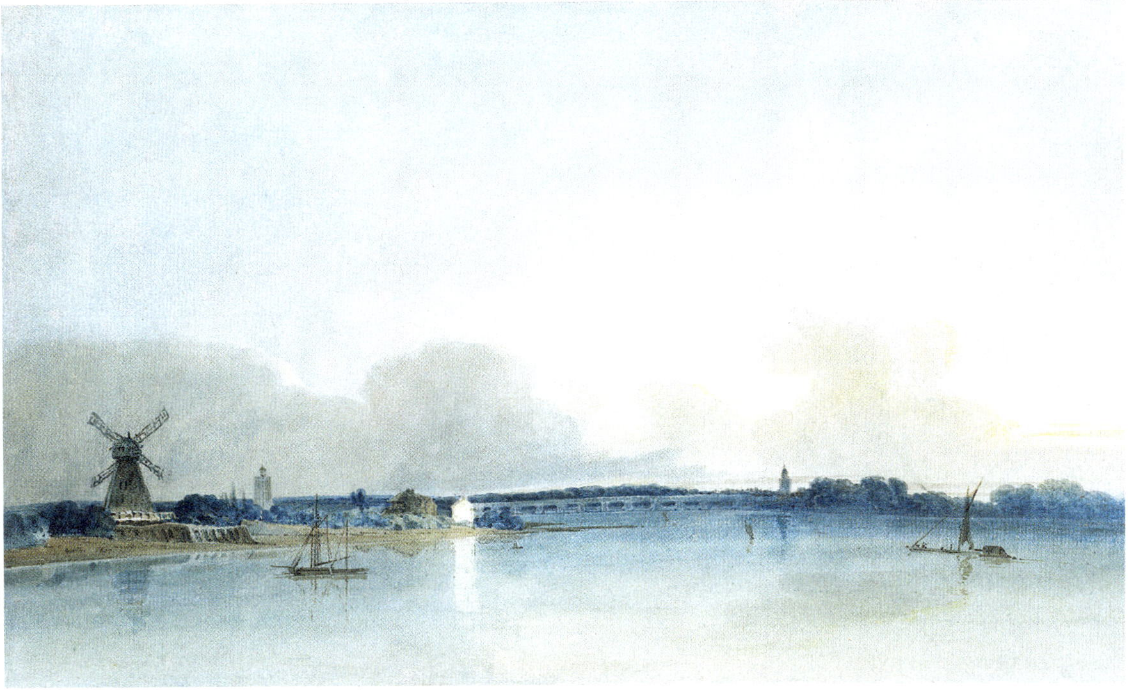

↑ Thomas Girtin, *The White House at Chelsea*, 1800, watercolour on paper, 29.8 × 51.4 cm (11¾ × 20¼ in.), Tate

say – such, such were the joys, when we were girls and boys. For there is a 'nostalgia' in Constable's art, but it is acknowledged, not concealed: personal, not political. He is backward-looking in the same way as his contemporary Wordsworth is in his autobiographical poem *The Prelude*. For Wordsworth, a childhood adventure in a boat was one of the experiences that made him who he is:

> *No sooner had I sight of this small Skiff,*
> *Discover'd thus by unexpected chance,*
> *Than I unloos'd her tether and embark'd...*

The boys messing about by the river in Constable's painting of Flatford Mill are enjoying the rural childhood, and its closeness to nature, that he said inspired him to paint. He claimed it was such 'scenes of his boyhood' that 'made him a painter'. If we look at his paintings in that light we find them full of children who are at home in the natural world. The young shepherd who drinks from a stream in *The Cornfield*, from 1826, is communing with the earth, literally drinking from it. Looking at the painting in the National Gallery, in the heart of London, we too drink

– for the light and space, the air and colours of this masterpiece are like being taken far from the city, out into the fields, to be refreshed.

The Cornfield is a consummate vision of the living world. Everything is connected in a breathing organism. Today we might say Constable has captured Gaia – for everything in this scene, including agriculture, is linked in an ecosystem. It is that sense of connection that makes Constable such a Romantic. He is a great observer, but never coldly objective. His feel for the landscapes in which he grew up is worshipful. This country lane is sacred: trees quivering in the breeze, clouds falling in soft white cascades, the golden band of the cornfield, the grassy verge of the mottled lane, those wild flowers in the trees' shade – all are intertwined and warmed by the pulse of life.

This poetry is rooted in science. Constable's most audacious oil sketches are his studies of different types of cloud formation – paintings of nothing but vapour in the sky. They float to us from an age when meteorology was young. Constable's *Study of Cirrus Clouds*, painted quickly and acutely one day in about 1822, is at the forefront of the science as well as the art of its time. Luke Howard, a skygazing pharmacist, first classified 'cirrus', in addition to 'cumulus' and 'stratus', 'cirro-cumulus' and 'cirro-stratus', clouds in 1802. These newly categorized phenomena are painted meticulously by Constable. His cloud paintings show what kind of artist he is: a true empiricist.

The subversive Lockean belief that all knowledge is the result either of sensory experience or our reflections upon it creates as many headaches for art historians, apparently, as it does for philosophers. The idea that a painter can simply respond to reality is held by many thinkers on art to be impossible. For we do not see the world innocently, they argue. Far from looking at nature with an open eye, painters peer through the veil of tradition. Even to conceive a particular scene as a 'landscape' is to match it up with the conventions of landscape art.

This habit of making the world conform to pictures of it was consciously practised in Georgian Britain, as a leisure activity. William Gilpin's writings on the 'picturesque' were bestsellers. Travellers to the Lake District or Tintern Abbey were encouraged to have an imaginary picture frame in their heads and apply it to ruins, parks and mountains. The young Jane Austen jokingly cites Gilpin as one of the 'first of men' in her *History of England*, written in 1791 when she was 16. She also suggests ironically that Henry VIII's abolition of the monasteries 'and leaving them to the ruinous depredations of time has been of infinite use to the landscape of England…'.

→ John Constable, *The Cornfield* (detail), 1826, oil on canvas, 143 × 122 cm (56 ⅓ × 48 in.), National Gallery, London

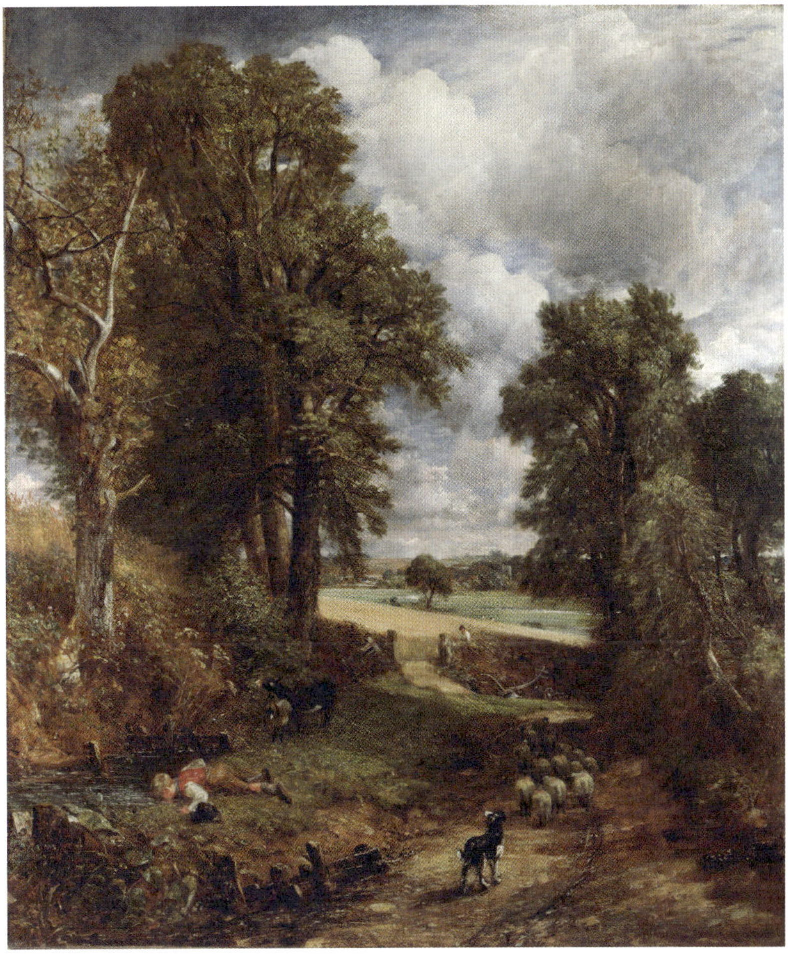

Constable's art is one long rebellion against this fashion for forcing nature to be picturesque. As a young painter he made a trek to Cumberland to try to fit the mould by painting picturesque lakes and mountains, but failed to be moved, for, as his nineteenth-century biographer C. R. Leslie recounts:

> *...his mind was formed for the enjoyment of a different class of landscape. I have heard him say the solitude of mountains oppressed his spirits.*

The countryside that Constable loved to paint, with its real-life details of farming, waterways and milling, is a very long way from the romantic

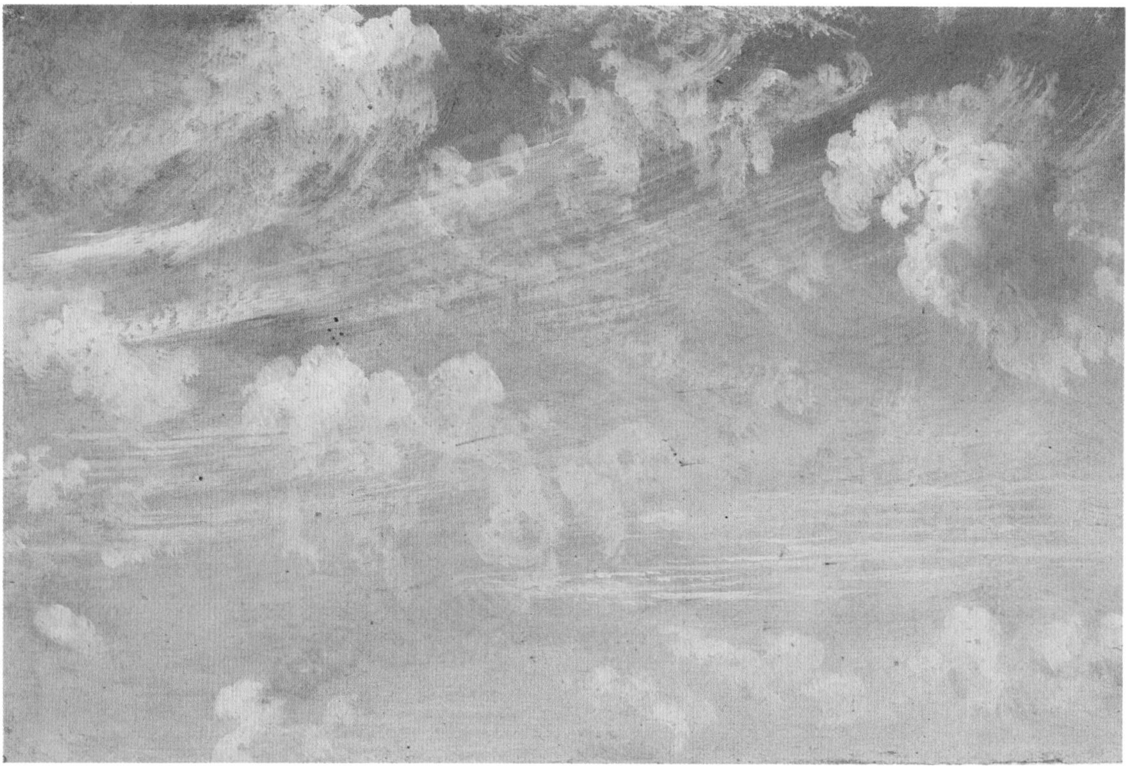

scenes defined as picturesque by readers of Gothic fiction or the works of Gilpin. This does not mean that Constable has no artistic models. He met the eminent collector George Beaumont – his future patron – as a youth through some clever social engineering by his mother. Beaumont showed him a landscape by Claude at their very first encounter. While a student at the Royal Academy, Constable made copies not only of Claudes but also of landscapes by Jacob van Ruisdael and Rubens. Yet when we look at his cloud studies, where are the patterns and paradigms he learned from these masters?

None of the Old Masters had ever painted anything like his oil sketches of the clouds overhead. It would be absurd and irrelevant to look for echoes of Baroque paintings in his white streams of sky vapour. What they do resemble are modern photographs of cloud formations, for in these studies Constable preserves useful information about nature. We can recognize these cloud specimens in the same way we still recognize the finches and fossils Charles Darwin collected on the *Beagle*.

↑ John Constable, *Study of Cirrus Clouds*, c. 1822, oil on paper, 11.4 × 17.8 cm (4½ × 7 in.), Victoria and Albert Museum, London

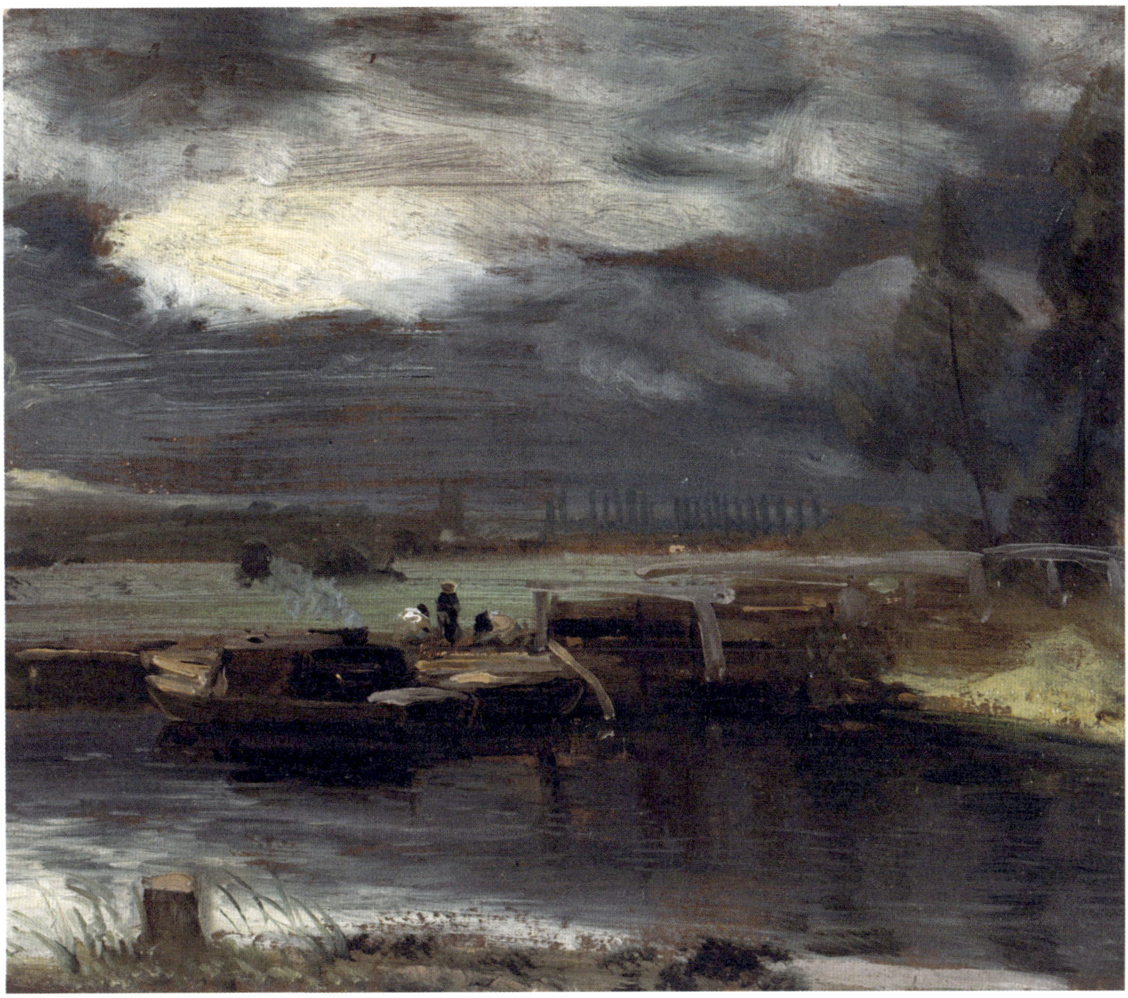

↑ John Constable, *Barges on the Stour with Dedham Church in the Distance*, c. 1811, oil on paper laid on canvas, 26 × 31.1 cm (10 ¼ × 12 ¼ in.), Victoria and Albert Museum, London

That same scientific outlook that made Constable paint clouds infuses all his oil sketches. His little open air paintings focus on details, not the big picture: on real moments, not idealized evocations. *Barges on the Stour with Dedham Church in the Distance*, from circa 1811, has an impulsive immediacy as if the paint is still wet: the quickly daubed figures mooch under that rainy sky. Once again we see that Fuseli had a point. Rain scours Constable's world. It is a rain both real and inward. Like the nature poets of his time, he finds analogies for his feelings in sky and fields and sea. There is rain in Constable's soul. Revisiting his boyhood scenes he can always find some consolation, the mysterious comfort that radiates from his grand pastoral *The Hay Wain*, but in

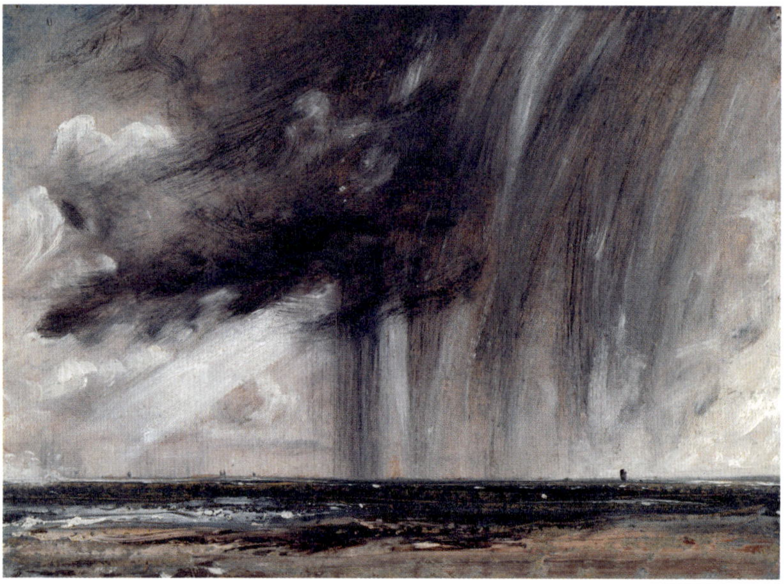

← John Constable, *Rainstorm over the Sea*, c. 1824–28, oil on paper laid on canvas, 23.5 × 32.6 cm (9 ¼ × 12 ⅝ in.), Royal Academy of Arts, London

London or on Hampstead Heath or beside the sea his memories desert him and the damp gets to his bones. His oil sketch *Rainstorm over the Sea* beats the artists of the sublime and the tourists of the picturesque at their own game. It is the kind of storm that really can whip up the sea from nothing – even on Brighton beach, where Constable painted this in the 1820s. It looks as if he started calmly, patiently painting the view from the beach, mapping the sea in accurate perspective and detailing sailing ships. Then, as he works, the sky changes, the clouds darken and burst. Constable too explodes in energy, covering his brushes in black and white and slashing, dashing down the wet streaks of a massive downpour. Water cascades on water, the sky punishes the earth. It is mythic and monstrous, yet real. He conveys the weight of the storm, the gravity of this phenomenon. It is a weight on his heart.

No landscape painting in the world is more eloquent about its maker's inner state than Constable's masterpiece *Sketch for 'Hadleigh Castle'*. This is a full-scale study for one of the big 'six-footer' canvases that he prepared, slowly and laboriously, for exhibiting at the Royal Academy. As he works up its mottled grey surface, Constable finds himself directly translating his feeling into colour and texture. The paint is astonishingly free: Stubbs or Wright, though not Gainsborough, would have been baffled by the way Constable allows individual brushstrokes to make their stabbing, thudding impact.

Maria, his deeply loved wife, died in November 1828. This vast echo chamber of his heart was painted in the immediate anguish of that loss. Nature provides not a shred of consolation, the futile vapours of the sky hold no hope. Hadleigh Castle stands shattered and ugly, the bereft antithesis of a picturesque ruin. Its broken battered bones watch over the ghastly landscape of the Thames Estuary. In the flatness below it, land, water and sky blur miserably. The marshy waterlogged earth does not have any firm division from the unspectacular sea. Birds bleakly loiter in a joyless scrawl of cloud. It is a primeval scene of sorrow. The world, robbed of all meaning, has returned to its swampy origin.

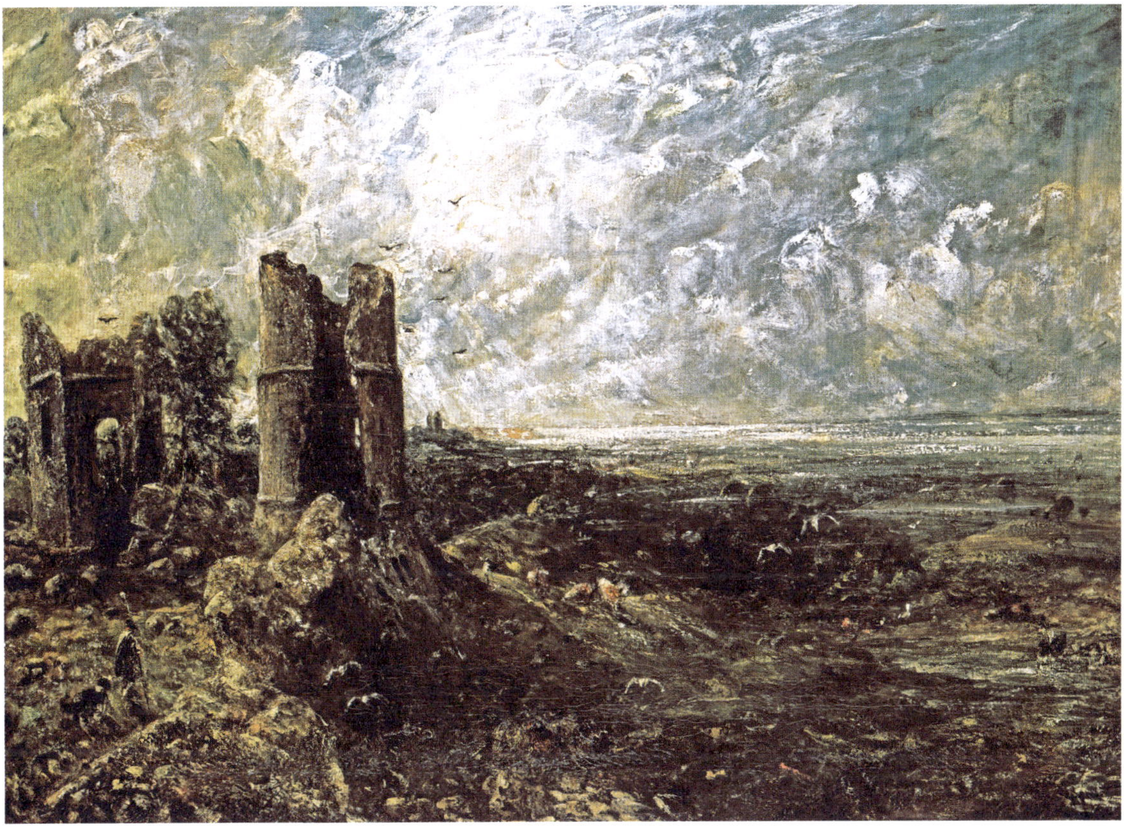

↑ John Constable, *Sketch for 'Hadleigh Castle'*, c. 1828–29, oil on canvas, 150.7 × 195.1 cm (59 ⅓ × 76 ⅘ in.), Tate

Albion

Blake and Constable share a singular experience. Neither travelled abroad. Constable once took a sea voyage around the south coast of England. Blake left London for a few years for the more pastoral setting of Felpham in West Sussex. That was as geographically adventurous as either of them got. This lack of curiosity about other climes was by now atypical for British artists. Stubbs and Wright, Reynolds and Wilson all went to Italy while hardier souls sailed to the South Pacific, spanned the Atlantic, or worked in India. It is not as if either artist had no eye for European art. Blake yielded to no one in his passion for Raphael and Michelangelo. He furiously annotated his copy of Reynolds's *Discourses*, raging against the Royal Academy president for – among other sins – praising the colours of Rubens; true greatness of art, he insisted, must follow the sharp designs of Raphael, not the flabby colours of Baroque painters. Yet unlike Reynolds he had never seen Raphael's frescoes in Rome, and never would.

If it was partly the poverty of a working artisan that stopped Blake seeing Europe, what was stopping Constable? He, too, looked intently at European art. Yet he finds feeling and truth outside art, in nature itself – as nature looks in the mutable and middling light of southern England. This is made all but explicit in one of Constable's greatest paintings: his *Cenotaph to the Memory of Sir Joshua Reynolds*. This painting from the final decade of Constable's life is a memorial to more than one person. Its invincible atmosphere of grief refers not only to Reynolds but, more personally for Constable, to his supporter the connoisseur Sir George Beaumont, who put up this monument to Reynolds on his Leicestershire estate before his own death in 1827. It is also, inevitably, scarred by Constable's widowerhood. Like a rich deep note on a cello, this painting sucks in every grief going – add your own – and makes it resonate. I seem always to have seen it on dark rainy autumn afternoons, but that cannot be true – the painting's mood is so irresistible it creates its own climate.

English nature eclipses European art in this painting. Flanking Reynolds are stone busts of the same two art heroes revered by Blake: Raphael and Michelangelo. They face each other, sombre visages across a damp forest clearing, mute under the towering trees, the recesses of the wood beyond, or the gaze of the stag that has stopped to look at us, held by the gravity of this place and its feelings of time, ambition and death.

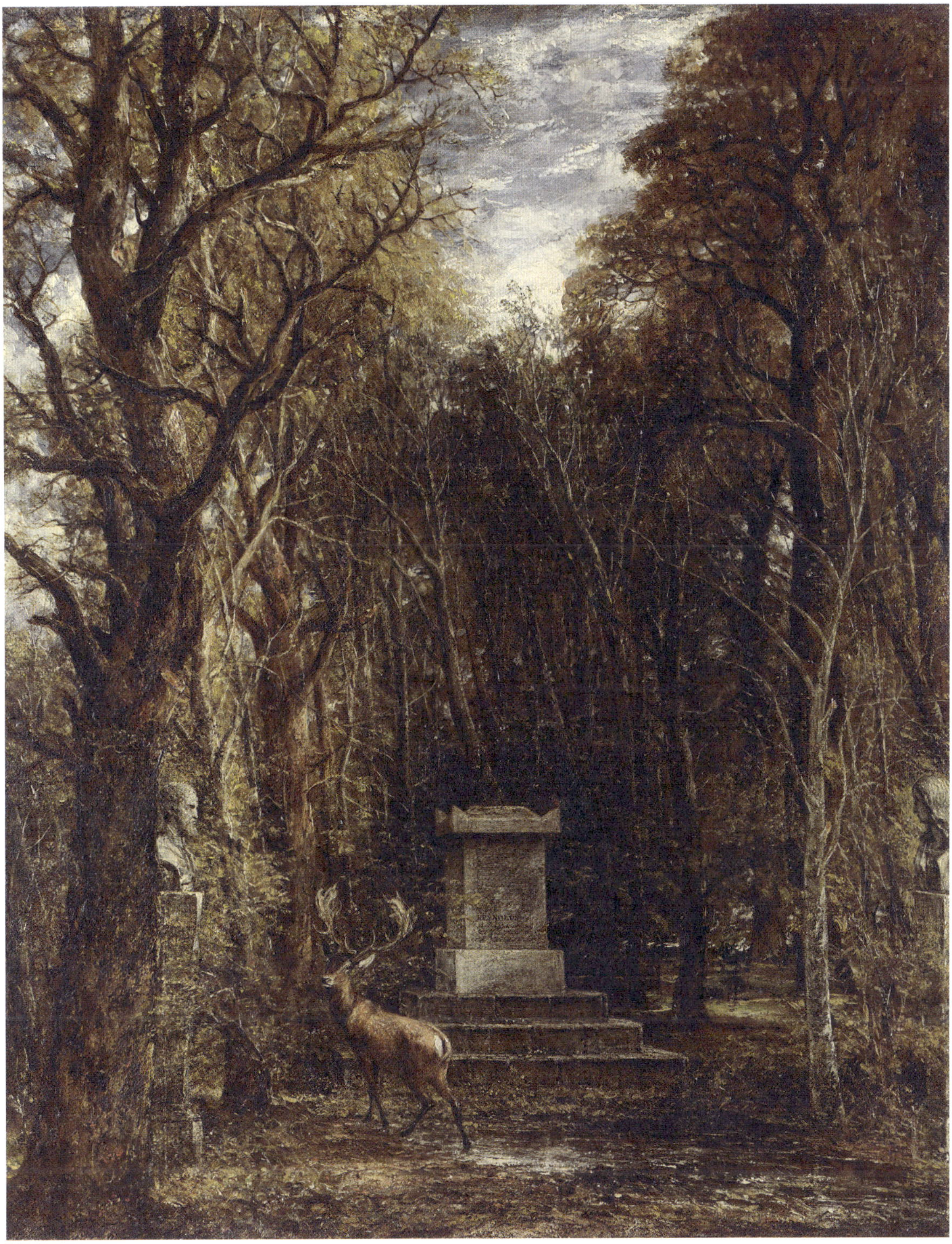

↑ John Constable, *Cenotaph to the Memory of Sir Joshua Reynolds*, 1833–36, oil on canvas, 132 × 108.5 cm (52 × 42¾ in.), National Gallery, London

Empiricism? The word no longer seems so applicable. Constable paints an expressive vision of a pastoral monument in which the message of mortality seeps from carved stone into the very web of nature. This is muddy, brown misery. The painting itself is a matted, morose object, the size and shape of a gravestone.

The models for Beaumont's monument, and for this painting, are the classical tombs that grace the seventeenth-century paintings of Poussin and Claude. While those monuments are chanced on by shepherds in Arcadia or loom in the Roman countryside, this painting translates their frozen grief from classicism to Romanticism and from the Mediterranean world to a cold dank Britain. It anglicizes melancholy.

This British introspection is shared by Blake. In his later prophetic writings he broods not on a global revolution but specifically on the fate of 'Albion', the ancient Britain whose soul is fought over by cosmic forces of good and evil:

And did those feet in ancient time
Walk upon England's mountains green.

The 'radical' Blake and his 'conservative' contemporary Constable share a fixation on their native land. Their nationalist introspection reflects the perils, anxieties and intense shared consciousness of Fortress Britain.

For the French Revolution led to the most dramatic age of national struggle Britain had ever seen. War with France began in 1792 and continued with only brief respites until final victory at the Battle of Waterloo in 1815. Even before the brilliant, ruthless and culturally minded general Napoleon took power in France in 1799, its revolutionary armies proved a match for their enemies. In Britain, the pro-French radicalism of the 1790s was in short supply by the first decade of the nineteenth century. Napoleon was admired only by a tiny minority. Patriotism built imaginary walls and the practical impossibility of travelling to continental Europe created real barriers. After the wars ended, the patriotism they forged never went away. Britain's radicals and reformers, campaigning for changes that came with the Great Reform Act in 1832, spoke a language of earthy Britishness and rural nostalgia, from the campaigning countryman William Cobbett, author of *Rural Rides*, who called London 'the Great Wen', meaning a monstrous cyst, to the Luddites and Swing rioters who protested the coming of mechanization and defended customary ways against an increasingly brutal modernity.

Like the machinery-smashers, Blake and Constable fix their eyes on Britain's past. In his most intensely wrought illuminated book, *Jerusalem: The Emanation of the Giant Albion*, which took him from 1804 until 1820 to write and illustrate, Blake imagines the austere megaliths of Stonehenge enlarged to a colossal, dwarfing scale. Fascination with this ancient site had increased ever since the antiquarian William Stukeley studied Stonehenge and the atmospheric Avebury in wildly illustrated books published in the early 1740s. Stukeley wrongly attributed these stone circles to the Celtic Druids – in reality they were built by Neolithic people much earlier – but the idea of ancient Druidic temples in the British landscape was an elixir to the Romantic age. For Blake, Stonehenge is the mythic heart of Albion, the towering sacred place of a land uniquely fought over by Satan and Christ. Constable sees it with less enchanted eyes. His 1835 watercolour of the stones on Salisbury Plain is, needless to say, a lot more accurate than Blake's fantastic vision. It is observed from life – well, not life exactly, for this is a morbid musing on the desolation of dead stones. Still stunned by grief for his wife, he responds with measured but eloquent passion to the lonely site of Stonehenge. A wall of sky scarred and scuffed as if by life's blows broods over the inhuman plain. Megaliths lie fallen or dumbly survive in their original positions, like imprisoned souls who cannot cry out. This is a gathering of ghosts.

Constable had visited Stonehenge while staying with his friend John Fisher, the Bishop of Salisbury. His most self-consciously 'national' paintings are his visions of Salisbury Cathedral. In *Salisbury Cathedral from the Meadows,* which he showed at the Royal Academy in 1831, he sets the formidable Gothic spire of this

↓ William Blake, object 5
Stonehenge (from Milton: A Poem), 1811, coloured etching, 23.7 × 17.6 cm (9 ⅓ × 7 in.), New York Public Library, New York

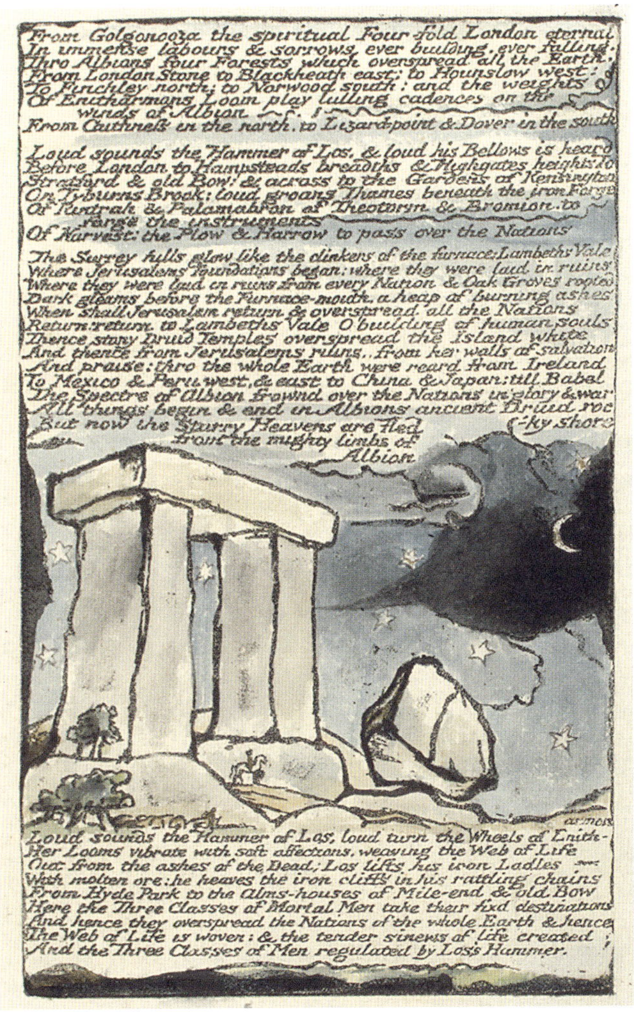

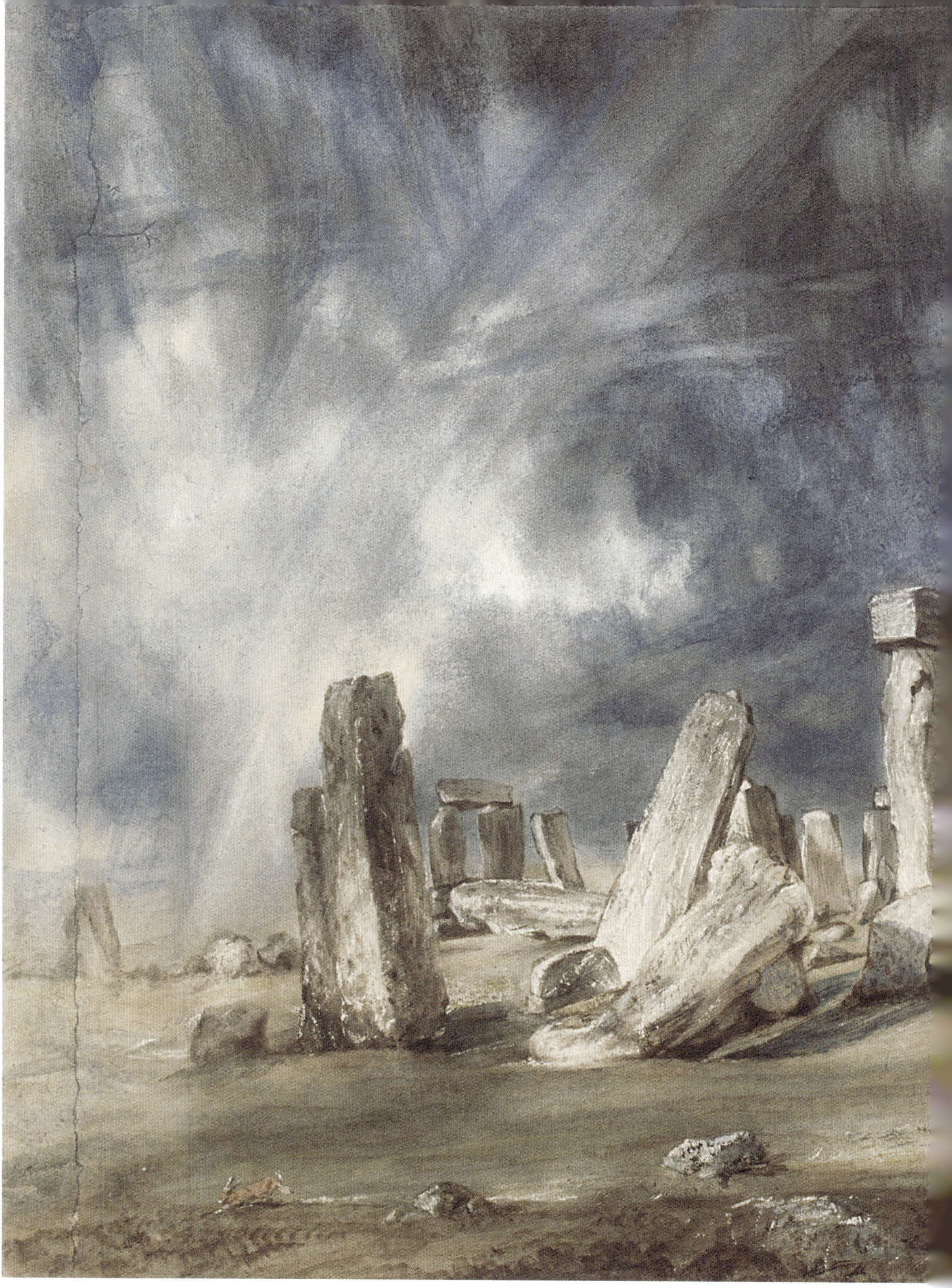

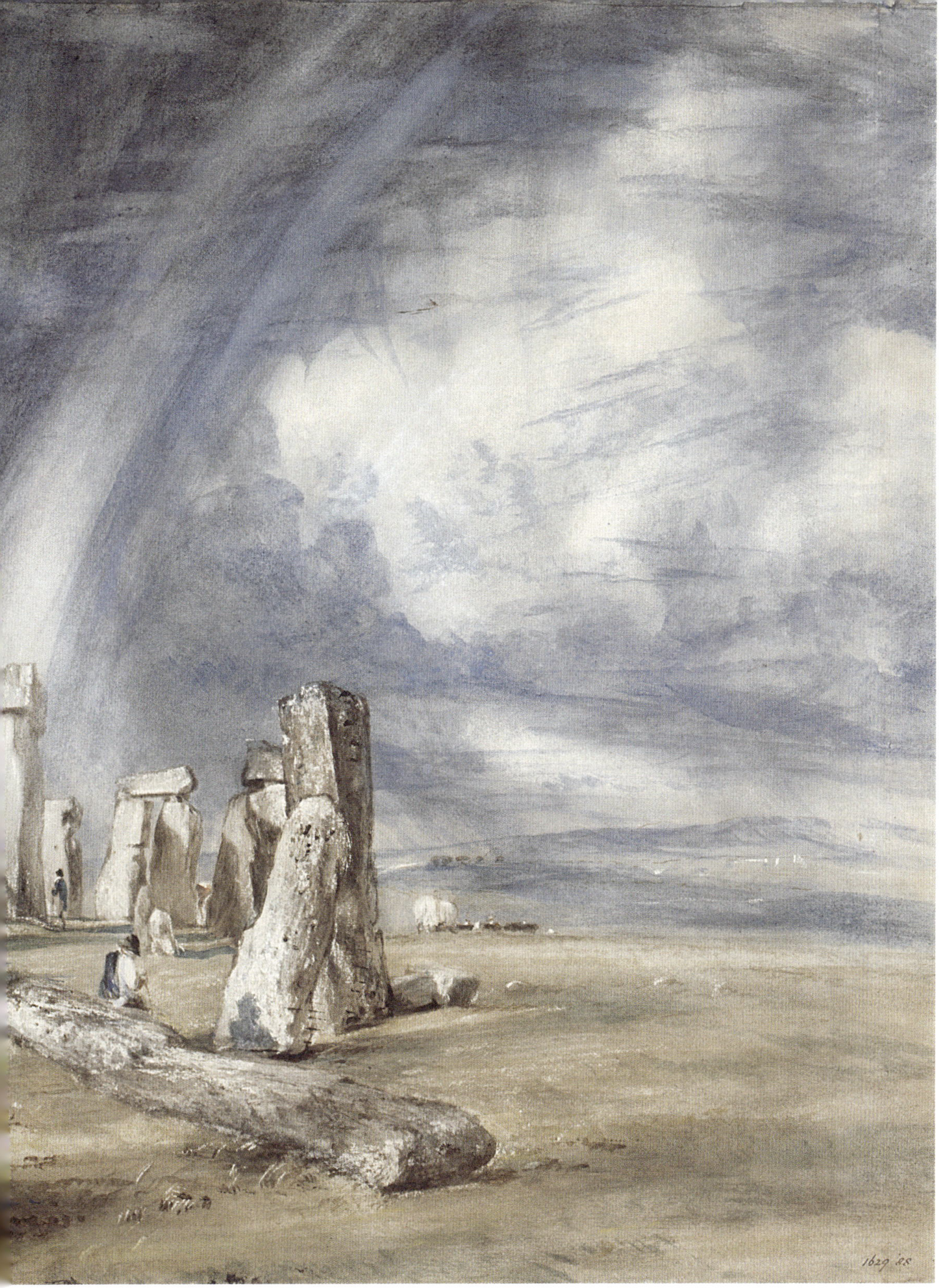

↑ John Constable, *Stonehenge*, 1835, watercolour, 38.7 × 59.7 cm (15 ¾ × 23 ½ in.), Victoria and Albert Museum, London

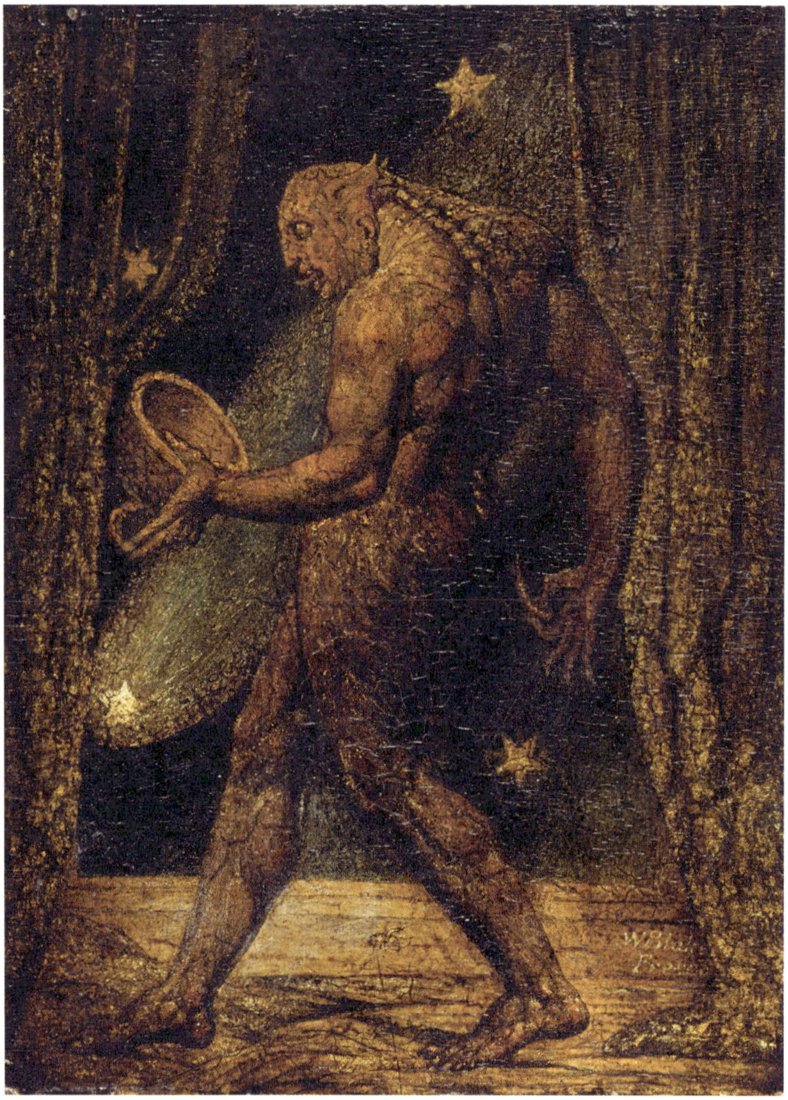

← William Blake, *The Ghost of a Flea*, c. 1819–20, tempera and gold on mahogany, 38.2 × 32.4 cm (15 × 12 ¾ in.), Tate

great medieval building against a menacing sky whose coal-dark intensity is leavened by the magic of a rainbow. This is another painting in which every fierce brushstroke is a battering pulse of sensibility. Perhaps the rainbow symbolizes the kindness of his friend Fisher when he was crippled by grief; perhaps it represents a religious rhapsody. Perhaps it means nothing. The colours of the rainbow resolve into an accurate spectrum. Isaac Newton would assent to it.

Constable is the most factual of all artists. It is not that he is never influenced by other art, or that he is always faithful to appearances. In fact, he is a free, expressive handler of great dollops of paint. Yet he never paints mythological scenes, or historical scenes, or anything that has not been before his eyes. From clouds to cornfields, he paints what he sees – ideally with the motif in front of him as he works quickly in a small oil sketch. Even the bigger canvases he created to show at the Royal Academy relentlessly return to the scenes he has sketched. His art embodies an astonishing urge to be honest. Constable refuses to make anything up. Out of this pedantry comes a poetry that more than equals Blake.

The cussed prophet Blake, who would die in 1827, poor but surrounded by a small group of intense young fans who would carry his legend into the Victorian age, cast one final snook at the empiricism of Locke and Newton. One day he told his admirer John Varley he had seen 'the ghost of a flea'. At Varley's urging he looked again, saw it, and portrayed it from the life. Hooke had shown the appearance of a flea under the microscope (pages 34–35). Blake depicts its inner being as seen with his third eye.

Blake's circa 1819–20 painting *The Ghost of a Flea* convinces you he really has seen this dreadful monster. For it carries an almost nauseating conviction. Constable's truth is poetic. Blake's poetry is true.

7. The Assumption of the Dragon

I have to prove to them that there are more things in heaven and earth than are dreamed of in their philosophy, and that the truth of nature is a part of the truth of God...
John Ruskin, *Modern Painters*, Volume I (1843)

'What a book a Devil's Chaplain might write on the clumsy, wasteful, blundering low & horribly cruel works of nature!'
Charles Darwin, writing to J. D. Hooker (1856)

The Speed of Light

The old man died still thinking of the sun: so much is clear. Some time during his last hours in a house overlooking the River Thames at Chelsea, the painter Joseph Mallord William Turner spoke of the star at the centre of the solar system whose brightness he had made peculiarly his own. Perhaps he exclaimed, as the most sensational record has it: 'The sun is god!'

Or maybe he merely said, if we believe a more prosaic account, that he would like to paint the sun again. Whatever his precise words, it seems the sun still blazed in Turner's mind in the days before his death on 19 December 1851, as it always had.

The last words of Turner may not matter that much. What should mean more to us is the living master's last exhibition of new paintings at the Royal Academy in the year before his death, for he unveiled four stupendous and utterly strange paintings in the Academy's annual exhibition in May 1850 that are his true last testament.

These paintings are not that large, by his standards, but they open windows on infinite spaces carved by sunshine. The titles, given by Turner, reveal that they illustrate one of his favourite books, Virgil's *Aeneid*, the great epic poem composed in Latin in the late first century

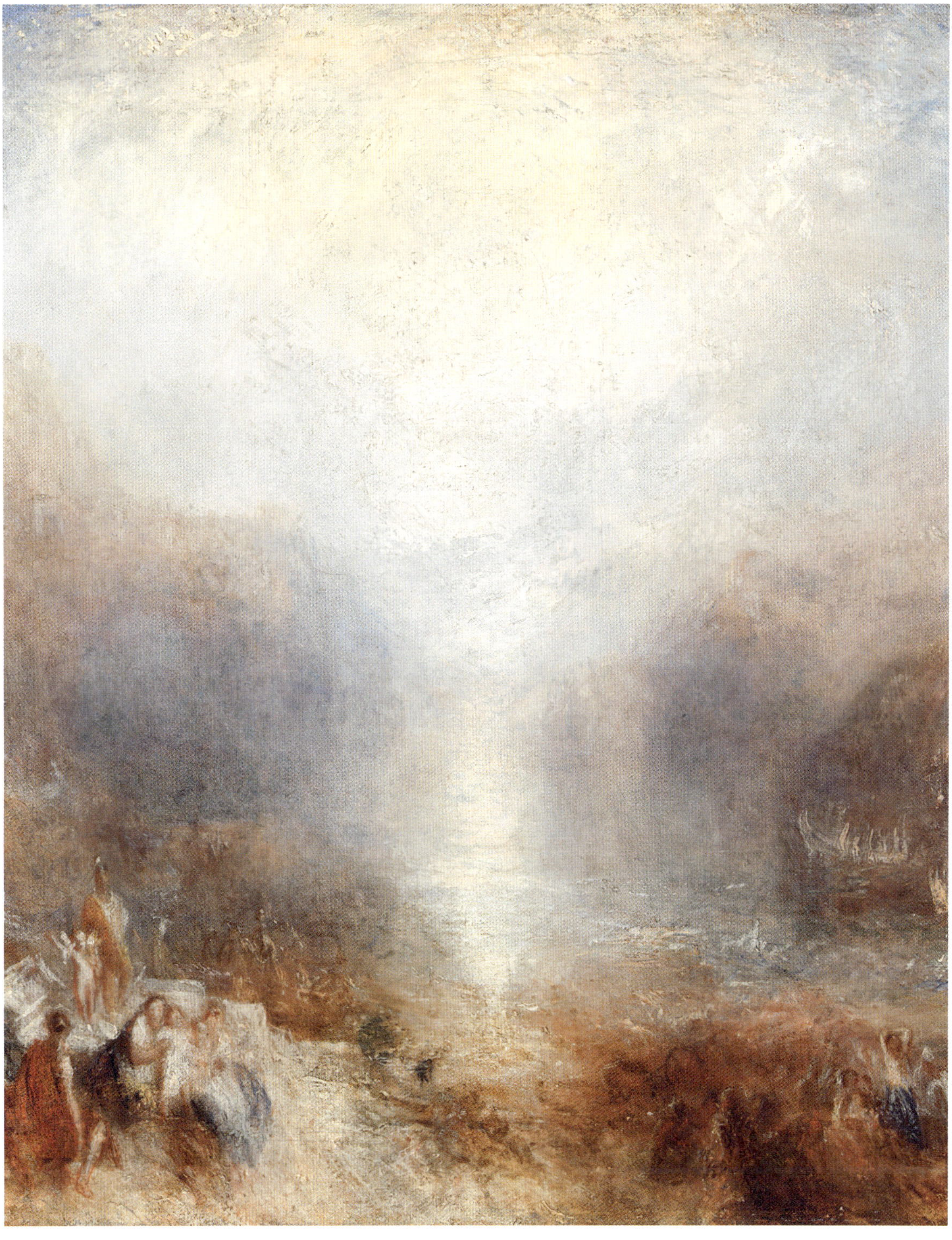

↑ J. M. W. Turner, *Mercury Sent to Admonish Aeneas* (detail), exhibited 1850

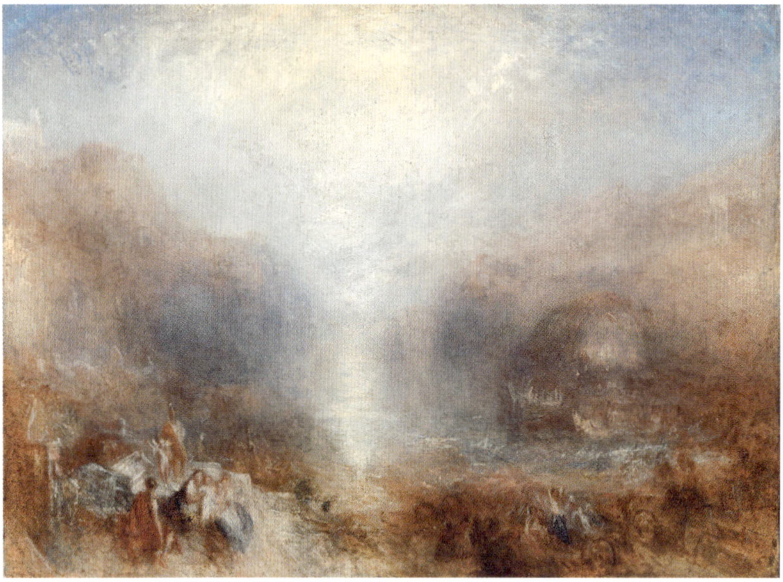

BCE that tells of the adventures of Aeneas, leader of a band of refugees from the destroyed city of Troy, as he journeys to Italy. What fascinated Turner from the moment he read a translation of the *Aeneid* – for he had only a rudimentary schooling and had certainly never been taught Latin – was the tragedy of Dido, queen of Carthage, who fell fatally in love with her guest Aeneas and killed herself when he sailed on in pursuit of his destiny. This doleful love story is full of historical portent, for the North African city-state of Carthage was Rome's main rival for dominance of the Mediterranean until Rome obliterated it in the second century BCE.

Turner's choice to unveil four paintings from the *Aeneid* in 1850 at the very end of his epic career was the climax to a lifetime's brooding upon Carthage, and seeing eerie analogies between ancient and modern history. Four decades before, in 1812, the year Napoleon made the fatal mistake of invading Russia with its vast spaces and cruel winter, Turner exhibited *Hannibal and his Army Crossing the Alps*, in which the tiny figures of the Carthaginian general and his army are dwarfed by a great arch of paint, a swirling storm of iron-grey and snow-white that is about to crush them. One of the elephants that Hannibal famously used in his invasion of Italy is glimpsed as a distant silhouette against sickly yellow light under the cascade of nature's violence. Three years after that, in 1815, the year of Napoleon's final defeat at the Battle of

↑ J. M. W. Turner, *Mercury Sent to Admonish Aeneas*, exhibited 1850, oil on canvas, 90.2 × 120.6 cm (35 ½ × 47 ½ in.), Tate

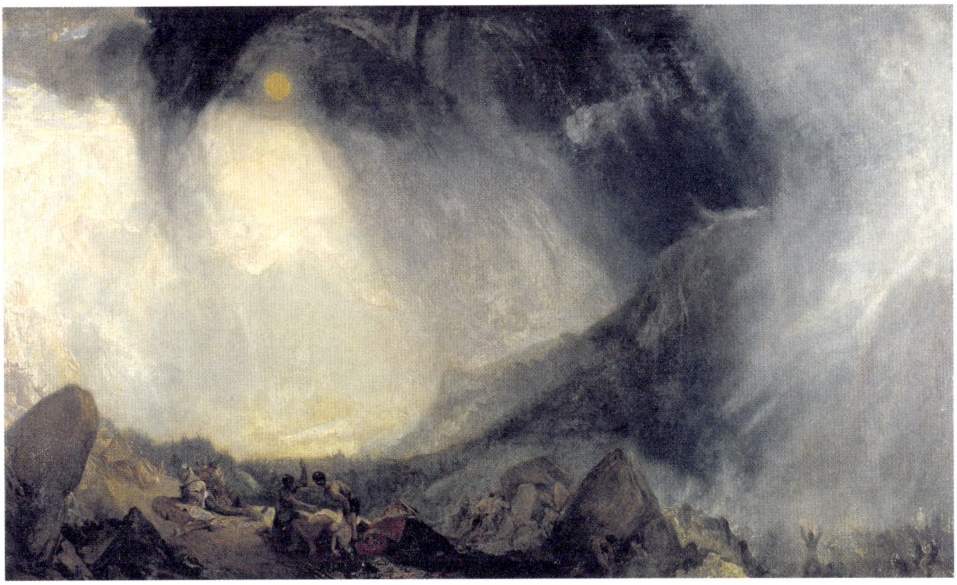

Waterloo, Turner revealed his majestic vision *Dido Building Carthage*, in which the woozy pinnacles of an opulent yet doomed imperial city glow and shimmer in the brightness of the morning sun.

These are pictures that pulsate with wild colour and painterly freedom yet they are, unquestionably, pictures – detailed scenes whose figures make sense and whose landscapes unfurl in precise perspective. The illustrative abundance of *Dido Building Carthage* includes boys watching a toy boat on the luminous waters, a sculpted frieze recalling the Elgin Marbles, which had been on display in London since 1807, and a towering reinvention of classical architecture that is all the more impressive given he had not yet been to Italy.

It is a lot less easy to see the paintings Turner exhibited in 1850 as 'pictures'. Without their accompanying texts it would probably be impossible to guess what they are about at all, and even with these titles given by Turner, it is impossible to 'read' them in the same way as *Dido Building Carthage*. Thus in *Mercury Sent to Admonish Aeneas*, we can make out a crowd of figures, but there is no architectural detail to speak of and the landscape has been reduced to vague forms floating in a world of pure colour. The potency of Turner's light has become here an enveloping field, a numinous glow pervading the centre and upper parts of the canvas. Tiny ships are scorched by its weird incandescence, bodies irradiated by it.

↑ J. M. W. Turner, *Snow Storm: Hannibal and his Army Crossing the Alps*, exhibited 1812, oil on canvas, 146 × 237.5 cm (57 ½ × 93 ½ in.), Tate

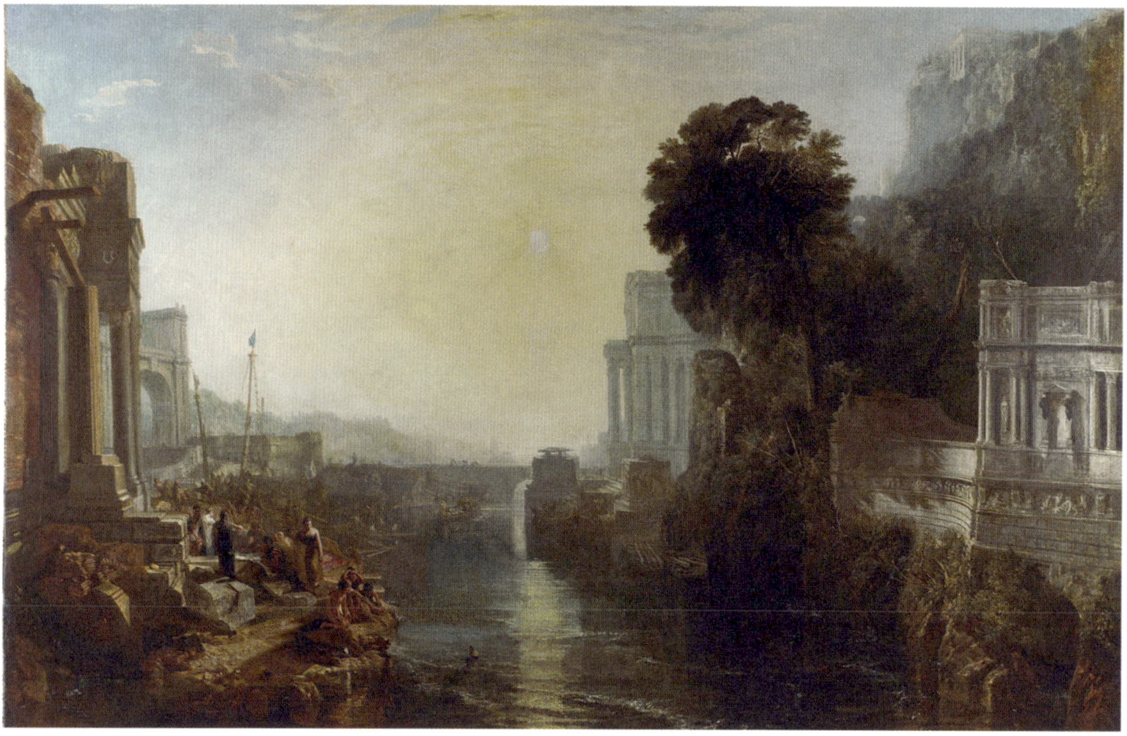

Astonishingly, this bold rejection of almost everything a painting was expected to be in the middle of the nineteenth century does not deprive *Mercury Sent to Admonish Aeneas* of expression, emotion or intellect. In the *Aeneid* the messenger god Mercury is sent to remind the lovestruck Aeneas that he has a destiny to fulfil. Those ships blazing in the ether, that crowd stunned by the sun, convey the tragic pain and mighty grandeur of this moment, the melancholy of duty and the awe of history, in a terse poetic language of stark symbolism that is heightened by the mystery of colour, just as an opera's libretto is transfigured by waves and spirals of sound.

Turner has created an abstract work of art. More remarkably still, he chose to exhibit it.

Some authorities would love to demolish the idea that J. M. W. Turner's late paintings are 'abstract'. Perhaps their scepticism is an understandable backlash against an overenthusiastic twentieth-century tendency to draw premature parallels between this giant of the Romantic age and such later artists as Claude Monet or Mark Rothko: or perhaps it is merely excessive and myopic scholarly caution. Paintings

↑ J. M. W., Turner, *Dido Building Carthage*, 1815, oil on canvas, 155.5 × 230 cm (61⅕ × 90½ in.), National Gallery, London

such as *Norham Castle: Sunrise* that were still in Turner's studio when he died certainly look 'abstract' to us and cannot really be enjoyed as anything else: let their unfettered light work its mysterious enchantment, see the hints of a cow or a castle as symbolic entities in a work of rhapsodic visual music, and these late paintings are modern masterpieces. Yet should we be cautious of such enjoyment and instead sniff that *Norham Castle* is merely an 'unfinished' underlay of a painting?

Turner's own decision to exhibit four paintings at the Royal Academy in 1850 that are among his most abstract experiments ought to silence that dreary doubt. These canvases break with all the conventions of clarity, pictorialism and 'finish' of his age, yet they cannot be dismissed as an old painter's unfinished daubs. They are his considered public statements, his painterly last words. They reveal the revolutionary nature of Turner's genius. His vision reaches far ahead of his own time into extremes of modernism that there were not yet any words to describe. Abstraction, Expressionism, even Abstract Expressionism – how did a painter born in the eighteenth century imagine such freedoms?

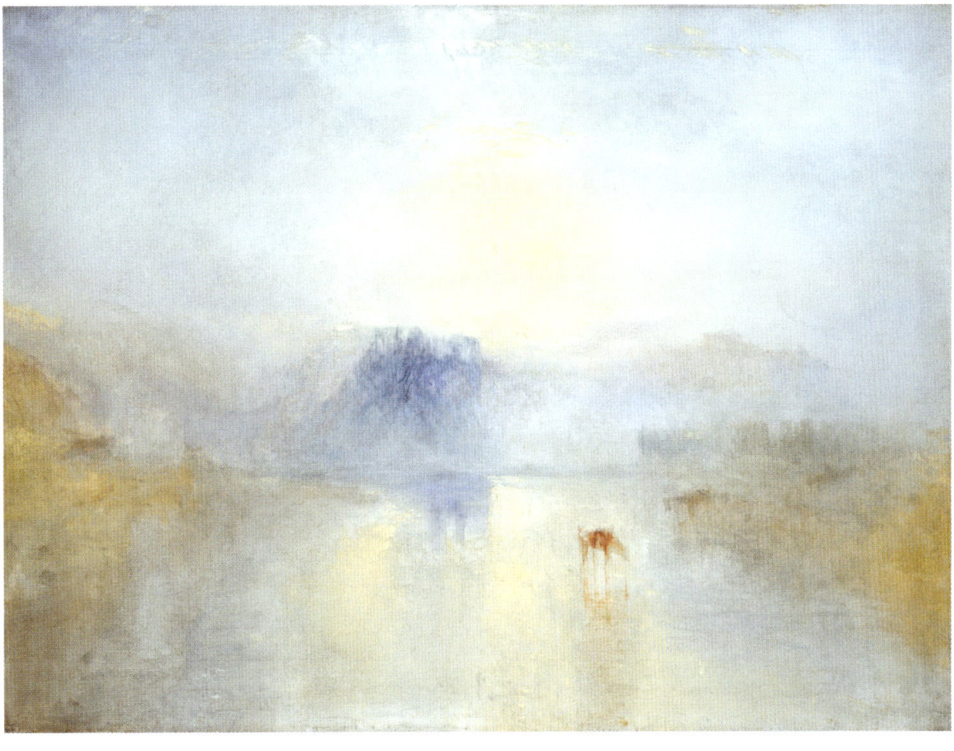

↑ J. M. W. Turner, *Norham Castle: Sunrise*, c. 1845, oil on canvas, 90.8 × 121.9 cm (35¾ × 48 in.), Tate

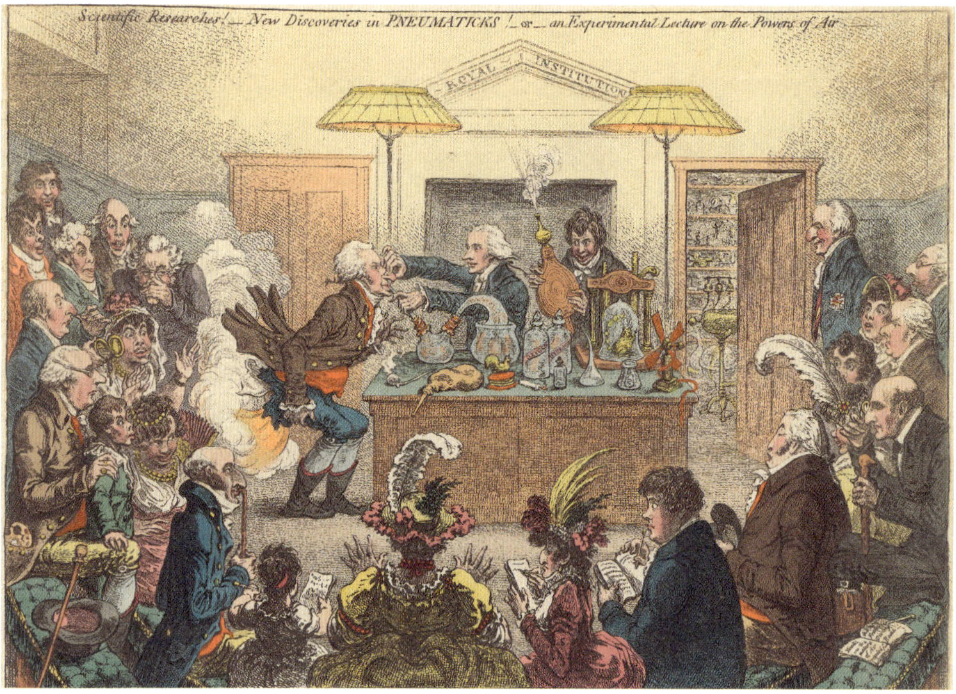

The answer starts with the very fact that he was, indeed, born in the eighteenth century – in 1775, in Covent Garden, where his father had a barber's shop. Turner was the last great artist of the English Enlightenment. His vision is the consummation of its daring fusions of art and science. The best analogy in his own time for what his late paintings do can be found in the work of a scientific contemporary and fellow child of the Enlightenment.

Michael Faraday was born in 1791 into an even humbler London family than Turner's. He too had only a basic schooling before being apprenticed to a bookbinder who luckily encouraged his curiosity and efforts to educate himself. Faraday fell in love with science in an age when science was gripping imaginations more explosively than ever, literally. Public experiments, especially in flammable chemistry, were all the rage in the early 1800s. James Gillray's 1802 print *New Discoveries in Pneumaticks!* depicts a public experiment in which nitrous oxide is being given to a willing subject. The assistant with a diabolical grin on his unpatrician face is Humphry Davy, who seized London's scientific stage during the Napoleonic Wars with a mixture of charismatic lecturing and dazzling discoveries, becoming the star of the Royal

↑ James Gillray, *Scientific Researches! New Discoveries in Pneumaticks! Or, an Experimental Lecture on the Powers of Air*, 1802, hand-coloured etching, Yale University Libraries, New Haven

Institution, founded in 1799 with an emphasis not only on pure research but on popularizing science. The interesting effects of laughing gas were among Davy's signature experiments.

Faraday got a job as Davy's assistant at the Royal Institution in 1813 and was to become an equally brilliant popular lecturer. Like Turner, he lived far longer than such early nineteenth-century contemporaries as Davy and John Constable, to become a Victorian. In 1852, the year after Turner died, he made a series of 'drawings' that show what happens around a magnet. It is an experiment anyone can do: scatter iron filings on paper over a magnet and see the patterns they make. Faraday preserved these patterns under wax to create extraordinary artworks.

Faraday's drawings show mysterious curves radiating in space. These abstract patterns display an order, a structure, but it is much more elastic and uncanny than the mechanics of Newton.

The research that produced these drawings also led Faraday to invent the electric motor and the transformer, and so start the electrification of the world. Yet looking at his beautiful drawings it is clear that his discoveries went way beyond the practical or prosaic. What are those strange pulsing effects that surround a magnet?

Faraday had discovered a new kind of invisible yet omnipresent physical phenomenon – a 'field'. He saw that electrical currents also produce a field around themselves. His experiments with motors and

→ Michael Faraday, Magnetic field drawings, 1851, paper, iron filings, wax, Wellcome Library, London

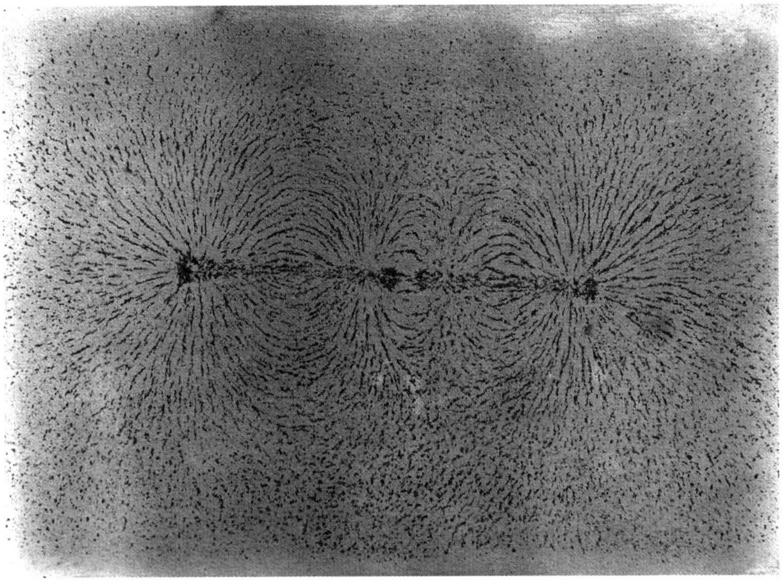

induction depend on his most extraordinary discovery of all, that the magnetic and electric fields are connected and can be transformed into one another: moving magnets generate electricity, and electricity creates magnetism. He saw that both these enigmatic phenomena are aspects of a single phenomenon, the electromagnetic field, which pervades the whole of space.

The consequences of this insight would ultimately end the Newtonian age. Faraday had no mathematical training and preferred to think visually rather than numerically – as in his evocative drawings of the invisible electromagnetic field. In 1865 the Scottish physicist James Clerk Maxwell, an exceptional mathematician, published *A Dynamical Theory of the Electromagnetic Field*, in which he translated Faraday's experiments into the language of equations. In place of beautiful drawings he invented what have been called his 'beautiful equations'. Maxwell's calculations proved that light itself is an electromagnetic wave with the same velocity as other kinds of electromagnetism. Some historians of science see it as a very short step from there to Einstein's theories of special and general relativity. Einstein used Maxwell's field equations to develop and prove his fundamental new concepts of space and time. He kept pictures of three scientific heroes in his study: these Einsteinian icons were Newton, Faraday and Maxwell.

What has this got to do with Turner?

It is surely not too much of a stretch to see some parallel between the radiant fields of light that fill the painter's later canvases and Faraday's radiating abstract patterns of electromagnetism. It might even be conceded that somehow Turner sees mysteries in light that were to be unlocked and analyzed by physics in the wake of Faraday's experiments.

As it happens, Turner and Faraday knew each other well. These two self-educated stars of the early nineteenth-century cultural scene often met at the dinners and clubs typical of the age, where Turner also met the science writer Mary Somerville. Faraday's brother-in-law George Barnard, himself an artist, thought the basis of their friendship was a common fascination with light. He remembered Faraday's frustration with the way most artists failed to look properly at the sky and its changing luminosity:

> *Storms excited his admiration at all times, and he was never tired of looking into the heavens. He said to me once, 'I wonder you artists don't study the light and colour in the sky*

more, and try more for effect.' I think this quality in Turner's drawings made him admire them so much.

Barnard tells it blandly, but the fact that Faraday, whose discovery of the electromagnetic field was to transform the very concept of light and pave the way for the most mind-boggling ideas of modern physics, was drawn to the numinous, melting, electric skies of Turner is revealing. Intuitively or consciously, Faraday felt drawn to Turner's fields of light.

The attraction was mutual. Barnard recalled that Faraday and Turner first met at a *conversazione* – a cultured evening gathering – at the home of the lithographic printmaker C. J. Hullmandel in the 1820s. Faraday stayed in touch with Turner and 'often had applications from him for chemical information about pigments...'.

So the supreme colourist of British art sought regular advice from one of Britain's greatest scientists. This was not at all surprising, for painters in the Romantic age were intensely conscious of both the physics and the chemistry of colour. Newton's *Opticks* was still the bible of the spectrum. The scientific analysis of light was written, or rather painted, into the creed of the Royal Academy, to whose Schools the teenaged Turner was admitted as a student in 1789. On the ceiling of the Academy's Council Chamber in its rooms at Somerset House, London, were four specially commissioned allegorical pictures by the renowned Neoclassicist Angelica Kauffman, one of only two women Academicians in the eighteenth century (the other was Mary Moser). The Swiss-born Kauffman was a close friend of the German polymath Johann Wolfgang von Goethe, who challenged Newton's understanding of colour in his 1810 book *Zur Farbenlehre* (*Theory of Colours*). Goethe, who had travelled around Italy looking closely at paintings with Kauffman, claimed that our experience of colour cannot be reduced to the clarity of the Newtonian spectrum. Turner was to invoke his ideas in his 1843 painting *Light and Colour (Goethe's Theory)*. In the painting *Colour* that she created for the Royal Academy in 1778–80, however, Kauffman is strictly Newtonian. She depicts a female artist limning Newton's spectrum in the sky: art, science and nature are one as the artist's brush produces the rainbow.

Kauffman's four allegories of the 'Elements of Art' commissioned for the ceiling of the Council Chamber also showed *Invention*, *Composition* and *Design*, yet the Royal Academy in the late eighteenth century was notoriously fixated on colour in particular. Blake loathed the Academy and despised its first president, Sir Joshua Reynolds, for reasons that included its blindness to his genius and its shabby treatment of such contemporaries as the Irish visionary history painter James Barry; the ultimate outsider of British art was never going to rub along with the insiderist Academy. Yet Blake's most intellectual critique was that the Academicians put colour above design. For him, the true tradition of art in which he and Barry worked was descended from the clear line of Raphael. He was horrified that the likes of Reynolds and Gainsborough emulated instead such soft suggestive masters of colour as Titian and Rubens: 'Reynolds and Gainsborough blotted and blurred...'.

The splenetic notes Blake added to a surviving early copy of Reynolds's *Discourses on Art* mock the colouring of Titian, so admired of the Royal Academicians, as mere trumpery:

Venetian, all thy Colouring is no more
Than Boulster'd Plasters on a Crooked Whore.

Blake was not wrong to think the grand painters of the Royal Academy were fatally addicted to Titian's colours. When a young painter called Ann Jemima Provis claimed in 1796 to have discovered an old manuscript containing the lost colour recipes of Titian and his fellow Venetian masters, Benjamin West, who succeeded Reynolds as president of the Royal Academy, was one of the leading painters who fell hook, line and sinker for her scam. In Gillray's satire on the scandal, *Titianus Redivivus; or – the seven-wise-men consulting the new Venetian oracle*, Provis balances on top of a rainbow – what else? – while painting a grotesque portrait of the ghostly, naked Titian before an admiring audience. As she works, three nude women hold up her long green skirts to reveal the pink rags below while a muddy, murky pseudo-rainbow – the false rainbow of her fakery – shoots its ugliness onto her canvas.

Reynolds had died in 1792 so he was spared the shame of being embroiled in this highly publicized hoax, but his own pursuit of perfect colours had severe consequences for his art. Many of his paintings have deteriorated badly, with faces that look pale, blueish and ghastly. This is because he experimented boldly with pigments in a failed attempt to rival the old Venetians. *Three Ladies Adorning a Term of Hymen*, a rare masterpiece by him from 1773, whose rich colouring has survived and that successfully melds his commercial work as a portraitist with the high ideals of history painting that he preached, revels in the chromatic brilliance of nature as the Montgomery sisters hang a gorgeous garland of flowers, a flow of pinks, reds, whites and blues, on a shrine of the Greek marriage god.

→ James Gillray, *Titianus Redivivus; or – the seven-wise-men consulting the new Venetian oracle*, 1797, hand-coloured etching, Yale University Libraries, New Haven

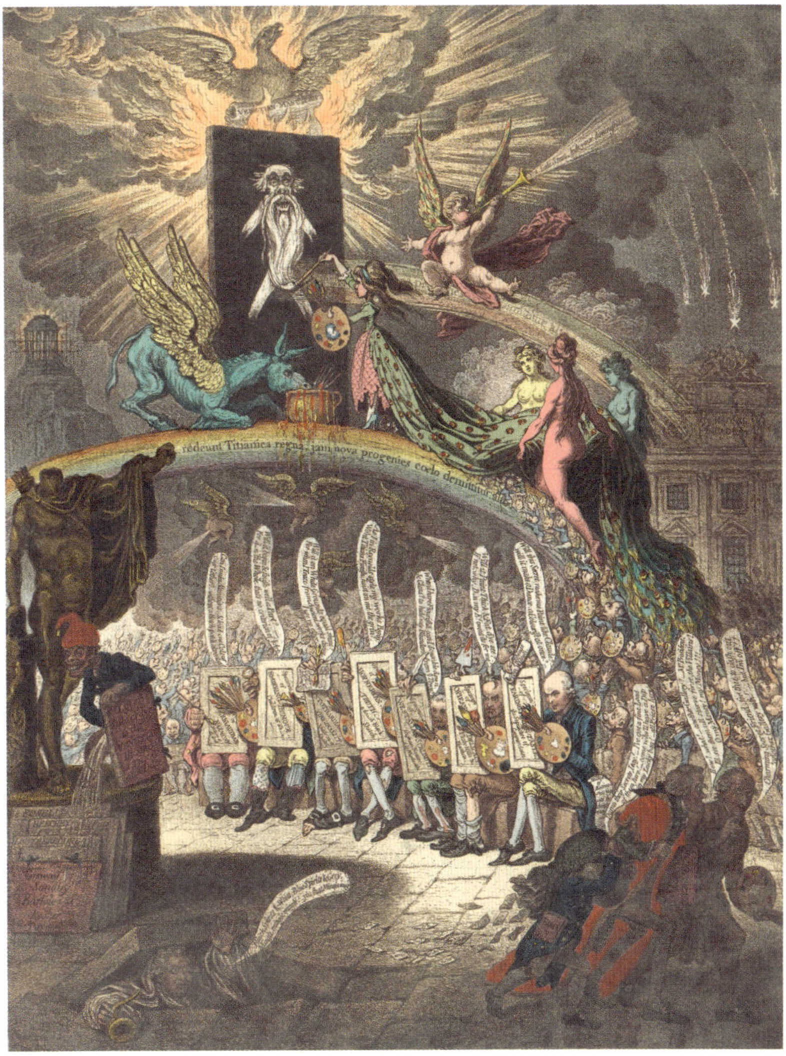

Mary Moser, who was Kauffman's fellow Royal Academician, specialized in painting flowers in the style of Dutch still lifes. Was there a connection between women and the Georgian passion for colour in painting? Blake and Gillray suggest, in a highly pejorative and misogynist way, just that. It needs rephrasing. The eighteenth-century Britain in which Turner grew up was, compared with the black-clad Puritans of the previous century or the equally black-addicted Victorians, both colourful and foppish. People wore bright colours and makeup. Male as well as female fashion came in all the colours of the rainbow, if not more. In art, spectacular colour has often been associated with women – Titian, Giorgione and Veronese in sixteenth-century Venice were not only great colourists but also enthusiasts of the female nude – yet it has also been associated with the exotic novelties of global trade. Venice in the Renaissance was Europe's most powerful trading empire, importing intensely coloured spices and fabrics from Asia. Perhaps the Georgian urge to reproduce Venetian colour was no coincidence. Britain was now a global trading power where the colours of the world could be enjoyed. Exploration and empire enriched the palette of the national imagination.

One glaring example of how empire came in colours was the vogue for the brightly coloured feathers of tropical birds. In a 1773 portrait by Reynolds of Lady Cockburn, her red and blue pet macaw steals the show. Soon fashionable Georgians would start wearing such gorgeous feathers themselves. The idea may have come from encounters with cultures in which feathers were a form of adornment. In Johann Zoffany's painting *The Death of Captain James Cook, 14 February 1779*, one of the doomed explorer's Hawaiian attackers wears a blazing red feathered helmet: this is not a fanciful addition by Zoffany but an accurate rendering of a real object brought back from Cook's expeditions and still in the British Museum today. Benjamin West's sensationally popular 1770 history painting *The Death of General Wolfe* similarly has a Native American bright-red feather headdress.

Perhaps from looking at Oceanic and American headgear or perhaps just to rival the bird world, British women in the late eighteenth century started sporting feather headdresses of their own that gave satirists a treat. One of the theatre-goers in Thomas Rowlandson's 1789 print *Comedy Spectators* wears yellow, pink, blue and white feathers in her hair. Not everyone laughed. The painter George Romney was plainly in love with Emma Hamilton, the young wife of William Hamilton, portraying her again and again in ever-varying poses and costumes. In one of his pictures she wears a single, stylish pale-blue feather while Vesuvius erupts behind her.

All this flirtatious Georgian passion for flowers, feathers and Titianesque beauty may seem a long way from the mighty Romantic palette of Turner. Yet when he died in 1851 his hyper-serious Victorian champion, the art critic John Ruskin, discovered something that shocked him. As executor of Turner's will he was looking forward to diving into his hero's vast artistic legacy, bequeathed as a gift to the nation. What he did not expect was to see, for the first time, the erotic art that Turner enjoyed creating. It turned out that Turner was a true child of the eighteenth century who freely indulged his appetites by getting women to pose naked for him.

Titian's secret and Turner's secret were not unrelated. The Georgian age with its materialist outlook shared the libertinism of Renaissance Venice as well as its love of colour. Out of this pagan moment in British culture came one of the most sensual painters of colour who has ever lived.

When he asked Michael Faraday in the 1820s to advise him on the chemistry of pigments, Turner was taking the same experimental interest in how to create colours that had driven Reynolds to wreck many of his portraits and West to believe in a fake manuscript. He clearly picked a better adviser. Yet is it really possible that Faraday's daring science helped inspire the freedom and strangeness of Turner's late art?

Of course it is the wrong question. It is not so much that Faraday taught Turner, or vice versa – why should not the painter's fields of light help Faraday imagine the nature of electricity? – as that both were thinking equally radically about some of nature's grandest facts. Beyond their fascination with light they had something else in common. Both were empiricists in the British scientific spirit whose bold insights came out of exact observation. Faraday did not pluck electromagnetism out of the ether. He found it by experiment. By trial and error, this persistent practical scientist revealed fundamental facts that led to a new understanding of the natural world.

In just the same way, Turner's late vision is the fruit of a lifetime's looking. It is completely correct to see abstraction in his art – yet it is a special kind of abstraction. Even in his wildest, most obscure paintings, Turner never imposes arbitrary colours on nature. Instead, he becomes over his lifetime ever bolder and more experimental in painting what he has understood about light through endless looking.

Turner stared into the sun more persistently than any other artist in history. It is true that he is not an observational artist of nature in the same way as Constable: his trees, lakes and especially people often seem like figments of a dream. Yet what gives his art its unique power is the relentless observation of sunlight that sets the mind on fire. Turner, like Faraday, reveals natural wonder by looking hard.

A lifetime's looking straight at the sun burns in one of his greatest paintings.

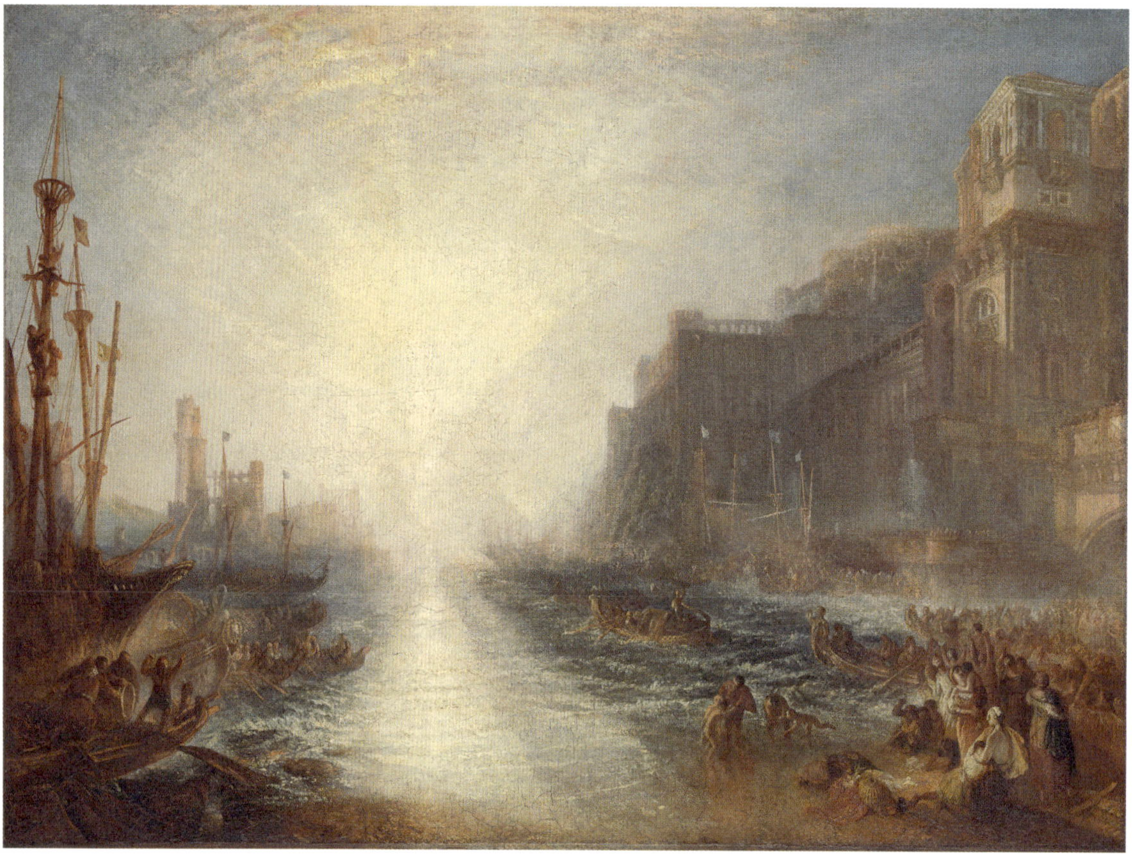

Regulus, begun in 1828 and reworked in 1837, tells the story of a Roman general captured by Carthage – yet another instance of Turner's interest in this lost empire – who had his eyelids removed after he failed in the mission on which his captors sent him. Regulus returned to Carthage as an act of honour, knowing he would be killed. His torture, by literally having his eyes opened, is an extraordinary theme for an artist to choose, portraying vision as agony, the sun as death. Turner makes the horror of staring helplessly into the North African sun without being able to close your eyes not only imaginable but tangible. Your own eyes hurt looking into the terrible sunlight that spreads across the canvas like a white-hot pool of molten metal, scorching everything, turning solid objects into pure light. Turner's eyes penetrate your mind without mercy.

↑ J. M. W. Turner, *Regulus*, 1828, reworked 1837, oil on canvas, 89.5 × 123.8 cm (35 ¼ × 48 ¾ in.), Tate

The Terrible Lizard

The creature that basks hideously on top of a mountain, breathing fire, in Turner's 1806 painting *The Goddess of Discord Choosing the Apple of Contention in the Garden of the Hesperides* has appalled and perplexed observers since the nineteenth century. There is something formidably alive and real about this sprawling reptile with its open mouth and spiny back. It seems it could suddenly smack its tail out of the painting and send the onlooker flying. Of course it is just a painted beast. Yet as Ruskin observed, it is seen in such distant perspective, lying across the heights of the Atlas Mountains, that its real size must be up to three-quarters of a mile long. Still, it is not the size or sublimity of this dragon that is most puzzling. It is the fact that Turner appears to have portrayed a prehistoric monster five years before the discovery of the marine reptiles of the Jurassic age and 36 years before their terrestrial contemporaries got the name 'dinosaurs'.

In 1811, five years after Turner exhibited this painting, a family of impoverished rock-hunters who lived in Lyme Regis on the Dorset coast found the petrified head of a similarly outlandish ancient creature. The Annings had for years been supplementing Richard Anning's meagre income as a cabinetmaker by selling the coiled-snakelike ammonites that they found on the shore to tourists. After their father's death in 1810 his children Mary and Joseph worked even harder to find curios to sell. The following year Joseph came across something incredible: the skull of what would duly be named an 'ichthyosaur', a dolphin-like reptile that swam in ancient seas. With its huge platelike eye and long toothy snout it was not exactly like any living creature, yet looked as if it could be related to the crocodilians. A few months later Mary Anning discovered the rest of the animal's fossilized skeleton. She would spend the rest of her life seeking out similar remains, providing stupendous specimens for the new science of palaeontology, making an enormous contribution to human knowledge in spite of severe poverty and a minimal education.

Her finds came as British science turned its eyes increasingly to the secrets of the rocks. Geology boomed in the early 1800s, helped along by the practical imperatives of the Industrial Revolution. Coal was the fossilized residue of ancient forests, and ferns and other vegetation from the Carboniferous era were frequently found in it. Looking closely at the earth was also encouraged by the excavation of Britain's growing canal network. It was through his profession as a

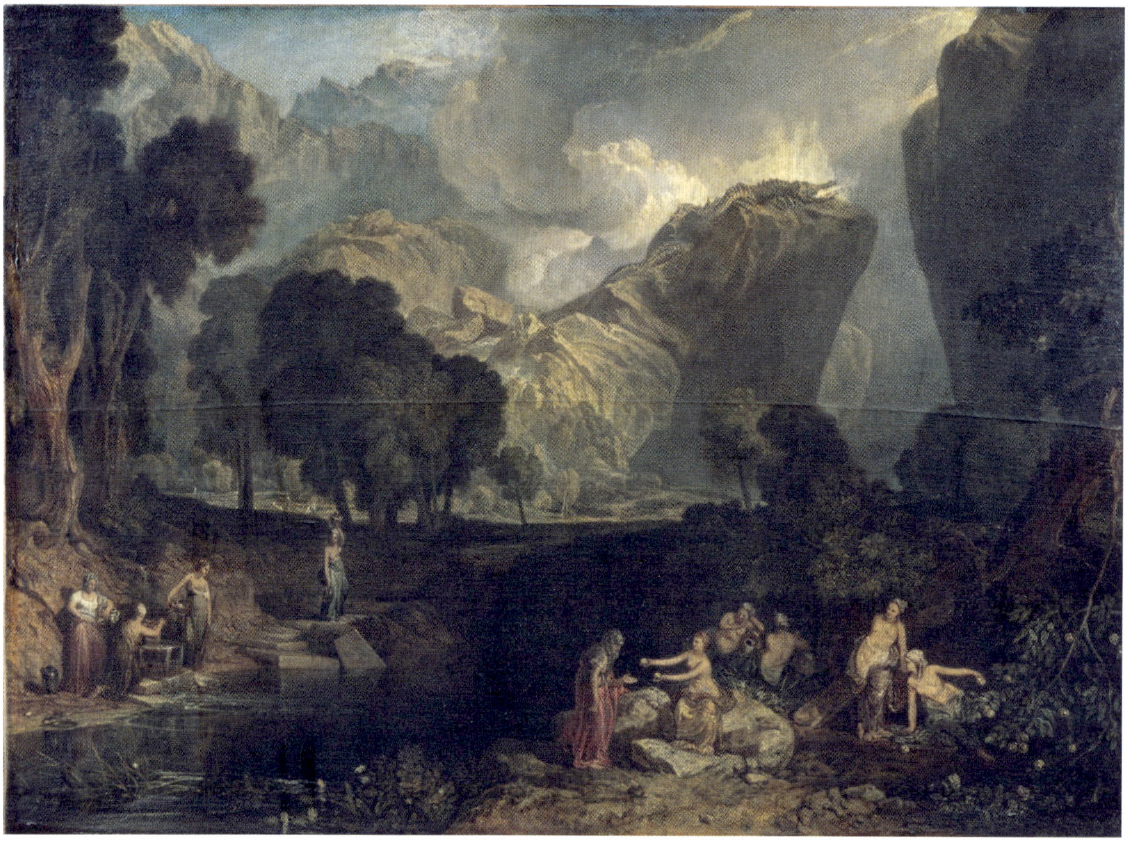

↑ J. M. W. Turner, *The Goddess of Discord Choosing the Apple of Contention in the Garden of the Hesperides*, exhibited 1806, oil on canvas, 155.3 × 218.4 cm (61⅛ × 86 in.), Tate

surveyor of coal and canals that William Smith came to understand the layering of different ages of rock and to map these geological 'strata' in the British landscape in 1815.

Inquisitive eyes were constantly looking downward. In 1824 the fossil-loving clergyman William Buckland described the giant bones of an ancient land-walking reptile that he had found in Oxfordshire, to which he gave the name *Megalosaurus*. It was the first genus of non-avian dinosaur to be named. Gideon Mantell, a shoemaker's son from Lewes in Sussex who trained as a doctor, studied the records written in the stones in his moments of spare time. In the early 1820s he collected the bones and teeth of a creature that in 1825 he would name, amid fierce and continuing controversy, *Iguanodon* – another genus of dinosaur. One of the most brutal critics of Mantell's prehistoric reptile was the leading anatomist of the day, Richard Owen, who insisted it must be a mammal in spite of the similarity between its teeth and those of living lizards.

Owen was a lot more welcoming of the fossils of extinct South American mammals brought back by a young scientist in 1836 from his voyage of discovery aboard HMS *Beagle*.

Charles Darwin had graduated from Cambridge just a few months before joining the *Beagle* in 1831 as a naturalist as well as 'gentleman companion' to its captain, Robert FitzRoy. Its mission was to survey the southernmost Americas for the Royal Navy. Born in Shropshire in 1809, a country boy who preferred riding and shooting to studying, Darwin was expected to become a doctor in the tradition of his well-off family. Instead, it was the natural curiosity of his grandfather Erasmus Darwin that burst out in him. At Edinburgh University he was nauseated by medicine but keen on collecting along the Scottish shore. At Cambridge, where his family – who had shied from the atheism of Erasmus to adopt respectable if unfelt Christian ways – hoped he would prepare for a soft living in the church, his collections grew and so did his engagement with science. The university's leading geologists rated him and recommended him for the *Beagle*.

The fossils he found in South America were just some of the vast haul of specimens he collected on his eye-opening voyage, for Darwin proved a natural explorer. He took every chance to vanish from the *Beagle* on long, dangerous expeditions in the company of trigger-happy gauchos and ranchers who laughed at the idea the Earth was spherical. His ability and enthusiasm for hunting won him friends: he was always quick to shoot and catalogue a monkey. He was also an outstanding fossil hunter: when local people told him about a farm where giants' bones lay, he travelled there and found fossils of a giant mammal that would be identified by Owen as *Toxodon*.

When Darwin showed his *Toxodon* to Owen, the dogmatic anatomist was busy reorganizing the museum of the Royal College of Surgeons in London, which had grown out of the eighteenth-century collections of John Hunter. Fossils were now numerous and spectacular enough to start their career as star museum exhibits. It was Owen who saw this. Today he is often seen as the villain of palaeontology who persecuted the unhappy Mantell, yet Owen also pioneered the public display of fossils and made them popular. In 1842 he came up with a catchy name for the most glamorous group of extinct reptiles – 'Dinosaurs', or 'Terrible Lizards'. By then his museum at the Royal College of Surgeons was displaying huge reassembled fossil skeletons in a completely new way to awe and astonish the London public.

Turner imagined his terrible lizard at the very beginning of the golden age of fossils, when Lyme Regis was better known for blustery walks on the Cobb than antediluvian monsters. How did he prophesy the discovery of a lost world of giant reptiles?

I am not the first to see a precocious vision of prehistory in his 1806 painting. Contemplating it in the late 1850s, Ruskin found the fossil-like quality of the monster in the *Garden of the Hesperides* impossible to ignore:

> *The strange unity of vertebrated action, and of a true bony contour, infinitely varied in every vertebra, with this glacial outline; – together with the adoption of the head of the Ganges crocodile, the fish-eater, to show his sea descent (and this in the year 1806, when hardly a single fossil saurian skeleton existed within Turner's reach), renders the whole conception one of the most curious exertions of the imaginative intellect with which I am acquainted in the arts.*

The modern Turner authority John Gage also notes that the monster resembles 'the crocodile-like *Ichthyosaurus*...'.

Yet how was that possible?

Turner did not share the inward-looking nationalism of his contemporaries Blake and Constable – neither of whom, as we have seen, ever travelled abroad. Seeing the world was admittedly not easy (at least for a civilian) during the wars with France that raged with only brief breaks from Turner's teenaged years until 1815, when he was 40. Nor was he exactly blind to the British landscape. He tramped the country seeking out every castle, waterfall and mountain vista he could find. Before getting into the Royal Academy Schools, the teenaged Turner worked as an architectural draughtsman producing watercolour views of British buildings such as Fonthill Abbey. He never lost that appetite for British scenery, and started his regular landscape-hunting tours with trips to the West Country in 1791 and North Wales in 1792. His early paintings gave the public of the Romantic age exactly what they wanted: picturesque beauty laced with sublime shudders. He unveiled *Buttermere Lake* at the Royal Academy in 1798, the same year that Wordsworth and Coleridge published their collection *Lyrical Ballads*; it shares not just the Wordsworthian setting of the Lake District, which Turner had visited the previous year, but the more blasted passions of Coleridge's verse. Like the ancient mariner, the

painter seems to have looked into icy waters of terror. Lake Buttermere is black and leaden, a mirror of the mountains above. The sunlight in the valley beyond does not so much lighten as heighten its foreboding.

Clearly, Turner had none of Constable's reluctance to satisfy people's taste for such scenes. Nor did he attempt the same raw fidelity to what was before his eyes. His empiricism is different. Only a few oil sketches painted in the open air by him survive. Instead of trying to show nature exactly as he saw it, he drew endlessly wherever he travelled, then synthesized this visual information in grand paintings created at his London studio.

Is he, then, an observational painter at all? Yes, and in a profound way. To see this we only have to compare him with Romantic artists who did not subject themselves to the discipline of the real.

Turner learned a lot about the popularity of swirling spectacle from Philip James de Loutherbourg, who not only enjoyed parallel

↑ J. M. W. Turner, *Buttermere Lake, with Part of Cromackwater, Cumberland, a Shower*, exhibited 1798, oil on canvas, 88.9 × 119.4 cm (35 × 47 in.), Tate

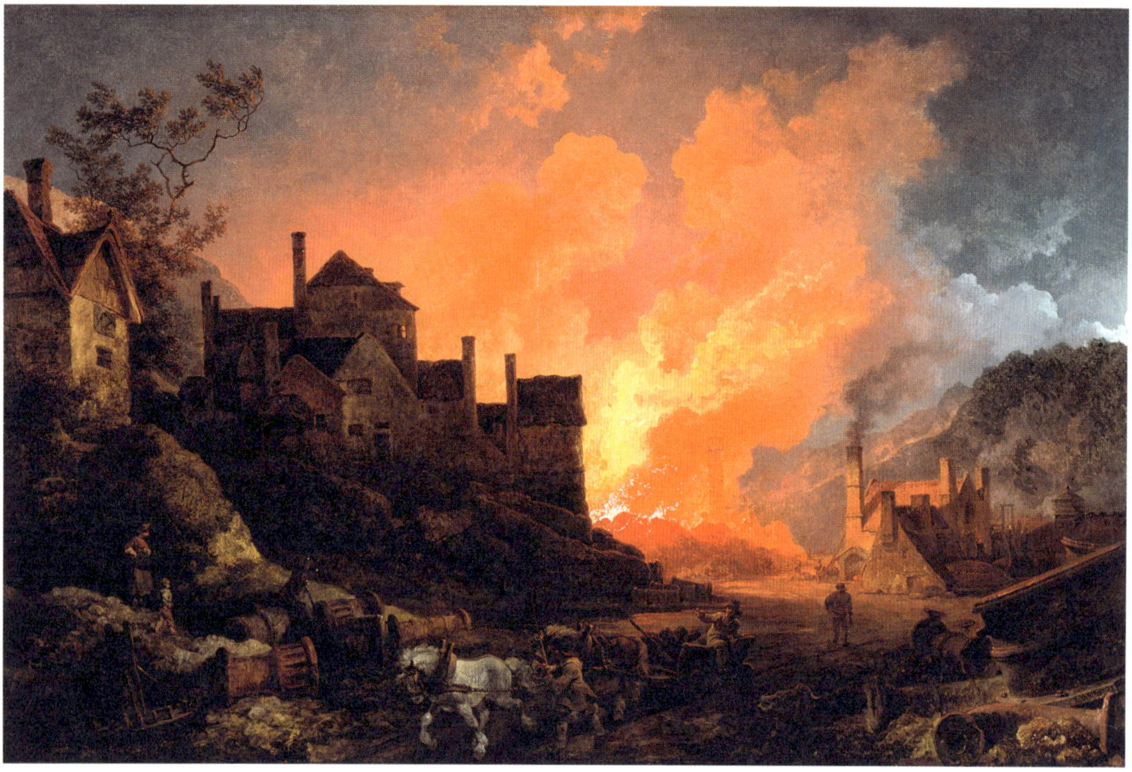

↑ Philip James de Loutherbourg, *Coalbrookdale by Night*, 1801, oil on canvas, 68 × 106.7 cm (26 ¾ × 42 in.), Science Museum, London

careers as chief set designer for the Theatre Royal, Drury Lane, and as a landscape artist, but combined them to invent a kind of landscape cinema. Visitors to Loutherbourg's 'Eidophusikon' (meaning 'nature's image') at Leicester Square in 1781 were promised:

> *Various Imitations of Natural Phenomena, represented by moving pictures, invented and painted by Mr Loutherbourg, in a manner entirely new.*

They were treated to a misty dawn scene in Greenwich Park, a sunset on the Bay of Naples, the moon rising over the Mediterranean, and the grand finale: a shipwreck in a violent storm. It was all Turneresque stuff, and while Loutherbourg's cinematic experience is no more, his surviving oil paintings fully share Turner's appetite for the sublime. His 1801 canvas *Coalbrookdale by Night* is a dazzling image of the new power of industry as a satanic show of smoke and flame. Yet as a study of light, it goes no further that Wright had done: there is none of Turner's

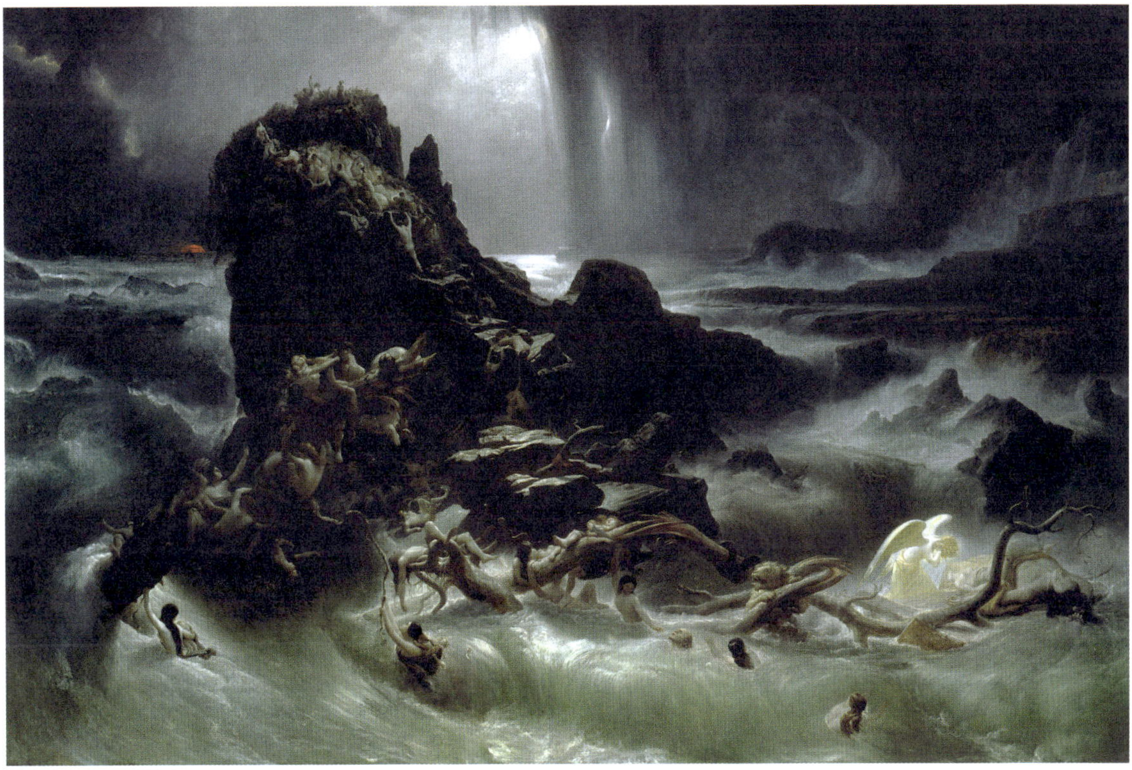

↑ Francis Danby, *The Deluge*, exhibited 1840, oil on canvas, 284.5 × 452.1 cm (112 × 178 in.), Tate

complex atmospherics. Loutherbourg just has not looked as closely. The same goes for Francis Danby, a boldly imaginative Romantic born in Ireland in 1793 who made a home among the gorge scenery of Bristol. Danby's 1840 painting *The Deluge* has Turner's energy and exhilaration but no one could call it a realistic study of the natural world. By contrast, even in his intensely imagined 1796 concoction *Fishermen at Sea*, the 21-year-old Turner takes time to depict an almost heartbreakingly real row of trees in the moonlight, swaying icons of earthbound safety so near yet so far from the imperilled fishing boat.

The tension between reality and fantasy that shudders in Turner made him one of the world's truly great artists. It also meant his imagination and curiosity could not be sated forever by Welsh ruins or the Lake District. In about 1798 he painted a captivating Italian scene before he had ever seen Italy: the light and space of *Aeneas and the Sibyl, Lake Avernus* come from dreams of art, as Turner pays homage to the classical visions of Claude and Wilson. It also cannot have harmed him, with aristocratic patrons nostalgic for their youthful Grand Tours before the French Revolution. The following year Lord Elgin offered the up-and-coming artist a once-in-a-lifetime chance to go to Greece on an archaeological expedition: the western Continent might be barred by war but the Royal Navy could get ships to the Balkans. This was the year –1798 – that Nelson blew up the French flagship at the Battle of the Nile and established British control of the Mediterranean.

Turner wanted too much money, so his chance to paint Elgin's workers ransacking the Acropolis fell through. When a temporary peace broke out between Britain and France in 1802, however, he seized his chance and got a boat to Calais. It was a terrifying crossing, if his painting *Calais Pier*, done the following year, is anything to go by. People crawl about nauseously on the fragile wooden jetty while boats stuffed with bodies lurch on the hurling, spewing sea: Turner's grasp of nature is never surer than when he paints the motion of saltwater. The dark surface of the English Channel stretches taut like a skin as it is pressed outwards by the invisible forces within it. Pushed up into towering ridges, it shatters into whiteness.

The seasick artist soon got over his rough crossing to explore France and Switzerland. His 1810 painting *The Fall of an Avalanche in the Grisons* is a thrilling riff on the new kind of mountain scenery he saw – a bit more dangerous than Buttermere. Yet he also spent several weeks in Paris, studying art in the Louvre, which had been turned from a royal palace into a museum by the Revolution and filled with the spoils of France's recent conquests as well as expropriated royal treasures. He met artists including the former Jacobin and signatory of Marie-Antoinette's death warrant, Jacques-Louis David, who was now at work on a heroic portrait of Napoleon riding a mighty horse over the Alps.

It was on this trip that Turner executed his earliest surviving example of erotic art – an unknown woman naked in bed. It is worth stressing again that he was a Georgian sensualist, not a Victorian prude. He had a mistress, Sarah Danby, back in London and had probably fathered his first illegitimate child, Evelina, in 1801.

As well as mountains, art and sex it seems highly possible Turner did something else on his first trip abroad. He looked at a famous fossil.

In 1793 the Revolution established a Museum of Natural History in Paris. Its home was the former Royal Garden that had been growing herbs and other useful plants since the seventeenth century. Before the Revolution this had been the intellectual playground of the Enlightenment naturalist the Comte de Buffon: now its professors included the palaeontologist Georges Cuvier, who argued that a series

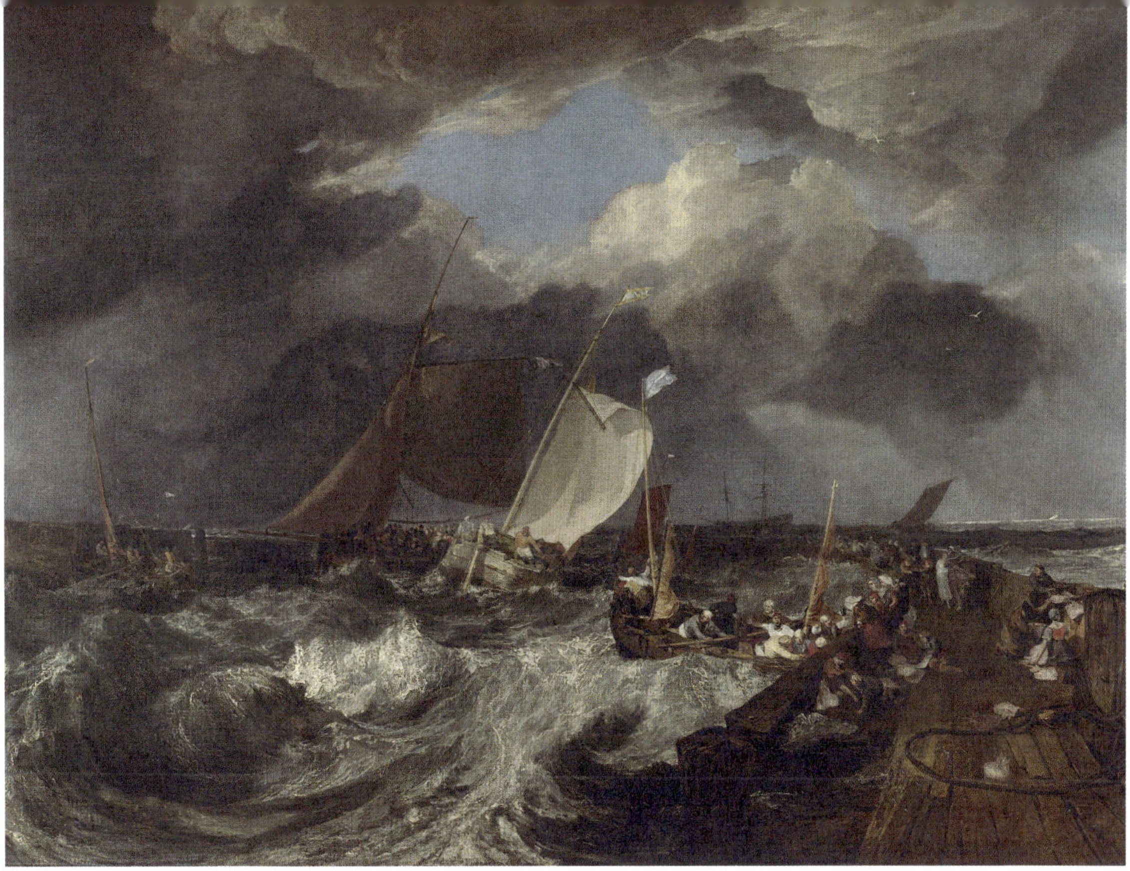

of catastrophes had made waves of species extinct and identified both the prehistoric mammal *Megatherium* – whose fossils Darwin later found – and the flying reptile *Pterodactylus*.

Cuvier also studied a strange fossil that had been discovered by quarry workers near Maastricht in Holland in the eighteenth century: a massive skull studded with terrifying teeth. This fearsome object was so renowned that just as the armies of revolutionary France collected works of art for the Louvre, they also coveted this geological treasure. Its owner hid it when Maastricht was occupied by a French army, but a bribe of 600 bottles of wine secured it as a spoil of war and in 1794 it was brought to the Museum of Natural History in Paris, where it has been on display ever since.

It was a wonder, a treasure – the order to seize it referred to the 'famous skull'. It seems entirely likely that it could have caught the eye of an English visitor in 1802.

Parisian scientists argued fiercely about it. Was this toothy head that of a whale? No, surely it was a giant crocodile. This is how Cuvier's colleague Barthélemy Faujas de Saint-Fond interprets it in a book illustrated not only with the skull but also with a living crocodile

↑ J. M. W. Turner, *Calais Pier*, 1803, oil on canvas, 172 × 240 cm (67¾ × 94½ in.), National Gallery, London

→→ J. M. W. Turner, *The Fall of an Avalanche in the Grisons*, exhibited 1810, oil on canvas, 90.2 × 120 cm (35½ × 47¼ in.), Tate

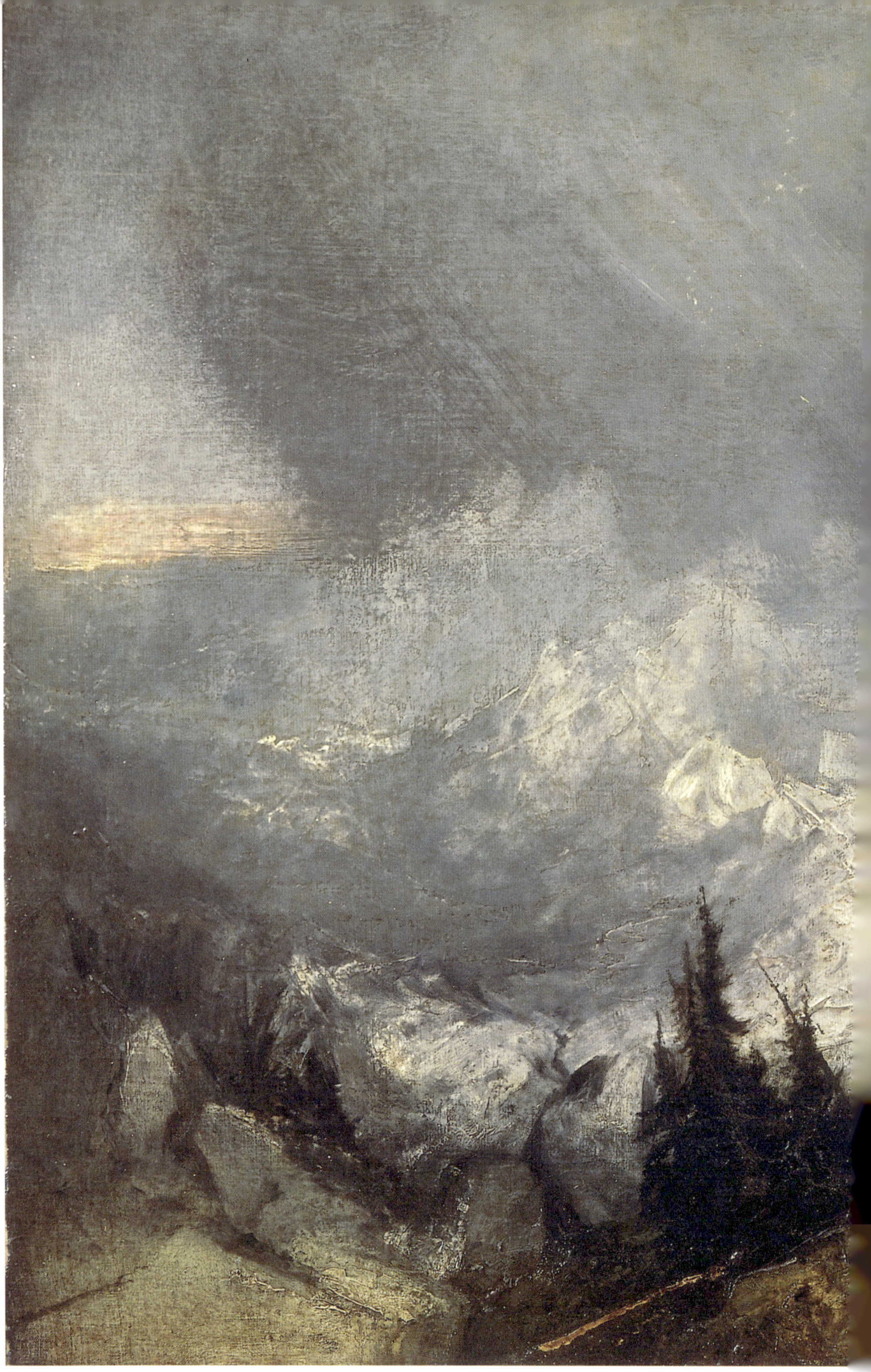

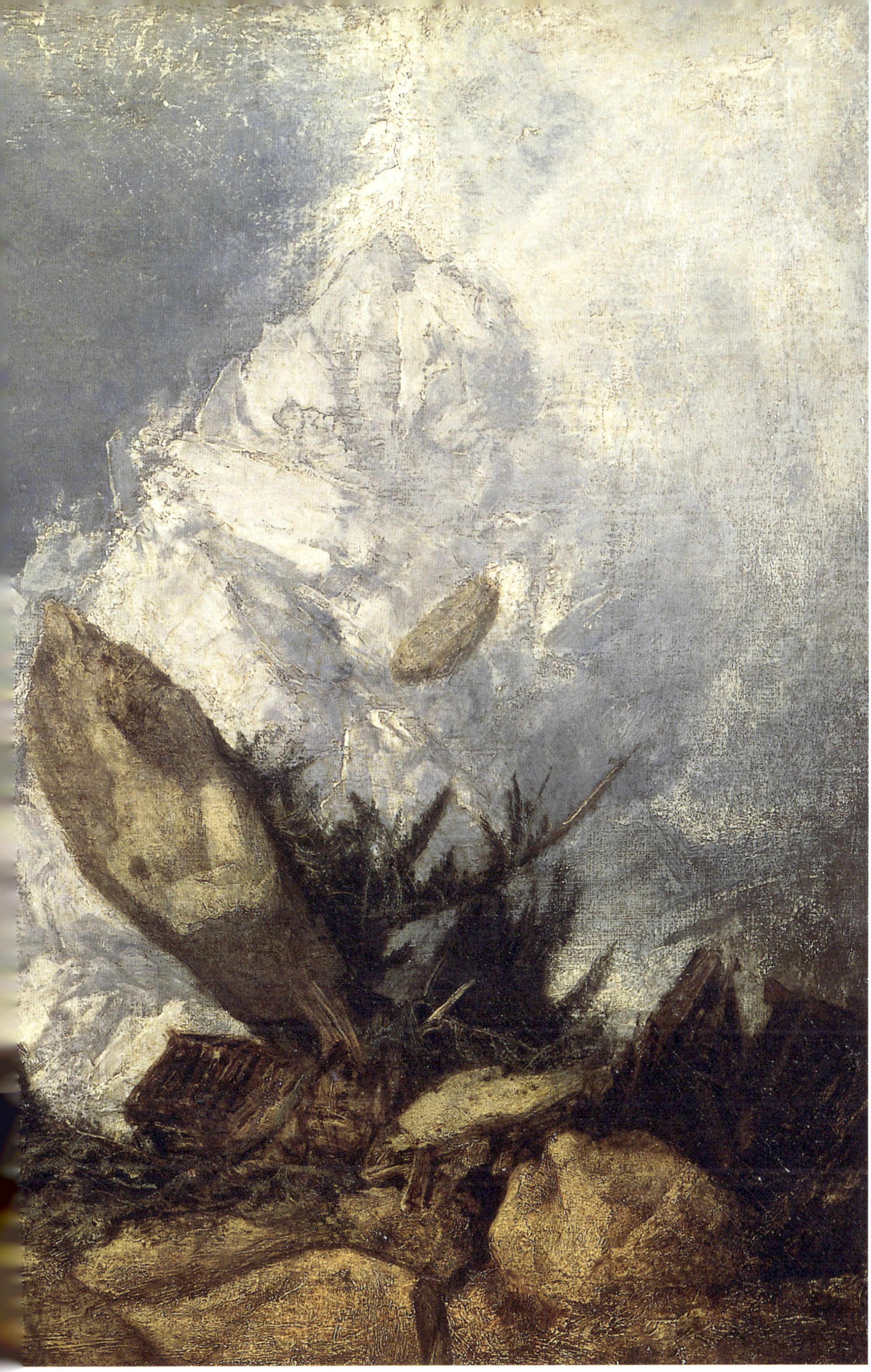

for comparison. Cuvier would recognize the Maastricht monster as a marine reptile and in the 1820s it would get its name: the mosasaur.

Did the Maastricht fossil inspire Turner's crocodilian creature in the *Garden of the Hesperides*? That makes a lot more sense than his somehow 'foreseeing' the discovery of the ichthyosaur. It also offers a direct glimpse of his self-taught intellectual openness. After sitting by Turner at a Royal Academy dinner Constable praised his 'wonderful range of mind'.

A crocodile with a skull of this size would be nearly 12 metres (40 feet) long – not quite the three-quarters of a mile imagined by Ruskin, but monstrous enough to inspire Turner's undeniably fossil-like, mountain-living crocodile.

The fact that the skull came from a mountain could have helped suggest the image painted by Turner. There are of course no mountains in the Netherlands like the ones on which he set his creature, but the discovery was described as having taken place on a 'mountain' and Faujas de Saint-Fond's illustrations vividly convey this.

It is, above all, the stony aura of Turner's monster that confirms its palaeontological pedigree. It seems to grow out of the rock: it is flinty, craggy, ossified. Ruskin conveys this in speaking of its 'bony contour', its 'glacial outline'.

But why might Turner in 1806 have looked back on his 1802 trip to Paris? *The Goddess of Discord Choosing the Apple of Contention*

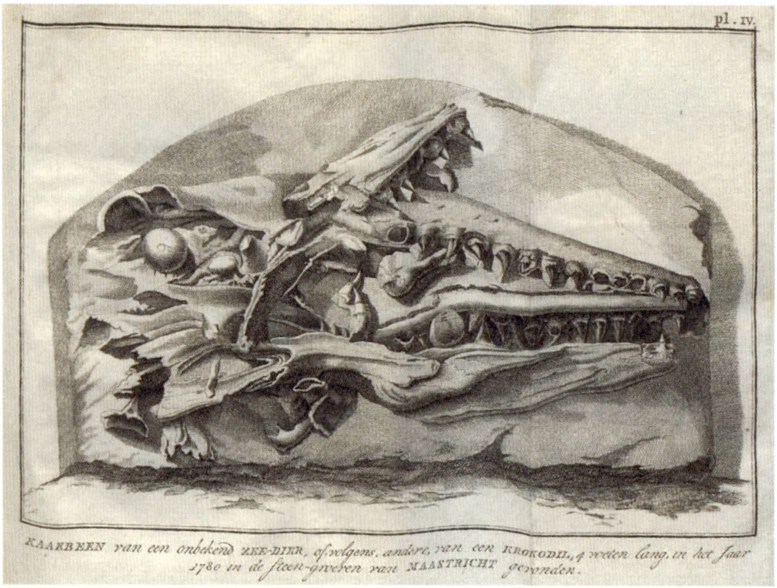

↑ Barthélemy Faujas de Saint-Fond, the Maastricht mosasaur skull from *Histoire Naturelle de la montagne de Saint-Pierre de Maestricht*, 1798–1803, Naturalis Biodiversity Center, Leiden

in the Garden of the Hesperides is a pessimistic vision of history, set in a primordial landscape where a prehistoric monster exudes timeless, brainless ferocity. The violence of the reptilian beast on its mountain is a mirror of the human violence premeditated below.

This scene from Greek mythology is set in the garden below the Atlas Mountains in North Africa where the three Hesperides – the nymphs of evening – looked after a tree of golden apples guarded by the dragon Ladon. This is Turner's terrible lizard. The apple the goddess chooses is the one that Paris, prince of Troy, will later award as a prize in a beauty contest between the goddesses Aphrodite, Athene and Hera. By giving it to Aphrodite, in return for her promise to make the most beautiful woman on earth fall in love with him, he will spark the bloodshed of the Trojan War.

In early 1806 the death of Pitt and the return of Charles James Fox to government as a liberal, positively Francophile foreign secretary raised the fluttering possibility of peace with Napoleon. The negotiations were secret, but Fox's presence in government made an end to war plausible. It came to nothing; by the summer there was no prospect of any let-up. Did Turner long for a peace so he could travel again?

His painting bleakly demolishes such fond hopes. Humans will always make war, as surely as nature breeds monsters with mouths bigger than their brains.

The Hammers of the Geologists

John Ruskin's interpretation of Turner's monster in the fifth and final volume of *Modern Painters*, published in 1860, does not stop at comparing it with fossil saurians. That is just one of the almost surreal thoughts he expresses in gushes of apocalyptic prose and fantastic erudition. For Ruskin, the dragon Ladon is a hideous image of evil that he pursues through the circles of Dante's *Inferno* down to his own time, finally concluding that Turner has painted nineteenth-century Britain's true god – Greed – basking monstrously, hoarding its golden apples. While earlier ages painted the Assumption of the Virgin Mary, Turner has created a blasphemous image of an all-consuming beast:

> *This is no irony. The fact is verily so... here, in England, is our great spiritual fact forever interpreted to us – the Assumption of the Dragon...*

It is probably fair to call him a disillusioned man when he wrote this.

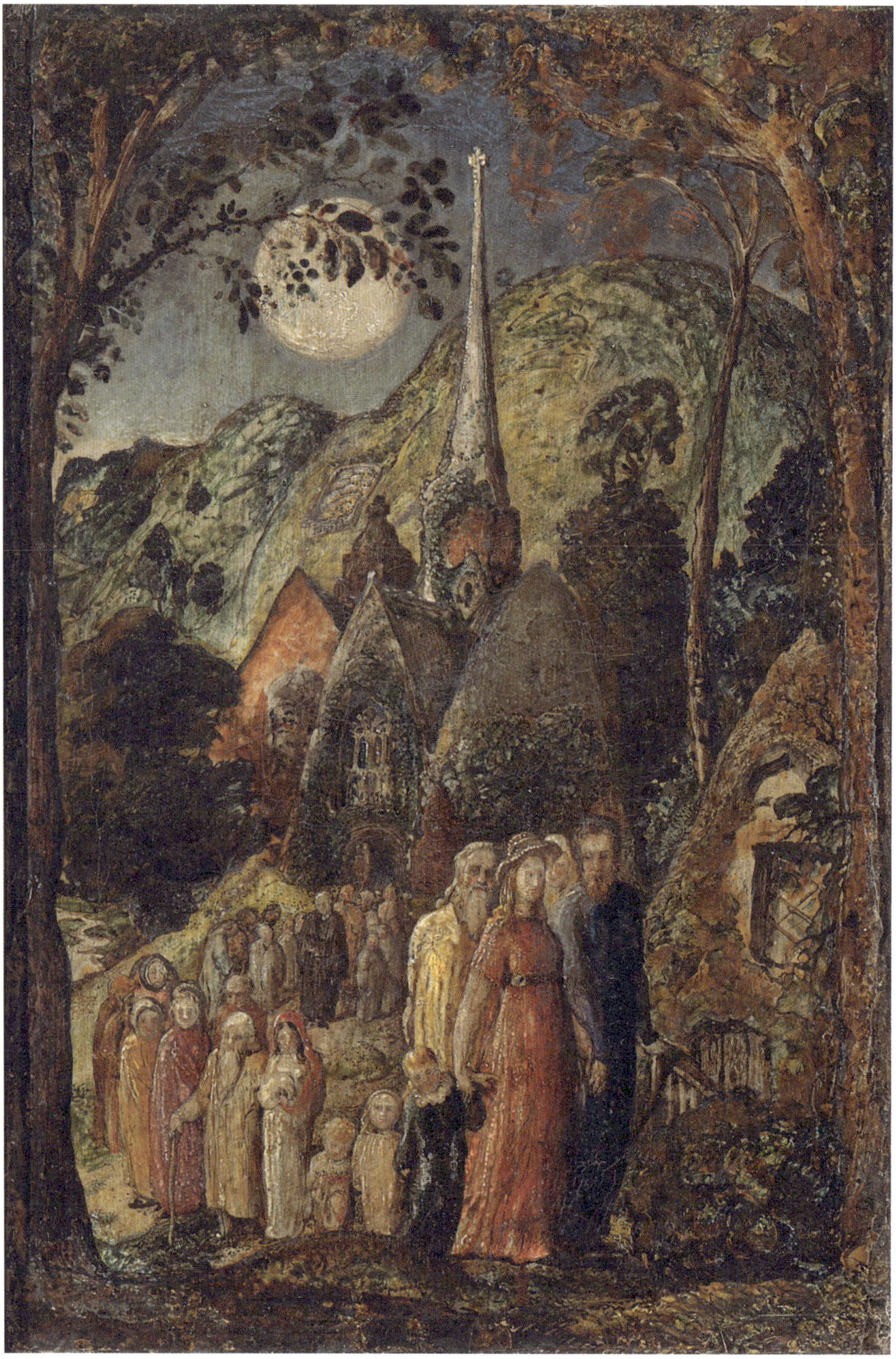

↑ Samuel Palmer, *Coming from Evening Church*, 1830, tempera, chalk, gold, ink and graphite on gesso on paper, 30.2 × 20 cm (11⅘ × 7⅚ in.), Tate

By the time he reached these thoughts, Ruskin had dedicated much of his life to the genius of Turner. Even in the despair that fills his chapter 'The Nereid's Guard', he reaffirms his hero worship of 'The greatest son of our England, in the first half of the nineteenth century'.

Since 1843 he had been championing Turner as the most insightful of all painters of nature in volume after volume of his immense book spanning not only the history of art but also meteorology, geology and oceanography. The early volumes of *Modern Painters* are joyously scientific. Ruskin began his project because he was horrified by crude attacks on Turner that mocked his colours as mad hurlings of mustard or curry powder. He wanted to refute the notion of Turner as some facile abstractionist and prove him a deep analyst of nature.

Compare the glassy blue skies of old landscape artists with Turner's rich atmospheres, he urges: which is more truthful? Turner alone has got close to capturing the flux of clouds illuminated by the sun.

In these ecstatic early volumes Ruskin is convinced not only that Turner reveals the truth of clouds, light and water, but that in so doing he shows us the face of God. As a genuine scientific enthusiast who explored Alpine glaciers and practised geology, he does not simply summon up scientific facts to prove Turner's accuracy. He advances what amounts to a Christian vision of science as the decoding of God's great book.

Ruskin has become notorious for his eccentricities – which are today more familiar than his writings. His marriage to Effie Gray ended after he failed ever to make love to her. Then he fell in love with a child called Rose La Touche, who as a young woman would die insane. Yet in searching for God in nature he was not being odd at all, merely typical of his age. A square Anglo-Saxon church tower nuzzles the trees in Constable's masterpiece *The Cornfield*, heightening the sense of religious communion that pervades this painting. With similar spirituality Samuel Palmer's 1830 painting *Coming from Evening Church* portrays a procession of Blake-like country folk emerging from a parish church that nestles in a mystic vale. Palmer, born in 1805, was enraptured by Blake's engravings. In this rhapsodic, dreamlike painting done in Shoreham in Kent he pipes his own song of innocence.

There was a strongly Christian dimension to the love of nature that enthused the early nineteenth century. The title of William Paley's 1802 book *Natural Theology: or, Evidences of the Existence and Attributes of the Deity, Collected from the Appearances of Nature*, speaks for itself. Paley's argument that the intricacy of natural forms reveals the beauty

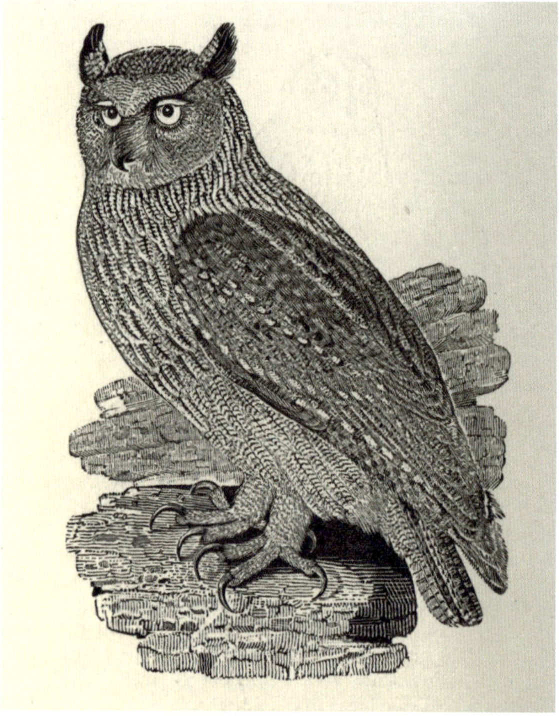

of God's design did not satisfy all Christians: the faith-based Methodists rejected rational Christianity as being vulnerable to rational critique. But in the Romantic age a deepening respect for the countryside and its creatures fed a warm feeling that God's love glows in misty sunsets and flutters in the wings of birds. Thus the avian woodcuts of the Tyneside-born ruralist Thomas Bewick were widely loved for their acute, characterful portraits of a beady-eyed owl, an elegant redshank and other British wildfowl.

Yet Bewick filled his rural world with nasty surprises for the sentimental. One of the deflating vignettes dotted among his books portrays an old man contemplating a gravestone in front of a ruined parish church with no glass in its windows and no roof. Such troubling glimpses of unredeemed reality in Bewick's art – another of his woodcuts is of a suicide hanging from a tree – reveal the danger of using the pastoral as a source of religious feeling. Look too closely at the working world of the British countryside and it is full of horses waiting to be knackered, wretched bands of wandering entertainers, exhausted labourers having to smash stones for a living and crippled veterans of the wars – to peer into a few more of Bewick's vignettes.

Ruskin was no prosaic Paleyite. He was drawn to the transporting paintings of Turner because he saw in them an incantatory, drunken worship. He criticized Constable for never staring at the sun with eyes wide open:

> *There is strange want of depth in the mind which has no pleasure in sunbeams but when piercing painfully through clouds...*

In Turner he could drink the sunbeams straight, no chaser necessary.

The child of a wealthy, cultured sherry merchant and his Evangelical wife, Ruskin was brought up to love art and Christ equally. Evangelicalism within the Church of England, with its advocacy of passionate personal faith constantly expressed through demeanour and action, reshaped the manners and morals of the elite in the early

↑ Thomas Bewick, *Eagle Owl*, c. 1797, white-line wood engraving, 11.6 × 8.2 cm (4 ½ × 3 ¼ in.), University of California Libraries

nineteenth century, making the libertines and dandies of the Georgian age look old. Young Ruskin was a Victorian in the making who was born in the same year, 1819, as Victoria herself. Even as she took the throne in 1837, however, the divine light was going out of nature.

In July of that very year, just weeks after Victoria's coronation, Charles Darwin started a secret notebook on what he called at this early stage the 'transmutation of species'. Since getting home from his voyage aboard HMS *Beagle* the year before and showing his collections to authorities such as Richard Owen, he had begun to reflect more extensively on the complexity and variety of the life he had seen. He was now convinced that species did not stay the same throughout time according to a heavenly design. Slowly but surely through long ages, they evolved.

One encounter that led him to the rudiments of his great theory that year casts a light on the relationship between art and science at the dawn of the Victorian age. Darwin gave more than 450 bird specimens that he had collected on his voyage to the Museum of the Zoological Society in January 1837. He did not yet understand the significance of all of them, but the beady eye of the ornithologist John Gould soon spotted something strange about a group of finches Darwin had found on various islands of the Galapagos archipelago. They were all similar, not to mention drab in their brown feathers, but as Gould studied the varying lengths of their beaks he identified 13 species. Darwin was to deduce that they shared a common South American ancestor, yet had evolved differently to adapt to the conditions of each Galapagos island.

Gould's eye for variation was not only that of a naturalist, but also that of a draughtsman. Together with his wife, Elizabeth, he illustrated his own books on taxonomy with precise and accurate renderings of the birds he catalogued. It was, then, the keen gaze of a scientific artist that helped Darwin comprehend the evolutionary wonders of the Galapagos.

It would take Darwin another 22 years to publish his theory. The work he did in those years would make *On the Origin of Species*, when it finally appeared in 1859, a devastatingly powerful attack on tradition and the most severe blow in history to religious thinking. For he had spent his intervening life amassing evidence, not in a dogmatic, rhetorical way to bolster an argument, but with genuine curiosity and openness. Darwin is the greatest of all empiricists. You know he would find the facts he relates addictive even if they disproved his case. Facts about pigeon-breeding, bees, gardens in winter. Facts he gathered in the Galapagos and others found through experiments and strolls in the peace and calm of Down House, his country home south of London.

Ruskin did not need to wait for Darwin's book to see where all the fossils discovered in the first half of the nineteenth century were irrevocably leading a conscientious mind like his. By 1851 he was confessing:

> *If only the Geologists would let me alone, I could do very well, but those dreadful Hammers! I hear the clink of them at the end of every cadence of the Bible verses.*

For a mind so infused with faith to accept the evidence of the geologists' hammers showed courage. It also made Ruskin more far-seeing than many scientists. For the fascinating interplay between faith and empiricism in the golden age of fossils was not – yet – a question of artistic imagination versus hardheaded science. Many scientists were just as convinced as Ruskin that to know nature was to see God. Faraday, raised in the dissenting Sandemanian sect, was one. So was William Buckland, who hoped that his pioneering research in palaeontology could not only be reconciled with Genesis but would provide positive evidence of the biblical flood. In 1819 he told the Geological Society he had actually found 'the Evidence of Recent Deluge' – that is, Noah's flood – in southern England. Buckland was no crank, but a great excavator of a past more remote than he wanted it to be.

Given how slowly science itself accepted the disturbing evidence exposed by the geologists' hammers, it is remarkable how honestly Ruskin listened to their banging.

Yet one wide-ranging thinker had long seen nature as a godless, restless world. Ruskin's early vision of Turner as a painter of God's design was woefully misplaced. There is precious little evidence of religious belief in Turner's art. The only gods he seems to take seriously are those of ancient Greece, and they are provocative and morose.

As his doubts took hold, Ruskin turned his eyes to the monstrous reptile in Turner's *Garden of the Hesperides*, for this godless beast broods over a scene that pictures history as absurd and the gods as cruel. The apple from the Hesperides will result in mass slaughter. Divine plan? This is casual divine mass murder. The tranquil poses of the figures express the banality of the decision.

Turner puts his sardonic laughter at the madness of the gods even more directly into his 1818 painting *The Field of Waterloo*. In the

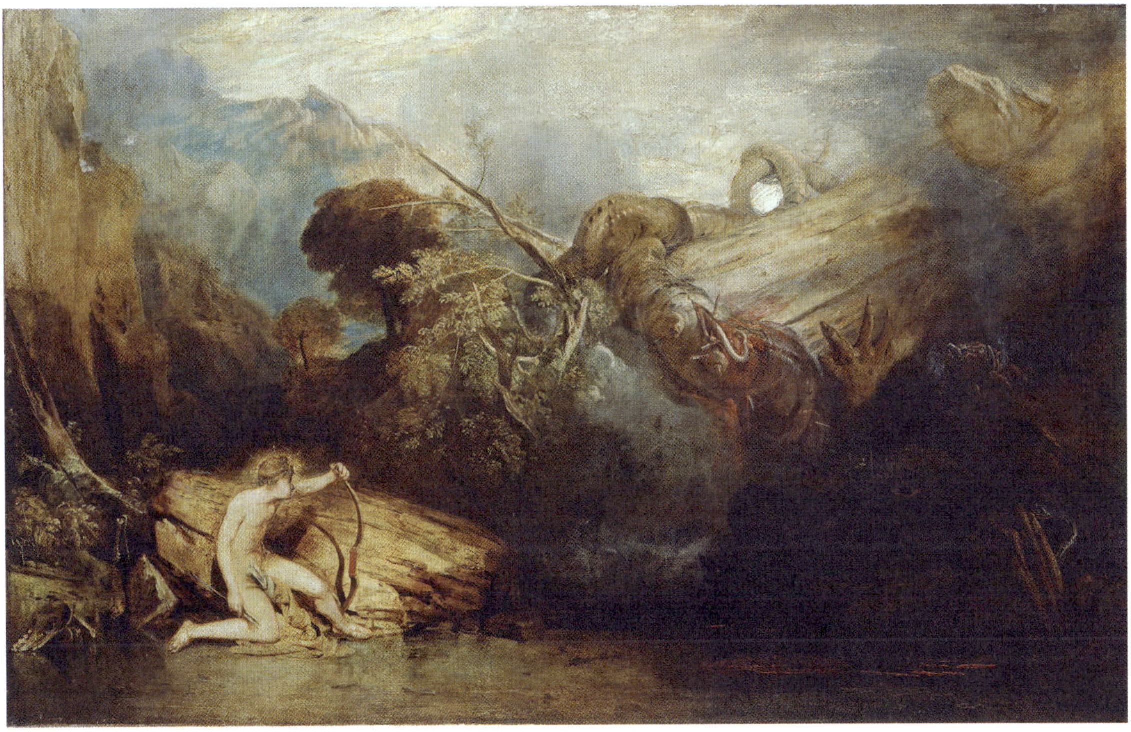

↑ J. M. W. Turner, *Apollo and Python*, exhibited 1811, oil on canvas, 145.4 × 237.5 cm (57¼ × 93½ in.), Tate

white light of a flare we behold a gruesome heap of human bodies. French, British and Prussian bodies are hopelessly entangled. There is no glory, no redemption here. This is less a protest against war than an expression of Turner's pessimistic view of human history as a doomed struggle for order and sanity in a nature fundamentally uninterested in us.

Apollo and Python, exhibited at the Royal Academy in 1811, is on the face of it a vision of progress and ascent. The god Apollo radiates light as he rests after killing the reptilian monster Python. This primordial beast that lived at the centre of the Earth was, in Greek mythology, slain by the god of music, healing, light. In other words this is a painting of civilization triumphing over the primitive, bestial, prehistoric past. Yet something is not quite right. Our eyes are drawn away from Apollo's blinding light, into the complex shadows where not one but many monsters can be made out. Even as the scaly coils of Python breathe their last, the sepulchral gloom in the lower right part of the painting is breeding new monsters, new attacks on sanity and civility. History here is not a confident upward progress but an endless

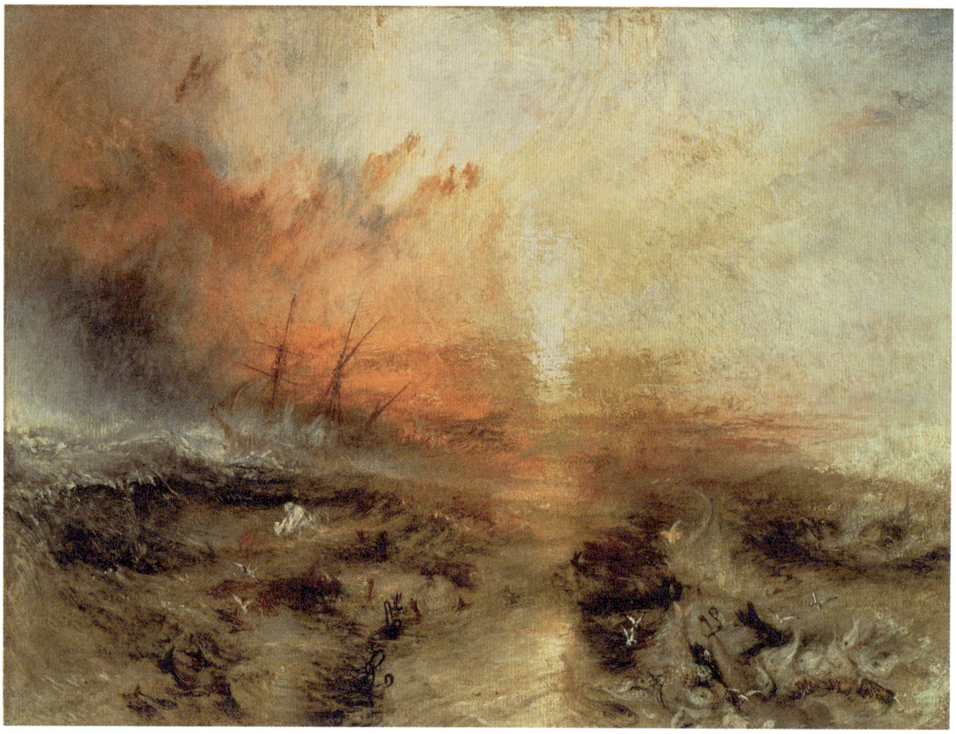

↑ J. M. W. Turner, *Slave Ship (Slavers Throwing Overboard the Dead and Dying, Typhoon Coming On)*, 1840, Oil on canvas, 90.8 × 122.6 cm (35¾ × 48¼ in.), Museum of Fine Arts, Boston

struggle against the slimy things in the corners of our minds. The primeval is always with us.

Where did Turner get such a subtle and ambitious understanding of mythology? One friend who shared his expansive interest in the ancient world was the architect Sir John Soane. They first met in 1792, and the seriousness of their intellectual dialogue is obvious from the fact that Turner imitated Soane's austerely poetic style in his own design for a Thameside villa, which the increasingly well-off artist began building the year after he painted *Apollo and Python*. In 1826, seven years after his first visit to Italy, he painted a view of the Roman forum intended for the museum Soane was creating in his house at Lincoln's Inn Fields. Soane's museum is an intricate artwork, well-loved today, that, like Turner's paintings, casts doubt on human progress. Its central space, illuminated brightly from above by a skylight, is filled with fragments of classical sculpture that seem to bear witness to the triumph of the Apollonian spirit of civilized reason. Peer down below into the crypt, and the sarcophagus of the Egyptian pharaoh Seti I lies open. Descend into the Stygian gloom and you find the 'Monk's Parlour', a suitably atmospheric setting in which to read Gothic novels. The gloom of the primeval is just as human as the brightness of civilization. Python must have its due.

Turner's most devastating vision of an unloving universe is *Slave Ship (Slavers Throwing Overboard the Dead and Dying, Typhoon Coming On)*. Here the once calm waters have turned to a seething hell. This nightmare of the high seas unveiled at the Royal Academy in 1840 looks back at a real event of the slave-trading eighteenth century when, in 1781, the captain of the slave ship *Zong* chose to throw sick and dead slaves overboard so that he could claim the insurance money. Turner depicts this as a ruthless bid to lighten the load by a slave ship fighting for survival on a tilting, slippery sea, as the white spume of a storm bursts at it out of a blood-tinged sky. A chained leg rises from the water. Hands of the doomed rise from the lurid silky surface of the Atlantic's boiling cauldron. Unearthly, perversely beautiful colours – purple, ivory, silver – twinkle around the lost souls and sharks.

Who could design this world? Turner deliberately piles up horror on horror, cruelty on cruelty, in this chilling philosophical meditation on the struggle to survive. The slaves we see drowning and being eaten alive were kidnapped, chained, held in subterranean dungeons in West African forts, then stuffed into the cargo deck of the *Zong*. Now the sailors have thrown them into the sea like so much shark bait. Yet the ship itself may not survive the storm. Turner was familiar with Théodore Géricault's *Raft of the Medusa*, which portrays people cast adrift on a raft, driven to cannibalism to survive. Here he imagines an even more pathetic extreme of human behaviour on the unforgiving sea.

It is the equivalent in painting of a confession Charles Darwin was to make in 1860:

> *But I own that I cannot see, as plainly as others do... evidence of design & beneficence on all sides of us. There seems to me too much misery in the world.*

8. The Mirror Crack'd

I didn't like British art at first. You have to get used to it...
Vincent van Gogh,
letter to Theo van Gogh, 1874

Glass Houses

In his final year, 1851, J. M. W. Turner witnessed something remarkable. He went to Kensington to see the colossal building site where a glass pavilion was being raised to house an exhibition of all the arts and industries of the modern world – a titanic display that would live up to its name, the Great Exhibition. Turner must surely have found the unique structure designed by Joseph Paxton to house this technophile jamboree entrancing, for it was the three-dimensional equivalent of his own paintings of light.

The best way to get an idea of its appearance today is to visit Kew Gardens, whose Victorian Palm House has miraculously survived when its rivals are long gone. Built in 1844 to house the tropical plants and trees that were constantly being brought back to Britain by adventurous botanists who explored the empire and beyond, seeking sensual orchids and practical crops such as the rubbery juices of rainforest trees, this is a hypnotic place. Nineteenth-century illustrations of the Crystal Palace – as Paxton's exhibition hall was to be known – cannot convey the evening sun catching its curved translucent surfaces, the endlessly changing natural light within, the unreal lightness of a cathedral of glass, that can still be enjoyed in the Palm House at Kew, where overhanging foliage adds cool caverns of shade to set off the dance of sunshine.

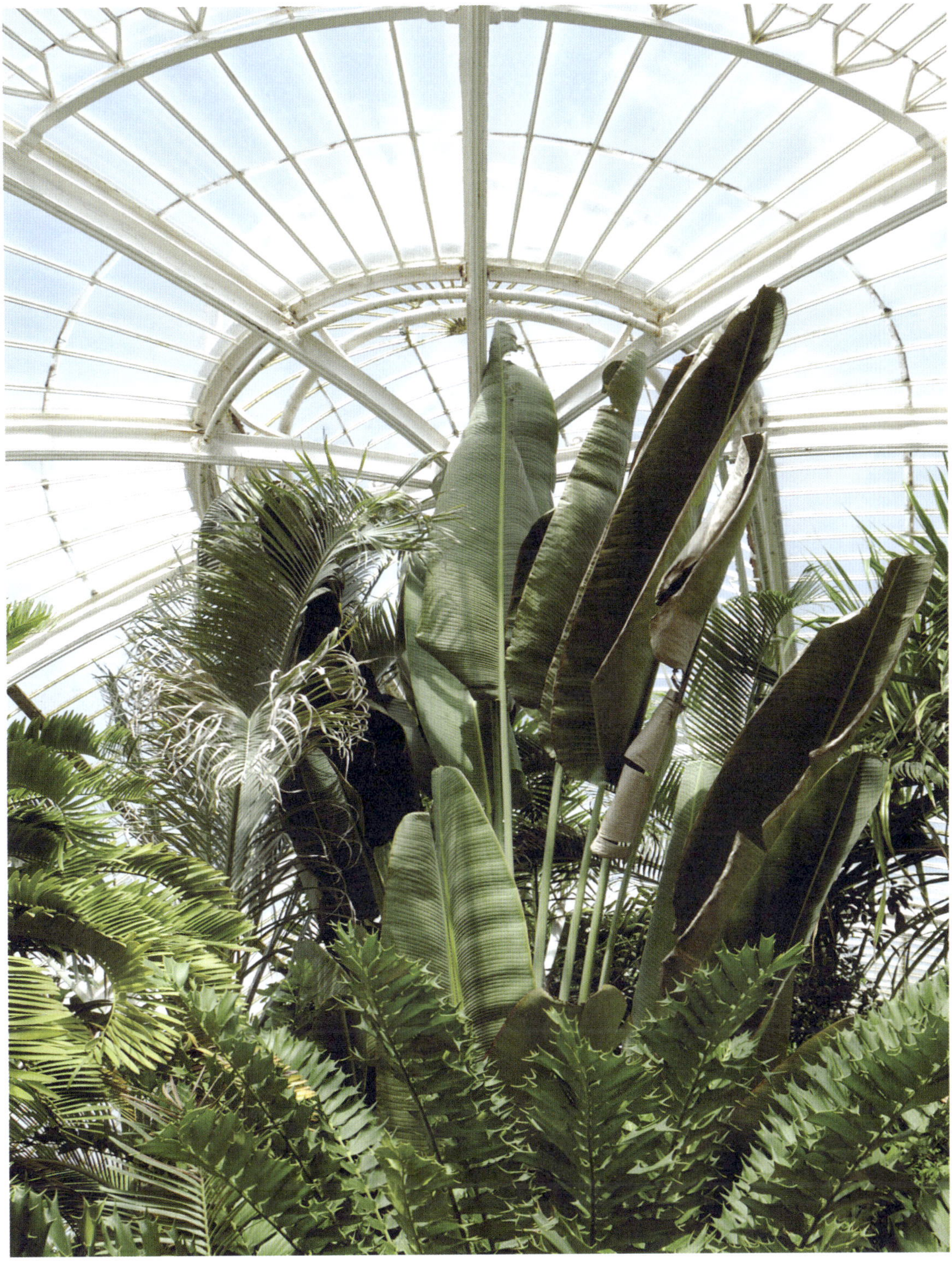

↑ Decimus Burton and Richard Turner,
Palm House, 1844
Kew Gardens, London

Glasshouses evolved fast in the age of Turner. An early example of crystal ambition was raised for the Duke of Devonshire at Chiswick House, before the Devonshires went on to commission a much bigger conservatory for the gardens of their grandest dwelling at Chatsworth House in Derbyshire. Its architect was Paxton, who created this architectural wonder as part of his duties as the duke's head gardener. When the planners of the Great Exhibition struggled to find a suitable design to house their mega-event, Paxton proposed an immense glasshouse enlarged from his Derbyshire conservatory. The development of these novel translucent structures was a case of science bringing beauty into being, for collections of exotic plants were central to Victorian natural history. One of Darwin's closest scientific friends was Joseph Hooker, who would become director of Kew. Hooker settled down to this job after a series of daring global journeys, including a botanical mission to the Himalayas, where he collected seeds of the rhododendron. Hooker's book *Rhododendrons of Sikkim-Himalaya*, published in three volumes in 1849–51, has precise yet delicate illustrations by Walter Hood Fitch that make it easy to see why Victorian Britain fell for this flower from the far-flung borders of the empire.

The scintillating garden structures out of which the Crystal Palace blossomed embodied the cutting edge of science in fabric as well as function, for here was an unapologetic architecture of the modern age, with curving walls of glass suspended on slender iron frames mirroring a new world of steam trains and boats, suspension bridges, tunnels, factories and – not least – photography.

Turner sampled this last invention near the end of his life, visiting the daguerreotype portrait photographer J. J. E. Mayall to learn more about the mysterious new scientific method of capturing light on a silvered copper plate of which he had heard. It was big of Britain's greatest painter to be interested in an invention that might make his own art obsolete. The photographic pioneer Henry Fox Talbot, for one, who set up his camera in the heart of the English landscape at picturesque Lacock Abbey in Wiltshire, saw his salt-paper and calotype (using paper coated with silver iodide) methods as replacing the artist's hand with that of nature. He emphatically entitled the book of still and silent photographs of rural England that he published in the mid-1840s *The Pencil of Nature*. The pictures within, he boasted, were 'impressed by the agency of Light alone, without any aid whatever from the artist's pencil.'

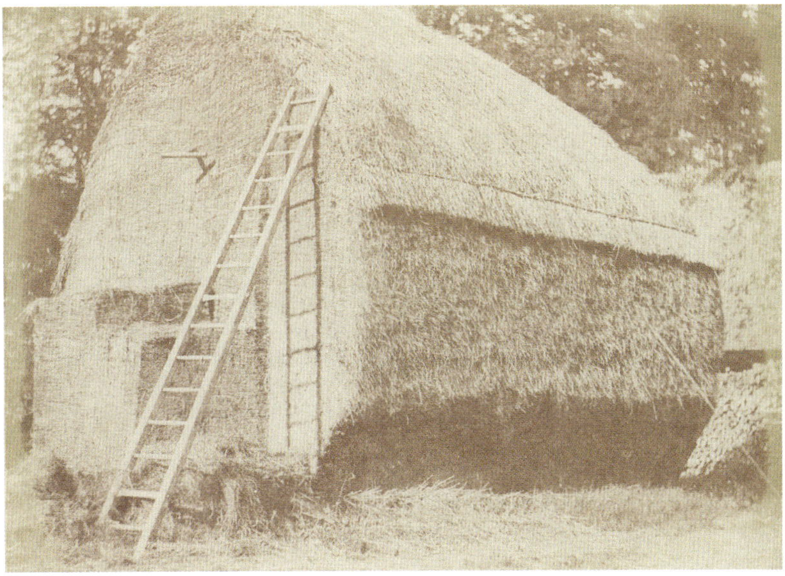

→ William Henry Fox Talbot, *The Hay Stack*, 1840, salted paper print from paper negative, 16 × 20.7 cm (6 ⅓ × 8 ⅙ in.), Metropolitan Museum of Art, New York

Turner was not afraid of this new magic. Photography was one more wonder of an age of dynamic progress driven by the application of science. For the genius of Joseph Paxton and the miracle of photography were both typical of an era when engineers and inventors created unprecedented marvels. From Thomas Telford's Pontcysyllte Aqueduct of 1805 to Isambard Kingdom Brunel's Clifton Suspension Bridge, which was begun in 1831 though not completed until the 1860s, the lifetime of Turner saw bold and often resplendent transformations of the landscape by the architecture of industrialism.

Turner had his eyes open to industry's accelerating transformations. As early as 1815, in his painting *Crossing the Brook*, he had depicted water-driven industrial workings not as scars but as embellishments to the sublime landscape of the Tamar Valley in Devon. Three decades later he painted a vision of Brunel's Great Western Railway, a canvas whose hissing, scalding celebration of the Industrial Revolution is the most ecstatic futurist manifesto ever created by a British artist.

In *Rain, Steam and Speed – The Great Western Railway* a locomotive hurtles out of empty space, as if flying towards us across the powerful brick buttresses of Maidenhead bridge. People in the wet, rainy recesses of the scene wave up at the rocketing train as if they were hailing a balloonist or a space traveller. The blaze of its fire and the black sheen of its ironwork make the train more real than the woozy world through which it moves. One could almost imagine that the swirl of rain and mist are hurtling past while the train itself stands still. Once again Turner's vision leaps forward like a locomotive into new realities, as if he were depicting relativity, a universe in which there is no stable absolute space whatsoever. 'Speed', to which his title emphatically refers, was a new thing on the Earth in 1844. No one before the nineteenth century had ever travelled faster than a horse could gallop. Turner paints not just the miracle but the strangeness of speed. The rain-filled atmosphere into which the hurtling train's steam dissolves is vague and empty, a kind of nowhere. It is as if the train's speed has torn through a veil in time and propelled it into the shapeless void of the future. Why do the people watching the train look so ethereal? They are ghosts, looking out of the stationary, rooted world of the past at a train vanishing into the unknown future.

So much was new, and so much had suddenly gone forever. The world had never before changed in a human lifetime as much as it did in that of Turner – that is, between 1775 and 1851. Britain was the furnace of this revolution in technology, powered by Newtonian science. The first experimental steam trains ran in the 1780s when he was a child; the first public railway line, the Stockton and Darlington, opened in the late 1820s. By the time he painted *Rain, Steam and Speed*, the Great Western was whizzing people to Bristol for business and pleasure. Britain was getting smaller: the sublime vistas of Snowdonia and the Lakes that he had once trekked to see were easy to get to now.

Society too had been remade. The end of the Napoleonic Wars in 1815 left unfinished business between the landowning political class and the rest of society, for which the 1832 Reform Act provided a semi-democratic release of steam. Further Reform Acts in 1867 and 1884 would widen the franchise bit by bit. Yet when Turner painted *Rain, Steam and Speed* there was no shortage of tension in an edgy, divided Britain. The Chartist movement was challenging elite complacency with its demands for working-class political representation. In 1845, a year after *Rain, Steam and Speed*, the German bourgeois Friedrich Engels published *The Condition of the Working Class in England*, based on what he had seen in Manchester while helping to run his family's mill there. It was not only revolutionists who criticized the inequalities of the world's first industrial society. The Conservative MP and author Benjamin Disraeli diagnosed a dangerous gulf between rich and poor in his 1845 novel *Sibyl, or The Two Nations*.

While such 'condition of England' novels – also being penned by Elizabeth Gaskell and, of course, Charles Dickens – pondered injustice, the Anti-Corn Law League was campaigning for a free market. Its leaders claimed that new cities such as Manchester – where the League started – were being done down by the protectionist Corn Laws, introduced in 1815 to prevent cheap foreign corn from undermining British agriculture and its ultimate beneficiaries, the landowners. These duties on imported corn kept bread prices in the cities artificially high, so the campaign against the Corn Laws united working-class radicals with middle-class free-trade evangelists. In 1846 Robert Peel, a Conservative prime minister defying his own party's perceptions of its class interests, repealed the Corn Laws in a symbolic triumph for industrial capitalism and its ideal of unrestricted commerce.

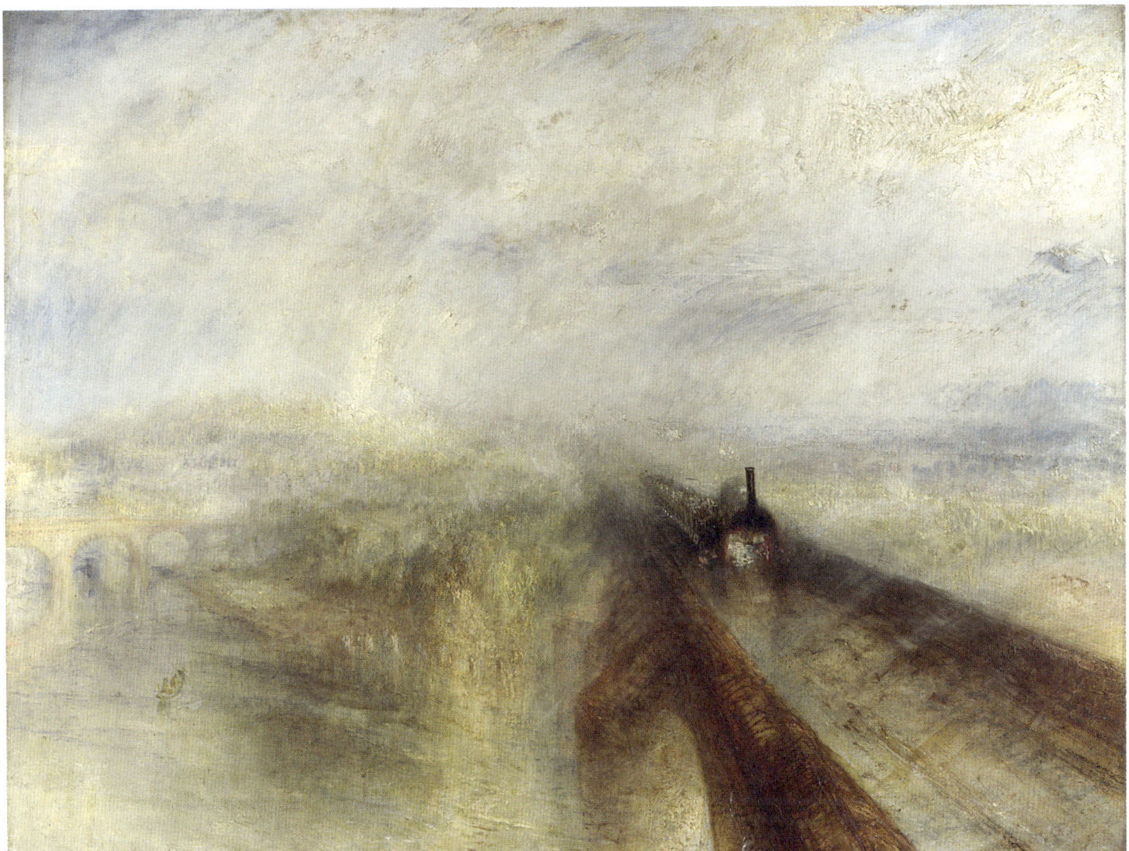

↑ J. M. W. Turner, *Rain, Steam and Speed – The Great Western Railway*, 1844, oil on canvas, 91 × 121.8 cm (35⅘ × 48 in.), National Gallery, London

With the classes of the new Britain consciously competing for power in this way, to a degree that persuaded Engels and his refugee friend Karl Marx that all nations would soon succumb to similar struggles, it might seem the Crystal Palace projected an image of a society about to shatter into fragments under its own internal contradictions.

The Victorian mind certainly seems to be cracking and splintering in the art of John Martin. His 1852 painting *The Destruction of Sodom and Gomorrah* is a stupendous vision of God's wrath descending on the cities of the sinful in the shape of a seeping veil of red smoke and yellow flame that sucks the wicked into its unimaginably hot vortex. Like the furnaces of an ironworks or a locomotive's blazing coals, this sublime blast from heaven fills the mind with terrible delight. Martin is a true painter. The fire that falls on Sodom shares the abstract freedom of late Turner in its great smear of crimson, pink and gold.

Yet far from being a pessimistic prophet of Victorian Britain's doom, Martin was at the cutting edge of its avant-garde of engineers and inventors. He claimed he dedicated at least two thirds of his energy to

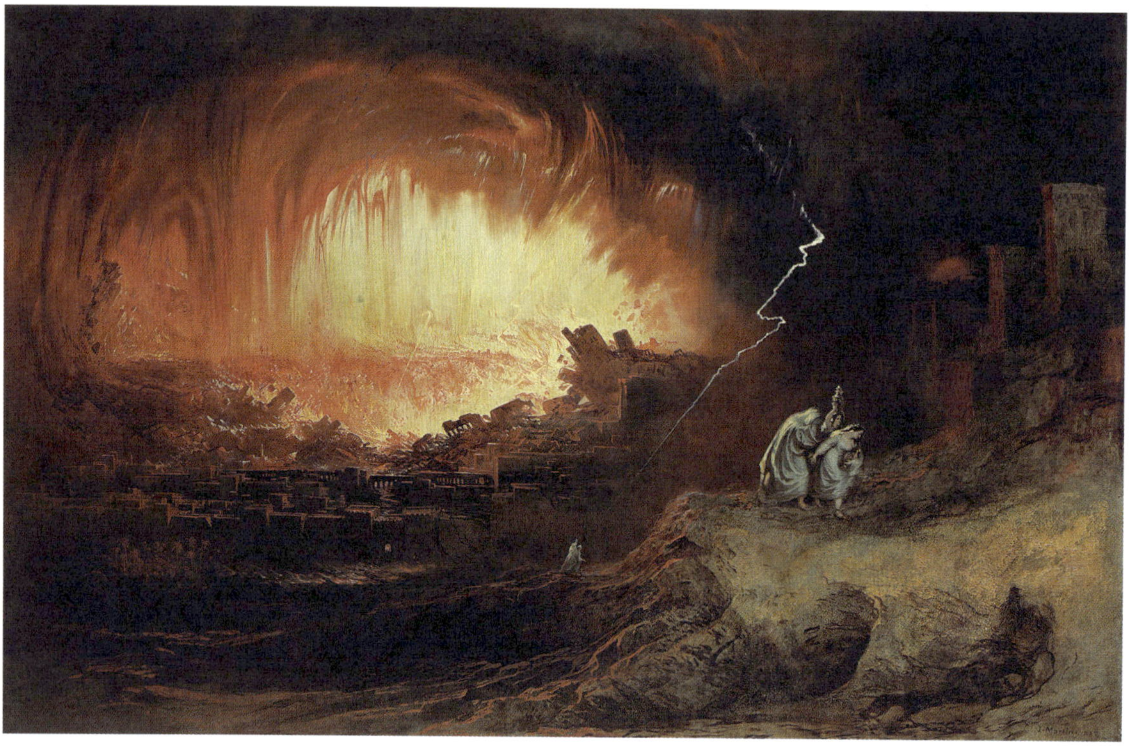

↑ John Martin, *The Destruction of Sodom and Gomorrah*, 1852, oil on canvas, 136.3 × 212.3 cm (53⅔ × 83⅗ in.), Laing Art Gallery, Newcastle

engineering projects – even though they tragically came to nothing. His frenetic blueprints for a more modern world included a circular railway designed to speed people around London and an – urgent – scheme to give the capital a healthier water supply. In 1836 Martin's friend Turner sat on a committee to assess the visionary inventor's plan to give London decent water. It impressed the eminent gathering but never came to fruition. Martin was respected. Brunel took him seriously enough to invite him to witness a time trial on the Great Western Railway – did he describe this exciting spectacle of steam and speed to Turner? One admirer of Martin's mixture of artistic imagination and scientific curiosity was the palaeontological pioneer Gideon Mantell, who commissioned him to depict the prehistoric world inhabited by the dinosaur *Iguanodon* as a frontispiece to his 1838 book *The Wonders of Geology*. Prehistory was a strange realm where empiricism needed fantasy to help it put flesh on its fossilized bones. Martin's watercolour design for Mantell's book is called *The Country of the Iguanadon*. It deploys his instinct for the sublime and marvellous to create a majestically visceral drama of dinosaurs fighting tooth and claw in a primeval landscape.

It was typical of the entrepreneurial Martin that he showed his apocalyptic paintings at the Great Exhibition in 1851, among delights of art and industry that ranged from bark canoes to Colt revolvers. Oil paintings hung next to Native American masks above Ottoman rugs, as they might in an antique shop. The India section included, naturally, a stuffed elephant. Endless curiosities were packed together like desirable goods in a vast emporium – appropriately, since this was a celebration of global commerce and its domination by the British Empire.

Looking at images of polite crowds enjoying this cornucopian department store of an exhibition, it is apparent that Britain had not been blown apart by class conflict after all. No Chartists threw stones at the Crystal Palace. In 1848, revolution had swept across continental Europe – but Britain was unshaken. London became a refuge for revolutionaries like Marx who fled their countries after the Springtime of the Peoples faded. Victorianism was suddenly triumphant, the power and wealth of Britannia universally acknowledged, as the trade cycle turned from the slump of 1847–48 to a bullish boom that started in 1850. British cotton, already a motor of growth, entered a golden age. Employees in this key industry were to double in the 1850s. The age of capital and of the world's most advanced capitalist economy had well and truly arrived.

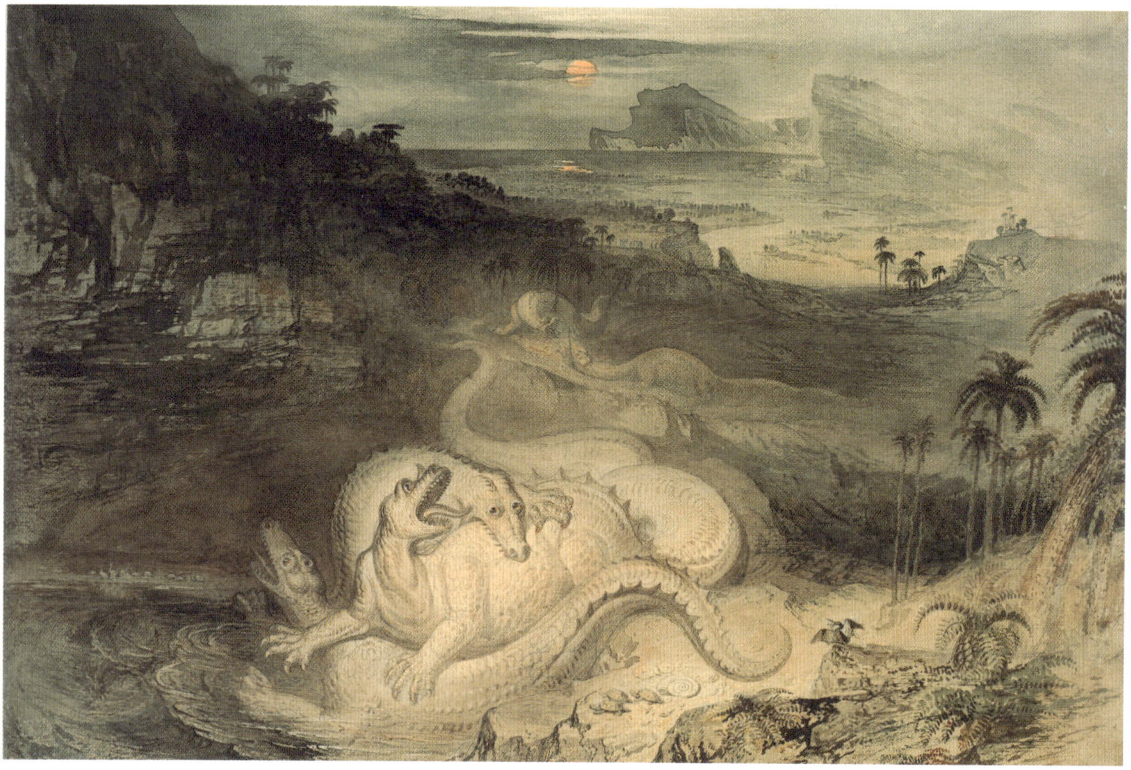

↑ John Martin, *The Country of the Iguanadon*, 1837, watercolour on paper, 30.2 × 42.6 cm (11 ⅝ × 16 ¾ in.), Museum of New Zealand Te Papa Tongarewa, Wellington, New Zealand

For Turner, who died at the end of 1851, with his secret companion Sophia Booth at his side, and Martin, who like him was born in the eighteenth century and would die in 1854, the dawn of the Victorian age had been a rollicking train ride into the future, head-spinning but also thrilling. The Crystal Palace was a glittering consummation of the belief in science held by these children of the Enlightenment. If we could only look up from its cluttered stands to see the sun glint on its glass roof we might be able to free ourselves from the condescension of posterity and recognize why old man Turner needed to drag himself along to see it.

Yet the modernity of Paxton's Crystal Palace did not foretell Britain's cultural future at all. The Great Exhibition was a brash high-water mark of raw confidence in technology that would soon become a byword for bad taste. Its steel and glass optimism was not to be repeated. It would take American, Austrian, German and Italian architects at the start of the twentieth century to once again celebrate the industrial world. The death of Turner in the very year of this precociously modern occasion was appropriate, for nineteenth-century Britain would not produce another artist so alive to the new. Nor would it produce a painter half so good.

The world's first industrial society was, inevitably, the first to see the dark side of being modern. Black smoke and stinking slums haunted the Victorian imagination. Sensitive souls turned away, to dream of a green past. Art closed its eyes to science and all the ugliness it was making.

Gothic Nature

The shape of Britain's artistic future was not twinkling above the heads of the more than six million people who visited the Great Exhibition but was on view in a display that, amid all the products of industry, proposed an artistic return to the age of monks and nuns, knights and serfs.

In this part of the Crystal Place straight-limbed statues in carved Gothic niches towered over their bonneted admirers. An entire cathedral altar glowed with yellow gilding and crimson hangings. Gold and silver church vessels were displayed in a glass case with a spire-like summit, while beyond it soared an actual spire, encrusted with knobbly detail, rising past the upper galleries towards the glass sky.

The Medieval Court expressed the vision of its curator, Augustus Welby Pugin, the most influential architect of the Victorian age, whose passionate assimilation of the Gothic style of the fourteenth century would inspire many variations up to the century's end. Flying buttresses, gargoyles, pointy arches and bunched pilasters were back. The scale and ambition of Victorian Gothic dwarfed precedents like Strawberry Hill and Soane's crypt. From the medievalist space rocket that is the Scott Monument in Edinburgh to the still more stupendous Albert Memorial in Kensington, it made its extravagant and wilful mark on Britain.

Pugin shaped the most extreme Gothic vision of all at the very heart of the British Empire. The old Houses of Parliament burned to the ground in 1834, giving Turner a terrific chance to paint reflections of apocalyptic fire in the Thames. It was Pugin who, as deputy to the more conventional senior architect Charles Barry, ensured that it became an immense accumulation of intricate medieval touches. He also expressed his romantic dream of renewal in evocative pieces of furniture and sacred sculptures.

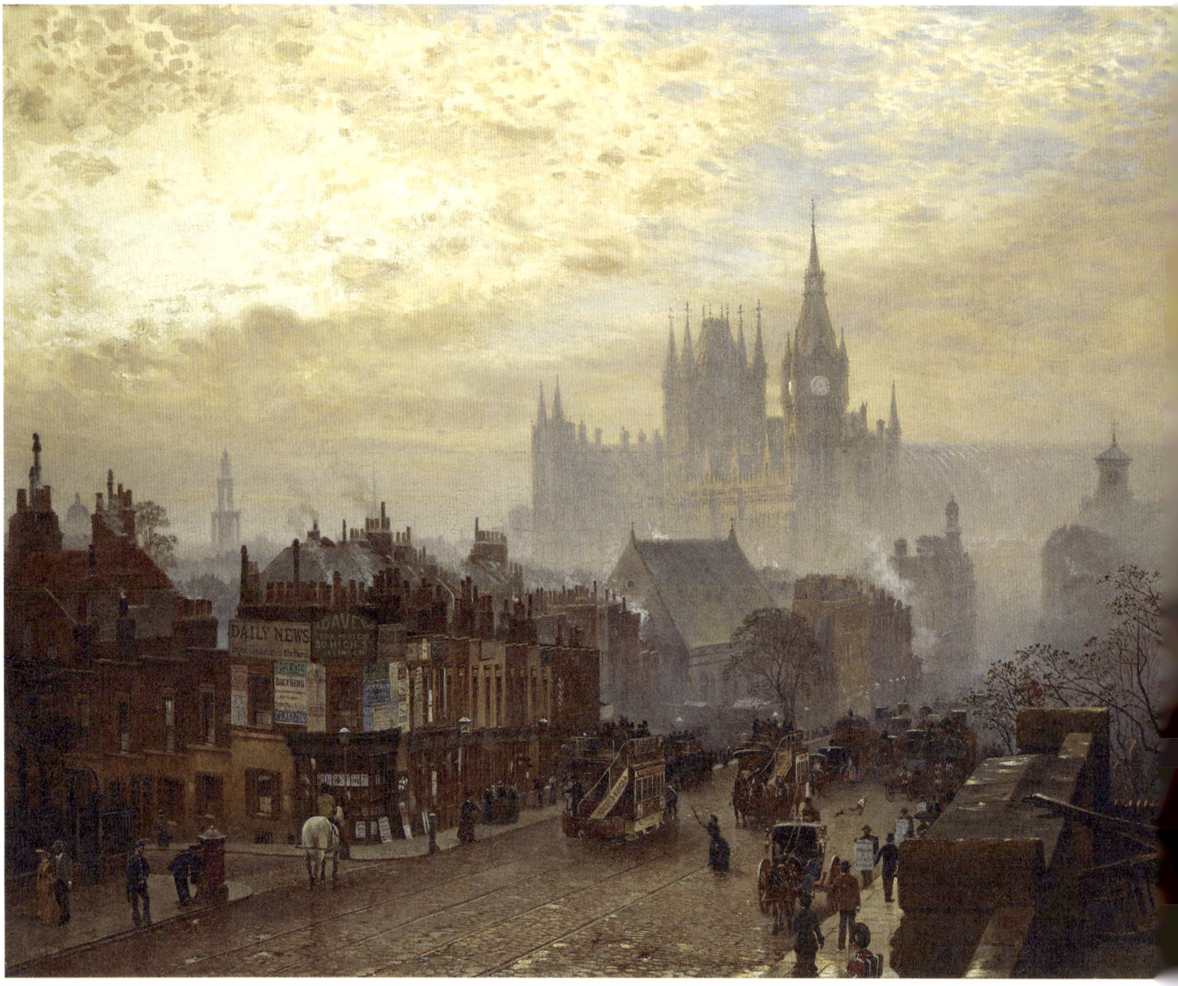

The Gothic was not just a style for Pugin but an expression of his Catholic faith – more than that, a way to recapture Britain for his faith. He was trying, in a rapidly modernizing society, to revive fourteenth-century Christendom.

The effort killed him. The Medieval Court at the Great Exhibition was Pugin's finest hour. Exhausted and overwrought, in 1852 he had a mental breakdown and was incarcerated for a time in Bedlam. By the autumn of that year he was dead, at 40.

Why did the Gothic style so obsess and delight Victorian Britain? In the year Pugin died, Karl Marx made the striking observation, in his essay 'The Eighteenth Brumaire of Louis Napoleon', that it is

↑ John O'Connor, *From Pentonville Road Looking West: Evening*, 1884, oil on canvas, 32 × 19 cm (11 5⁄8 × 7 1⁄2 in.), Museum of London, London

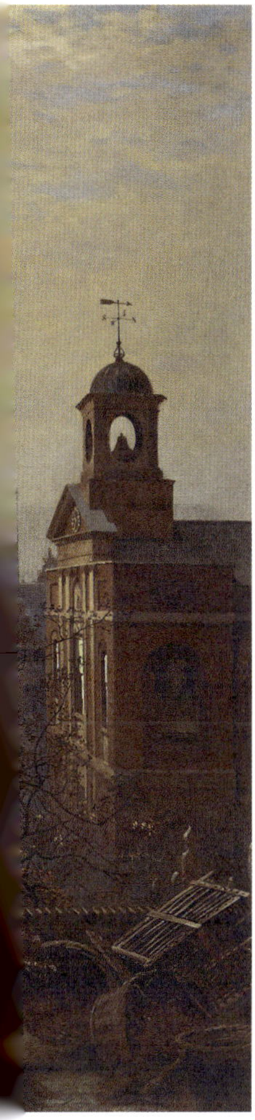

precisely when people are being hurtled fastest into the future that they borrow most brazenly from the past:

> *The tradition of all dead generations weighs like a nightmare on the brains of the living. And just as they seem to be occupied with revolutionizing themselves and things, creating something that did not exist before, precisely in such epochs of revolutionary crisis they anxiously conjure up the spirits of the past to their service, borrowing from them names, battle slogans, and costumes in order to present this new scene in world history in time-honoured disguise and borrowed language.*

Nineteenth-century Britain may not have produced the kind of revolution Marx predicted, but it was speeding like Turner's train away from all known human customs and traditional ways. It is almost comically apparent how Gothic architecture swathed the new in the past. Was it essentially an attempt to romanticize and decorate the brutality of industrialism? That certainly might seem to be what is going on at London's St Pancras railway station, where in John O'Connor's 1884 view of it from Pentonville Road, the Grand Midland Hotel sprouts up gratuitously like a fifteenth-century Flemish palace from an iron and glass hall whose shameful practicality it gloriously obscures.

That is one way of seeing it. Yet as the successful reawakening of St Pancras in the twenty-first century proved, Victorian Gothic has strengths that have outlived the nineteenth century. Once again the forceful mind of John Ruskin intrudes. In 1851, the year Pugin created his Gothic installation in the Crystal Palace, Ruskin published the first volume of an enthusiastic exploration of the 'grey, shadowy, many-pinnacled image of the Gothic within us'.

Ruskin's *The Stones of Venice* is both a highly opinionated guide to an Italian city to which, in the steam age, more and more people could travel, and a manifesto for the Gothic revival. It is an edgy, subversive hymn to primitivism that anticipates some of the most radical impulses of twentieth-century art. For Ruskin embraces what he calls the 'savage' nature of medieval architecture, accepting that it:

> *...is rude and wild: but it is not true, that, for this reason, we are to condemn it, or despise. Far otherwise: I believe it is in this very character that it deserves our profoundest reverence.*

Not only is the spirit of Gothic savage, irrational and disordered – the work of a 'Disturbed Imagination', even, says Ruskin, as if portraying both himself and Pugin – but it has a raw and vital sense of the natural world. For Ruskin this is crucial. He has not forgotten his belief that art must embrace nature's wonder. The title of *The Stones of Venice* is not casually chosen. This is a book that bulges with geology. Mountains and glaciers glower and rumble through it. When theorizing the essence of the Gothic style, Ruskin even compares himself with a scientist, using chemicals to purify a mineral.

Gothic buildings emulate the wildness and scale of nature itself. Their abundance is organic. We can see this, even without Ruskin to tell us. That is what makes Victorian Gothic so pleasurable. It brings a welcome unweeded oasis into the cities where it still stands. But what side does it take in the great argument over the laws of nature and their divinity, or lack of it, that boiled to a head when Darwin published *On the Origin of Species* in 1859?

The twisted spirit of the Gothic Revival is entwined with the tendrils of a period perplexed and gripped by the tree of life. It longs for a nature in which God's hand will be made visible again. At a time of doubt, it aches for the age of the triumphant church. As such it is the expression of a split in Victorian culture not so much between art and science as between Godly versus Darwinian science.

It took a Victorian scientist who was just as brooding and intense as any prophet of the Gothic Revival to weaponize this style in a last-stand war against evolution.

When the Great Exhibition ended, the Crystal Palace was left empty in Kensington Gardens. It was too beautiful to simply be demolished. Instead it was carefully disassembled and re-erected on top of a hill in Sydenham in South London, where it became the crowning glory of a winding park. That glowering creationist authority on dinosaurs, Richard Owen, had an inspired idea to add to the entertainments of this green space. Under his direction and according to the reconstructions of ancient reptiles pioneered by Mantell and himself, the sculptor Benjamin Waterhouse Hawkins created the first ever full-scale replicas of dinosaurs. These Victorian beasts, which still crawl over the lake islands of Crystal Palace Park long after the glass building itself has gone – it burned down in 1936 – are made of concrete with an audacity that blends science, art and the ingenuity of the Industrial Revolution. Like the deep railway cutting where trains to the park stop, they communicate the grandeur of the first industrial age. A massive *Iguanodon* standing heavily on all fours has a spike on its nose like a rhino: in modern reconstructions this has become a thumblike claw. *Iguanodons* themselves are today pictured as bipedal, as is *Megalosaurus*, which in 1852 Dickens imagined hulking on all fours through London:

> *As much mud in the streets, as if the waters had but newly retired from the face of the earth, and it would not be wonderful to meet a Megalosaurus, forty feet long or so, waddling like an elephantine lizard up Holborn Hill.*

The *Megalosaurus* of *Bleak House* invades Holborn at the very moment Hawkins was building his concrete recreation of it in the South London park.

One advantage of depicting dinosaurs as gigantic 'waddling' lizards with immense bellies was that Owen was able to preside over a banquet inside the mould used to create the *Iguanodon* at New Year, 1853. Hawkins had faithfully set his image of dinosaurs into concrete. The dinner in the *Iguanodon* was a sensational news story, the inanimate menagerie a great success. Yet this was just the beginning of Owen's instinct for fusing science and art.

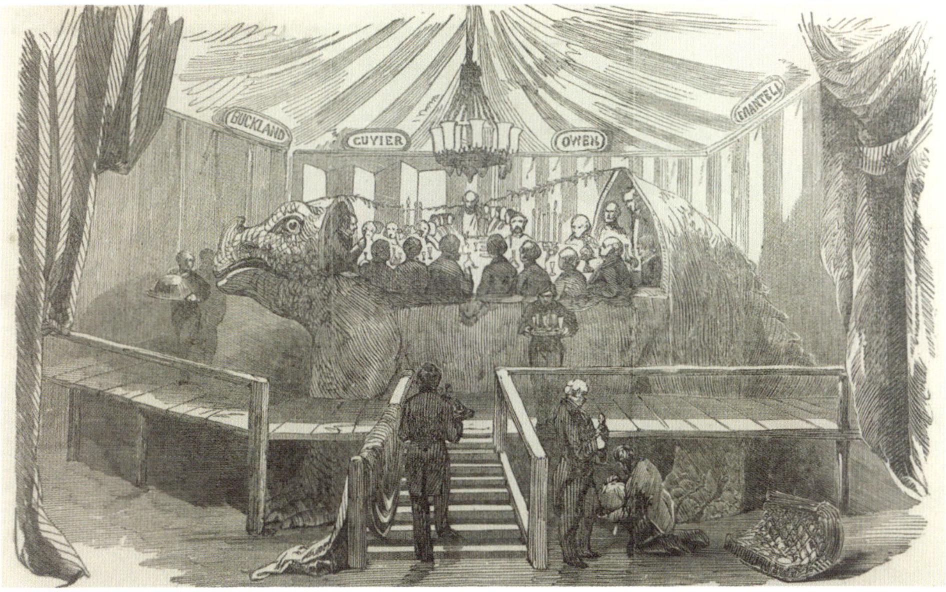

↑ Wood engraving from the *Illustrated London News*, 7 January 1854, showing 'Dinner in the Iguanodon Model, at the Crystal Palace, Sydenham', British Library, London

In 1856 he took over the natural history collections of the British Museum, and immediately began campaigning for them to be rehoused in a specialist museum of natural history. Paris, as we have seen, already had such a museum. At the British Museum, specimens amassed since the time of its benefactor, Hans Sloane, looked like leftovers from an archaic cabinet of curiosities. It was not good science or good museology. Owen's eye for display saw a vision of a great new museum that would show the wonders of nature with real beauty and magic – a veritable 'cathedral of nature'.

That religious image was not chosen lightly. When *On the Origin of Species* appeared in print Owen became stridently involved in the controversy over Darwin's devastatingly patient, richly researched masterpiece. He got embroiled in a fierce dispute about the relationship between human and ape brains with T. H. Huxley, 'Darwin's bulldog', who vowed that 'before I have done with that mendacious humbug I will nail him out, like a kite to a barn door, an example to all evil doers'.

Mendacious humbug he may have been, but Owen was also a champion of popular science who lived to see his greatest creation, the Natural History Museum in South Kensington, open to the public in 1881. It was, and is, not only a treasure house of science but also an architectural and artistic masterpiece that truly resembles a medieval cathedral.

Gargoyles of pterosaurs squat on its façade. In the lofty central hall, monkeys crawl over columns and arches. There is a vertigo-inducing bridge and galleries, soaring vistas, stained-glass windows – everything Ruskin or Pugin could demand of a Gothic building, although with semicircular arches that give it a Romanesque twist. In fact Ruskin had anticipated the idea of a medievalist science museum when he advised on the decoration of the Oxford University Museum of Natural History in the 1850s. Oxford's collections of fossils and stuffed fauna were housed in a building inspired, under Ruskin's watchful eye, by early French Gothic monasteries.

The Natural History Museum takes Oxford's Ruskinian ethos to ecstatic extremes in a vast and complex image of nature's superabundance. Its designer, Alfred Waterhouse, used terracotta to create its many moulded creatures, allowing for their replacement with fresh copies. These playful animal portraits are framed by the grace of arches and columns in a way that stresses the interconnectedness of life. The great regular medievalist structure of the main hall embodies

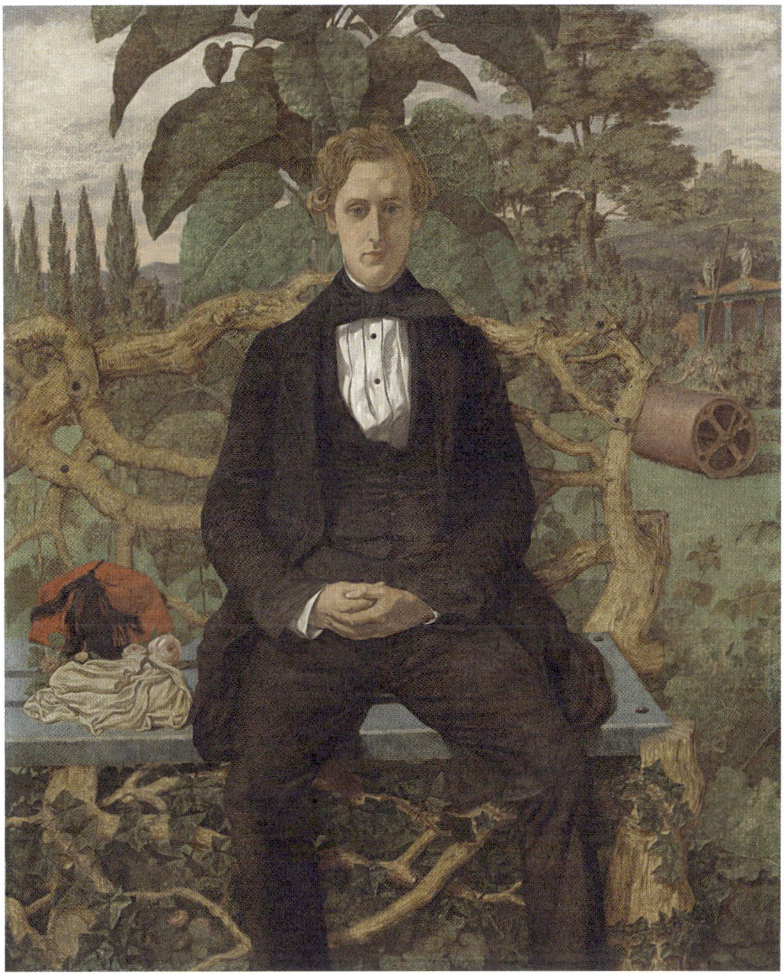

→ Richard Dadd, *Portrait of a Young Man*, 1853, oil on canvas, 60.6 × 50 cm (23 5⁄8 × 19 2⁄3 in.), Tate

the principle of natural history itself, that the infinite variety of nature can be comprehended and its hidden patterns discovered. Owen's creationist intentions no longer seem to matter to the twenty-first century crowds delighting in the museum. Yet it is a monument to the anguished paroxysms of the Victorian mind. For what could be stranger and more perverse than a museum of science covered in gargoyles?

The art of Richard Dadd, perhaps.

The natural world looked chaotic and sinful from Bedlam – the Bethlehem Royal Hospital – whose maltreatment of patients Hogarth had once satirized. Bedlam was still Britain's leading mental hospital and it was where the painter Richard Dadd was confined after murdering his father in 1843. Dadd thought his father was the devil, so he stabbed him on a country path near their Kent home. He had been a highly promising young artist with a penchant for Arab scenes until, on his way back from a trip to Egypt, Syria and Turkey, he started hearing the voices of ancient Egyptian gods who warned him of the Pope's enmity.

After being caught and judged insane, Dadd spent the rest of his life in Bedlam and later Broadmoor, where he died in 1886. It is unlikely that he followed the news about evolution. In fact his doctors reported that he never regained much intellectual coherence at all. Yet in the paintings his kindly carers encouraged him to make – contrary to the cliched image of the cruel Victorian asylum – he deliriously explores the very themes of order and disorder in nature that saner people were debating in packed meetings. The subject of his 1853 painting *Portrait of a Young Man*, perhaps a member of staff at Bedlam, sits on a Gothic garden seat whose tangled wooden structure resembles the roots of a deranged tree of life. A giant tropical leaf seems to burst out of his head. Nature is disturbingly lavish in this vision of Bedlam's garden. The young man in his crumpled suit does not look too healthy either. A heavy iron roller on the lawn suggests an attempt at order yet also the possibility of crushing violence.

Dadd worked on his most ambitious painting, *The Fairy Feller's Master-Stroke*, in Bedlam from 1855 to 1864 as the implications of evolution were unravelled outside the hospital walls. Like Darwin peering closely at his garden to see the tiny yet complex lives of earthworms, or, chart the mortality levels among garden birds that looked so decorative to believers in intelligent design, this painting enters a hidden nature of enlarged secrets. Fairies move among giant daisies. Acorns dwarf them. Dadd's microscopic exactitude makes this monstrous garden uncannily real as well as unmistakably insane.

The pressures on Victorian minds made madness so immediate that it became a deliberately feigned, comically hallucinatory state in the curiouser and curiouser genre of Nonsense. A brooding, intelligent baboon gazes out of John Tenniel's picture of the animals waiting for Alice to give them prizes after taking place in the Caucus Race in Lewis Carroll's *Alice's Adventures in Wonderland*. Carroll sketched his own drawings in the manuscript of his discombobulating nonsense masterpiece, but when it was published in 1865 its illustrations were by the brilliant *Punch* cartoonist Tenniel. It seems to be Tenniel who added the slightly sinister allusion to an ape, for the text only specifies crabs and various birds. Yet there is something drolly anti-Darwinian about

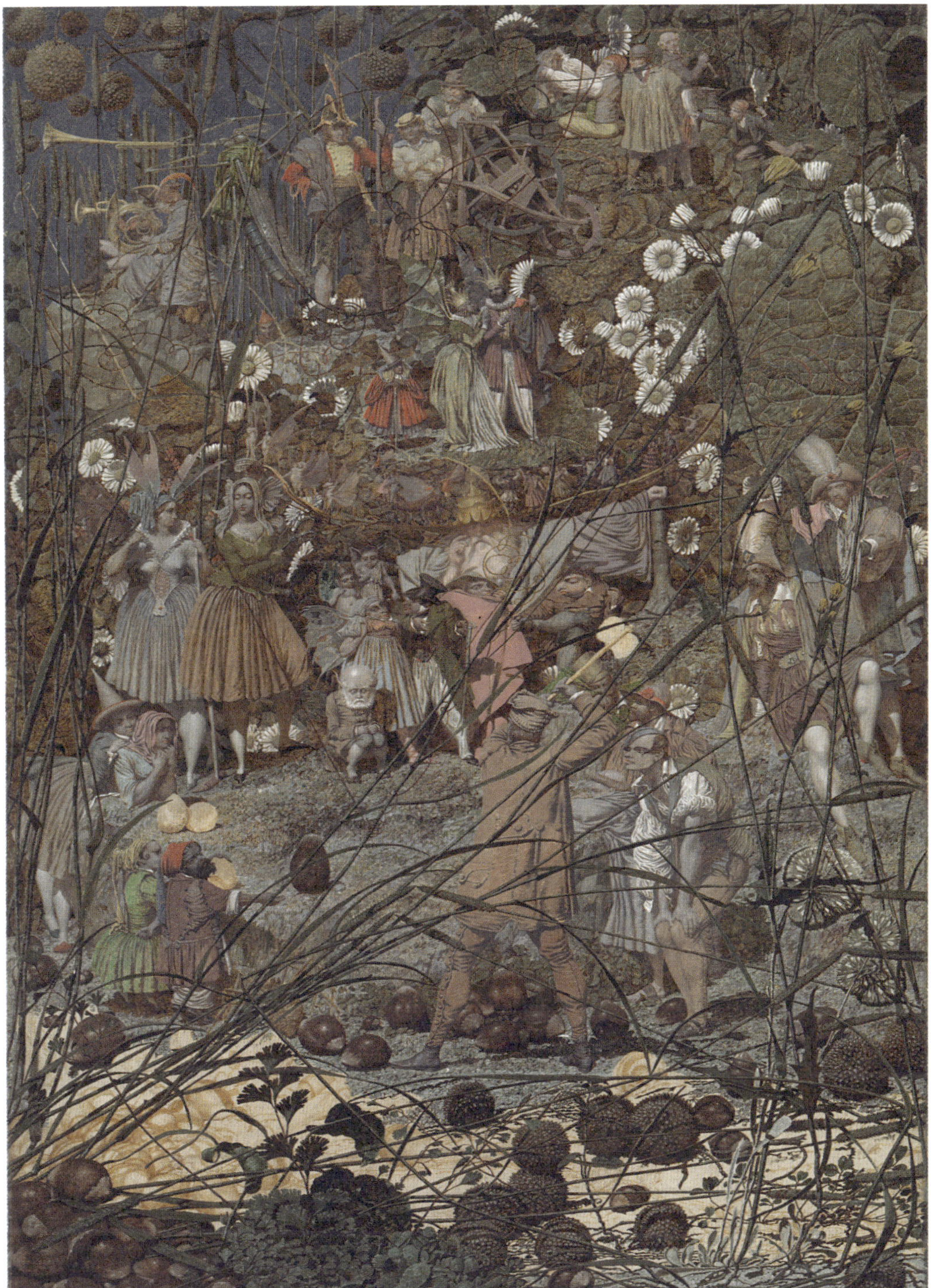

↑ Richard Dadd, *The Fairy Feller's Master-Stroke*, 1855–64, oil on canvas, 54 × 39.4 cm (21¼ × 15½ in.), Tate

the Caucus Race. Darwin's concept of natural selection saw life as a struggle to survive in which arbitrary birth mutations can prove useful and be passed on if they give competitive advantages. Yet the animals who run the Caucus Race refuse the very idea of competition and insist they should be rewarded equally. The Dodo pronounces: '*Everybody* has won, and all must have prizes.'

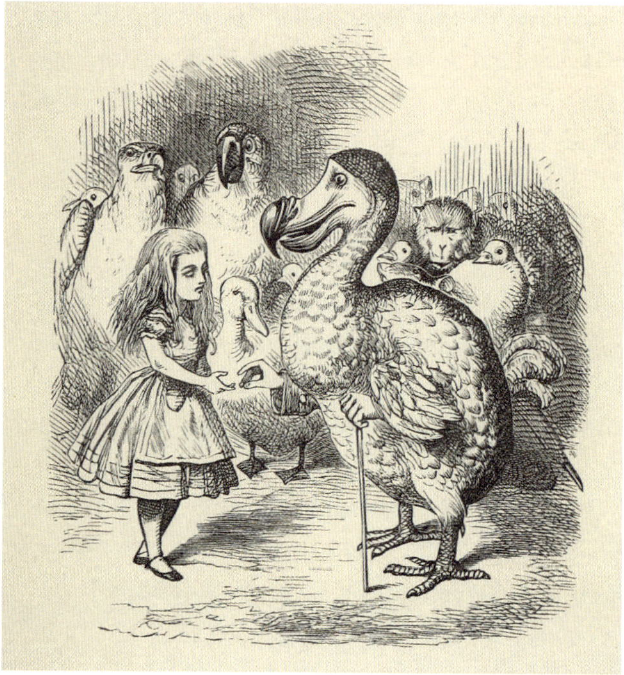

This is a rich joke on the tangled arguments of the Victorian age – political, economic, moral as well as scientific – but in Tenniel's image it gets an unmistakable evolutionary twist from the presence of a human-looking ape. And at the heart of his picture is the Dodo, an extinct species that *Alice in Wonderland* was to make just as famous as those other great Victorian icons of evolution, the dinosaurs.

The Oxford University Museum of Natural History possessed, and still does, a rare, near-complete skeleton of a dodo. Oxford also inherited, from the collection of curiosities of the seventeenth-century gardener John Tradescant that was the seed of its Ashmolean Museum, a painting by the Dutch Golden Age artist Roelant Savery that appeared to portray a dodo from life. European visitors to Mauritius had made this island bird extinct before 1700, so Savery's painting and the Oxford bones were valuable fragments of evidence.

Lewis Carroll, aka the Reverend Charles Dodgson, lecturer in mathematics and fellow of Christ Church, Oxford, perhaps took direct inspiration from the university's dodo relics. It is obvious anyway that Tenniel has studied the Savery painting. But while carefully reproducing what was thought to be the real appearance of the dodo, he connects this near-mythic beast with Gothic sculpture, giving it spiky feathers that seem carved out of stone, like the stylized plumage of a heraldic beast. It is an image of unchanging archaism and medievalist pomposity: an officious animal that does not even know it is extinct.

Carroll's fellow inventor of nonsense, Edward Lear, needed no illustrator, for he was himself a talented artist. Lear's early art was aimed squarely at lovers of science and nature. He started out as a

↑ John Tenniel, 'Alice and the Dodo with other animals looking on', from *Alice's Adventures in Wonderland* by Lewis Carroll, 1865, Boston Public Library

teenager sketching exotic birds at London Zoo, and in 1832 published an ambitious work of visual natural history called *Illustrations of the Family of Psittacidae*, a set of 12 prints of opulently coloured parrots. It was clearly an attempt to emulate the American bird artist John James Audubon, and got him patronage and commissions in the same scientific vein until failing eyesight forced him to give up the precision of natural history to travel, paint, and pen limericks.

In 1871, the year that Darwin published his analysis of human evolution, *The Descent of Man*, Lear brought out *Flora Nonsensica*, a series of drawings of made-up plants with Latin names that parody Linnaean classification. The blooms of Manypeeplia Upsidownia are, as its name specifies, many people hanging upside down from its sagging stalk. Cockatooca Superba is a plant with the head of a cockatoo.

Yet the most influential Victorian art movement was a self-proclaimed Gothic revival in painting that started in 1848, when a group of young artists led by John Everett Millais, Dante Gabriel Rossetti and William Holman Hunt formed the Pre-Raphaelite Brotherhood. As their name announced, they proposed to turn the clock back to a time before the birth of the Renaissance master Raphael – that is, to before 1483. That meant shedding all false sophistication to paint with a primitive authenticity and innocent faith.

↓ Edward Lear, 'Manypeeplia Upsidownia', from Lear's *Flora Nonsensica*, 1871, glass lantern slide, 8.25 x 10.16 cm (3 ¼ x 4 in.), Library of Congress

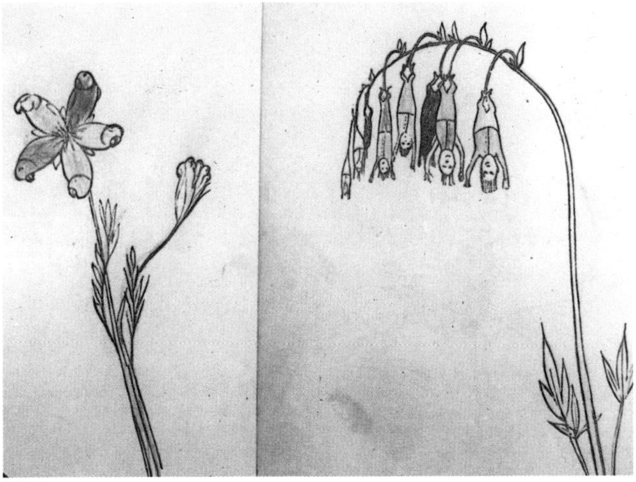

Hunt was by far the most faithful to this ideal. His 1852 painting *Our English Coasts* is like a stained-glass window, glowing with sacred light, lurid with mystic fire. Who made the sea so brilliantly turquoise, the grass so brightly emerald? A loving God. Compelled by medievalism to push his poesy over the edge from subtle spirituality to ludicrous allegory, Hunt dwells melodramatically on a flock of sheep who have strayed from the Lord their shepherd towards the abyss. Yet the colour of the sea, the precariousness of the cliff and even descendants of the sheep can still be found on the coast near Hastings where he set this memorable landscape. It is at once empirical and holy.

The same bizarre mixture of acute observation and symbolic revelation casts a ghastly atmosphere over his masterpiece *The Scapegoat*. Executed between 1854 and 1856, in the painting God's golden light catches compassionately in the sleek hairs of a poor creature that has been cast out as the bearer of a community's sins. It stands there dumbly stoic, yet is there a reprobate glint in its eye? The purple mountains, yellow sky and barren white salty desert are images not of the outer world but of inner suffering.

The Scapegoat looks forward to the art of the Norwegian Modernist Edvard Munch, whose 1893 painting *The Scream* similarly finds echoes of inner angst in a morbid vision of nature. Both paintings match Ruskin's description of the 'grey, shadowy, many-pinnacled image of the Gothic within us'. At its most imaginative, Pre-Raphaelitism was one of the first European modern movements, insisting on the power of internal vision years ahead of the subjective Symbolist art of Munch, Odilon Redon and Gustave Moreau. In his poignant and troubling 1854–56 painting *The Blind Girl*, for instance, Millais powerfully contrasts the detailed, exact landscape we look at with the unknowable mindscape of the blind young homeless woman who casts her head back as if in ecstatic vision. We see the rainbow, a miraculous visitation in the sky. She apprehends – perhaps – an equivalent inner revelation.

The Blind Girl creates a complete mystic landscape, from the birds in the field – recalling Christ's words in Matthew 6:26 – to the echo of Italian paintings of the Madonna in the way the girl's head is piously covered. Yet like *Our English Coasts* and *The Scapegoat* it was painted in the 1850s just a few years before the publication of *On the Origin of Species*. Evolution, as we've seen, was already in the air, the

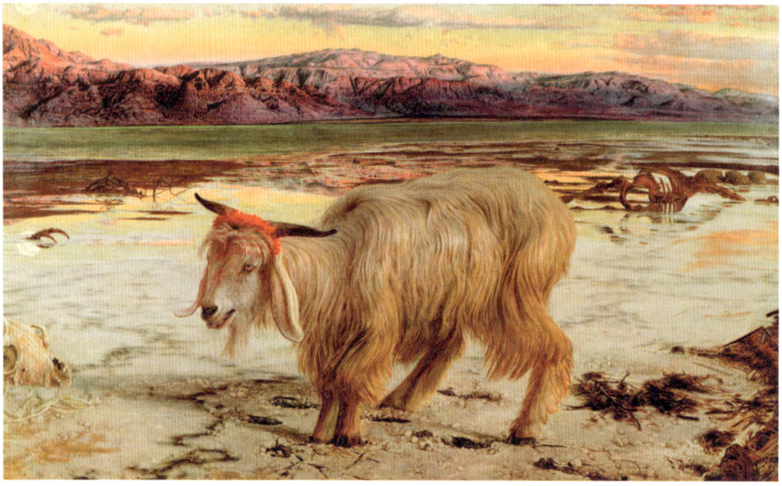

↑ William Holman Hunt, *The Scapegoat*, 1854–56, oil on canvas, 86.5 × 139.8 cm (34 × 55 in.), Lady Lever Art Gallery, Port Sunlight, National Museums Liverpool

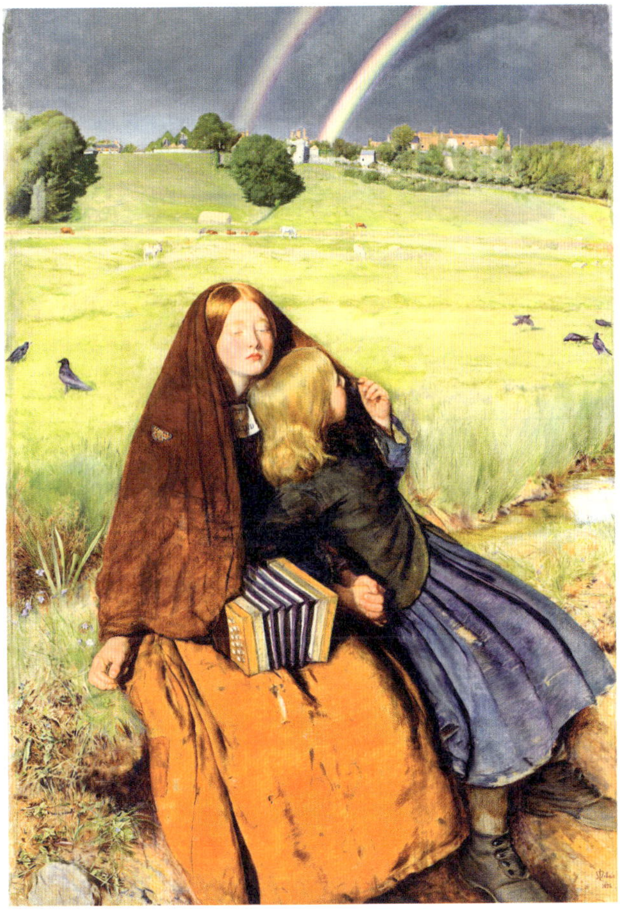

↑ John Everett Millais, *The Blind Girl*, 1854–56, oil on canvas, 81 × 62 cm (31⅚ × 24⅖ in.), Birmingham Museums and Art Gallery

hammers of the geologists knocking loudly at the door of faith's decaying church. It marks a caesura in the intertwined story of British art and science that just when scientific evidence was about to deliver its most powerful blow to religion, the most avant-garde artists of the day were reasserting a Christian aesthetic in which nature overflows with sacred symbols. The effect was not so much to answer Darwin as to make art and science alien to one another.

It also pitted art against industry and modernity. Long gone were the days when Wright of Derby had hobnobbed with Midlands industrialists and shared their Enlightenment faith in humanities' progress through technological improvement. The Gothic spirit in Victorian art is in flight from the industrial age and angry at its injustices. Where have the vagrant sisters in *The Blind Girl* wandered from? Perhaps they come from the slums of London or Manchester, trekking in their rags in search of relief from the horrors of urban poverty. Here in the countryside, it seems, they may find God's charity. The village on the horizon is marked out by His rainbow as a place of humanity and hope.

Ruskin led the way, as usual. His championing of the Gothic in *The Stones of Venice* explicitly contrasts the more communal and natural way of life he ascribes to the Middle Ages with the cynicism and brutality of the modern world. He sees the Renaissance classical style not just as bland but as evil: a moral crime, the architecture of self-satisfied Florentine merchants and of Victorian banks. The revulsion at commerce and longing for a more just society was to shock some Victorians when Ruskin applied it directly to them in a series of essays that started to appear in the *Cornhill Magazine* in 1860. His consciousness of inequality seems to have been intensified by his 'unconversion' from Christianity, for if the poor were not to be rewarded in heaven, why should they not get justice on earth?

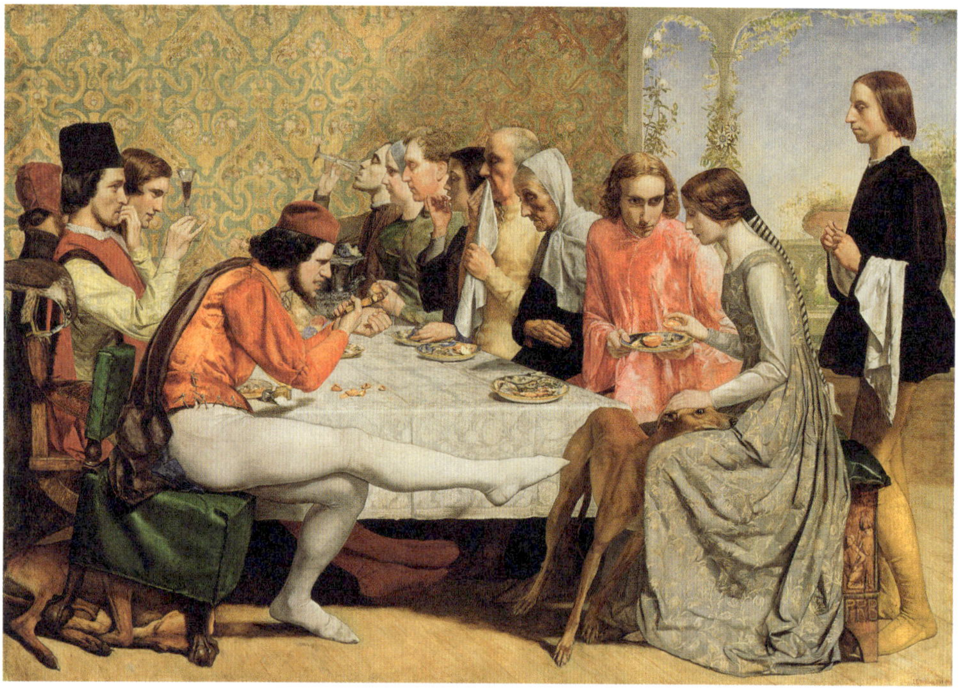

Readers of the *Cornhill* were so upset by Ruskin's essays that the series was cut short. He published his anti-capitalist manifesto as a book instead. *Unto This Last* came out in 1862, five years before Marx's *Das Kapital*. Both books attack the science of political economy founded in Enlightenment Edinburgh by Adam Smith. For Ruskin, political economy is not a true science but a pseudo-science, because it deliberately excludes such human passions as altruism, love and generosity from its grim analysis of a world driven by competition and greed:

> *Of course, as in the instances of alchemy, astrology, witchcraft, and other such popular creeds, political economy has a plausible idea at the root of it. 'The social affections,' says the economist, 'are accidental and disturbing elements in human nature; but avarice and the desire of progress are constant elements. Let us eliminate the inconstants, and, considering the human being merely as a covetous machine, examine by what laws of labour, purchase, and sale, the greatest accumulative result in wealth is obtainable....*

↑ John Everett Millais, *Isabella*, 1848–49, oil on canvas, 103 × 142.8 cm (40 ½ × 56 ⅕ in.), Walker Art Gallery, Liverpool

The art of Millais is full of anti-capitalist implications. In his 1849 scene *Isabella*, a gathering of hard-faced medieval Florentine burghers shows scant sympathy for the young heroine and her lover, who is shortly to be murdered by her brothers. One brother fastidiously holds up his glass of wine as if calculating its volume and cost per fluid ounce. Opposite him sits a row of pinched hypocrites with the faces of Poor Law guardians. By contrast, his 1849–50 picture *Christ in the House of his Parents* is a study of a communitarian carpenter's workshop that matches Ruskin's idyll of medieval craft.

No wonder Ruskin saw the PRB – to use the initials with which, embracing the anonymity of the Gothic artisan, members of the Pre-Raphaelite Brotherhood sometimes signed their works – as fellow travellers. Yet when he befriended Millais he found out the hard way how far they were from being medieval ascetics. In 1853 Millais went with Ruskin and his young wife, Effie, on holiday to Glenfinlas in Scotland. The idea was that Millais would paint a portrait of Ruskin against a rugged setting of rock and water, and the polymathic art critic would hone his favourite young painter's understanding of geology. The portrait did get done, but not before Effie, tortured by Ruskin's refusal to have sex with her, had fallen in love with Millais. On their return to London she left him, divorcing in 1854 on grounds of 'incurable impotency'. Millais and Effie Gray married the following year.

Looking again at *The Blind Girl*, why do the ragged outcasts it portrays have such glossy, glowing hair? It is a jarring detail that undercuts the painting's compassion. Somehow, while trudging the lanes and sleeping in hedgerows, Millais' paupers have managed to carefully wash and comb their brilliant locks. This is surely a cunning bid for the sympathies of his audience. The Pre-Raphaelites may have started in the 'hungry Forties' but they became well-known at the height of the mid-Victorian boom. An expanding art market served by such dealers as Thomas Agnew, who began his business, significantly, in Manchester, before opening a London branch in 1860, and the expansion of collecting beyond the aristocracy into the new merchant and industrial elite, made Victorian art big business. Even when painting poverty, the Pre-Raphaelites knew how to please and seduce that audience.

The past might be a form of resistance. It could also be a place to escape. In an age when evangelical Christianity made the sexual openness of eighteenth-century art impossible, the archaic fantasy worlds of Victorian art offer a less direct and more perverse eroticism.

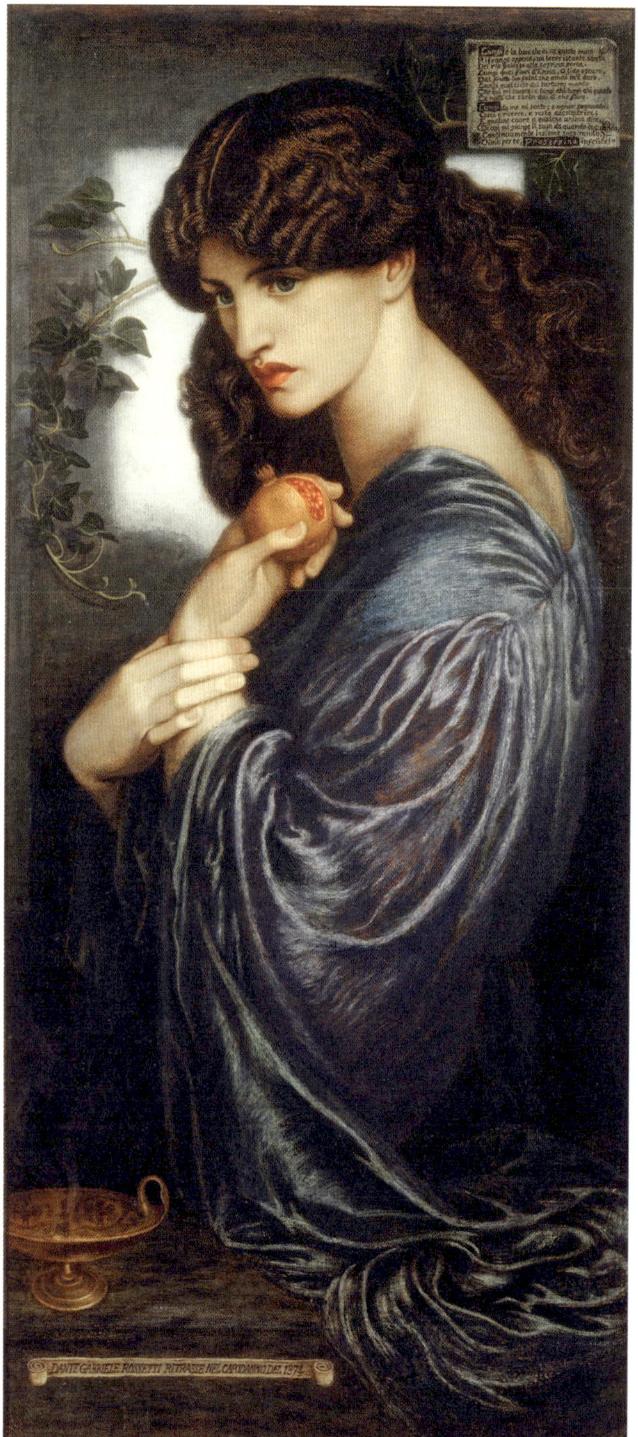

← Dante Gabriel Rossetti, *Proserpine*, 1874, oil on canvas, 125.1 × 61 cm (49 ¼ × 24 in.), Tate

No artist since Leonardo da Vinci had fetishized hair quite so passionately as Rossetti. He also liked luscious lips, and tended to shade his images of Eros with intimations of death. The full kinky orchestra sounds its throbbing notes in his 1874 painting *Proserpine*. In classical myth, Proserpina, daughter of Ceres, was abducted by Pluto, the god of the underworld, and trapped in his subterranean realm. Eventually Pluto agreed to let her go, on condition she had not eaten. Sadly she had tasted a pomegranate, so she was doomed from then on to spend only one half of the year in the land of the living, and the other in the realm of the dead. Rossetti makes from this myth of the seasons a portrait of mystery and desire. The red flesh of the opened pomegranate is ripely sexual, the rich auburn hair of his model a river of passion, her eyes vast orbs of unease.

The same model, with red hair this time, plays a dying beauty in Rossetti's 1869–71 work *Dante's Dream*. Here the medieval poet Dante dreams that he visited his beloved Beatrice on her deathbed. Rossetti gives the scene a sepulchral splendour, as Beatrice, pale and lifeless in her tomb, is kissed by the red angel of Love. Poppies carpet the dark earth as Dante contemplates the dead object of his desire.

The eroticism of Rossetti unleashes appetites for which Pugin and Ruskin saw no place in their edifices of Gothic virtue. The past obsesses Victorian art yet its meanings are far from fixed. Historical costume offered an almost limitless wardrobe of identities that opened increasingly subversive secret doors. In 1873 the Oxford scholar Walter Pater published his *Studies in the History of the Renaissance,* a slim volume whose staid title belies the luxuriant sensuality of its prose and the bold hedonism of its message. Pater inverts Ruskin, praising the very individualism that revolted Ruskin in the Renaissance. Instead of socialism he advocates an amoral existence of pure aesthetic intensity: 'To burn always with this hard gemlike flame, to maintain this ecstasy, is success in life.'

It is easy to see from Rossetti's paintings of morbid beauty how one road out of the mid-Victorian Middle Ages led to the Aesthetic Movement, whose manifesto Pater penned under the guise of art history. Like the prophets of the Gothic Revival, aesthetes in the late nineteenth century wanted to change the world and remake themselves. Art for Art's Sake was not an excuse for idleness. It was a demanding ideal. In a series of captivating photographs for which he posed on a visit to New York in 1882, Oscar Wilde comes across as a living work of art, expressing his idea of the Life Beautiful in every detail of clothing and demeanour, from his stockings to his languid gaze.

The dream of replacing industrial squalor with an Arthurian social utopia blazed on even as Wilde was cracking wise. The woman who posed for Rossetti as Proserpine was Jane Morris, wife of a would-be Pre-Raphaelite artist, William Morris. As his paintings make plain, Rossetti was her lover. As well as his Proserpine she was his Beatrice, although in *Dante's Dream* he combines her face with the russet hair of Elizabeth Siddal, who in 1852 had spent months posing in a bath so Millais could paint her as Ophelia. Siddal died in 1862, so the afterglow of her in *Dante's Dream* adds to its truly Gothic tincture of eroticized death.

While Jane Morris and Rossetti were pursuing their affair like Lancelot and Guinevere, William was on a road that would lead him to Marx. The political vision of William Morris is far better known today than that of Ruskin, who is often portrayed simply as a repressed Victorian weirdo, yet it is far less original. In his political writings, including his utopian work *News from Nowhere*, he bolts Ruskin's vision of a medieval craft society to the Marxist ideology that was gathering disciples on the edge of the late nineteenth-century labour movement. Where Morris was far more original was in finding an aesthetic solution to some of the glaring limitations of Pre-Raphaelite art.

For all the memorable image-making of which these Victorian idealists were capable, their paintings are earthbound. They aspire to the ethereal and seek to be visionary: in 1847, a year before he helped found the Brotherhood, Rossetti bought one of William Blake's notebooks, allying the Pre-Raphaelite movement with the Victorian rediscovery of British art's great anti-empiricist. Yet for all the stress that such paintings as *The Scapegoat, The Blind Girl* and *Proserpine* place on symbolism and poetry, they are prosaically, obsessively empirical. Every strand of hair has to be depicted with glistening precision. Ophelia must be surrounded by exact and accurate flowers and weeds painted with mechanical fidelity. Why does the cult of the Pre-Raphaelites dwell so voyeuristically on their models? Because they always painted from the model, painstakingly, laboriously portraying real people in fancy costume as if unable to make anything up.

Where is the inspiration that Blake said comes from inside? These Victorian artists are painfully torn between a conscious desire to be Blakean and an unbreakable belief in empirical observation. The tradition of hard looking that had produced such brilliance in the age of Constable has become, for them, a prison.

Morris found a way to break out of that prison into an Avalon of abstraction. His only surviving figurative painting, *La Belle Iseult*, exhibits all the faults of the Pre-Raphaelites to an alarming degree. Painted in 1858 with the model Jane Burden, who would become Jane Morris when they married the following year, it is a slightly absurd gathering of medievalist details weighed down by a banal ordinariness in the way he handles paint. Morris remained faithful to the same romantic dream of the Middle Ages all his life but found better ways to express it. Iseult has an illuminated book of hours in her bedroom: in 1896 at the very end of his life Morris would recreate the book arts of the Middle Ages in a beautiful edition of Chaucer illustrated by Edward Burne-Jones, who shared his dream of a chivalrous, noble, strangely passive medieval age.

The Kelmscott Chaucer was the culmination of Morris's lifelong efforts to renew the arts and crafts, or rather the Arts and Crafts. Ruskin had called for a revival of good honest work, a rediscovery of craft that could free the labourer from inhuman mechanical wage slavery. In his attempts to return the manufacture of carpets, wallpapers, furnishings, tiles and stained glass to the pre-industrial age, Morris attempted seriously to realize this dream. Unfortunately Morris & Co was just a drop in the ocean of modern industry. The exquisite designs Morris came up with enhanced the lives of well-to-do aesthetes rather than having any impact whatsoever on working-class liberation. Yet there is no denying the visual power of the repeated arabesques and orotund symmetries of the patterns that proliferate in his prints. Morris takes Gothic nature into the realm of the non-objective. He transforms flowers and foliage into vortices of colour that intertwine forever . His medieval vision is pure and unblemished and you can get lost in it, like a knight wandering into an endless forest.

Even Victorian photography fell under the dreamy spell of the past. To get themselves taken seriously as artists, pioneering photographers turned away from tedious reality to portray fey faerie girls in costumes of yore. The melancholy, nostalgic vision of the poet laureate, Alfred, Lord Tennyson – which inspired a castle-full of Victorian paintings, from Millais' *Mariana* in 1851 to *The Lady of Shalott* by John William Waterhouse in 1888 – also provided the experimental photographer Julia Margaret Cameron with copious material. Cameron was more than a fan of Tennyson's work: she befriended him, and in 1860 moved in next door to his home on the Isle of Wight so she could be close to her literary hero. In 1874 she created a series of staged photographs to illustrate a new edition of Tennyson's disconsolate verse sequence *Idylls of the King*.

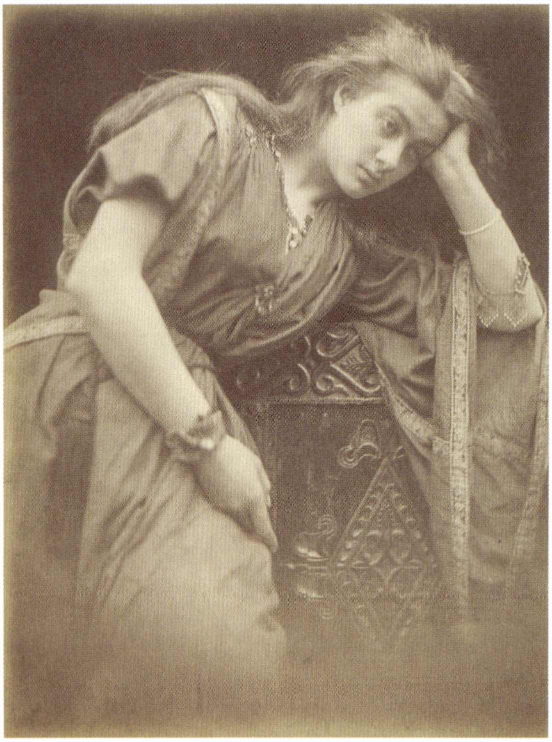

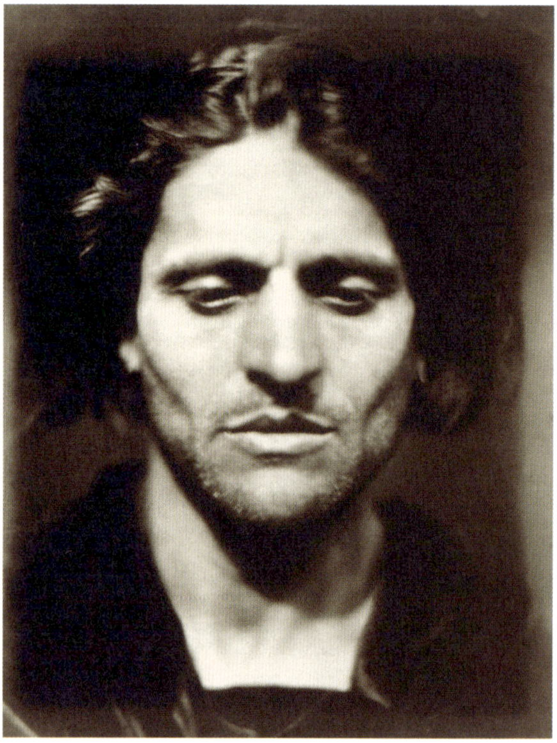

To a twenty-first-century eye these pictures resemble stills from an early silent film as people pose dramatically in robes, veils, frocks and armour. Yet the camera cannot help letting raw reality intrude. It is interesting to compare Cameron's photograph of Tennyson's Mariana with Millais' painting. Both pictures evoke the uneasy boredom of a Victorian woman confined within the home by a society of fixed gender roles.

Tennyson's poem is a depressed meditation on a single image in Shakespeare's *Measure for Measure* of 'Mariana in the Moated Grange', a line that for the Victorian poet suggests infinities of dreariness. Cameron quotes Tennyson in her photograph's subtitle:

> *She said, 'I am aweary, aweary,*
> *I would that I were dead!'*

While Millais in full Gothic mode elaborately imagines the interior of Mariana's moated grange and expresses her frustration in a peculiarly elaborate arch of her back, as if she were imitating a flying buttress,

← Julia Margaret Cameron, *Mariana*, 1875, albumen silver print, 35.6 × 27.9 cm (14 × 11 in.), J. Paul Getty Museum, Los Angeles (84.XO.732.1.2.8)

↑ Julia Margaret Cameron, *Iago, study from an Italian*, 1867, albumen silver print, 35.6 × 27.9 cm (14 × 11 in.), The National Media Museum, Bradford

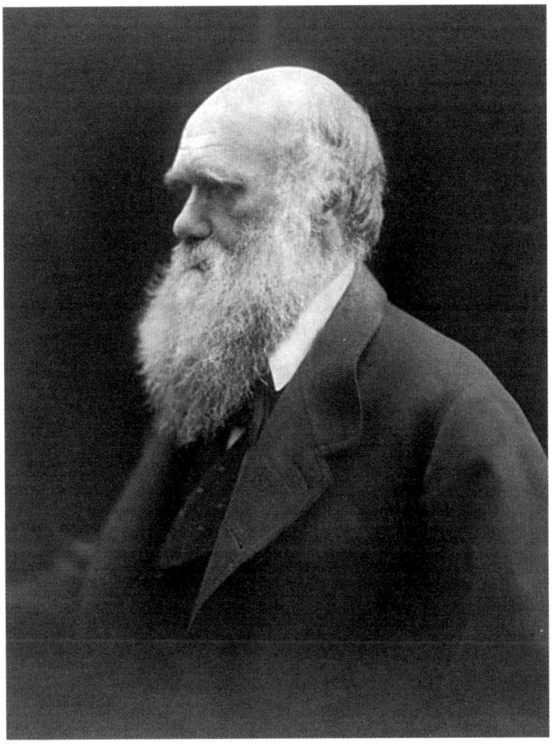

↑ Julia Margaret Cameron, *Charles Darwin*, 1868, albumen silver print, 29.3 × 23 cm (11½ × 9 in.), Library of Congress Prints and Photographs Division, Washington, D.C.

Cameron's model stares glumly into space, her head on her hand, her hair wild. Her misery is much more simply expressed than in the painting. For all her fancy dress the effect is lumpen and grimly real.

Given the manifest weaknesses of Victorian painting, Cameron picked the right time to assert that photography is an art. Her best pictures are more haunting than most British paintings of her time. Her eye for the stark poetry of the human face is particularly refreshing after looking at the pretentious art of the Pre-Raphaelites. Take her 1867 picture *Iago, study from an Italian*. It preserves a romantic male face in passionate close-up, eyes downcast, hair tousled, stubble catching the silvery light. This is a picture of an unnamed model, but Cameron's interest in character and talent for befriending celebrities enabled her to create enduring images of some of the most famous faces of her time. Her awe at the power of light itself shines in her portrait of her friend the astronomer Sir John Herschel as a superbly savage old man, with a bright iridescence of hair, his features as remotely cratered as the moon. By the time Cameron took this picture in 1867 she had known the old lion Herschel for more than 30 years. She was born in Calcutta, the daughter of an East India Company man, and her life was that of a Victorian globetrotter who spanned the British Empire. In 1836 she met Herschel in South Africa, where he was living near Cape Town to survey the southern stars. The young Charles Darwin also visited him in that same year when the *Beagle* was anchored at the Cape. It was Herschel who first sent examples of photographs to Cameron and told her about this new way to capture nature's light. Photography might be able to create art, but it was rooted in science – and somehow Cameron's camera has a special sympathy for scientific faces.

In 1868 Darwin, by now one of the most famous (and infamous) people alive, rented Cameron's home on the Isle of Wight for a six-week holiday. She did not miss the opportunity to photograph him. Darwin looks almost like a waxwork of himself in her uncanny profile image. He is a specimen in a jar, his oddly simian features preserved for close and detailed study. Yet the camera's dissection is kind. Cameron preserves the shyness and sensitivity of this controversialist recluse.

The natural world studied with such subversive acuity by Darwin proliferates in Victorian art and architecture in ornate and even surreal ways. From concrete dinosaurs to strayed sheep, the tension between faith and geological discovery throws up odd and unusual forms – freaks, you might say, of cultural evolution. Evolutionary anxiety is at its most hauntingly explicit in the Scottish artist William Dyce's painting *Pegwell Bay, Kent - a Recollection of October 5th 1858*. Set on the eve of Darwin's bombshell book and painted, it seems, between 1858 to 60 as the debate it brought about raged, it is a geological reverie. Dyce's family collect sea shells in front of cliffs whose precisely rendered strata speak of the immense, newly appreciated age of the Earth and the millions of years through which, according to Darwin, life has evolved. Is that slow process of adaptation all there is to the wonder of nature? A comet streaking through the luminous sky might be a sign from God that reassures the artist otherwise. Yet the sacred landscape is full of disturbing fossils. This painting is in two minds. The cathedral of nature has been invaded by a devil's chaplain.

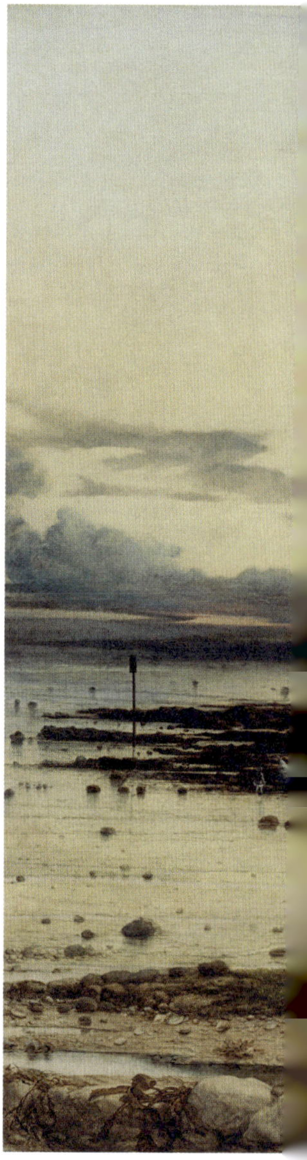

→ William Dyce, *Pegwell Bay, Kent - a Recollection of October 5th 1858*, c. 1858–60, oil on canvas, 63.5 x 88.9 cm (25 x 35 in.), Tate

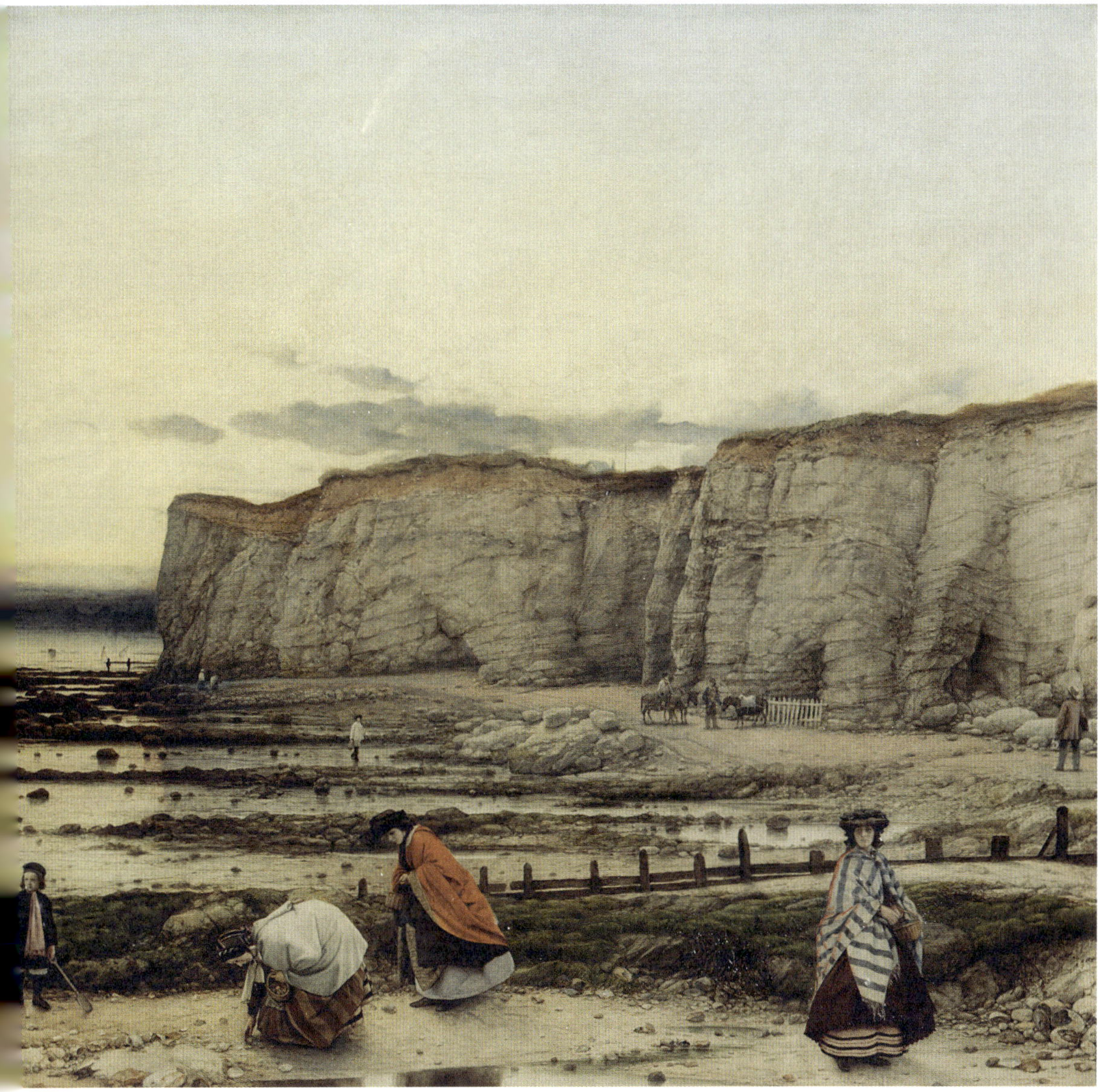

9. Fireworks

What are the roots that clutch, what branches grow
Out of this stony rubbish?

T. S. Eliot, *The Waste Land*, 1922

Cockney Rebels

The madness that destroyed Pugin, made a murderer of Dadd and is wittily kept at bay by the art of Edward Lear caught up with Ruskin in the 1870s. In Venice at Christmas 1876 he started seeing things and by 1878 he suffered his first full mental breakdown. Periods of alternating illness and lucidity dominated his life from then on and silenced him from 1889 until his death in 1900. He was not institutionalized, but survived in forgotten seclusion in his own home, supported by an ample inheritance from his wine merchant father.

As Ruskin was losing his mind he looked in perplexity at a new kind of art. In 1877 at the Grosvenor Galleries in London he saw James Abbott McNeill Whistler's painting *Nocturne in Black and Gold: The Falling Rocket*. Dapples of metallic paint, sparks of pigment are scattered through the greenish darkness of this sensual night scene. Except is it a 'scene' at all? Whistler's louche creation flirts with the abstract. Like a late Turner, it exults in light and colour for their own sake. It is free from rules, free from morality.

Ruskin could not see the affinity with Turner, or recapture the critical daring of his youth. He was appalled by the casual aesthetic fireworks of Whistler's *Falling Rocket*. He denounced it in terms depressingly similar to the attacks on Turner that he had given so much of himself to refute:

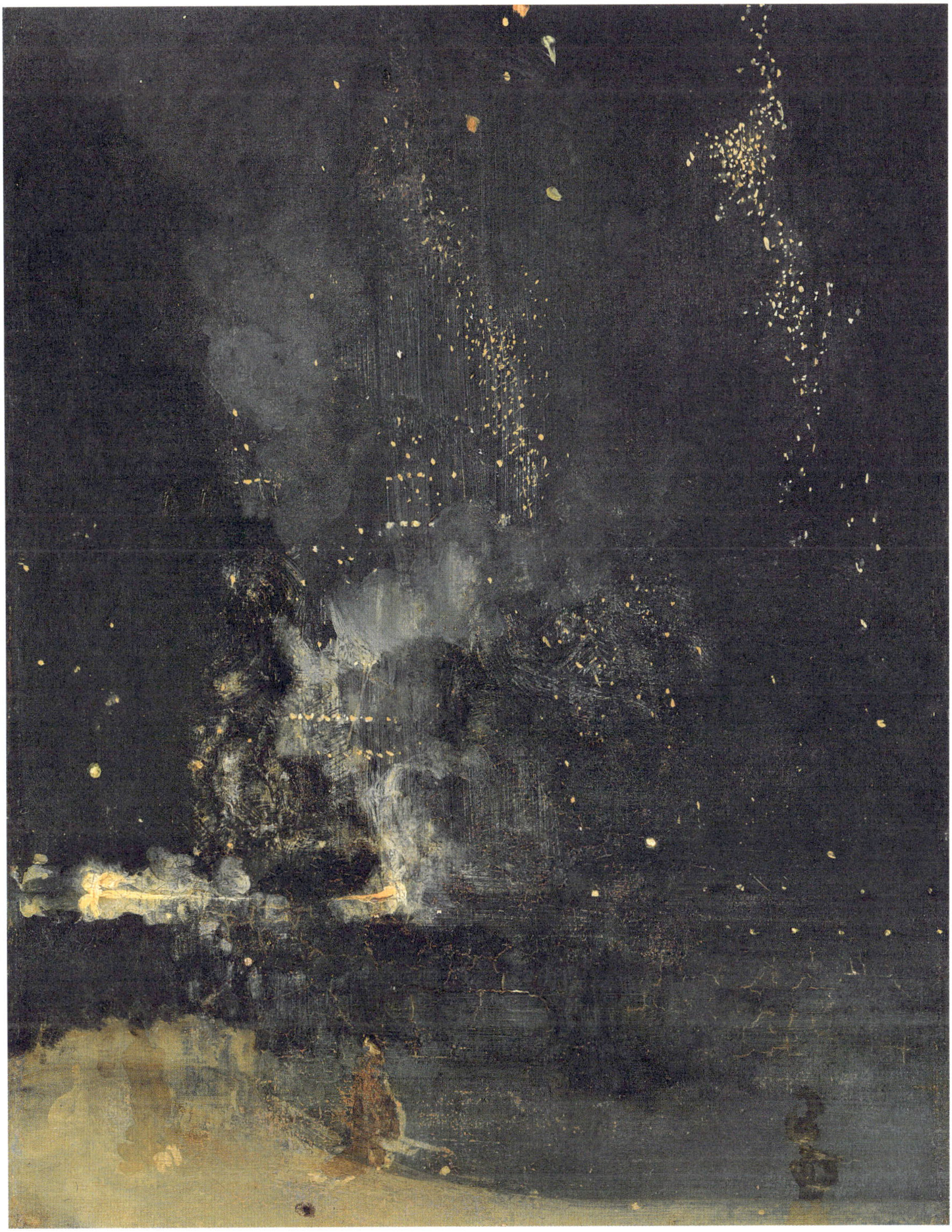

↑ James Abbott McNeill Whistler, *Nocturne in Black and Gold: The Falling Rocket*, 1875, oil on panel, 60.3 × 46.7 cm (23 ¾ × 18 ⅜ in.), Detroit Institute of Arts

> *For Mr Whistler's own sake, no less than for the protection of the purchaser, Sir Coutts Lindsay ought not to have admitted works into the gallery in which the ill-educated conceit of the artist so nearly approached the aspect of wilful imposture. I have seen, and heard, much of cockney impudence before now; but never expected to hear a coxcomb ask two hundred guineas for flinging a pot of paint in the public's face.*

Ruskin refused to see anything but chaos and fraud in Whistler's daub. There was something utterly dishonest in this pretentious work of art, he claimed, something that went beyond mere lack of merit. Whistler was a posturing con-man, throwing paint in Victorian England's face.

Whistler sued for libel. By the time the case came to trial in November 1878, Ruskin was too ill to appear. Whistler performed brilliantly in court, as was only to be expected of this swashbuckling avant-gardist. He was not, of course, a cockney. Born in New England in 1834, he spent part of his childhood in Russia where his father was working as a railway engineer, part of it in England, before going back to the United States to train as an army officer at West Point, until he was expelled by the future Confederate general Robert E. Lee, partly because of his non-regulation curly hair. Whistler's curls as well as charisma are preserved in Henri Fantin-Latour's 1864 painting *Homage to Delacroix*, in which this American in Paris makes the French artists around him look like shy students and dull professors. With his long black coat and dashing stance, turning to look at us as if someone has just dared him to a gunfight, he resembles a Wild West character. As he gave evidence in his lawsuit against Ruskin, reported *The Times*, this Doc Holliday of the art world nonchalantly explained his idea of abstract painting:

> *Mr Whistler said that a picture was to him throughout a problem, which he attempted to solve ... 'An Arrangement' was an arrangement of light, form and colour.*

It was not the best way to convince a Victorian court of his seriousness. Yet he received applause when Ruskin's lawyer asked if he thought the two days' labour he had spent on his *Nocturne* was worth 200 guineas: 'No,' Whistler dramatically replied; 'I ask it for the knowledge of a lifetime.'

The outcome was a technical win for Whistler but a moral defeat: he was awarded only a farthing's damages. Ruskin felt injured too, and resigned his Slade Professorship in Fine Art at Oxford in protest.

Beyond Whistler's glittering sparks in the erotically dark night lay a new artistic world. This migratory American had dared to show London what his friends in Paris were uncovering. For Whistler was au fait with a French avant-garde that was reinventing the very nature of art. Those serious-looking men around him in Fantin-Latour's group portrait were not such dullards after all. They include the ginger-bearded Édouard Manet, whose coolly observed paintings were putting modern life onto canvas with a new kind of sophisticated directness, and Charles Baudelaire, whose long grey hair and need to sit down suggest the dissipated lifestyle behind his shockingly explicit 1857 poetry collection *Les Fleurs du mal*. In his essay 'The Painter of Modern Life', published in 1863, Baudelaire provided a manifesto for the art of Manet, who that same year painted his unsentimental modern nude *Olympia*.

To look from Ruskin and Tennyson to Manet and Baudelaire is to open a window. The fog clears. Why was French art suddenly so far in advance of British?

One answer is, surely, Victorianism. That tangle of Evangelical Christianity, moral scruple and high-mindedness was an enchanting mental undergrowth, yet in it art suffocated. Who can respect the evasive perversity of Rossetti after beholding the audacious, almost insolent factuality of Manet?

The moral claustrophobia of the Victorian age surely played a part in crushing visual delight. All delight. In 1895 Oscar Wilde made the same mistake as Whistler, his rival for the leadership of the Aesthetic Movement, when he sued a pillar of society. The Marquess of Queensberry had abused Wilde over his affair with Lord Alfred Douglas, Queensberry's son. Wilde's decision to sue Queensberry was catastrophic. The defence threatened to reveal detailed evidence of his homosexuality, his case collapsed, and he himself was prosecuted. In May 1895 he was sentenced to two years' hard labour for 'gross indecency'. When he was released from Reading Gaol in 1897 he went to live on the Continent.

Wilde's aestheticism was perfumed with the sinful atmosphere wafting over from France. His 1890 novel *The Picture of Dorian Gray* acknowledges that debt. The experimental sensualist Dorian, in his search for satiation that gradually turns his portrait in the attic into a grotesque image of a corrupt old satyr while he himself remains pristine, is inspired by Joris-Karl Huysmans's 1884 book *À rebours (Against Nature)*, which in turn teems with references to contemporary French art, especially the ripely decadent paintings of Gustave Moreau. Paris returned Wilde's admiration. Shortly before he was jailed, Henri de Toulouse-Lautrec painted a compassionate portrait of him in the audience at the Moulin Rouge.

Wilde wrote his play *Salomé* in French; it was first performed in Paris in 1896, while he was in prison, having been banned in Britain by the Lord Chamberlain for presenting biblical personages on stage. The first English publication of *Salomé*, in 1894, was illustrated by a young British artist whose libidinal vision more than matched that of his French contemporaries. Aubrey Beardsley's prints create a black-and-white world of depraved suggestiveness and, in his most explicit works, phallic riot, that translates the misty sensuality of Moreau into hard-edged eroticism. His illustrations to a privately printed edition of *Lysistrata*, the ancient Greek comedy by Aristophanes in which Athenian women stage a sex strike to stop a war, are rampant fantasies in which human flesh is both hideous and desirable. Women display bounteous breasts, hips and buttocks defined by neat black lines; immense phalluses are measured; a bottom is sensually washed. The carnal is rendered as moments of touching, stroking, assessing, with a cold, aesthetic regard.

Beardsley makes all sexuality look perverse, all his people alien, but he confesses to being the most freakish of his characters in a portrait of himself immersed in a vast bed that he drew in 1894. Its inscription reads like a piece of decadent French poetry:

> *PAR LES DIEUX JUMEAUX TOUS LES*
> *MONSTRES NE SONT PAS EN AFRIQUE.*
> ('By the twin gods, not all the monsters are in Africa.')

This self-styled 'monster' is in fact an enigma. Was he homosexual, heterosexual or not sexual at all? One theory is that he committed incest with his sister. Beardsley resembles an invented character from a fin-de-siècle fiction, an artist of the obscene and the beautiful whose hedonist art hides the mystery of his true nature behind black curtains and preposterous hairstyles. No one has ever made black-and-white so erotic: the depth of his shadows and brightness of his empty spaces give every scene a sinister glamour that makes you shudder. This precocious sexual visionary died of tuberculosis in 1898, at the age of 25.

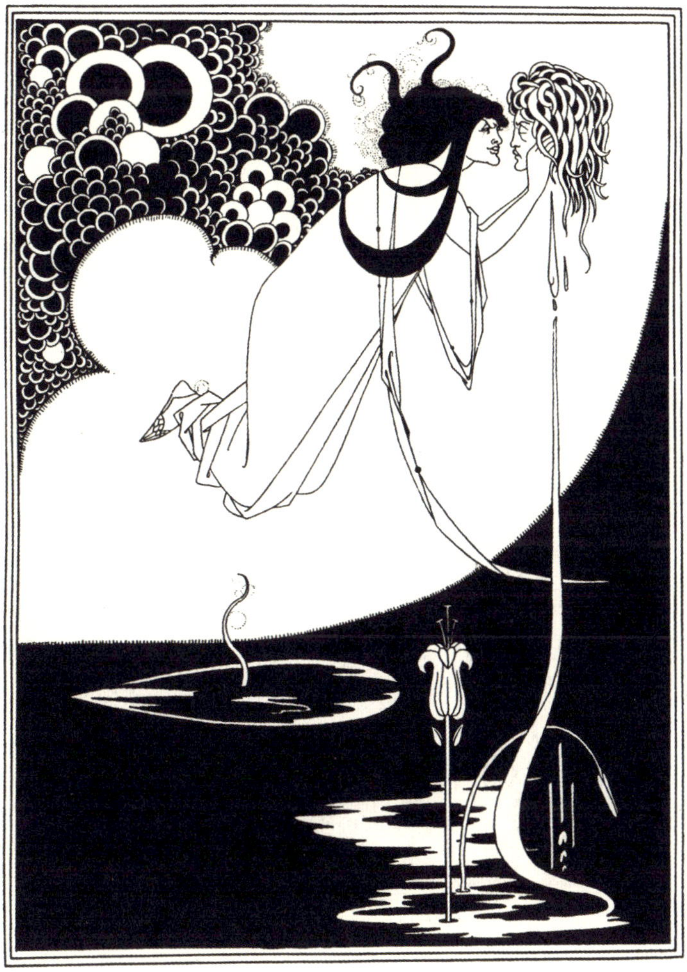

→ Aubrey Beardsley, *The Climax*, illustration to *Salomé* by Oscar Wilde, 1894, Private Collection

Beardsley's understanding of the erotic power of ink comes from looking at Japanese woodblock *Shunga* prints. In this enthusiasm he is a fully paid-up member of the European avant-garde. Japanese art bewitched the first modernists. It was abstract and freely coloured, a bold structure of shapes that helped detach the imagination from centuries of Western habit. In Manet's 1868 portrait of the radically naturalist writer Émile Zola, a print of a wrestler by Utagawa Kuniaki II is pinned above his desk along with works by Velázquez and Manet himself. Van Gogh displays the same reverence for Japanese art in his *Self-Portrait with Bandaged Ear*, painted in 1889. Behind his wounded, blue-eyed stare hangs the print of Mount Fuji by Sato Torakiyo that hung on his wall in Arles.

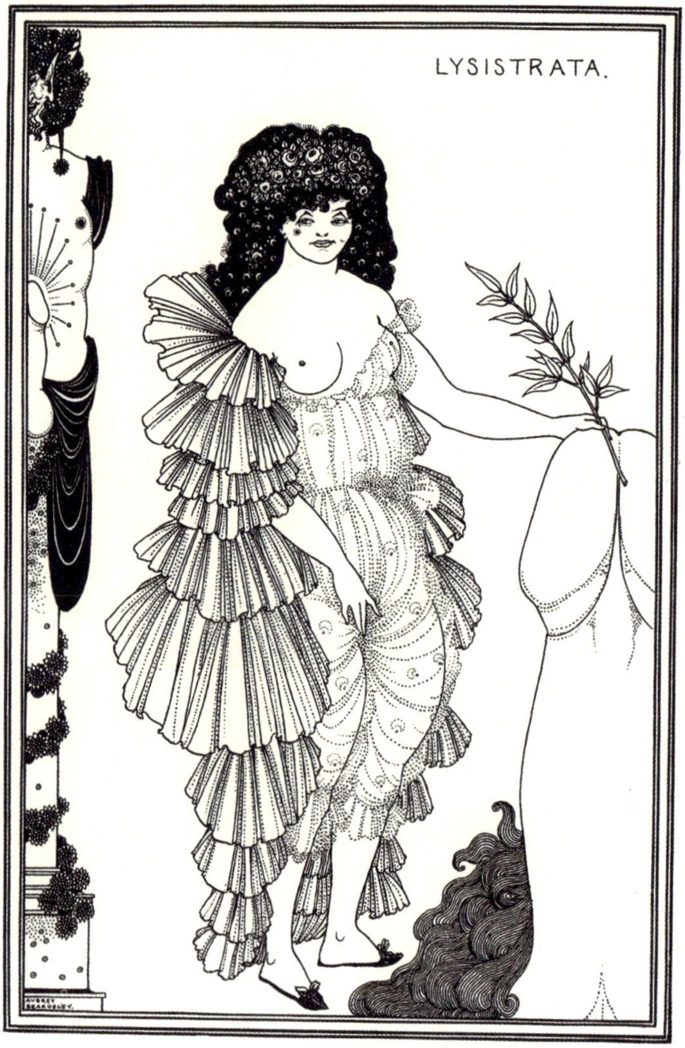

← Aubrey Beardsley, *Lysistrata Shielding her Coynte*, illustration to *Lysistrata* by Aristophanes, 1896, Private Collection

Yet the first Western artist who incorporated Japanese aesthetics directly into his own work was Whistler. The formal 'Arrangements' that he defended in a London court are his interpretation of the stylized 'floating world' of Japanese prints. His 1871 work *Arrangement in Grey and Black No. 1* – 'Whistler's Mother' – is a provocative manifesto for Japanese-style abstraction, 'arranging' his own mother in her black dress and pale bonnet in a manifestly artificial pattern of coloured shapes. The way she rests her feet above the ground is another echo of Japanese sophistication.

Whistler's portrait of his mother boldly sets the liberty of art against the confines of Victorian morality. A puritan sits like a living work of art, in front of curtains that shimmer like starlight. This American wizard's confrontation with Ruskin was a long overdue reckoning with British morals. He had been teasing the British since the 1860s by mixing the conventions of Pre-Raphaelite art with an insouciant abstract licence. His 1862 painting *Symphony in White, No. 1: The White Girl* is a portrait of a Pre-Raphaelite beauty with flaming red hair. Any echo of Rossetti is, however, dissolved by its ethereal play of pale hues, the model's white dress floating before a white curtain as she stands on a cream-coloured fur.

She is Whistler's Irish lover, Joanna Hiffernan, who also modelled nude for Gustave Courbet. It is probably her genitalia we see in Courbet's 1866 painting *The Origin of the World*. That secret history heightens the irony with which Whistler provocatively glided between avant-garde Paris and stern Victorian England. In his realist painting *Wapping*, painted in 1860–64, the redheaded Hiffernan plays a prostitute drinking with two sailors – or is one of them a bohemian? – on a Thameside balcony. Wapping, at the heart of the East London docklands in this age when the river was crowded with merchant shipping, was notorious for its sex industry. Turner had owned a pub there and Ruskin believed he went 'a-Wapping' at the weekends to indulge his passion for erotic art.

Whistler's *Wapping* shares the unsentimental modern eye for easy leisure that Manet brings to bear on the amorous picnic in his painting *Le déjeuner sur l'herbe*, which in Paris in 1863 was rejected by the same Salon jury that turned down *The White Girl*. Both paintings appeared, instead, in that year's famous new Paris institution, the first Salon des Refusés.

In the East End of London, Whistler looks with calm, uncritical perceptiveness at the olive-green and grey river, the red wood of masts, the dappled forms of people on the Thames and the purple smoke on the horizon. It is a brilliantly sensual and alive depiction of the river as a crowd of mobile coloured forms that is both flowing and solid, free and observed. We are a million miles from the airless closed garden of the Pre-Raphaelites. This London looks alive – sexuality and all.

It is through the injection of Parisian modernity that British art regains some of its lost joie de vivre. For the spirit of Georgian empiricism, from Hogarth to Turner, was never pedantic. It was a pleasure in looking, a feel for the world. That sensibility still breathes in the sleazy docklands of Whistler's *Wapping*. Was it a knowledge of his adventures downriver that made Ruskin call this New Englander a 'cockney'?

For Whistler was intimate with the Thames. The river life we see in *Wapping* is mapped in detail in his etchings of Rotherhithe, the Pool of London, Limehouse and other haunts where he portrays East Enders drinking, working and watching the river. By the 1870s he distilled these detailed observations of Thames life into near-abstract visions of London's river as a watery dream of colour turning the great city into unreal reflections. In 1871 he painted *Nocturne: Blue and Silver – Chelsea*, a breath of moonlight shimmering in space. The thin blue veil of the river passes city lights and shadowy buildings that are reflected on its creamy pale surface. A single wispy person stands on the near bank. Whistler has painted his symbolic signature, a butterfly, in a way that undercuts the reality of the scene entirely: it is not a reproduction of the world, this trompe-l'oeil insect tells us, but a painting: an arrangement of colours.

Whistler shows his contemporaries how painters can defy the camera. No camera could make this. Painting can survive the photographic age by becoming proud of its own artifice. Paradoxically, this defiance of Victorian art's pedantry and workaholism allows him to capture the experience of the river, and of the city. *Nocturne: Blue and Gold – Old Battersea Bridge*, painted in about 1872–75, is one of his most 'Japanese' creations. The tall wooden support and bamboo-like curve of the bridge make it look very like bridges that appear in Japanese prints such as Hiroshige's *Moonlight at Ryogoku*. The curt cropping of the image is also strikingly Japanese. Yet the shadowy forms of people passing over Battersea Bridge and the twinkle of lights along the river make this a real moment in the life of London.

The art of Walter Sickert is a lot more grimily 'cockney' than Whistler's riverine reveries. Sickert was taught by Whistler in the early 1880s before visiting France for himself and meeting Edgar Degas. For many people Degas is the artist of ballet dancers and horse races, an easily palatable Impressionist. In reality his art is coolly voyeuristic and intensely carnal. Degas is an uncompromising observer of modern life and a hypnotic student of the nude. Sickert learned his lessons well.

Born in Germany in 1860, Sickert came to live in Britain as a child, and perhaps his outsider status encouraged his appetite for wearing disguises and losing himself in urban crowds. He acted as a

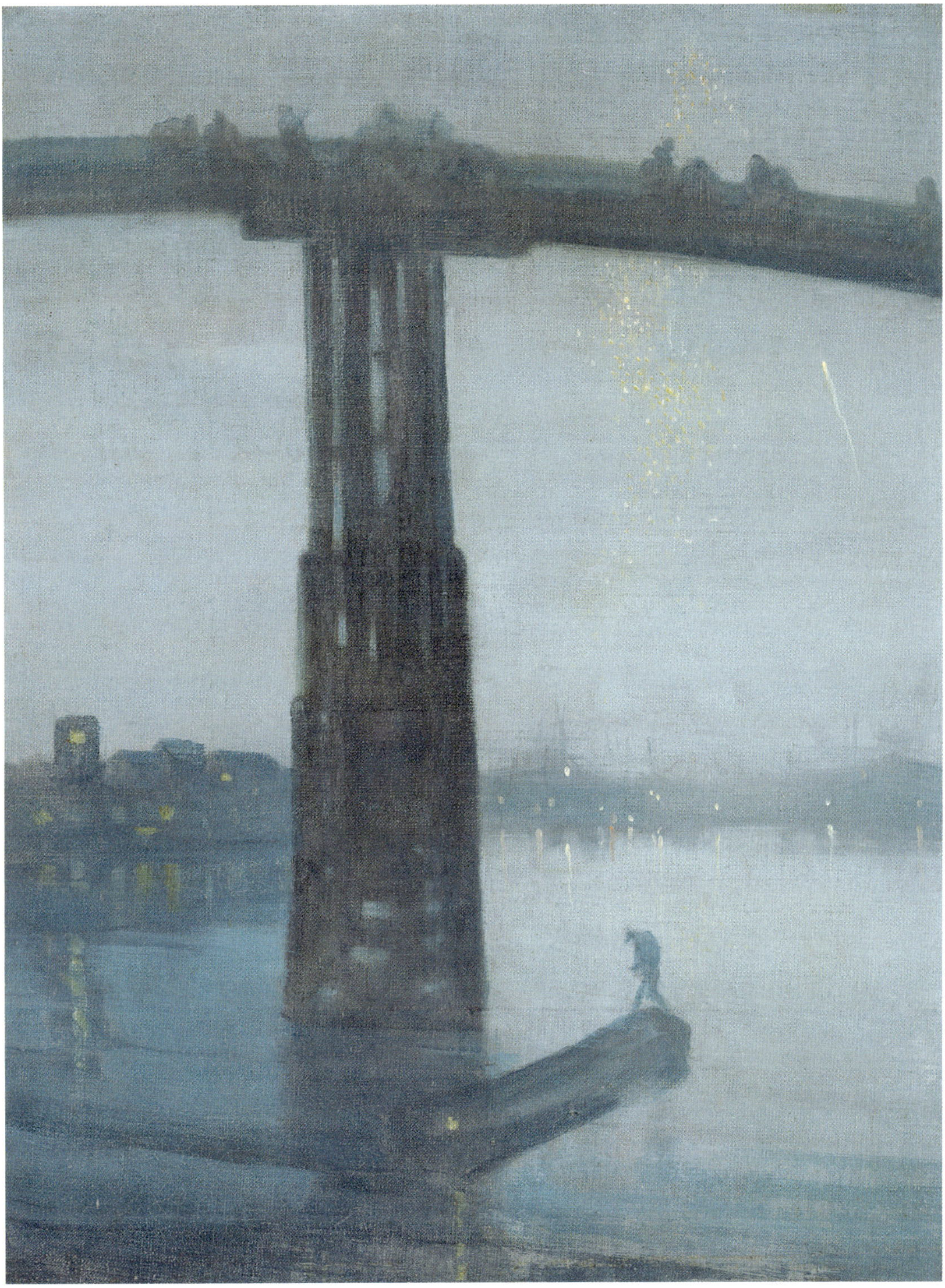

↑ James Abbott McNeill Whistler, *Nocturne: Blue and Gold – Old Battersea Bridge*, c. 1872–75, oil on canvas, 68.3 × 51.2 cm (26 ⅝ × 20 ⅛ in.), Tate

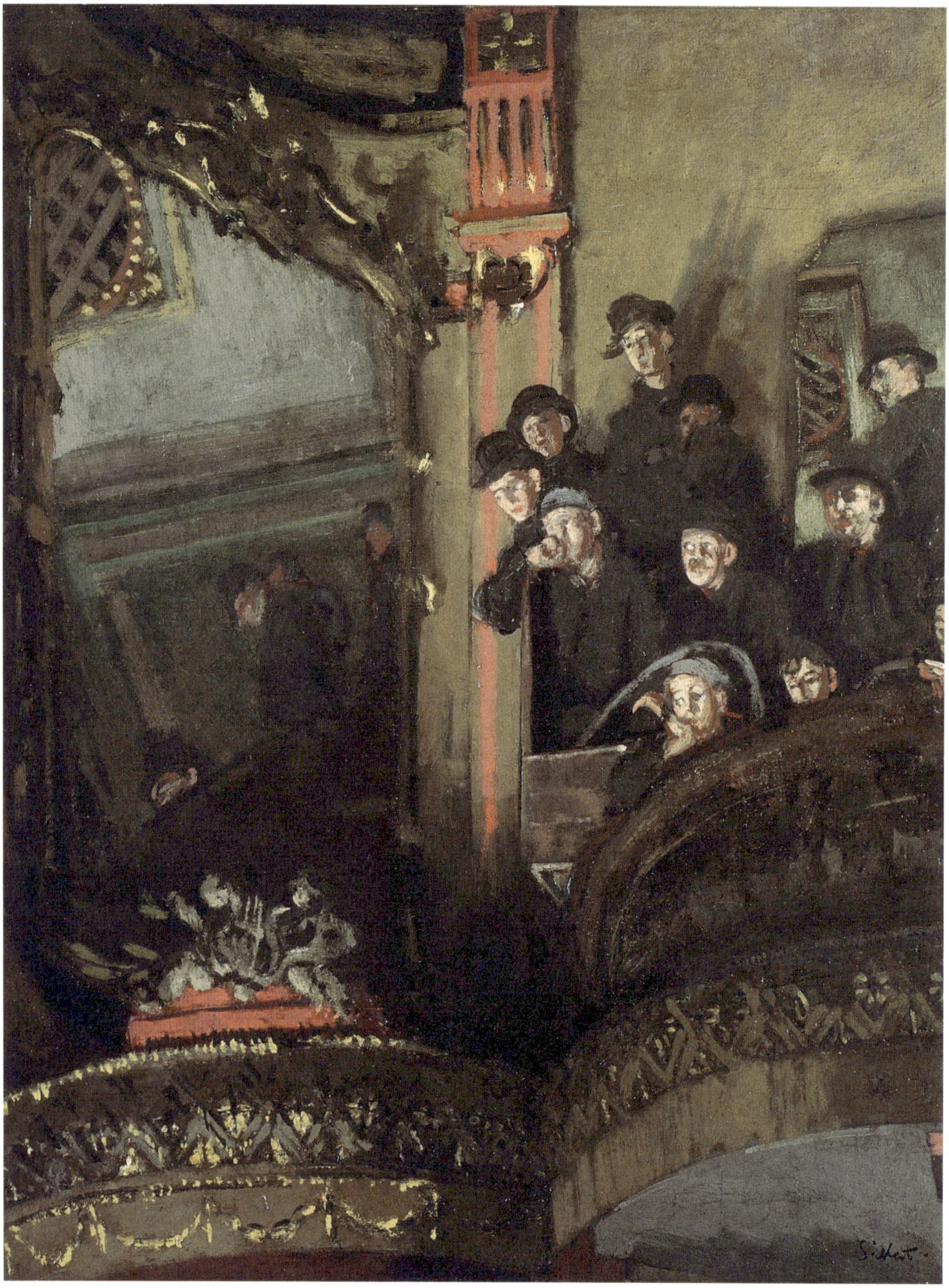

↑ Walter Sickert,
The Old Bedford, 1895,
oil on canvas, 76.3 × 60.5 cm
(30 × 23⅘ in.), Walker Art
Gallery, Liverpool

young man with Henry Irving, the titanic theatrical personality who inspired his business manager Bram Stoker to invent Dracula in 1897. Some see Sickert's masquerading as sinister. A bizarre myth has even grown up that identifies him with Jack the Ripper, the serial killer who murdered five women in Whitechapel in 1888.

Needless to say, Sickert was not Jack the Ripper. He did, however, have something in common with Dorian Gray. The aesthete anti-hero of Wilde's novel is drawn to London's working-class entertainments. He falls in love with an actress who wows East End audiences in low-rent performances of Shakespeare. She ends up dead. Come to think of it, Sickert might also be fingered as the good doctor's demonic alter ego in Robert Louis Stevenson's 1886 tale *The Strange Case of Dr Jekyll and Mr Hyde*.

For like these fictional characters of the fin-de-siècle, Sickert was drawn to London's rowdy venues and cheap rooms. His art is an unromantic, disabused vision of the metropolis. Manet and Degas painted French cafés and concerts. Sickert preserves an archetypally British entertainment, the music hall. He was to see these institutions fade in his own lifetime from being the soul of popular culture to its waning yesteryear tradition, for he lived until 1942. His favourite was the Bedford Music Hall in Camden Town, North London. He painted and drew it again and again, observing its seedy opulence, delighting in its weird ornate decor, marvelling at the alien, engrossed faces of audience members. Sometimes the faces seem drugged and idiotic, stupefied by the spectacle before them. Yet the crowd precariously balanced high up in the gods can easily become dangerous, angry, aroused. Raw animal emotion and desire glare from dark eyes among the gilded cupids and caryatids.

Performers themselves have a pathos and vulnerability. Minnie Cunningham stands alone on the darkened stage of the Bedford, in 1892, in red dress and hat. Sickert, however, sees drama outside the walls of the music hall as well as within. His paintings have a narrative quality very different from French Impressionism. They belong in a British realist tradition that goes back to Hogarth. Like those of Hogarth, the stories Sickert tells, or suggests, are rarely reassuring.

A drunken husband totters in a bowler hat in his 1911 painting *Off to the Pub*. His wife sits frozen by rage and humiliation. In his more detailed domestic scene *Ennui*, painted in about 1914, a couple cannot even look at one another. Immense sadness and threat hang in the air along with the invisible aroma of the man's cigar, while the woman stares fixedly into a corner.

Sickert sees human beings in an almost clinical way. The men he portrays in the upper balcony of the Bedford Music Hall gawping or raging at the acts below resemble excited apes. The fractured couples whose mutual torment he analyzes look like cornered animals. His unsentimental paintings of modern life are in an empirical tradition of anthropological art with their roots in Hogarth's 'modern moral subjects'. And they have a surprising intellectual fellow traveller: Charles Darwin.

In his 1872 book *The Expression of the Emotions in Man and Animals*, the theorist of evolution turns his eyes on photographs and drawings of human and animal faces to analyze the similarity between the ways human beings express joy, fear, anger and sorrow and emotional signs in other animals, especially apes. Many of the illustrations are photographs taken to record pathological behaviour in the Parisian mental hospital La Salpêtrière. Just as artists including Toulouse-Lautrec and Picasso appear to have studied photographs from the Salpêtrière, so Darwin draws on this strange archive of human suffering.

Yet he also finds himself thinking of the eighteenth-century British prints he had examined in his university days, when he spent happy hours looking at art in the Fitzwilliam Museum, Cambridge. In an enthusiastic footnote he pays homage to Hogarth as a scientific observer of the human face:

> *In an engraving of one of Hogarth's wonderful pictures, passion is represented in the plainest manner by the open glaring eyes, frowning forehead, and exposed grinning teeth.*

Which Hogarth print is he remembering? This vivid description could fit quite a few. In the same passage Darwin quotes a description of a crowd in *Oliver Twist*:

> *Dickens, in speaking of an atrocious murderer who had just been caught, and was surrounded by a furious mob, describes 'the people as jumping up one behind another, snarling with their teeth, and making at him like wild beasts'.*

When it came to portraying the society around him in vividly visual characterizations, Dickens was indeed the Hogarth of his age. The original illustrations to his novels by 'Phiz' and other artists are Hogarthian vignettes in their own right. George Cruikshank's illustrations to *Oliver Twist* are obvious tributes to the eighteenth-century artist; in his depiction of feeding time in the workhouse, open mouths and staring eyes say it all.

Of course it was not for sensitive references to Hogarth and Dickens as like-minded observers of the human scene that people read Darwin's book in 1872. It was for fresh insults cast by Victorian Britain's most subversive thinker at the sacred supremacy of the human form divine. Those insults are not hard to find. The very title of *The Expression* puts human beings on a level playing field with 'lower' creation. Darwin uncompromisingly argues that not only do other animals have emotions like our own, they also have similar ways to display them. The image from Hogarth he recalls is as much animal as human. Glaring eyes, frowning forehead, grinning teeth: it reads like a description of an angry ape. Hogarth sees the animal in us. Darwin conversely exhibits the human in the animal in a drawing that he commissioned for *The Expression* from Thomas William Wood, of a 'Chimpanzee disappointed and sulky. Drawn from life ...'. With its face turned away huffily as it purses its lips in self-pity, the chimpanzee shows a poignant similarity to human moodiness.

The Expression of the Emotions in Man and Animals was published just a year after Darwin's most sensational book, *The Descent of Man, and Selection in Relation to Sex*, came out in 1871. In this most explicit of his works he hammers the last nails into creationist human arrogance and Victorian prudery alike. Not only does he argue trenchantly that human beings are closely related to other apes, but for good measure he makes it clear that sex is the driving force of nature.

Sickert's strange paintings make a lot more sense if we see him as a Darwinian student of the ape in us. He shares that shocking evolutionary view of human society with the Polish sailor Józef Teodor Konrad Korzeniowski, who took the name Joseph Conrad when he settled in Britain and began writing novels in English. Conrad saw an immense variety of human interactions and habits on his voyages, and became a firm believer in an evolutionary understanding of social existence. Having sailed to the Far East, his bedside bible was *The Malay Archipelago* by Darwin's friend and rival Alfred Russel Wallace. This 1869 book is dedicated to Darwin, to whom Wallace deferred when it turned out they had both independently theorized evolution.

Like Darwin, Wallace applies evolutionary theory not just to animals but also to people. He tells of his pathetically doomed attempt to make a pet of a baby orang-utan (whose mother he had shot) and has a keen eye for the complexity of social worlds. His account of dockside life in Singapore is far from the stereotype of an insular Victorian Englishman:

> *The harbour is crowded with men-of-war and trading vessels of many European nations, and hundreds of Malay praus and Chinese junks... All about the streets are sellers of water, vegetables, fruit, soup, and agar-agar (a jelly made of seaweed), who have many cries as unintelligible as those of London. Others carry a portable cooking-apparatus on a pole balanced by a table at the other end, and serve up a meal of shell-fish, rice, and vegetables for two or three halfpence...*

Wallace detects a close resemblance between the noisy street life of Singapore and the traditional 'cries' of London's street sellers. Conrad makes that same cross-cultural comparison between the Far East and London in his 1907 novel *The Secret Agent*. Its characters include a chief of detectives who previously commanded the colonial police in Malaya and who applies anthropological lessons from Wallace's book to his work in London.

For this was the apogee of empire. The shock of the Indian Rebellion – or 'Mutiny' as Britain called it – in 1857 had led to the government dismissing the East India Company and assuming direct control of Britain's imperial pearl. Red patches on the globe spread rapidly, and empire became central to British self-perceptions. This was partly because it was now something to defend, a secret economic weapon in an increasingly competitive world. The total dominance of the global economy that Britain enjoyed at the time of the Great Exhibition was challenged in the later nineteenth century. The Industrial Revolution was imitable after all. The victory of the modernizing North over the agrarian, slaveholding South in America's Civil War from 1861 to 1865 paved the way for spectacular economic growth by the USA. Closer to home, Germany's unification in 1871 unleashed an economic giant as well as overturning the balance of power in Europe.

In 1900, Britain was still the world's top economy, but the dynamism of Germany and America could not be ignored. Empire too was now a rivalrous field. European nations raced to grab colonies all over the world. Conrad's *Heart of Darkness*, published in 1902, is a cumulatively horrifying account of the brutal reality of empire, a cynical process of exploitation and rapacity hypocritically disguised as a work of virtue. It starts with a pleasure cruise downriver towards the mouth

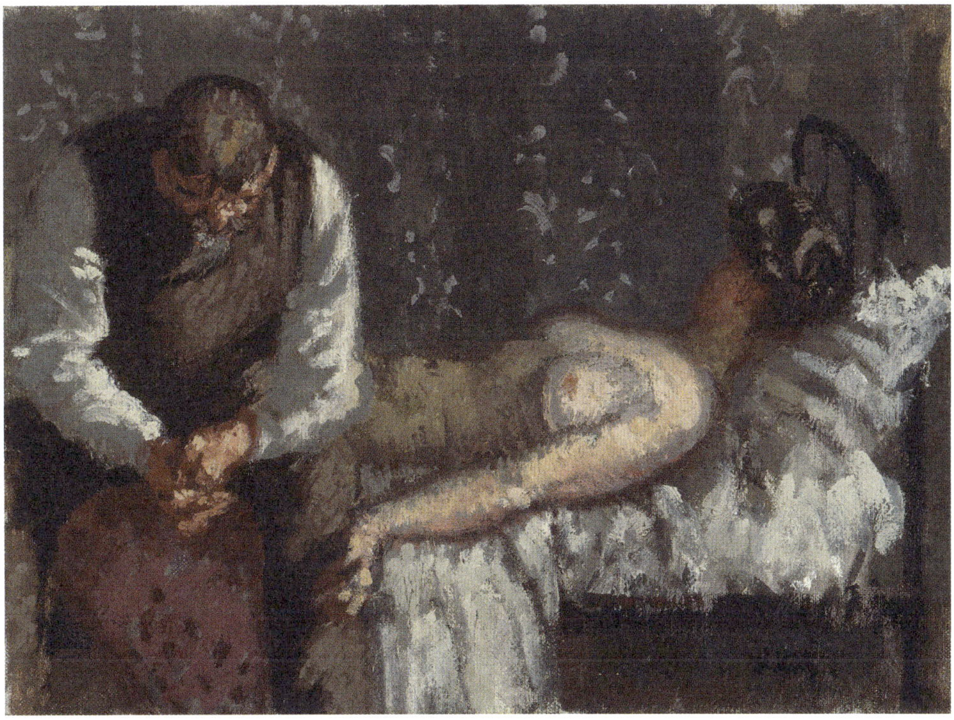

of the Thames, whose participants, stalled by the tide, find themselves contemplating 'the biggest, and the greatest, town on earth'.

London, the monster city at the heart of the world's greatest empire, was nothing if not that in 1902. Yet the veteran sailor Marlow, whose adventures have included a journey to the viciously inhumane rubber plantations of the Belgian Congo, has a mordant turn of mind:

> *'And this also,' said Marlow suddenly, 'has been one of the dark places of the earth.'*

He is referring to a time when Roman soldiers shivered among alien British tribes, but the story Marlow tells will leave a troubling possibility – that the modern metropolis of empire is the true 'heart of darkness'.

London is a dark place indeed in Sickert's paintings. The most intimidating of all his urban scenes are four paintings to which he gave the collective title *The Camden Town Murder*.

In 1907 Emily Dimmock, who worked as a prostitute, was murdered in Camden, the same London district where Sickert attended the Bedford Music Hall. She had had her throat cut by a man she took

↑ Walter Sickert, *The Camden Town Murder, or What Shall We Do for the Rent?*, c. 1908, oil on canvas, 25.6 × 35.6 cm (10 ⅛ × 14 in.), Yale Center for British Art, New Haven

home after a night at the Eagle pub. The crime became a newspaper sensation, and in 1908 Sickert provocatively associated four paintings of unromantically painted nudes in seedy bedrooms with this shocking crime.

The most disturbing of the series is *The Camden Town Murder, or What Shall We Do for the Rent?*

It looks as if the woman who lies prone on a bed, her head turned away and her throat prominent, really may have been murdered by the man who sits beside her in despair, his head lowered, his meaty hands clasped in anguish over a bloodlike blanket or apron on his knees. Did those thick hands throttle the woman, whose arm, we suddenly notice, is awkward, stiff and corpselike? The implicit violence is matched by Sickert's brutal handling of paint. His rough creation of the woman's flesh in creamy coarse daubs of meatlike colour resembles early paintings of murder, rape and prostitution by Cézanne. Apart from that subtle avant-garde antecedent, this is a new kind of nude. Sickert does not idealize, or even eroticize – at least in a conventional sense – his cruelly empirical study of the human animal. It is the beginning of the unsentimental Darwinian depiction of our nature that would become Britain's most original contribution to modern art.

The Real Thing, Revisited

On the 10th of March, 1914 suffragette Mary Richardson took out a hatchet she had smuggled into the National Gallery on Trafalgar Square and repeatedly slashed one of the most celebrated European paintings of the nude, the 'Rokeby Venus' by Velázquez.

Was Richardson's attack a critique of the way this painting offers up silky female flesh for the male eye? It is probably anachronistic to attribute feminist theories of the gaze that emerged long afterwards to this early twentieth-century iconoclast. In fact Richardson put her case in terms that belong firmly to her time:

> *I have tried to destroy the picture of the most beautiful woman in mythological history as a protest against the Government for destroying Mrs Pankhurst, who is the most beautiful character in modern history. Justice is an element of beauty as much as colour and outline on canvas. Mrs Pankhurst seeks to procure justice for womanhood, and for this she is being slowly murdered...*

Yet there is no avoiding the symbolism. Women for millennia had been the subjects of art, not its creators. Women artists have so far been rare in this story because while it was hard to stop Jane Austen and George Eliot from writing – all they needed was pen and paper – the rigorous training expected of pre-modern artists and the rarity of access to that specialist education for women made the likes of Artemisia Gentileschi and Angelica Kauffman few and far between.

The Suffragette movement sought votes for women at a time when centuries of gender injustice were becoming hard to hide or explain. Sickert's paintings of domestic stress share with Conrad's 1907 novel *The Secret Agent* a sense that something is very wrong in the British household. *The Secret Agent* exposes an apparently respectable lower middle-class marriage as a sham on every level. Mr and Mrs Verloc support their conventional home life with proceeds from a porn shop – except that is a sham too, for Adolf Verloc is really an agent provocateur working for a foreign government. When his secret profession explodes into chaos and death, his wife Winnie, who never loved him, is driven like a character in Greek tragedy to stab him to death.

The 1884 Reform Act that recognized working-class voters did so by enfranchising all male householders – a bizarre decision that literally made Britain a patriarchal society, with Daddy in charge. Young upper-class men who were not yet householders were disenfranchised, while educated middle-class women had less political power than men they might regard as social inferiors. It was a wildly unstable situation and the Suffragettes fought it with spectacle and shock.

Gwen John took a quieter route. The life of this haunting Welsh painter reveals the tribulations women had to endure to become artists at the start of the twentieth century. John trained alongside her charismatic and, at the time, hugely acclaimed brother Augustus at the Slade School of Art, which became Britain's leading art college in the 1890s and 1900s – and the only one that admitted women. The Johns were not a wealthy family. After squatting in London, Gwen John hustled her way to Europe, and after living rough became an artist's model in Paris. It was the old story. Having sought to be an artist, John became merely someone (something?) for male artists to look at – just like Whistler's and Courbet's model, Joanna Hiffernan, just like the women who modelled for the 'Rokeby Venus' in the seventeenth century and for Sickert's *Camden Town Murder* in 1908.

Even more stereotypically, John's modelling led to a relationship with a male artist – the revolutionary sculptor Auguste Rodin. As

Rodin's lover for ten years she saw the art of Paris up close. When she settled in the French village of Meudon she painted with a fervent, solitary intensity that has some of the gravitas of Cézanne's portraits but perhaps owes just as much to still lifes in the Louvre by the eighteenth-century master of silence, Jean-Siméon Chardin.

Girl in a Green Dress, painted some time between 1915 and 1925, typifies her sombre concentration on women observed alone in moods of contemplation. There is a dignified autonomy to John's art, a validation of inner states. In her 1918–19 painting *The Convalescent*, a young woman sits absorbed in a letter, with a pot of tea beside her. There are echoes of the seventeenth-century artist Jan Vermeer in its study of a moment of pure unfettered introspection.

If Mary Richardson's attack on the 'Rokeby Venus' might seem to have some kind of cogency as a precocious manifesto of feminist aesthetics, it is a lot harder to see why Mary Wood (real name Mary Aldham) selected John Singer Sargent's portrait of the novelist Henry James for a Suffragette attack in May 1914. She went for it with a meat cleaver, which certainly livened up the Royal Academy summer show that year. What was so particularly patriarchal about this serious portrait of a cerebral novelist?

Wood said she chose it for its economic value:

> *I have tried to destroy a valuable picture because I wish to show the public that they have no security for their property nor for their art treasures until women are given ... political freedom.*

Art was big money in 1914. Everything was big money. The early twentieth century was a plutocratic age when business profits soared and the wealthy lived it large. Rival empires and international tensions of the age seemed like ripples on the surface of what had become a truly global economy, with London as arguably its central cash nexus. The economist John Maynard Keynes famously remembered that in these years a – presumably well-heeled – Londoner could purchase:

> *...by telephone, sipping his morning tea in bed, the various products of the whole earth, in such quantity as he might see fit, and reasonably expect their early delivery upon his doorstep.*

Who needed Internet shopping when we had an empire?

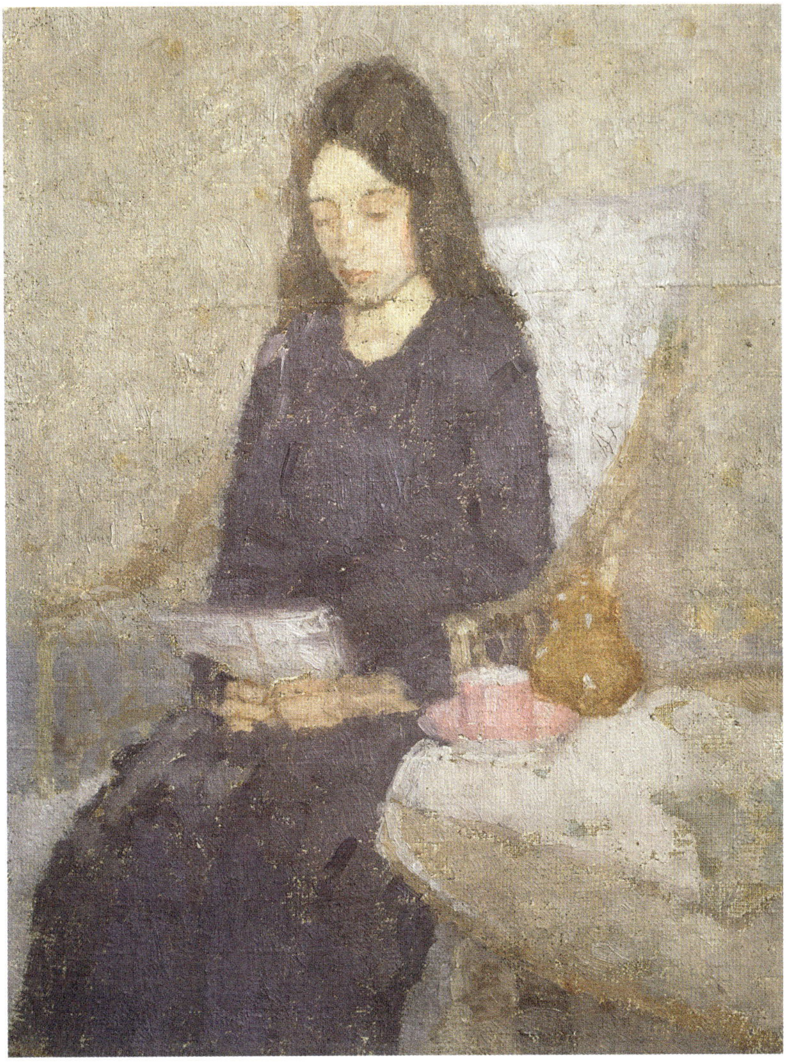

Another thing this inhabitant of plutocratic London might do was commission a portrait from John Singer Sargent.

This American abroad, born almost literally in a suitcase in 1856 to wealthy, wandering, expatriate Yankee parents who happened to be in Florence at the time, had a life that could easily have been invented by his friend Henry James. After a childhood spent touring Europe he trained as a painter in Paris, where he knew and admired Monet, without ever becoming anything as wild as an Impressionist. Sargent understood French avant-garde art, learned from it, yet painted portraits whose

↑ Gwen John, *The Convalescent*, 1918–19, oil on canvas, 33.7 × 25.4 cm (13 ¼ × 10 in.), Tate

formality and grandeur give them the swagger of Van Dyck or Rubens. The results are brilliantly provocative and alive. Sargent, like Sickert, is an anthropologist of modern life. Where Sickert portrays the London working class with the eye of an ethnographer reporting from the edge of empire, Sargent studies the rich and powerful with equal acuity.

Sargent, like Sickert, is also intensely theatrical. One of the reasons his portraits are so vivid and memorable is that he sees everyone as a 'character' – in the sense both of someone arresting, and of a personage on stage. For Sargent the empirical truth of a person is not simple. To get at it you have to dramatize something about them. His paintings are costume dramas in which we are invited to see heroes and villains, women of fortune and men with secrets.

It would be tempting to speculate on Lord Ribblesdale's secret. In Sargent's 1902 portrait this archetypal aristocrat poses in hunting clothes with his riding crop in his hand. With his top hat and long black coat, his hard gaze and potent stance, Ribblesdale appears the essence of an English 'milord', as Sargent's French friends might say, who has stepped straight out of a fantasy of English depravity by Maupassant. His whip might suggest, in such a story, *le vice anglais*. Yet any hint of sadism is subterranean. The conscious symbolism of the whip Sargent has him hold seems to be political, for Ribblesdale whipped for the Liberals in the House of Lords from 1896 to 1907.

In his 1892 story 'The Real Thing', Henry James adopts the voice of an artist who works as an illustrator for magazines and books. When an immaculately dressed and well-mannered English upper-crust couple visit his studio he believes at first they have come to commission a portrait. This is exciting, for 'I couldn't get the honours, to say nothing of the emoluments, of a great painter of portraits out of my head.'

But no, the impressive couple want him to pay them as models. They suggest that as gentlefolk they are perfectly equipped to pose in scenes that feature people of their rank. They are after all 'the real thing'.

Yet as the artist attempts to use them in his illustrations to a luxury edition of the works of a famous novelist, he finds something is not quite right. His usual, working-class models can actually play the parts better. Being the real thing is not enough to look like it in art. The couple are no good at playing what they in reality are.

James's story has subtle fun with the notion that art can never portray reality. The most real-seeming image is a fiction. The artist transforms and invents. Reality is endlessly elusive.

→ John Singer Sargent, *Lord Ribblesdale*, 1902, oil on canvas, 258.4 × 143.5 cm (101¾ × 56½ in.), National Gallery, London

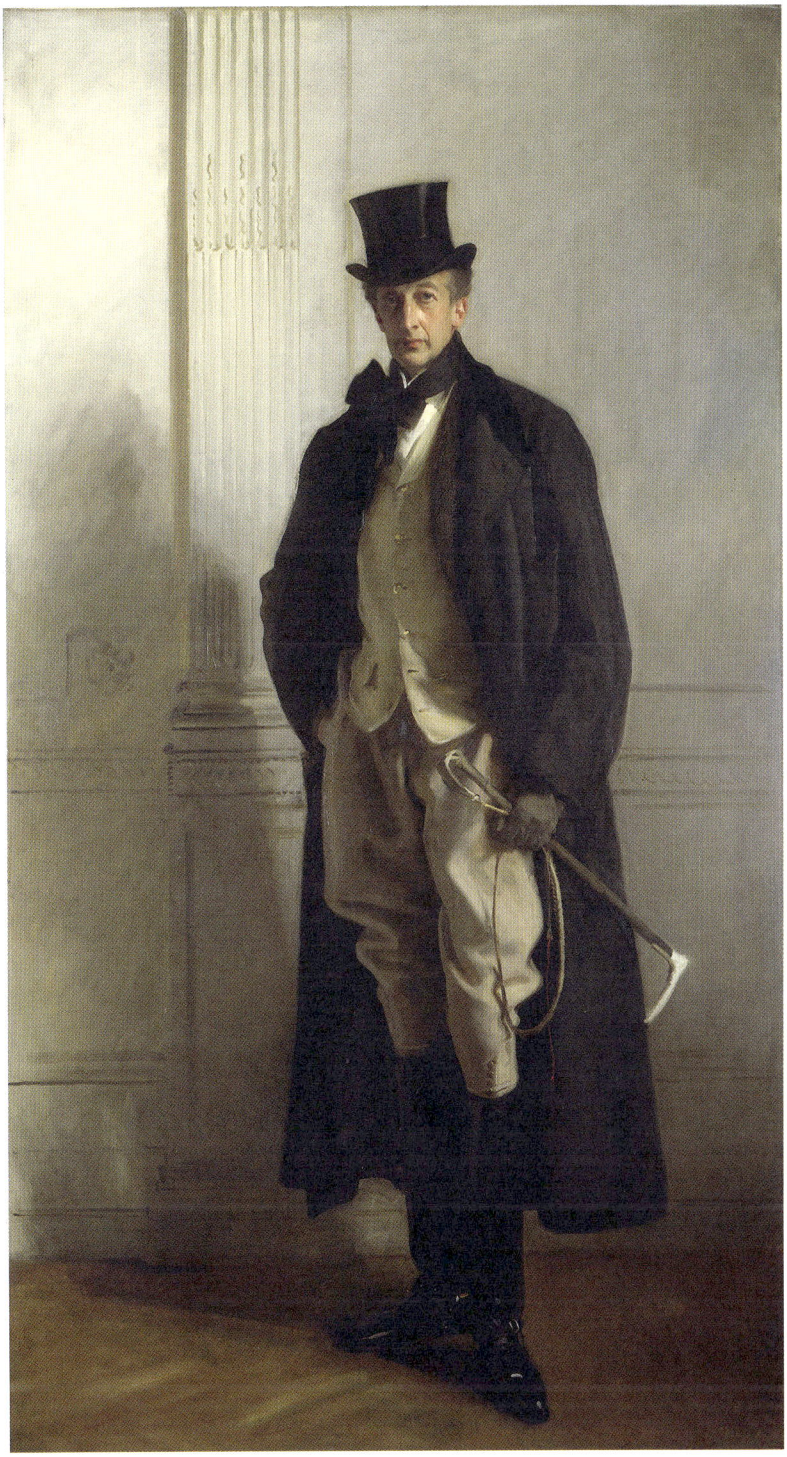

Sargent is almost certainly the model of the 'great painter of portraits' that James's narrator has it in mind to become, for James and Sargent had been friends since the 1880s and admired one another. James understood the sophistication and nuance of his friend's art and saw he was much more than a society flatterer. The narrator of 'The Real Thing' explains that his true purpose is to portray 'character':

> *I might only be a presumptuous young modern searcher: but I held that everything was to be sacrificed sooner than character.*

The trouble with his new genteel models is that they cannot act out or suggest characters: they are simply themselves. The real thing gets in the way of the characterful thing.

Character is subjective, a fancy. It is what Sargent excels at in painting. Nowhere does he convey it more efficaciously than in the full-length portrait of Arthur James Balfour commissioned in 1908. Balfour had been Conservative prime minister from 1902 until he resigned in 1905 (he was still leader of his party). He was also a philosopher, whose world-weary cynicism is encapsulated in the title of his book *A Defence of Philosophic Doubt*.

Sargent captures all that, and more. The tall, sinuous, silver-haired statesman leaning against a classical pilaster as if it were a fireplace stretches out long, willowy fingers like a Wildean aesthete. He looks at the world out of sagging, tired, knowing eyes. The thin black shape of his body against creamy stone, stalked by his own sinister shadow, adds to the sense of exquisite style and taste, the impression that we are seeing not a prosaic politician but a master of the parliamentary arts.

Balfour really did play politics as an ironic philosophical game, as Sargent exquisitely suggests. In 1906 the Liberal Party won a landslide election victory. Under the leadership of Herbert Asquith, the radical minsters David Lloyd George and Winston Churchill started ambitious social reforms that were the first stumblings towards a welfare state. Balfour, however, played the Conservatives' trump card – a permanent majority in the aristocratic House of Lords. Their Lordships vetoed so much legislation that a direct confrontation between the lower and upper houses, people and aristocracy, erupted. The eloquent lawyer Lloyd George, whose sense of injustice was formed in the mountains of North Wales in a rural society with callous, remote landlords, led the democratic attack on inherited wealth and power. In July 1909 he made a passionate speech in Limehouse in London's East End, attacking the landed class in words of revolutionary fire:

> *...the landlord is a gentleman who does not earn his wealth. He does not even take the trouble to receive his wealth. He has a host of agents and clerks to receive it for him. He does not even take the trouble to spend his wealth. He has a host of people around him to do the actual spending for him. He never sees it until he comes to enjoy it. His sole function, his chief pride, is stately consumption of wealth produced by others.*

The House of Lords crisis was not the only firework that exploded in these years of rage and panic. As we have seen, the campaign for women's votes felt like an assault on the patriarchal foundations of the age. Another crisis coming to a head was the fate of Ireland. In the late nineteenth century, Irish demands for self-rule dominated British politics. John Bull's oldest colony, whose violent subjugation in the reigns of Elizabeth I and Oliver Cromwell was a dress rehearsal for colonies further afield, suffered famine and hunger-driven emigration amid Victorian prosperity that drove a growing fury.

The great Victorian Liberal leader William Gladstone was converted to Irish Home Rule in his old age and introduced two bills to enact it in 1886 and 1893. Not only did they fail in Parliament but the Liberal Party split as the Birmingham politician Joseph Chamberlain and his allies formed the Liberal Unionist Party, opposing Home Rule, which joined with the Conservatives to form the Unionist government of 1895 to 1905.

Gladstone's second Home Rule Bill had been vetoed by the House of Lords; the curbing of that House's powers in 1911 paved the way for a new Liberal Home Rule Bill in 1912. This brought Unionists to the brink of civil insurrection. The Ulster politician Edward Carson, who in his career as a barrister had crushed Oscar Wilde's case against the Marquess of Queensberry, rallied Northern Ireland's Protestants to fight 'the most nefarious conspiracy that has ever been hatched against a free people'. By 1914 he agreed plans to procure guns for the coming struggle. The new Conservative leader, Andrew Bonar Law, himself an Ulsterman, strongly sided with Carson's Ulster Unionists in what looked like a lurch towards civil war.

These were strange days. George Dangerfield's provocative classic of history writing *The Strange Death of Liberal England*, first published in 1935, argues that Britain was on the edge of revolution and civil war in the years from 1906 and 1914, as liberalism, not just as a party but as an ideology of free trade, human rights and the moderate rule of reason, was killed by modern forces unleashed in democracy's dangerous dawn.

Most political historians today judge Dangerfield's thesis histrionic and sensational. Yet it is curiously illuminating of British art on the eve of World War I. For to judge from the images and manifestos issuing from London's art world, the apocalypse was truly at hand.

The Killing Machine

It surveys the world curiously and warily, leaning its long smooth helmet-snout forward as if to identify the last surviving human specimens on a ravaged battlefield. For the last war has come, and the future belongs to this machine.

The aerodynamic head, shaped like a spacecraft, balances on a long girder-like neck that protrudes from a tapered torso ribbed with metallic hoops. Below this artificial rib cage, a vertical void like a secret recess in a tomb contains the creature's child. This being must contain organic life after all, for it holds this fleshy offspring within it. Are we looking at a cyborg into which we humans are destined to evolve? If so, it is a hermaphrodite cyborg. As well as the baby in its steel belly it rests its long shapely mechanical legs on a massive industrial drill whose piercing machinery seems to emerge from its loins and extend its male sexual prowess. It is a phallocratic androgyne designed to leap across the wastelands of the future like a robot kangaroo on its giant pounding drill.

When the artist David Bomberg saw it in the studio of the American-born sculptor Jacob Epstein in Lamb's Conduit Street, London, in December 1913 it stood nearly 2 metres (7 feet) high. Its plaster body posed on a real miner's drill propped by three spider-like legs. Today this first version of Epstein's sculpture *The Rock Drill* exists only as a ghostly black-and-white photograph. It is like seeing a fading document of some real metal monster that terrorized London in the early twentieth century. If it looks, for all its strange menace,

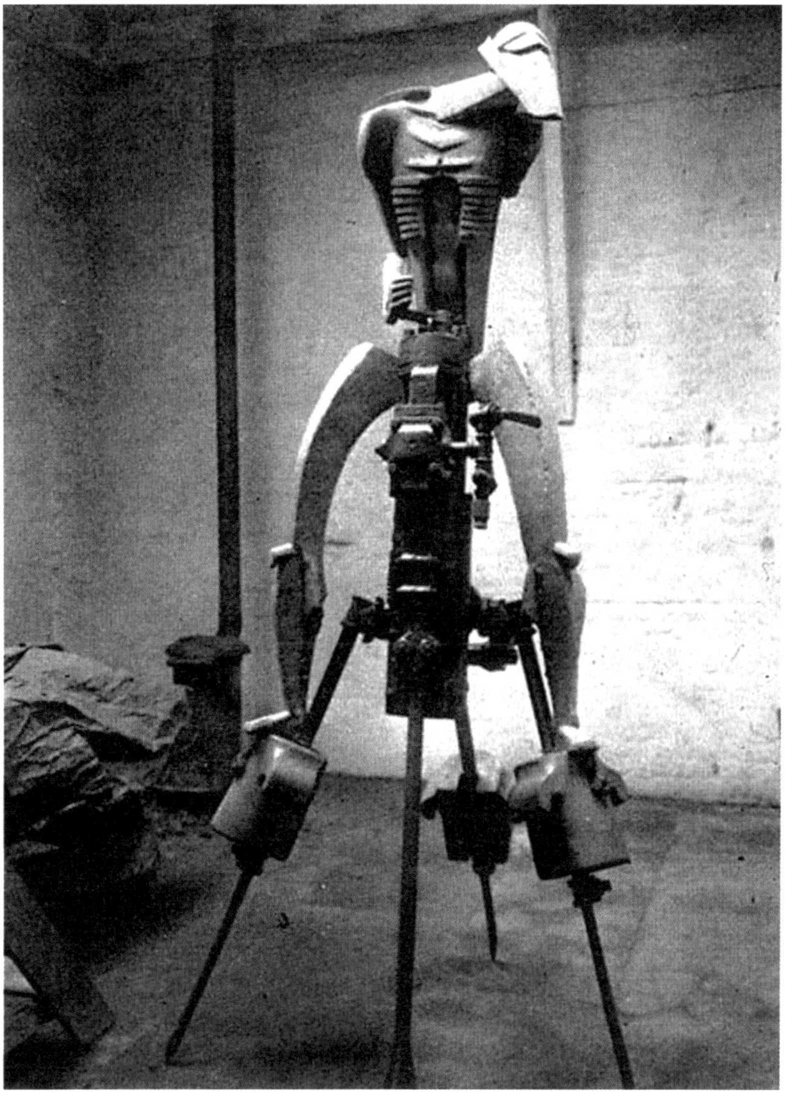

familiar, that is because it helped to create the visual language of science fiction we still use. It is one of the first ever attempts to imagine a post-human mechanical being. Cyborg or autonomous machine, *The Rock Drill* was created seven years before the Czech writer Karel Čapek invented 'robots' with his 1920 science fiction play *R.U.R.* Epstein himself, remembering his most audacious creation, compared it with an earlier science fiction masterpiece, Mary Shelley's *Frankenstein*:

↑ Jacob Epstein, *The Rock Drill*, 1913, black-and-white photograph of lost work, Birmingham Museum and Art Gallery

> *It was in the experimental pre-war days of 1913 that I was fired to do the rock drill, and my ardour for machinery (short-lived) expended itself on the purchase of an actual drill, second-hand, and upon this I made and mounted a machine-like robot, visored, menacing, and carrying within itself its progeny, protectively ensconced. Here is the armed, sinister figure of today and tomorrow. No humanity, only the terrible Frankenstein's monster we have made ourselves into.*

Epstein was talking with hindsight, but the 1913 photograph of his lost masterpiece completely justified his incendiary description of it. The creature's visored head has not a trace of a human visage, no means of expressing emotions even if it had them. From its throbbing phallic drill to its cold surveying gaze it embodies threat. With its open womb revealing its humanoid 'progeny', *The Rock Drill* seems to have evolved from us. Like a Dalek, its newborn will be cradled in steel, fortified by electronics, deprived of emotion and turned into a living machine.

The vision that lurked on the edge of the Bloomsbury district where London's avant-garde was centred in 1913 prophesied the end of humanity. It also expressed with precision the anxieties of its moment. Just as the Suffragette movement was making gender political and summoning up suppressed anxieties of sexual identity, Epstein created this mechanical androgyne from the future. And at the very moment that British politics appeared to be robotically ploughing towards civil war in Ireland, Epstein created this post-human war machine, perfectly adapted to modern conflict.

Jacob Epstein already had a reputation for danger and disruptiveness. Born in New York in 1880, the son of Jewish refugees from Poland, he had studied in Paris before settling in London and becoming a British citizen. In 1908 he was commissioned to create a monument for the tomb of Oscar Wilde in Paris. Epstein's memorial defiantly asserts the 'love that dare not speak its name' – in fact, it celebrates all sexual love. It is a thrusting horizontal angel of desire, phallically moving forward into the future just as *The Rock Drill* thrusts itself downward at an earth it assaults.

Even in a Paris that was home to Picasso and Matisse, the tomb sculpture of Oscar Wilde caused ructions. Its nudity was thought so outrageous it was at first covered with a tarpaulin. Then plaster was used to smother the angel of love's huge testicles. Much later, they would be stolen.

Epstein's eroticism was partly inspired by the sensuality of Indian art. He and his friend the sculptor Eric Gill were the first British artists to seriously seek creative inspiration from cultures ruled by the British Empire. Throughout the nineteenth century, artistic treasures from India, Africa and further afield had been reaching Britain. The East India Company had even opened its own museum of India's art as early as 1801. Yet the idea of learning a new way to see from non-Western art was unimaginable: these exotic objects were at best collectables.

Paris looked with different eyes. It is time to catch up with the waves of artistic revolution pulsating from the French capital.

The French avant-garde was drawn to non-European art as early as 1893, when Paul Gauguin painted Oceanian sculptures in the background of his portrait *Ancestors of Tehamana, or Tehamana Has Many Parents*. In 1906 André Derain painted *The Dance*, a wild vision of a primal Arcadia that includes a figure covered in blue tattoos. The following year Picasso painted *Les Demoiselles d'Avignon*, a scything, aggressive, diamond-hard vision of a gathering of pink prostitutes among blue and white lozenges of colour. Two of the women appear to have African masks for faces. At the same time, Derain, Picasso and Matisse were studying 'primitive' art in the Trocadéro in Paris and starting to collect it. The cult of the 'primitive' was born.

Art untainted by European intellectual habits helped artists to escape their straitjacket of supposed knowledge and common sense. The completely unexpected ways in which African wood carvers created images of the human face liberated Picasso to make outlandish faces of his own. This was the moment when avant-garde art became not simply challenging but completely unrecognizable to eyes schooled in convention. In 1910, Picasso and Georges Braque embarked on a series of experimental canvases in which they tried to extend the discoveries of Cézanne, who had searched for the underlying structure of the visible world. Their portraits and still lifes became fractured monochrome kaleidoscopes of shaded planes, in which drawings of circles, musical notes or eyes gave the smallest of handholds to the befuddled beholder.

Braque and Picasso kept their adventure quiet, sharing their quest at first with just a few friends and supporters. This was committed research, whose goal was not shock or celebrity but a new way to see. Nevertheless word got out. The strange new art was nicknamed 'Cubism'.

Ambitious young artists started practising it as a style, without the same rigour or restlessness. Cubistic paintings of bicycle races and the Eiffel Tower created a marketable image of the new. Suddenly modernism was an idea that could be waved like a banner. In 1909 the Italian poet F. T. Marinetti published a manifesto in the French newspaper *Le Figaro* for his new Futurist movement. He called on the young to attack the past, reject sentiment, praise speed, even glorify war. Futurism had no art style to start with, but the broken mirror of Cubism pointed a way to a fast, warping aesthetics of energy and change.

In 1913, the year Epstein created *The Rock Drill*, all these forces came together in a constellation of revolutionary works of art. At a moment of epoch-making artistic change, *The Rock Drill* stands in all its sinister glory shoulder to shoulder with a dazzling parade of modern masterpieces.

On 29 May 1913, the premiere of Igor Stravinsky's ballet *The Rite of Spring* caused a near-riot in Paris. With its story of human sacrifice danced violently by Nijinsky to jagged swoops and blades of sound, *Rite* hurled primitivist atavism and Cubistic dissonance at its wealthy audience. That same year the Futurist artist Umberto Boccioni created his sculpture *Unique Forms of Continuity in Space*, a striding figure whose motion leaves flanges and waves of energy behind it and sends beams of power ahead, so that instead of an enclosed body we see the trace of human movement in the ether. Meanwhile Picasso and Braque were now into the 'Synthetic' phase of Cubism, pasting real newspaper clippings into still lifes such as Picasso's 1913 collage-drawing *Bottle of Vieux Marc, Glass, Guitar and Newspaper*. After visiting Picasso's studio, the future Russian Constructivist Vladimir Tatlin also created his first relief object, *The Bottle*, in 1913.

Like these experiments with collage and found materials, Epstein's 1913 version of *The Rock Drill* used a real object taken directly from the world: a powerful mining drill, no less. It was more substantial than a piece of newsprint and Epstein made no attempt to make it into 'art'. Instead the robot he sculpted in plaster is granted a share of the drill's reality. The name of the work is simply the name of the apparatus: this is the rock drill, come to life.

The artist with whom Epstein's vision has most in common is Marcel Duchamp. In 1913 this former Cubist fixed a bicycle wheel on top of a kitchen stool to create a confounding cyclopean object. Like *The Rock Drill*, Duchamp's *Bicycle Wheel* uses real parts of the world around him. In fact it was Duchamp's first 'readymade'. Yet it is not just a taste for the found that Epstein shares with Duchamp.

The previous year, 1912, Duchamp had sequestered himself in Munich to think about perspective and plan an ambitious work, *Large Glass*. It was to be a mechanical ballet mapped out in empty space with domestic machines, including a chocolate grinder, as characters and sex as its theme. Duchamp's *Large Glass* would take years to create and even longer to interpret. At the heart of it was a joke about machines and sex. Duchamp, like Epstein, was creating science fiction. He was prophesying a future in which machines would fall in love and their desires would fuel a new kind of ethereal cosmic beauty.

Duchamp and Epstein were both haunted in 1913 by the beauty and strangeness of machines. Epstein remembered it as a brief infatuation: 'my ardour for machinery (short-lived) expended itself on the purchase of an actual drill, second-hand.'

He jokes about the sexual perversity of it all – his 'ardour', he says, 'expended itself' in buying a throbbing mighty rock drill. Epstein's 1913 masterpiece is truly at the drilling edge of its time. It shares with Duchamp a science fiction vision of sexualized machines replacing the worn-out human animal. Yet it is scarier than Duchamp's intellectual jests. It is evil. It threatens our very existence.

Mechanical monsters had already invaded London once. At the end of the nineteenth century their spaceships landed in Surrey, and they stalked on spindly metal legs across the capital, killing without mercy. In H. G. Wells's 1898 novel *The War of the Worlds* these killing machines were piloted by Martians. *The Rock Drill* could be their heir. For it too is a fiction, a story. Epstein, like Sickert and Sargent, is a fabulist and this is an entertainment for the end of the world.

The Rock Drill, in its original monstrous heroism, was the masterpiece of a dynamic moment in British art when Futurists and Vorticists each offered disconcerting, brutal images of the machine age.

In June 1914 the grand, gilded interior of the London Coliseum shook to the discordant sounds of Luigi Russolo's *intonarumori*, noise machines bristling with loudspeakers that he claimed were the future of music. In his 1913 manifesto for a Futurist 'Art of Noises', Russolo declared that Futurism wanted to replace the cosy harmonies of orchestral music with a riotous imitation of modern urban sounds:

> *...the eddying of water, air and gas in metal pipes, the grumbling of noises that breathe and pulse with indisputable animality, the palpitation of valves, the coming and going of pistons, the howl of mechanical saws...*

For 12 nights in 1914, curious audiences flocked to the Coliseum to be provoked, amused or outraged by Russolo's Art of Noises. It was part of a Futurist invasion of London that also saw the movement's leader, Marinetti, give sensational readings and speeches in bookshops and cafés, performing poems whose spiky grammar and bomblike booms praised the joy of war.

In 1912 Marinetti had gone enthusiastically to war. When Serbia, Bulgaria, Greece and Montenegro attacked the crumbling Ottoman Empire he rushed to report on this brief conflict for an Italian newspaper. After experiencing all the sound and fury of modern armaments in an assault on Adrianopolis – today's Edirne in western Turkey – he composed his Futurist war poem *Zong Toomb Toomb*. When he performed it at the Doré Gallery in New Bond Street, London, in 1914 he used wooden boards and hammers to recreate the noise of battle:

> *...2,000 grenades thunder of applause Quick*
> *quick what enthusiasm...*

The First Balkan War was just a far-off little struggle, with no larger implications for western Europe, many might have thought. Yet Marinetti saw and heard the future in it.

In June 1914 *The Observer* published an article that Marinetti co-wrote with the British Futurist painter C. R. W. Nevinson, urging British artists to develop 'a cult of strength and... moral and physical courage, the strong virtues of the English race'.

The Vorticists were not keen on taking advice from an Italian. The true spirit of the new, they claimed, was not continental but thoroughly British. Their leader, the artist and writer Percy Wyndham Lewis (he preferred to drop the Percy), aimed for the same kind of aggressive charisma as Marinetti himself. In photographs from the time his cigarette-smoking, loose-haired stylishness looks defiant and brash. His friends included the American poet Ezra Pound, who later remembered him as the romantic 'd'Artagnan' of their little group.

Pound fondly recalled the small printshop in Harlesden, northwest London, that coped with the brilliantly disruptive typesetting of *Blast*, the magazine-cum-manifesto whose first issue (of two) Wyndham Lewis edited in 1914. It was actually the wordsmith Pound who suggested a suitably spiralling, surging, menacing name for their movement: Vorticism. How exactly Vorticism differed from Futurism

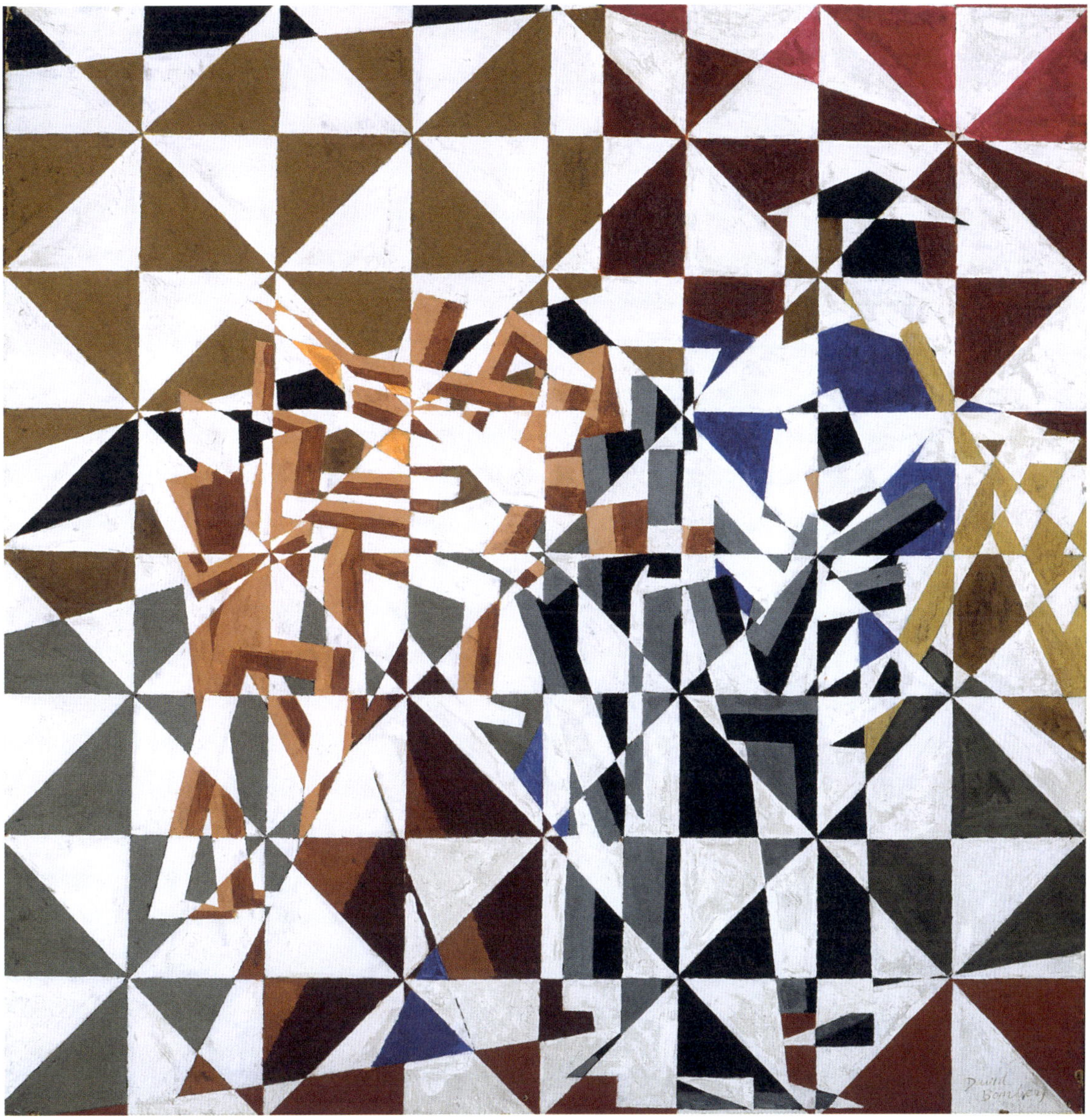

is a subtle mystery, but it claimed to be more truly modern than any continental movement. After all, declared *Blast*:

> *The Modern World is due almost entirely to Anglo-Saxon genius – its appearance and its spirit.*

↑ David Bomberg, *Ju-Jitsu*, c. 1913, oil on board, 76 × 76 × 3.5 cm (30 × 30 × 1⅓ in.), Tate

The rantings of Futurists and Vorticists in the London art world were part of a riotous conversation among artists and poets about how to be modern, which happened mostly in the area between St Pancras and the British Museum. Since 1905 a circle of intellectuals and creative types had met, debated and made love to each other in Bloomsbury. Wyndham Lewis worked briefly at the Omega Workshops in Fitzroy Square, founded in 1913 by the Bloomsbury Group's star art critic Roger Fry, who ran it with the painters Vanessa Bell and Duncan Grant. It produced lovely curtains, cushion covers and upholstery in the bright colours of Cézanne and the Fauves. Yet this version of French modern art was already old hat in 1913. Bell and Grant were happy to paint a safe, timid after-image of French Modernism. Only very rarely, as in his painting *The Tub* dating from about 1913, does Grant come close to capturing some of the primitivist fire of Picasso's *Demoiselles d'Avignon*.

You have to side with Wyndham Lewis when he rejected this pale British copy of modern art, walking out on the Omega Workshops to open his own Rebel Art Centre on nearby Great Ormond Street. He was one of a generation of troublemakers. In 1913 the Slade School of Art – which also happened to be in Bloomsbury – expelled the Jewish East Ender David Bomberg for being artistically disruptive. His painting *Ju-Jitsu* probably from that year shows why his conservative teachers had a problem. It is an explosion of tubular bodies inside a grid of interconnected triangles, as if a bomb has gone off in a tile factory.

Epstein aside, the most gifted and original artist of this rebel moment was a young French sculptor who moved to Britain in 1908 and, in an unusual gesture for a time when the avant-garde seemed obsessed with 'virility', took the surname of his girlfriend, Sophie Brzeska. The art of Henri Gaudier-Brzeska has a compacted power. He was a fully paid-up Vorticist who contributed to *Blast*. Pound called him 'the most complete case of Genius I have ever encountered' – high praise from someone who knew Duchamp and was a close friend of T. S. Eliot.

In his masterpiece *Bird Swallowing a Fish*, begun around 1913, a bishop's mitre appears to be digesting an artillery shell. This is a vision of nature for the machine age – a nightmare of animals as mechanical beings. The bird is alien, monstrous, its appetite robotic and unconscious. Its beak engulfs an equally robotic fish whose eye stares emptily at its own death.

After Pound introduced Wyndham Lewis to his young poet friend T. S. Eliot, the student writer submitted a poem to *Blast*.

Wyndham Lewis rejected 'The Triumph of Bullshit' for being too vulgar, with its repeated chorus, 'For Christ's sake stick it up your ass'.

Perhaps that rejection reveals the limits of British modern art, even at this ambitious moment. For it suggests that Wyndham Lewis was not so different from the genteel Bloomsbury set after all. *Blast*, as Pound admitted, was read by almost no one. All the noise and clatter of Vorticism and Futurism was confined to a small network of London galleries and a few newspaper articles. Yet these prophets of the machine age had an uncanny intimation of the terrible fate that was about to overtake their generation.

The tragedy that unfolded in the summer of 1914 was a complex accident rather than an act of will. There was something robotic about the descent into war through the thoughtless unfolding of treaty clauses and railway timetables. The assassination of Archduke Franz Ferdinand of Austria-Hungary by Serbian nationalists on 28 June 1914 might have led to nothing in particular. Instead, Germany supported Austria and encouraged it to take tough measures, Russia stood up for Serbia, France supported its ally Russia, and Germany started putting war plans into action because it needed to move fast to survive a struggle on two fronts. Britain defended Belgium. Thus the Great War started. Yet it was not so much its causes as its nature and consequences that mattered.

The war broke out at a moment when technological development guaranteed it would prove unprecedented in its ferocity and slaughter. Firepower had overtaken traditional tactics without the tacticians knowing. Cavalry were obsolete and in infantry attacks thousands of men could be rapidly mown down. Only by sheltering in muddy, disease-ridden trenches could soldiers on the Western Front reduce their vulnerability to shells and machine guns. From 1916 poison gas added to the suffering. The visions of Futurists and Vorticists were apposite; the world really did become a death machine in August 1914. Yet the martial spirit of the avant-garde that year also shows why war attracted so many enthusiastic volunteers.

Nevinson, friend and follower of Marinetti that he was, volunteered for an ambulance unit and painted Futurist visions of soldiers dehumanized by machines, an abstract ballet of harsh geometries. His 1915 painting *Bursting Shell* sees a terrible beauty in war. The coruscating light of an explosion radiates in cosmic colours, changing and transforming everything forever. We do not know where we are or what is happening to this smashed world. Is the shell bursting

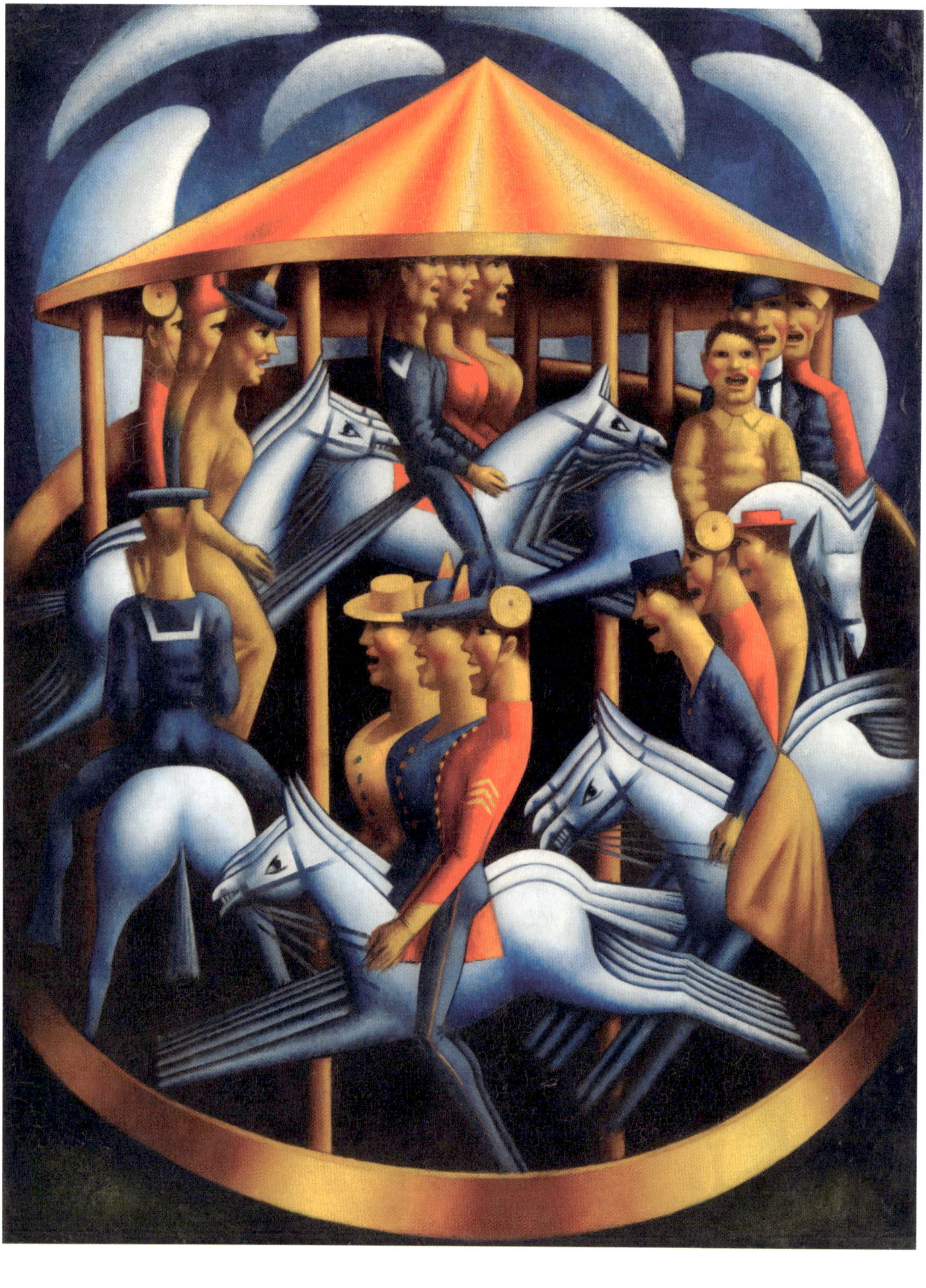

↑ Mark Gertler, *Merry-Go-Round*, 1916, oil on canvas, 210 × 162 cm (82 ⅝ × 63 ¾ in.), Tate

in a tunnel or pit, or are we seeing the world spin as we ourselves are blown up? Wyndham Lewis sees soldiers as robotic puppets in his 1919 painting *A Battery Shelled*. They stumble across a churned-up battlefield like broken mechanisms, abstract stick-men. Yet this is not quite what it seems. A group in the foreground are more characterful. They stand pensively, reflecting on the shattered Vorticist battlefield. Why are some human and others not? This painting lets us into the psychology of war. Enemy soldiers and even comrades can seem distant, remote, unreal. In war, you save yourself by effacing fellowship with others.

Even the home front seemed inhuman and manic. Mark Gertler's 1916 painting *Merry-Go-Round* depicts soldiers in uniform among the mad adult participants in a pointlessly rotating fairground ride. Their faces are brutalized masks, their individuality willingly sacrificed to a savage, inane herd instinct.

War did not immediately make gentle humanists of Britain's technophile avant-garde. Yet as it wore on, their armour disintegrated. Nevinson's 1916 painting *The Doctor* abandons any Futurist joy in the abstract patterns of war. Here he shows not the bursting shell but what it does to human bodies. His lack of cheap conventional sentiment means he does not conceal the humiliation and grotesqueness of the wounded men's suffering. One is having shrapnel picked out of his posterior. This would be comic if it were not so catastrophic.

Nevinson's style became more realist as his illusions about war gave way to straightforward compassion. His 1917 picture *Paths of Glory* is an unvarnished study of two dead soldiers face down in a tangle of barbed wire. Nevinson looks hard at the lumpen shapes of their bodies, the bluntness of death as a physical fact.

Henry Tonks did not have to change his style to portray the war's truth. This most empirical of observers was a qualified surgeon who operated in London hospitals and lectured in anatomy, before going to evening classes in art in his spare time, and discovering a talent that led to a spectacular change of career as a senior teacher at the Slade School of Art. With his professional experiences, he was not impressed by young rebels and took part in expelling Bomberg.

When the war began, Tonks returned to medicine and by 1916 was invited to work with the pioneer of facial reconstruction Harold Gillies, who asked him to draw portraits of the disfigured soldiers he was treating. These pastels are unique documents. They are utterly honest, yet the fact that they are made by a human hand gives them a compassion no clinical photograph of these men could communicate.

For Tonks always sees the human being inside the ruined face. We look with dismay at what has been done to these young men. The red open holes where eyes once were, the mouths that are gashes, the holes for noses. Yet instead of horror, Tonks turns our feeling to sympathy. He is the good doctor as artist, his science a work of humanity and love.

Henri Gaudier-Brzeska did not get a chance to mature. He was killed on the Western Front in 1915.

As for Epstein, he maimed *The Rock Drill*. His 'ardour for machinery' was gone. He reduced his triumphant cyborg to a one-armed bronze stump of its former self, a wounded killer with a broken heart.

A Heap of Broken Images

We Are Making A New World, says the sardonic title of a terrifying Western Front landscape that Paul Nash painted in 1918. Not one tree has been spared. Black stubs of life are stuck like gibbets into a ground reduced to a patchwork of holes and tumour-like mounds. The stuttering survival of such a deformed and injured earth is an insult in itself. Nature is no longer a lush reassurance but at best the ugly rose garden of a home for shellshocked convalescents. Nash shares this nausea at the persistence of life with T. S. Eliot's 1922 poem *The Waste Land*:

> *April is the cruellest month, breeding*
> *Lilacs out of the dead land.*

Neither Nash nor Eliot believe the world was healed by the Armistice signed on 11 November 1918.

World War I did not end in 1918. Instead it left unresolved crises and tensions and a peace treaty, signed at Versailles in 1919, that seemed to invite bitterness. Anyway, that was how the German nationalist right used it, accusing the victors of penalizing Germans, dismissing the new Weimar Republic as the work of 'back-stabbing' politicians who had supposedly betrayed an undefeated army.

The Russian Revolution in 1917 created the spectre of a communist state that, according to the extreme right, justified replacing 'feeble' capitalist democracy with a bold new ideal of nationalistic dictatorship. Italy became the first of these new dictatorships when Benito Mussolini led his fascist blackshirts into Rome in 1922. Marinetti, a keen supporter, sought to make Futurism the art of the fascist state.

→ Henry Tonks, *Reconstructive Surgical Procedures, Portrait of a Serviceman*, 1916–18, pastel on paper, 27.8 x 20.3 cm (11 x 8 in.), Hunterian Collection, Royal College of Surgeons, London

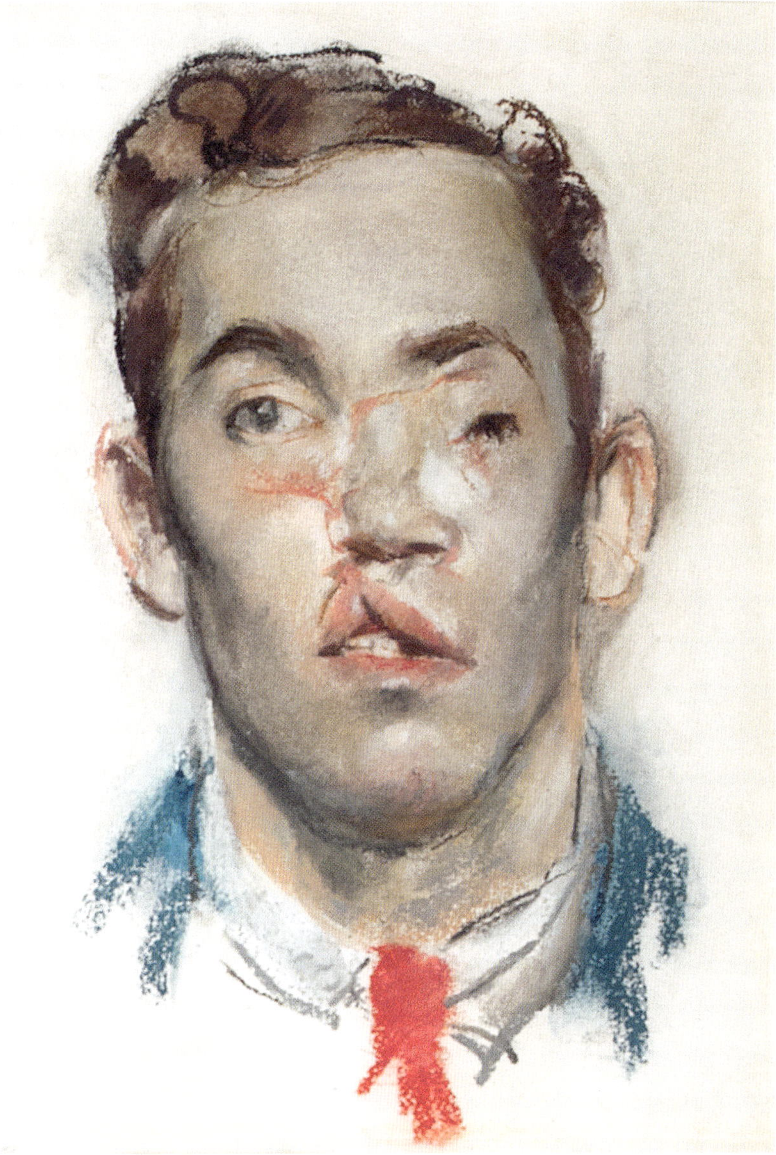

The 1929 Wall Street Crash plunged the world into an economic depression that deepened Europe's crisis of democracy. In 1933 Adolf Hitler became chancellor of Germany and quickly established a Nazi totalitarian state founded on racial hatred.

Some of Britain's most provocative modernists were drawn to the fascist and Nazi attack on democracy. In 1931 Wyndham Lewis published an enthusiastic book about Hitler. Pound met Mussolini in 1933 and was impressed. He was to become a wartime radio propagandist for fascist Italy.

In 1936 a civil war started in Spain when General Francisco Franco led his armed forces from North Africa to attack the democratic Spanish Republic. Wyndham Lewis sided with Franco. He translates the war to a quixotic vision of the Spanish Middle Ages in his painting *The Surrender of Barcelona*, finished in 1937. Yet for a younger generation of artists, that political choice was unimaginable. Instead it was Picasso's *Guernica*, a mural-scale painted protest against the bombing of the Basque town of Gernika by Hitler's Luftwaffe on behalf of Franco, that caught imaginations.

In 1939 *Guernica* went on view at the Whitechapel Gallery in London's East End. This black-and-white vision of terror and suffering that Picasso had painted to show in the Spanish Republic Pavilion at the 1937 Paris International Exhibition distills how modern art changed after 1918. The despair of the war seemed to the Paris art scene to demand a 'return to order'. Even Picasso started emulating the classical composure of Ingres. The human figure returned to the centre of art, as if the inhumanity of the age demanded an artistic reassertion of its fleshy vulnerability. In Picasso's 1923 painting *The Pipes of Pan*, two disarmingly near-nude young men share a gentle moment of contemplation and peace, their exposed skin a sign of intimacy.

Yet as the body was rediscovered so was the psyche. The poet André Breton had served in the war as a medical orderly. His experience with shellshocked soldiers led him to read the works of Sigmund Freud, who in fin-de-siècle Vienna had invented a new science of dreams and desire. Breton was transfixed by Freud's claim that our unconscious is the true secret landscape of the mind, a wild forest of symbols where sexuality rules. Freud showed how the unconscious manifests itself in dream images, verbal slips and jokes. Breton and his poet friends tried to find ways of letting the unconscious write their poems. His first Manifesto of Surrealism, issued in 1924, argues that 'automatic' creativity is the royal road to poetic genius and liberty from bourgeois reason.

Picasso never joined the Surrealist movement, but its ideas helped him break out of his 'classical' phase into a furious synthesis of neo-Cubistic visual violence, mythological grandeur and rampant sexuality. *Guernica* is the supreme masterpiece of this period. It witnesses war as a living nightmare, in images that have the lucidity of a waking dream. As he reads the newspaper – as the painting's lines of newsprint and monochrome resemblance to a 1930s press photograph suggest – a sequence of fragmentary images flash up. A woman with a dead baby in her arms. A burning house. A screaming horse.

For some British artists the 'call to order' after World War I was more than a return to a traditional aesthetic. It was a call from God. Stanley Spencer paints a folkloric lost idyll of obscure customs, prayers and hymns. His England is comic, tumultuous, and Christian. In 1915, as war raged across the world, he started a painting of a peaceful sun-blessed scene beside a shimmering, wind-ruffled river. *Swan Upping* depicts a ritual held on the Thames every summer by representatives of the monarch and the Dyers' and Vintners' companies of the City of London to establish ownership of swans, 'upping' a certain number from the river to mark them as City birds while the monarch's were left unmarked.

Spencer paints this curious, archaic ritual (which takes place to this day) in a curious, archaic style. His bright palette, boldly shaped spaces and roly-poly figures are rooted in the fifteenth century. The early perspective paintings of Piero della Francesca and Paolo Uccello echo in his heraldic vision. The young artist had to leave *Swan Upping* unfinished in his bedroom in the Thameside village of Cookham, where he was born in 1891, when he enlisted in the Royal Army Medical Corps in 1915. He served with the Field Ambulance in Macedonia before joining the infantry in 1917 to fight for his country. In the last months of the war his older brother Sydney was killed on the Western Front.

The stupendous suffering of the war seemed to demand a supernatural response. Angels, ghosts, the Last Days. Thus it was said by some that an angel appeared to protect British troops at the Battle of Mons in 1914, and spirits of dead soldiers were claimed to have been photographed among Armistice Day crowds at the Cenotaph in the 1920s.

In 1923 Spencer started a cycle of paintings for a memorial chapel in Burghclere, Hampshire, that combine the boisterous perspectives of Uccello with a medieval Last Judgement in which the dead awaken. White crosses tumble out of the altar wall painting, piling and cascading in a fervent carnival of prayer. This is the resurrection of the soldiers, the unburial of the lost.

In *The Resurrection, Cookham*, painted between 1924 and 1927, all the generations awaken as the tombs in Spencer's parish churchyard yield up their prisoners. All shall be redeemed in an enchanted pastoral England of flowers and white-robed angels. Christ has defeated science. Magic has returned. Spencer has reached back in time, past Blake, past

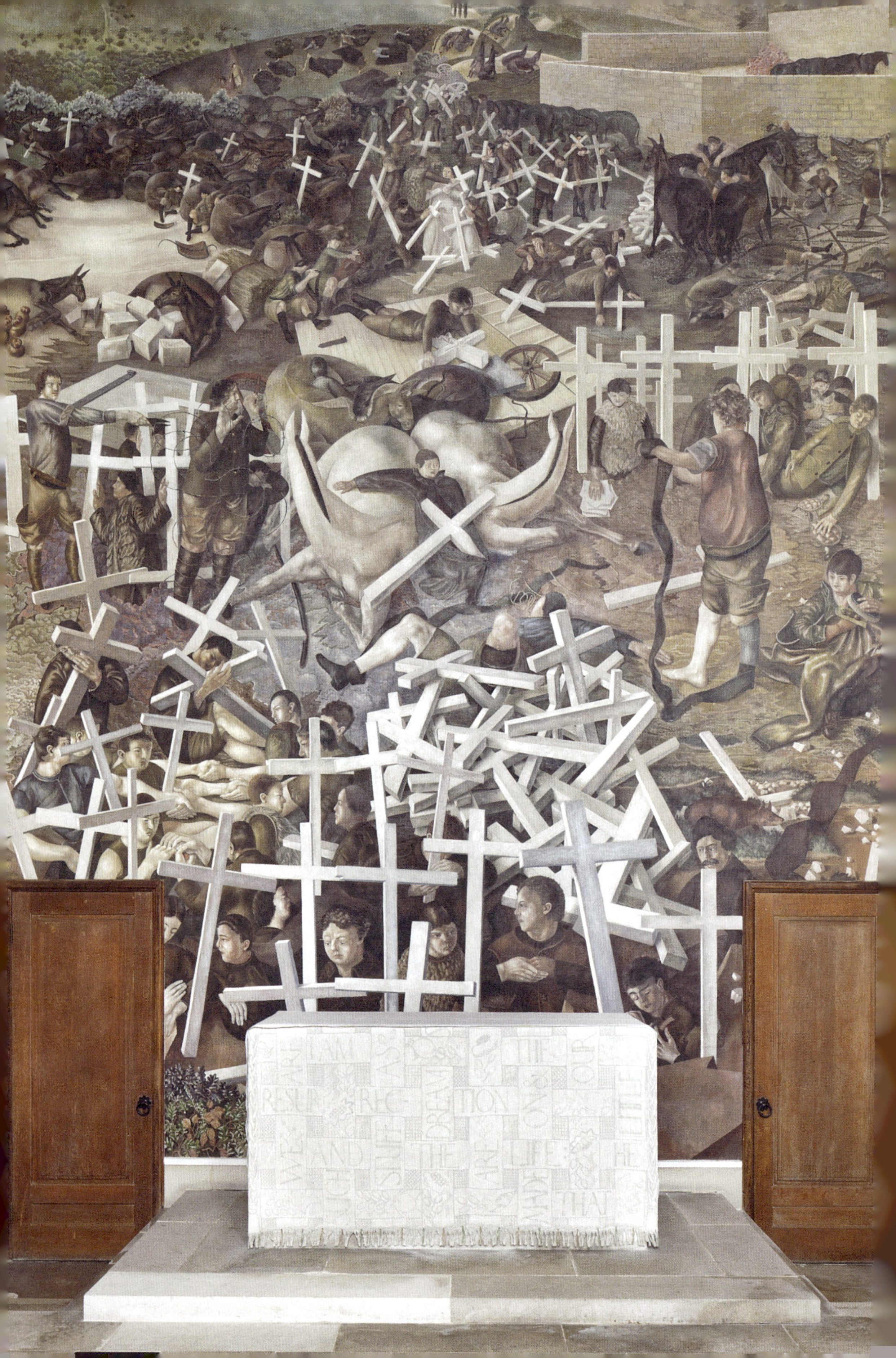
WE ARE
I AM
AS
THE
OUR
RESUR
REC
DREAM
TION
ON
LITTLE
SUCH
AND
STUFF
THE
ARE
LIFE
MADE
HE
THAT

the Reformation itself, to repaint the lost Dooms of Britain's whitewashed parish churches (pages 26–27).

Fifteenth-century depictions of the Passion of Christ by Donatello and Rogier van der Weyden also haunt the memorial art of Charles Sargeant Jagger, who fought at Gallipoli and on the Western Front and survived to sculpt the Royal Artillery Memorial at Hyde Park Corner, with its unlikely rendition of a huge howitzer gun in marble. The monstrous image of a massive modern artillery piece, rendered in the sculptural material used by Phidias and Michelangelo, exposes the way mechanized war and industrial modernity have ruptured the very fabric of nature and made artistic beauty a thing of the past. Christian images of suffering well up in the figurative scenes that surround the big gun. Jagger's bronze relief *No Man's Land*, created in 1919–20 as he directly translated recent gory memory into art, includes the figure of a half-naked soldier crucified sideways on barbed wire, decaying in full view of his comrades with his bare legs compressed together like those of Christ in a painting by Matthias Grünewald.

The Welsh artist and poet David Jones survived three years in the trenches, fighting in the Royal Welch Fusiliers from 1915 to the end of the war, an experience preserved by his war epic *In Parenthesis*, published in 1937. In the aftermath of war he turned to Christ, converting to Roman Catholicism in 1921. In his 1925 painting *Sanctus Christus de Capel-y-ffin*, a Christ with the emaciated bony carnality of medieval carvings is crucified among the bare hills and winter trees of Wales.

Jones painted this convincingly primitive icon after staying at a former monastery at Capel-y-ffin in Powys, where his mentor Eric Gill had set up one of a series of spiritual retreats-cum-artistic communes with his family under the rubric of his own lay order called the 'Guild of St Joseph and St Dominic'. Gill's 'visionary' activities included sexually abusing his daughters, a crime his diaries would bring to light long after his death. He also had sex with his dog. It was this cult leader, as he might be called nowadays, who led Jones towards Catholicism, having converted to it himself in 1913, the same year he agreed to sculpt *The Stations of the Cross* for Westminster Cathedral, the new central church of Catholicism in Britain. Gill's marble relief carvings tell the story of the Passion in stark chunky scenes that would not be out of place in a thirteenth-century French monastic church.

Gill was not just a Catholic artist but a would-be social seer in the style of Ruskin and Morris. He wanted to take society back to a medieval communalism in which wage slavery was replaced with the

← Stanley Spencer, *The Resurrection of the Soldiers*, 1928–29, oil on canvas, 640.5 × 526.1 cm (252 ⅛ × 207 ⅛ in.), Sandham Memorial Chapel, Burghclere, Hampshire

honest creative toil of the carpenter and stone mason. The Victorian idealism that turned its back on the modern world was very much alive in his Guild of St Joseph and St Dominic. As the sceptical socialist George Orwell summed up Gill's politics:

> *True civilisation, Gill thinks, can only return when people choose their own work and do it in their own time, and when they are conscious of being free agents while possessing a common body of [Christian] belief... a return to peasant ownership, hand production, and in general, to an idealised version of the Middle Ages.*

Yet Gill was also an apostle of sex. In the 1900s he and Epstein revered the joyously sensual art of India. His engravings and carvings are full of triumphant embracing couples whose rapture might be more appealing if we did not know of his incestuous abuse.

This worship of sex was shared by one of Britain's most radical modern writers. D. H. Lawrence's 1928 novel *Lady Chatterley's Lover* was immediately banned in Britain. Yet its steamy story of an affair between an upper-class woman and a gamekeeper is not just a pornographic potboiler. It expounds Lawrence's vision of a modern Britain desiccated by snobbery and parched by industrialism, where only desire can bring new life. In 1929 this vision took a highly carnal form when he showed his erotic paintings at London's Warren Gallery. Crowds came, and so did the police. Twelve thousand people saw what *The Observer* branded a 'frankly disgusting' show before 13 of Lawrence's crudely painted but undeniably salacious pictures were seized.

With such simmering cults of free love stoking the intelligentsia it is not surprising Surrealism found fans in Britain.

In René Magritte's 1937 painting *Not To Be Reproduced*, a young man with slickly combed, shiny hair stands with his back us, looking into a mirror. We might expect to see his face in the mirror, but instead we see, uncannily, the back of his head. This enigmatic figure is a portrait of the English art collector Edward James, one of Surrealism's most enthusiastic patrons. Visitors to his West Sussex home could sit on a luscious red sofa designed by Salvador Dalí in the shape of Mae West's lips. James financially supported Dalí for part of the 1930s and also helped publish the Surrealist journal *Minotaure*. He was generous to Magritte too, but the Belgian artist's portrait suggests that his benefactor was a hard man to know or love.

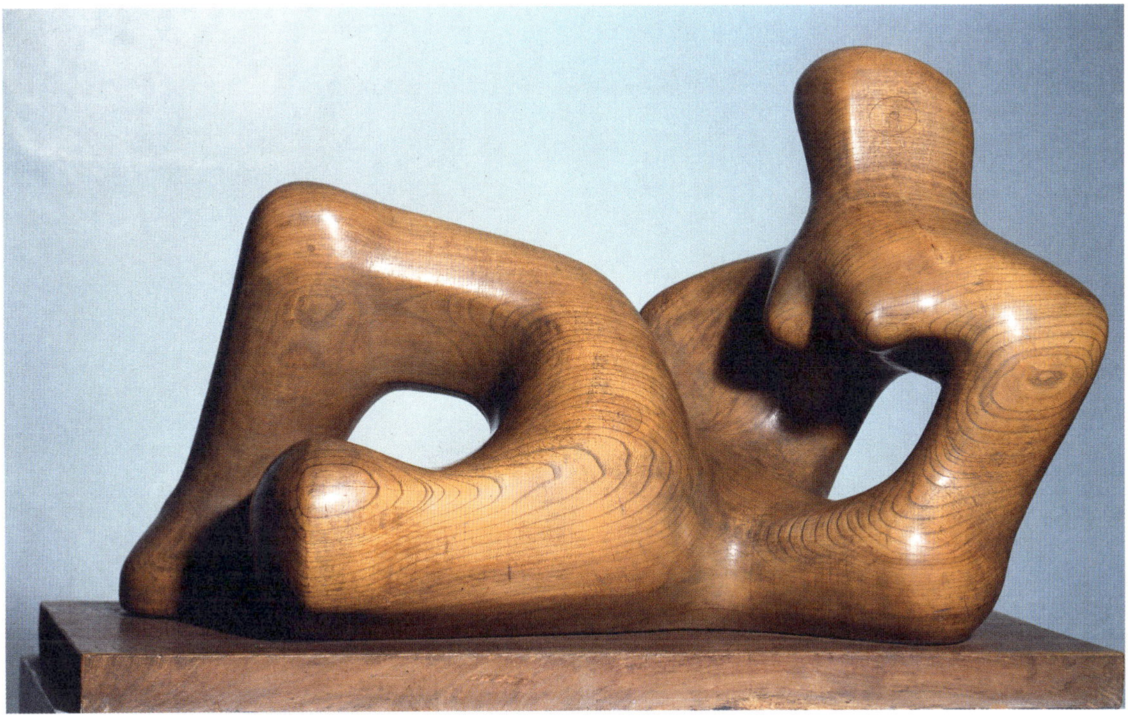

↑ Henry Moore, *Reclining Figure*, 1936, elmwood, 64 × 115 × 52.5 cm (25⅕ × 45¼ × 20⅔ in.), The Hepworth Wakefield, West Yorkshire

James's taste for these dream artists was not shared by Orwell, who called Dalí 'a dirty little scoundrel'. Yet Surrealism appealed to several strands of Britishness. It had a sense of humour, an asset in winning over the self-consciously witty British in what was, after all, the age of P. G. Wodehouse. It could even be seen as a modern version of the eighteenth-century Gothic style that Britain had invented; Breton idolized Matthew Lewis's depraved 1796 novel *The Monk*.

Surrealism reverberates in 1930s British art like a pebble thrown in a stagnant pond. Fully paid-up British members of the movement included the painters Leonora Carrington, Roland Penrose and Conroy Maddox. The best British example of 'pure' Surrealism is probably Eileen Agar's object *Angel of Anarchy*, created between 1936 and 1940. It is a romantic image of the blind dreamer, lost in sensuous reveries of silk, peacock feathers and animal hide.

Yet Surrealism echoed far beyond the group's orthodox followers. Agar often went to look at African art in the British Museum with her friend Henry Moore. Born in 1898 in Castleford, Yorkshire, Moore was a stupendously ambitious artist. In an age when modernism seemed confined to the margins of British life he conceived of dreamlike images of the human form on a heroic scale. He was on the committee of the International Surrealist Exhibition in 1936 – best known for Dalí's near-fatal attempt to give a lecture while wearing a deep-sea diving suit.

Moore's 1936 work *Reclining Figure* is a disconcertingly shaped elmwood carving of a woman whose curvy stance creates huge voids between her legs and under her breasts. Are these incongruities tricks of the eye or acts of sculptural violence?

At another pole of 1930s British art there are Surrealist echoes in purportedly conservative society portraits. Meredith Frampton's icily accurate 1935 painting, *Portrait of a Young Woman*, might appear merely upper class and snobbish. Yet with its unexplained array of objects – the cello, the books, the woman's perfect white shoes – it resembles an uneasy dream.

Surrealism had a seductive resonance that took it far beyond the confines of the art world. Alfred Hitchcock's silent film *The Lodger*, released in 1927, portrays London as a city of glittering lights, dance girls and perverted serial killers. *The 39 Steps*, released in 1935, comes much closer to Surrealism proper. It tells an adventure story that feels like a dream. A man meets a glamorous spy who is murdered in his flat, sending him on a madcap train journey to Scotland. One dream image follows another. He has to pose as a politician and make an unscripted speech. He gets handcuffed to a young woman who loathes him. He recognizes the true villain because part of his finger is missing.

Hitchcock is one of Britain's greatest modern artists. Where Moore and Agar were essentially emulating the latest thing from Paris – just compare Moore's nudes with Picasso's infinitely more alive metamorphic sculptures and paintings of the early 1930s if this seems dismissive – Hitchcock created his own authentic dream art. In 1945 his affinity for Surrealism would become official, and marketable, when Dalí devised a Freudian dream sequence for his Hollywood film *Spellbound*.

Surrealism's appeal was political as well as aesthetic. It was fun, but also, claimed the Trotskyist Breton, revolutionary. Picasso, Joan Miró and other Surrealists supported the Spanish Republic, even if the sly Dalí hedged his bets. Yet it was more than that. The descent of Europe into irrational, hateful politics made reality itself seem to buckle. The propaganda and cynicism of the age of dictators created a 'surreal' world. In 1938 the news magazine *Picture Post* employed the German montagist John Heartfield to create a cover satirizing Prime Minister Neville Chamberlain's claim to have obtained Hitler's promise of 'peace for our time'. Heartfield's image of winged elephants gently flying upward captures the unreality of it all.

It wasn't only Surrealists who were committed to the Spanish Republic. Barbara Hepworth, born in Wakefield, Yorkshire, in 1903, had studied alongside Moore at Leeds School of Art. In 1938 she created *Project (Monument to the Spanish Civil War)* to mourn the defeat of the Republic and the sacrifice of the international volunteers as well as Spanish fighters who had made a stand against the fascist tide. Hepworth and her husband, Ben Nicholson, saw salvation in pure abstraction. This was the most spiritual and ethereal vanguard of the 1920s and 1930s, pioneered by such artists as Piet Mondrian and Wassily Kandinsky. While Nicholson is a dry, dull imitator of the European modern greats, Hepworth carved images of genuine beauty. The more abstract her work the more it seems a magical act of self-expression by nature itself, with curvy pierced forms that seem to have been created by the sea slowly eroding cliffs to sculpt caverns and fantastic overhangs. Hepworth said sculpture should be 'an act of praise, an enduring expression of the divine spirit'.

She can certainly salve, if not save, your soul. Her art is as calming as a good walk in an unspoiled landscape. Her studio in the Cornish resort of St Ives is a peaceful, ascetic place far from the madding crowd – and free today, in its clean light, from any sign of the fire in which she died in 1975. Her small carvings are indoors, with colossal bronze versions of her works in the restful garden. On a nearby promontory one of her elliptical forms is posed so as to frame a view of the grey sea through green bronze.

In 1939 Chamberlain's policy of appeasing Hitler crashed to earth and a new world war started that would kill 80 million. Britain's heroic role would be that of a dogged survivor, refusing to give up after the fall of France and keeping the last flame of democracy in Europe alive until Hitler's invasion of Russia led to disaster for the Third Reich. It was an achievement of stolidity, not genius. British art from the 1920s to 40s largely shares that stolidity. It is tame and dull. Moore and Hepworth were not great modernists. Compared with the darkness and danger of continental Surrealism the British version was superficial. Yet who would swap being British in 1940 for any other nationhood? The radical thinking that made continental art so powerful in this era was at the same time irresponsible, callous, addicted to extremes.

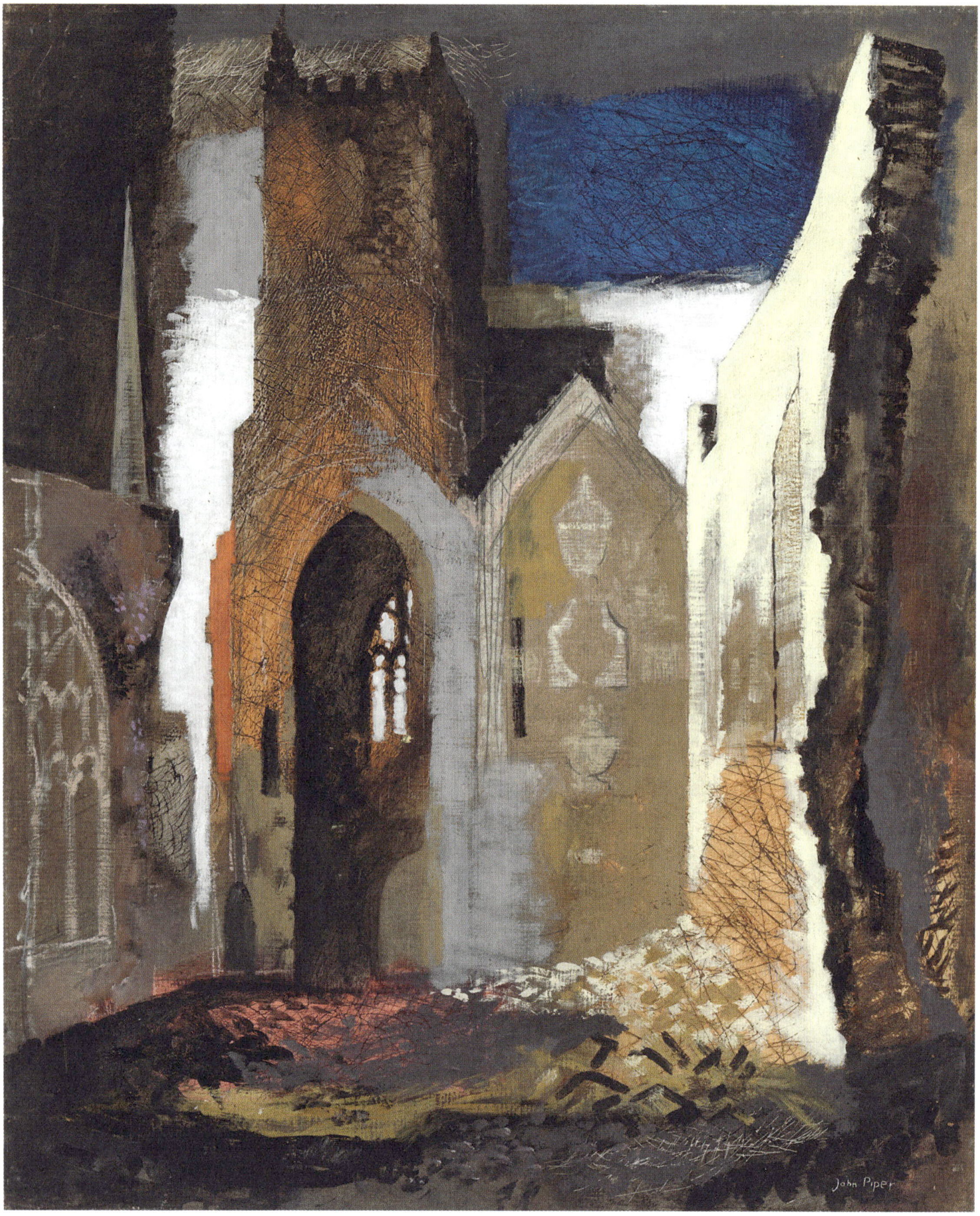

↑ John Piper, *St Mary le Port, Bristol*, 1940, oil and pencil on canvas and wood, 76.2 × 63.5 cm (30 × 25 in.), Tate

Orwell, who was so revolted and disturbed by Dalí's embrace of those extremes, sat down in early 1941 with bombs falling around him to define Britishness. As a socialist who supported the war effort, who chose patriotism over pacifism in England's moment of peril, he attempts in his essay 'The Lion and the Unicorn' to identify the national spirit. He starts with the self-evident:

> *Here are a couple of generalisations about England that would be accepted by almost all observers. One is that the English are not gifted artistically...*

It was indeed a view accepted 'by almost all observers' at the time. In the age of Picasso few considered Britain a great artistic nation. Outside the tiny artistic communities in London and St. Ives it was fashionable among educated Britons to reject modernism itself as a continental pose. 'What are pictures for?' asked the sporting painter Alfred Munnings, who sneered at Picasso, answering: 'To fill a man's soul with admiration and sheer joy, not to bewilder and daze him.'

Munnings was a friend of the wartime Prime Minister, Winston Churchill, who painted for a hobby. Churchill was far from philistine. He studied the French Impressionists and cherished art as a salve for the soul. Still, it was no job for a man. It was, rather, fine relaxation and therapy, as the title of Churchill's book *Painting as Pastime* makes clear.

In Britain, the ultimately modest fate of art in the modernist era might be encapsulated by the career of John Piper. This painter who started out as a pale imitator of continental abstraction and surrealism reverted by 1939 to a pastoral pleasure in the British landscape. The Blitz was to prove his finest hour. His melancholy paintings of bombed-out churches glow with patriotism and love of place. In the rubble, red embers burn like the last dying sparks of a fallen firework.

10. Memo from Turner

I'll tell you this: the only performance that makes it, that really makes it, that makes it all the way is the one that achieves madness.

Turner, played by Mick Jagger, in *Performance*, 1970, directed by Nicolas Roeg and Donald Cammell

So that the artist may be able to open up or rather, should I say, unlock the valves of feeling and therefore return the onlooker to life more violently.

Francis Bacon, interview with David Sylvester, 1962

The Pit

Blindfolded, perching, hunched, with long phallic necks on stumps of bodies, propped on pieces of pointless furniture, isolated in red sterile rooms, they twitch and howl. They might be medieval gargoyles, ancient Greek harpies or monsters from science fiction. In fact they are personifications of a world at war.

Francis Bacon painted *Three Studies for Figures at the Base of a Crucifixion* in 1944. These tragic chunks of grey mutilated flesh with eyeless faces screaming in the red airlessness of their hell convey the true violence and horror of the 1940s with a blunt accuracy that eluded Henry Moore. No one with ideals, no one with a belief in humanity, could look so directly into the abyss that was Europe in 1944. Bacon has no fine sentiments. He does not offer any humanist counterbalance to his vision of the damned. His disdain for virtuous convention allows him to collect a menagerie of the bereft from Europe's darkest hour and exhibit these beasts without comment.

Born in Dublin in 1909, the son of a racehorse trainer, Bacon gambled and dabbled in chic modern interior design in 1930s London

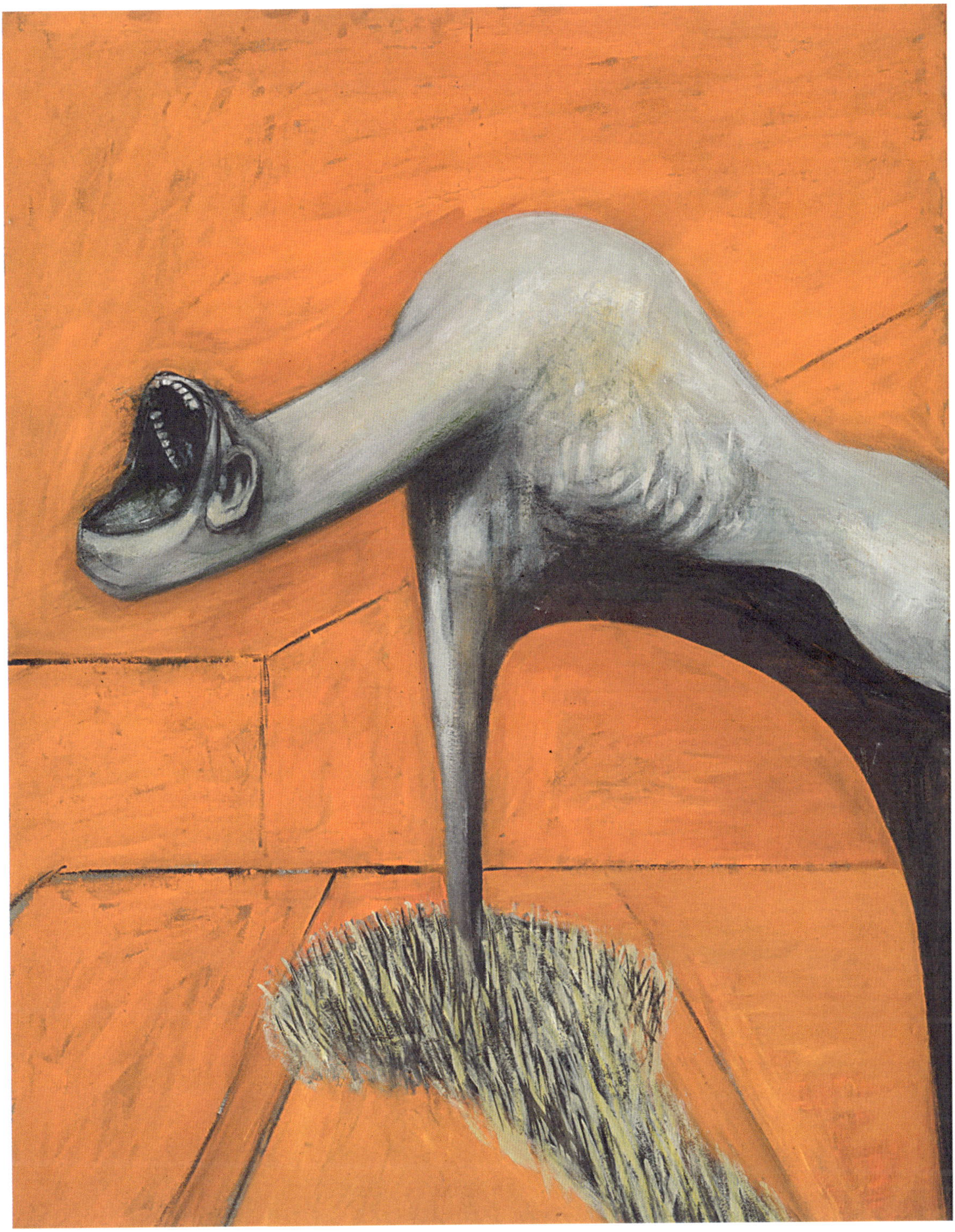

↑ Francis Bacon, *Three Studies for Figures at the Base of a Crucifixion* (detail), 1944

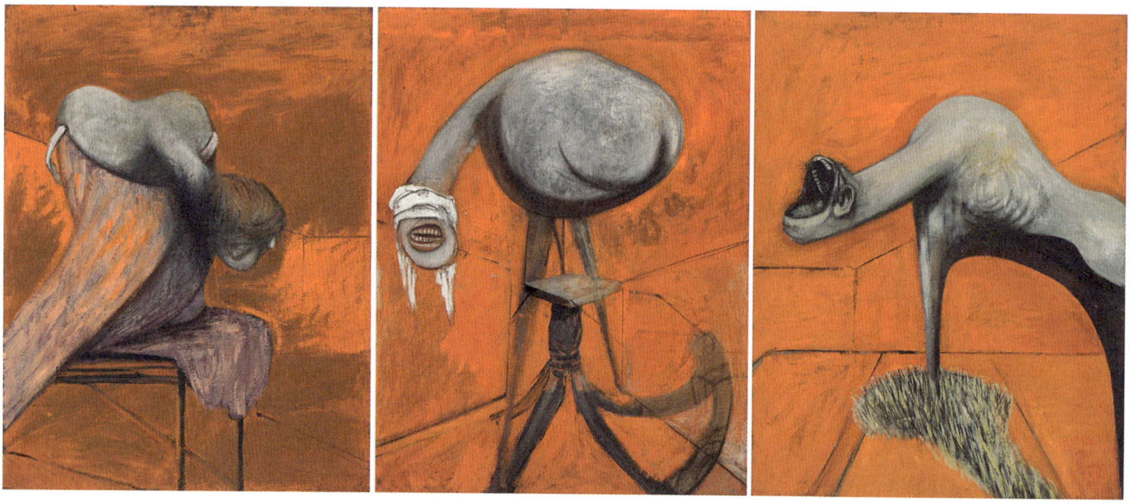

↑ Francis Bacon, *Three Studies for Figures at the Base of a Crucifixion*, 1944, oil and pastel on fibreboards, each panel 94 × 73.7 cm (37 × 29 in.), Tate

before starting to make paintings that spin Surrealism into new satanic realms. A lost early work appears to have been a painting of Hitler getting out of a car.

You can always make a case for art. You can see it as social history, or take pleasure in the biographical eccentricities of its creator, sentimentally celebrate the parochial or delight in portraits of the famous. In all these ways we justify the second-rate. This kind of special pleading is very tempting in a history of British art because, after Turner's death in 1851, there was so little genius and so much mediocrity. It is important to be clear. With Bacon, British art comes alive at last. After nearly a hundred wasted years it rediscovers the grotesque comedy of Hogarth and Gillray, the painterliness of Turner, the poetry of Blake.

Above all, this new art is real. However hellish and fantastical Bacon's beasts might be in *Three Studies*, they have a hideous carnal undeniability. They exist. A perverse suggestiveness emphasizes that monstrous facthood. These things have not been painted so much as released.

Only Bacon, amoral denizen of the London night, seemed able to see his time for what it was. In drinking dens and at the roulette wheel he glimpsed the demons that had brought human civilization close to its demise. If the world did not end in 1945 that was only from the perspective of the lucky. It did end for the many millions who lost their lives in the most murderous of all wars. Britain could be proud of the honourable part it had played. Yet with approximately 400,000 deaths it also had less to mourn than a country such as Poland, where civilian mortalities alone totalled 6 million. As well as suffering such losses, the countries of Eastern Europe, conquered early in the war by Nazi Germany and treated as colonies for the Reich's benefit, became the killing grounds of the Holocaust. Hitler 'prophesied' in January 1939 that if 'international Jewish financiers' were to start a world war it would result in 'the annihilation of the Jewish race in Europe!'

Did rumours of mass murder in Eastern Europe – of shootings in forests and trains bound for Auschwitz – reach Bacon in his demimonde, or was it just intuition?

A desolate sense that we are just animals bound for slaughter, lonely pieces of flesh in a godless void, seems a reasonable conclusion to have drawn once photographs and films from the death camps were widely seen at the end of World War II, and after two atomic bombs were dropped on the Japanese cities of Hiroshima and Nagasaki in August 1945. It was more thoughtful, anyway, than the cosy myth of World War II that still confuses and deludes Britain today, dwelling on our finest hour yet forgetting its true context of global horror.

There is no danger of self-congratulation in front of Bacon's flesh-crawling shudders of paintings.

In 1953 he painted a portrait of an isolated monkey. The purple rump of the benighted creature in *Study of a Baboon* points sulkily towards us as the forlorn creature turns from the shadows of its cage to bare its teeth in a howl. It seems to be nothing but a flash of white canines in a mist of bruise-blue, white and red, a being made entirely of hostility and pigment. Paint for Bacon is a means of making bodies, but he has no wish to organize those bodies into grand, confident figures. Instead he conveys fragments of perception, glimpses of skeletal and muscular structure in a velvet frenzy of suggestive colour. He is a malevolent impressionist of carnal form.

Exact anatomical observation is the basis of Bacon's cruel depictions. He did not need to dissect a horse, as George Stubbs had in the eighteenth century, to see inside bodies (pages 68–70). The twentieth century was his anatomy lesson. A still of a screaming bespectacled nurse from Sergei Eisenstein's Russian revolutionary film *Battleship Potemkin*, an old photograph of a paralysed child attempting to crawl, pictures of Nazis, monkeys and wrestlers were strewn about his studio, and their images minced into the meat of his art. Yet out of this obsession with the flesh he creates curiously ethereal depictions that are ultimately not of the body at all but of the human self, which

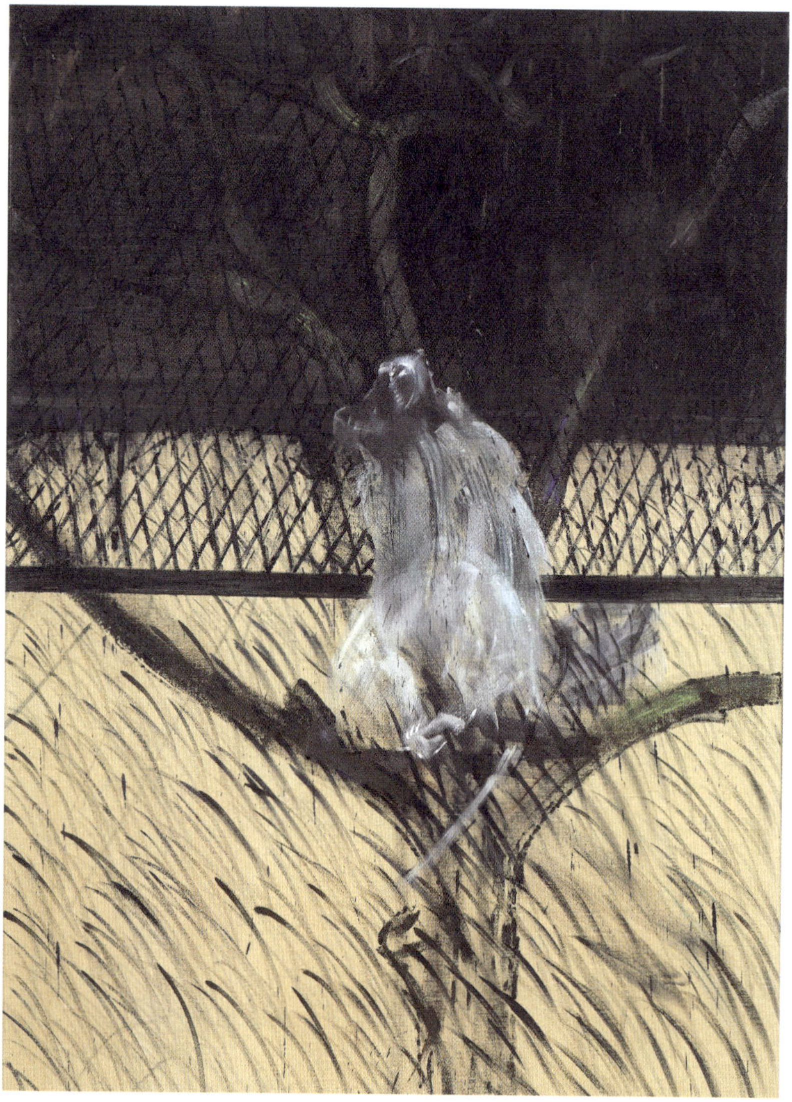

← Francis Bacon, *Study of a Baboon*, 1953, oil on canvas, 198.3 × 137.3 cm (78 × 54 in.), Museum of Modern Art, New York

in his art is always suffering or dying or imprisoned or barely there at all. The man in his 1945 painting *Figure in a Landscape*, for instance, is vanishing before our eyes. His trousered legs have almost entirely dissolved, leaving just a headless torso in a suit, sitting in a chair, with one hand clenched in determination. From the strength of this fist and the breadth of his jacket we perceive a man of affairs, a forceful character – but his suit opens to reveal a void within. This is the shadow of a great man, the wraith of a once-potent personage.

In a 1946 work simply called *Painting*, a similarly absent person is little more than a big toothy mouth gaping idiotically under an umbrella in a gallery of hanging meat. The figure that haunts this atrocity exhibition is surrounded by a slick circle of chrome railings, like the substructure of a modernist table. Bacon's youthful experience designing Art Deco interiors before the war never left him. Many of his paintings are set in horribly stylish rooms with odd pieces of tubular furniture, elegant daybeds and blinds – as here in *Painting* – to shut out the world and turn a room into a private theatre of extreme behaviour.

The spiralling railings that appear in these early paintings and were to become one of his most recurring props are ambiguous in use. They might be supports for the failing flesh of his pitiable people, armatures for their decaying forms, like the structure that seems to prop up the last remnants of the fading *Figure in a Landscape*. Or they might hint at imprisonment, enclosure, the narrow perimeter of a restricted existence.

That theme of imprisonment becomes explicit in the series of paintings that made Bacon one of the most internationally famous artists of the postwar age – his 'popes'. These portraits of men enthroned inside glass boxes grew out of traces of transparent vitrines that he started drawing around anguished isolated beings in such works as *Head I*, painted in 1947–48, in which a dire fusion of a noble human head with an ape's snarling jaws is exhibited inside a rectangular display case. *Head VI*, done in 1949, forms a clearer, more confident, more mysterious image. This time it is not a monster but a man of God who is sealed inside a glass chamber just big enough to hold his grey howling face and purple-mantled shoulders. The disappearance of the upper part of his head in a sooty mist of black pigment helps him fit under the low ceiling of the box. His eyes are dark voids, his mouth a pit of terror.

Why has Bacon sealed the pope inside a glass cage? It is not so much an attack on Catholicism as a love letter to painting. The pope's cape is a gorgeous ruched array of purple, set off by the ashen streaks of black that rain down vertically. This painting is not simply a bleak scream of despair. It aspires to create a modern version of the great portraits of the Old Masters that capture the human condition with timeless authority.

In about 1650 the Spanish court painter Diego Velázquez, on a visit to Rome, painted a portrait of Pope Innocent X that is a work of uncanny power. Painting a portrait of the pope was a chance to rival the greats, to spread your fame by proving yourself equal to the likes of Raphael and Titian. Velázquez rose to the challenge. His Innocent X looks out of his portrait angrily, threateningly. This is a portrait that bursts out of its frame, a painting that crosses the border between art and life.

Bacon's paintings of popes are interpretations of it. His 1950 *Study after Velázquez* or the 1953 *Study after Velázquez's Portrait of Pope Innocent X* make that explicit. But Velázquez's Innocent X is a potent character imposing himself on the world. Bacon seals him in glass and rains down bars of blackness between him and us, or paints his face as

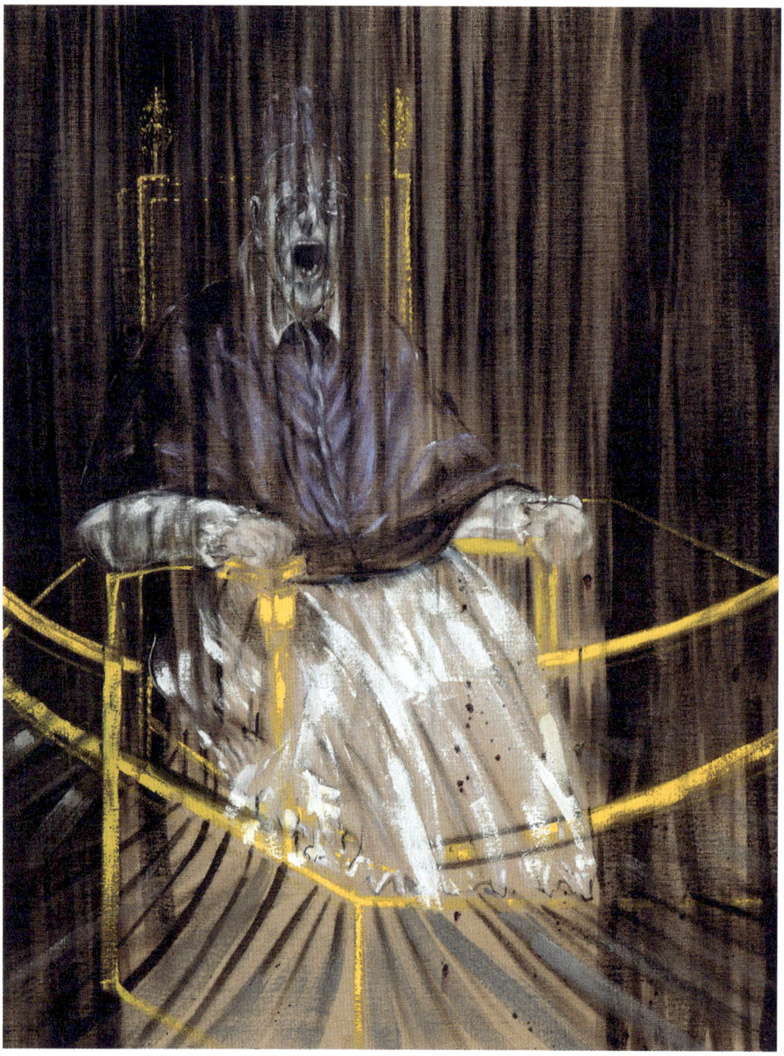

← Francis Bacon, *Study after Velázquez's Portrait of Pope Innocent X*, 1953, oil on canvas, 153 x 118 cm (60 ¼ × 46 ½ in.), Des Moines Art Center, Iowa

a blue blur looking outward with would-be authority but succeeding only in seeming querulous. A portrait of power has become a study in failure.

The pope is a father figure, Il Papa. Bacon had a difficult relationship with his real-life father. The future artist said he discovered that he was homosexual when he was young, in encounters with grooms in the family stables. When his father caught him in his mother's underwear there was hell to pay. Do his tragicomic paintings of Il Papa take revenge on his papa?

It is at any rate the kind of explanation that might have appealed to Lucian Freud's grandfather. The boy who was to become Bacon's friend and rival was born in Berlin in 1922, the grandson of the Viennese doctor and founder of psychoanalysis, Sigmund Freud. Unlike Sigmund, who stayed in Vienna until he had no choice but to leave, Freud's parents moved with their family to Britain when Hitler became chancellor of Germany in 1933. Lucian Freud was a wild kid and a gifted painter. What his early works share with Bacon is a desire to unsettle and perturb, to break the glass wall between art and life.

Freud's 1950–51 painting *Girl with a White Dog* portrays his first wife, Kitty Garman, with a dog resting its long snouty face on her lap. She wears a pale green dressing-gown pulled back to expose one shoulder and breast. The painting seems a dialogue, perhaps a tense one, between artist and model. How much of herself will she let him paint? She places her right hand on her still-covered left breast, as if protectively. Yet this gesture becomes an intimate key to the painting's power. It may seem at first that Freud in this early work is almost pedantic in his efforts to reproduce the appearances of things. Blue veins under pale skin, the pink of the dog's ear, the pattern of the cover on which she sits – is there anything the artist has not stared at and meticulously put down on canvas? Yet the effect is not illustrative. To look at the way Garman holds her breast is to feel the weight of it in her hand, and from there you start to sense her anatomical presence. You are drawn to her frail collarbones and the reflections of a window frame in her eyes. This is not just an accurate painting. It is one that exhibits the complete physical reality of another person – her life force, even.

Freud shares Bacon's fascination with the human figure, the vulnerable and irreplaceable self. Yet where Bacon dramatizes this frail essence in paintings that are prisons or torture chambers, Freud prefers to study real people in natural light, with a relentless dedication to the act of looking.

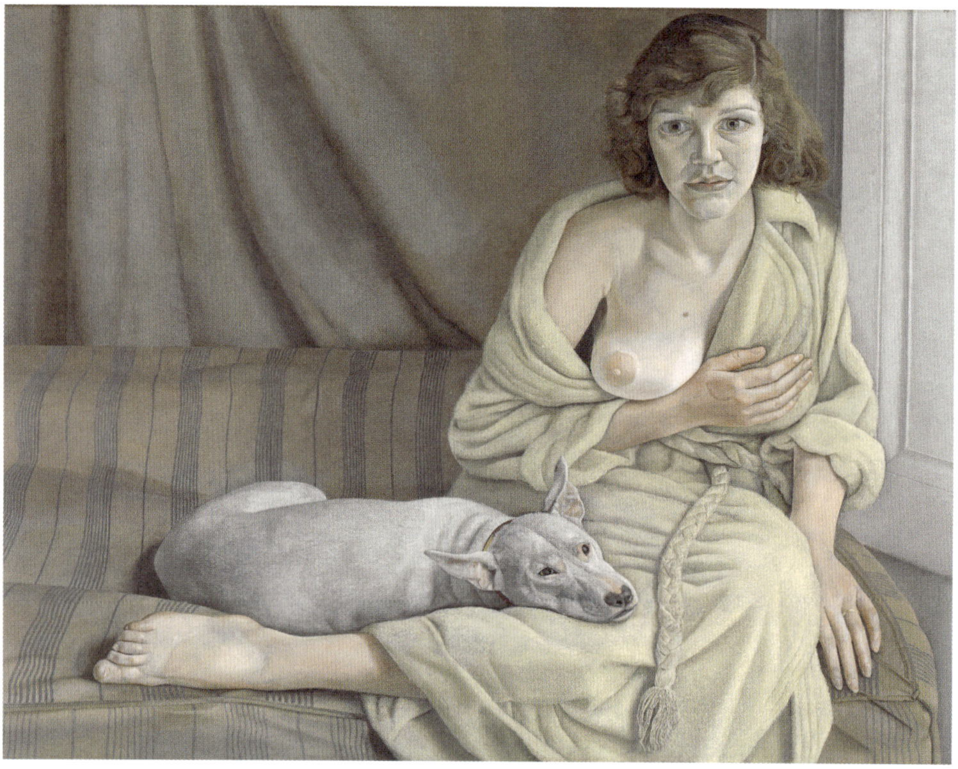

Truly, Freud's compulsion to observe is extreme. He seems to be trying to look so hard at Kitty Garman and her dog that he can preserve every nuance of skin colour, the blotches in her pallor, the ruffle of each hair. Why would an artist in the 1950s want to mimic the world so closely? Has this young man not heard of modern art? For Freud no ideas or images seem to matter except the ones in front of his eyes. We can be confident the dog really did hunker down like that, and Garman really did wear that modest robe. For Lucian Freud never seems to have made anything up in his life.

Other than some early experiments in light Surrealism – in his 1944 exercise *The Painter's Room* a yellow and red giraffe sticks its head in through the window – Freud never painted made-up scenes. No screaming popes for him, no Potemkin references, no narratives of any kind except those suggested by the singularity of who he is looking at and his relationship with them.

Freud is the most sincerely empirical British artist since Constable. Perhaps far more sincere. For his commitment to the evidence

↑ Lucian Freud, *Girl with a White Dog*, 1950–51, oil on canvas, 76.2 × 101.6 cm (30 × 40 in.), Tate

of sensation alone was never to waver. No expressionism, no confessions. If Freud only paints what he sees, where does imagination enter his art?

Girl with a White Dog provides the answer. This painting does not just record facts. It creates a mysterious living encounter. Kitty Garman is placed before us as a tense and conscious being. By looking, Freud fills the blank page of his imagination. He imprints people on it.

Frank Auerbach too came to Britain as a child. He also was born in Berlin, in 1931, to middle-class Jewish parents. They either would not or could not emigrate in time. In 1939 they sent him alone to Britain, packing, along with items he would need immediately, things for when he grew up. He was never to see his murdered parents again.

Auerbach's early paintings have a savage innocence, a feral energy, the sense of being hewn out of the shattered concrete of a ruined world. In 1953–54 he painted a reclining nude that looks like a classical muse buried in the ash of Pompeii and cast in grey plaster by archaeologists. The excavators have recovered the ripe, almost Rubens-like, wide-hipped body of this woman, yet far from being conventionally eroticized she lies in a black morass of funereal earth. Still, she is carnal, she is vital, she has a body. Auerbach feasts visually on her flesh even as he fights the weight of melancholy that imprisons her. This is a painting of life defying death, desire surviving in the darkest hour.

Estella West, the model for this painting, which he called simply *E.O.W. Nude*, appears repeatedly in Auerbach's paintings, becoming a figure of elusive power. In 1955 he portrayed her face as a kind of radioactive trace in a thick storm of massed-up oil paint. It is like finding an old photograph of someone who was loved once, in the charred skeleton of a bombed and abandoned house. Nude, or as a sorrowful head, 'E.O.W.' becomes for Auerbach a heroic figure, the embodiment of enduring vitality and conscience, a person who deserved to be painted, monumentalized, preserved.

Where Freud in the 1950s painted with almost hallucinatory exactitude, Auerbach from the start piles up the colours in thick funeral banquets of expressive impasto. Yet these artists, who were to become lifelong friends, share something essential. Both insist on the artist's duty to observe. Both are fiercely loyal to the seen (and felt) world. They paint specific people, specific places, with a fierce belief that this is the basis of any honest art. If the realism of Freud makes that instantly apparent, you do not have to look at many paintings by Auerbach to understand that he too is almost obsessively committed to the truth of perception.

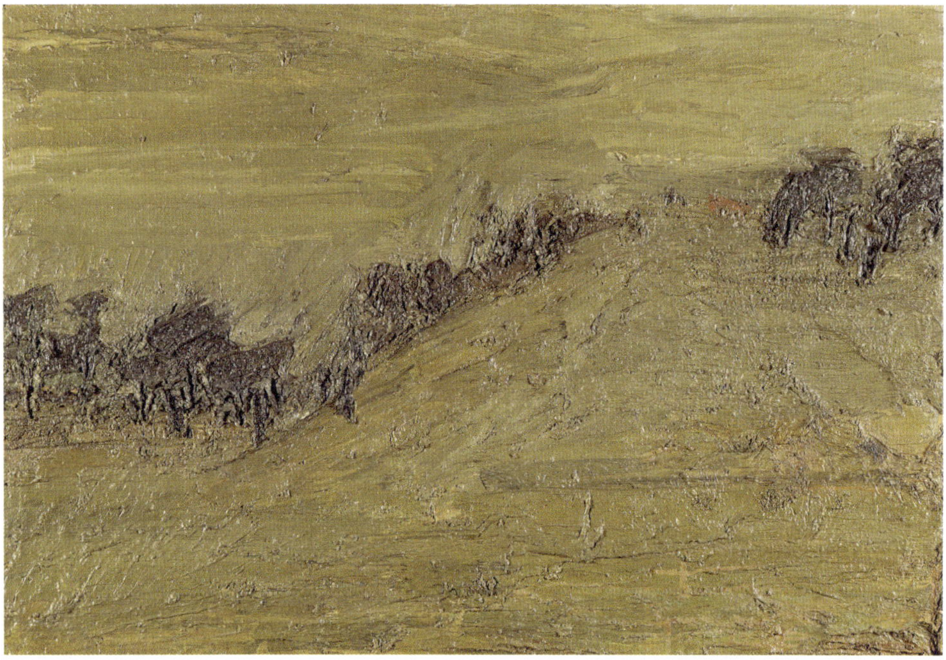

That became apparent when he began to paint landscapes. The raw, almost naive quality of an early venture into this very English genre, his 1960 painting *Primrose Hill, Winter Fog*, is disarming. As he gazes on muddy winter light floating over some khaki-coloured smears of trees on the crest of this hill in North London, his emotion seems to spill out in a sudden intuition of what it was that so moved Gainsborough and Constable when they painted nature. What you cannot know from this one haunting response to place is how many times he would return over the next six decades to paint Primrose Hill, as well as his other favourite North London motif, Mornington Crescent and its environs. Auerbach's most striking characteristic as a painter is the way he keeps faith with what he looks at. If a face or a place is worth painting it is worth painting over and over and over again. For each time the artist sees something new. His theme becomes the inexhaustibility of experience. To look well is always to see a new colour in nature or a new expression in a head.

Empiricism returns to the forefront of British art in these artists' trenchant insistence on the mystery of the real. They paint as if their lives depended on paying attention to the particularities of the world around them, as if to record a person or a city was to save the world.

↑ Frank Auerbach, *Primrose Hill Winter Fog*, 1960, oil on canvas, 86 × 122 cm (33 ⅝ x 48 in.), Fitzwilliam Museum, University of Cambridge

That sense of urgency is shared by Leon Kossoff, who was so close to Auerbach in the 1950s and early 1960s that sometimes they seem to be twins. Kossoff was born in London in 1926 to Jewish parents who had come from Russia. Like Auerbach he paints with stupendous sensual freedom yet rigorous loyalty to facts. As postwar London was rebuilt, with bombed wastelands left by the Blitz filled by new houses or offices, and old buildings replaced by more 'modern' ones, the two artists became fascinated by the great seeping open wounds of building sites that seemed to be everywhere in the always-changing capital. In Kossoff's 1961 painting *Building Site, Victoria Street*, pink mud oozes from the opened earth as if the city were made of human flesh. In Auerbach's 1962 work *Rebuilding the Empire Cinema, Leicester Square*, gory, blood-red girders criss-cross above a pit that seems bottomless, a muddy trench dug deep into the past. Wherever you look, the morass of caked-up paint slides into melancholic depths. You can smell the excavated soil speckled with disintegrated bones.

It would be an insult to Auerbach, an orphan of the Holocaust, to view his long life as a painter as entirely shaped by the crimes of Nazism. Yet, it would be misleading to ignore the sense of history that gives *Rebuilding the Empire Cinema, Leicester Square* such heft and horror.

This stupendous painting's macabre excavated void shares its vision of London with a classic of British science fiction that was broadcast by the BBC in the winter of 1958–59. Nigel Kneale's serial *Quatermass and the Pit* was set around a London building site where workers digging deep in the past's mud have uncovered early human skeletons next to what seems to be an unexploded bomb but turns out to be a Martian spacecraft. All human history has been manipulated by Martians, who sowed the seeds of our violence and irrationality. Kneale later said his story of evil buried in the ancestry of humans was an attempt to understand the Holocaust, from which his wife, the author Judith Kerr, was a child refugee.

Auerbach's painting that sees melancholy, not futurism, in a 1960s building site, and Kneale's science fiction story that reveals human history to be cursed at the root, glimpse ghosts and graves in the technocratic glass of a new Britain.

It was a Britain tantalized by visions of the future while struggling to recover economically from World War II and the Depression that had preceded it. The most universally loved symbol of the new was television. The first British TV broadcasts had reached a tiny audience in the 1930s, but the live coverage of the coronation of

Queen Elizabeth II in 1953 was seen by nearly 20 million people. That same year, Kneale's first Quatermass serial was also broadcast as the BBC set out to entertain and educate with everything from serious drama to *Come Dancing*, which had first aired in 1950.

The changes that to Kossoff and Auerbach looked like one more cosmetic facelift on an ancient, murderous earth struck others as the birth of a completely new world with new kinds of truth, or perhaps no truth at all. Richard Hamilton's 1957 painting *Hommage à Chrysler Corp.* suggests not only that modern consumerism is destined to transform the material world but that its myths will replace reality with ad-land's eroticized fantasy world. In his curvy collection of painted fragments, the opulent lines of a pink-painted American car merge with the semi-visible shape of a naked woman whose red lips float in nothingness. The painting has a glistening chrome frame to add to its ironic beauty, yet it has an unfinished elusiveness: reality vanishes like a fast car speeding by.

The previous year Hamilton had participated in *This Is Tomorrow*, an exhibition at London's Whitechapel Gallery that included a cardboard cutout of Robby the Robot from the science fiction film *Forbidden Planet*, looming over a still of Marilyn Monroe in *The Seven Year Itch*. Hamilton designed the exhibition poster, a collage that sardonically asks: 'Just what is it that makes today's homes so different, so appealing?'

The answers include canned ham, a television, a reel-to-reel tape recorder, a lollipop, a vacuum cleaner and a black and white rug – pasted into Hamilton's parodically ultra-modern interior with its picture window looking out on a cinema across the road.

Yet it is not the images in this collage that make it so new, so memorable, as much as the way they are combined. It is one thing to create a montage of colliding fragments – a genre of art invented by the German Dada movement at the end of World War I – and another to use them to create a viable, inhabitable world. Hamilton uses the Renaissance science of perspective to create a collage picture with a deep interior space, a room that is real and solid – yet not real at all. The view of the Earth from space that floats where the ceiling should be undermines the illusion, as does the fantastical perspective of the staircase that makes the woman who is vacuuming it appear tiny. Hamilton's collage is more than a collection of pop icons. It is a comic vision of a new kind of world, open to the rest of the planet, literally – as the Earth hangs above the room – and figuratively – as mass communications burst into this unprivate space: comics, TV, taped music, the cinema just outside the window.

Little wonder the people who live here have no inhibitions. The man of the house has nothing to hide. He looks as if he has just stepped out of a bodybuilding magazine, as of course he has. He flexes his muscles and sports his lollipop while a woman perches on a comfy chair wearing nothing but a lampshade.

Hamilton has created a virtual reality, but his attitude to it is ambivalent. This place undeniably has its attractions – erotic, material, cultural – but the people who live there seem to be either crude monsters or, in the case of the tiny woman vacuuming the stairs, enslaved by technology. Is this brave new world a utopia or some fresh hell?

The hint that it is hellish becomes all the stronger when we recognize its affinity with the nightmares of Francis Bacon.

Hamilton, who was born in London in 1922, is generally seen as having more in common with Marcel Duchamp than with Bacon. He was working in the 1950s on a 'typotranslation' – a visual as well as literal translation – of Duchamp's *Green Box*, a collection of notes that explore the ideas behind *The Bride Stripped Bare by Her Bachelors, Even,* the obscure mythological picture on glass that Duchamp left 'definitively unfinished' in 1923. Hamilton's epic piece of Duchampian research was published in 1960. It is not hard to discern the fruits of his studies in *Hommage à Chrysler Corp.*, with its icily humorous conflation of sex and cars. Duchamp had explored such cybernetic, autoerotic themes in mechanistic paintings and early 'readymades' before World War I. In *The Bride Stripped Bare*... he creates an absurd science fiction world of sexualized machines expending themselves in lugubrious mechanical gestures and self-stimulating fantasies. Hamilton suggests in his pioneering 'Pop' art that we are now, in 1956, entering this utopia or dystopia, that people are becoming pumped-up robots of advertising-exacerbated desire.

'Most of our people have never had it so good', the Conservative prime minister, Harold Macmillan, put it in a speech in 1957 that hailed the coming of the consumer society.

Hamilton's admiration for Duchamp was to culminate in 1966 with his precise recreation of *The Bride Stripped Bare*... itself. Duchamp signed this loving homage to validate it as a '*copie conforme*' of his enigmatic masterpiece. Yet in reality Hamilton is as much the heir of Bacon as of Duchamp.

The perplexing room Hamilton creates in his 1956 collage is a Pop version of the rooms in Bacon's paintings, with their peculiar furnishings and air of sterility. The parallels are exact. Hamilton

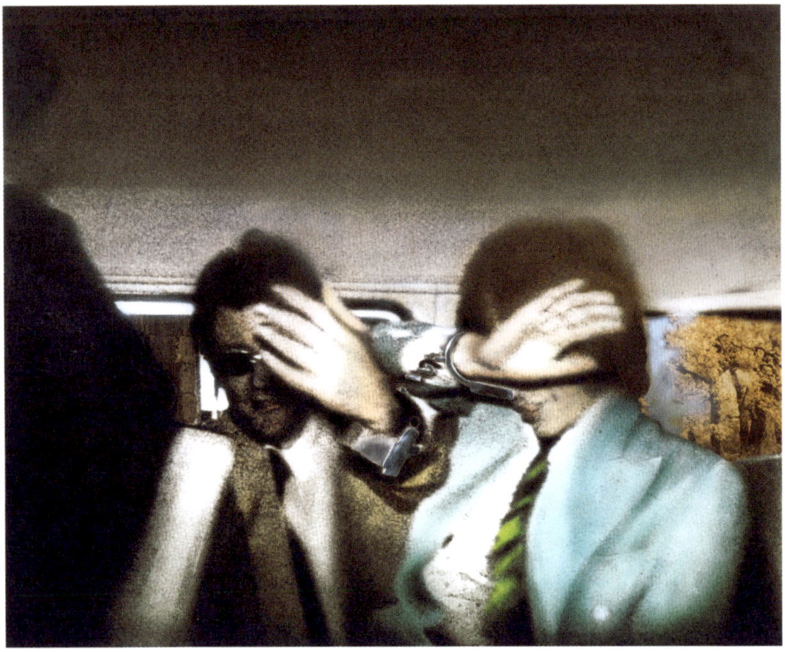

← Richard Hamilton, *Swingeing London 67*, 1968–69, acrylic paint, screenprint, paper, aluminium and metallized acetate on canvas, 67.3 × 85.1 cm (26½ × 33½ in.), Tate

decorates his interior with modern chairs and tables not so very different from Bacon's daybeds and glass tables. Even the splotchy black and white rug and orange upholstery recall Bacon's nauseating colour clashes. The principal inhabitants of this unreal space are two nudes, just like the bodies that cavort and suffer in Bacon's paintings.

If there were any doubt of Hamilton's Baconianism, the series of paintings he made of Mick Jagger in the back of a police van confirm how painterly his vision is, and how much he shares Bacon's sour eye.

On Sunday 12 February 1967, police raided a party at Redlands, the country home of Rolling Stones guitarist Keith Richards. They seized incense sticks that were claimed to be concealing the smell of cannabis, pudding basins containing ash, and four tablets belonging to Jagger containing amphetamine sulphate and methamphetamine hydrochloride. Hamilton's interest in the case was partly piqued by the involvement of his own art dealer, Robert Fraser, who was arrested alongside Jagger and charged with possessing heroin.

Swingeing London 67 is derived from a newspaper photograph of Fraser and Jagger handcuffed together, which Hamilton screenprinted onto canvas before adding lurid, electric colours – the bright blue of Jagger's jacket, the green and black stripes of his ironic establishment tie, the pink of his unmistakable lips; a faecal brown smear behind him, the dead cream colour of the van roof, the (real) metal shine of the handcuffs. The photographic image he has chosen (for as Duchamp said, an artist may 'choose' anything as a readymade) is haunting, when recoloured and redefined in paint, because it shows both men refusing to reveal their eyes. As Jagger covers his eyes with his hand, the flash light bursts brightly on his open palm and the glinting cuffs, while Fraser looks at us from behind half-visible shades.

The van forms a sinister enclosure, like one of Bacon's rooms or even like the walls that close in on the characters in Hogarth's progresses. The colours too have Bacon's sickly sensuality. *Swingeing London 67* portrays a new kind of hell – gaudy and hallucinatory.

I Can See for Miles

Hogarth's moral satires haunted young David Hockney, albeit in a way that induced a glad smile, as he reflected in autumn 1961 on the trip he had just taken to the USA. It was, to judge from the work of art that records it, an eye-opening visit, intoxicating, liberating. Born in 1937 in Bradford, Yorkshire, Hockney trained at the Royal College of Art in Kensington, where he was still a student when he took his transatlantic trip. That September he began etching the story of his adventure in an updated version of *A Rake's Progress* (page 67). His trip begins cautiously with a visit to a religious gathering as he tries to get the measure of New York. Then his skinny bespectacled self-portrait as the rake discovers the gay scene. Eventually, like all good rakes, he runs out of cash. The final scene, Bedlam, pictures insanity as a crowd of identically dressed young men in jeans all listening to pop on earphones – Hockney being a lifelong lover of classical music.

By 1964, Hockney would move to Los Angeles to enjoy the American freedom he had discovered and to paint a utopian – yet real – world of hedonism, beauty and swimming pools. In his 1966 painting *Peter Getting Out of Nick's Pool*, a nude shows his pink round buttocks as he pulls himself in a leisurely fashion out of water whose deep blue is slowly rippled by wavy lines of white. Even without knowing the painting's story – it portrays Peter Schlesinger, with whom Hockney was in love – you cannot miss its intimacy and frankness.

Hockney is as much a painter of the real as Freud or Auerbach – no screenprinted news images for him, no Duchampian jokes, just painting and printmaking based on empirical drawing. Yet the truth he chose to reveal was courageous and subversive in a Britain that did not decriminalize homosexual relations until 1967 – and then only between two men over the age of 21. Right from his early works, when still a student, Hockney had no inhibitions about honestly depicting gay life.

But his art was much more than a celebration of a subculture that was just emerging from the shadows. The light of California, its tall anencephalic palms, low buildings, patios, eggshell skies, pools that both heighten the sensuality of a nude and create a distance between watcher and watched – these perfectly distilled elements of his personal pastoral realm create enigmatic poems of the pursuit of happiness. Is *A Bigger Splash* a happy painting or a sad one? The upward rush of white water in Hockney's renowned 1967 painting hangs ghostlike in the air, frozen by art. The diver has vanished underwater. Apart from the splash, the hot day is completely motionless. Palms, sky, the surface of the pool – an impersonal stillness prevails. Is this the beginning or the end of something? The splash might be the start of a story or its final sentence.

Pleasure became legal in 1960s Britain. It was not just that liberal laws – including the 1967 Sexual Offences Act, the legalization of abortion, the abolition of the death penalty and the easing of divorce – modernized the legal system. These changes followed and tried to keep up with a much broader embrace of youth, freedom, self-discovery, hedonistic exploration and chemical experimentation. Even where laws remained punitive, attitudes were tolerant. 'Who breaks a butterfly on a wheel?' asked *The Times* of the Rolling Stones drugs bust.

Art is a sensory indulgence. It flourishes in libertarian times and shrinks in puritan eras. British art was far more inventive in the hedonistic Georgian age than under the moral strictures of Victorianism. In the 1960s it once again burst its confines. Artists literally demanded more space. In 1962 the young sculptor Anthony Caro left the formality of plinths behind and sent his welded steel construction *Early One Morning* out onto the gallery floor to occupy the real world. Caro's expansiveness was, like Hockney's pleasure-seeking eye, a response to the big open spaces of America. Or rather, in his case, to the cinemascope scale of modern American art, for Caro's sculptures are three-dimensional attempts to rival the almost limitless-seeming two-dimensional fields of colour created by modern American painters such as Jackson Pollock and Mark Rothko. Yet nothing reveals the difference between American and British art, and the empirical peculiarities of the English, more than the contrasting national feelings for abstraction.

Once, American art had been part of British art. In the eighteenth century, it seems as valid to call John Singleton Copley's *Watson and the Shark* a British painting as an American one. Even after the War of Independence, American artists remained in the British shadow. John James Audubon published his epic of nature art *The Birds of America* in London and Edinburgh from the 1820s. Later in the nineteenth century Whistler and Sargent gravitated to London's wealth. Yet as American art became distinctively 'American', it was much readier than its British parent to depart from observation and explore the sublime frontier of the abstract. The nineteenth-century writers Edgar Allan Poe and Herman Melville both imagined, in their fictions, unearthly abstract paintings. When American art finally leapt

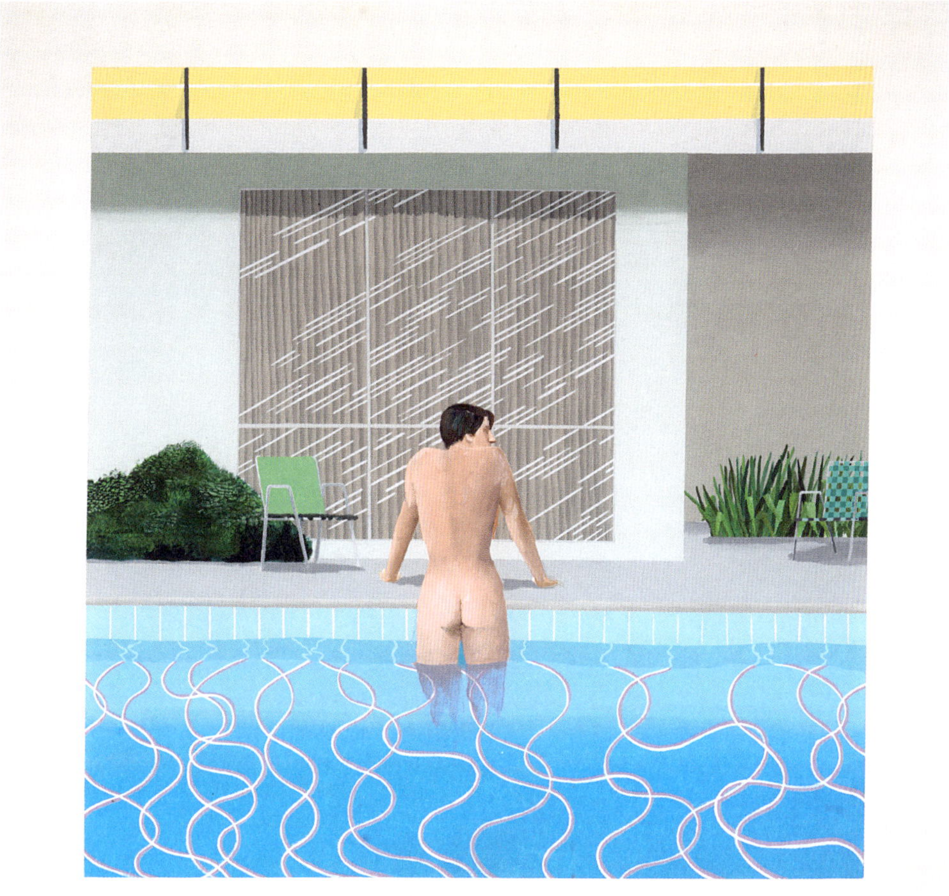

↑ David Hockney, *Peter Getting Out of Nick's Pool*, 1966, acrylic on canvas, 152.4 × 152.4 cm (60 × 60 in.), Walker Art Gallery, Liverpool, © David Hockney

into global consciousness after World War II, it was the completely non-representational paintings of the Abstract Expressionist movement that put it there.

British artists found their freedom intoxicating yet hard to emulate. The empirical belief in fidelity to nature that runs through British art like 'Brighton' through a stick of rock is not mere 'conservatism', as we have seen. It reflects a theory of perception and knowledge that originates in the Scientific Revolution. British artists who embraced the spatial adventure that was Abstract Expressionism could not resist rooting it in reality, grounding it in nature. The Cornish painter Peter Lanyon – who was actually born in St Ives, unlike so many artists who moved there – found a direct equivalent in nature for the free, broad, vertiginous visions of Pollock when he took up gliding in 1959. In paintings such as *Thermal*, with its powerful gusts of white and blue, he creates abstract-seeming records of what it was like to fly. In 1964 his pursuit of the same lofty world once painted by Constable and Turner led to his death after his glider crashed.

Frank Bowling, born in Guyana, was at the Royal College of Art at the same time as Hockney but became fascinated by the sheer scope of American-style abstract painting. Even so, he could not leave reality behind. On the contrary, his abstract art uses colour to speak of Caribbean history. His 1968 painting *Who's Afraid of Barney Newman?* parodies the famous vertical 'zips' of one of the most renowned Abstract Expressionists, but in green, yellow and red, the colours of the Pan-African flag, with maps of Guyana and South America stencilled into what seems a bright, worn banner.

Bridget Riley found another way to anchor her art in reality. Her abstract paintings are genuinely abstract. They contain no hidden images or echoes of nature. These are Britain's most exhilarating answer to the visions of Pollock, Newman and Rothko: spacious, dynamic, free. And yet they insist on scientific fact. Riley's paintings of the early 1960s are optical experiments. They challenge the eye to make sense of carefully calculated, exactly designed waves and spirals that replace the poetic sublimity of American abstraction with an empirical experiment conducted upon the person lured into their striking patterns.

Even in reproduction, her 1963 painting *Fall* creates confusing effects as you move your eyes over it. The waves that pulse over its surface seem to expand into real space, then to shrink: it is never still (unless you keep your eyes absolutely still), but constantly surging and

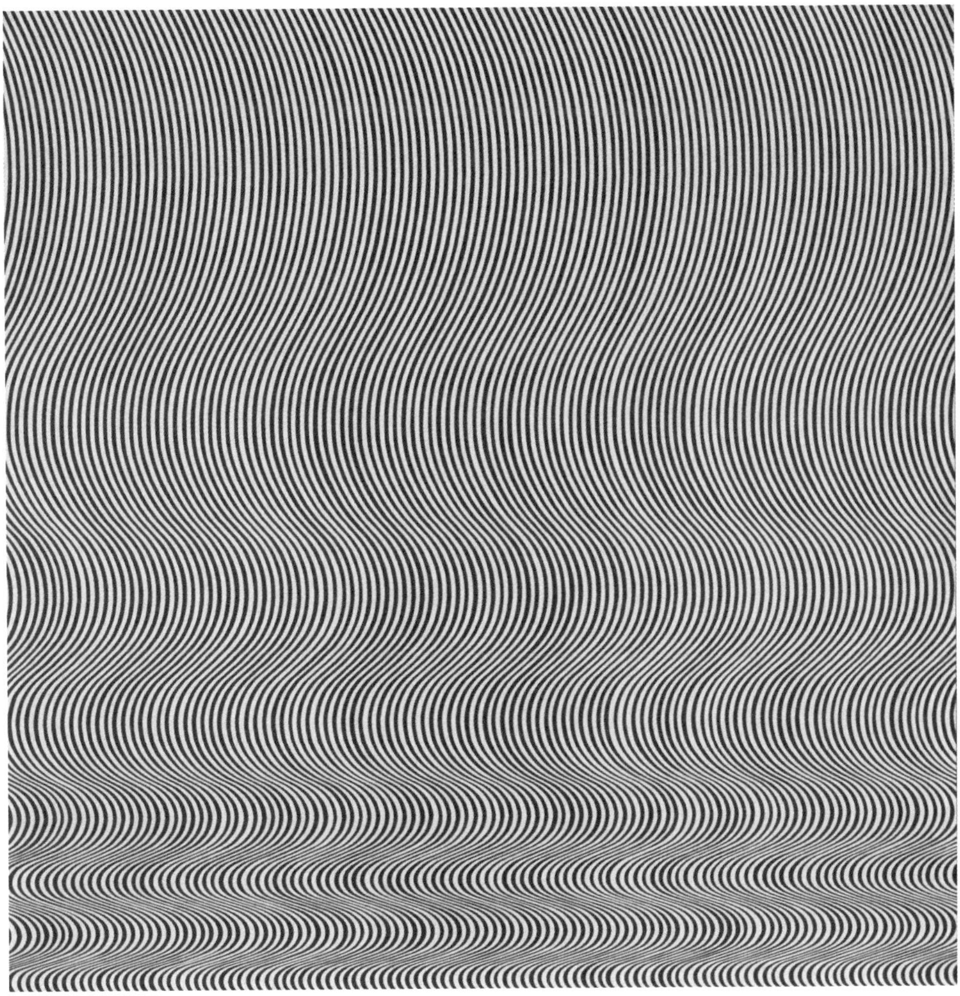

vibrating like a real, dynamic entity, like the sea or clouds. This movement is of course illusory. It happens in the head of the onlooker. This is a truly scientific work of art, an analysis of the nature of perception itself. Rather than showing us something, Riley shows us the mechanics of how we look.

Born in 1931, this most conscious and intellectual of British painters studied the Post-Impressionist landscapes of Seurat, with their optical networks of coloured dots that resolve into objects, as she took her imaginative journey from observation to abstraction. Yet Riley is a romantic disguised as a rationalist. Her early career after graduating from the Royal College of Art in 1955 was interrupted by

↑ Bridget Riley, *Fall*, 1963, polyvinyl acetate paint on hardboard, 141 × 140.3 cm (55 ½ × 55 ¼ in.), Tate

a severe breakdown: seeing Pollock's art at the Whitechapel Gallery in 1958 must have been an emotional as well as artistic medicine. Her empathy for America's abstract painters – troubled characters all – can be felt in the sublime momentum that is released by her apparently controlled art.

This tension between control and passion, design and ecstasy that makes Riley such a surprising and profound artist can be seen at its most acute in her 1961 work *Movement in Squares*. In many ways this is a triumph of technocratic cool. It looks like a chessboard folding inward. Yet follow that fold and your mind seems to be led into infinity, into a warp in time and space. Reality plummets into this bottomless rift. The imagination takes off for a journey into unknown dimensions. The pattern of black and white squares may seem disciplined yet it creates delirious visions that are as relentlessly seething as Turner's seas, and as inward as Coleridge's drug-induced reverie in his 1797 poem 'Kubla Khan':

> *Five miles meandering with a mazy motion*
> *Through wood and dale the sacred river ran,*
> *Then reached the caverns measureless to man...*

Riley surely never intended her paintings to be seen as drug-induced odes to the highs of later 1960s youth culture, yet she mirrors its ethos. Psychedelia was, like her art, simultaneously scientific and romantic. It was an experiment in seeing. By taking the right chemical, or by looking at Riley's art, you could perceive new realities.

That quintessentially 1960s application of what prime minister Harold Wilson called 'the white heat of technology' to release ethereal visions of heaven and hell was given spectacular visual form at London's Roundhouse in 1966 when The Who, Cream and The Move played in front of swarming screens of lurid colour created by the artist Gustav Metzger. These Liquid Crystal Environments, as the artist called them, used heat-sensitive substances sandwiched between glass slides, sensitive to heat applied from a projector, to create intense, multifarious colours that waxed and waned, warped and melted in an arbitrary cosmic dance like luminous abstract paintings.

The Who's guitarist and songwriter Pete Townsend first encountered Metzger when a student at Ealing College of Art. The visionary art guru had already inspired the band to smash their instruments on stage in the spirit of his conception of 'Auto-Destructive

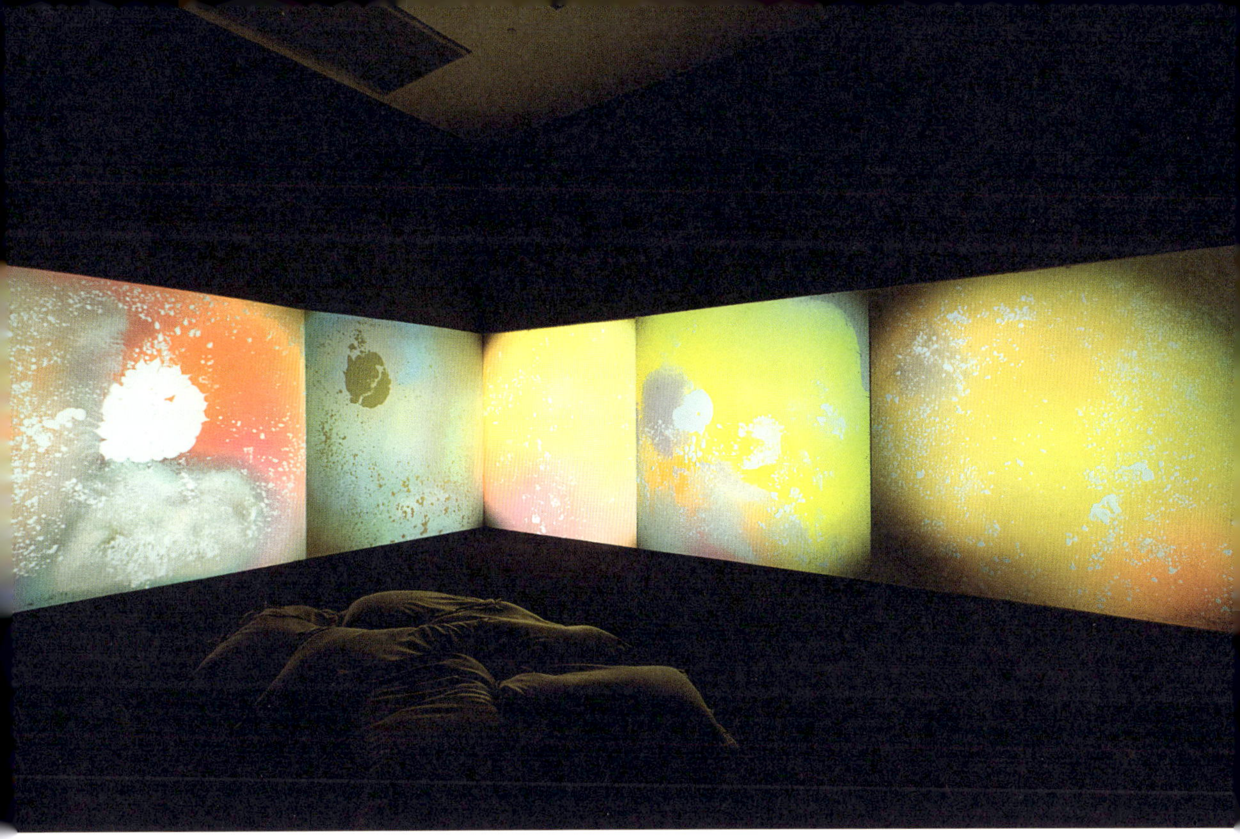

↑ Gustav Metzger, *Liquid Crystal Environment*, 1965, remade 2005, 5 control units, liquid crystals and slide, 35 mm, 5 projections, colour, duration: 22 min, dimensions variable, Tate

Art'. This was arguably the first attempt to truly bring the spirit of Dada to Britain. While British artists had emulated Futurism and Cubism in the early twentieth century, they did not show much interest at the time in Dada, the movement that started in Zurich in 1916 as a protest against the slaughter of a generation on the Western Front, and spread in 1918 to cities as various as Berlin, Cologne, Paris and New York – but emphatically not London. Dada dared to reject art itself, to use a Rembrandt as an ironing board, put a moustache on the Mona Lisa. With collages and montages, crazed acts and enigmatic gestures, it mocked, satirized and scorned the ideals of high culture whose bankruptcy it believed World War I to have exposed.

Richard Hamilton brought the ideas of Duchamp, Dada's most charismatic wit, to Britain, but it was Metzger who imported the movement's anger and savage disdain. He had good reasons to be angry. Born in Nuremberg in Germany in 1926, he witnessed, as a Jewish child, the parades the Nazi Party held each year in this medieval city. In 1939 he was brought to Britain by the Kindertransport. His parents and all his family were murdered in the Holocaust. Metzger's concept of Auto-Destructive Art was a rejection of beauty, complacency, even modern life itself. In 1961 an audience on London's South Bank saw him demonstrate his technique of Acid Action Painting: clothed in protective gear that looked sinister and post-apocalyptic, he threw acid at a suspended sheet of nylon, burning it to nothing. It was a savage parody of Jackson Pollock.

In September 1966 Metzger staged the Destruction in Art Symposium at the Africa Centre in London's Covent Garden, a pioneering festival of disruption and provocation that rejected all received ideas of what art should be. The British artist John Latham set fire to a tower of books outside the British Museum and the Vienna Actionist Hermann Nitsch explained his aesthetic of ritual violence. Among these parades of hippy machismo and revolutionary rhetoric, the Japanese artist Yoko Ono's performance *Cut Piece* stood out for its introspection. She knelt down, for two nights in a row, at the Africa Centre and invited the audience to cut off her clothes bit by bit. This violence was meant to be disturbing, a symbolic assault on Ono's person, a troubling enactment of power.

Ono followed up *Cut Piece* with a London exhibition at the Indica Gallery, which was visited that November by John Lennon. He was initially underwhelmed by the weird works on view, but softened when he had to climb a ladder to read the word YES on the ceiling. Soon Ono and Lennon were not just lovers but artistic collaborators – in fact they managed to merge the two when they celebrated their 1969 wedding with a Bed-In for Peace. Lennon's new passion for avant-garde art spilled into The Beatles' 1968 White Album, with its fan-dividingly radical track 'Revolution 9', and a completely blank cover 'designed' by Richard Hamilton, proving himself more than equal to the conceptual art revolution.

'Concept' or 'Idea' art crystallized out of many strands of the 1960s avant-garde and was an international phenomenon, yet it took on a distinctive flavour in Britain. The fact that it was promoted by the most intellectual of The Beatles – and blamed for their breakup – catapulted this crazy new kind of art into the pop arena. It even invaded television sets when Monty Python liberated screens in 1969 with Terry Gilliam's opening sequence of the painted foot of Bronzino's Cupid crashing down on the title to the sound of a fart. Yes, conceptual art could be funny.

Two students who met on the Advanced Sculpture course at St Martin's School of Art in London in 1967 saw this just as clearly as the Pythons did. George Passmore was born in Devon in 1942, Gilbert

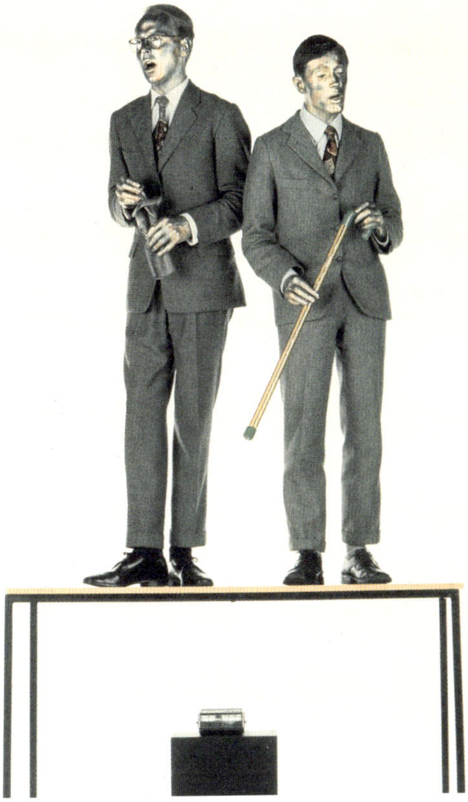

↑ Gilbert and George, *The Singing Sculpture*, 1970

Prousch in the Dolomites in Italy in 1943: both were country boys, and their intense relationship was nurtured by a mutual awe at the magnificence and quirkiness of London. They took long walks together through the city and started to see these rhapsodic perambulations as 'art'. Their St Martin's contemporary Richard Long was also pioneering the idea that a walk might be a work of art. While hitchhiking from his native Bristol to London in 1967 he went into a field in Wiltshire and walked it back and forth in a perfectly straight line until he left a long narrow mark – a trace of his passing that was environmentally tactful and intended to vanish. *A Line Made by Walking* survives today only as a black-and-white photograph.

It was archetypally English to give conceptual art this pastoral twist. Once Constable had hiked the fields to sketch, now Long would walk the landscape as a non-invasive artistic gesture. This was the era of free rock festivals, when psychedelia embraced (and littered) the countryside: the Isle of Wight Festival started in 1968, Glastonbury in 1971.

Gilbert and George too went walking in the country to pose for their dreamlike series of leafy, almost Gainsborough-like drawings, *The General Jungle*. In these big sketches composed, like Renaissance cartoons, of multiple sheets joined together and designed to fold neatly into a travelling case, the two artists are seen in smart suits leaning against a gate, walking among trees, brooding by water. Their sayings are neatly written by the slow summer scenes:

> *WE BELIEVE THAT LOVE is the PATH for a Better WORLD of ART in which GOOD & BAD GIVE WAY for GILBERT and GEORGE TO BE.*

In these self-portraits Gilbert and George seem unanchored in time, like vagrants lazing in a park. They took that uncanny sense of disengagement from time into realms of lugubrious science-fiction slapstick when they painted their faces bronze and silver, stood on a table in their 'responsibility suits', and danced slowly to a record of the 1932 Flanagan and Allen music hall song 'Underneath the Arches'.

They had become 'living sculptures'.

Are You Angry or Are You Boring?

The morning after was ashen. Bad head, bad memories. In their 1972 'drinking sculpture', *Balls: The Evening Before the Morning After*, Gilbert and George map a night at Balls Brothers wine bar, Bethnal Green, London, in fragmentary images of booze, bar pumps, wooden fittings and their own blurred faces. It is a record of getting drunk, losing control, giving in to the dangerous god Bacchus. In the same year they filmed themselves downing a bottle of gin – that most Hogarthian of drinks.

Far from being an abstract intellectual game, conceptual art, as practised by Gilbert and George, provided new ways of putting raw life into art. What better way to empirically apprehend reality than by making reality itself the 'art'? Their self-consciously British conceptualism had a tough, intimate, everyday eye for the grotesque. That was what drew them to the then almost derelict neighbourhood of Spitalfields in London's poverty-stricken East End. In the late 1960s they settled on Fournier Street, close to Hawksmoor's Christ Church, among Jewish clothes factories and dilapidated eighteenth-century houses. They have lived there ever since. In their 1975 series of photo-pieces *Dusty Corners* they pose among the antiquated, unrestored rooms of their home. Once again they look lost in time, grey-suited ghosts in the grubby corners of the past.

It was a time for tough reckonings. Francis Bacon woke up to a much worse hangover than one bottle of gin can give you. Far from receding from view in the 1960s as the avant-garde staged its bed-ins and singing sculptures, the painter of tortured flesh reached new heights. His style opened out into a louche, decadent version of the Baroque that captured the feel of the world he inhabited – a 'gilded gutter life' in the words of his friend Dan Farson, in which he moved between East End drinking clubs, West End oyster bars and functions attended by Princess Margaret. His 1966 nude portrait of his friend, the model Henrietta Moraes, lying on a bed with her feet towards the onlooker, her hips, buttocks and breasts bulging, her skin a crazy patchwork of pinks, greys and blacks and her face a smashed-up mask, rivals the late works of Picasso (who was still alive). Women often brought out the best in this most homosexual of painters. His 1967 *Portrait of Isabel Rawsthorne Standing on a Street in Soho* captures not only her pugnacious presence, a masked Picasso Demoiselle in a black dress, but also the Soho setting where Bacon's nights were fuelled by champagne and seafood.

In 1963 Bacon met – in a pub, naturally – a small-time criminal from the East End called George Dyer. Photographs show him as a handsome character with a sharp, distinctive profile, which was to haunt Bacon's art.

Bacon's lover may have looked like – and carried a whiff of the sinister glamour of – more successful 1960s East End villains such as the Kray twins and Charlie Richardson, but he lacked the painter's high tolerance for alcohol. The boozy lifestyle that fed Bacon's imagination gradually turned Dyer into a wreck. As their relationship decayed, Bacon shrugged and paid for Dyer to drink as much as he wanted. In autumn 1971, they went to Paris for Bacon's most prestigious exhibition to date, a retrospective in the spectacular setting of the Grand Palais, which gave him a chance to shine in the city that, for a man who had grown up in the 1920s, was still very much the capital of art.

Two days before the exhibition was due to open, Dyer killed himself. A conspiracy kept the news quiet until after Bacon's big day. Any cynicism he showed in the immediate aftermath of Dyer's death – from a drug overdose, while sitting on the toilet – is, however, eclipsed by the power of the paintings he made in his lover's memory. *Triptych, May–June 1973* imagines, and makes horribly immediate, the physical facts of Dyer's suicide. As he broods in the central panel, a batlike, vampiric shadow of evil thoughts emanates from his pummelled purple form. In the right-hand scene he vomits into a sink after taking an overdose. To the left he slumps on the toilet. These images emerge from a black doorway framed by walls the colour of dried blood. It is like a scene from a tragedy too bleak to be written.

Bacon himself is in the right panel of *Triptych August 1972*, a violet wraith remembering his lover. An equally ethereal Dyer sits in the left-hand scene. In the centre, their bodies contort together in a vision of ecstasy and rage. O that this too, too solid flesh would melt.

Even David Hockney was painting scenes of disillusion in the early 1970s. Jack Hazan's 1974 documentary film *A Bigger Splash* caught

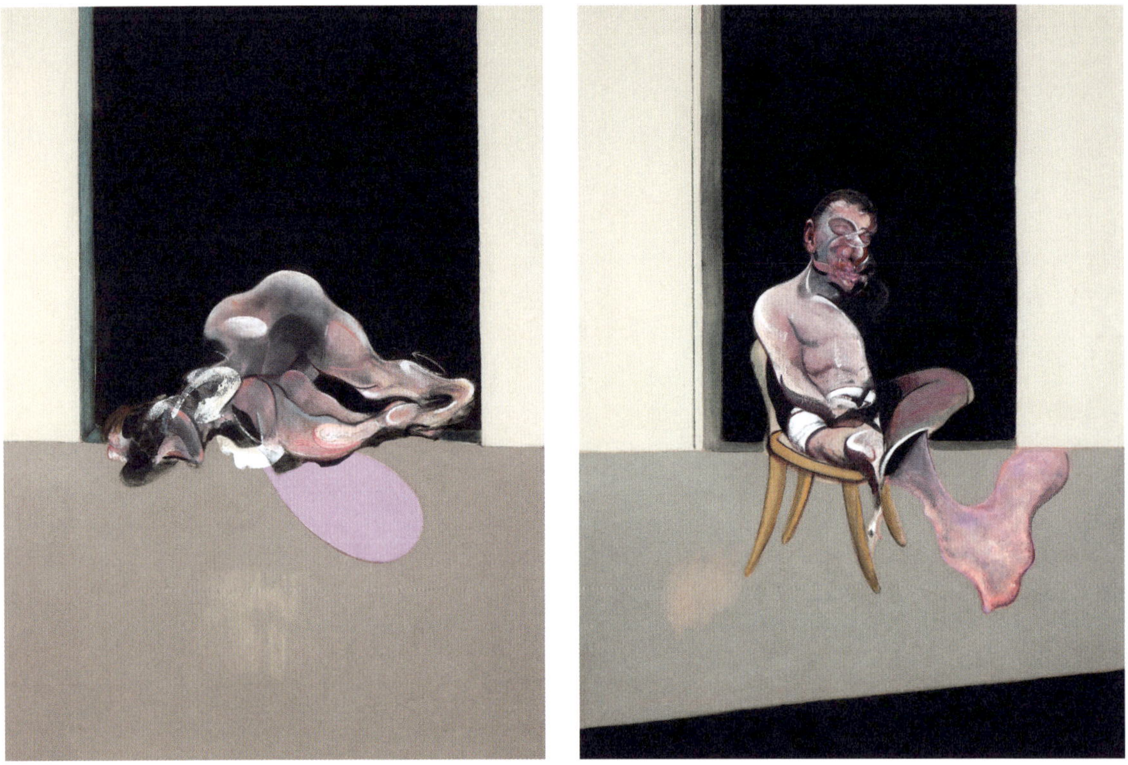

the painter at a time of crisis after his lover Peter Schlesinger left him. Hockney's spookily beautiful 1972 painting *Portrait of an Artist (Pool with Two Figures)* is a document of their break-up. Schlesinger stands in a pink jacket and pale lime trousers gazing down at a near-nude male swimmer whose pale form is refracted by the dazzling translucent hues of the water. Beyond, a dreamlike vista of green, purple and blue hills, like some vast operatic set, adds to the sublime, disturbing stillness of this moment of frozen desire.

A similarly haunted calm hangs in the warm, empty air of Michael Andrews's 1974 painting *Lights VII: A Shadow*. A balloon is passing over a beach by a rich aquamarine sea on a summer's day, but we cannot see it. We only observe the shadow of the balloon, precisely etched as a darkness on the bright sand. British art has come full circle. Andrews paints reality with the precision of an empiricist, yet something eludes him. Life is elsewhere. Truth is unknowable. The numbed unease of this masterpiece makes it the perfect work of British 1970s art, an image that seems to belong on the cover of every post-LSD concept

↑ Francis Bacon, *Triptych August 1972*, 1972, oil and sand on canvas, each panel 198 × 147.5 cm (78 × 58 in.), Tate

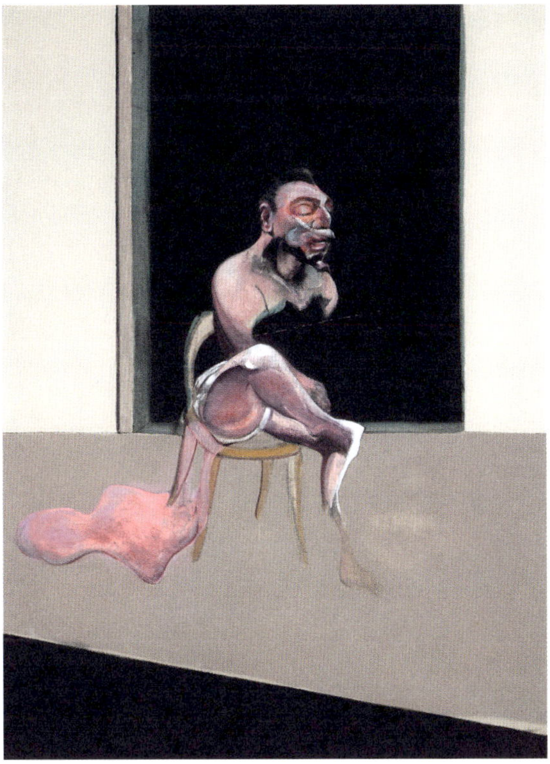

album recorded by a band that had crashed to earth, wealthy and bereft: 'How I wish, how I wish you were here.'

Throughout the cultural revolutions of the postwar era, British political and economic history had veered between the utopian and the dismal. High hopes were born in 1945 when a Labour Party promising fundamental change won a landslide victory. It delivered on its bold manifesto in a way rarely matched. The new National Health Service transformed British life. Welfare 'from the cradle to the grave' made society infinitely kinder. Industries were nationalized and the empire started to be dismantled, with a hasty departure from India in 1947. A decade later Ghana would become the first African republic to gain independence from Britain.

Yet as rationing continued and the government could not seem to rekindle an economy shattered by war, Winston Churchill won his final victory, at the 1951 general election. The Conservatives would stay in power for the next 13 years, in spite of Churchill's deterioration and the catastrophic attempt by his successor Anthony Eden in 1956 to reassert Britain's place in the world by attacking the Suez Canal. Under Harold Macmillan, the Conservatives reaped the fruits of an economy finally starting to deliver a consumer revolution that had come much earlier in the USA.

It turned out to be consumer goods – television sets, record players, tape recorders, mopeds, mini-skirts, drugs – that generated a sense of change and freed Britain from old constraints. Yet under this buzz of novelty the economy was staggering. Britain had lost its imperial markets, was on the brink of losing its heavy industries, and seemed caught in an unhealthy trap of inflation and poor productivity. Harold Wilson's Labour and Edward Heath's Conservatives appeared equally befuddled by what looked increasingly like tragic national decline. In 1968 Enoch Powell gave a speech that chucked the petrol of racial paranoia onto the bonfire of post-imperial crisis.

Essentially, Britain after 1945 failed to find a recipe to modernize itself. The husk of the greatest power of the nineteenth century was not easy to reinvent as a post-industrial, post-colonial economy. Cities that lost their busy ports or smoking factories had no idea how to start again. The warehouse flats and waterside cafés of the future were as yet unimagined. Instead, the state attempted to make Britain 'modern'. For the 1945 government that meant a planned economy and central control of industry. Later came tower blocks, flyovers, comprehensive education and nuclear power. None of it drove away the spectre of decline. By the 1970s every recipe for renewal looked threadbare. An atmosphere of violence crept into miserable city centres. In Northern Ireland this meant armed conflict. The failure to secure improved civil rights for Catholics in the late 1960s led to riots, followed by the rebirth of the Irish Republican Army and a small but savage civil war on British soil.

Gilbert and George saw this deterioration from their street-level vantage point in the East End. Their increasingly ambitious pictorial works composed from photographs of themselves and others became a mirror of a society on the edge, bristling with graffiti, insults, urban rage. Their 1977 picture *Cunt Scum* features these words, photographed from scrawled graffiti, juxtaposed with a variety of anxious Londoners: a policeman, a TV crowd, people crossing the road, homeless men sitting on a pavement. Race, class, poverty and power all pulse in this tapestry of the capital. Most of all it has an atmosphere of menace, a foreboding of imminent mayhem.

In another 1977 picture, in which fragmentary glimpses of a restless, dangerous, powder-keg city are flanked by prophet-like monumental images of Gilbert and George themselves, are the painted words:

ARE YOU ANGRY OR ARE YOU BORING?

This graffiti could easily have been written by one of the 'punks' whose youth revolt that same year shocked a Britain unable even to enjoy Queen Elizabeth II's Silver Jubilee in peace. To promote the Sex Pistols' incendiary 1977 single 'God Save the Queen', artist Jamie Reid collaged words cut from tabloid newspapers across a black strip where he had removed the Queen's eyes from her portrait. It was all set against the Union Jack. Dada was now the stuff of teenage rage on working-class estates.

For a generation of future artists who grew up in the 1970s it was easy to pick up avant-garde ideas from record covers or the BBC's *Top of the Pops*. Tracey Emin, a teenager in 1970s and 80s Margate with a catastrophic school attendance record and a brutally early experience

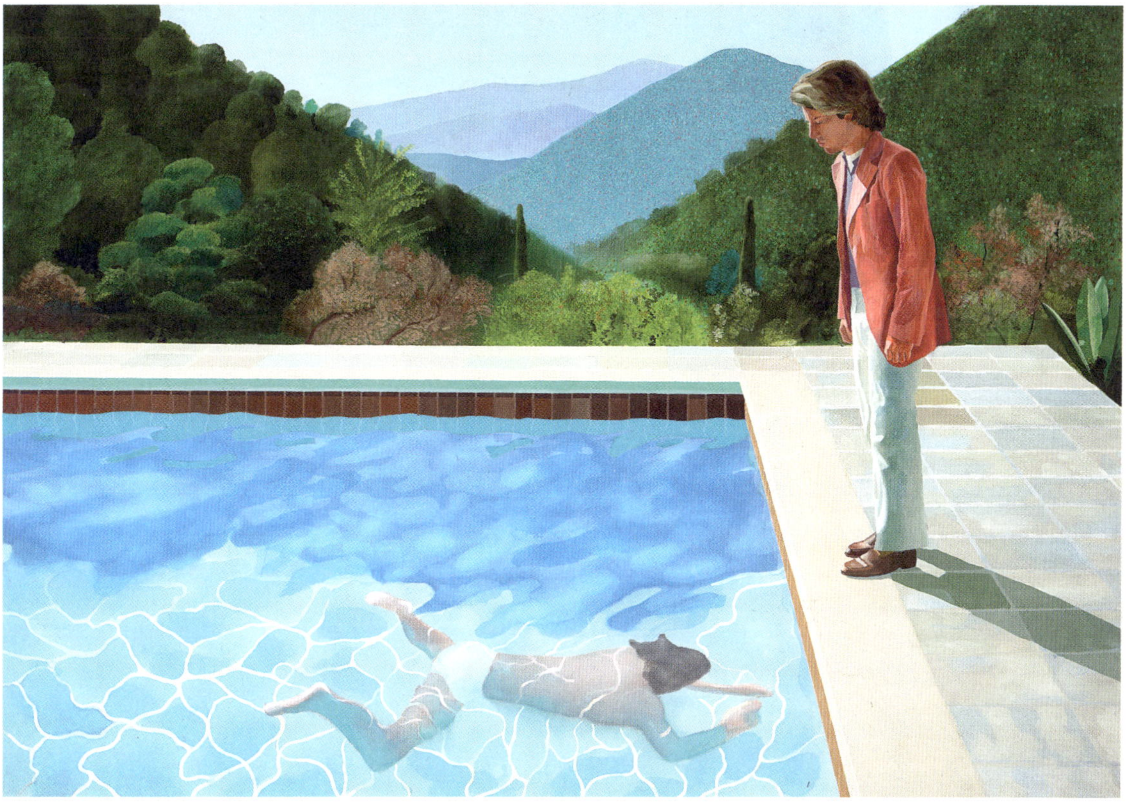

↑ David Hockney, *Portrait of an Artist (Pool with Two Figures)*, 1972, acrylic on canvas, 213.36 x 304.8 cm (84 x 120 in.), Private Collection, © David Hockney

of casual sex, discovered the existence of German Expressionist art from David Bowie's poses on his album sleeves. Ever since the early 1960s, pop culture and art had enjoyed a special relationship in Britain. For the generation that grew up in the scabrous shadow of punk, that relationship would be one of provocation and calculated shock. Yet by the time their artistic rebellion took off, the Britain of their childhoods would be remade.

Richard Hamilton's painting *The citizen*, created in 1981–83, is his most powerful homage to Bacon. Like so many of Bacon's paintings, it uses the multi-panelled forms of medieval art: it is a diptych. Like Bacon's rooms, this prison cell is a scene of carnage. The inside of a body has exploded outward. The prisoner has daubed his own tiny, barren living space with faeces that curl in strangely creative spirals and arabesques. Amid this art of disgust and refusal, a bearded, long-haired man gazes at us out of dark, shadowed eyes. With his bare upper body covered only by a blanket he looks Christlike.

In 1981, ten Republicans at the Maze Prison in Northern Ireland starved themselves to death in a hunger strike. They were demanding to be treated as political prisoners rather than criminals. Hamilton's political sympathies were with the prisoners, yet his painting seems ambivalent. There is something terrifying in this man's intensity and consciousness of his own martyrdom. His piercing presence recalls lines W. B. Yeats had written after the Easter Rising in Dublin in 1916:

Too long a sacrifice
Can make a stone of the heart.

This is also a picture with an absent other.

Margaret Thatcher, elected as Conservative prime minister in 1979, showed her iron in the way she refused a single concession to the hunger strikers. To her critics it was proof of her inhumanity. To her fans it revealed qualities that made her the most effective prime minister since – they would say Churchill – but perhaps it should be the 1945 government's quietly successful Clement Attlee.

Taking on the miners and anyone else who defied her ideal of free market economics, Thatcher transformed British society. The age of nationalized industries was over. The market was god.

The market meant money, and one thing you can do with money is buy art.

Journal of the Plague Years

In 1990 Leon Kossoff painted – and not for the first time – the church at the end of Gilbert and George's road. The elaborate mass of Hawksmoor's Baroque invention, with its pyramid spire that seems full of secret symbolism and Masonic significance, leans at a crazy angle across the thick painterly mass of the almost square, nearly 2 metre (6 ft 6 in) tall work. Its outlines appear to have been scoured into the encrusted surface with all the desperation of a man remembering this church as he stares into the horizon on some desert island; it might be a painting made by Robinson Crusoe to remind himself of early eighteenth-century London. Below the church, below the lamps of Fournier Street, passers-by and derelicts all seem equally vulnerable, the living ghosts of a city whose streets bleed history.

Kossoff said he wanted to preserve this bit of old London before it was swallowed by commercial development. He painted *Christ Church, Spitalfields, Morning* with a keen awareness 'that time is short, that soon the mass of this building will be dwarfed by more looming office blocks and overshadowed…'.

At the same moment, a much younger artist was trying to achieve a similar act of preservation in, what some thought, a more extreme way. For in the same year Rachel Whiteread, born in 1963, managed to make a plaster cast of an entire room of an old house, 486 Archway Road, in North London. It was exactly the kind of house, the kind of street, that might be seen through tear-stricken ridges of colour in a painting by Kossoff or Auerbach. Yet instead of picturing it, Whiteread created a three-dimensional replica of the volume of a Victorian front room. In other words she solidified its air, its space.

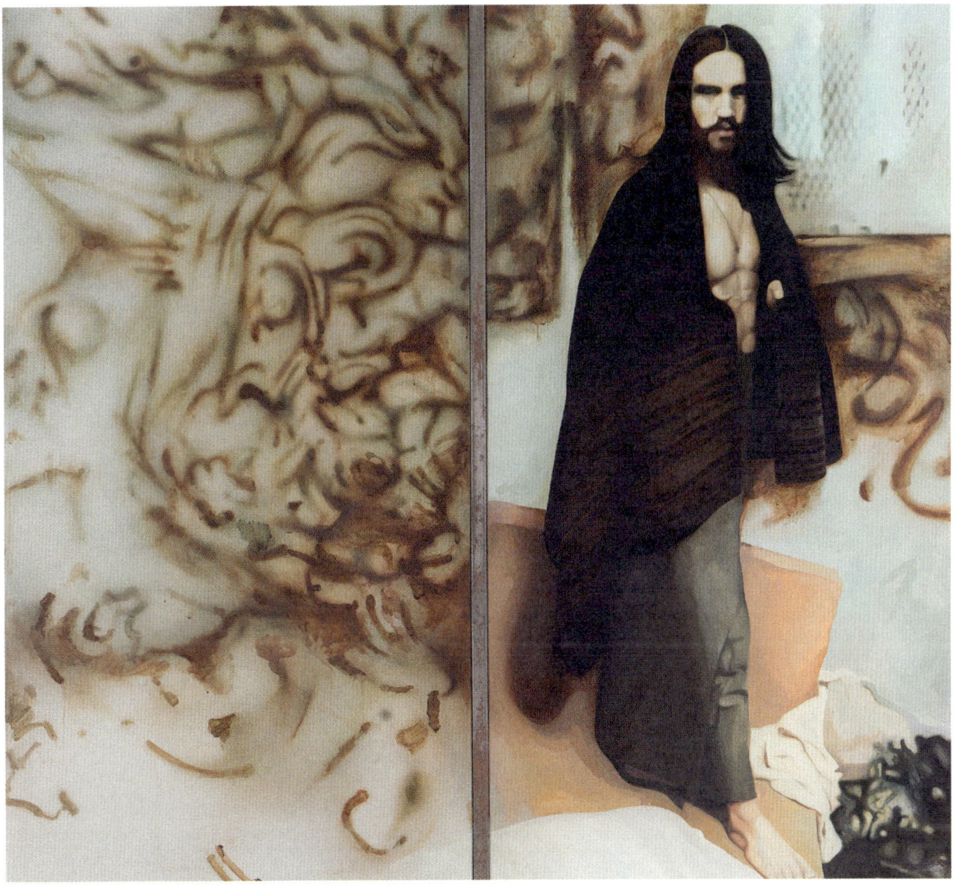

↑ Richard Hamilton, *The citizen*, 1981–83, oil on two canvases, each 200 × 100 cm (78¾ × 39⅓ in.), Tate

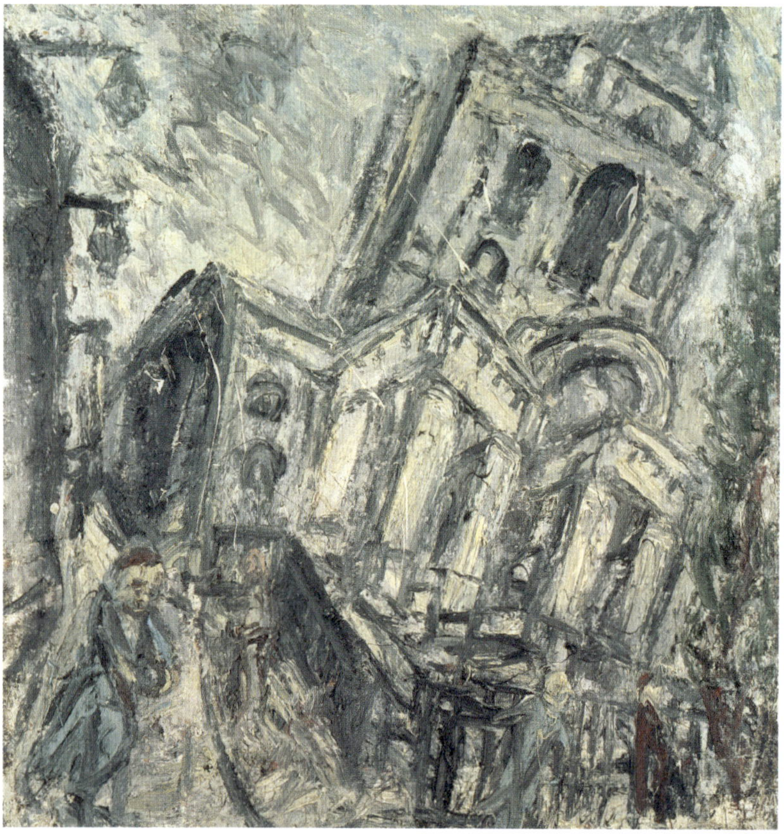

Walking around the big block of white plaster that resulted, you find yourself pondering the unknown moments lived here. History records barely any of the human story, it becomes apparent. Cups of tea, kisses, arguments, an old man gazing out of a window – all the silent joys and sorrows of vanished London lives are held safe inside this sepulchral cast. Impressions of doors, windows and fireplaces are clues to the untold stories it cherishes. *Ghost*, as Whiteread called her time capsule, is a monument to the sheer entropy and redundancy of the everyday, the immense amount of reality we forget from second to second.

Ghost was bought by the advertising mogul and Conservative Party campaign veteran Charles Saatchi. In 1992 he put it on display at his gallery near Swiss Cottage, North London, in the first of a series of exhibitions called *Young British Artists*. Thus history is made. Far from seeing any shared melancholy in the London visions of Kossoff

↑ Leon Kossoff, *Christ Church, Spitalfields, Morning*, 1990, oil paint on board, 198.6 × 189.2 cm (78 1⁄6 × 74 2⁄5 in.), Tate

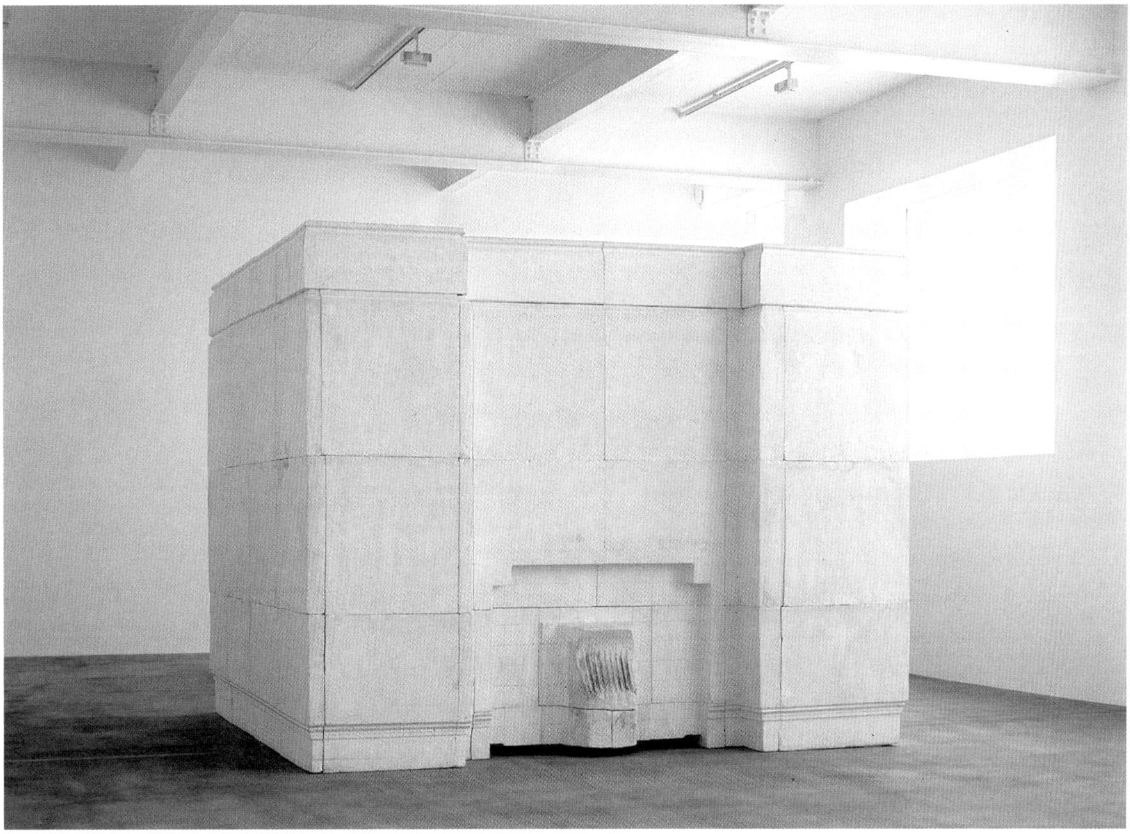

↑ Rachel Whiteread, *Ghost*, 1990, plaster on steel frame, 269 × 355.5 × 317.5 cm (105 7/8 × 140 × 125 in.), National Gallery of Art, Washington, D.C.

and Whiteread, we swallow a myth of generational revolt. In the 1990s, the instant accounts all say, a rebel generation of Young British Artists, or YBAs, who grew up with punk and were taught market values by Thatcherism, rejected the painterly intensity and skill of their elders and instead made 'artworks' (as opposed to staid old Works of Art) from found stuff, with little apparent effort, conceived for maximum impact to make them rich and famous.

The truth is much more interesting. At the beginning of the 1990s a new seriousness gripped British art. A mood of introspection, a preoccupation with life's fragility, among some gifted artists young and old, brought forth a rare crop of imaginative works of art, all in the space of a few years, mostly in one city: London.

This golden moment of British art was a brief, brilliant revival of the fascination with science and attention to raw empirical facts on which British art was founded in the age of Hogarth and Gainsborough.

Damien Hirst's early art has obvious similarities with the public experiments of the Scientific Revolution. His grotesquely brilliant 1990 installation *A Thousand Years* is a none-too-subtle allegory of life, death and the universe contained inside a glass vitrine with a heavy steel frame. Countless maggots and flies spend their entire life cycle sealed inside this small artificial insect cosmos. Feeding on a rotting cow's head and dishes of sugar and water, instinctively reproducing new generations of imprisoned maggots, the flies arguably have all they need. That does not mean they have everything they want.

The tragicomedy of it is that to get to the tasty cow's head, the flies must enter a second section that also includes a glowing blue electric insect-killer. They could stay in the safe area where they started out as maggots, and where sugared water provides sustenance. Instead they are drawn to glamour, excitement, flavour – and their deaths. The stench of decaying meat lures them to a sizzling end.

Joseph Wright of Derby had painted *An Experiment on a Bird in the Air Pump* (page 123). Hirst's installation is the experiment itself, offered as art. *A Thousand Years* presents an entire natural history, turning living animals into art. As it develops, the swarming flies look like an abstract field of oscillating black dots. You feel the flesh, the exoskeletons, the maggots' pulp when you gaze in appalled fascination at this grisly creation. What if it really did go on for a thousand years? How might this doomed insect society evolve?

For Hirst's next jaw-dropper, an Australian fisherman was paid to catch a tiger shark so it could be displayed in a 5.5 metre (18 ft) long tank filled with formaldehyde. When it was fresh, the shark looked alive. It swam like white death through the empty space of the Saatchi Gallery. This illusion was aided by the refractive qualities of the liquid inside the tank, for when you walked towards its front end an optical shift made the predator appear to leap forward.

Hirst's feats were not only works of horror. His monstrous vitrines were accompanied by cabinet displays that mimic the classificatory systems of science. We have seen how, in the eighteenth century, the precise animal portraits of Stubbs mirrored the new principles for classifying the natural world with which Carl Linnaeus put natural history on a scientific footing. Hirst's cabinets do not so much parody Linnaeus as create their own aesthetic taxonomy. His 1991 piece *Forms Without Life* is an arrangement of beautiful and exotic sea shells on white melamine shelves. The glistening pearly interiors and gothic spiked exteriors of these natural creations are ravishing, yet all these hard remains have one thing in common: the soft animals that inhabited them are dead.

Why were London artists fixated on death all of a sudden? One of the Four Horsemen is pestilence. The HIV/AIDS epidemic that began in the 1980s terrorized Western urban populations and took a high toll among artists. Hamad Butt, who graduated from Goldsmith's College a year after Hirst in 1990 and whose promising work shared his fascination with medicine and chemistry, died from an AIDS-related illness in 1994. A look at mortality statistics tells a chilling tale. Deaths from AIDS in Britain increased throughout the early 1990s to peak in 1995, the year Hirst won the Tate Gallery's Turner Prize. In other words, the years when British art was most obsessed with death coincided precisely with the worst years of the AIDS crisis.

Many things have been said about Hirst's death imagery. It is often dismissed as glib – especially when he later unveiled his

↓ Damien Hirst, *The Physical Impossibility of Death in the Mind of Someone Living*, 1991, glass, painted steel, silicone, monofilament, shark and formaldehyde solution, 217 × 542 × 180 cm (85 ⅖ × 213 ⅖ × 70 ⅚ in.), installed in the *Young British Artists I* exhibition at the Saatchi Gallery, 1992

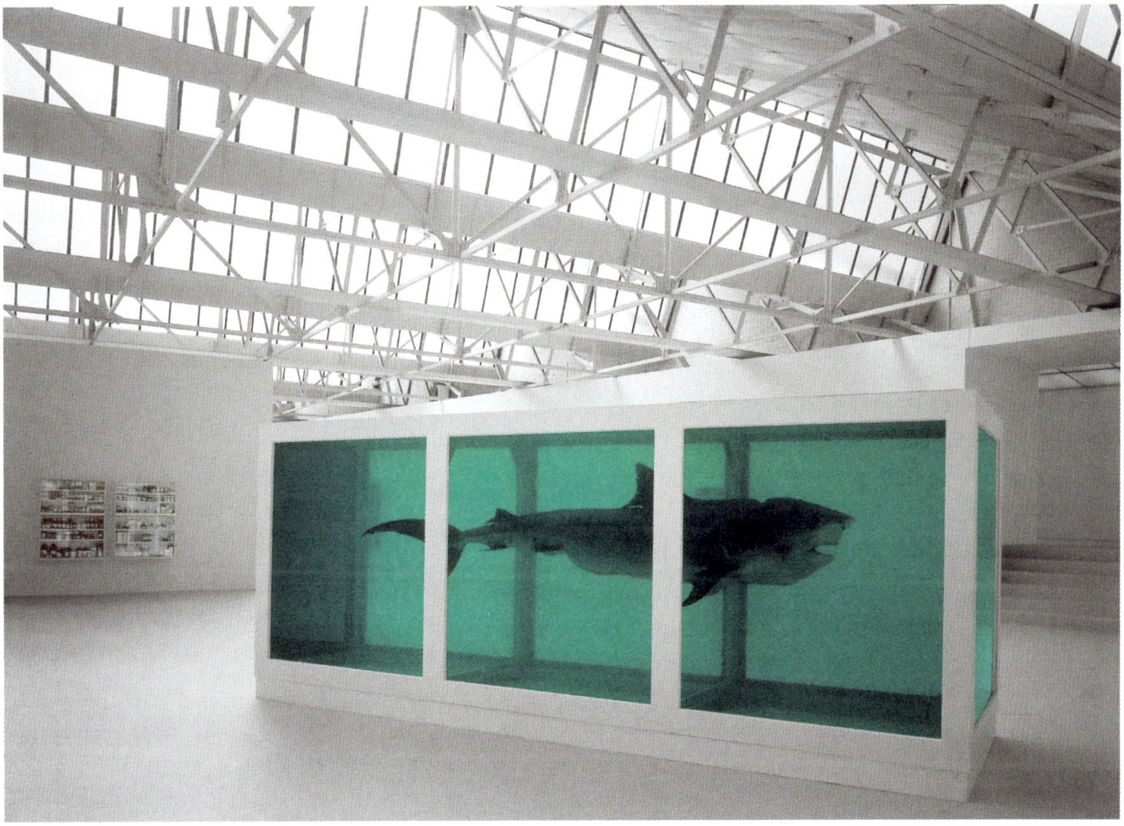

diamond-encrusted skull *For the Love of God*. Yet an epidemiological view of art history suggests that all the dead animals and funereal casts in early 1990s art may have been as direct a response to the immediate presence of death as Holbein's *The Ambassadors*, painted in an earlier age of human vulnerability by an artist who died of plague.

But it was an older artist who responded most explicitly to the mortality crisis. In 1991, Howard Hodgkin collaborated with American writer Susan Sontag on an illustrated edition of her story about AIDS, *The Way We Live Now*. It was a natural extension of his work. Hodgkin's fiery yet tender paintings are elegiac in spirit. Memory turns to colour in his apparently abstract, yet in reality richly diaristic, evocations of people, places, times.

He started out as a Pop artist of sorts in the 1960s, yet reached his finest period in the 1980s and 90s when what had earlier seemed an uncertainty about whether he wanted to paint reality or not matured into a wondrously free and acutely poetic use of colour to tell hidden tales of modern life. Most of his elusive confessions were painted very slowly, often over several years, as every touch of colour became laden with significance. Hodgkin clearly spent as much time brooding over his paintings in the London light that fell into the secret skylit well of his studio near the British Museum as he did painting them. The title of his 1988–93 work *When Did We Go to Morocco?* suggests a memory already distant, a long-ago holiday with an old flame: yet the fierce reds and oranges that cavort and gyrate in it glow with unquenchable sensory recall. He may not remember what year they went to Morocco but he remembers how it felt.

That concentration of sensual feeling leaps out of his 1993 painting *After Degas* with the intensity of a dancer's pirouette, or of making love. Two great blasts of fleshy colour manage to create, in the simplest possible sweeps of translucent oil, within a frame he has painted a cool green, the double sense of human bodies and rapid motion. It is a swoon of desire.

By contrast, in her 1992 sculpture *Two Fried Eggs and a Kebab*, Sarah Lucas, born in 1962, reduces flesh to an obscene caricature. Two real fried eggs are laid on a table to take the place of breasts. A greasy kebab is the table-woman's vagina. Being a table, she lies there passively. On the table stands a photograph of this very image, like a sentimental pornographic ideal.

There could hardly be a harsher update of Hogarthian realism. Lucas sees heterosexual love with even fewer illusions than Hogarth's

Before and After (page 57) in her 1994 piece *Au Naturel*. A man and a woman in bed are reduced to two melons and a bucket beside a cucumber and a couple of oranges on a filthy mattress. Artistic celebrations of the nude are mocked and scorned here as so much pretentious erotica. You want a nude? It's just a few pieces of fruit and a bucket, mate. Lucas manages to turn demotic English obscenity into memorable art.

When Hirst won the Turner Prize in 1995 – at his second attempt: he had been shortlisted in 1992 – his fellow contestants included Mona Hatoum, born in 1952 to a Palestinian family in Beirut. In the Turner exhibition, she showed *Corps Étranger*, a video made by inserting an endoscopy camera inside her own body to record wet pink images of her interior.

Helen Chadwick, born in 1953, achieved a similarly intense evocation of our fleshy selves in 1989 with a series of disconcertingly sensual photographs of artfully arranged pieces of meat, lubricious still lifes that find in red raw beef a mirror of our inmost being.

In other words, it was not some sterile Duchampian revolution in 'conceptualism' and 'the readymade' that made British art striking in these years. That revolution had taken place long ago: its heroes were Richard Hamilton and Gilbert and George. The use of found objects

→ Sarah Lucas, *Two Fried Eggs and a Kebab*, 1992, table, fried eggs, kebab, photograph, 151 × 89.5 × 102 cm (59⅖ × 35¼ × 40⅙ in.), Private Collection

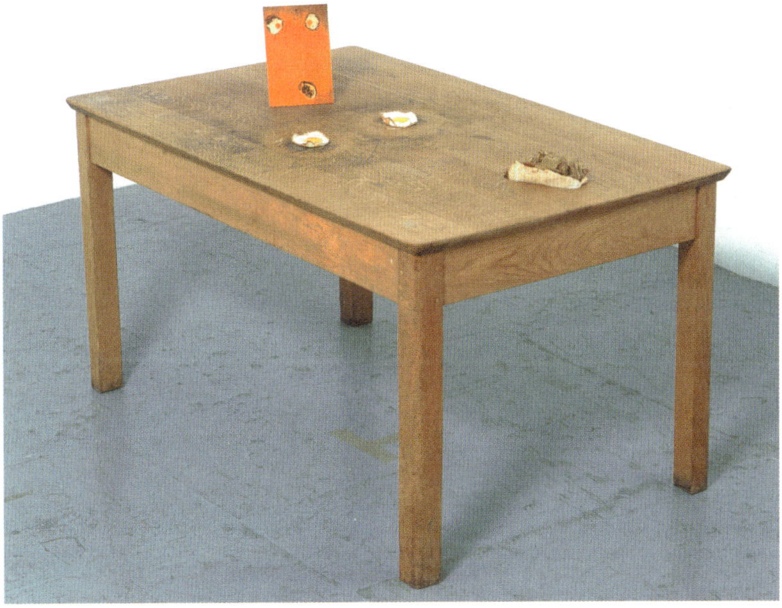

was routine in the work of the 1980s British sculptors Tony Cragg, Bill Woodrow and David Mach. What was different and special as the decade changed was a new ferocity, a savage readiness to look life and death in the eye, a fixation on – often literally – meaty content.

Francis Bacon's bloody nightmares hung over it all. Hirst's debt to the butcher of Soho was obvious and openly proclaimed. His isolated animals enclosed in glass tanks gleefully emulate Bacon's popes in their glass booths. It is equally easy to see echoes of Bacon in Hatoum's innards and Chadwick's 'enfleshings'. Bacon died on 28 April 1992, yet his vision had never been more alive. In their 1995 sculpture *Zygotic Acceleration, Biogenetic, De-Sublimated Libidinal Model (Enlarged x 1000)*, Jake and Dinos Chapman give Bacon's mutations of the human form a science-fiction spin, melting together a crowd of trainer-wearing girl mannequins so they seem to have evolved into one creature with one consciousness – literally, a generation from hell. The most shocking exhibit in *Freeze*, an exhibition staged by Hirst in an East London warehouse in 1988 when still a student, was Mat Collishaw's *Bullet Wound*, an enlarged colour photograph of a bloody red hole in a human skull: exactly the kind of photo Bacon kept in his studio at 7 Reece Mews in Kensington, from which to derive inspiration.

None of these artists was Bacon's legitimate successor. That title passed instead to the carnal expressionist's close friend Lucian Freud. The two painters had socialized together and watched one another's work for decades. Their portraits of each other reveal an intense mutual affection and respect. After Freud's precisely observed, deadly serious 1952 portrait of Bacon was stolen in Germany in 1988, he would make a Wanted poster for it that seems as much a lament for Bacon as for the painting. Bacon's portraits of Freud hint at something still more fervent. It seems reasonable to think he was a little bit in love with the younger man.

Yet they are very different artists. Bacon gets at the truth of human vulnerability and the despair of loss through spectacular, sensationalist excess. His art hits at reality until emotion and truth bleed out of a numbed shell – 'to unlock the valves of feeling and therefore return the onlooker to life more violently', as he put it. Freud never lets go in that fantastical way. He never departs from visible facts at all. He is the least imaginative of all great artists – at least by a conventional popular understanding of what 'imagination' is.

John Locke in the seventeenth century had offered an alternative concept of imagination. For him, our imaginations can only be fed by

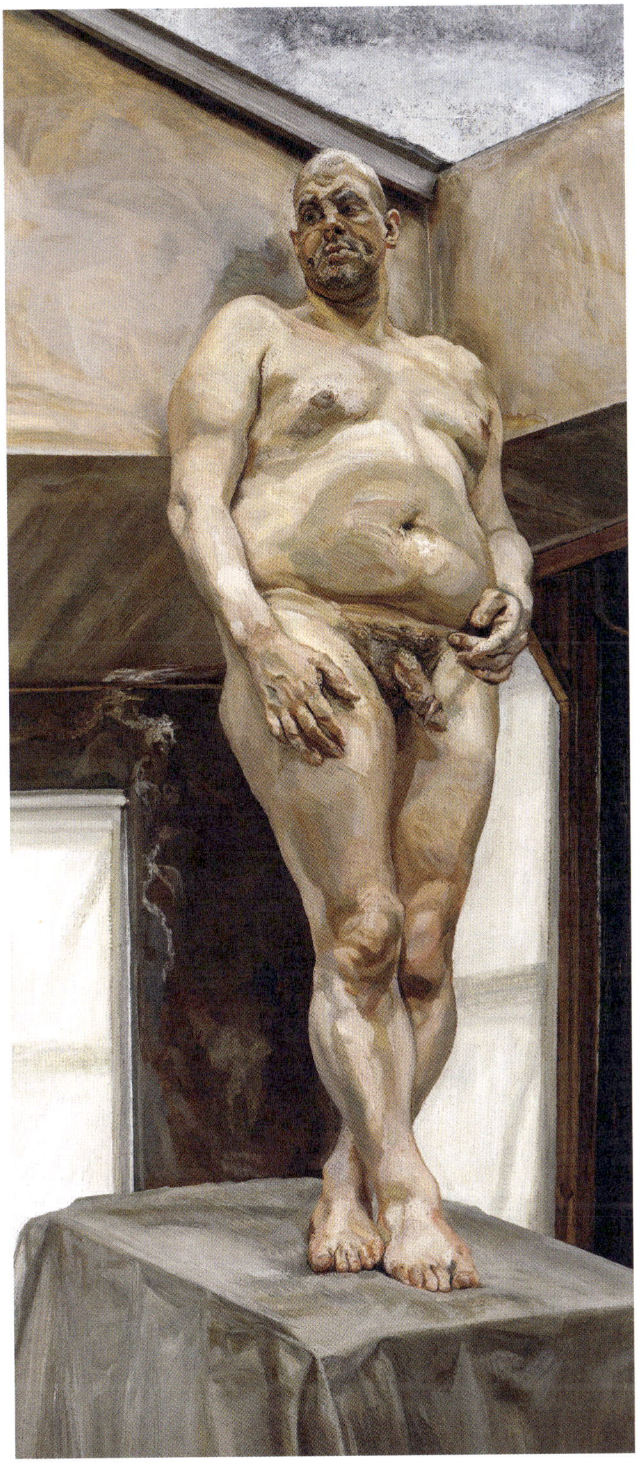

our observations. It is the information of reality that sets us imagining.

Freud never departed from the ruthless Lockean empiricism of his early art. Portraiture remained at the absolute centre of his work. Sometimes he looked out of the window of his studio in Paddington, West London, to paint a cityscape or a garden scene. He also painted animals superbly. The idea of making anything up clearly struck him as somewhat immoral. His sole theme was the reality he observed. Staring hard, turning to his canvas with his brush, then staring again: that was art, for Freud.

We see this process, interrupted for a moment by the painter's absence, in a photograph taken in Freud's studio by his friend Bruce Bernard in 1994. A big, shaven-headed man stands on a high makeshift plinth that is clearly intended to make him even more colossal. It brings his head almost level with the lowest side of the studio's sloped glass roof. While he poses there, the artist seems to have slipped out for a cup of tea. Close to the camera looms a nearly finished painting of the exact view we see.

Exact, but not pedantic. Freud's empiricism had not relented one jot since he painted his early hallucinatory replicas of big-eyed girls, but his feel for paint had evolved. By the time he painted *Leigh Under the Skylight* in 1994, his surfaces were mottled and rough, his theme no longer the clothed individuals he portrayed in works such as his Pinteresque 1984–85 painting *Two Irishmen in W11*, but the naked human creature. Freud's late style was saturated in the history of the human body as a painterly motif. He had looked long at, not just flesh,

↑ Lucian Freud, *Leigh Under the Skylight*, 1994, oil on canvas, 297.2 × 120.7 cm (117 × 47 ½ in.), Private Collection

but the techniques with which such masters as Titian and Rubens made it come alive.

Bernard's photograph shows how deeply Freud assimilated Titian's approach to painting. British art has a long-standing affinity for this towering figure of the Venetian Renaissance. Eighteenth-century artists obsessed over the 'secret' of his colours and Blake raged against his bad influence; English and Scottish country houses were full of Titian's canvases, most of which have migrated into public collections. When, near the end of Freud's life, the National Galleries of Scotland and the UK launched a joint campaign to buy two great Titians for the nation(s) from the Duke of Sutherland, he spoke up in support of the campaign to purchase both *Diana and Actaeon* and *Diana and Callisto*. A few years earlier he explained his passion for these paintings to his friend Martin Gayford; how he adored:

> *...the way the drapery flung over the branch to the right of Diana and Callisto, and the curtain to the left of Diana and Actaeon, were both obviously done at the last minute out of pure joie de vivre. (The paint is very thin and you can see through to what was painted before.) These two Titians are intimate yet also grand. I can't say which I like the most, but I would love to have one hanging on my sitting room wall, though I'm not sure it would fit.*

Titian painted directly from life, with naked models posing for him. He did not work from preparatory drawings; paint responds spontaneously to flesh in his sensual nudes. We see in Bernard's photograph how Freud worked in the same way. To pose for him was a committed collaboration. He wanted your body for his eyes to feast on.

At the start of the 1980s Freud made a prolonged study of Titian's two paintings of the goddess Diana and her all-female retinue. Like Freud, the Venetian lover of women had started out with a crisp, clear attention to detail. By the time he painted *Diana and Actaeon* his touch was much more fleeting, poetic, suggestive. The bodies of Diana and her companions are so intimately made of light and shadow you seem to feel their shivers from inside.

This was the kind of rawly spontaneous, roughly handled (in every sense), powerfully lit nude that Freud set out to create in the 1990s.

Leigh Bowery was a stupendous model. Born in Melbourne, Australia, in 1961, this performance artist, punk singer, nightclub impresario, fashion hero and gender radical became an underground icon of the London club scene who took the flamboyant 1980s pop culture of New Romanticism to surreal extremes. Bowery dressed in tight-fitting multicoloured costumes that did not so much feminize his body as deliberately accentuate its bulges to invent a totally new gender. This science fiction self-transformation into an almost post-human being was sometimes accentuated by covering his head with a giant featureless sphere of taffeta or silk. He wore PVC skirts, clinging silk dresses that covered his entire body including his hands, a fake pregnancy bulge, masks, giant hats and the occasional Nazi helmet. In performances at clubs and art galleries he appeared to give birth to his friend and collaborator Nicola Bateman, who was so small she could hide up his skirts. On stage with his band Minty, he simply screamed into the mic in performances of chaotic Dada abandon.

How did Freud, an 'establishment' figure in his sixties, team up with this star of the subculture? He knew – and portrayed – Welsh bohemian Cerith Wyn Evans, born in Llanelli in 1958, who worked with the director Derek Jarman on *Caravaggio* and other films before becoming the most mature member of the Young British Art movement. After Freud saw one of Bowery's live-birth performances at the gallery of his dealer Anthony d'Offay, Wyn Evans introduced them. It was the beginning of a brilliant partnership.

Bowery's readiness to display his body, his complete lack of inhibition, pleasure in his own corpulence, and ability to communicate his very being physically, helped Freud create naked portraits that are heroic, truthful, and full of feeling. These paintings isolate a human figure and laud him, using textures at once subtle and harsh to make Bowery live forever on canvas.

In one sense, however, Freud undoes Bowery. He paints this man who loved to masquerade without even the shred of a costume. A costumed performer is stripped to reveal a naked everyman. Bowery clearly understood this and collaborated with it. As it turned out, he had every reason to seek the timeless permanence Freud could give him. He would die of an AIDS-related illness at the end of 1994.

Leigh Under the Skylight is at once an act of naked empirical observation and an exploration of the mythic, the superhuman. As Bernard's photograph shows, Freud falsifies nothing – only the angle of the skylight is perhaps a little lower in the painting than in reality. Yet he has posed Bowery for maximum effect, to give his sheer height and girth the most sensational aspect. It is a vision of the extreme. Freud has in fact got Bowery to pose in a way that evokes the Farnese Hercules, an ancient statue by the Greek artist Glykon that was found in 1546 in the Baths of Caracalla in Rome. This musclebound antiquity is an almost grotesque image of human massiveness, portraying the hero Hercules as a kind of monster. The brooding look in Bowery's eyes and the ripples of his loose flesh give him a touch of that monstrosity in Freud's painting, but the whole point is that he is real: a rare wonder truly observed.

Like Stubbs painting *Zebra* (pages 93 and 95), Freud is astounded by Bowery. Realist painters have often dwelt on physically exceptional people. In the seventeenth century, Velázquez portrayed dwarves at the Spanish court and Jusepe de Ribera sought out and portrayed a southern Italian peasant woman with a full black beard.

Yet Freud stops short of a freak show. The size of Bowery is daunting when you stand in front of this picture, but it is heroic, too. The ultimate effect is to make him real. Scale in art is a strange thing. Most art is smaller than life. To seem alive, it needs to explode into our consciousness with great force. Size therefore does matter, and Bowery's size makes him formidably real.

Freud's 1991–92 painting *Naked Man, Back View* gorges on the abundance of Bowery's flesh. His back is a carnival of fatty texture. Colours from gristly white to oily grey shape its dimpled contours. Bright light casts brown and pewter shadows on his lower spine. His buttocks are pressed into the smooth white surface of the luxury stool he squats on.

If Hirst isolated a shark for quasi-scientific scrutiny, Freud here holds up human corpulence for similar study. Hunched so that only one eye is partly visible, Bowery is like an imprisoned animal, a sulky Darwinian chimp. Freud's small 1991 painting *Leigh Bowery* takes an altogether more intimate view. It catches its subject asleep and homes in on his gentle tranquility, the suddenly soft, feminine way he rests his huge head on his shoulder as he slumbers. We get an intense feeling of what it is to paint someone 'from life'. It seems almost as if Bowery's unconsciousness has imparted some sleepy kindness to Freud's brush.

And the Bridegroom, painted in 1993, shares that slumberous benevolence. It is a nude portrait of Bowery and Nicola Bateman resting side by side on a bed in Freud's studio. Its title was prophetic, for although Bowery was gay he married Bateman the following year. Freud revels in their unlikely partnership. Bateman's pale body seems tiny beside Bowery's tawny hulk. What is their true relationship?

She puts her leg over his in easy closeness as they lie in intimate yet autonomous accord.

Bowery clearly understood Freud's fascination with scale, for he introduced him to another friend, Sue Tilley, who had worked at his nightclub Taboo and was now a benefits supervisor at Charing Cross Job Centre in central London. That is how Freud describes her in his 1995 painting *Benefits Supervisor Sleeping*. Straight from his heroic rediscovery of the male nude, he directly revisits the Venuses of Titian, Velázquez and Rubens. Tilley lies on a sofa, like so many female nudes down the centuries, but her body shape is anything but conventional. Her immense breasts sag and her belly flops forward as she rests a meaty arm on the back of the sofa. Her thighs are equally generous. Freud relishes this copiousness as she sleeps, letting his eyes drink in the sheer quantity of her. She is a specimen and a myth. Her sheer reality pours out of the painting. She is a human marvel. Aren't we all?

The Road to Dismaland

Some of Freud's paintings of Bowery and his circle went on view at London's Whitechapel Gallery in autumn 1993. You could walk from this remarkable exhibition to Grove Road, Mile End, where something equally exceptional loomed in the chilly October air. With the help of art facilitator Artangel, Rachel Whiteread had cast in concrete the entire interior of 193 Grove Road before removing the bricks, windows, roof tiles and doors of the house like the rind of an orange.

It seems unbelievable that two such intense and outstanding responses to modern life – Freud's naked portraits and Whiteread's inside-out house – could both be seen in London's East End simultaneously. What a profuse and complex artistic moment this was. Yet unstoppable forces of publicity, marketing, money and fame were already conspiring to efface that richness, deny that variety, reducing British art's new energy to crass populism, crude commerce and empty rhetoric.

Instead of paying attention to the meanings and ambitions of British art in one of its great moments, its supposed patrons and protectors encouraged a narrow, dishonest marketing of coolness and youth. The initial source of that shallow myth was Saatchi. As recently as 1990 his gallery had put on an exhibition of Freud, Hodgkin, Auerbach and more, and the most popular, permanent exhibit at his

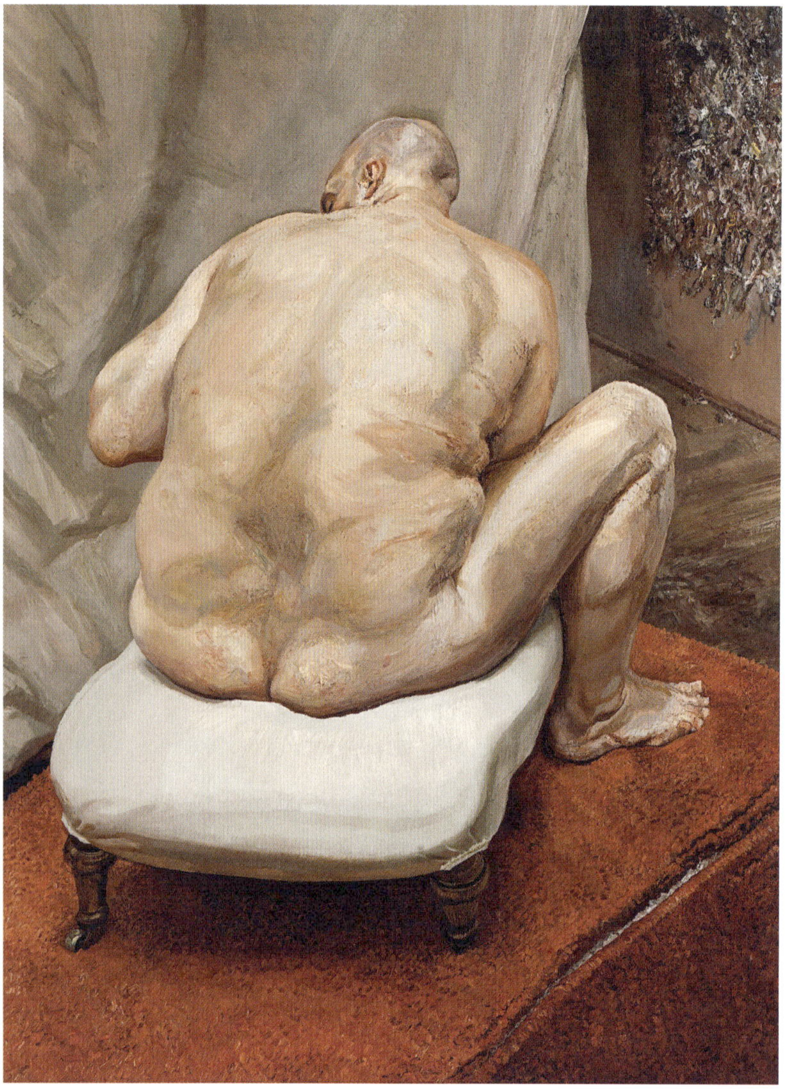

← Lucian Freud, *Naked Man, Back View*, 1991–92, oil on canvas, 182.9 × 137.2 cm (72 × 54 in.), The Metropolitan Museum of Art, New York. Purchase, Lila Acheson Wallace Gift, 1993 (1993.71)

gallery was Richard Wilson's inkily beautiful 1987 installation of sump oil, *20:50* – yet another work that proved that the macabre aesthetic of the time straddled artistic generations. Yet from 1992 Saatchi identified himself exclusively with Young British Artists of the Hirstian school, putting on a series of group shows with this name. This aggressive transformation of taste into hype culminated with *Sensation*, a blockbuster survey of Saatchi's collection of YBAs at the Royal Academy in 1997.

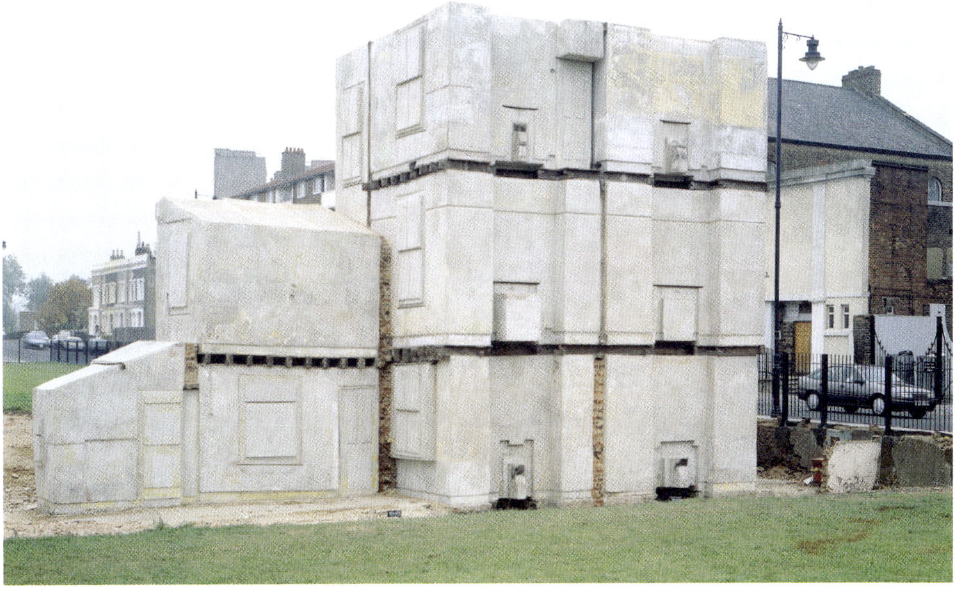

The Tate Gallery had meanwhile joined the marketing drive by making its annual Turner Prize a stage for Young British Art. First awarded in 1984 and a bit confused in its early years – it could even be awarded to non-artists for good cultural works – the Turner had become a prize for artists under 50 in 1988. This made it a perfect platform for the myth of generational revolt. Yet what was the rationale for excluding older artists? It implied different standards of judgement, and was ultimately patronizing to artists whose success on this stage was achieved by excluding 'established' talents that might dwarf them.

Whiteread was the winner of the prize in 1993. She was not up against Freud, however. He was way too old.

That meant audiences who came to the exhibition of this increasingly popular prize at the Tate that autumn received a distorted view of what was happening in British art: a narrow fiction. As a fiction it was highly effective. The Turner became identified with novelty and outrage. When Whiteread won, she was also awarded a prize as Britain's 'worst' artist by the Dadaistic K Foundation. The local council played a prank of its own by refusing all pleas to preserve *House*. It was demolished in January 1994.

↑ Rachel Whiteread, *House*, 1993 (193 Grove Road, London E3, destroyed 1994)

The Turner Prize in the 1990s became a bizarre mix of high-mindedness, pretension and crude populism – a successful cocktail. What got lost was any real sensitivity to the value and purpose of art. What had all this noise got to do with a serious sculpture like *House*, and what was really gained by pretending it was inherently more 'contemporary' than Freud's radical naked portraits of bohemian Londoners?

It can be argued that Freud's paintings of Bowery and Tilley were much closer to the pulse of alternative culture than anything created by the YBA movement, if movement it was. Although they had grown up in the age of punk and new wave, and assimilated punk's Dada tactics into their aesthetic of shock, they were not in the least allied to any wider pop movement. Their art was made for the gallery, not the street. When Hirst did make a foray into pop music it was to record a beery soccer anthem called 'Vindaloo' with the group Fat Les. This mediocre stunt was not exactly Andy Warhol's Velvet Underground, or Peter Blake's cover for *Sergeant Pepper's Lonely Hearts Club Band*.

That did not stop Young British Artists being celebrated alongside such groups as Blur, Oasis, the Spice Girls and Pulp in the supposed rebirth of 'Cool Britannia'. It was fitting that *Sensation* took place in the same year that Tony Blair's New Labour achieved its first landslide election victory. Born in the dying years of Conservative rule, the ballsy new conceptualism became a symbol of the more modern, progressive yet market-friendly Britain that New Labour promised.

One group of artists – like Hirst's Goldsmiths contemporaries, more a network of friends than an '-ism' – saw the YBAs as commercial sellouts and Saatchi stooges. They rejected this branding of youth in favour of a more conscious and passionate engagement with aspects of British popular culture. Jeremy Deller, born in 1966, was not a trained artist. Instead, he studied art history at the Courtauld Institute and Sussex University, an academic background that helps explain the clarity of his purely conceptual art. This suburban southerner was fascinated by northern working-class history and music. In 1997 he persuaded Stockport's Williams Fairey Brass Band to play a concert of specially arranged acid house dance anthems. Deller saw this as a utopian allegory of the history of the north, and drew a diagram to prove it. Then in the mild early summer of 2001, with the support of Artangel, he brought battle to an English field. Working with groups of Civil War re-enactors as well as people who had been there, he restaged an epic struggle between police and pickets that took place at Orgreave in 1984 during the Miners' Strike. Deller's *The Battle of Orgreave* was a haunting work of art on a stupendous yet human scale. As police charged on horseback down Orgreave high street it felt as if not just the class conflicts of the 1980s but the seventeenth-century Civil War or the medieval Wars of the Roses had come back, to bloody British soil.

Deller's artworks are like history paintings with real people as his brushes. Yet do the people involved express their memories and feelings, or his? There was a kind of genius in getting so many people to bring the Miners' Strike back to life, but it was a manipulative achievement, in which everyone ultimately helped Deller tell history as he saw it.

Chris Ofili, born in 1968, was innocent of any such moral complexities, as he worked in the more individual art of painting. He was in fact the only painter to win the Turner Prize in the 1990s, getting it in 1998 for his neo-pop romps featuring a black superhero called Captain Shit as well as collaged images of cultural heroes, painted blobby dots that parodied 'primitive' art, and lashings of glitter. But wait – there was a 'shocking' readymade element too. They rested on balls of elephant dung. Ofili's 1997 work *Double Captain Shit and the Legend of the Black Stars* demonstrates the Hogarthian comic robustness of Ofili's carnivalesque myth-making. Yet his subsequent career revealed how hard it was to be a serious artist – let alone a painter – in an art world intoxicated by celebrity. His ambitious installation *The Upper Room*, a version of the Last Supper with monkeys playing the disciples that took from 1999 until 2002 to complete, lacked the energy of his earlier street-pop. That did not stop the Tate from buying it, which caused the wrong kind of outrage as he was a trustee at the time. Since 2005 his main base and inspiration has been Trinidad, where his paintings have become deliberately quieter, more elusive. This is also where his friend and artistic ally Peter Doig, born in 1959, makes his home. Doig's 2001 painting *100 Years Ago (Carrera)* creates an aching and oppressive sense of emptiness and stillness as we look into the eyes of a somehow sinister canoeist on a dead calm sea. Beyond him is the bleak rocky mass of a prison island off Trinidad. In the magic unreality of Doig's dreamscape, this is an utterly real place, accurately depicted, where all too real lives are miserably eked out.

Martin Creed, born in 1968, also moved far from London, to a small island off Sicily, yet proved one of the most adept players of the celebrity art game – a star of anti-stardom whose drily comic manner made his alternative rock recordings as characterful as they are frankly enraging. His works of art, all numbered, range from a piece of paper crumpled into a ball to videos of people being sick. The one that won him the Turner in 2001 was *Work No. 227: The lights going on and off.* Depending on how whimsical you are feeling, this can seem either a sublimely simple demonstration of the fragility of life – the lights may go out any minute – or a stupefyingly pretentious bit of nothing.

If you are in the mood for it, Creed's art insists in ways that range from the ascetic to the gross that, as he puts it in his white luminous sign, *Work No. 232*, 'the whole world + the work = the whole world'. In other words, life is much bigger than art. A work of art is just an addition to reality, not a transcendence of it. It is another twist on British empiricism. Locke might agree, if he could get past the cute mock profundity of these glowing words, presented as if they are as profound as an Einsteinian equation.

Deller and Creed set out to bring conceptual art closer to life, to make it part of the whole world, yet they have created themselves as brands just as astutely as Hirst. The world is only in their art in the ways they choose to put it there. Was there any room left in British art as the twentieth century ended for a messier, more dangerous, less predictable engagement with 'the whole world'?

One artist who genuinely could not disentangle her art from reality was Tracey Emin. Raised in the dilapidated south coast resort of Margate, she started out amid plenty. Her Turkish father was a successful hotelier. Soon the relationship between her parents failed, the business ended and her father moved to London. Emin became so wayward that she barely attended secondary school at all. Instead, as she has related in her art and writings, she spent her time around the seafront, drinking, dancing and having sex. In spite of this dangerous life she showed a strong artistic talent that got her into college to study fashion, then printing, and finally an MA in painting at the Royal College of Art.

Yet Emin abandoned paint and became the most eloquent of the Young British Artists. She told her boyfriend, the painter and poet Billy Childish, that he was 'Stuck, stuck, stuck' doing old-style art. This gave rise to the Stuckist Movement, a group of campaigners against conceptualism whose belief in painting was unfortunately not matched by any great talent for it.

Emin meanwhile was making tents and telling stories as art. However, she was different from others in the 1990s conceptualist wave. Instead of neatly fabricating, or commissioning, objects, photographs or videos that stood coolly separate from their inventor, she was compulsively regurgitating her own life. Her brutal adolescence, her unhappy relationships, her abortion – all were reported in videos, installations and drawings.

She was the first of the YBAs to become a household name. In 1997 a debate about the Turner Prize on Channel 4 was completely derailed by Emin's drunken outpourings before the assembled male critics. She later claimed it was caused by painkillers for a severe hand injury, but it launched her into the spotlight as a genuinely outrageous bohemian character, a punk artist. In fact Emin was far more of a true bohemian than some of her professionalized contemporaries. Yet she was also too real to turn this into a TV persona: a genuinely troubled and unhappy person, scarred by the experiences she recounted.

When Emin created her installation *My Bed* in 1998, it had a noose hanging over it. By the time it appeared in the Turner Prize

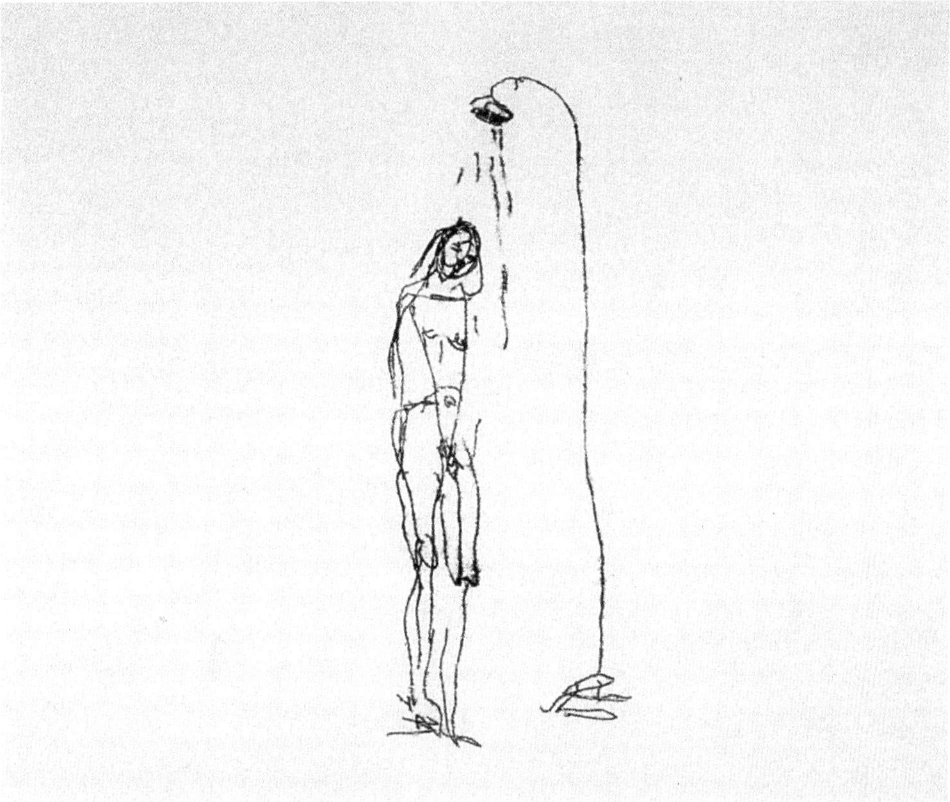

↑ Tracey Emin, *Sad Shower in New York*, 1995, monoprint on paper, 42 × 59.3 cm (16 ½ × 23 ⅓ in.), Tate

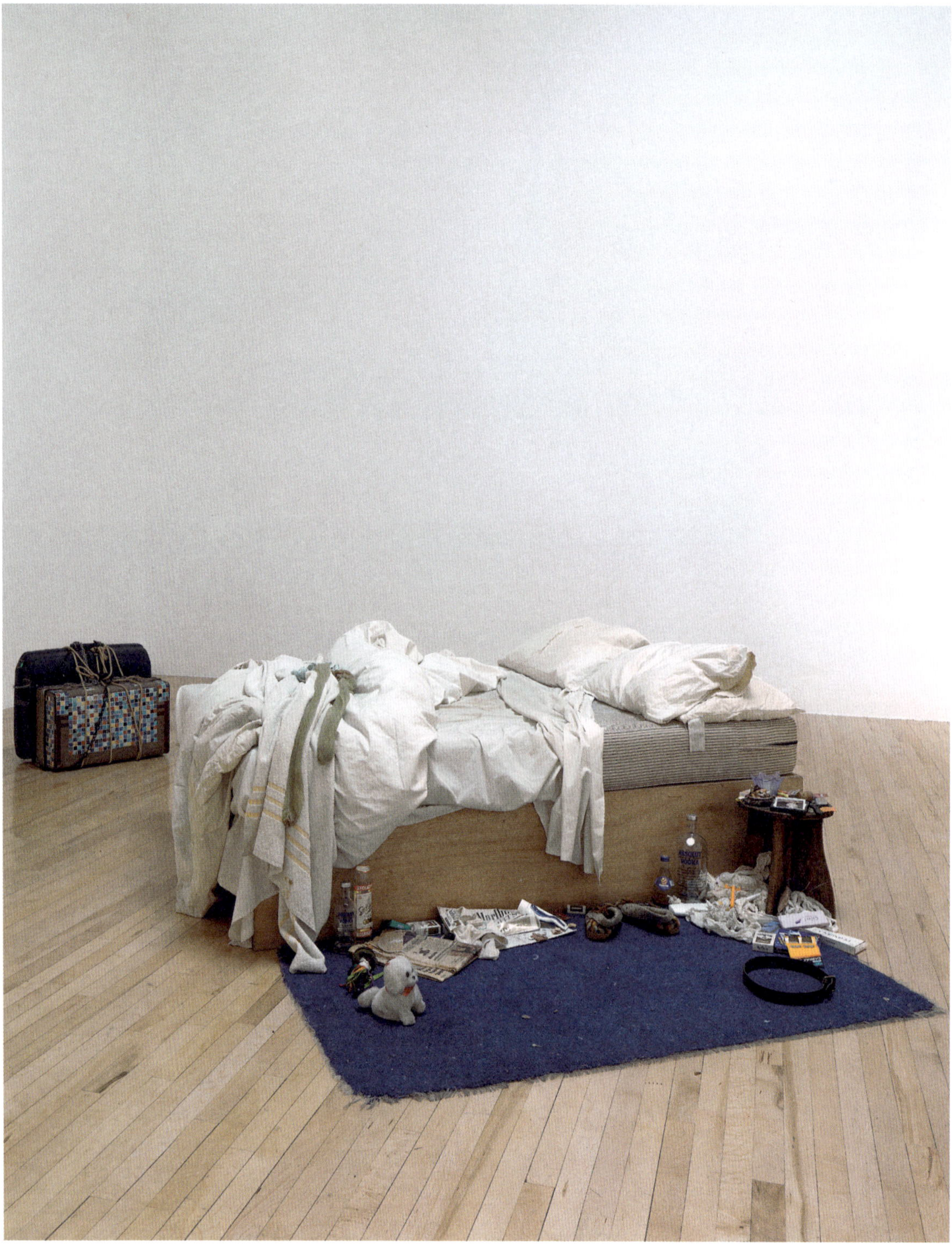

↑ Tracey Emin, *My Bed*, 1998, box frame, mattress, linens, pillows and various objects, dimensions variable, Installation photograph from the 1999 Turner Prize exhibition, Tate

exhibition at the Tate the following year, this explicit reference to suicide had been edited out. The crowds who came to see it were instead fascinated or outraged by tampons, tights, ashtrays, vodka bottles, dirty sheets, drugs legal and illegal – all evidence of a life in disarray. Emin's monument to an emotional slough of despond was the purest of readymades, a blunt document of unvarnished reality. It was a Hogarthian progress towards destruction told in trivia. A plaster, a pill, a pillow to cry on.

With time, this came to look like the most enduring conceptual artwork of the 1990s. Emin helped to ensure that: when it subsequently entered the Tate Collection on long-term loan, she took responsibility for recreating it every time it went on view. It was her bed, after all – part of her.

This intense relationship with what she saw as a monument to her past epitomized what made Emin seem an increasingly serious artist. To document your whole life in your thirties might be a stunt, but keep it up into your fifties and it becomes unquestionably authentic.

Emin lives so absolutely in her own emotions and memories that she is able to feel haunted and agonized even as a very wealthy woman with a portfolio of homes around the world. It took guts to move on from her highly saleable conceptual works to return to painting. Her savagely personal drawings and sensual canvases take the eroticism and desperation implicit in *My Bed* and make it overt. She may not be the most sophisticated of painters, yet the same unedited projection of herself that makes her early work memorable gives her canvases a ferocious presence.

Emin's raw paintings and sketches have almost the scabrous crudity of street art. In another life (without the houses and helicopter hires) she might have been a graffitist. A craving for that kind of genuine art from below made the most popular artist in early twenty-first century Britain neither her, nor Hirst, nor even the omnipresent TV pundit and potter Grayson Perry, but a West Country-born street artist going by the pseudonym Banksy.

In 2006 he painted an illicit mural on the side of a sexual health clinic in Bristol that portrays a naked man dangling from the ledge of a window by one hand. The window is drawn with enough stark shadowy depth to give it a three-dimensional reality, as is the anything but prepossessing nude man. From the window a cuckolded husband in a suit searches for the elusive lover. Beside him shivers a woman in her underwear.

A naked man, a window, a woman, a cuckold, a dirty joke. Hogarth would love it.

If only it was typical of Banksy's oeuvre. His immense international fame, however, had more to do with instantly understandable, populist political stunts than Hogarthian humour. His glib satirical gestures such as having a boy shine Ronald McDonald's clown shoes outside branches of the burger chain in New York were just the entertainment people craved in the discontented Western world in the unhappy decade after the market crash of 2008. He was not so much an artist as a revolutionary prankster. In the summer of 2015 he opened his own theme park – known as Dismaland – for just five weeks in the Somerset seaside resort Weston-super-Mare. There was a seedy-looking castle, inside which Cinderella's coach had crashed and the paparazzi crowded round her dead body, while attendants were trained to look as sullen as possible.

It was a media sensation, but wandering around I felt genuinely dismal. The fair was full of political jokes with easy targets and no cultural depth. The Cinderella tableau typified the easy, knowing shallowness of it all.

Local people queued to get in and thronged the dodgy rides. Everyone apparently lapped up the relentless critiques of capitalism. Then, less than a year later, North Somerset voted by 52 per cent to leave the European Union, exactly reflecting the national result in the referendum in June 2016. Perhaps Banksy's politics made less impact than his celebrity.

Populist art did not only come from the political left. In the summer and autumn of 2014, vast crowds gathered at the Tower of London to see an installation in its moat of hundreds of thousands of red ceramic poppies. Devised by artists Paul Cummins and Tom Piper, this memorial to Britain's World War I dead aroused intense responses.

The pop conceptualism of the 'official' art scene seemed completely dwarfed by such mass phenomena. Since the late 1990s Britain had embraced art on a spectacular scale. It started when Antony Gormley's colossal winged figure the *Angel of the North* was unveiled on the edge of Gateshead in 1998. Was it a monument to industry, a religious vision, or an empty totem of northern pride? Perhaps it succeeded as public art precisely because it was, for all its size, bland enough for each onlooker to give it a personal meaning.

Two years later Tate Modern opened on London's Bankside, across the river from Wren's masterpiece, St Paul's Cathedral. It had

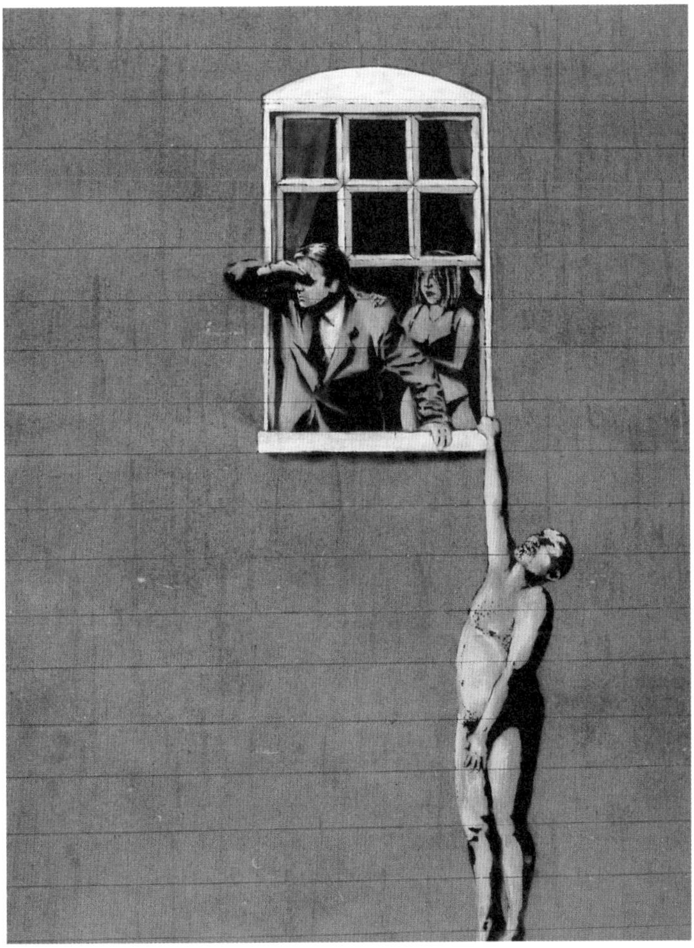

↑ Banksy, *Well Hung Lover*, 2006, Frogmore Street, Bristol

an instant impact on British art, not least because there was very little British art in it. A decade of excitement in British art ended, oddly, with its being shunted to the sidelines. For the old Tate Gallery became Tate Britain and was never to be anything like as popular as its cooler, more spectacular sibling.

Tate Modern created a new kind of art experience, which was more about the architecture, scale and vibe of the place than anything on display. The only works that rivalled the place itself were the expansive installations commissioned for its immense rectangular Turbine Hall. Anish Kapoor's 2002 sculpture *Marsyas* was a tapered blood-red horn that ran the entire length of the cavernous space. In ancient Greek mythology the satyr Marsyas challenged the god Apollo in a musical contest and, for his hubris, was flayed alive. Kapoor appeared to have created a sculpture out of the satyr's bloody pelt.

Kapoor, born in Mumbai in 1954, was, like Gormley, happy working on an outsized scale in the public sphere. His hypnotic feel for intense colour, whether the red and purple of eviscerated flesh or a deep heavenly blue in which you struggled to measure space and depth, enabled him to create art of sublime effect.

Britain had an appetite for art, sublime or otherwise, that galleries, even one as big as Tate Modern, could no longer contain. A plinth for an equestrian statue on the northwest side of Trafalgar Square had long stood empty. No longer. A programme of contemporary art commissions put a variety of sculpture there. Marc Quinn's statue of artist Alison Lapper was an almost kitsch marble sculpture commissioned from Italian workmen, yet it made a huge emotional impact because it was a heroic image of a disabled body.

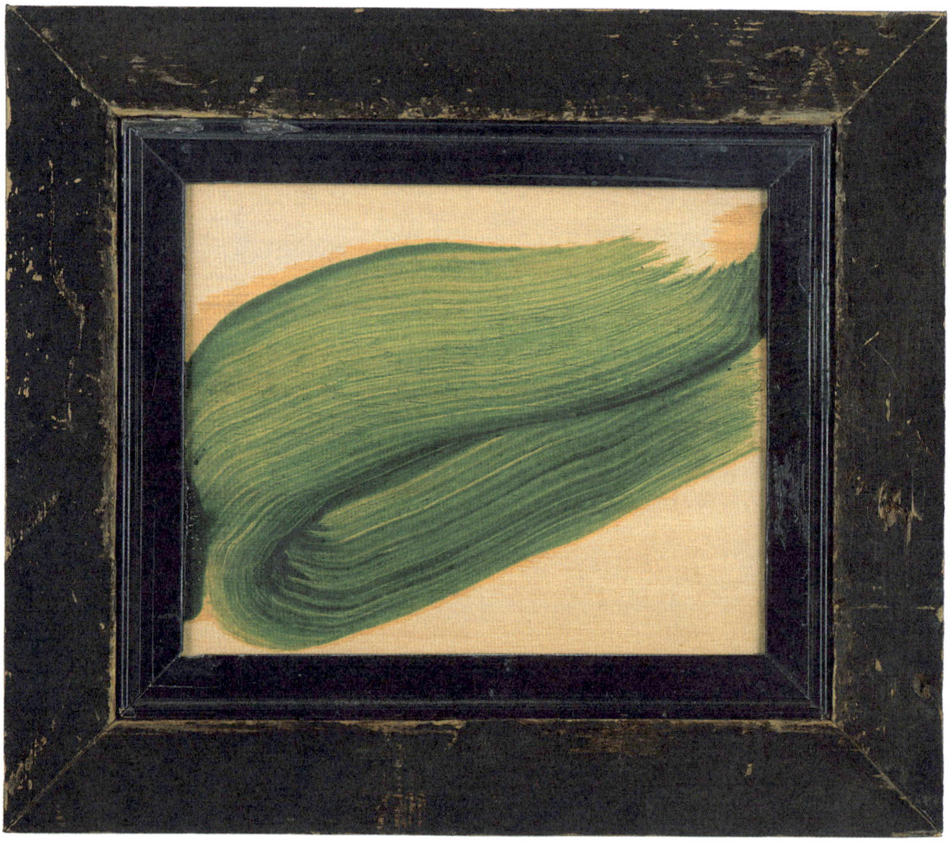

While public art was creating images that got everyone talking, the Frieze Art Fair was keener to get everyone buying. This chic festival of the global art market was held in Regent's Park, London, every autumn from 2003 onwards. London had become an international centre for buying and selling art, with galleries such as Gagosian and Hauser & Wirth opening branches in rivalry with Jay Jopling's White Cube.

Walking around the sophisticated art supermarket that was Frieze, it was easy to see why people preferred Banksy to any artist lauded by the self-congratulatory and superficial epigones of the art world.

Yet there were artists in this age of sensation who still trusted their sensations. Tacita Dean's moving 2006 work *Crowhurst* was created from a photograph she took of a (reputedly) 4000-year-old English yew tree. So ancient it needs sticks to prop it up, this

↑ Howard Hodgkin, *Leaf*, 2007–9,
oil on wood, 25.1 × 28.9cm (9 ⅞ × 11 ⅖ in.),
Gagosian

gnarled and twisted hulk seems conscious. It seems human. The things it has seen, the stories it could tell.

Dean has used white gouache to isolate and emphasize the image. Somehow this hand-painted addition infinitely increases its expressiveness. We feel her feelings. *Crowhurst* is a work of art to look at while listening to the music of Elgar, an elegy for nature and for a land with a long, long history.

British art in the end is a simple thing. It is naive. The best British artists did little more than look, yet in their looking they were honest and could be unexpectedly profound.

In 2007–9, Howard Hodgkin painted a leaf. Although he meditated over it for two years, it is one simple sweep of green, a leaf expressed in fresh, wet, dewy colour. It is as if he has preserved life itself in this sigh of love.

I would give all the riches in Dismaland for it.

Bibliography

Burke, Edmund. *A Philosophical Enquiry into the Origin of Our Ideas of the Sublime and Beautiful*, 1757.

Cannadine, David ed. *The Penguin History of Britain*, London: Penguin, 1997-.

Clark, Kenneth. *The Gothic Revival : An Essay in the History of Taste*, London : Constable & Co., 1928.

Dabydeen, David. *Hogarth's Blacks: Images of Blacks in Eighteenth Century English Art*, Manchester: Manchester University Press, 1987.

Danchev, Alex ed. *100 Artists' Manifestos: From the Futurists to the Stuckists*, London: Penguin, 2011.

Duffy, Eamonn. 'The Stripping of the Altars' in Theological Studies, vol. 54, part 4 (1993), pp. 739-741.

Evelyn, John. *Memoirs of John Evelyn comprising his Diary, and a Selection of His Familiar Letters*, edited by William Bray, London: Henry Colburn, 1818.

Farson, Daniel. *The Gilded Gutter Life of Francis Bacon*, London: Century, 1993.

Gatrell, Vic. *The First Bohemians: Life and Art in London's Golden Age*, London: Penguin, 2014.

Gage, John. *J.M.W. Turner: A Wonderful Range of Mind*, New Haven/London: Yale University Press, 1987.

Gayford, Martin. *Man With a Blue Scarf: On Sitting for a Portrait by Lucian Freud*, London: Thames and Hudson, 2010.

Gombrich, E. H. *Art and Illusion: A Study in the Psychology of Pictorial Representation*, London: Phaidon Press, 1960.

Graham-Dixon, Andrew. *A History of British Art*, London: BBC, 1996.

Hockney, David. *Secret Knowledge: Rediscovering the Lost Techniques of the Old Masters*, London: Thames and Hudson, 2001.

Hogarth, William. *The Analysis of Beauty*, 1753.

Holmes, Richard. *The Age of Wonder: How the Romantic Generation discovered the Beauty and Terror of Science*, London: Harper Press, 2011.

James, Henry. *The Real Thing, and Other Tales*, New York/ London: Macmillan and Co., 1893.

Jardine, Lisa. *On a Grander Scale: The Outstanding Life of Sir Christopher Wren*, London: HarperCollins, 2002.

——. *The Curious Life of Robert Hooke: The Man who Measured London*, London: HarperCollins, 2003.

Klingender, Francis. *Art and the Industrial Revolution*, London: Noel Carrington, 1947.

Locke, John. *An Essay Concerning Human Understanding*, 1690.

Pepys, Samuel. *Diary*, part published London 1825; full publication, edited by Robert Latham and William Matthews, London: G. Bell & Sons, 1970-1983.

Porter, Roy. *Enlightenment: Britain and the Creation of the Modern World*, London: Penguin, 2000.

Pevsner, Nikolaus. *The Englishness of English Art*, London: BBC, 1955.

Roberts, J.M. ed. *New Oxford History of England*, Oxford: Oxford University Press, 1992-.

Ruskin, John. *Modern Painters*, 5 vols, London: Smith, Elder & Co., 1843-60.

Shapin, Simon and Schaffer, Simon. *Leviathan and the Air-Pump: Hobbes, Boyle and the Experimental Life*, Princeton: Princeton Universtiy Press, 1985.

Stubbs, George. *The Anatomy of the Horse*, London: 1766.

Uglow, Jenny. *The Lunar Men: The Friends who Made the Future*, London: Faber, 2002.

——. *Mr Lear: A Life of Art and Nonsense*, London: Faber and Faber, 2017.

Walpole, Horace. *Anecdotes of Painting in England*, London, 1762-80.

Wilde, Oscar. 'The Picture of Dorian Gray', *Lippincott's Monthly Magazine*, July, 1890.

Wootton, David. *The Invention of Science: A New History of the Scientific Revolution*, London: Allen Lane, 2015.

Credits

Laurence King Publishing Ltd, the author and the researcher wish to thank the institutions and individuals who have kindly provided material for use in this book. Numbers below are page numbers. While every effort has been made to trace the present copyright holders we apologize in advance for any unintentional omission or error and will be pleased to insert the appropriate acknowledgement in any subsequent edition.

Cover © The National Gallery, London/Scala, Florence
Frontispiece © Tate, London 2019. © R. Hamilton. All Rights Reserved, DACS 2019

Page 7 © Mark Wallinger. Courtesy Hauser & Wirth; **11** © Museums at the Royal College of Surgeons; **13** © The Lucian Freud Archive/Bridgeman Images; **15 & 16** © The National Gallery, London/Scala, Florence; **19** Photo Scala, Florence/ bpk, Bildagentur für Kunst, Kultur und Geschichte, Berlin ; **21** © Her Majesty Queen Elizabeth II, 2019/Bridgeman Images; **22** Bridgeman Images; **23** © Her Majesty Queen Elizabeth II, 2019/Bridgeman Images; **25** The Metropolitan Museum of Art, New York; **26** © C B Newham/Alamy Stock Photo; **27** Seamus Heaney, 'Leavings', *Field Work*, Faber and Faber Ltd and Farrar, Straus, and Giroux, LCC. All Rights Reserved; **32** Bridgeman Images; **34-35** Duke University Libraries, Durham, NC ; **36** Wellcome Collection CC BY 4.0 ; **40** Reproduced by kind permission ofthe Syndics of Cambridge Library (MS Add.3975 p. 15); **44-45** © Jo Miyake/Alamy Stock Photo; **47** © Museum of London; **49** © akg-images/Erich Lessing; **53** Photo: Jigsaw Design & Publishing; **58 & 59** © The National Trust Photolibrary/John Hammond/Alamy Stock Photo; **61** Yale Center for British Art, Paul Mellon Collection (B1981.25.1428); **64** The Metropolitan Museum of Art, New York. Gift of Sarah Lazarus, 1891 (91.1.140); **66-67** Courtesy of the Trustees of Sir John Soane's Museum, London/Bridgeman Images; **69** Royal Academy of Arts, London/Bridgeman Images; **73** Coram in the care of the Foundling Museum, London/Bridgeman Images; **78-79 & 81** © The National Gallery, London/Scala, Florence; **84** Yale Center for British Art, Paul Mellon Collection (B1981.25.1443); **85** Wellcome Collection CC BY 4.0 ; **88 & 89** Royal Academy of Arts, London/Bridgeman Images; **90** Bridgeman Images; **93** Yale Centre for British Art, New Haven. Paul Mellon Collection (B1981.25.617); **95** Yale Centre for British Art, New Haven. Paul Mellon Collection (B1981.25.617); **97** The Iveagh Bequest, Kenwood House, London/© Historic England/Bridgeman Images; **99** Dulwich Picture Gallery, London. William Linley Bequest, 1835/Bridgeman Images; **105** © The National Gallery, London/Scala, Florence; **106** National Gallery of Art, Washington D.C. Ferdinand Lammot Belin Fund (1963.6.1); **108** Bridgeman Images; **110** © Pictures from History/Bridgeman Images; **112** National Maritime Museum, Greenwich, London. Acquired with the assistance of the Heritage Lottery Fund; The Eyal and Marilyn Ofer Foundation (formerly known as the Eyal Ofer Family Foundation); The Monument Trust; Art Fund (with a contribution from the Wolfson Foundation); The Crosthwaite Bequest; The Sackler Trust; Sir Harry Djanogly CBE; The Hartnett Conservation Trust; Sheila Richardson and Anthony Nixon; The Leathersellers' Company; Gapper Charitable Trust; Genevieve Muinzer and others.; **114** Bridgeman Images; **117 & 119** Derby Museum and Art Gallery/Bridgeman Images; **123** © The National Gallery, London/Scala, Florence; **125** akg-images/Erich Lessing; **128** © Tate, London 2019; **130** © AF Fotografie/Alamy Stock Photo; **132** Bridgeman Images; **134** © The National Gallery, London/Scala, Florence ; **135** © Tate, London 2019; **136-137** akg-images; **138-139** © Tate, London 2019; **142-143** © The Trustees of the British Museum; **145** © The National Gallery, London/Scala, Florence ; **147** Library of Congress, Washington, D.C.; **149** © Tate, London 2019; **150** © Tate, London 2019; **152** Yale Center for British Art, New Haven. Paul Mellon Collection (B1992.8.4(17)); **155** Yale University Libraries, New Haven. Beinecke Rare Book & Manuscript Library (11811407); **156** Yale University Libraries, New Haven. Beinecke Rare Book & Manuscript Library (11811434); **158** Yale University Libraries, New Haven. Beinecke Rare Book & Manuscript Library (11861199); **160** New York Public Library. Henry W. and Albert A. Berg Collection of English and American Literature; **161t** New York Public Library. Henry W. and Albert A. Berg Collection of English and American Literature; **161b** Library of Congress, Washington D.C. Lessing J. Rosenwald Collection; **162** Bridgeman Images; **163** The Metropolitan Museum, New York. ; **164-165** Detroit Institute of Arts/Founders Society Purchase with funds from Mr. and Mrs. Bert L. Smokler and Mr. and Mrs. Lawrence A. Fleischman/Bridgeman Images; **167** Bridgeman Images; **168** Library of Congress, Washington D.C. ; **170** Bridgeman Images; **172** © Victoria and Albert Museum, London; **173** © Tate,

London 2019; **175** © The National Gallery, London/Scala, Florence; **176 & 177** © Victoria and Albert Museum, London; **178** © Royal Academy of Arts, London. Photo: John Hammond ; **179** © Tate, London 2019; **181** © The National Gallery, London/Scala, Florence ; **183** New York Public Library, Rare Books Division (b14163872); **184-185** © Victoria and Albert Museum, London; **186, 189, 190 & 191** © Tate, London 2019; **192** © The National Gallery, London/Scala, Florence; **193** © Tate, London 2019; **194** Yale University Libraries, New Haven. Beinecke Rare Book & Manuscript Library (11861127); **195** Wellcome Library CC BY 4.0 ; **199** Yale University Libraries, New Haven. Beinecke Rare Book & Manuscript Library (11860665); **202, 204 & 207** © Tate, London 2019; **208** SSPL/ Getty Images; **209** © Tate, London 2019; **211** © The National Gallery, London/Scala, Florence; **212-213** © Tate, London 2019; **214** Naturalis Biodiversity Center, Leiden; **216** © Tate, London 2019; **218** University of California Libraries; **221** © Tate, London 2019; **222** Museum of Fine Arts, Boston, MA. Henry Lillie Pierce Fund/Bridgeman Images; **225** © Patricia Spinelli/Alamy Stock Photo; **227** Metropolitan Museum of Art, New York. Gift of Jean Horblit, in memory of Harrison D. Horblit, 1994 (1994.197.2 [5]); **229** © The National Gallery, London/Scala, Florence; **230** © Tyne & Wear Archives & Museums/Bridgeman Images; **232** Museum of New Zealand Te Papa. Gift of Mrs Mantell-Harding, 1961 (1992-0035-1784); **234-5** © Museum of London; **237** British Library (Add MS 50150, f. 225) ; **239** © Tate, London 2019; **241** © Tate, London 2019; **242** Boston Public Library; **243** Library of Congress, Washington D.C.; **244 & 245** Bridgeman Images; **246** Walker Art Gallery, National Museums Liverpool/Bridgeman Images; **248** © Tate, London 2019; **252l** J. Paul Getty Museum, Los Angeles (84.XO.732.1.2.8); **252r** Photo by SSPL/Getty Images; **253** Library of Congress Prints and Photographs Division Washington, D.C.; **254-5** © Tate, London 2019; **257** Detroit Institute of Arts /Gift of Dexter M. Ferry Jr./Bridgeman Images; **265** © Tate, London 2019; **266** Walker Art Gallery, National Museums Liverpool/Bridgeman Images; **272** Yale Center for British Art, Paul Mellon Fund (B1979.37.1); **275** © Tate, London 2019; **277** © The National Gallery, London/Scala, Florence; **281** Archive PL/Alamy Stock Photo/© Tate, London 2019; **287 & 290** © Tate, London 2019; **292** T. S. Eliot, 'The Wasteland', Faber and Faber Ltd; **293** © Museums at the Royal College of Surgeons; **296** National Trust Photographic Library/ John Hammond. © The Estate of Stanley Spencer/Bridgeman Images; **299** The Hepworth, Wakefield. Purchased with aid from the Victoria and Albert Purchase Fund, Wakefield Corporation and Wakefield Permanent Art Fund (Friends of Wakefield Art Gallery and Museums), 1942. © Reproduced by permission of The Henry Moore Foundation & DACS 2019; **302** © Tate, 2019. © The Piper Estate/DACS 2019; **305 & 306** © The Estate of Francis Bacon. All rights reserved. DACS 2019. Photo © Tate, London 2019. ; **308** Museum of Modern Art, New York. James Thrall Soby Bequest (1198.1979). © The Estate of Francis Bacon. All rights reserved, DACS/Artimage 2019. Photo: Prudence Cuming Associates Ltd; **310** Des Moines Art Center, Nathan Emory Coffin Collection. © The Estate of Francis Bacon. All rights reserved. DACS 2019. Photo: Prudence Cuming Associates Ltd; **312** © Tate, London 2019; **314** Bridgeman Images. © Frank Auerbach, courtesy Marlborough Fine Art; **318** © Tate, London 2019. © R. Hamilton. All Rights Reserved, DACS 2019; **321** Photo Richard Schmidt. © David Hockney; **323** Photo © Tate, London 2019. © Bridget Riley 2019. All rights reserved; **325** © Tate, London 2019. © Estate of Gustav Metzger; **327** © Gilbert & George. Courtesy White Cube; **330-331** © The Estate of Francis Bacon. All rights reserved, DACS/Artimage 2019. Photo: Hugo Maertens; **333** Photo: Art Gallery of New South Wales/Jenni Carter. © David Hockney; **335** © Tate, London 2019. © R. Hamilton. All Rights Reserved, DACS 2019; **336** © Tate, London 2019. © Leon Kossoff; **337** National Gallery of Art, Washington, D.C. Gift of The Glenstone Foundation (2004.121.1). © Rachel Whiteread. Photo: Mike Bruce. Courtesy of the artist and Gagosian; **339** © Damien Hirst and Science Ltd. All rights reserved, DACS/Artimage 2019. Photo: Courtesy Saatchi Gallery; **341** © Sarah Lucas. Courtesy Sadie Coles HQ, London; **343 & 348** © The Lucian Freud Archive/ Bridgeman Images; **349** © Rachel Whiteread. Photo: Sue Omerod. Courtesy of the artist and Gagosian Gallery.; **353** © Tate, London 2019. © Tracey Emin. All rights reserved, DACS 2019; **354** © Tate, London 2019. On long term loan from The Duerckheim Collection 2015. © Tracey Emin. All rights reserved, DACS 2019; **357** © Keith Ramsey/Alamy Stock Photo; **358** © The Estate of Howard Hodgkin. Image courtesy Gagosian.

Index

Note: titles of art works, books, magazines, etc are given in italics; page numbers in italics refer to illustrations.

Acknowledgements

I'd like to thank all at Laurence King for their enthusiasm and energy in creating this book. Laurence King, Marc Valli and Kara Hattersley-Smith boldly commissioned it. Donald Dinwiddie has expertly seen it through to publication, calmly negotiating text and image as did Philip Contos at an earlier stage. Julia Ruxton's picture research and the design by Sonya Dyakova and Vanessa Green have made the book beautiful. Angus Hyland and Alexandre Coco designed the sublime cover. Fiona Livesey and Jantien Abma have been great to work with on publicising and marketing it. Julian Bell kindly read and commented on the manuscript. *The Guardian* has given me many opportunities to think about British art, from visiting galleries and collections from St Ives to Orkney to interviewing artists, including Richard Hamilton, David Hockney, Howard Hodgkin and Gilbert and George. The artist I talked to most when I was working on this book was Tracey Emin, who has given me many insights into art, life and their relationship. My biggest debt, more than ever, is to my wife Sarah whose sensitivity has illuminated this book and my life.